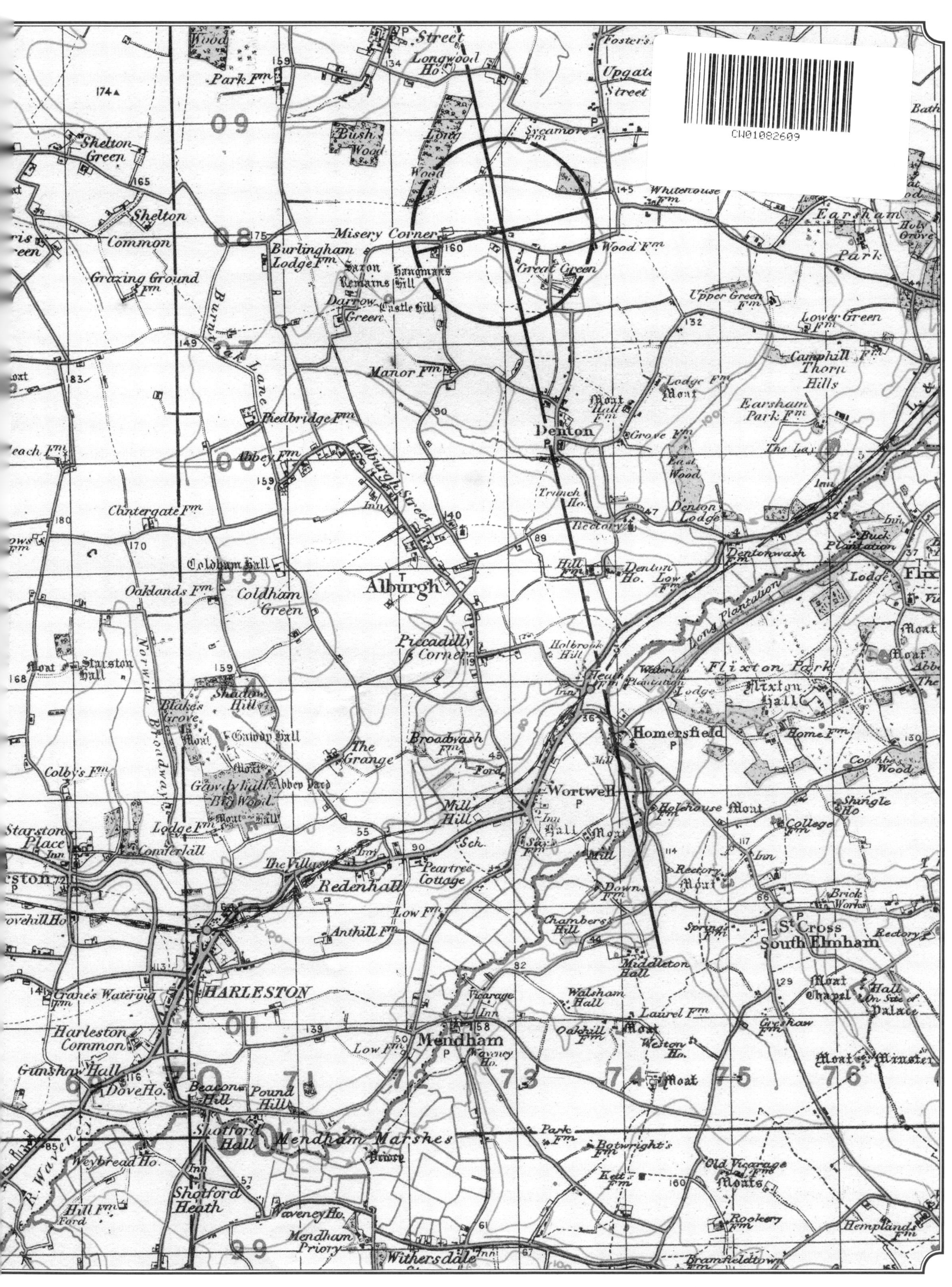
Street
Longwood Ho.
Park Fm
Wood
Foster's
Upgate Street
Bath
174
159
134
09
Bush Wood
Long Wood
Sycamore Fm
Shelton Green
165
Shelton
Common
145
Whitehouse Fm
Earsham
Holy Grove
Park
08
175
Misery Corner
160
Wood Fm
Burlingham Lodge Fm
Saxon Remains
Hangmans Hill
Great Green
Grazing Ground Fm
Darrow Green
Castle Hill
Upper Green Fm
Lower Green Fm
132
Burnthouse Lane
149
183
Manor Fm
Camphill Fm
Thorn Hills
Lodge Fm
Moat
Moat Hill Fm
Piedbridge Fm
90
Denton
Earsham Park Fm
Grove Fm
The Lay
Abbey Fm
Alburgh Street
159
Each Fm
East Wood
Trunch Ho.
Inn
Denton Lodge
Clintergate Fm
180
140
Rectory
89
47
Dentonwash Fm
32
Buck Plantation
Inn
170
Coldham Hall
Hill Fm
Denton Ho.
Low Fm
Lodge
Flix
Oaklands Fm
Alburgh
Coldham Green
Long Plantation
Moat
Piccadilly Corner
119
Holbrook Hill
Moat
Starston Hall
159
168
Heath Fm
Waterloo Plantation
Flixton Park
Flixton Hall
Lodge
Norwich Broadway
Blake's Grove
Shadow Hill
Gawdy Hall
Inn
36
Homersfield
Home Fm
130
The Grange
Broadwash Fm
45
Colby's Fm
Moat
Ford
Mill
Coombe Wood
Gawdyhall Big Wood
Abbey Yard
Moat Hall
Wortwell
Mill Hill
Holehouse Moat
Shingle Ho.
Starston Place
Lodge Fm
Inn
Hall
Moat
College
Coniferhall
55
Sch.
117
Inn
Sax Fm
Mill
114
The Villa
Inn
90
Peartree Cottage
Rectory
Moat
Redenhall
Downs Fm
66
Brick Works
Low Fm
Chambers Hill
Spring Fm
St. Cross South Elmham
Rectory
Anthill Fm
44
Middleton Hall
113
82
129
Grane's Watering Fm
HARLESTON
Vicarage
Walsham Hall
Moat
Chapel
Hall
On Site of Palace
Inn
Laurel Fm
58
01
139
Oakhill Fm
Moat
Grishaw Fm
Harleston Common
50
Low Fm
Mendham
Weston Ho.
Waveney Ho.
Moat
Minster
Gunshaw Hall
116
70
71
72
73
74
Moat
75
76
69
Dove Ho.
Beacon Hill
Pound Hill
Park Fm
R. Waveney
Shotford Hall
Mendham Marshes
Priory
Botwright's Fm
85
Weybread Ho.
Inn
Kett Fm
Old Vicarage Fm
Moats
57
160
Shotford Heath
Hill Fm
Ford
Waveney Ho.
Rookery Fm
Hemplands Fm
Mendham Priory
61
99
Withersdale
Inn
67
Bramfieldtown

THE

WAVENEY VALLEY RAILWAY

TIVETSHALL TO BECCLES

Tivetshall Junction station from the south on 1st September 1951, with the signal box on the west side of the Down main line controlling all points and signals at the station. The main line crossing gates have been opened after the passage of a Down train whilst the lorry is waiting for the second barrier to be cleared on the separate Waveney Valley level crossing across the single branch line. The line in the immediate foreground leads to the Up reception line located parallel and east of the Up main line. Note the signalman has yet to return the Down starting signal to danger. *H.C. Casserley*

THE
WAVENEY VALLEY RAILWAY
TIVETSHALL TO BECCLES

PETER PAYE

Lightmoor Press

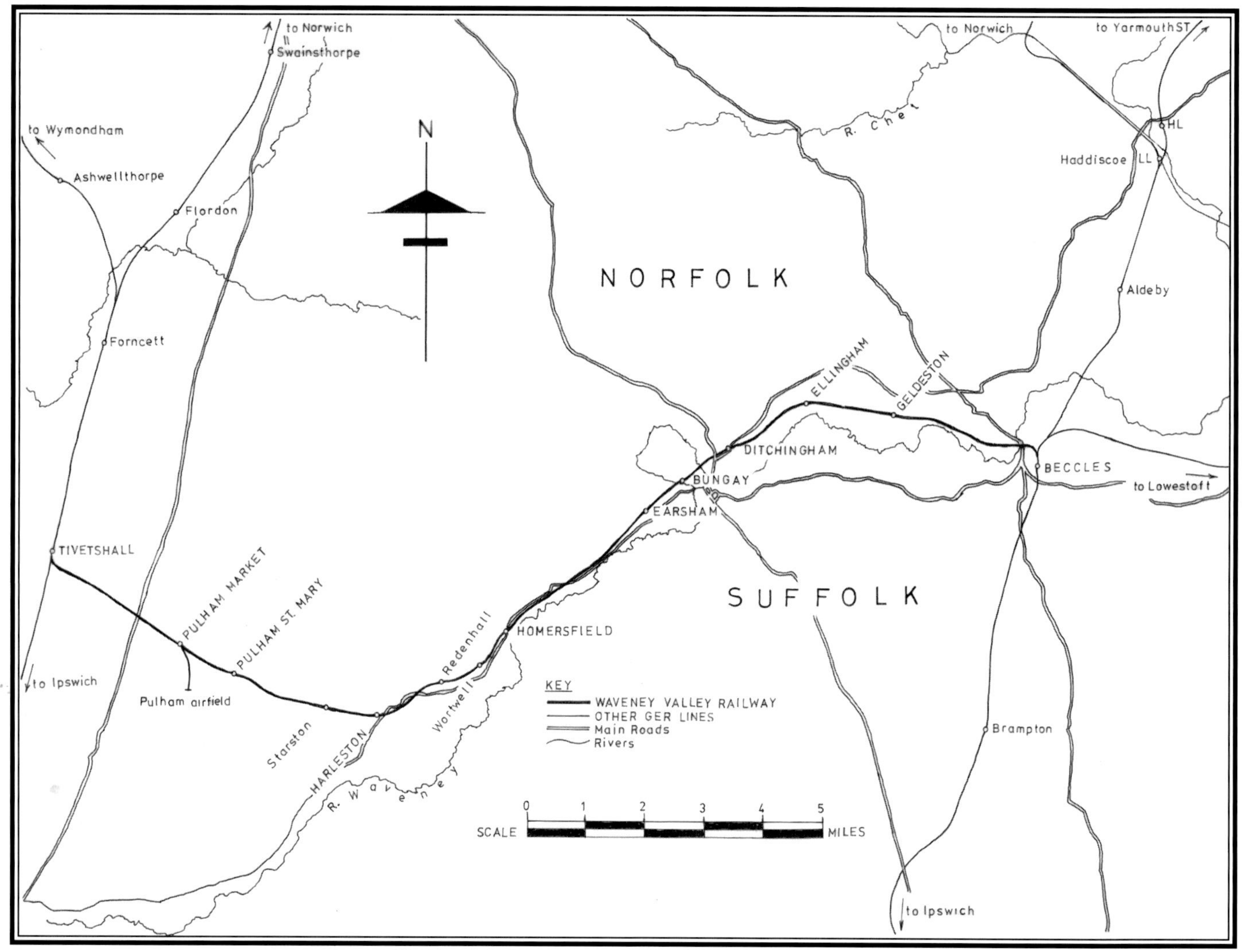

Map showing the Waveney Valley Branch in context with the neighbouring lines. The Up direction is Beccles to Tivetshall.

Designed by Nigel Nicholson

British Library Cataloguing-in-Publication Data. A catalogue record for this book is available from the British Library

ISBN 9781 911038 58 0

LIGHTMOOR PRESS

Unit 144B, Lydney Trading Estate, Harbour Road, Lydney, Gloucestershire GL15 4EJ

www.lightmoor.co.uk

Lightmoor Press is an imprint of Black Dwarf Lightmoor Publications Ltd

Printed in Poland; www.lfbookservices.co.uk

Contents

'F4' Class 2-4-2T No. 67167 approaching Pulham Market with the morning Tivetshall to Beccles train in July 1952. The short headshunt to the goods yard is to the left. *Dr I.C. Allen*

'J15' Class 0-6-0 No. 65469 waits at Harleston with a Down goods train after shunting the yard. The guard can be seen in the ' six foot' checking the consist of his train. Note the station footbridge No. 1178 at 6 miles 25 chains spanning the line and connecting the Up and Down platforms. *Dr I.C. Allen*

Introduction

A GENTLE BREEZE BLOWS ON this fine summer morning, swallows dip and dive in the azure blue sky as passengers gather at a small wayside station on a single-track branch line to await the arrival of their train. Few buildings surround the railway with a backcloth of open fields but a church clock chiming is evidence of habitation. It is market day and for many in this rural community it is the one outing of the week. Pigeon baskets are arranged on the platform along with a barrow containing parcels and a couple of milk churns awaiting despatch as people converse and pass the time of day with their neighbours and friends. The conversation is briefly interrupted by the clang of bells from the signal box and within a short time the porter-signalman scurries from the building, down the steps to open the gates at the adjacent level crossing. He then returns to pull the levers to clear the signals as some latecomers, including a young lady with a pram, arrive. An engine whistle warns of the approach of a locomotive with tall stovepipe chimney hauling three elderly corridor coaches, pulling into the platform before the brakes are applied. All appears pandemonium as passengers, pigeon baskets, parcels *et al* are hurried aboard, doors slam and the guard and station staff exchange pleasantries. The Westinghouse pump on the locomotive pants away to restore air pressure to the braking system as the guard, satisfied that all is correct, sounds his whistle and waves the green flag to the engine crew who acknowledge with a wave. A shriek of the whistle and the 2-4-0 tender locomotive eases her coaches into motion. A passenger waves a last goodbye to a friend on the platform as the train disappears round a curve in the line. The signals clatter to danger and the level crossing gates are again opened for road traffic to cross; soon all is rural bliss, the swallows barely inconvenienced by the temporary commotion.

The scene changes, to a loop line beside the same single-track branch; it is early on a dank and dull November day. Military lorries are arriving on the adjacent concrete roadway as servicemen in drab uniform gather in small groups beside the line, huddling against the vehicles for protection from the northerly wind. Barely a word is spoken and in chorus there is no bird song but in the background there is the rumble of large aircraft lifting their heavy cargo into the sky. A locomotive whistle sounds announcing the approach of a train, which after a momentary pause for the points to be changed, pulls off the main single line into the siding. Only a slight glare from the firebox door lights the arrival but a tarpaulin cover between the engine cab and tender shields the temporary illumination. As the train shudders to a halt, organised unloading commences. The shadowy figures begin a well-drilled routine, small hoists are brought alongside the open wagons as the side doors are dropped open. The contents are heavy and handled with much care for the train is loaded with bombs and ammunition destined for local military airfields, ultimately for use against Hitler's Germany, for these are the dark days of World War Two. Lorries are loaded and the convoy of vehicles grind their way into the semi-darkness as the deadly cargo is taken to adjacent airfields and bomb dumps. The military officer in charge checks all has been unloaded and signals that the empty train can continue its journey. As the daylight increases the guard ensures the points are set for the main single line and the locomotive eases the empty wagons away from the siding.

Such scenes register the two extremes of traffic handled by the Waveney Valley Branch of the Great Eastern Railway, later London & North Eastern Railway and then British Railways (Eastern Region). From sylvan setting to essential involvement in the defence of the realm, this rural line following for much of its path the border between the counties of Norfolk and Suffolk, and serving but a cluster of villages and small towns nestling in the shadow of their spiritually protective parish churches, would be considered the quintessential railway backwater. The county of Suffolk owes much of its natural charm to its rivers, especially the Stour, Deben, Orwell and Waveney. The Waveney, which constitutes the greater part of the northern boundary with neighbouring Norfolk rises between South Lopham and Redgrave, and flows by Hoxne, Mendham and Flixton to Bungay where it makes a horseshoe curve before flowing on to Beccles, via picturesque locks at Wainford, Ellingham and Geldeston. A little way below Burgh St. Peter the Waveney, forsaking Suffolk, flows into Norfolk, where it joins Oulton Dyke, a wide navigable channel, ultimately connecting it to Oulton Broad and the North Sea.

The cultivation of land by the plough had for generations been the main industry in this part of the country, but agriculture and animal husbandry was dependent on good transport for farmers and growers to get their produce and beasts to markets. The old Norfolk and Suffolk tracks and roads were gradually improved and in the late-18th and 19th centuries turnpike roads were established. Carrier's carts, however, were slow and ponderous on their journeys, with many delays incurred during wet or adverse weather. Often produce rotted en route, animals suffered and all earned poor prices at Ipswich, Norwich and other provincial markets. The advent of the railways in East Anglia brought drastic improvements and after initial scepticism there was urgent desire for communities to be served by the new lines.

Not all benefited from the new mode of transport, however, as the proposed trunk route from London to Yarmouth had only reached Colchester when opened by the Eastern Counties Railway in March 1843. Inhibited from progress because of lack of funds, the section thence to Ipswich was opened by the Eastern Union Railway in June 1846 and on to Bury St. Edmunds in December of the same year. In the meantime the ECR had recovered and reached Norwich another way. By taking over the Northern & Eastern Railway, which had opened to Bishop's Stortford on 16th May 1842, the line was then extended to Newport in July 1844 and finally via Cambridge and Ely to Brandon to join up with the Norfolk Railway route to Norwich opened throughout on 30th July 1845. The Norfolk Railway had opened between Yarmouth and Norwich on 30th April 1844. Pressure from businessmen and landowners saw the EUR link from the junction at Haughley to Norwich open on 7th November 1849. East Suffolk was served by the Haddiscoe, Beccles & Halesworth Railway, opened in December 1854 and then, renamed as the East Suffolk Railway, extended to Woodbridge to join up with the EUR branch from Ipswich on 1st June 1859. The area between these routes was thus devoid of railways and a scheme, which hoped to alleviate the problem, envisaged a cross-country route from Yarmouth to Diss via Ditchingham and Bungay, thus forming a more direct route from the coast to the capital by circumnavigating Norwich. The promoters succeeded in obtaining an Act of Parliament on 25th June 1847 but the necessary capital failed to materialise. Thus the leading businessmen and traders of the small market towns of Harleston and Bungay, aggrieved that their communities would suffer economic depression, decided to promote their own railway. They met with greater success and Parliamentary authority for the Waveney Valley Railway was obtained on 3rd July 1851. The line commenced at Tivetshall, an intermediate station on the EUR Ipswich to Norwich main line a few miles north of Diss, with the aim of serving Bungay and ultimately Beccles to connect with the East Suffolk line. The railway, worked by the ECR, which had taken over many lines in East Anglia, initially opened to Harleston on 1st November 1855 but the operator immediately complained the service was operating at a loss and relationships were fraught. The WVR, constantly short of resources, was forced to seek further Parliamentary aid for finances to extend the line to Bungay and as relationships deteriorated decided on independent operation from 15th September 1860, just before the extension opened on 2nd November 1860. This situation remained even when the ECR combined with other undertakings to form the Great Eastern Railway from 7th August 1962. By then the WVR had obtained powers to extend the line from Bungay to Beccles, with the undertaking being absorbed by the GER on completion to the junction, which was achieved on 2nd March 1863.

The new regime took steps to improve facilities and services and quickly arranged for some trains to work through from Norwich to Beccles and return, with a few trains limited to operating between Tivetshall and Beccles. The management also rationalised the infrastructure – deciding that for such a rural location the railway was endowed with too many stations – by closing Redenhall and Starston with effect from 1st January 1866 and Wortwell on 1st January 1878. The cross-country branch then led a peaceful existence save that during World War One a long siding was laid from Pulham Market station to serve a Royal Naval Airship Station, whilst passenger services were withdrawn as an economy measure from Earsham (from 22nd May 1916 until 1st August 1919) and from Geldeston (from 22nd May 1916 until it was reopened as an unstaffed halt on 14th September 1916, gaining station status again on 14th September 1919).

Solemnity returned after the war until the outbreak of World War Two. Initially little changed but as hostilities progressed the establishment of Royal Air Force and United States Air Force fighter and bomber bases transformed the area. From a peaceful existence the branch was open day and night as additional sidings and facilities were opened for the military at Earsham, Ditchingham and Ellingham. Train-loads of armaments and bombs destined for the airfields were delivered day and night, augmented by deliveries of aviation fluid en route to Ellingham. The Air Station at Pulham Market saw much increased activity as an RAF base for equipment. Into this maelstrom passenger services continued as local markets flourished as best they could and military personnel journeyed to and from their bases.

The end of hostilities in 1945 found consignments of unused armaments being transferred away to military compounds as passenger services returned to normal, but gradually as petrol rationing eased and road transport increased so the numbers of people travelling by train decreased and many services conveyed few passengers. The branch freight was handled by two services on weekdays only: one operating from Norwich to serve the western section of the branch and the other from Beccles serving the eastern section, the two trains meeting to exchange traffic at Harleston. So drastic was the fall in passenger traffic that services were withdrawn on and from 5th January 1953. Freight facilities continued, but to reduce operating costs the route was converted to a Light Railway under the order dated 15th November 1954. The abolition of some level crossings, with trainmen opening and closing the barriers at others, failed to arrest the transfer of goods to road transport and on and from 1st February 1960 the line was severed by closure of the Harleston (exclusive) to Bungay (exclusive) section. A general review of all freight routes in East Anglia resulted in the closure of Bungay to Ditchingham on 3rd August 1964. Ditchingham to Beccles officially closed on 19th April 1965 but remained operational for contractual purposes until August of the same year. Then, on and from 18th April 1966, services were withdrawn from Tivetshall to Harleston.

In this volume I have attempted to provide the fascinating history of the rural cross-country railway on the Suffolk/Norfolk border and details have been checked with available documents, but apologies are offered for any errors which might have occurred.

Peter Paye
Bishop's Stortford

1

Beginnings: A Railway from Tivetshall to Harleston

The advent of the railways in East Anglia began in earnest with the incorporation of the Eastern Counties Railway on 4th July 1836. With a share capital of £1,600,000 the company was granted powers to construct a 126 mile line from Shoreditch in East London to Norwich and Yarmouth via Chelmsford, Colchester, Ipswich and Eye. All but £58,100 of shares had been sold by September and there was great concern that only a twelfth of the total share capital raised was of local origin. In late March 1837 construction commenced at the London end only, as incomplete negotiations with landowners prevented a concurrent start planned between Norwich and Yarmouth. The troubles continued as landowners along the route of the proposed railway demanded high compensation. By October 1838 forty per cent of the capital had been called but only nine miles of railway were under construction. With creditors pressing, only urgent action prevented total ruin, and in April 1839 Lancashire proprietors, who had taken a great stake in the undertaking, forced a decision to terminate the line at Colchester.

The first public trains ran from a temporary terminus at Mile End to Romford on 20th June 1839, with extensions each end to Shoreditch and Brentwood opening for traffic on 1st July 1840. In the meantime the ECR Directors called in Robert Stephenson for engineering advice, but he could only confirm that a further £520,000 was required to complete the railway to Colchester. Mutinous shareholders were almost bludgeoned into meeting the call for shares whilst application to Parliament for a further £350,000 share capital was made in 1840. With the combined assets and borrowing powers sanctioned in a further Act in 1840, construction of the final section was possible. Inclement weather in 1841 caused delay and damage to earthworks, but eventually the line was opened for goods traffic on 7th March 1843 and for passenger trains on 29th March. The 51 mile line had take seven years to construct at a cost of nearly £2½ million and the works at £1,631,300 had exceeded the original estimate for the whole project from London to Yarmouth.

The decision of the ECR to terminate its project at Colchester was a matter of grave concern to the merchants of Ipswich, Norwich and Yarmouth, who were fearful of isolation from the growing railway network. A number of ECR shareholders in Suffolk and Norfolk, alarmed at the slow progress and decision of April 1839, obtained a decree nisi in the Bail Court to force the fulfilment of the company's contract with the public, but this was nullified in 1840 when Parliament refused to extend the ECR powers beyond July of that year. Undaunted, local factions then planned a railway linking Norwich and Yarmouth, and this received the Royal Assent in 1842 to be followed the next year by a projected line from Norwich to Brandon. Such developments caused consternation to the Ipswich traders and businessmen, and these were aggravated by the ECR planning a possible extension to join up with the Norwich and Brandon line at Thetford, with the main line by-passing Ipswich altogether.

Representations against such proposals fell on deaf ears and so the merchants and tradesmen from Ipswich produced their own scheme for a line linking the town with the ECR at Colchester, based on plans submitted by Peter Schuyler Bruff of 22 Charlotte Street, Bloomsbury, London, who had already worked on surveys for the initial ECR route. The leading advocate was John Chevallier Cobbold of the wealthy Ipswich banking and brewing family, who was a member of the original ECR Board of Directors. As well as connecting Ipswich with Colchester, the promoters of the scheme also intended to pursue the idea of a railway running north to Norwich, and a new company entitled the Eastern Union Railway, was incorporated on 19th July 1844. The railway, 17 miles in length, was designed by Joseph Locke, with Peter Bruff, who had moved to Ipswich, as resident engineer.

Meanwhile the ECR route to Thetford was abandoned but a group of businessmen in Bury St. Edmunds were concerned their town would also be isolated from the railway network and suffer economic depression. Having met with ECR Directors in February and found they were unwilling to extend the line beyond Colchester, the townsfolk promoted their own line, the East & West Suffolk Railway. They were advised the EUR would not oppose such a venture provided the route went from Bury St. Edmunds to Ipswich via Hadleigh and did not interfere with the direct line from Ipswich to Colchester.

The development of railways in Suffolk and Norfolk was then the subject of a special study by the Railway Department of the Board of Trade. The Diss & Colchester Junction scheme, which commenced from an end-on junction with the ECR at Colchester before proceeding via Hadleigh, Stowmarket and Eye to Diss to join up with a branch from Diss to the Norwich and Brandon line of the Norfolk Railway, came in for scathing criticism for by-passing Ipswich, the chief market and industrial town in Suffolk. In the report finally published on 4th March 1845, full support was given to the EUR scheme to Ipswich and for the extension to Norwich.

North of Ipswich the tract of land towards Bury St. Edmunds finally received the attention of railway developers, and on 21st July 1845 the Act authorising the construction of the Ipswich and Bury St. Edmunds Railway received the Royal Assent. With an initial capital of £400,000 the new concern appeared nominally independent. It was, however, an extension of the EUR, boasting no fewer than six EUR Directors out of a total of fifteen on the board. The Ipswich & Bury Railway also occupied the same head office at Ipswich and had the same engineer, secretary and contractor as the EUR. The official opening of the 26¼ mile route took place on

Monday 7th December 1846 with passenger services commencing on Christmas Eve.

In the meantime, on Monday 1st June 1846 the EUR had opened for goods traffic pending the official Board of Trade inspection. General Pasley duly conducted this on 4th June and the official opening took place on 11th June 1846, passenger traffic commencing on 15th June, by which time £270,000 had been expended on works between Colchester and Ipswich.

On the same day as the ECR was incorporated in 1836, a rival company, the Northern & Eastern Railway, received the Royal Assent to build a line over the 53 miles from Islington to Cambridge with a share capital of £1,200,000. Like the ECR, the N&E ran into financial and purchasing difficulties, and it was not until 1839 that construction commenced and only then with the sanction of the ECR. To save money, the N&E route was diverted from Tottenham via Stratford where running powers were allowed into the ECR Shoreditch terminus. Like the ECR the new line was built to a gauge of 5 feet and, despite the abandonment of the route north of Bishop's Stortford by Act of Parliament in 1840, the railway had reached the Hertfordshire town on 16th May 1842, at a cost of £25,000 per mile. In 1843 the N&E secured an extension Act for a line to Newport, some 10 miles nearer Cambridge. On 23rd December of that year, however, the ECR agreed with the company a 999 years lease from 1st January 1844. Once the lease was in force the ECR obtained powers for a line linking Newport to the Norwich & Brandon Railway at Brandon on 4th July 1844. The N&E was converted to the standard gauge of 4 feet 8½ inches in the late summer of the same year and after a formal opening the previous day, the whole line from Bishop's Stortford to a temporary terminus at Norwich Trowse commenced public service on 30th July 1845.

ANNO DECIMO & UNDECIMO

VICTORIÆ REGINÆ.

****

Cap. lxiv.

An Act to empower the *Norfolk* Railway Company to make a Railway from the *Lowestoft* Railway near *Reedham* to join the *Norwich* Extension of the *Ipswich and Bury Saint Edmunds* Railway near *Diss*, with a Branch therefrom to *Halesworth*. [25th *June* 1847.]

WHEREAS an Act was passed in the Fifth and Sixth Years
of the Reign of Her present Majesty, intituled *An Act for* 5 & 6 Vict.
making a Railway from Great Yarmouth *to* Norwich *in* c. 82.
the County of Norfolk, whereby a Company was incorporated under
the Name of "The *Yarmouth and Norwich* Railway Company:" And
whereas another Act was passed in the Seventh and Eighth Years of
the Reign of Her present Majesty, intituled *An Act for making a* 7 & 8 Vict.
Railway from Norwich *to* Brandon, *with a Branch to* Thetford, c. 15.
whereby a Company was incorporated under the Name of the "*Norwich and Brandon* Railway Company:" And whereas an Act was
passed in the Eighth and Ninth Years of the Reign of Her present
Majesty, intituled *An Act for the Consolidation of the* Yarmouth and 8 & 9 Vict.
Norwich *and* Norwich and Brandon *Railway Companies, and for* c. 41.
[*Local.*] 9 *T* *authorizing*

Front page of the Norfolk Railway, Reedham & Diss Branches Act of 25th June 1847.

The EUR, having absorbed the Ipswich & Bury Railway on 9th July 1847, commenced their extension to the north; following surveys by Joseph Locke the railway was built from Haughley Junction, north of Stowmarket, direct to Norwich via Diss but by-passed Eye some three miles to the west of that town. The line was opened in stages, initially for goods traffic to Finningham from 7th June 1848, then to Burston for goods on 11th June and passengers from 2nd July 1849, with completion to Norwich Victoria by 7th November 1849.

While the main routes from London to Norwich via Cambridge and Ipswich were now established, a vast acreage of East Suffolk was devoid of railways. This was rectified when a local venture, the Halesworth, Beccles & Haddiscoe Railway, obtained powers to construct a line connecting the river ports of Halesworth and Beccles with the Reedham to Lowestoft line of the Norfolk Railway. The following year it was empowered to enter into a working agreement with that company and subsequently opened to goods on 20th November and passenger traffic on 4th December 1854.

Within three months of the line from London via Bishop's Stortford, Cambridge and Ely to Norwich opening on 30th July 1845 a meeting was called at Yarmouth Town Hall to examine why it took seven hours to travel by rail from Norwich to London compared with the four hours from Exeter to London, nearly twice the distance. The outcome was a proposal for a Waveney Valley & Great Yarmouth Railway, the line joining the embryonic EUR line from Colchester to Norwich near Diss, serving the valley as well as enhancing Yarmouth's importance. This scheme was successor to the previous year's ill-fated Diss, Beccles & Yarmouth promotion. If the Ipswich to Bury scheme failed to reach Diss, the new Yarmouth Company proposed to build its own line to Haughley. Palmer, the Mayor, hoped Yarmouth would be the Liverpool of the east coast whilst other speakers pointed out that Southampton's trade as a port had risen from 200,000 tons a year to over 3,000,000 tons after the coming of the railway. Despite the brave talk no decision was made on progressing the scheme pending the development of other railways in the area. Local finances were scarce in East Anglia and already the ECR had had to rely on heavy support from Lancashire. Opposition came from the Norfolk Railway, which had been formed on 30th June 1845 by the amalgamation of the Yarmouth & Norwich and Norwich & Brandon railways. Another scheme mooted was a line from Bungay to Yarmouth following the lower Waveney Valley as part of a Suffolk South Coast Railway. Yarmouth fishing interests hoped to distribute their wares to the villages and towns but again nothing came of the plans.

Despite the initial opposition on 23rd October 1846 a meeting was held at the Star Inn at Yarmouth to promote the Waveney Valley & Yarmouth Railway. Under the chairmanship of R. Hammond it was agreed to seek authority for a railway from the Norfolk Railway at Reedham, passing by way of Beccles and Bungay to join up with the EUR, together with a proposed branch line from Bungay to Harleston. The Norfolk Railway was to create new stock for the venture of 2,000 shares at £20 each. Progress was rapid for the plans and prospectus were deposited with the Clerks of the Peace for Norfolk and Suffolk on the last day of November, by which time the Waveney Valley & Yarmouth scheme had been absorbed by the larger party.

The Norfolk Railway, Reedham & Diss Branches Act authorising the construction of the line received the Royal Assent on 25th June 1847 (10 and 11 Vict cap lxiv) and granted the company powers to raise £430,000, of which some shares were to be made available to the shareholders or script-holders of the Waveney Valley & Great Yarmouth Railway, together with borrowing powers not exceeding one third of the amount of the share capital authorised by the Act. The statute sanctioned the building of a railway commencing by a junction with the Lowestoft Railway in the parish of Raveningham in the County of Norfolk and terminating with the line of the Norwich Extension of the Ipswich & Bury St. Edmunds Railway as authorised to be made, in the parish of Palgrave in the County of Suffolk. The Act also gave powers for a branch railway commencing in the parish of Beccles in the County of Suffolk near the north-east side of the town of Beccles and terminating in the parish of Halesworth and Holton or one of them near the town of Halesworth in the County of Suffolk. Clauses xvi, xvii, viii, xix and xx stipulated requirements when crossing the River Waveney, whilst clause xxiii granted the Ipswich & Bury St. Edmunds Railway, later EUR, running powers over the completed line.

Level crossing were authorised in the following parishes, at which the company was required to maintain stations or crossing keeper's lodges.

Parish or Hamlet	Road Numbers
Palgrave	68
Stuston	4
Scole	8
Billingford	6
Thorpe Abbots	22
Brockdish	1 and 30
Needham	75 and 90
Redenhall with Harleston	46, 51, 78 and 111
Wortwell	2, 58 and 96
Alburgh	1
Earsham	49, 70, 82 and 102
Ditchingham	16 and 35
Broome	1
Ellingham	14, 20 and 29
Geldeston	11
Gillingham	49
Beccles	1, 7, 13, 29 and 41
Toft Monks	32 and 38
Thurlton	14
Weston	14

Three years were allowed for the compulsory purchase of land and five years for the completion of works, with actual construction work commencing twelve months after the passing of the Act.

Unfortunately the grandiose plans came to nothing and whilst Beccles and Bungay had water transport by 1850, only Diss had railway connections. In the same year the EUR management deposited plans for a line from Tivetshall to Bungay, there dividing with one branch going on to Beccles and Reedham and the other to Halesworth, but nothing came of the venture. Local landowners, farmers and tradesmen of Harleston and district were distraught at the possible loss of trade and in December 1850 a meeting was arranged in the Corn Hall at Harleston to engender support for a branch line to Tivetshall on the EUR Ipswich to Norwich line. The promoters advertised their intention to introduce a bill to construct a railway from Tivetshall to Bungay and from there to Beccles with branches from Bungay to Halesworth and from Bungay to the Lowestoft Railway at Raveningham. In the cold light of day, however, these ambitious schemes were severely pruned.

The plans and books of reference were deposited with the Clerk of the Peace for the County of Norfolk and his counterpart for the County of Suffolk, and with the various parish councils through which the line was to pass on the last day of November 1850. The Waveney Valley Railway Act 1851 (14 and 15 Vic cap lxvi) received the Royal Assent on 3rd July 1851 and authorised the building of a railway commencing at or near the Tivetshall station of the Eastern Union Railway in the Parish of Tivetshall St. Margarets in the County of Norfolk and passing through the parishes or places of Tivetshall St. Mary, Pulham St. Mary Magdalene, Pulham St.

ANNO DECIMO QUARTO & DECIMO QUINTO

VICTORIÆ REGINÆ.

****

Cap. lxvi.

An Act for constructing a Railway from the *Tivetshall* Station of the *Eastern Union* Railway to *Bungay* in *Suffolk*. [3*d July* 1851.]

WHEREAS the making of a Railway from the *Eastern Union* Railway at *Tivetshall* to *Bungay* in *Suffolk* would be of great public Advantage: And whereas the Persons hereafter named, with others, are willing, at their own Expense, to construct the said Railway, but they cannot do so without the Authority of Parliament: May it therefore please Your Majesty that it may be enacted; and be it enacted by the Queen's most Excellent Majesty, by and with the Advice and Consent of the Lords Spiritual and Temporal, and Commons, in this present Parliament assembled, and by the Authority of the same, as follows:

I. That "The Companies Clauses Consolidation Act, 1845," "The Lands Clauses Consolidation Act, 1845," and "The Railways Clauses Consolidation Act, 1845," as far as the Provisions of those Acts are not altered or otherwise provided for by this Act, shall be incorporated with and form Part of this Act. Provisions of 8 & 9 Vict. cc. 16. 18. & 20. incorporated with this Act.

II. That in citing this Act for any Purpose it shall be sufficient to use the Expression "The *Waveney Valley* Railway Act, 1851." Short Title.

[*Local.*] 11 *B* III. That

Front page of the Waveney Valley Railway Act of 3rd July 1851.

Mary the Virgin, Starston, Redenhall-cum-Harleston, Wortwell, Alburgh, Denton and Earsham all in the County of Norfolk and Bungay Holy Trinity in Suffolk to terminate in the last-named parish in a field near the road leading from Bungay to Halesworth.

The line was authorised to cross the following public roads by level crossings.

Parish	Road Numbers
Tivetshall St. Margarets	6a, 16, 19, 29 and 45
Tivetshall St. Mary	3
Pulham St. Mary Magdalene	20
Pulham St. Mary the Virgin	26 and 36a
Starston	18
Redenhall-cum-Harleston	12 and 59
Wortwell	1, 36 and 69
Alburgh	1
Earsham	12, 28, 37, 42 and 49
Bungay Holy Trinity	13

By clause xix of the statute the company was required to build stations or lodges for crossing keepers at all these crossings, or

ANNO DECIMO SEXTO & DECIMO SEPTIMO

VICTORIÆ REGINÆ.

Cap. cxliv.

An Act to enable the *Waveney Valley* Railway Company to extend their Railway from *Bungay* to *Beccles*. [4th *August* 1853.]

WHEREAS an Act was passed in the Session of Parliament held in the Fourteenth and Fifteenth Years of the Reign of Her present Majesty, called "The *Waveney Valley* Railway Act, 1851," and by that Act the *Waveney Valley* Railway Company were incorporated, and were authorized to make a Railway from the *Eastern Union* Railway to *Bungay* in *Suffolk*: And whereas the Company are proceeding to carry into execution the Powers of the said Act: And whereas the Extension of the said Railway to join the *Halesworth, Beccles, and Haddiscoe* Railway at *Beccles* would be of great public Advantage: And whereas Plans and Sections of the proposed Railway showing the Line and Levels thereof, and also Books of Reference to the Plans, containing the Names of the Owners or reputed Owners, Lessees or reputed Lessees, and Occupiers of the Lands through which the said Railway will pass, were deposited in the Month of *November* last with the Clerks of the Peace for the Counties of *Suffolk* and *Norfolk*: And whereas the said Company are willing to make the said Railway, but they cannot do so without the Authority of Parliament: May it therefore please Your Majesty that it may be 14 & 15 Vict. c. lxvi.

[*Local.*] 27 *N* enacted;

Front page of the Waveney Valley Railway Extension Act of 4th August 1853.

failing that provide a proper person to superintend the operation of the gates. In the event of failure to abide by these rules the company was liable for a penalty of £20 for every offence and a daily penalty of £10 thereafter for every day the offence occurred. The following clause advised that the Commissioners of Railways could at any time require the substitution of crossings by bridges. Construction at the junction at Tivetshall was to be agreed by and to the satisfaction of the Engineer of the Eastern Union Railway and was not to interfere with the works of that railway without prior consent. By clause xxii the works were to be completed within four years of the passing of the Act.

Clause xxvi provided for the mutual working agreement of traffic between the Waveney Valley Railway and the Eastern Union Railway, whilst the following clause required the EUR to afford all reasonable accommodation and facilities at their stations for the booking of passenger and goods traffic to the new railway especially at Tivetshall. Clause xxviii granted powers for the two companies to enter into mutual contracts.

The Act authorised the raising of £80,000 to finance the building of the railway, the capital being raised in 3,200 shares of £25 each, together with borrowing powers of £26,666 once the whole of the capital had been subscribed for and the sum of £40,000 actually paid up. Four years were allowed for completion of works. The initial Directors of the company were Samuel Bignold, John George Hart, Peter Bruff, William Warwick Hawkins, John Wright, John Chevallier Cobbold and Augustus Adolphus Hamilton Beckwith, five of whom were also Directors of the EUR. Edmund Ayres, Secretary to the WVR, was also the EUR Company Secretary.

The chief engineer was Peter Bruff, also engineer of the EUR, later elected as a Member of Institute of Civil Engineers in 1856, whilst Alexander Ogilvie, a Scot who had been born in 1812 and trained under the Bridgemaster of Cheshire, was appointed as engineer of the WVR under Bruff's direction. Later Ogilvie in partnership with Thomas Brassey not only constructed the Waveney Valley line but with others was involved with the construction of the Portsmouth Direct Line, the Runcorn Viaduct over the River Mersey, and Great Eastern lines from Sudbury to Shelford and Bury St. Edmunds, as well as the first section of the Tendring Hundred Railway from Colchester Hythe to Wivenhoe. Much of his subsequent work was chiefly in Argentina but in about 1860 he purchased Sizewell House from Richard Garrett, the Leiston engineer, and it remained his home until he passed away in 1886.

The initial sale of shares was encouraging but little actual construction work was achieved as members of the board thought the existing scheme too restrictive and plans were soon developed to extend the line eastwards as originally proposed. Again the Plans and Books of Reference were distributed to the Clerk of the Peace for the County of Norfolk and his counterpart in the County of Suffolk on the last day of November 1852.

The Act authorising the WVR Company to extend their line from Bungay to Beccles received the Royal Assent on 4th August 1853. The statute, the Waveney Valley Railway Extension Act (16 and 17 Vic cap cxliv) authorised the company to build a line commencing by a junction with the authorised line of the Waveney Valley Railway at the termination at Bungay in the parish of Bungay Holy Trinity in the County of Suffolk and passing through the parishes of Bungay Holy Trinity, Mettingham, Shipmeadow and Barsham, all in the County of Suffolk, and Gillingham in the County of Norfolk to terminate in the parish of Beccles in Suffolk by two junctions with the Halesworth, Beccles & Haddiscoe Railway.

The statute authorised the company to construct level crossings over turnpike and public roads in the following parishes: Bungay Holy Trinity, roads No's 9 and 46; Mettingham, roads No's 59, 72 and 87, and Beccles, roads No's 14, 18 and 40. A carriage road was also to be constructed linking roads No's 72 and 87 on the north side of the railway in the parish of Mettingham within the limits of deviation. Gate lodges or stations were to be built alongside each of the level crossings. Two years were allowed for the compulsory purchase of land and five years for the completion of works. The work at the junction of the railway with the Halesworth, Beccles & Haddiscoe Railway at Beccles was to be made under the direction and to the satisfaction of the engineer of that company; neither was the Waveney Valley construction to interfere with the works, rights, privileges and powers of the Halesworth Company.

In carrying the railway over the River Waveney the company was required to construct bridges over the waterway to the satisfaction of the Commissioners appointed under the Great Yarmouth Haven Bridge & Navigation Act 1835 and the subsequent improvement Act of 1849, such bridges spanning the full width of the river at the point of intersection so as to leave the waterway without obstruction and the height from the river at high tide to the underside of the bridge no less than 8 feet 6 inches. The construction of embankments over the low land at each end of each bridge was to include openings, culverts or drains to ensure the free flow of any flood or back water to obviate any obstructions to the navigation. Before commencing any bridge work the company was required by clause xv of the statute to deposit plans at the Admiralty Plan Office for the approval in writing of the Lord High Admiral of the United Kingdom of Great Britain and Ireland or his commissioners. The following clause required such bridgework to be completed according to plans submitted unless subsequent alterations were authorised as agreed by the Admiral. During construction of any bridge over the River Waveney the railway company was to arrange for lights to be exhibited for the navigation and guidance of vessels from sunset until sunrise and once construction was completed good and sufficient lights for navigation and guidance of any shipping. The Lord High Admiral or his commissioners could from time to time order a local survey or examination of any of the works and if any such bridge or structure was abandoned the same office could order the demolition or part demolition so as to restore the site to its former condition.

To finance the works of the extension the Waveney Valley Company was authorised to raise an additional sum of £40,000 in £25 shares with borrowing powers of £9,000 once the whole of the new capital had been subscribed and half actually paid. Unfortunately for the promoters of the railway, investing members of the public declined to take up shares and no firm action was taken on progress until December 1853 when a local committee was established at Harleston. A contract was subsequently awarded for constructing the line but only as far as Harleston. Once the contract was awarded, contractor's men took possession of the required property and a narrow brown swathe advanced across the fairly level terrain bounded by the Beck, a tributary of the River Waveney. The formation was fenced off as progress was made towards the Pulhams, Starston and on towards Harleston. Few engineering problems were encountered so that the railway was relatively cheap to construct, costing £6,500 per mile for the first six miles.

Away from WVR affairs, but hugely important to the minor company, was the initial relationship between the EUR and ECR which was good. However, this eventually soured with the extension of the EUR line from Haughley to Norwich, which finally reached the cathedral city in December 1849 in direct competition with the ECR route via Cambridge. A revenue pool for the London to Norwich traffic was negotiated but the ECR required unjustifiable ratios to which the EUR objected. By March 1851 the rift was extreme and subsequently the ECR declared its intention of destroying the EUR traffic, and through bookings to Colchester were refused except at rates totally punitive to the Suffolk company. The ECR even resorted to sending goods traffic to their own railheads before carting commodities across-country by road to EUR destinations. The effect was disastrous to the EUR, for although receipts increased, expenses also mounted from 49 to 60 per cent and by 1853 the capital debt of the company could not be supported. Thus on rather forced terms the working of the EUR was taken over by the ECR on and from 1st January 1854 under a tripartite agreement made on 13th December 1853, also involving the Norfolk Railway; the ECR shared profits on the ration 5 to 1 to 1 with the other companies, after deducting expenses at the actual rate on its own lines and 46 per cent on the EUR and Norfolk lines. The EUR objected to some of the terms but, subject to only minor adjustments, the arrangements were ratified by Act of Parliament dated 7th August 1854 (17 and 18 Vic cap ccxx).

To the east of the embryonic WVR and also of strategic importance was the Act of Parliament obtained on 3rd July 1854 authorising the Halesworth, Beccles & Haddiscoe Railway to change its name to the East Suffolk Railway with powers to extend to Woodbridge to connect with the projected EUR Ipswich to Woodbridge line, plus branches to Leiston, Framlingham and Snape Bridge. Samuel Morton Peto, who was a leading advocate of the ESR was also involved with construction of the WVR together with Thomas Brassey.

The Board of Trade inspection of the East Suffolk Railway took place on 20th November 1854 when goods traffic commenced, but the inspecting officer required remedial work, which was soon completed and the line was re-inspected on 25th November 1854 before opening for passenger traffic on 4th December.

In the meantime the WVR Directors were finding it difficult to raise capital and construction slowed until sufficient funds could be made available to finance the further purchase of permanent way materials. The decision was then made to approach the ECR and EUR for the possible leasing of the company to enable continuing construction of the railway.

At a meeting of the ECR and EUR joint committee on 6th March 1855 the Secretary reported the Bill for the WVR had been deposited and included provision for the lease of the railway to the ECR. A month later, on 5th April 1855 the ECR solicitor was asked to closely watch the progress of the bill through Parliament to ensure nothing prejudiced the interests of the company. It was further reported the WVR was to have running powers over the EUR and in return the EUR running powers over the WVR. Arrangements were being made for the WVR to be worked for 50 per cent of the gross receipts. It was stressed, however, that the local company was required to complete their line to Bungay by 5th December 1855 and the ECR was not bound to work the line until it was opened to that town. By now the EUR was in financial difficulty, the ECR was dominant in East Anglia and landowners on the WVR route were asked to accept paid up shares in payment or to rent the required land to the company for up to ten years.

The Waveney Valley Railway Act 1855 (18 and 19 Vic cap clvii), which received the Royal Assent on 23rd July 1855, granted the company powers to extend the period for the compulsory purchase of land and completion of the railway to 4th August 1856. Clause ii of the Act permitted owners, occupiers and parties aggrieved by the extension of time to have compensation for additional damage.

By the end of August the railway was completed and the engineer advised the line was ready for inspection. The Secretary duly advised the Board of Trade in early September and Lieutenant Colonel George Wynne conducted the official Board of Trade inspection of the railway from Tivetshall to Harleston on 24th September 1855. He found the single line, 6 miles 22 chains in length, commenced from a siding at the EUR Tivetshall station, and it was from that siding that the passenger trains were to be worked. There was also a connection between the WVR and the Up main line but as it was only to be used occasionally Wynne recommended the points be kept locked and only opened when required. He also opined:

> *although the arrangement may not be so convenient it certainly would be safer if this communication between the main line and the branch was to be made from the down line and I would suggest this for consideration on the Engineer of the Company.*

ANNO DECIMO OCTAVO & DECIMO NONO

VICTORIÆ REGINÆ.

****

Cap. clvii.

An Act for extending the Times granted to purchase Lands for the Part of the *Waveney Valley* Railway between *Bungay* and *Beccles*.

[23d *July* 1855.]

WHEREAS by "The *Waveney Valley* Railway Act, 1851," the *Waveney Valley* Railway Company thereby incorporated were authorized to make a Railway from the *Eastern Union* Railway to *Bungay* in *Suffolk*; and by "The *Waveney Valley* Railway Extension Act, 1853," the Company were authorized to extend the said Railway so as to join the *Halesworth, Beccles, and Haddiscoe* Railway at *Beccles*: And whereas the Time granted by the secondly-mentioned Act for the Purchase of the Lands necessary for the Works thereby authorized will expire on the Fourth Day of *August* One thousand eight hundred and fifty-five, and the Time granted for the Construction of the said Works will expire on the Fourth Day of *August* One thousand eight hundred and fifty-eight, and although Progress has been made by the Company in constructing their Railway to *Bungay*, yet the Company have not yet been able to commence the said Extension to *Beccles*; and it is expedient that further Time should be granted to them for purchasing Lands for that Purpose: But inasmuch as these Objects cannot be effected without the Authority of Parliament,

[*Local.*] 28 *M*

Front page of the Waveney Valley Railway Act of 23rd July 1855.

The inspector noted the bridges were substantially constructed, the permanent way well laid and *'other works connected with the safe working of the line completed'.* Wynne recommended the sanctioning of the opening of the line, having been handed a letter from the engineer undertaking that the line would be worked by one engine in steam.

Edmund Ayres, the WVR Secretary, wrote to the ECR from his office at Ipswich on 26th September advising that the government inspector had authorised the opening of the line and his Directors wished to commence services on 1st October. The subject was discussed at the ECR/EUR joint meeting the following day when the Secretary reported that despite repeated applications he had not received copies of the WVR agreement until 25th September. After a brief discussion it was agreed the opening of the line would be postponed pending further enquiries.

Ayres replied on 29th September that the agreement between the two companies was to commence on 1st October and the late delivery of the working agreement was onerous.

> *I had a meeting with the directors of the WVR on the 18th instant at which the solicitor reported that in consequence of copies of the agreement furnished to your solicitor nearly two years since and having been mislaid – duplicates were prepared and delivered early in the day on 19 September prior to the meeting of the Traffic Committee and at your request the WVR solicitor waited in your offices several hours in case further information was requested. The company was so anxious to open the line that the WVR secretary wrote to the engineer to give information regarding the condition of the line, which might be required on 20 September. The engineer stated on the previous day he had a meeting with the ECR General Manager, Mr Moseley upon the contents of the agreement and duplicates were handed to him. Under the circumstances the agreement furnished to your solicitor two years ago and considered and acknowledged under the amalgamation agreement of the ECR and Norfolk Railway assumed the resolution was passed by the ECR board on 27 September was passed in entire ignorance of the facts.*

He reiterated the BOT had sanctioned the opening of the line on and from 1st October and as only one locomotive was required to work the traffic he pressed for reconsideration as the delay in opening was depriving local traders who were complaining of hardship and loss to their businesses. The subject was discussed by the ECR board on 4th October and the following day J.B. Owen, the ECR Secretary, replied dismissing who was at fault and stating the ECR would now consider the agreement and not the EUR and reminded the WVR Directors that his company was not bound to work the line until Bungay was reached which was scheduled for 31st December. If the ECR/EUR amalgamated company was to work the Tivetshall to Harleston portion of line it was to be upon new terms irrespective of the agreement. The ECR solicitor was instructed to take the opinion of counsel regarding the working liability of the WVR at 46 or 50 per cent or at cost.

On 9th October 1855 Edmund Ayres replied, *'regretting the disposition of the ECR'* in departing from the basis of the agreement made with the EUR. In future the company would refuse to negotiate with the ECR Directors and only negotiate with their EUR counterparts! At the EUR board meeting held at Ipswich on 12th October the Secretary reported of the dispute between the ECR and WVR regarding the opening on 1st October because the line to Bungay was unfinished. He reported that work on the Harleston to Bungay section was now proceeding after the state of the money market and difficulty with landowners had effectively delayed construction and caused the completion date to be deferred until the summer of 1856. The EUR Directors asked the Secretary to reply to the ECR expressing regret and that there appeared to be a desire to depart from the spirit of the agreement with the WVR. In the letter sent the following day the ECR Directors were asked to reconsider the opening of the Tivetshall to Harleston section of line without delay.

At their meeting on 16th October 1855 the ECR Directors' meeting heard from solicitors regarding the working cost of the WVR and suggesting any loss be shared by the three companies ECR, EUR and WVR as per the agreement which had not been put to counsel. The General Manager reminded the Directors that Tivetshall to Harleston, 6½ miles in length, was ready to open to traffic; work on Harleston to Bungay section, 7 miles, had commenced as land sales had been negotiated, and Bungay to Beccles, 7 miles of single line, was in abeyance. At Beccles the East Suffolk Railway offered accommodation to Norwich, Yarmouth, London and Peterborough, and as soon as that company completed the line to Woodbridge it would provide a second outlet for traffic from Beccles reducing the proposed WVR route to third choice. The distance from London to Tivetshall was 100 miles and from Tivetshall to Norwich 13½ miles. The routes from London upon completion of the WVR via Haddiscoe, Norwich and the EUR to Beccles 134¾ miles; London to Beccles via Ipswich and Woodbridge 108 miles; London to Beccles via Tivetshall and WVR 120 miles; Beccles to Peterborough via Haddiscoe, Norwich and Ely 105 miles, Beccles to Peterborough via Tivetshall, Bury and Newmarket 103¼ miles; Beccles to Peterborough via Tivetshall, the EUR and Norwich 97¼ miles; Beccles to Peterborough via Tivetshall, East Suffolk line, Woodbridge, Ipswich and Newmarket 140½ miles. Bungay, the next important town was at present without a railway and had one road coach daily to Norwich each way with an ECR waggon running four days a week to and from Tivetshall. Bungay was the centre of an agricultural district and enjoyed the facility for transit of heavy goods via the Bungay Navigation in connection with coastal vessels connecting to Yarmouth and Lowestoft and on to London and the north. The rates of carriage would have to be reduced to meet the competition. Harleston was a busy little market town 6½ miles from Tivetshall relying solely on land transport. The populations of the towns served or soon to be served by the WVR were Harleston 1,509, Bungay 3,841 and Beccles 4,398, making a total of 9,748. According to the agreement the revenue to be earned by the existing line was divided 50 per cent to the Waveney Valley Company and 50 per cent ECR which included permanent way maintenance. Should the expenses exceed 50 per cent the EUR and Norfolk companies would doubtless claim two-sevenths of the Waveney Valley traffic brought on to the main line notwithstanding that the ECR had lost 5 per cent or more in working the junction at Tivetshall. The solicitor was of the opinion that when the WVR opened throughout to Beccles the 50 per cent of gross receipts would be insufficient to cover the working charges and interest on capital of the rolling stock utilised. He also inferred that the running powers over the EUR granted to the WVR in the Act of Parliament might be used to disadvantage against the ECR.

On 30th October 1855 it was announced the WVR Directors and shareholders were disappointed the section of line to Harleston had not been opened. The shareholders were advised that on the previous Friday and Saturday a deputation had met with the EUR Directors and asked for that company to work the line, but as the board had parted with their rolling stock it was not possible to work the line. The Secretary had written to the ECR but as no reply had been received it had been agreed between the EUR and WVR to cancel the opening. However as the ECR Directors had decided to work the line on the original fixed terms of 50 per cent of gross receipts, these terms were to be irrespective of the agreement. The WVR Directors wrote asking the ECR to work the line for a period of twelve months by which time the extension to Bungay was expected to be completed and opened on the terms settled by Robert Stephenson, acting as arbiter, or if preferred by the ECR

Earsham level crossing No. 64 looking south along station road with the Down starting signal standing sentinel by the gates. The edge of the canopy on the station platform is to the right.
Author's collection

board upon a fixed percentage of goods receipts, the figure to be agreed. It was now desirous to open the line as soon as possible.

On 2nd November 1855 Owen replied and expressed regret in not replying earlier because of pressure of work. He iterated the ECR company had never refused to ratify the earlier agreement but the percentage cost of working the 6 mile line was more than for working a greater mileage. The company did not wish to go to arbitration but desired to make a profit out of the line before the opening to Bungay. The Directors therefore agreed to the ECR working the line at cost price for a period of twelve months until the Bungay extension was completed.

The WVR Company was quite adamant on the EUR agreement that the line from Tivetshall to Harleston was to open on 1st November. The ECR, however, refused to operate on the terms proposed as the line was unfinished to Beccles. Harleston to Bungay work had commenced but landowners were being difficult and it was not expected to open until the summer of 1856. A letter from the WVR to the ECR dated 30th October 1855 again expressed dissatisfaction on the non-opening of the line from Tivetshall to Harleston. The EUR had been asked to work the railway but as they had no rolling stock they were not legally bound to operate. The Bungay line agreement would be cancelled and it was suggested the ECR operate the WVR for a period of twelve months until the Bungay section was completed, when the agreement would be terminated.

Frustration set in and on 17th November 1855 Ayres advised he had consulted the Directors that they had no objection to the ECR fixing the maximum percentage at 75 and to seek arbitration if this was unacceptable. Ayres reiterated the line from Tivetshall to Harleston was ready for immediate use. Two days earlier on 15th November 1855 it had been announced a meeting would be held the next Friday regarding the WVR agreement and on 23rd November the letter dated 17th November proposing the revised working agreement of 75 per cent ECR and 25 per cent WVR was accepted by the ECR board.

The WVR finally opened their line between Tivetshall to Harleston on 1st December 1855 with three intermediate stations: Pulham Market, Pulham St. Mary and Starston. Each station had attractive brick buildings of a standardised pattern, probably to the design of Peter Bruff EUR Engineer and Frederick Barnes Ipswich Architect; similar designs were used on the Tendring Hundred Railway at Great Bentley, Hythe and Kirby Cross. Harleston at the time had a weekly market on Wednesdays as well as three annual fairs: one for sheep, another for Scottish cattle sales, the third for general items. A gas works had been erected in town in 1840. The initial timetable offered six mixed trains in each direction calling at the intermediate stations only if required, with the ECR providing the locomotive and rolling stock out of the allocation allotted to the EUR. It was originally intended the EUR would work the line for 50 per cent of receipts but with the absorption by the ECR the new company as expected operated the line at 75 per cent of receipts and even retained the balance to settle disputed debts. The local Directors were infuriated and Ayers subsequently submitted an official complaint. The ECR Directors considered this at their meeting on 13th December 1855 and were reminded the company was working the line for 75 per cent of gross receipts. After due consideration they decided to retain the rate but agreed to provide two-weekly accounts to the WVR board. On the same day, in connection with the conveyance of Royal Mail to Harleston, Bungay and Beccles, it was agreed that GPO guards would be allowed to travel from Tivetshall to Harleston paying the fare as Second Class passengers but with no liability to the ECR.

'J15' Class 0-6-0 No. 65471 makes heavy weather of a permanent way special train approaching Bungay whilst en route to Beccles. *Dr I.C. Allen*

2

Extension to Bungay

THUS THE NEW RAILWAY SETTLED down to provide a service to the local community, but on 3rd April 1856 the ECR considered a letter received from Mr Ayres, the WVR Secretary, dated 12th March 1856 complaining of the lack of furniture at Pulham St. Magdalen (*sic*) station and claiming the ECR company should provide the furniture as part of the agreed plant to enable efficient working of the line. The letter was passed to the ECR solicitor for action and on 8th April he replied to the effect that the WVR was not bound to provide moveable items of equipment under articles 3, 4, 6, 8 and 9 of the agreement dated 17th September 1852. On 22nd March 1856 a dispute also arose with regard to the weighing machine supplied to Pulham Market station, as to whether the WVR was liable to provide fixed assets at their cost price. The ECR Directors at their meeting on 1st May 1856 authorised the provision of furniture required under a temporary agreement.

ANNO DECIMO NONO & VICESIMO

VICTORIÆ REGINÆ.

****

Cap. cxxix.

An Act to revive and extend certain of the Powers of the *Waveney Valley* Railway Company with relation to their Railway. [29th *July* 1856.]

WHEREAS by "The *Waveney Valley* Railway Act, 1851," (14 & 15 Vict. c. lxvi.) the *Waveney Valley* Railway Company were incorporated, and were authorized to make a Railway from the *Eastern Union* Railway to *Bungay* in *Suffolk*: And whereas the Company have completed and opened to the Public so much of the Railway as is situate between the *Eastern Union* Railway and *Redenhall-cum-Harleston*, but they have not purchased all the Land which is required for constructing, nor have they as yet constructed, their Railway between *Redenhall-cum-Harleston* and *Bungay*, but the Powers granted to the Company by the said Act for the compulsory Purchase of Lands and for making the said Railway having expired, it is expedient that those Powers should be revived and extended: And whereas by "The *Waveney Valley* Railway Extension Act, 1853," (16 & 17 Vict. c. cxliv.) the Company were authorized to extend their Railway from *Bungay* to *Beccles*, and the Fourth Day of *August* One thousand eight hundred and fifty-five was the Time limited by the same Act for the compulsory Purchase of Lands by the said Company, which Period was extended by "The *Waveney Valley* Railway Act, 1855," for a

[*Local.*] 22 *N* Year;

Front page of the Waveney Valley Railway Amendment Act of 29th July 1856.

All was not well on the new railway for on 23rd July 1856; the ECR Traffic Committee were advised that the Secretary of the WVR had written complaining of the poor train service provided but the Superintendent said in his opinion there were sufficient trains to meet the requirements except on Mondays when a connecting service from Harleston to Tivetshall to connect with a London train was to be restored. The Secretary replied to the WVR that his company was quite prepared to put on additional trains provided they were remunerative.

The local company were finding it extremely difficult to finance the undertaking and were again forced to go to Parliament. The Waveney Valley Railway Amendment Act 1856 (19 and 20 Vic cap cxxix) received the Royal Assent on 29th July 1856 and noted that the Company had not purchased all the land or completed construction of the line between the parishes of Redenhall-cum-Harleston in the County of Norfolk and Bungay Holy Trinity in the County of Suffolk. Clauses I and II of the statute revised the time for compulsory purchase of land referred to in the Waveney Valley Railway Act 1853 to 31st August 1857, and for land mentioned in the 1855 Act to 31st August 1858. The latter date was also the revised date for the completion of the railway.

On 7th August 1856, James Robertson, the Superintendent, advised the ECR Directors that Archdeacon Bouverie of Harleston with others had complained of the recent timetable alterations to the Harleston to Norwich services. He had suggested the provision of a train between 9.00am and 11.00am but the Superintendent reported that revenue earned by the noon Down train in May and June was 15s 2d equal, to the rate of one halfpenny per train mile whilst earnings on the 1.00pm Up train including the ECR proportion was £15 0s 10d equal to 11¼d per train mile. Because of the poor earnings of the former both trains had been withdrawn from the timetable on 1st July 1856. The subject was again raised at the Directors' meeting on 4th September when the Superintendent reported continuing complaints from Harleston travellers and suggesting that the trains be terminated at Norwich Victoria, which was almost unused. The WVR Secretary had also written on 7th August regarding the poor services provided by the ECR and the lack of trains. Traffic was not greater on the branch because of the limited facilities offered and Ayres considered additional trains could have been operated as the engine lay idle in steam on the branch for many hours. He stated the agreement with the EUR and temporarily adopted by the ECR was that best endeavours would be made to develop through and local traffic for which the ECR would receive three-quarters of the receipts. There had been no restoration of the Monday morning service from Harleston to connect with the London train at Tivetshall and it was quite hopeless to expect an increase in traffic unless reasonable facilities were offered. In mitigation, the Traffic Superintendent countered that earnings on the new Harleston branch line were extremely poor. In the two months of May and June 1856 four trains were operated in each direction making eight trains in all. Of these eight trains, four recorded abysmal receipts: the 12.00 noon Down earning a total of 15s 2d, earnings of 0½d per train mile; the 8.10pm Down £1 1s 2d, at 0¾d per train mile; the 1.00pm Up £15 0s 10d at 11¼d per train miles; and the 9.15pm Up train £6 9s 11d at 4¾d per train mile. The Monday morning train from Harleston to Tivetshall had in fact been reinstated during the month of August, the fault lying with the printer who had omitted it from the printed and exhibited timetables!

On 17th September 1856 the WVR Directors advised the ECR board that they wanted a split in the presentation of receipts between local and through traffic passing to and from the branch stations and stations beyond Tivetshall, the split between coal and goods traffic gross tonnage, and details of the number of passengers travelling from each station. The solicitor advised the ECR Directors on 18th September 1856 that the agreement between the EUR and the WVR was now binding to each company. On the same day the board considered a letter dated 12th September received from Mr Ayres the WVR Secretary complaining that only local traffic receipts were credited to the branch and through traffic was not credited. He also considered the branch timetable was extravagant because of the inconvenient times of the ECR which caused the lack of through traffic to and from their line. The WVR had a right to expect a more convenient service for their trains and cited from Harleston to Norwich there was no through service from 7.35am until 3.20pm without entailing a two-hour wait at Tivetshall. In the reverse direction there was no service before 3.15pm which did not entail a similar wait at the junction station. It was desirous that these bad arrangements were rectified by a train which connected with the 11.20am Up train from Norwich, which instead of standing nearly two hours at Tivetshall could run to Harleston and return to connect with the Down Parliamentary train offering an arrival at Norwich at 1.30pm. The Directors requested Robertson the Superintendent to advise.

At the Directors' meeting held on 2nd October 1856 the ECR Superintendent reported that the revised timetable showed a morning train departing Harleston at 7.35am instead of 9.00am with an earlier arrival time in Norwich at 8.50am instead of 10.20am. It was noted that late running incurred by main line services resulting from delays sustained at five other junctions en route culminated in trains being well behind schedule at Tivetshall Junction. As the report on the branch was still awaited the Superintendent was instructed to carry out the WVR company suggestions and on 14th October reported additional services were to depart Tivetshall at 12.00 noon for Harleston and return at 12.50pm for Tivetshall, both connecting with mainline services to and from Norwich.

After further correspondence regarding branch traffic the Directors on 21st October 1856 invited Ayres, the WVR Secretary, to inspect the operating and terminals financial records for the six months ending 30th June 1856. By 11th December 1856 the dispute on freight charges reached crisis point and Mr Moseley, the ECR General Manager, was instructed to report at the next Directors' meeting.

Early in 1857 a public meeting was held at Bungay to urge for the extension of the WVR from Harleston to Bungay. The *Suffolk Chronicle* reported that as the line from Tivetshall to Harleston had cost only £6,500 per mile to construct, it had proved one of the *'cheapest lines in the Kingdom'*. The extension was seen as important providing a cross-country link to the coast, Bungay and Earsham having important mills served by the Waveney navigation. Completion of the route by Thomas Brassey was seen as a means of securing an important east–west route to join up with the line being constructed to Beccles by Sir Morton Peto. After detailed discussion the promoters advised that £15,000 would be required from the local inhabitants, with the company finding the balancing amount.

At the WVR proprietors' meeting held at the end of February, the gathering was informed that company matters were far from satisfactory. The *Suffolk Chronicle* reported on 3rd March:

> *Traffic arrangements had not been as satisfactory as they might have been, either as regards passengers or goods. By the discontinuance of market tickets, a considerable loss had been sustained by the company despite the directors remonstrating against the policy adopted by the Eastern Counties directors.*

The traffic conveyed over the line to 30th June 1856 was stated to amount to £942, from which the ECR deducted 75% for working expenses, leaving £235 to the credit of the company, *'which they had not yet received'*. On 1st April 1857 the WVR complained of high rate charges for conveyance of coal from Tivetshall to Harleston, whilst later in the month, following complaints from the station master, the toilets at Pulham Market station were repaired. Then on 2nd September authority was given for the toilets at Pulham St. Mary to receive similar treatment.

During the ECR Directors' meeting on 7th August 1857 the Secretary presented a letter from Ayers, the WVR Secretary, regarding a charge of £370 5s 10d for conveyance of materials from the EUR at Ipswich and also for materials used on the construction of the WVR. Outstanding claims for £125 and £245 for work executed in 1854 and 1855 were also submitted. The matter was passed to Mr Moseley for investigation and it was resolved the charge for carriage would be reduced from 1¼d to 1d per ton per mile.

Early in September 1857 the ECR advised the WVR Secretary that £178 14s 8d was outstanding for conveyance of materials and by 16th of the month the money had been received. In return a cheque for £500 was sent to the WVR as apportionment of traffic receipts. In the same month the WVR complained that charges for sulphuric acid traffic from Thetford to Harleston for Mr Pashley were too high when compared to road transport. On 30th September it was agreed to reduce the price to 14s 0d per ton, a comparable figure to road transport.

The *Suffolk Chronicle* for 26th September 1857 reported that a committee appointed at a public meeting at Bungay in January 1857 had met a deputation from the EUR and ECR and learned that the Directors had made a conditional contract with Brassey and Ogilvie for completing the line to Bungay. They had also arranged for the necessary amount of capital for that purpose, namely £8,000, reduced from £15,000, and if this sum was supplied by the district, immediate steps would be taken to continue the line to Beccles. A sub-committee was formed to obtain the subscriptions.

A public meeting was subsequently held at Bungay at which the EUR was represented and the sub-committee duly reported that the Town Reeve and Feoffees had resolved to offer land at Earsham in exchange for stock. Peter Bruff, the WVR engineer, stated that Mr Childs was in error saying the company must make the line in its own defence, as the interests of the EUR and ECR were now identical and it was a matter of no importance upon which line the traffic was placed. He concluded the Harleston people had raised the sum necessary to build the line from Tivetshall to Harleston and he thought there ought to be no difficulty in Bungay raising the sum required.

The subject of rates chargeable for the conveyance of grain was considered in the autumn of 1857 and after learning on 28th October 1857 that rates from Tivetshall to Chester were £1 5s 10d per ton, and to Burton £1 per ton, charges raised at the branch station were considered excessive. After due deliberation the ECR goods manager agreed to the grain rates from Pulham Market to Burton-on-Trent being reduced to £1 1s 8d per ton from November 1857.

The WVR Secretary advised the ECR that arrangements had been made with a contractor to handle cartage and delivery at Harleston. At the same time, book-racks and shelving were required in the goods office and authority for their provision was made on 17th March 1858. Within a month the appointed contractor had reneged on his agreement including cartage to and from Bungay and he was duly relieved of his contract.

On 13th May 1858 the ECR Directors discussed the bill enabling the WVR to alter the route of their proposed line between Bungay and Beccles where the company had intended constructing the line on the Suffolk side of the River Waveney but the offer of cheaper land purchases in Norfolk led to the abandonment in favour of running the railway along the northern bank. On 3rd June the solicitors advised against objection as the new line was to the ECR's advantage and on 14th June at a special meeting at the London Tavern the ECR shareholders approved of the plan. The Bill for the new route was thrown out by the House of Lords in June 1858 on the representations of hostile landowners, who claimed the company had no capital available for the works, having been unable to issue a single share, and the powers to reach even Bungay were about to expire.

After several months of wrangling over apportionment of receipts, agreement was finally reached on 23rd June 1858 wherein the Waveney Valley Company was to have mileage and terminal charges for Tivetshall to Harleston, the ECR mileage and terminals for London to Tivetshall whilst the connecting coach service from Harleston to Halesworth was allocated to the road contractor.

The WVR requested the provision of a set of buffers for Harleston goods shed and also reported the crane in the shed was in need of repair. Authority was duly given by the ECR for the buffers and repairs to the crane on 15th September 1858. Three days later, on 18th September, the 5.00pm train from Harleston to Tivetshall collided with a flock of turkeys, killing one bird and injuring another. It was discovered the birds had entered railway property through a broken fence on the farmer's land and the railway company was absolved from responsibility. Later in the month it was reported that problems had occurred at Tivetshall as the branch engine was unable to top up with water through lack of supply from a water tank. On 29th September authority was given to transfer the water tank from nearby Diss, where the tank was surplus to requirements, to Tivetshall at a cost of £100. At the same meeting it was agreed that Mr Gibbons, timber merchant of Ipswich, could hold a timber sale in Harleston station yard provided the vendor paid a sum of £2 for the facility.

Further demands for improvements to infrastructure came at the end of October 1858 when the WVR reported that cattle pens were required at Pulham Market, where livestock traffic had increased rapidly, whilst a gate was required at the boundary between railway property and Mr Smith's maltings at Harleston. Authority was duly given for the provision of the pens and gate on 27th of the month.

By 6th January 1859 the ECR Directors agreed that costs of any opposition to new schemes, including the Waveney Valley line, should be borne by the three companies, the ECR, EUR and Norfolk Railway, with the ECR paying 5/7th of the total. On 18th of the month the WVR reported that Harleston goods office required alterations because of the necessity to employ additional staff brought about by steadily increasing traffic. On 3rd March 1859 Sir Samuel Bignold, Chairman of the WVR, applied for free passes over the ECR for the company engineer and his assistant, but after the ECR solicitor had considered the legal ramifications the request was declined on 17th March.

On 25th May 1859 the station master at Starston passed away and immediately after the funeral his widow applied to become station mistress, in all probability so that she could remain in the station house. The matter was considered on 8th June 1859 but as the lady had no railway knowledge or experience the application was refused. In the late spring of 1859 the WVR management were highly critical of the ECR that Bungay goods traffic was being conveyed by road to Beccles for onward transit and not via Harleston and Tivetshall. The matter was quickly rectified and from 27th June all traffic was routed via Harleston, although the ECR failed to inform the WVR officially until 14th September.

The early years were not easy for railway staff as relations with the local populace were often fraught with animosity between the two parties. On one occasion a local squire used to delight in incurring the displeasure of the local station master in charge of the station where he alighted, by deliberately walking along the track (after the train had departed) as a short cut to his residence. In response to the admonition of the railway official he replied, *'This part of the line is mine and I shall do what I like with it. Your company haven't paid me for it yet!'*

On Wednesday 1st June 1859 the East Suffolk Railway opened their line from Halesworth to Woodbridge, linking with the EUR line from Woodbridge to Westerfield opened on the same day, thus allowing access to Ipswich and providing another outlet for traffic off the WVR.

The Waveney Valley Railway Act (22 and 23 Vic cap cxv) of 13th August 1859 noted the railway had been opened between Tivetshall and Harleston for some time but that the company were unable to complete the line to Bungay because the time limit for the powers of compulsory purchase of land had expired. The statute by clause III revived the powers granted in The Waveney Valley Railway Act 1856 for a period of six months from 13th August to enable the company to obtain land between the parishes of Redenhall-cum-Harleston and Earsham. Clause VII authorised the company to construct a railway commencing with the authorised line at or near a public road in the parish of Earsham and passing through or into the parishes or places of Earsham, Bungay or Outney Common, Holy Trinity Bungay and St. Mary's Bungay, all in the County of Suffolk and terminating in the parish of Ditchingham in the County of Norfolk at or near Day's Corner, in a public road leading from Ditchingham to Mettingham. The company was authorised to construct a level crossing over road No. 12 in the parish of Earsham. A station or crossing keeper's lodge was to be provided by the level crossing and trains were not permitted to stand on the crossing when stopping at the station or when shunting any future adjacent siding. Clause XI decreed that at a future date the Board of Trade might require the level crossing to be substituted by a bridge.

The Act specified the powers for compulsory purchase of land were limited to a period of one year from the date of the statute, whilst the period for the completion of works was two years.

Meanwhile in early August 1859 Mr Banham the owner of a maltings at Tivetshall made application for a siding some 130 to 150 feet in length to serve the premises. The matter was considered on 17th August and finally approved on 28th September at an estimated cost of £120 to £130.

On 1st September 1859 the ECR Directors refuted the claim made by Ayres for re-ballasting. The 1855 agreement stated the ECR was to work the WVR at 75 per cent of gross receipts and the claim for £150 to £200 was not acceptable. The Harleston to Bungay section was almost completed and all accounts were to be settled before that section of line opened. It was agreed detailed accounts would be sent to Ayres. Then on 6th September 1859 the *Beccles & Bungay Weekly News* reported the half yearly meeting held at Ipswich where WVR shareholders were advised the extension of the line to Bungay would soon be completed. Once the extension was opened to traffic it was the intention to request a revised working agreement with the ECR amending the operation to 50 per cent of the gross receipts.

ANNO VICESIMO SECUNDO & VICESIMO TERTIO

VICTORIÆ REGINÆ.

****

Cap. CXV.

An Act to enable the *Waveney Valley* Railway Company to extend their Railway from *Harleston* to *Bungay* and *Ditchingham*; and for other Purposes relating to the same Company.

[13th *August* 1859.]

WHEREAS an Act was passed in the Year One thousand eight hundred and fifty-one "for the making of a Railway from "the *Tivetshall* Station of the *Eastern Union* Railway to "*Bungay* in *Suffolk*," whereby the *Waveney Valley* Railway Company (in this Act referred to as "the Company") were incorporated: And whereas the Powers of that Act have been amended and enlarged by Three subsequent Acts, by One of which, namely, "The *Waveney Valley* Railway Extension Act, 1853," the Company had Power to extend their Railway from *Bungay* to *Beccles*, but they have never exercised such Power, and the same has now lapsed: And whereas the Company have long since completed and opened so much of the Railway as is situate between the *Eastern Union* Railway and *Redenhall-cum-Harleston*, and they are also in possession of the greater Part of the Land which they require for the Construction of their Line towards *Bungay*, and have made great Progress in constructing the same, but they are unable to complete that Part of their Railway because their Powers for the Purchase of Lands by Compulsion have expired, and it is expedient that such

14 & 15 Vict. c. lxvi.
16 & 17 Vict. c. cxliv.
18 & 19 Vict. c. clvii.
19 & 20 Vict. c. cxxix.

[*Local.*] 19 *E* Powers

Front page of the Waveney Valley Railway Act of 13th August 1859.

The shortening daylight hours and approaching winter heralded a complaint from passengers changing at Tivetshall of the poor lighting on the Up platform used by the WVR branch trains. The ECR duly authorised the provision of additional lamps on the platform on 12th October 1859. Later in the month it became necessary to employ additional staff at Harleston to handle the ever-increasing grain traffic. Despite the assurance made by the ECR that all Bungay traffic was being routed via Harleston, local staff reported a considerable number of goods consignments were still being conveyed via Beccles and thence by road. The chairman was asked to investigate on 26th October and reported back on 8th November that goods conveyed via Beccles amounted to less than 13 tons, thus losing the WVR £1 2s 5½d. The ECR solicitor requested the WVR to issue definite instructions as the future routing of traffic.

By early November 1859 local staff reported that the WVR Company goods office at Harleston was in a dangerous state. Remedial work authorised for completion earlier in the year had never been completed and the ECR Secretary was instructed to inform the WVR of the condition of the building and ask what repairs were to be made.

By 8th December 1859 the ECR Directors had read the draft of the bill for the extension of the WVR from Bungay to Beccles and noted W.H. Kitton of Norwich was the solicitor acting for the company. Then on 22nd December 1859 the ECR board considered a letter from Ayres regarding the share of traffic receipts from the WVR, and also the fact that no payments had been received because of the ballast dispute. The company required interest payment on the traffic revenues and non-receipt had resulted in the delay to the Harleston to Bungay work, which was blamed on the ECR. Mr Dawson of the Railway Clearing House was delegated to check the traffic accounts at the EUR offices at Ipswich. The ECR was agreeable to Dawson checking the books and agreed to future accounts being sent to the RCH for audit. Dawson duly checked the accounts on 1st January 1860 and raised queries regarding the WVR 75 per cent mileage and demurrage charges and terms of receipts with the ECR. On 1st February Moseley was asked to draft a reply explaining the arrangements.

In the meantime on 18th January 1860 the ECR board were advised that Sir Edmund Lacon, the brewer, had complained of the shortage of wagons for his barley traffic and the Superintendent was instructed to take remedial action to improve matters. Evidently the supply of rolling stock proved sufficient for no further complaints were made.

A public meeting was called at Bungay on 13th March 1860 to consider what measures were desirable for the railway to cross Outney Common. When the line was projected, the WVR Engineer had pledged it would run along the upper edge of the common. It now appeared the railway company intended to divert the line across the *'best portion'* of the common thus placing Bungay station a greater distance from the town. The *Beccles & Bungay Weekly News* reported *'it had even been stated that it was intended to have no station at all at Bungay!'* The meeting unanimously carried the resolution that the railway be carried on a route more to the south and that *'it is essential to the interests and comfort of the public that there shall be a station at the end of Broad Street'*. The resolutions were passed to the WVR Directors. They, however, had other problems for yet again, on 14th March 1860, the poor condition of Harleston goods office and urgent need for repair was raised, with complaints that this was the sixth time the issue had been reported!

On 15th March 1860 the ECR was advised of a letter received from Ayres saying that work had started on the Harleston to Bungay section of line as of that date and the line beyond Bungay was planned for opening in December. As the traffic accounts to 31st December 1859 were still under investigation the ECR replied agreeing to work to Earsham at 75 per cent of gross receipts. By 29th March, E. Ayres had replied stating the distance from Tivetshall to Earsham was 12 miles and the proposed cost of working was 50 per cent, but the ECR reiterated 75 per cent. Ayres advised his Directors of the disputed Tivetshall to Earsham line working costs and mileage. The ECR on 26th April asked their engineer for working costs of the present line and estimate costs of the working to Bungay. As no answer was received from the ECR, Ayres wrote again with the threat the WVR would work the line themselves from 1st July 1860. The board on 10th May 1860 asked Sinclair to report on the working of the WVR.

The WVR Secretary raised the question of the working arrangements and apportionment of receipts again in May 1860 and Sinclair duly reported to the ECR board on 23rd of the month that the 50 per cent of gross earnings only applied after the line was open to Bungay. Construction work was half a mile short of the site of Bungay station and agreement for the reduction from 75 per cent to 50 per cent was for the completed line within a given time and neither had transpired. The matter was placed in the hands of the Parliamentary and Project Committee for further investigation.

On 6th June 1860 the ECR announced that terminal charges for coal and minerals would be fixed at 4d per ton but the WVR were dissatisfied and requested 6d per ton, which was declined. On the same day the Railway Clearing House was instructed to continue deducting 75 per cent of gross receipts as the ECR share of earnings but the Committee strongly objected to this interference in rate fixing.

For months feelings in Bungay had been running high regarding the course of the projected railway; townsfolk wanted the line to run south of Outney Common bringing the station within the town boundary but the WVR management wanted to bisect the common. The *Ipswich Journal* added to the furore, reporting there was *'nothing more salubrious and beautiful than the remarkable peninsula caused by the loop of the river'*. Peter Bruff assured the authority that the desired conditions would be met and the owners of Outney Common intimated in late March 1860 that they would settle with the railway company on favourable terms, if not the price for land would be higher. The Directors decided in April they would not put the station where the townsfolk wanted it and claimed they were responding to the request not to pass over the land occupied by the National School. Thus by 16th June 1860 the railway construction had reached the western edge of the common, but such was the animosity felt in the district that few shares were taken up locally.

The problems raised over the re-routing of the railway at Bungay necessitated the company to yet again seek further parliamentary approval. The Waveney Valley Railway Act 1860 (23 and 24 Vic cap clvii) received the Royal Assent on 23rd July 1860 and noted that despite the passing of various Acts the line was only being operated between Tivetshall and Harleston. Construction of the remainder had reached Earsham, within one mile of Bungay, and the company was extending construction on to Ditchingham as authorised in the 1859 Act. However, powers granted in the 1853 Extension Act for the construction of the line between Bungay and Beccles had expired. The new statute by clause IV granted powers to the company to construct a line from the termination of the authorised line at Day' Corner in the parish of Ditchingham in the County of Norfolk and pass through the parishes of Broome, Ellingham, Geldeston and Gillingham in the County of Norfolk and Beccles in the County of Suffolk to terminate by a junction with the East Suffolk Railway at or near the passenger station in the parish of Beccles.

Level crossings were authorised over road No. 28 in the parish of Ditchingham, road No. 1 in the parish of Broome, road No. 27 in the parish of Ellingham, road No. 43 in the parish of Geldeston and public highway No. 14 in the parish of Beccles. Before opening the line to traffic the company was also to maintain a good and convenient footway or bridge, 5 feet in width under or over the railway by the side of Northgate Street (road No. 14) in the parish of Beccles and lower the parish road No. 25 in the parish of Beccles to enable the thoroughfare to pass under the railway. This road was to be no less than 20 feet wide with headroom of not less than 9 feet and inclinations on each approach of not less than 1 in 20. Stations or crossing keeper's lodges were to be provided adjacent to each of these crossings, whilst the BOT could at any time require the substitution of any crossing by a bridge.

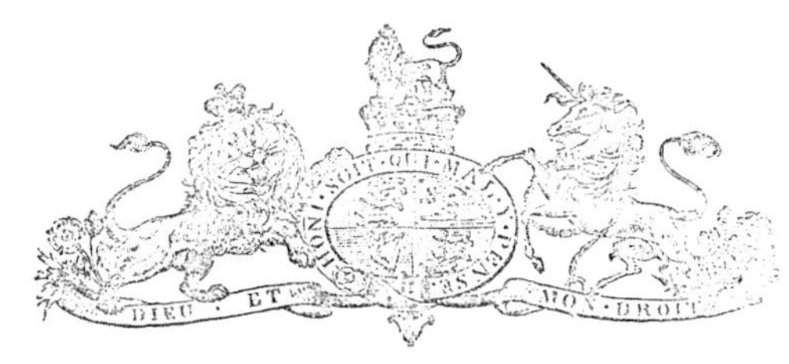

ANNO VICESIMO TERTIO & VICESIMO QUARTO

VICTORIÆ REGINÆ.

Cap. clvii.

An Act for the Extension of the *Waveney Valley* Railway from *Bungay* to *Beccles* in *Suffolk*.
[23d *July* 1860.]

WHEREAS an Act was passed in the Year One thousand eight hundred and fifty-one, called "The *Waveney Valley* Railway 14 & 15 Vict.
Act, 1851," and by that Act the *Waveney Valley* Railway c. lxvi.
Company (in this Act referred to as "the Company") were incorporated for the making of a Railway from the *Tivetshall* Station of the *Eastern Union* Railway to *Bungay* in *Suffolk*, and they have in fact constructed a Railway which has long been open for Traffic from *Tivetshall* to *Harleston*, and they have also nearly completed the Construction of so much of the Remainder of the said Railway as lies between *Harleston* and a Place in the Village of *Earsham* within One Mile of *Bungay*: And whereas by "The *Waveney Valley* Railway Act, 1859," the Company 22 & 23 Vict.
were empowered to extend their Railway from the said Place in *Earsham* c. cxv.
across *Bungay Common* to *Day's Corner* in the Parish of *Ditchingham* near *Bungay*, and they are now constructing such Extension: And whereas by "The *Waveney Valley* Railway Extension Act, 1853," the 16 & 17 Vict.
Company were authorized to extend their Railway from *Bungay* to c. cxliv.
Beccles; but no Part of such Extension has been made, and the Power to make it under that Act has expired; and it would be advantageous to the

[*Local.*] 25 *Y* Public

Front page of the Waveney Valley Railway Act of 23rd July 1860.

Clause IX of the statute required all works at Beccles to be made under the direction and superintendence of the engineer of the East Suffolk Railway, whilst the following clause required the WVR not to interfere with the works or take any lands of the East Suffolk Railway without prior written agreement. The erection of signals and the appointment of signalmen to control the junction between the two lines was to be under the exclusive management and regulation of the ESR, and any expense incurred was to be repaid by the Waveney Valley Company every six months. Any dispute between the two companies was to be determined by the BOT or an arbiter appointed by them.

Clause XIV stipulated that the bridge spanning the River Waveney constructed by the Company was to be of only two openings. Before commencing works on the bridge, clause XV required the Waveney Valley Company to submit plans, sections and working drawings to the Admiralty for the approval of the Lord High Admiral of the United Kingdom of Great Britain and Ireland. During construction of the bridge, reportedly with three 50-feet openings, each 8 feet 6 inches in height, the company was required to maintain a light from sunset to sunrise for the navigation and safe guidance of vessels, and after completion of the structure lights on or near the centre of the bridge in perpetuity for the same purpose. In the event of neglect to exhibit the lights the company was liable to a fine of £10. Clause XVII stipulated that the bed of the river where it passed under the bridge was to be kept in a good navigable state at the cost to the company. No deviation to the course of the river was to be made or the banks altered without the consent of the Admiralty. Any other works affecting the River Waveney were not to be constructed without the consent of the Admiralty and works constructed without such consent could be altered by the Admiralty at the expense of the Waveney Valley Company. Lastly, if any of the works were abandoned or fell into future decay the Admiralty had powers to remove the works and return the site to its former condition with costs recoverable from the railway company. The statute granted the company three years from the date of the Act for compulsory purchase of the necessary land and four years for completion of works.

The dispute with the ECR over working arrangements finally reached crisis point in the summer of 1860 and on 16th August, the WVR Directors gave notice they intended to work the line independently from 15th September 1860. The ECR promptly offered to reduce the working arrangement on the entire Tivetshall to Beccles line when that line was ready for passengers to 50 per cent but this was refused. At a meeting of the ECR Directors on 30th August the Directors were advised of further correspondence from Ayres regarding the outstanding ballasting issue and also the completion to Bungay for 50 percent of the operation. As the ECR had not reduced from 75 per cent for the short section Tivetshall to Bungay the WVR had no alternative to work the line independently. A further letter from Ayres on 25th August raised the question of the station staff between Tivetshall and Harleston and also the stores in hand, furniture, ticket machines, time bills and account books. He stressed the same rates and fares would be maintained. The ECR Directors replied that Maynard the solicitor would assist the WVR in any way possible to operate the services, even arranging for the transfer of station staff. All stores and equipment would be valued, the total sum being mutually agreed by 13th September. The account books would pass to the ECR and station charges were to

The ornate frontage of Harleston station in the early 1900s. The building bears similar Italianate architecture to that on the smaller stations. The covered footbridge connecting the platforms can be seen in the background. *Author's collection*

be arranged by the respective traffic managers. On 13th September the valuation of stores and equipment was agreed at £200 17s 9d and the ECR advised the WVR they would work the services until midnight of 15th September 1860.

In the meantime, on 12th September the ECR General Manager reported that a pass for the WVR manager Mr Brown had been declined. The conveyance rates for the transport of his furniture from London to Harleston had been referred to Mr Moseley whilst the use of ECR grain sacks by the WVR was declined. As a numbertaker was required at Tivetshall to record the numbers of wagons transferring between the main line and the Waveney Valley line, it was decided the RCH should provide the person. Whilst several other disputes were dealt with, Ayres reported he had sold surplus WVR stores and ticket cases, and submitted a cheque for £150 and another for £5; it also being noted with concern that owing to the shortage of materials all rails had been lifted from the sidings at Harleston for use on the running line! Instructions were subsequently issued that the track in the goods yard was to be replaced by second-hand rails.

On 26th September 1860 the ECR Superintendent requested instructions as to whether the WVR Company were to be supplied with ECR horse boxes and carriage trucks if application was made. It was decided vehicles could be supplied if any could be spared. Construction of the final section of line commenced in the summer of 1860 and Peter Bruff employed his eldest son William as assistant. William married Louisa, the daughter of Edmund Ayres, whilst the contract was in progress. Brassey and Ogilvie were again appointed contractors for the final thrust to Beccles.

Having been advised the works on the section of line from Harleston to Bungay were completed, Colonel William Yolland duly inspected the second section of the WVR on 26th October 1860. The line, 6 miles 44 chains in length, commenced at Harleston and terminated at a temporary station at Bungay. Sidings but no passing places had been provided at some of the intermediate stations and the width of the formation except at stations was 16 feet. The inspector noted the one overbridge on the line constructed of brick in cement and lime had a 26 feet square span and 27 feet 3 inches skew span. Of the four underbridges, two had brick abutments and wrought iron girders, whilst the other two were brick in cement and lime. The longest span on one of the underbridges was 25 feet on the square and 46 feet 10 inches on the skew. In addition to the underbridges there were three timber viaducts of short lengths with small openings. Yolland found the bridges and viaducts were well constructed, but the iron girder bridge with the 46 feet 10 inches span showed a strain of 5¾ inches per square inch on the sectional area with a rolling load and 1 ton per foot, which was somewhat excessive of inspecting officer's requirements. The deflections on the outside girders under the load of two locomotives, one lightweight and the other heavy, was 7⁄16 of an inch. The girders appeared to be well constructed and sufficiently strong for the rest of the permanent way, which was not adopted for high speeds or very heavy engines. The inspector concluded in his report:

I do not need to mention that the deflections observed is that of the outside girders as the roadway on the siding at Harleston over this bridge was not completed and the central girder was not in consequence tested but it is somewhat stronger by calculation than the outside girder.

During his inspection the Colonel noted goods and passenger stations, protected by station and distant signals, had been erected at Homersfield, Earsham and Bungay, and stopping places for passenger trains only at the level crossings at Redenhall and Wortwell, these being protected by stop signals. He noted that there were no unauthorised level crossings although the road over authorised No. 37 crossing was not advised as such in correspondence sent to the BOT. Yolland also remarked on the lack of engine turntables, especially where the WVR made a junction with the EUR at Tivetshall, but was not aware of any conditions stipulated when the line opened between Tivetshall and Harleston using one engine in steam. He was, however, concerned to find that up to the time the ECR ceased working the line, some two months before the inspection, the ECR operated the services with tender engines which were required to run tender first in one direction, considered an unsafe practice. Although the WVR was now working the line independently with a tank locomotive he had had occasion to comment of similar illicit workings on the Market Harborough & Northampton Railway. *'I may remark that the WVR and its extensions when completed will form a cross communication between the EUR at Tivetshall and the ESR at Beccles and these stations should be supplied with engine turntables'*. Pending the completion of the line between Bungay and Beccles, Yolland was prepared to forego the stipulation for turntables at Harleston and Bungay on the express stipulation that engine turntables were provided at Tivetshall and Beccles.

In the meantime the line may only be worked by tank engines and that every train should stop at all passenger stations and stopping places between Harleston and Bungay viz Redenhall, Wortwell, Homersfield and Earsham by which means the speed will especially be limited.

Yolland thought the line to be in fair order but he was unhappy with some deficiencies in the permanent way and asked that some fang bolts replace dog spikes. Clocks were required to be placed at each station so that they could be seen from the platform, whilst the gatekeeper's lodge had yet to be provided at the Earsham public road crossing No. 37. The WVR engineer attending the inspection advised that land had been purchased for the lodge to be erected but in the meantime a wooden hut would be provided. Certain point switches at Bungay also required double rodding. As Yolland was of the opinion the remedial work could be completed in the course of a few hours and the Chairman and Secretary had advised the line would be worked by one engine, the inspector was prepared to sanction the opening of the line between Harleston and Bungay.

The railway from Harleston to Bungay opened for traffic on 2nd November 1860, with the intermediate stations at Homersfield and Earsham being reported as being simple temporary *'comfortable and convenient'* timber structures. The *Suffolk Chronicle* for 3rd November reported, *'the extension of the line from Harleston to Bungay was opened for traffic yesterday (Friday). Bungay, hitherto somewhat isolated for want of railway communication, is now supplied with that desideratum'*. The *Ipswich Journal* added that *'work was to start immediately on the line to Beccles'*. Other intermediate stations between Harleston and Bungay at Redenhall and Wortwell were subsequently opened for traffic in January 1861.

On a winter's morning with snow still carpeted on parts of the platform, 'J15' Class 0-6-0 No. 65471 pulls into Bungay with the first Down Norwich to Beccles through train. The land behind the Up platform had been put to good use, being used as allotments by station staff. *Dr I.C. Allen*

The view from Beccles South signal box looking towards the station in October 1911. The brick-built goods shed, which had capacity for the storage of 100 quarters of grain, is prominent on the Down side of the railway with GER wagon stock stabled on the siding parallel to the Down main line, including, a high-sided open, a single bolster, a converted ballast wagon without its sides and a furniture truck. The advertisements on the side of the goods shed encourage the purchase and consumption of Lipton's tea. *GERS/Windwood 1350*

3

Opening to Beccles and Great Eastern Railway Takeover

At a meeting between the ECR and WVR on 7th November 1860 it was decided to equate the goods and coal rates on the line and the extended line was to be included in the Harleston district. It was also suggested that fares from stations between Bungay and Harleston to Norwich would be fixed as the same rate as from Harleston to Norwich by the ECR and it was agreed that the ECR would receive their proportion. The WVR representative reported the WVR was still owed 50 per cent of the through booking revenue for the four weeks ending 17th October 1860. By 21st November 1860 traffic returns had still not been received from the Railway Clearing House and the Secretary was instructed to request the details as a matter of urgency. On Monday 10th November the first accident occurred on the branch when a train collided with the level crossing gates at Five Acre Lane, west of Earsham, after the crossing keeper failed to open the barriers in time.

At a further meeting between the two company officials on 5th December the WVR representatives complained of delays incurred at Tivetshall station because of poor siding facilities and Sinclair was asked to investigate. A request that all coal traffic from Peterborough would be charged to Tivetshall, for the WVR company to take over at the junction for onward transit was agreed. The WVR requested a fares reduction from Bungay to London to prevent passengers travelling by road the 9 miles to Halesworth to join a train on the East Suffolk line and the ECR Chairman was asked to investigate. Following many complaints from passengers the ECR promised to erect canopies over the platform at Tivetshall, with Sinclair providing costs. A fortnight later, on 16th January, Sinclair provided estimates for the provision of 60 feet long canopies at Tivetshall on the branch and Up platforms costed at £150 and the Down main platform at £60.

On declaring independence the WVR resorted to hiring a locomotive and coaching stock from outside sources and initially relationships with the ECR were fairly amicable, but on 19th December 1860, when the company requested the ECR to carry out repairs to the locomotive, matters came to a head when it was realised locomotive maintenance staff would be required to carry out repairs at either Harleston or Bungay and the request was declined on 2nd January 1861. A fortnight later the request for a reduction in the cost of through fares was declined at a meeting on 16th January 1861. The WVR also requested a reduction in the cost of the conveyance of coke from Lowestoft from 5s 2d to 3s 7d per ton and from Ipswich 4s 6d down to 3s 3d per ton, but these were also declined.

At a meeting between the two companies on 30th January 1861 Sinclair reported the ECR had loaned a tank locomotive to the WVR as their own engine was under repair. Then on 14th February 1861 Ayres, the WVR Secretary, wrote to the ECR regarding the possible purchase of a locomotive but after consideration by the board the Secretary was instructed to reply that none was available. The impasse regarding motive power for the operation of the railway could not be allowed to continue and the WVR resorted to purchasing a small tank locomotive from Sharp, Stewart & Company of Manchester to maintain services.

On 13th March 1861 the ECR agreed to erect a loading gauge at Tivetshall to obviate delays to traffic interchanging between the main line and the WVR. At the same meeting the WVR, frustrated by ECR inaction, announced they were cancelling all through rates for coal traffic and charging rates from Tivetshall.

Then on 28th March correspondence from the WVR declared the company officials objected to the statement of traffic revenue for period 1st January to 15th September 1860. After yet more bickering it was agreed at a meeting on 24th April 1861 that as the Tivetshall goods traffic was worked by the ECR then that company would receive terminal credit. At the same meeting it was announced that the contract for the erection of two canopies at Tivetshall had been awarded to R. Hood who had tendered at £118 18s 0d.

The Waveney Valley Railway Act 1861 (24 and 25 Vic cap clxxi) received the Royal Assent on 22nd July 1861 and authorised the company to increase its borrowing powers by a sum not exceeding £4,334 and to reorganise the capital by re-issuing forfeited shares with preference shares giving a dividend not exceeding £5 per cent per annum and also converting the mortgage debt into debentures.

In July the WVR was asking for the provision of ECR sacks for grain traffic but were curtly refused and told to purchase their own supply. Later in the year, on 9th October 1861 consideration was given to the provision of a shunting horse at Tivetshall to assist with the smooth outsorting of wagons for the branch but it was later agreed an animal would only be provided during the harvest period. At the meeting on 4th December 1861 the WVR finally accepted the ECR claim for costs of providing the horse and the Railway Clearing House was advised accordingly. On the same date it was agreed to reduce Norwich to Bungay fares to those charged below Harleston in order to compete with charges from road coaches.

The New Year did not get off to a good start for on 29th January 1862 Mr Guyton's cow was run over and killed by a train after the gate of an occupational crossing was left open near Tivetshall. Guyton claimed compensation but this was declined as Guyton's cowhand admitted having left the gate open after driving the herd across the line an hour or so earlier to the incident.

With a view to an amicable settlement in the approaching amalgamation bill the ECR agreed with the EUR that they would pay preference charges and that they would receive £1 per cent on their ordinary stock from 1st January 1863 and two fifths of the increase of the ECR dividend over 3 per cent in all future half years.

On 13th March 1862 it was announced that negotiations were proceeding on a similar scale with the WVR.

On 29th May 1862 it was agreed the future combined company when formed would give to the EUR £50,000 stock of the Waveney Valley company on completion of that line; the terms of the takeover valued at £110,000, apportioned in £30,000 preference stock, £40,000 debentures, with £40,000 being paid to shareholders, 45 per cent of this being GER 4½ per cent stock. By 5th June 1862 it was announced the WVR Directors had agreed terms.

Having leased or taken over the working of all major railways in East Anglia, the ECR was the principal party to a scheme being prepared for the amalgamation of the Eastern Counties, Eastern Union, East Anglian, Newmarket and Norfolk railways into a new undertaking to be known as the Great Eastern Railway. The Act sanctioning the amalgamation, the Great Eastern Railway Act 1862 (25 and 26 Vict cap ccxxiii), received the Royal Assent on 7th August 1862 but took effect retrospectively from July of that year.

As construction of the railway neared completion traders at Beccles expressed concern of the possible delays to road traffic along Ravensmere and Northgate caused by the low clearance of the bridges. It was pointed out that Northgate Street was provided with a level crossing but the petition for a crossing at Ravensmere was refused. With the imminent opening of the Bungay to Beccles extension of the WVR, Sinclair reported on 12th November 1862 that it was desirable to install a siding to accommodate twelve wagons and also a turntable at Beccles. Authority was agreed at an estimated cost of £300.

The *Beccles & Bungay Weekly News* for 6th January 1863 reported that a locomotive had traversed the railway between Bungay and Beccles for the first time the previous Thursday: *'With exceptions of a few irregularities the state of the line is thoroughly satisfactory'.* On the previous Saturday the connecting points at Beccles had been permanently installed.

At the meeting of the GER Traffic Committee on 21st January 1863 the General Manager and Superintendent were delegated to provide all necessary station equipment on the WVR stations Bungay to Beccles inclusive, whilst Sinclair was instructed to make arrangements to commence working the line on receipt of the BOT certificate. At the same meeting the Post Office intimated they wished to use one train for the conveyance of the Royal Mail in each direction on the new railway throughout between Tivetshall and Beccles. The Directors agreed to the proposal subject to no deductions in annual payment, the exception being £62 per annum in respect of services on the WVR.

The WVR Secretary on 14th February 1863 gave notice to the BOT that the extension of the line from Bungay to Beccles was ready for inspection, a copy of the correspondence being sent to the GER, wherein it was hoped the railway would open on and from

General view of Bungay goods yard from Outney overbridge with 'J15' Class 0-6-0 No. 65460 profusely leaking steam as it shunts a rake of covered vans into the dock siding. The lengthy Down and Up loop lines are in the foreground with Bungay signal box to the left. No. 65460 later appeared in the film 'Postman's Knock' starring Spike Milligan, shot at West Mill on the St. Margaret's to Buntingford branch in 1961.

Dr I.C. Allen

1st March. Colonel William Yolland duly carried out the BOT inspection of the Bungay to Beccles extension of the WVR on 21st February 1863. He arrived at Beccles by special train at 12.45pm and accompanied by Peter and Willam Bruff, the engineers, Mr Fenn, the WVR land valuer, and Mr Boys, agent to the contractor, travelled to Bungay where lunch was taken. The inspection special then returned to Beccles and at every bridge the locomotive reversed over the span to test the structure. At the bridge spanning the River Waveney, a second engine was attached so the pair could test the spans for deflections. Yolland found that the section offered for inspection was 6 miles 34 chains in length with overbridges, underbridges and viaducts constructed for a single line of railway. The width of the formation on the level was 16 feet and there were two underbridges and two overbridges in addition to two viaducts and a number of timber culverts. Two of the overbridges and one underbridge were constructed of brick whilst the other underbridge had brick abutments and wrought iron girders, the largest span being 20 feet 3 inches on the skew. Yolland found one of the viaducts 37 yards in length was constructed entirely of timber and the second of 72 yards span was partly constructed of timber on piling and partly of continuous wrought iron girders. The two openings of 72½ feet span rested on timber piles and all were sufficiently strong whilst the large opening exhibited a moderate deflection. From Bungay three stations had been provided, at Ditchingham, Ellingham and Geldeston, all with sidings and the line terminated by a junction with the GER East Suffolk line at Beccles station.

The inspector reported the line was in good order but noted there was an unauthorised level crossing of a public road at Ditchingham. The railway officials attending the inspection advised Yolland that the crossing was constructed in deference to a protest the Directors received from the local authority, magistrates and residents against an overbridge. The Directors were, however, willing to build the bridge within a definite time period if they were unsuccessful in obtaining the legislation for the level crossing.

Yolland noted the permanent way on the line was of light construction but was sufficient for local traffic worked at moderate speed with *'not over heavy engines'*. Clocks had yet to be put up at the various stations so the face could be seen from the platform, whilst the distant signal at Ellingham required repositioning to bring it within view of the signalman. One or two of the timber bridges required additional work and the engineer Peter Bruff promised immediate attention. At the time of the inspection Yolland had not received in writing the undertaking as to the mode of working the single line but understood the railway was to be worked by the GER using Train Staff and Ticket. Arrangements were being made to operate the services from Norwich to Beccles, where engine turntables were already installed. In his report, Yolland noted the Company Directors were anxious to open the line for traffic on 1st March 1863 but because of the incompleteness of the works and the presence of the unauthorised level crossing he refused the opening between Bungay and Beccles because of the *'danger to the public'*.

The proposed opening of the Bungay to Beccles section, and ultimately the entire line for through traffic from Tivetshall to Beccles, was overshadowed by preparations for the celebration – with sports and fireworks, and much free food and drink for the local inhabitants – of the marriage of the Prince of Wales to Princess Alexander of Teck on 10th March 1863. However, following correspondence with the BOT and confirmation that all remedial work had been completed, the line from Bungay to Beccles opened to traffic without formality on 2nd March; the *Ipswich Journal* reporting it *'hoped the published timetable was only temporary'*.

On 4th March 1863 the Railway Clearing House and stations within the immediate area of the railway were advised that with effect from 2nd March 1863 the WVR had been taken over by the GER as per the agreement dated 29th July 1862 and that trucks and sheets lately belonging to the smaller company were to be dealt with as GER property. On the same date Sinclair was instructed to value the WVR in its entirety including rolling stock, after it was revealed that altogether some £170,000 had been expended in making the 20-mile line.

The WVR had barely settled down under its new ownership when on 5th March 1863 the 4.10pm Tivetshall to Beccles mixed train comprising a locomotive hauling five trucks and three coaches became derailed on the newly opened portion of line. The engine after derailing ran down the embankment followed by the five wagons but fortunately the carriages at the rear of the formation remained on the rails and no passengers were injured. The local enquiry into the accident concluded that the timetable allowed insufficient time for proper operation, especially of mixed trains, and on 18th March the Traffic Committee was advised that

ANNO VICESIMO SEXTO & VICESIMO SEPTIMO

VICTORIÆ REGINÆ.

****

Cap. cxc.

An Act to amend "The *Great Eastern* Railway Act, 1862," and to confer Powers in reference to the Undertakings of the *Great Eastern*, the *Waveney Valley*, the *Lynn and Hunstanton*, and the *Bishop Stortford, Dunmow, and Braintree* Railways; and for other Purposes.

[21st *July* 1863.]

WHEREAS by "The *Great Eastern* Railway Act, 1862," the *Great Eastern* Railway Company (herein-after called "the Company") were formed by the Amalgamation of several previously existing Companies, and the Acts relating to those Companies respectively were consolidated and amended: And whereas it is expedient that the Provisions of the recited Act with respect to the Redemption of the Preference Creditors or guaranteed Stocks of the Company should be amended, and that the Company should be empowered to redeem such Stocks otherwise than at Par: And whereas the Capital of the *East Anglian* Railways Company (One of the Companies amalgamated by the recited Act) at the Time of the Amalgamation consisted of One million three hundred and twenty thousand nine hundred Pounds consolidated 25 & 26 Vict. c. ccxxiii.

[*Local.*] 32 *D* Stock,

Front page of the Great Eastern Railway (Additional Powers) Act of 21st July 1863.

arrangements had been made to allow services more running time on the branch.

The repercussions of the takeover continued well into the year and on 1st April the GER Directors were advised that a letter had been received from H.L. Hudson of Harleston stating the WVR had not paid him for the land at Harleston where the station was erected and there had been no conveyancing agreement between the two parties. The matter was placed in the hands of the solicitor to reach a settlement with Hudson. Later in the month, on 15th April 1863, the Superintendent reported the WVR was proving an operational inconvenience. The line was 19½ miles in length with twelve stations exclusive of the terminal stations at Tivetshall and Beccles and the booked journey time could not be performed in reasonable time in consequence of the great number of stopping points. It was already evident that some stations were little used and he recommended trains should discontinue calling at Starston, Redenhall, Wortwell and Earsham to obviate the problem. The Directors considered the proposals and recommended that the service would continue in the short term but the plan would be adopted after further investigation and a review of the stopping pattern with a view to reducing the journey time across the branch.

It was soon very evident that goods traffic handled at Earsham, where no siding existed, was insufficient to warrant the provision of a goods shed whereas the tonnage dealt with at the recently opened Geldeston was increasing. On 24th June 1863 the goods manager duly recommended the removal of the shed from Earsham to Geldeston provided the former WVR officials raised no objections. None was received by 21st July and the transfer was made the following autumn.

The Great Eastern Railway (Additional Powers) Act (26 and 27 Vic cap cxc) of 21st July 1863 concluded legalities between the two companies for by clause 8 of the statute the Waveney Valley Company was dissolved and incorporated within the GER and all WVR Acts were repealed. The GER adopted all debts of the former company and agreed to maintain stations or lodges at stipulated level crossings. Holders of WVR preference shares were to receive a similar holding in GER capital known as Waveney Valley No. 1 preference shares. The GER was to create £18,000 stock known as Waveney Valley No. 2 preference stock entitling holders to fixed dividends of £4 10s 0d per cent per annum. Every person who immediately before the passing of the Act was entitled to one or more of the £25 ordinary WVR shares was to receive £11 5s 0d of Waveney Valley No. 2 preference stock.

'F4' Class 2-4-2T No. 67158 departing from Homersfield with a Beccles to Tivetshall train on a winter's afternoon. Passengers are enjoying steam heating in the three-coach train, although two steam leaks are exposed in the cold air. *Dr I.C. Allen*

4

Consolidation and Retrenchment

THE GER AUTHORITIES WASTED NO time in rectifying omissions on their new acquisition, for on 12th August 1863 the Traffic Committee agreed to the construction of a new gatehouse at Northgate Street level crossing, Beccles, at a cost of £150, the contract finally being awarded to R. Warwick on 15th February 1864 after he tendered at £150 12s 0d. In the meantime, on 20th January 1864, authority was given to enlarge the stables at Beccles to accommodate two horses. On the same day, Sinclair reported to the Traffic Committee that he had contacted Peter Bruff regarding the valuation of the Waveney Valley Company rolling stock but as the company had ceased to exist Bruff declared he had no authority to provide such information. The Directors again instructed Sinclair on 17th February to proceed with the valuation using his own judgement.

With the arrival of the WVR and improvements on other lines serving Beccles the junction had become a place of some importance, a fact not overlooked by the local authority. In early April 1864, the Town Clerk of Beccles wrote to the GER Board complaining of the inadequacies of the station and asking what improvements were planned. The matter was discussed on 27th April and the Secretary was asked to inform the Town Clerk that *'the Directors have given instructions for alterations to be carried out'*.

On 31st August 1864 the Traffic Committee considered a letter submitted by the Town Clerk of Beccles bringing attention to a covenant by the GER Company to construct a bridge over the railway at Beccles station and for the better provision for the comfort and safety of passengers. The matter was put to Sinclair who stated that the whole station had to be remodelled and the bridge formed part of the work in the plans being prepared. By the 26th October 1864 the plans and estimates for the rearrangement and improvements at Beccles were announced at a cost of £7,600.

Although the GER had provided a service of six trains in each direction across the Waveney Valley Branch, the residents of Earsham wrote requesting that the connection off the 11.42am train from London might be stopped at Earsham. The Superintendent was asked to investigate and as a result of his findings the Traffic Committee requested the Secretary to advise that the company was unable to comply with the request as overall there were few passengers using the station.

After a prolonged period, on 1st September 1864 Sinclair provided his inventory of the valuation of the WVR rolling stock, fixed plant and stores amounting to £6,689 11s 6d – broken down to rolling stock £5,940 0s 0d, fixed plant and tools £52 3s 4d and stores £697 8s 2d. It was resolved that the amount was to be placed to the credit of the sum paid by the GER in respect of WVR liabilities and a copy of the valuation was to be sent to Mr Ayres.

On 23rd September 1864 the Tivetshall to Beccles branch had became the first GER route to be equipped with Train Staff and Ticket working for single line working. For ease of operation the line was divided into three sections: Tivetshall to Harleston, Harleston to Bungay and Bungay to Beccles. Unfortunately the safety of the line was marred by the second accident between Bungay and Beccles when the locomotive hauling the 4.50pm Bungay to Beccles train derailed as it passed over the bridge on the Bungay side of the factory near Ditchingham, later No. 1194, dragging with it eleven trucks and two passenger carriages for a distance of 70 yards before running down the embankment.

On 9th November 1864 a claim for £51 was made by Messrs Hazard, being the purchase money and interest on 13 rods of land taken by the WVR over and above that which had been agreed and paid for. Bruff reported to the Traffic Committee on the same day that the amount of land taken amounted to only 9 rods; a compromise was made and the matter amicable settled. Later in the month, on 23rd November authority was given for the provision of a small lock-up in the goods warehouse at Tivetshall to cater for increased traffic to and from the WVR.

On the night of 24th January 1865, Beccles Junction signal box was completely destroyed by fire causing serious operating problems with trains on the East Suffolk main line and the Waveney Valley and Lowestoft branches. Then the following day the 8.20pm train from Tivetshall to Beccles had an uneventful run as far as Earsham but as it set out in the darkness for the short run to Bungay the locomotive collided with two bullocks which had strayed onto the line. The animals were killed outright but as the locomotive pushed the beasts aside the sudden impact caused a carriage on the train to derail without damage to the vehicle or injury to passengers. Within days Mr Copeman, the farmer, was claiming £60 compensation for the loss of the bullocks, which he reported strayed onto the railway because of the poor condition of the lineside fencing. Liability was strenuously denied and on 1st February 1865 Copeman was advised in no uncertain terms that the railway company Directors absolved themselves from all liability. The matter was not laid to rest for on 25th March 1865 the Superintendent reported that a solicitor, C.C. Simmons, had submitted a revised claim on behalf of Copeman of £50 for the bullocks killed.

On 12th April 1865 the Traffic Committee was advised that Mr Crisp, a maltster of Beccles, was offering to transfer coal traffic, which was presently delivered by water transport, to rail. The lease of his premises expired at Michaelmas and if the railway company would offer him wharfage accommodation at Beccles station together with a short siding then transfer would take place. Sinclair was asked to provide the necessary estimates for the provision of facilities as the adoption of rail transport would be beneficial to the GER, the work being completed in September.

Since the opening of the WVR line the lack of facilities at Ditchingham had caused problems with the handling of increasing goods traffic; on 14th June 1865, Sinclair proposed the installation of an additional siding to obviate the problem at cost of £212 and the new work was authorised by the Traffic Committee on the same day.

At the end of June 1865 some inhabitants of Beccles and the surrounding villages sent a petition to the GER asking for a train to

Postcard view of Harleston station front, circa 1906.
John Alsop collection

be run between Beccles and Halesworth on Tuesdays in connection with the 2.30pm train off the Waveney Valley line. On 4th July the Superintendent was asked to investigate whilst on the same day a request was made to provide waiting rooms on the proposed new station at Beccles. Sinclair and Robertson were asked to comment but on 2nd August declined the request for the connecting service. Earlier, on the morning of 12th July 1865 the roof of the pump house at Beccles station was discovered on fire. The fire engine from the town attended and only the roof was damaged.

On 16th August 1865 it was revealed the GER had land surplus to requirements at Beccles, which it was thought might provide a suitable site for a granary or coal wharves. The goods manager was instructed to offer the site to interested local parties on payment of an annual ground rent. Later in the month on 30th the Traffic Committee considered a letter from the Mayor of Beccles complaining that the proposed station was not of sufficient importance for the place. Sinclair was asked to estimate for the provision of a *'very large'* station to meet the requirement but in the meantime all progress was to be deferred pending the visit of Directors to view the site. No further action was taken but on 6th December 1865 the GER Executive Committee recommended the Traffic Committee take an *'early opportunity'* to visit Beccles station and arrangements were duly made for a visit to be made in the spring of the following year. In the meantime, minor alterations were made at Beccles, H. Norfor receiving the contract on 9th November 1865 after tendering at £200, later increased to £312 on 21st December.

On 23rd May 1866 the Land Agent reported that two pieces of land at Ditchingham were conveyed in June 1863 to Mr Warne as freehold, the land being copyhold with no enfranchisement made to the company. Warne was now asking the GE company to execute a deed of redemption to complete the title agreement and the matter was passed to the law clerk. On the same date the Land Agent reported that in accordance with the minutes of the EUR company and the WVR company of 30th March 1865, Messrs Hazard and M.R.R. Wood were arranging payment of £100 in respect of 1 rood and 12 perches of additional land taken from the late Mr Umpleby's estate in the Aldburgh and Denton parishes. The original claim was for £151 15s 0d as the quantity of land was 2 acres 0 rods and 22 perches and the price was £200. There was also a further claim from Messrs Leach of £27 7s 10d for solicitor's correspondence which Hazard might be able to reduce if settlement was agreed.

For some time the GER Directors were concerned that receipts at certain stations on the East Anglian line and the WVR were little in excess of expenditure and were therefore considered unprofitable. The Directors broached the subject on 20th June 1866 when the WVR results for the previous twelve months made sorry reading and future traffic growth was considered negligible.

	Receipts £	Expenditure £
Redenhall	93	86
Starston	94	80
Wortwell	86	80
Earsham	166	80

The expenditure included wages, stores and taxes only. The Superintendent recommended closure and included Earsham as it was only three-quarters of a mile distant from Bungay station. He also recommended closure of Pulham Market station as it was only three-quarters of a mile from Pulham St. Mary station. After considerable discussion the Traffic Committee finally endorsed the closure of Redenhall and Starston stations, which were close to Harleston, with effect from 1st August 1866. Ever watchful of the expenditure incurred on the branch the company also received annual reports of coal consumption at stations and were shocked to learn on 20th August 1866 that for year ending 30th June 1866 excess usage had been reported at Pulham St. Mary where 7 tons 6 cwt was consumed, almost double the average consumption. The station master was duly admonished and advised that station masters were not supplied with coal for private use.

On 19th November 1866 two heifers straying onto the line between Ellingham and Ditchingham were killed by a passing train. From enquires it transpired the animals had strayed onto the railway through occupational gates which had been left open by a boy who had been sent by his master to fetch two cows. At a meeting on 21st November the law clerk was asked to see what action could be taken against the master of the boy who had left the gate open, whilst Davis, the engineer, was to report on the provision of spring locks on the gates to obviate future incidents.

The question of the provision of the electric telegraph on the Waveney Valley line was raised at a meeting of the Traffic Committee on 27th February 1867. After due discussion the Secretary was instructed to prepare an order if no order existed, the work to be completed as soon as possible, but no action was taken.

The steady increase in traffic on the East Suffolk line to and from Yarmouth and Lowestoft, especially with longer trains and the necessity to accommodate the Waveney Valley Branch trains at the main line platforms, caused considerable congestion at Beccles at certain times of the day. The Superintendent monitored the situation over a number of weeks and found that the Waveney Valley Branch train was compelled, at considerable inconvenience to all other traffic movements, to cross the main line before entering a platform. At the Traffic Committee meeting on 27th April 1867 the Superintendent recommended the lengthening of the existing platforms by 50 to 60 feet and the provision of a separate dock platform for the Waveney Valley Branch trains to obviate the crossing of the main lines. The Directors approved of the scheme and asked the engineer to prepare plans and report on the estimated cost. On 22nd May the lengthening of the platforms was agreed after the engineer quoted the cost at an estimated £250 and this was confirmed by the board on 4th June.

Despite the provision of a siding at Ditchingham, in 1865 the goods manager and local station master requested the provision of an extension to accommodate addition vehicles; on 7th May 1867 the work was agreed at a cost of £28 10s 4d.

On 10th May 1867 the GER Directors were informed that a saving of £85 had been effected by the Traffic Department for the sixteen weeks ending 20th April 1867 by the closure of five stations in 1866, including Redenhall and Starston. It was thought additional savings could be effected by further closures, especially when stations were adjacent to one another. Three stations on the branch had been investigated together with their earnings for 1866.

	Station to the West and Mileage		Station to the East and Mileage		Total Traffic		
					£	s	d
Wortwell	Harleston	2	Homersfield	½	114	19	1
Earsham	Homersfield	3¼	Bungay	¾	169	7	2
Ellingham	Geldeston	1½	Ditchingham	1½	350	9	8

It was noted that level crossings existed at all these stations, each costing an extra £30 to £40 per annum to work. Five days later, on 15th May the Directors announced that consideration would be given to the closure of additional small stations without detriment to traffic but none on the Waveney Valley line.

The Great Eastern Railway (Additional Powers) Act 1867 (30 and 31 Vic cap cix) of 15th July 1867 recorded the cancellation of two bonds dated 12th January 1854 and 28th February 1854 for the sum of £8,000, given by the WVR to the Treasury for non-completion of works. The statute also confirmed, by clause 42, that it was lawful for the GER to maintain a single-track railway as constructed across the Bungay to Norwich road (No. 17 in the 1859 WVR Act) in the parish of Ditchingham.

In the late spring of 1867 concern was expressed at the lack of water supplies available at Tivetshall, especially after footplate staff complained it was impossible to fully replenish the locomotive side tanks or tender tanks on engines working the Beccles branch services. After due investigation the engineer on 18th July 1867 estimated the cost of enlarging the well serving the water tank at between £10 and £20. It was 20th November 1867, however, before authority was given for work to commence at a vastly increased price of between £500 and £600. This was to incorporate capacity to top up the tanks of locomotives working main line services and included the transfer of a redundant tank at Diss, where the water supply was disused. It was also agreed that the crossing keeper at Tivetshall could pump water in addition to his operational duties.

Whilst major alterations were made, minor items also required attention and after complaints from the crossing keeper and his wife it was agreed on 13th August 1867 to provide Beccles crossing gatehouse with an oven at a cost originally quoted at £4 14s 6d but revised in February 1868 to £5 16s 10d. One is left to wonder what happened in the intervening period.

In August 1867 the Electric Telegraph Company wrote to the GER, saying the company had been approached by parties at Bungay and Harleston to supply telegraphic communication along the Waveney Valley line and asking if the GER Company was prepared to pay rental on the capital. The request was considered at a meeting on 14th August 1867 and despite being raised in February was curtly declined. Within two months, however, growing pressure both from local people and railway officers stressing the benefit of the communication forced a rethink and on 9th October 1867 the question of the electric telegraph between Tivetshall and Beccles was passed to the Chief Officer for approval.

Early in 1868 a Mr Leather, who provided much traffic for the railway, requested the permission to construct a granary on railway land at Pulham St. Mary. The matter was discussed at a meeting on 8th April 1868 when the goods manager reported he was in favour of the scheme and the site was available. The work was duly sanctioned provided Leather paid the full costs of construction and annual rental of £20.

At the meeting of the Traffic Committee on 29th July 1868 the law clerk advised that an ejection threat had been made regarding a claim for £200 for a portion of land on the Waveney Valley line. He was unaware how the matter stood as papers were missing, but suggested and received approval to offer the claimant £100 in settlement without prejudice. Then on 2nd August 1868 it was revealed the land upon which Beccles station was built was in dispute of GER ownership. It was noted the East Suffolk Railway had built the station and the GER land agent advised on 15th August they wished to purchase three portions of land, but on 26th August Peter Bruff claimed the owner of approximately one acre was Sir Morton Peto. The law clerk and land agent were instructed to list all deeded properties and arrange for purchase of the disputed land.

On 20th August 1868 the GER Directors considered the claim received from Mr Ogilvie amounting to £15,215 8s 11½d for the additional work incurred on construction. The action had been referred to an arbiter with J.S. Crossley, Civil Engineer of the Midland Railway representing the GER, J.H. Tolme representing Ogilvie with T.E. Harrison of the North Eastern Railway as umpire. The basis of the claim was the loose manner in which the contract vesting the WVR into the GER had been drawn up and J.S. Valentine had been asked to unravel the claim and counter claim. After the Secretary had given a resume of the history of the line and reported the findings, it was agreed to pay settlement at £7,200 with the accrued interest of £2,000 to £3,000 waived. Then on 21st October Peter Bruff submitted a letter requesting £1,000 for outstanding services rendered after the takeover. A cheque was forwarded to the law clerk for his agreement before it was passed to the engineer.

On 27th January 1869 the law clerk advised the board he was pursuing company servants living on the Woolingham Estate at Beccles where staff in receipt of a salary were living rent free in property with a rental value. He cited three staff: Inspector Blue earning a salary of £150 per annum living in a house with rental value of £20 per annum; Inspector Brown £150 in a house valued at £14 per annum, and Inspector Tyler also earning £150 in a house worth £12 per annum. It was agreed the solution to the problem was to increase the salary of each man by £15 per annum and charge the appropriate rent.

Further problems were encountered on the Woolingham Estate where flooding had occurred. Sir Charles Clark's pumping engine was clearing water from GER property, but other remedial action had to be taken and on 17th February 1869 the engineer advised the excavation of a new culvert and a bridge to obviate the flow of water. Pumping appeared unsuccessful for on 3rd March it was suggested timber openings be inserted into the embankments at a cost of £100. A fortnight later it was reported a long stretch of the Waveney Valley line near Beccles was unfenced and cattle could stray on to a field owned by the GER and thus gain access to the permanent way. Authority was given for a fence to be erected as quickly as possible and for owners of cattle to be prosecuted if their cattle strayed on the line in future. At the same meeting a sum of £202 outstanding was paid to Thomas Brassey for works rendered on the WVR, whilst the costs of the Beccles drainage increased to £336 5s 0d. On 7th April the engineer was instructed to proceed with the drainage.

The subject of surplus railway land came on the agenda when on 9th June 1869 Mr Jeck's offers to purchase half an acre of land at Beccles was considered. The land agent was instructed to negotiate and by 30th June Jeck's land agent considered the £60 asking price to be a fair sum and the transaction proceeded. As well as disposing of land the railway company was keen to acquire property, which was of some value. On the Waveney Valley line, 4 acres of severed land sought by a land agent for the supply of GER ballast for the permanent way was initially valued at £500 but the GER land agent successfully negotiated a reduced price of £300 and the deal was transacted. Then on 15th July 1869 GER land at Beccles was thought suitable for a siding for Mr Crisp's traffic; as the cost was estimated at £404 10s 0d the Superintendent and goods manager were instructed to visit the site and make recommendations. Before a visit could be made Mr Aldred of Lowestoft complained on 11th August of the delays incurred by passenger trains at Beccles because of the lack of sidings requiring additional shunting to clear the main line of vehicles. This time the Superintendent and engineer were asked to visit and report back to the board. Crisps siding was subsequently installed at a cost of £425 with annual rental of £15.

In early October 1869 R.B. Mosse of Hadenham Lodge, Bungay, wrote to the GER authorities complaining of the train arrangements between Bungay, Beccles and Lowestoft, whereby travellers were invariably detained between 30 minutes and two hours awaiting connections at Beccles. He expressed the *'great dissatisfaction in the district'* and advised there were even proposals for a competitive omnibus service. The Superintendent was asked to investigate and duly reported to the Traffic Committee on 27th October that the Waveney Valley line was a connecting link between the Eastern Union and East Suffolk lines and as only one train operated the service, connections could not be guaranteed. The expense of running an additional engine and rolling stock on the line could not be warranted and, he concluded, *'the present arrangements are generally convenient for the surrounding district as can be arranged*

Johnson 'Little Sharpie' 2-4-0 tender locomotives were regularly used on the Norwich to Beccles train services via the Waveney Valley. Here the first of the class, No. 1, dating from October 1867, stands at Wymondham awaiting its next duty. The locomotive was placed on the duplicate list as No. 01 before withdrawal in 1913. *LCGB/Ken Nunn*

with one engine and with regard to the economic working of the line'. Mosse was duly advised accordingly.

At the close of the year the Traffic Committee considered a complaint from a Mr Andrews on 8th December 1869 regarding a culvert at Beccles near London Road crossing being partially blocked, which after heavy rain caused his parents farmhouse known as Gravel Pit Cottage to be flooded to ceiling level. The law clerk was instructed to investigate liability and on 22nd December he reported the GER company was not liable. However, the railway company response was not accepted and the matter was raised on 23rd November 1870 when it was reported the cottage had been flooded on a number of occasions beginning in 1857. The law clerk was again asked to investigate and although his report is not recorded, on 4th January 1871 the engineer was asked to quote the cost of remedial action and take all necessary action to obviate the problem.

After yet further complaints regarding of the lack of communication on the branch, the Electric Telegraph Company was finally asked to provide estimates and advised on 19th January 1870 the cost of providing the telegraph on Waveney Valley line was £286. The Directors initially recommended the matter be placed in abeyance but when reminded that provision of the asset had been constantly curtailed or cancelled, had a change of heart and approved of the scheme. Then on 29th April 1870 it was agreed to remove the cattle pens at Pulham St. Mary goods yard as they were no longer used, and extend the siding in the vacant space at a cost of £8.

At the end of June 1870, Steward, Patterson & Finch, brewers of Norwich wrote to the GER General Manager advising they had applied for a licence for a *'new and commodious house'* abutting the line at Tivetshall station which they had built *'for the purpose of a refreshment room for the comfort of passengers arriving at the junction together with large stables'* and asking the GER company to endorse the application for the licence. Robertson, the Superintendent, reported on 6th July that the inn would supply the accommodation required at Tivetshall Junction and fully supported the opening of the establishment. The Directors duly endorsed the petition and passed the document to the goods manager to negotiate with the brewers.

In August 1870 Mr Edwards of Homersfield made application to erect an open-sided coal shed measuring 30 feet by 15 feet for his coal traffic in the station goods yard. The matter was considered on 31st August 1870 and, as the engineer and goods manager approved, authority was given for the building to be constructed, providing the work was completed to the satisfaction of Davis, the engineer, and with the rent fixed at £1 per annum.

Despite earlier attempts to improve locomotive water supplies at Tivetshall and Beccles the replenishment of engines was still far from satisfactory and on 6th July 1870 it was reported the well at Tivetshall had dried up and Beccles water was fouling and furring up locomotive boiler tubes. The matter was passed to the Locomotive Superintendent but because of his lethargic action was referred to the Deputy Chairman on 12th October; by 3rd November the pair advised that the necessary work to improve supplies at Tivetshall would cost £430 and at Beccles £160. On 3rd November 1870 it was also reported that on a recent date the 5.35pm Beccles to Tivetshall train had been delayed by a bullock on the line. The driver had managed to drive the animal off the track but this was the second occurrence of trespass by animals and the law clerk was asked to ascertain ownership of the livestock and institute proceedings.

At a meeting of the Traffic Committee held on 15th March 1871 the General Manager submitted a further letter from the Privy Council regarding the strict requirements of water supplies for cattle at stations. Doctor Williams, the author of the original letter submitted in August 1870, was of the opinion the water supply at Bungay was adequate for the present but would require improvements once the stations with poor facilities had been improved. The engineer was requested to implement a programme of improvements so that Doctor Williams could be advised when the work was completed. It was noted action had already been taken in response to Doctor Williams earlier letter regarding Beccles where a water supply for cattle had been laid on at a cost of £10.

As late as 27th April 1871 the GER Directors were settling conveyancing costs totalling £426 8s 0d incurred by the late Mr Kitton on behalf of the WVR in 1860 after his executors complained of outstanding payment. Settling outstanding WVR debts was not the only problem facing the GER officers, for on the night of 29th May 1871 the passenger and goods offices at Bungay was broken into – the former by the assailant smashing a pane of glass and the latter by forcing a bolt on the door of the goods shed. A total amount of 6s 10d in copper coins was stolen from the booking office. Concern was expressed that the station was isolated and no member of staff lived near the premises. Then on 7th June 1871 it was reported the wall backing on to the property of Sir Shafto Addair at Pulham St. Mary station was unsafe to cattle and after due consultation it was agreed to demolish the wall and replace the boundary by a rail fence and quick growing hedge.

The Waveney Valley route had enjoyed the benefits of the electric telegraph between stations for almost two years but the same could not be said for the main line between Beccles and Haddiscoe, which was without the facility; but on 3rd January 1872 work was sanctioned for immediate effect costing an estimated £75. Traffic on the Waveney Valley Branch continued to increase, but as facilities originally installed were inadequate, problems were being encountered. In mid January 1872 the goods manager reported the cattle pens at Beccles were too small and inconveniently placed for the increasing traffic handled at the station. The Traffic Committee acceded to his request for the removal of the pens and replacement by new facilities on 31st January 1872, after the engineer estimated the costs at £50. A fortnight later on 14th February 1872 a request was considered for a siding at Tivetshall to serve Gentel & Elliott's proposed maltings. After investigation the engineer estimated the cost of the siding at £129 on GER land and £250 on Mr Copeman's land. The matter was deferred due to difficulty negotiating with Copeman.

When Beccles Water Company required to construct an extension to their water main located opposite the GER tank in January 1872, the GER authorities readily agreed the necessary wayleave for the pipe to pass under the line, having initially been approached on 7th November 1870. In return, negotiations were made for an improved supply, which initially was not acceptable to the railway company but by 14th February 1872 the water company offered to supply at 7d per 1,000 gallons. The Locomotive Superintendent asked for this to be agreed and thus ensure improved watering facilities at the junction. Later in the year action was taken after the Beccles station master complained of lack of facilities and on 7th May 1872 approval was given for additional accommodation at the station master's house, comprising two rooms plus kitchen and a wash house at an estimated cost of £160. Sanction was deferred until 4th June 1872 when revised plans were drawn up at an estimated cost of £200. The revision was accepted and on 13th August 1872 the contract was awarded to R.A. King after he tendered at £230, subject to the work being completed in ten weeks.

Despite warnings in the local press regarding the dangers of trespassing on the railway, such edicts were totally ignored by countryfolk at their peril. On 1st October 1872 a branch train ran down a man named Riches who was using the branch line as a walking route; both his feet were cut off by the engine and he died instantly. Then on 5th March 1873, lad porter William Francis Weston was delegated to couple trucks in the goods siding at Ditchingham. After completing the operation he slipped and struck his head against a wagon buffer with such force that he died instantly. At the subsequent inquest a verdict of accidental death was recorded.

The question of the provision of a siding to Gentel & Elliott's malting at Tivetshall was resurrected on 8th October 1873 when revised estimates of £350 were considered inadequate. Fourteen days later, on 22nd October, the siding costs on GER land were £600 on Gentel & Elliott's land £200, with additional signalling priced at £400. With such high costs the matter was passed to the Superintendent for further investigation. By 25th February a revised price was agreed for the siding: £350 on Gentel & Elliott's land and £340 on the GER land; the installation was authorised subject to the usual 10 per cent annual payment.

In early December 1873 Mr Hartup of Bungay submitted a letter complaining that passengers travelling from Bungay to Norwich on the 2.30pm departure from Beccles were turned out of the train at Tivetshall to await a main line service from London and Ipswich. The empty carriages were then worked forward to Norwich to form the 5.00pm Down market train from Norwich to Beccles. His logical request that passengers bound for Norwich be allowed to stay on the branch train was raised at the meeting of the Traffic Committee on 17th December 1873. The Superintendent in correspondence turned down the request and stressed the present method of working was to be retained. However, the Chairman, Deputy Chairman and General Manager agreed to investigate further and overruled the Superintendent, deciding passengers could remain on the train for the non-stop run to Norwich.

As work progressed on the installation of the siding at Tivetshall it was realised the signals and points at the junction were not interlocked and the matter was the subject of attention at the Way and Works meeting on 10th March 1874. Development work was, however, deferred as other locations were considered more important.

After the wet weather during the winter months, farmers complained of the poor state of the cattle pens at Beccles where animals were slipping and sliding because of the muddy surface. On 6th May 1874 remedial drainage and paving was agreed at a cost of £37. Further complaints, this time from the station master at Wortwell concerning the lack of space in his accommodation, resulted in agreement on 1st July 1874 for an additional bedroom to be added to the station house at an estimated cost of £55. Along the line at Geldeston, authority was given on 4th November 1874 for a 36-inch GEM stove to be installed in the station house at a cost of £5.

Yet another complaint came when the Reverend G. Barrett was so enraged after he made a journey on the GER in 1874 that he penned a long letter to *The Times* which published it in full. Barrett wished to travel from Norwich to Beccles on a Saturday evening in December. He checked the timetables and found he could leave Norwich at 7.45pm, change at Tivetshall and take the Waveney Valley Branch train to Beccles arriving at 9.28pm. Unfortunately things did not go to plan. He caught the train from Norwich as scheduled and arrived at Tivetshall at 8.20pm but did not leave until 1.07am on Sunday morning and finally arrived at Beccles at 2.20am. Barrett complained of a *'sad lack of management skills'* by GER staff after detailing the sorry saga. The main line train reached Tivetshall almost to time where it was to connect with the Waveney Valley train from Beccles and convey passengers off that arriving service on to Diss, Ipswich and the south, whilst the branch train would return to Beccles with passengers from Norwich. However, on arrival at Tivetshall there was no sign of the Waveney Valley service so the main line train waited. At about 9.00pm news came that the branch train had failed at Harleston and as the branch was worked as a single line requiring the Train Staff to authorise movement through single line sections the assisting train could not proceed from Beccles until someone collected the Train Staff from the failed train. A member of the engine crew was sent by road to Beccles with the Train Staff and the breakdown train then departed for Harleston, collected the failed locomotive and returned to Beccles. Only after arrival at Beccles was a relief train sent across the branch to Tivetshall to pick up the stranded passengers.

Meanwhile at Tivetshall the passengers were feeling cold and miserable and the *Norwich Mercury* reported their plight: *'Those who have been unhappy enough ever to stop at Tivetshall will know what kind of place it is to be detained at for 5 hours on one of the most inclement nights we have had this year'.* The Reverend Barrett and most other waiting passengers were *'thoroughly frozen'* and at 11.00pm the main line train having waited 2 hours and 40 minutes departed to the south – so chaotic was the departure that it left without the guard giving 'right away', with the guard and some passengers stranded on the platform. All was not lost to the Reverend Barrett and his fellow travellers, for *'at 11.27pm our ears at Tivetshall were gladdened by the sound of the long expected train coming into the station'.* Many of those who wished to go the Beccles clambered aboard, leaving those who had arrived from Beccles and waiting to go to Diss and beyond *'wondering what to do'.* Barrett found himself a snug corner in a carriage and was dozing happily when he was disturbed by the sudden influx of cattlemen and farmers. Before they could all settle down station staff told them all to alight from the train as it had been decided to run the branch train to Diss to deliver passengers who had missed the main line train. So Barrett and the other unfortunate passengers were forced to wait another hour until the train returned from Diss. The journey from Norwich to Beccles had occupied six hours of the clergyman's life. He had only one solution – the Midland Railway should immediately build a line into Norfolk!

The gradual increase in traffic passing through, terminating or starting at Beccles necessitated additional coaching stock on passenger services, resulting in trains having to pull up at the relatively short platforms. After the Superintendent raised the subject of platform extensions at a meeting on 10th February 1875, the Directors deferred any decision until a subsequent meeting. In the short term, however, no action was taken.

After an approach from the local water board, authority was given on 20th October 1875 for a 12 inches diameter sewer pipe to pass under the line at the level crossing at Beccles, the necessary wayleave being issued with single line working in operation when necessary for the completion of the work. Along the line at Bungay, Mr Walker had applied for a new siding and after the application was passed to the goods manager for approval it was estimated the cost would amount to £300. On 29th December 1875 the engineer was instructed to investigate and report. However, it was 30th May 1876 before negotiations were completed, when it was revealed the siding would generate agreed annual traffic receipts of £14,000, but at a revised cost of £515 The matter was confirmed by the chairman of the Traffic Committee on 11th July and work was sanctioned the following day.

In the meantime, after misunderstandings concerning the loading of wagons, a survey found that loading gauges had not been provided in the goods yards at Pulham Market and Pulham St. Mary stations. The deficiency was rectified when authority was given on 11th January 1876 for the necessary equipment to be provided as a matter of urgency. Three days later, as a mixed train from Beccles was entering Tivetshall station on 14th January 1876, the locomotive and leading coaches brushed against the side of a wagon standing in a siding slightly foul of the running line. The locomotive was undamaged but two passenger coaches and the brake van were slightly grazed and a lamp iron broken. No passengers were injured and the accident was attributed to the signalman omitting to ascertain if the line was clear for the passenger train. Pulham Market station received further attention when authority was given on 2nd May 1876 for the provision of a lamp room and coal store at a cost of £15.

The Waveney Valley Branch sustained a spate of level crossing accidents in the autumn of 1876 which not only resulted in several staff being suspended from duty for short periods with a loss of pay but also kept the local civil engineer's carpenters busy. The first, on 18th September, occurred at Denton level crossing between Bungay and Homersfield, when the gates were run through and smashed by a special passenger train. Then on 23rd September a goods train demolished the crossing gates near Pulham Market after the gateman failed to open the barriers for the passage of the train. The gateman was again at fault when a passenger train collided with and smashed Crossingfield level crossing gates near Pulham Market on 12th October 1876, and yet again the crossing keeper was at fault when a goods train ran through and damaged Earsham level crossing gates on 21st December. In all cases the driver of each train was also reprimanded for not keeping a vigilant watch on the road ahead.

On 9th January 1877 the General Manager submitted a statement of traffic at stations where receipts in 1875 were considered inadequate. Four of the Waveney Valley Branch stations came under scrutiny: Homersfield with earnings of £2,782 13s 2d, Wortwell £149 13s 6d, Earsham £286 0s 11d and Ditchingham £3,602 2s 0d were considered candidates for possible closure. After due consideration it was decided no action would be taken until the Chairman of the Traffic Committee had visited the various lines to assess the situation.

During 1877 various improvements were made to branch stations although initially on 23rd January, when application was made for additions to the office accommodation at Beccles, costing £35, the work was deferred pending further investigation into the condition of the station buildings. Underbridge No. 1189 at 12 miles 50 chains between Bungay and Earsham was found to be deteriorating and on 3rd April 1877 a bridge renewal contract was awarded to T. Shaw who tendered at £620, subject to the work being completed in ten weeks. Then on 26th June 1877, approval was given for the cart road at Tivetshall to be ballasted at an estimated cost of £100 following complaints from farmers and merchants using the goods yard.

For some considerable period farmers using Ditchingham station had also complained of the lack of facilities for loading and unloading of cattle traffic. After investigating, the goods manager reported on 10th July 1877 there were two cattle pens at Bungay, less than a mile from Ditchingham, where the company failed to load more than one wagon a month. It was considered the space at Bungay could be better used for the handling of general merchandise and authority was duly given for the transfer of the cattle pens to Ditchingham to obviate the problem.

During a tour of inspection of the system, the Directors visited the Waveney Valley Branch on 24th October 1877, and in particular the stations considered for closure. It was judged earnings at Homersfield and Ditchingham were sufficient to warrant their retention whilst at Earsham it was found passengers from the village and surrounding area booked from that station in preference to Bungay and therefore the station would continue to remain operational. Wortwell station receipts showed no improvement and it was considered the station could be closed *'without injury to the public'*. The Superintendent was instructed to arrange for the closure to be effected at the start of the New Year and Wortwell station duly closed to all traffic on 1st January 1878, thus reducing the stations on the Waveney Valley line to eleven.

On 8th August 1877 the GER Directors had approved of the redemption of the Waveney Valley No. 1 and Eastern Union 5 per cent stocks. This was confirmed on 27th February 1878 when finalisation of the accounts regarding the takeover of the WVR was achieved by consolidating the company stocks once the EUR 5 per cent and WVR No. 1 stocks were redeemed. A letter from the London & Globe Insurance Company declining the WVR No. 1 stock at 4% was to be ignored.

During a random inspection early in March 1878, a travelling inspector of the Veterinary Department of the Privy Council was aghast to find the cattle pens at Harleston in a deplorable condition and unfit for the loading and unloading of livestock. By 27th of the month the Department had threatened legal proceeding against the GER unless the pens were so constructed that they could be properly disinfected. The Traffic Committee immediately instructed the engineer to arrange for the cattle pens at Harleston to be paved and improved, a programme which also involved improvements at twenty other stations where the cattle pens were also found to be sub-standard. Authority was tardy for sanction was not forthcoming until 30th July for the provision of water supply to the pens at a cost of £5.

The month of March saw authority for signal renewals and alterations at Tivetshall when sanction was given on 26th of the month for work costing £43 in connection with the provision of a ticket platform on the WVR branch at a cost of £107. The platform enabled tickets to be collected before passengers alighted at the main station to make their onward journeys. Then on 4th July 1878 a siding extension at Tivetshall was authorised at a cost of £50 after the goods manager complained of the lack of accommodation for wagons waiting emptying and loading. The increase in goods traffic also required an extension to the goods office at Beccles at a cost of £35 to accommodate additional staff.

Shortly after 9.00am on 25th July 1878 a ballast train departed southbound on the East Suffolk line from Beccles but unfortunately the load was too heavy for the locomotive and so about a mile from the station on Beccles bank the train was halted to allow some of the wagons to be detached to permit the engine to convey the first part of the train forward before returning for the remaining vehicles. Once uncoupled the offending wagons started to roll back down the gradient towards Beccles station but unfortunately in the intervening period the 7.10am special excursion train from Eye to Yarmouth via the Waveney Valley line had just pulled into the Up main platform to allow the engine to run round the train before departing for the coast. Whilst the engine was running round, thirteen loaded trucks of sand and a brake van having gained velocity on falling gradients and travelling at speed collided with the coaching stock. The excursion train was full of passengers and many received cuts and superficial injuries.

Major General C.S. Hutchinson was delegated to hold the inquiry into the accident and noted the collision had resulted in thirty-eight passengers receiving injuries. The thirteen wagons formed part of a sand train from Lowestoft to Stratford and had run back down gradients of 1 in 66, 1 in 88 and 1 in 133 after having been uncoupled from the front portion of the train about one and a quarter miles south of Beccles. In the passenger train the buffers of six carriages were damaged and the buffer rods bent. The body of one carriage was slightly damaged and another had a door broken. No vehicle was derailed but in the sand train two vehicles were damaged. From evidence, Hutchinson was of the opinion the collision was caused by the driver and fireman of the sand train not attending to the rule especially framed for their guidance under the circumstances in which they were placed; the ignorance displayed by the driver raised the question as to what means were taken to ensure the company's servants had a reasonable acquaintance with the rules. The inspector concluded:

The mere possession of a rule book is useless unless means are taken to ensure that its contents are fairly understood. Had the working of the points and signals at the south end of Beccles been concentrated in a cabin it is probable the collision might have been avoided as the signalman would then most likely have seen the runaway trucks approaching and have been able to turn them into a siding adjoining the up line, and it might be well to let these siding points in their normal position be open for the siding, so that any future runaways might be intercepted before the station and junction was reached.

The incident was reported in *The Times*, which recorded on 31st July that the driver and fireman of the ballast train had been suspended from duty.

The Directors on a tour of inspection on 1st and 2nd October 1878, as well as visiting Snape and the Southwold Railway called to view facilities at Beccles. The Superintendent advised that as a result of the accident in July, it was considered desirable the points running out of the Up line at the London end of the station required adjusting to divert possible runaways into a siding instead of the passenger station. The question of additional siding accommodation was also on the agenda. The visit had the desired effect for on 20th January 1879 authority given for additional sidings at Beccles at a cost of £230, to be followed on 26th February 1879 when sanction was given for the rearrangement of signalling at Beccles, Lowestoft Junction at a cost of £550. This was concluded on 26th March when the interlocking of signals and points was authorised at a cost of £850.

On 25th March 1879 the Directors were advised that the parish rates for the Tivetshall to Bungay section of line payable to local

Geldeston station 16 miles 57 chains from Tivetshall, view facing west with the 330 feet long platform on the Down side of the main single line. The main station building has been rendered and beyond that the goods shed is prominent in the goods yard. The signal box in the foreground was equipped with a 15-lever Dutton frame to control points and signals as well as the level crossing gate to the right. *Author's collection*

authorities amounted to Eastern Union Main £2,938 and Waveney Valley £739. Attempts to reduce these amounts proved fruitless after the law clerk advised the figures quoted were already reduced.

During improvements at Beccles it was found a certain amount of rearranging had to take place and on 14th June 1879 authority was given for the siding belonging to Mr May and adjacent coal stacks to be moved back to allow the installation of a new road and siding. The work was completed at a cost of £230.

Continuous heavy rain on 22nd July 1879 brought flooding to several places in Suffolk and Norfolk as rivers and streams overflowed and burst their banks. The Framlingham Branch was completely blocked and closed for one day when the rushing torrent of water damaged a culvert between Marlesford and Parham. The Waveney Valley Branch running close to the river was especially vulnerable and the line was flooded between Ditchingham and Bungay, and a bridge damaged between Bungay and Earsham. Trains were worked locally between Tivetshall and Earsham, and between Bungay and Beccles, with a horse omnibus connection from Earsham to Bungay from 22nd July until the evening of 24th July, after which the line reopened fully for through traffic. However, on the morning of 28th July the bridge between Bungay and Earsham was again reported unfit for traffic and the local working between Tivetshall and Earsham, and between Beccles and Bungay resumed until repairs were effected. As new works continued at Beccles, the original estimates were being exceeded and on 8th October 1879 further alterations were sanctioned at a cost of £1,600.

Major General C.S. Hutchinson duly carried out the BOT inspection of the rearranged and improved signalling at Beccles on 20th February 1880. The control of the points and signals had been concentrated in two new signal boxes, one at the north end of the station close to the junction of the Waveney Valley line and the second at the south end of the station. The inspector found the arrangements generally satisfactory but required the following alterations in the North signal box: levers No's 12 and 21 required interlocking; levers No's 4 and 21 required interlocking; levers No's 23 and 21 required interlocking, and levers No's 19 and 24 also required to be interlocked. A locking bar was also to be installed at the Up end of No. 19 crossover road and an interlocked signal was required for Down trains passing through No. 19 crossover. The South signal box Down home signal also required slotting by a lever in the North signal box. In the South signal box, Hutchinson required the Up end of No. 5 siding points to be worked by a separate lever and in their normal position to lie open for the siding so as to act as a runaway point in case of vehicles breaking away on the ascending gradient and running back towards the station. Hutchinson returned to the station on 28th April 1880 and found all remedial work has been completed.

Yet further complaints were made by farmers regarding the poor condition of cattle pens at the branch stations resulting in animals arriving at market in an undesirable condition. The solution was simple but the GER authorities were slow in reacting, until on 6th April 1880 the paving of the cattle pens at Pulham Market was agreed at a cost of £5 and at Ditchingham for the princely sum of £8 5s 0d.

The modernisation at Beccles was not fully completed in 1879 and it was realised that for some considerable time delays had been occurring at the station, especially when a locomotive was taking water as it prevented a second locomotive or train from entering the station. The Acting General Manager reported to the Traffic Committee on 3rd August 1880 that it was proposed to obviate delays by installing a second water crane at an estimated cost of £90 and duly received the necessary sanction for the work to proceed. After further investigation by the engineer, authority was sanctioned on 18th August for the sinking of a well and provision of new water cranes at a respective cost of £40 and £90. At the same time new urinals and toilets were to be provided on the station for the sum of £205. Later in the year, on 5th October, a wayleave was issued for Mr Edwards to install a water pipe under the railway at Harleston, the work being subject to supervision by local permanent way staff.

Although many of the branch services from Beccles continued through to Norwich some terminated at or started their journey back from Tivetshall. Complaints were voiced that passengers changing trains at the junction station to join main line or branch connections enjoyed few facilities when waiting for trains, especially if the connections were delayed. Thus, on 1st February 1881, authority was given for the provision of improved waiting rooms and associated toilets at a cost of £520. On 15th February the contract was awarded to R. Skipper who tendered at £531. The Traffic Superintendent was also concerned that the length of the platforms was inadequate so that trains conveying additional coaches had to draw up twice to allowed passengers to alight. On 5th April 1881 sanction was given for the platforms to be lengthening at a cost of £130, the Down main from 200 feet to 280 feet, the Up main from 280 feet to 370 feet and the Up back platform from 280 feet to 365 feet.

Alterations continued apace at Beccles as the improvements of the past few years highlighted yet further anomalies which hindered the smooth flow of traffic through the station. To obviate some of the operational problems on 2nd August 1881 the provision of a new crossover road at the Yarmouth end of the layout together with two associated short sidings was authorised at a cost of £90, whilst additional sidings to the east of the line north of the station were sanctioned at a cost of £260 to ease the stabling of rolling stock which because of increasing traffic was becoming congested. The following month, on 20th September 1881 the Waveney Valley line water column at the Yarmouth end of the station was to be resited so as to provide water to engines on the main line as well as the siding, and thus enable the Down main platform to be lengthened by 40 feet. The latter work was authorised on 4th October 1881 at a cost of £75. A month later on 1st November, additional land was purchased at Bungay, Beccles and Tivetshall for the enlargement of the respective goods yards, the existing yards being cramped for room because of increasing traffic.

Work at Beccles continued into the New Year when authority was given for a new siding on the Up side to cross Corporation Road costing £30 and on 21st February 1882 it was revealed agreement with the local authority had been reached subject to a rental of £2 per annum for a period of twenty-one years. On 7th March 1882 additional expenditure was sanctioned when, before installation of the new siding, repairs were required to the private road costing £30. A week later, on 15th March 1882 a further fatality occurred when J. Bartlett was killed by a train at Pulham Market, as he was using the railway as a walking route.

For many months the train services on the Ipswich to Norwich main line incurred innumerable delays brought about by the lack of proper signalling. Finally after much debate, on 16th May 1882 the Directors agreed to the interlocking of the signals and points at Tivetshall, authorised at a cost of £5,620, the work including seven other signal boxes on the East Suffolk and Ipswich to Norwich main line.

At the Traffic Committee meeting on 5th September 1882 plans were to be prepared for yet further alterations at Beccles, including a new ladies waiting room and refreshment room on the Down platform, the positioning subject to agreement with the station master. Powers were also to be obtained in the next Parliamentary session to close the level crossing which bisected the platform. A proposal turned down by the Directors was for a service from Norwich to Beccles via Loddon as it was considered there was insufficient traffic to warrant the outlay.

During the protracted alterations at Beccles, opportunity was taken to alleviate problems every time a locomotive on the Waveney Valley service blocked the Down main line when running round its train. On 6th February 1883 the provision of a new crossover was authorised at a cost of £145 but it was 7th December 1883 before Major General C.S. Hutchinson inspected the alterations. He found a connection had been installed to enable the engine of a Waveney Valley Branch train to run round its stock without fouling the main line. The signals and points were correctly interlocked and worked from the existing North signal box and the inspector had no hesitation in authorising their use.

Although cattle pens had been in existence at Tivetshall for many years there was no water supply for animals in transit, but the omission was rectified on 1st April 1884 when authority was given for a water supply for cattle at a cost of £8. Then on 1st July 1884 sanction was given for an extension to the platform at Pulham Market to obviate trains pulling up twice. The increase in the length of rolling stock on the branch services found the 33-yard platform was inadequate so authority was given for a 10-yard extension at a cost of £10. In the autumn of the year the station master at Earsham complained bitterly of inadequate accommodation and after due investigation it was agreed on 18th November 1884 to provide a new booking office and new station master's residence at a cost of £350, the amount being readily agreed despite the station handling no goods traffic. After some dubiety the amount was ratified on 2nd December 1884.

The New Year found further work executed at Beccles when on 7th April 1885 the provision of four additional cattle pens was authorised together with two water hydrants for animal welfare at a cost of £150. Eleven days later, on 18th April 1885 the General Manager reported the lack of distant signals at Pulham Market, Pulham St. Mary and Earsham stations and it was estimated their provision would cost £234. The matter was considered but the lack of action brought complaints from footplate crews working the line, especially during the hours of darkness. The subject was raised later in the year on 18th August when the General Manager again reported there were no distant signals at Pulham Market, Pulham St. Mary and Earsham. In addition, at Ellingham the home and distant signals were old and too low. William Birt, the General Manager, recommended that proper signals be provided, the engineer estimating costs of provision at £234. The plan was duly sanctioned, the scheme being charged to the superintendent's fund.

Whilst the board members argued over the provision of signals on 5th May 1885, trap points were provided for Hudson's siding at Harleston at a cost of £40, whilst on 18th July 1885 Emma Drane was fatally injured when run down by a train at Pulham St. Mary as she crossed the line without noticing the approaching locomotive. The water supply to the cattle pens at Beccles was enhanced after work was authorised on 6th October 1885 at a cost of £25. Two years elapsed before further additions were made when on 18th July 1887 sanction was given for canopies to be erected over the platforms fronting the waiting rooms at a cost of £290. Later in the year, on 18th October 1887 it was agreed block working was to be introduced between Tivetshall and Beccles as an enhancement to the Train Staff and Ticket operation, the work costing £2,845 including four other schemes.

For several years the engine shed at Beccles was giving cause for concern and the growing importance of the depot and increased allocation of locomotives meant that the deteriorating conditions required urgent attention. Thus on 1st March 1887 the GER Directors were advised the engine shed was due for rebuilding at an estimated cost of £8,889. However, such an ambitious scheme was not required and, following drastic revision to the plans, a reduced figure of £2,150 was announced on 5th April. The subject was quietly allowed to lapse until early the following year when a decision was required and tenders sought. On 17th April 1888 a contract was finally placed with Bennett Brothers of Cambridge for a new two-road engine shed to the north of the station at a cost of £1,676, subject to the work being completed by 1st September 1888.

Yet further additions were sanctioned at Tivetshall on 7th February 1888 when the installation of trap sidings at a cost of £185 was agreed to. The work was completed in a short space of time, for Major General C.S. Hutchinson inspected the new siding connection with the Waveney Valley line at Tivetshall on 23rd May 1888. He found the connection was worked by properly interlocked levers in the existing signal box, which had a 32-lever frame now amended to 27 working and 5 spare levers. Certain alterations were necessary: No. 28 signal should interlock with levers No's 15 and 17 in either direction; lever No. 17 should bolt lock No. 18 points only in the normal position, whilst the signalman's diagram required altering to show the new connection. Subject to the requirements being rectified, Hutchinson sanctioned the use of the new siding.

The growth of cattle traffic handled at Bungay was cause for concern after farmers again complained of the poor state of the goods yard and facilities for the handling of animals in transit. Following deputations to the local goods manager it was agreed on 7th August 1888 to sanction the relaying of the roadway leading to the new cattle pens together with other minor improvements for animal welfare at a cost of £300, the work to be completed before the onset of winter.

After the signalling improvements at Tivetshall, Saxby & Farmer were awarded the contract for improvements at Beccles on 19th June 1888. Hutchinson returned to the branch on 23rd November 1888 when he inspected new works. The Major General noted the alterations at Beccles comprised the connections of a siding leading from the Waveney Valley line to the new engine shed. The connections were worked from the existing Beccles B (*sic*) signal box located at the Down or north end of the station, which contained a 45-lever frame with 41 working and 4 spare levers. Hutchinson found the majority of the work to his satisfaction, but No. 7 signal should lock No. 33 locking bar in either position, whilst No. 22 disc signal should be interlocked with No. 12 points when No. 23 points were in the normal position. The inspector also observed that the rails of the Up main line between the engine shed and B signal box were not properly bent to the required curve. Hutchinson duly approved of the use of the new connection subject to early completion of the remedial works. The year ended on a sad note when on 11th December 1888, a branch train killed platelayer Thomas Elsey, near Tivetshall.

5

Halcyon Years

As the last decade of the 19th century approached and railway traffic was increasing, the anomaly of the level crossing passing through the environs of Beccles station raised in 1882 now urgently required resolving; after approaches from the local authority, the GER board on 21st May 1889 approved of the alterations proposed by the corporation for a permanent bridge across the railway. Such action required Parliamentary approval and subsequently the Great Eastern Railway (General Powers) Act 1890 (53 and 54 Vict cap cviii), which received the Royal Assent on 25th July 1890, authorised the company to stop up an existing level crossing for carts, carriages and foot passengers and also the adjacent footbridge at Beccles. Clause 5q of the statute gave powers for the making of a new footpath commencing at a point 20 feet south-west from the foot of the western steps which led to the existing footbridge, the new path crossing the railway by a new bridge located about 50 feet northward of the existing footbridge and terminating at a point about 135 feet north-eastward from the eastern steps of the existing footbridge. The new footpath and bridge were to be a substitution for the existing level crossing and footbridge and once in place the company was authorised to remove the existing footbridge.

The required action was slow in materialising and it was 6th January 1891 before estimates were available. The Way and Works Committee readily sanctioned the proposed perambulator bridge at Beccles station to replace the level crossing leading from the town to a public promenade and pastureland at a cost of £1,116 together with £10 for the purchase of a small plot of land. By 5th May, tenders had been vetted and the contract was awarded to the Phoenix Foundry, Derby, for a sum of £3,057 10s 4d, which included bridgework at six other locations. The rearrangement took some time to complete and it was 30th April 1892 before the Directors visited Beccles to inspect the new bridge, which had been opened to the public for the first time on Easter Monday,18th April.

In the intervening period improvements had been made at Tivetshall where a new water column was provided for the branch platform, the work being authorised on 5th August for £92, whilst a pressure gauge for carriage gas lighting equipment at the junction was ordered at a cost of £151. On the same date, the Way and Works Committee agreed to the extension of the siding serving the Co-operative Society coal yard at Beccles at a cost of £86, the Society agreeing in return to pay an annual rental of £6. Further work at Beccles station included a sentry-type box for the ticket collector authorised on 2nd December 1890 at a cost of £35, a minor extension to the booking office costing £25, sanctioned on 2nd June 1891, and a new footwarmer house costing £80, authorised on 22nd December 1891.

The 1889 Regulation of Railways Act, as well as requiring block working on most lines also required the interlocking of points and signals; in accordance with the statute on 21st April 1891 the contract for the interlocking of points and signals, and provision of new signal boxes between Tivetshall exclusive and Beccles exclusive was entrusted to Dutton of Worcester. In the same month authority was given for the installation of additional sidings at Homersfield, the work to be carried out concurrently with the signalling programme. Opportunity was also to be taken to install passing places at Harleston and Bungay to provide greater flexibility when working the single line, as increased traffic had resulted in delays caused by the previous necessity of shunting trains at these places to let other services pass.

Major General C.S. Hutchinson subsequently conducted the BOT inspection of the alterations carried out at Ditchingham, Geldeston and Ellingham stations on 21st January 1892. At Ditchingham he found a portion of the siding connections had changed, the platform had been lengthened and signalling improved. The signals and points were now worked from a new raised signal box containing an 18-lever frame with 14 working and 4 spare levers. Along the line at Geldeston similar alterations were made including the lengthening of the platform, and signals and points were worked from a new signal box containing a 15-lever frame with 11 working and 4 spare levers. At Ellingham the position of the siding connections had also been altered and the improved signalling was worked from a new signal box containing a 15-lever frame with 11 working and 4 spare levers. Here the platform had been extended and the levels between the new and old portion were slightly different. Hutchinson found that the signals and points at all stations were properly interlocked and he recommended the new works be brought into use subject to the deficiency in platform height at Ellingham being remedied as a matter of urgency.

Major General C.S. Hutchinson again visited the Waveney Valley line on 5th July 1892 to inspect the new works and signalling arrangements at several other stations. He noted at Pulham Market an additional siding had been installed and the improved signalling was controlled from a new signal box containing a 17-lever frame with 13 working and 4 spare levers. He also noted the station platform had been extended and recommended the company lose no time in raising the level of the old part of the platform to the height of the new section. Hutchinson then visited Pulham St. Mary where he found improvements to sidings and signalling, the signals and points being worked from a new signal box containing a 15-lever frame with 11 working and 4 spare levers, where the interlocking was found to be correctly installed. On the same day the inspector also viewed the new arrangements at Homersfield and found that the new sidings were controlled from a new signal box containing a 20-lever frame with 16 working and 4 spare levers. The new works and interlocking at all locations was found to be correct and the inspector recommended the BOT sanction their use.

With all attention on signalling, on 19th April 1892 an order was placed with Eastwood, Swingler & Company for the provision of a footbridge connecting the proposed new Down-side platform with the original Up-side platform at Harleston to obviate passengers using the foot crossing; the work costing £1,695 4s 2d was combined with three other stations. Along the line at Beccles the growth in the conveyance of horse-drawn carriages and road vehicles had increased significantly, but gentry and farmers had complained of damage and delay incurred loading and unloading vehicles. The GER authorities were stung into action by the adverse publicity and on 4th October 1892 the provision of the new horse carriage dock was sanctioned at a cost of £350.

On and from 1st January 1893 Second Class accommodation was abolished on the branch train services. Major General C.S. Hutchinson inspected the new works at Bungay station on 10th February 1893 and found that the station had been made a passing place for passenger trains on the single line, by the provision of a new Down loop line and the construction of an associated Down-side platform. The sidings had also been rearranged and the signalling remodelled. The points and signals were worked from a new raised signal box containing a 25-lever frame with 18 working and 7 spare levers. Hutchinson found all work had been satisfactorily completed and recommended the use of the new facilities.

Six days later, on 16th February 1893 Major General C.S. Hutchinson inspected the alterations made at Beccles station. He found a new connection had been installed from a short siding to a dock line at the back of the Down end of the Down platform. The levers for working the new connection were interlocked in the existing Beccles North signal box containing a 45-lever frame, with 43 working and 2 spare levers. The inspector sanctioned use of the new connection subject to the new facing points being bolted before either No. 4 signal or No. 7 signal could be lowered, a requirement to be completed within two weeks. The GER engineer attending the inspection promised early rectification of the problem.

On Thursday 20th April 1893 the body of Frederick William Skipper, porter/signalman at Bungay aged 23 years, was discovered after a shunting mishap. At the inquest held the same day at the Kings Head Hotel, Bungay, the Coroner for the Liberty of the Duke of Norfolk, H.E. Garrod of Diss, initially heard evidence from station master John Haythorpe. He stated he was on the platform at 10.40am watching an engine shunting goods wagons to the siding. The deceased duty was to assist in the operation but he could not see the porter as the trucks took the curve into the goods yard. The duty of the porter was to keep outside the line of the trucks when being shunted. There was an eye on the side of the truck to which the rope was attached. After the trucks were uncoupled from the engine, Kerrison, the foreman porter, called to him that the deceased was lying across the rail apparently lifeless. A doctor was immediately summoned and pronounced Skipper dead. Asked as to the disposition of the porter/signalman the station master advised he was a steady and sober man and generally very careful. From the evidence given by Kerrison, the rope was attached to the engine and the other end to the couplings between the buffers on the leading truck, the deceased having put it there instead of on the side where there was an eye for such purpose. When the engine ran forward of the trucks the rope tightened and as the deceased was between the truck and the rope the rope frayed then broke and caught the deceased who fell across the rail where five wagons passed over his body before brakes were applied. The deceased was responsible for the accident for not having put the hook on the eye on the side of the truck. After hearing other minor evidence the jury returned a verdict of accidental death. Skipper was interred in

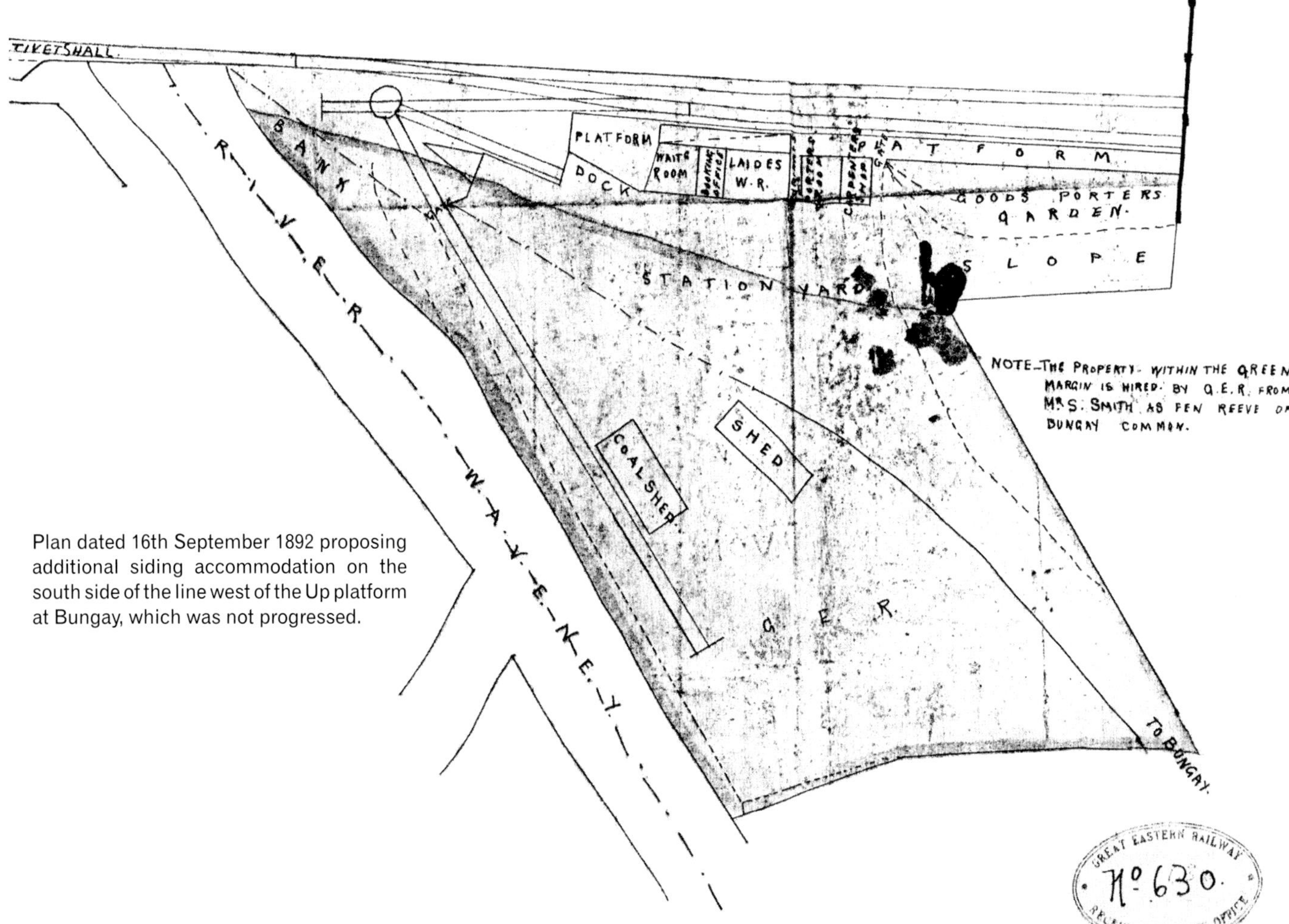

Plan dated 16th September 1892 proposing additional siding accommodation on the south side of the line west of the Up platform at Bungay, which was not progressed.

Ditchingham station from the approach road in the early 1900s with the Italianate station building to the left and signal box on the right. This contained an 18-lever Dutton frame controlling the signals and points at the station. It was abolished in September 1958. *Author's collection*

Holy Trinity Cemetery the following Monday, with the Reverend J.A. Fletcher and Reverend W. Boyce officiating. Prior to leaving the station, around thirty of his work colleagues from various branch stations assembled in the waiting room and were addressed by F.F. Chenery from St. John's Hall, Highbury. The coffin was borne by GER colleagues from the church to the grave and was followed by other friends and relatives.

The Great Eastern Railway (General Powers) Act 1893 (56 Vict cap lii), which received the Royal Assent on 9th June 1893, authorised the company to carry out widening and improvements at Beccles including north and south of the station and alongside the Lowestoft Branch. Clause 31 of the same statute authorised the purchase of land in the parish of Redenhall-with-Harleston, adjoining and on the south side of the railway immediately west of Harleston station. The GER wasted no time in taking action, for Harleston was to become the second passing place on the branch and on 4th July 1893 a contract was awarded to S. Brock & Sons for a new Down-side platform after the firm tendered at £620. The new works also included a revision of signalling and amendments to the track layout. Improvements were also made to the signalling at Tivetshall when new Up and Down advance starting signals were authorised on 5th September 1893 at a cost of £80.

On the morning of Monday 31st July 1893, Henry Baxter, an elderly man, was trespassing in the station yard at Harleston and, whilst leaning against the walls of the new cattle pen, received fatal injuries when he was crushed against the wall by the vehicles of a ballast train during shunting movements. An inquest held the same afternoon in the local Railway Tavern before the Coroner, H.E. Garrod of Diss, recorded the verdict of accidental death. Then on 27th December 1893 another fatality occurred when Edward Feek was killed by a train at Ingate Street level crossing, Beccles.

Major General C.S. Hutchinson conducted the BOT inspection of the alterations at Harleston on 9th February 1894. He found the new works comprised the construction of a passing loop, a new Down-side platform, changes to siding connections and a rearrangement of the signalling. The signals and points were worked from a new signal box containing a 42-lever frame with 35 working and 7 spare levers. Hutchinson found the arrangements to his satisfaction but required certain remedial work to be completed within one month: the steps at the Up end of the Up platform were to be replaced by a ramp; No. 14 disc signal was to precede No. 8 disc signal unless No. 12 points were pulled over, and the stock rail at No. 28 safety points was to be shortened. The GER engineer accompanying the inspector agreed the remedial work would be completed within the desired timescale.

Despite the numerous improvements made over the years at Beccles, to the operators the station formed a bottleneck to East Suffolk line services with consistent delays to all trains. Following discussions at board level it was imperative that action be taken and during a Directors' visit down the line on Friday 4th October 1895 the engineer was instructed to prepare plans for alterations at Beccles station Up side to enable Yarmouth and Lowestoft trains to enter at the same time. Little immediate action appears to have taken place save that on 4th February 1896 the General Manager reported to the Traffic Committee that Beccles was to be equipped with a gas storage holder to replenish coaches of main line and branch trains, with the tanks being replenished from a travelling gas tank wagon. However, the following day, 5th February 1896, it was announced that proposed new works costing £12,100 were needed because of the growth in London to Yarmouth and Lowestoft traffic (which had shown an increase of £10,414 in one year); the works to provide separate entrances to the station for trains from

Yarmouth and from Lowestoft, and increased accommodation for passengers on the Up side and goods on the Down side. The amount was readily agreed and commenced with a contract for new awnings and waiting rooms being awarded to W. Pattison of Whitehall on 8th April 1896 after the firm tendered at £1,489. As improvements progressed, so the contract for new signalling was awarded to Saxby & Farmer on 2nd June 1896; nine days later, on Thursday 11th June 1896, the Directors on a tour of the system again visited Beccles and approved of the new works on the Up side. The Down side accommodation was also to be considered, with the new accommodation including a refreshment room.

Lieutenant Colonel G.W. Addison conducted the BOT inspection of the major alterations at Beccles station on 6th November 1896. The alterations included the widening of the line to the east side of the railway for a distance of half a mile and the elimination of the former double junction with the Lowestoft single line. In consequence of the changes the Lowestoft Branch had a separate line leading to the back of the Up platform with connections to the Up main line south of the station and with the Up and Down main lines north of the station. The marshalling and goods sidings east of the railway had been rearranged and expanded, and a siding on the Down side of the railway south of the station had been remodelled and lengthened. The former Up-side platform had been abolished and replaced by an island platform 200 yards in length, on which were situated waiting rooms and gentlemen's and ladies' toilets. A new footbridge connecting the platforms had also been provided as a replacement for an earlier structure. Addison noted the provision of the new North signal box containing an 80-lever frame with 75 working and 5 spare levers, erected close to the former North signal box which had been abolished. One of the levers in the new signal box controlled a 2-lever frame at the level crossing gates north of the signal box and formerly locked from Lowestoft Junction signal box which had also been abolished. A new 38-lever locking frame with 34 working and 4 spare levers had also been installed in the existing South signal box. After inspecting the North signal box, Addison required that signal No. 38 could not be lowered until signal No. 36 had been cleared. The Up starting signal at the back of the Up platform required a duplicate arm to give the driver of a through train better sighting of the semaphore. At the conclusion of the inspection Addison required the GER to furnish details of curves and gradients of the new lines from the former Lowestoft Junction to the south of the station. He was concerned with the arrangements of Up home signals No's 13, 22 and 32, two of which pertained to the new line and were mounted on a signal post close to the old Up main line, and which might be misread by drivers; he requested the GER signal engineer to find a possible alteration to obviate the problem. On the same day Addison also inspected a long refuge siding which had been provided alongside the Bungay Branch; points were installed in the Waveney Valley line to give access to the siding and faced trains proceeding in the direction of Tivetshall. The points and associated signalling were worked from Beccles North signal box. Addison found the interlocking correct and arrangements satisfactory, and authorised use of the new works. No sooner had the inspector departed than authority was given on 1st December 1896 for an additional siding at a cost of £195.

*
15949

Great Eastern Railway.

Audit Office,
Liverpool Street Station,
3rd September, 1895.

Circular A.O. 615.

ELLINGHAM
AND
EASTON LODGE (NEW STATION).

With reference to the instructions which have recently been issued by the Traffic Departments as to the altered arrangements at Ellingham, and also respecting the course to be followed in regard to traffic with Easton Lodge, please note all Parcels Waybills to or from these Stations must be abstracted as under:—

GELDESTONE for ELLINGHAM
DUNMOW for EASTON LODGE

according as the traffic is to or from either of those Stations.

Goods, Coal and Cattle Invoices to or from Ellingham must be abstracted as "Geldestone for Ellingham."

Please acknowledge.

W. F. BECK.

GER Audit Office instruction of 3rd September 1895 regarding revision of invoicing of goods traffic for Ellingham.

The extension of gas lighting on GER rolling stock including branch lines required an increase in the fleet of vehicles conveying gas supplies from Stratford to the various filling points. On 28th July 1896 it was announced that five additional gas holder wagons would be required at a cost of £1,200, whilst the cost of fixing the necessary fixing holders, piping and one filling post at each of the designated stations amounted to £200.

Although not directly concerning the Waveney Valley Branch, on 19th May 1896 authority was given for the installation of water troughs in the main line, about a mile south of Tivetshall. The facility, costing £2,923, was required to enable locomotives hauling the Norfolk Coast Express from Liverpool Street to replenish their tenders and, by avoiding Norwich using the Wensum curve, to run directly to North Walsham, en route to Cromer and Sheringham.

Traffic continued to grow at Beccles and on 2nd February 1897 an extension to Elliott & Garrod's siding was authorised at a cost of £140. Then on 2nd March 1897 an instruction was issued advising that curves of 10 chain radius or less were to be equipped with check rails following a BOT instruction, these included the curve of the Waveney Valley and Lowestoft branches at Beccles and a short section of the Waveney Valley line at Tivetshall. Later in the year, on 2nd November, authority was given to provide a washhouse at Black Mill cottage at Tivetshall at a cost of £45 following complaints from the resident and the local health authority.

Winter was reluctant to leave in the New Year, for severe weather brought heavy snowfalls to East Anglia on 25th March 1898, resulting in a branch train being trapped in a drift blocking the line near Pulham Market. Only after considerable effort by permanent way staff was the train released and even then only by the driver finally charging the locomotive through the drift to force a way through.

Clause 22 of the Great Eastern Railway (General Powers) Act 1898 (61 and 62 cap Vict cap lxvi), which received the Royal Assent on 1st July 1898, authorised the company to purchase a piece of land and buildings in the parish and borough of Beccles on the west side of and adjoining the East Suffolk line immediately south of Beccles station. The acquisition was to enable further improvements to be made; in the intervening period an extension to Harleston goods office was sanctioned on 18th January 1898 at a cost of £65 to provide accommodation for additional staff brought about by increasing traffic. Along the line it was necessary to provide a granary at Homersfield and this was authorised on 20th September 1898 at a cost of £400; on the same day the company maintained the upkeep of their stations by awarding a contract to T. Hipperson for repairs and painting of Tivetshall station after the firm tendered at £115 11s 0d.

The Light Railways Act of 1896 was promoted to alleviate the distress of the agricultural depression by allowing inexpensive railways to be constructed in rural areas, with the proviso that those so constructed would be freed from the obligation to build to the high standards laid down by the Board of Trade for main lines. Section 5 of the Act stated that where the Board of Agriculture certified the provision of a light railway would benefit agriculture the Treasury might agree to the building of the line out of public money. The clause included the essential paragraph that, where *'a necessary means of communication would be established between a fishing harbour and a market, or that such a railway is necessary for the maintenance of some definite industry'*, then finance would be made available. Another significant feature was that *'application to the Light Railway Commissioners could be made by the County, Borough or District through which the railway was to pass, or by any company or individual'.*

Of the number of schemes advanced in East Anglia as a result of the Act, one had a close relationship with the Waveney Valley Branch. The South Norfolk Light Railway Order 1898, which received confirmation of the Light Railway Commissioners and the Board of Trade on 13th February 1899, authorised the building of a light railway from Trowse in the County of Norfolk to Beccles in the County of Suffolk. The original application was made through the Finance, Mines & Industries Association Limited, with the chief subscribers Sir Reginald W. Proctor Beauchamp Bart., Nicholas H. Bacon, John Holmes, John E. Crisp, Sir James Home Bart., W. Jefferson Woods, Freer Bargate, Arthur Knapp and Percival Deeley. The railway, 17 miles, 5 furlongs and 9 chains or thereabouts in length, commenced in the parish of Norwich by a junction with a siding on the Cambridge line of the GER at a point 350 yards or thereabouts measured in a south-easterly direction from the waiting room on the Up platform at Trowse station and terminated in a field in the parish of Beccles numbered 111, at a point 66 yards or thereabouts measured in a north-westerly direction from the north end of the Up side passenger platform at Beccles station by a junction with a siding to be constructed in such a position as agreed with the GER company. Of particular relevance was the approach to Beccles, for the light railway proposed to join the Waveney Valley line at a distance 6 furlongs 2½ chains or thereabouts measured in a westerly direction from the west abutment of the railway bridge over the River Waveney at Beccles, thence in an easterly direction following the course of the GER branch to its proposed termination.

The railway was to be built to standard gauge 4 feet 8½ inches and three years were allowed for the compulsory purchase of land and five years for the completion of works. All works associated with the GER at Trowse and Beccles were to be completed to the satisfaction of officers of the main line company, whilst the bridging of the River Waveney was to be constructed and completed for the protection of the Great Yarmouth Port & Haven Commissioners. No engine or vehicle with a greater weight then 14 tons was to run on the light railway and the speed limit was restricted to 25 mph, with 10 mph within a distance of 300 yards on the approach to and over level crossings and when passing over curves of 9 chains or less. The rails used on the railway were to weigh at least 60 lbs per yard.

The Light Railway Order authorised the promoters to raise £100,000 in £10 shares to finance the undertaking with borrowing powers of £33,000. Unfortunately the undertaking met with early difficulties and the promoters were forced to approach the Light Railway Commissioners for an extension of time to complete the line. This was duly authorised as the South Norfolk Light Railway (Extension of Time) Order 1902, passed on 21st August 1902, granting six years instead of the original three for the compulsory purchase of land and eight years instead of five for completion of the works. All was to no avail for the scheme ultimately drifted into oblivion.

The growth in the Waveney Valley Branch freight traffic necessitated improvements to the goods yard at Bungay, which were authorised on 7th February 1899 at a cost of £155. Following the purchase of additional land at Beccles a further round of improvements commenced beginning on 19th September 1899, when five additional yard lamps were authorised to aid staff in the

LIGHT RAILWAYS ACT, 1896.

SOUTH NORFOLK LIGHT RAILWAY ORDER, 1898.

ORDER

MADE BY THE

LIGHT RAILWAY COMMISSIONERS,

AND MODIFIED AND CONFIRMED BY THE

BOARD OF TRADE,

AUTHORISING THE CONSTRUCTION OF A

LIGHT RAILWAY FROM TROWSE, IN THE COUNTY OF NORFOLK, TO BECCLES, IN THE COUNTY OF SUFFOLK.

Presented to both Houses of Parliament by Command of Her Majesty.

LONDON:
PRINTED FOR HER MAJESTY'S STATIONERY OFFICE,
BY DARLING & SON, LTD., 1-3, GREAT ST. THOMAS APOSTLE, E.C.

And to be purchased, either directly or through any Bookseller, from
EYRE & SPOTTISWOODE, EAST HARDING STREET, FLEET STREET, E.C., and
32, ABINGDON STREET, WESTMINSTER, S.W.; or
JOHN MENZIES & Co., 12, HANOVER STREET, EDINBURGH, and
90, WEST NILE STREET, GLASGOW; or
HODGES. FIGGIS, & Co., LIMITED, 104, GRAFTON STREET, DUBLIN.

1899.

Front page of the South Norfolk Light Railway Order 1898 dated 13th February 1899.

Bungay station from the Down platform looking west, circa 1904. *John Alsop collection*

loading of trains during the hours of darkness. Then on 19th June 1900 sanction was given for alterations and extensions to the Down platform, and for a run round loop to be installed for the back platform road – the total cost including electrical work amounting to £1,695. On a visit down the line on 13th and 14th November 1900 the Directors again called in at Beccles and after discussion with local officers recommended the lengthening of the Down-side platform, alterations to the Down-side waiting room to make the accommodation larger with a window installed to face the approach road. As the work progressed, the Locomotive Superintendent requested improvements to water supplies for engines, as frequently motive power was changed there for the onward working. His request was acknowledged on 5th March 1901 when a new water storage tank and 3,000 gallons mushroom-type water crane was authorised at a total cost of £235, the final total being £238. Not to be outdone, the goods manager advised that additional goods accommodation was required in the form of extra sidings as the annual traffic handled totalled 37,965 tons. The Way and Works Committee and Traffic Committee readily agreed the outlay of £772 on 7th May 1901.

Sadly, in the intervening period, J.E. Skinner was fatally injured by a train at Homersfield on 25th October 1900; whilst walking along the track he became oblivious to the approaching locomotive. Lieutenant Colonel P.G. Von Donop duly carried out the inspection of the new works at Beccles on 12th May 1901 when he found that a new siding had been installed on the Up side of the Waveney Valley line with a connection at the existing end of that siding to the single branch line. The points and signals at the station end of the siding were worked from the existing Beccles North signal box containing an 80-lever frame with 77 working and 3 spare levers. At the Tivetshall end of the siding the points and signals were worked from a 12-lever ground frame, with 10 working and 2 spare levers, bolt locked from the North signal box. Von Donop found that the interlocking both in the North signal box and on the ground frame were correctly provided and recommended the use of the new connection. However, during the inspection the Lieutenant Colonel noted that a distant signal had been provided on the Waveney Valley line for the dock line at Beccles station. He advised the GER that it was unnecessary to provide such a signal and recommended its early removal; this was completed within days.

On 2nd July 1901 the contract for the water tank and crane at Beccles was awarded to Head Wrightson & Company at £150; by 17th September 1901 the platform extension and altered signalling was completed but above budget as the estimate was voted £1,657 but actual cost amounted to £1,786. Work at Beccles for the agricultural show was completed under budget, however, for on 5th November 1901 it was noted the additional work voted £772 had cost £595.

The programme of repairs and painting at stations continued when on 15th April 1902 work at Harleston was awarded to B. Rayner who tendered at £92 6s 3d. Two months later, on 4th June 1902, James Holden the Locomotive Superintendent requested the GER board that any future renewal of bridges should allow engines of 20 tons axle loading on any pair of driving wheels instead of 17 tons. After deliberation it was considered that many of the company's cross-country and branch lines would not require such expensive work as there was no immediate prospect of heavy engines being required; the Waveney Valley route was included in this category.

Yet further fatalities occurred on the Waveney Valley route when on 8th July 1902 C.H. Lee was hit by a train as he trespassed on the railway between Geldeston and Beccles. At the inquest a verdict of suicide was recorded. Then on 13th November 1902, a train ran down platelayer John Rudkin near Tivetshall as he was patrolling the line. It was thought the inclement weather prevented him hearing the approaching train. Another suicide occurred on 5th August 1903 when J. Gillman was hit by a train approaching Pulham Market.

Looking east from Outney occupational bridge towards Bungay goods yard and Ditchingham in October 1911. The Down and Up loop lines are to the left with a crossover connecting the two opposite the signal box. *GERS/Windwood 1335*

The view from Bungay signal box in October 1911, looking west through the arches of Outney occupational overbridge No. 1191 showing the Up platform beyond the structure. In the foreground is the Down loop line whilst the points from the goods yard throat lead to the Up loop line. *GERS/Windwood 1334*

Minor alterations were made at Tivetshall when authority was given for the extension of the Up siding to accommodate longer trains. Sanction came on 17th November 1903 at an estimated cost of £200 but the work was completed by 21st June 1904 at an actual cost of £148. Difficulties in identifying the position of trains led to complaints from Tivetshall signalmen and on 19th December 1905 authority was given for a bell contact to be placed on the Down advance starting signal to obviate the problem.

The repairs and painting of Beccles station carried out by F. Hipperson of Norwich, authorised on 18th April 1905 for £281 17s 7d, was completed by 3rd October at a cost of £133 17s 0d. Hardly had the paint dried when yet another scheme for a new station, costing £19,000, was aired. When the accountant reported to the board on the aggregate expenditure incurred over the recent years on the infrastructure, wiser counsels prevailed and on 20th February 1906 the proposed scheme was cancelled in favour of limited work costing a mere £608. Later in the year, on 3rd April 1906 it was announced that the 1906 Agricultural Show was to be held at Beccles when additional sidings costing £240 were agreed to handle the increase in traffic expected for the event.

At 11.20pm on 21st June 1906, Reliefman George Ayton received injuries to his left hand during a shunting operation at Harleston. At the subsequent inquiry the inspecting officer established that Ayton, aged 52 years, who was employed on an irregular hours basis, had been on duty for 14½ hours with 4½ hours interval during that period. On the day in question a carriage truck was being shunted into the cattle dock siding and shortly after, as the engine and four vehicles were drawn forward, the carriage truck started to run out of the siding. Instead of attempting to stop the vehicle by applying the hand brake, Ayton contrary to instructions attempted to halt the truck by placing his left hand against the leading buffer, and as the four vehicles were set back, his left hand was caught between the converging buffers. The inspector concluded that the accident was attributed to Ayton's own want of reasonable care and his total disregard of instructions.

Six days later, on 27th June 1906, Harleston was the scene of a fatal accident to 28-year-old Foreman Goods Porter Charles Blunderfield. At the enquiry into the mishap the inspection officer noted that the goods shed at Harleston was provided with a platform on each side of the siding to allow goods to be loaded or unloaded on either side of wagons. He learned, however, the offside platform was seldom used and that there was capacity for four wagons in the goods shed. On the morning in question a heavier than usual amount of goods traffic was returning from the Agricultural show and to keep the usual platform clear for that traffic, and at the same time avoid delay to ordinary inward traffic, Blunderfield arranged that a wagon of maize consigned to a local farmer should be offloaded on the offside platform. Unfortunately he failed to inform the staff employed and at about 1.20pm, during the absence of the farmer's men, Blunderfield gave instructions for the wagon to be drawn from the goods shed and replaced with empty wagons. As he stood by to superintend the work he momentarily forgot to ascertain if the door of the partly unloaded wagon containing maize had been lifted and consequently when the wagons were set in motion the door of the partly unloaded wagon slid along the platform and struck the end wall of the shed. As a result of the impact the brickwork was displaced causing the shed door to collapse on him, ultimately resulting in fatal injuries. Blunderfield survived to make a statement a few days after the mishap wherein he fully admitted the accident was due to his own momentary forgetfulness to which the inspecting officer agreed. Later in the year, F. Hipperson of Norwich continued their involvement with the GER when the firm was awarded the contract for repairs and painting at Tivetshall station on 2nd October 1906 after tendering at £95.

Heavy gales and continuous rain on 22nd February 1908 caused havoc to the GER services throughout East Anglia; the flooding and damage sustained at Beccles and Earsham severely delayed the branch services. Early the next year, on 19th January 1909, a train killed gateman W. Drane at Beccles after he opened the crossing gates but failed to get out of the way of the approaching service. The painting and repairs to branch stations continued, with A. Coe being awarded the contract for work at Harleston on 7th October 1909 for £128.

The BOT inquiry into the fatal accident to Porter Fisk at Ingate Street level crossing, Beccles, on 12th February 1910 revealed problems involved with the operation of level crossings for it established there had been several mishaps over the previous five-year period, at Ingate Street, Ingate Road, Cromwell Road, London Road and Northgate Street level crossings. After weighing up the evidence, the inspecting officer recommended the installation of distant signals interlocked with the gates to provide warning and protection. By September the BOT was pressing the GER for confirmation of action and as nothing had been done the Superintendent was asked to investigate and recommend a course of action. He duly reported to the Traffic Committee on 6th October 1910; distant signals were provided at Ingate Street and Ingate Road level crossings but not at London Road and Cromwell Road crossings as drivers of approaching trains had an excellent view. In the case of Northgate Street level crossing, located on the Waveney Valley line, the railway traffic was extremely light and it was not thought necessary to provide the distant signals. The Directors agreed to the provision of two single gates in lieu of the existing four gates at each of the crossings on the main line at a cost of £250 and electrical repeaters at a cost of £30 so that the crossing keepers were aware of the position of the distant signals. The crossing protection scheme had been completed by 15th June 1911 at a cost if £248 against an estimate of £210.

In the interim, the branch was flooded again on 9th December 1910 after heavy rain, and train services were disrupted for almost 24 hours until the water subsided. The deluge also affected the Snape and Framlingham branches as well as the Southwold Railway.

Lieutenant Colonel P.G. Von Donop was called upon to inspect the new arrangements regarding level crossings to the south of Beccles station and made his visit on 17th June 1911. He found that at Ingate Road and Ingate Street level crossings, gatemen had been employed to work the gates, each being advised by a bell fixed in the respective cabin when a train was in section. However, the crossings were not protected by signals and the only means of protection had hitherto been the red discs on the gates by day and red lamps mounted on the gates by night. The GER authorities, realising the potential for a disaster, had now provided distant signals in each direction of travel fully interlocked with the gates as a means of protection, the distant signals being readily identified with 'gate' distant arms visible to drivers of approaching trains. Von Donop was however far from convinced:

> *The provision of the these distant signals is undoubtedly a distinct improvement on the existing arrangements and they should certainly assist in preventing the gates being run through in future. As regards the down main line, the arrangements I consider to be satisfactory but in connection with the up main line there is one point to which attention must be drawn.*

He then elaborated that the Beccles South signal box Up advance starting signal was situated close to Ingate Road level crossing and although the new Up gate distant signal could not be lowered or cleared unless the advance starting signal was lowered and the gates across the public road, there was nothing to prevent the advance starting signal being lowered or cleared whilst the gates of Ingate Road and the adjacent Ingate Street were still across the railway! The inspector called for urgent alterations to remedy the defect. At the same time the Lieutenant Colonel also inspected London Road and Cromwell Lane level crossings and thought the driver's view from approaching trains was so good that he was not prepared to press for the provision of distant signals for the protection of these crossings. For their part, the GER operating authorities stressed they had

Trains crossing at Bungay station, circa 1912. *John Alsop collection*

issued instructions to drivers of the necessity to keep a good look out when approaching the crossings.

On 9th and 10th November 1911, during a visit down the line attended by the Chairman, General Manager and fifteen Directors and functional officers en route to Lowestoft, the party called at Beccles and approved the plan to convert the station master's house into a refreshment room. During discussions the hotel manager was instructed to see if the tea rooms could be provided upstairs, whilst the station master was to look for new house, possibly a GER building or failing that the local corporation was to be asked for land. The seats under the awning over the narrow Down platform were to be moved to the new booking hall to provide more space and the yard at the station entrance was to be paved. The Town Clerk, who was invited to attend, asked for the provision of a footbridge at Ingate Road level crossing, to which the General Manager replied it was customary for the local authority to contribute and he asked for a firm proposal.

Lieutenant Colonel Von Donop revisited Beccles on 30th January 1912 to view the alterations to Ingate Road and Ingate Street level crossings. He found that Ingate Road crossing gates were now locked from Beccles South signal box and interlocked with signals in both directions of travel. Ingate Street level crossing was protected by distant signals in each direction with the signals worked from a new 3-lever ground frame. The inspector was fully satisfied with these arrangements and found the interlocking was correct.

Following complaints regarding cramped accommodation by the station master at Ditchingham it was agreed on 1st February 1912 that the station master's house, booking office and waiting room were to be combined and a new booking office and waiting room provided at a cost of £172. The contract was subsequently awarded to G. Hipperson on 2nd May 1912 after he tendered at £149. In the same year the programme of painting and repairs to stations continued when on 7th March 1912 a contract was awarded to Watson & Kirby Limited for work at Homersfield for the price of £115, Bungay £166, Ditchingham £90 and Geldeston £100 respectively.

Throughout the line's existence, the Waveney Valley was always susceptible to flooding with the section between Homersfield and Bungay especially prone. The railway had suffered minor problems over the years and yet again, on 9th December 1910, excessive rainfall caused flooding between Geldeston and Bungay resulting in delays to all services. Other East Anglian lines affected included the Snape Branch, Framlingham Branch and the Southwold Railway. Then wet weather during August 1912 culminated in abnormal precipitation on 26th of the month causing considerable damage in many places when it was estimated 1,000 million tons of rainwater fell on Norfolk alone, but none more severe than on the Waveney Valley line. Inland lakes developed, including one 20 miles long and 2 miles wide between Tivetshall and Beccles. At Homersfield water came down the hills to the north of the station sweeping away the platform and the road in front of it, revealing the original road. Farms in the Harleston and Bungay areas were inundated and the River Waveney was described as a sinuous inland sea, with hay going down the river and wheat and barley disappearing by cart-loads. The railway suffered further misfortune when flood water moving like one great river more than a quarter mile across came down over Earsham Dam road and, swamping everything before it, poured across the line on the Earsham side of Bungay station, carrying away all ballasting and embankments, and leaving nothing but rails and sleepers suspended in the air. W.H. Hyde, the General Manager, reported to the Directors on 2nd October that traffic was working on all routes but the Waveney Valley Branch was still blocked at Earsham. The floods had seriously affected traffic receipts, especially the loss of corn and cattle traffic, which reduced by £24,000 in five weeks with an estimated overall loss of £40,000. The estimated cost of repairs was £2,000 with a further contingency plan of £6,700. For the period the branch was closed the GER organised a horse-bus and motor bus replacement service between Harleston and

Bungay. Norfolk County Council reported fifty-two road bridges and culverts were wrecked on the main roads. For 2½ days the city of Norwich, with six possible railway routes, was cut off and the Framlingham Branch and Southwold Railway were also affected.

On 25th and 26th October 1912 the Directors made another of their periodic visits down line, calling at Beccles where the alterations to the refreshment room were inspected before travelling on to Bungay and Homersfield where they noted the flood damage had been made good and everything was in working order.

During the early hours of 17th December 1912 at 4.00am a fire enveloped the maltings at Crisp & Sons premises at Beccles. The Lowestoft steam fire engine attended and was still at work on 19th December because of poor water supply to the pumps. As well as causing delays to railway services it was reported that nine wagons were damaged in the conflagration. The following year, on 3rd April 1913, Beccles station was repaired and painted under the periodic scheme for infrastructure refurbishment, the contract going to Morling Culham at £287 10s 0d. Just over a month later, on 20th May 1913 a train hit Platelayer F. Norman as he inspected the line between Earsham and Bungay and he sustained fatal injuries.

In the late summer of 1913 the Goods Manager reported the goods yard capacity at Ditchingham was insufficient for traffic, especially during the autumn when additional tonnage was despatched. There had been delays the previous year and he submitted a proposal for improved facilities to the Traffic Committee on 2nd October. The cost of the additional sidings and connections, including £100 for the purchase of land, was estimated at £1,203, consisting of £1,150 allocated to way and works and £53 for the electrical engineer. The installation was sanctioned provided the work was completed as a matter of urgency and it was noted the provision of the new facilities would eliminate the use of the tow rope during shunting operations. Lieutenant Colonel P.G. Von Donop inspected the new works at Ditchingham on 4th December 1913 and found that on the Up side of the station a new connection facing Down trains had been installed to serve additional sidings. The points and signals were worked from an 8-lever ground frame with 7 working and 1 spare lever, which was bolt locked from Ditchingham signal box. The interlocking was correct and the arrangements found to be satisfactory.

On 2nd April 1914 the contract for the repairs and painting of Tivetshall station was awarded to J. Read at a cost of £125. Their work proceeded apace but under the threat of mounting tension between factions in Europe. After Germany declared war on France and Belgium, Britain declared war on Germany on 4th August 1914 and within days the railway saw the departure of many men and some women who volunteered to serve with the armed forces; on occasions the branch station platforms were crowded as loved ones watched their departure and hoped for an early return. Sadly not all who departed returned to their native Norfolk or Suffolk.

On the outbreak of World War One the GER with other British railway companies came under Government control from the same date, under the powers of Section 16 of the Regulation of the Forces Act 1871, with the Railway Executive Committee taking control under the chairmanship of Herbert Walker, later Sir Herbert Walker of the London & South Western Railway. The Waveney Valley Branch services initially continued to run to pre-war timetables, but the issue of all excursion and cheap day tickets was suspended and all competition between companies cancelled. Goods traffic increased as additional produce from local farms was sent to towns and cities to make up for the loss of imported goods. Even hay was cut from railway embankments and sent to military stables. Several railwaymen also joined the colours and older men continuing in service or the recruitment of women ensured the temporary vacancies were covered.

It was deemed the Waveney Valley line was of military importance, being close to the East Anglian coastline, which would possibly bear the brunt of enemy hostilities. So concerned were the

Harleston station road frontage in August 1912 as passengers join the GER replacement bus service to Bungay after the line was damaged by flooding near Homersfield. Few passengers have occupied the lower deck of the bus and are evidently looking forward to the open top ride. The provision of the vehicle registration No. F 2441 and others from the Lowestoft allocated fleet must have resulted in reduced services to Oulton and Southwold. *Author's collection*

military and railway authorities of invasion that the branch was considered a second defensive line for the conveyance of troops and civilian personnel if the Germans managed to land their troops at Aldeburgh, Southwold or Lowestoft. For many months during this uneasy period an engine was kept in steam continuously 24 hours a day, 7 days a week, ready for instant action, with a second engine allocated to the branch at certain periods.

The Great Eastern Railway Act 1915 (5 and 6 Geo 5), which was passed on 9th June 1915, authorised the company to purchase land in the parish of Ditchingham in the rural district of Loddon and Clavering abutting on the north side of the line at Ditchingham station to enable the goods yard to be extended. The GER, serving mainly a rural community, was ever keen to promote ideas which would increase revenue. An exhibition train extolling egg and

Aftermath of the severe flooding, which occurred in Norfolk and Suffolk in August 1912. At Homersfield the beck burst its banks and the Waveney became a lake as the floodwaters rose. The original platform and permanent way are inundated but the station and signal box have escaped damage. Abnormal precipitation on 26th of the month caused considerable damage and it was estimated 1,000 million tons of rainwater fell on Norfolk alone, none more severe than in the Waveney Valley where inland lakes, including one 20 miles long by 2 miles wide, resulted in the river being described as 'a sinuous inland sea'. For almost two months the branch was operated as two sections from Tivetshall to Harleston and Bungay to Beccles with motor and horse buses covering the intermediate section. *Both John Alsop collection*

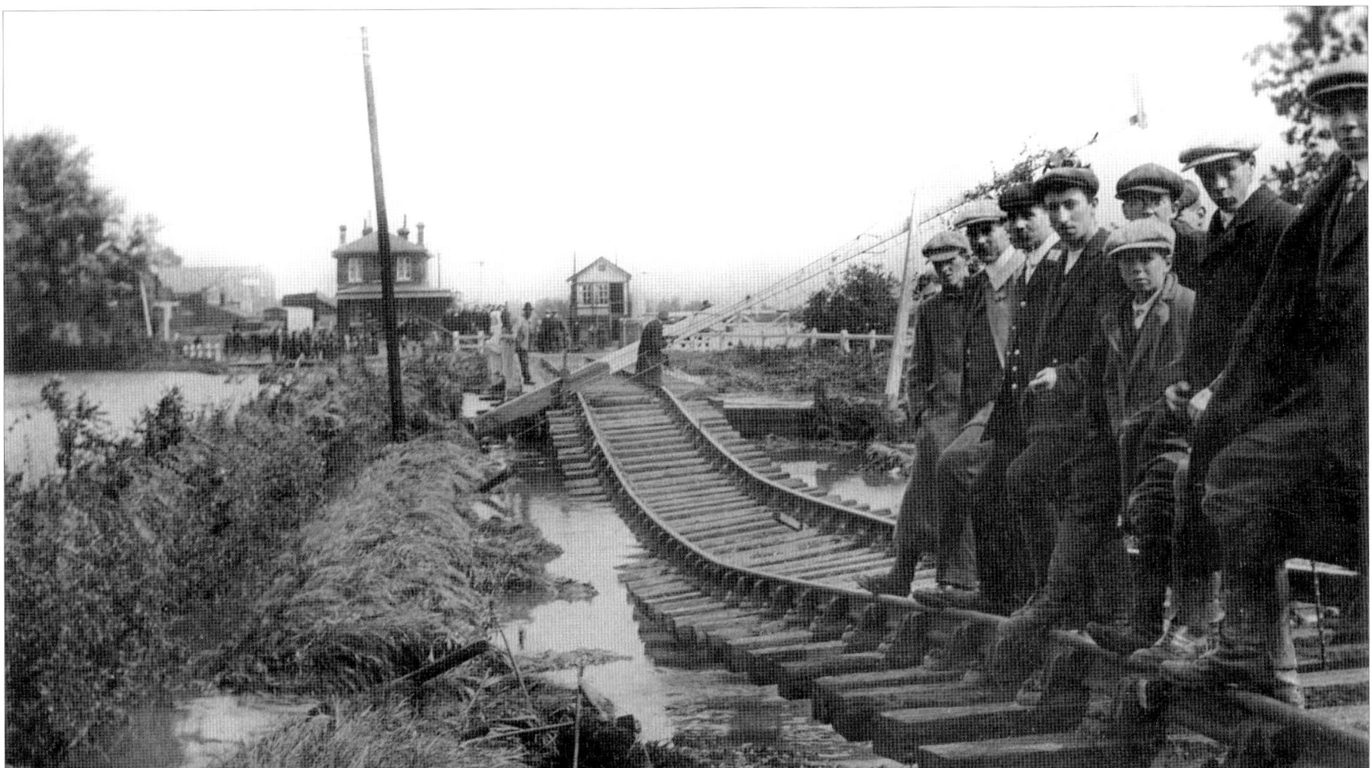

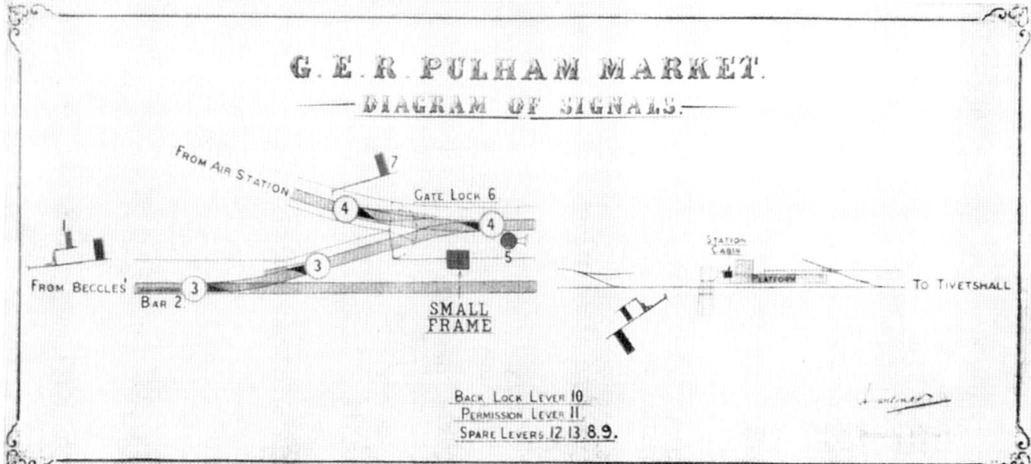

GER Diagram of Signals, Pulham Market Ground Frame 1916.

poultry farming was one of the publicity outlets and visited many locations in 1916. During the tour the train was stabled at Harleston to enable local farmers and landowners to view the latest techniques for improving breeding, as well as promoting rail traffic.

In 1912 the Admiralty had acquired 500 acres of land from three farms – Upper Vaunches Farm, Brick Kiln Farm and Home Farm – to the south of Pulham Market station. Thomas Gaze & Sons, surveyors and land agents, were given secret orders to purchase the property and civilian contractors under the supervision of the Air Construction Corps cleared and levelled the area for an airship station. The site did not become operational until 1915 when 100 Royal Navy personnel had established the station. Much of the material was brought by rail and initially conveyed to site by road from Pulham Market goods yard. A shed was erected in 1915 and a second a year later, both standing sentinel against the skyline. The station initially operated small non-rigid airships for patrolling the German Ocean (later known as the North Sea), the designated area being a line from Margate to Dunkirk in the south and Mablethorpe to the Dutch coast in the north, as well as engaging in combat with German Zeppelins. The first operational airship was launched in August 1916 and they soon acquired the nickname 'Pulham Pigs'. The first rigid airships arrived in April 1917 and were moored to 120 feet high mooring posts. In the same year the station was involved with parachute experimentation. To cater for the requirements of the air station and improve the supply facilities, a siding nearly a mile in length was installed from the branch at Pulham Market station to the nearby airfield, crossing in its path a public road. The Pulham Market station master assumed responsibility for all rail movements to and from the siding.

Lieutenant Colonel P.G. Von Donop conducted the BOT inspection of the new works at Pulham Market on 23rd February 1916. He found that on the Down side of the station, two facing connections had been made in the single line, one facing Down trains and the other facing Up services, both connections leading to a siding installed on the Up side of the line for the use of the Admiralty. The connection nearest the station was worked from Pulham Market signal box in which a new 22-lever frame had been installed with 20 working and 2 spare levers. The other connection was worked from a 13-lever ground frame with 11 working and 2 spare levers, the ground frame being released from the station signal box. Von Donop found the interlocking correct and being satisfied with the arrangements sanctioned the use of the connections. As a result of the installation, Pulham Market became a Train Staff station, with the line now divided into four sections: Tivetshall to Pulham Market, Pulham Market to Harleston, Harleston to Bungay and Bungay to Beccles.

With a view to making economies and staff savings, on 6th April 1916 the GER board agreed to the closing of a number of stations on and from 1st May. From that date it was planned to close Earsham (as prospective passengers could use Bungay station) and Geldeston, but only the former closed on that date and Geldeston station was closed to all traffic on and from 22nd May 1916. However, after complaints from the local population the latter station received a partial reprieve and reopened on 14th September for passenger traffic as an unstaffed halt. Because of the need for home-grown produce, Geldeston was reopened for goods traffic on and from 15th January 1917.

When nine-year-old Alice Alger, the daughter of a platelayer who lived in the cottage at Star level crossing Pulham Market, was walking home from school at midday on 9th February 1916, she noticed a ballast train approaching with the level crossing gates still across the railway. With no time to warn her parents she ran and opened one of the gates, and despite her weight and size, was in the act of opening the other gate when the engine hit the barrier. Alice was knocked off her feet but received only minor injuries to face and legs. Her action reduced the severity of the accident and her deeds were later brought to the notice of the GER management. On 19th May 1916 Alice, accompanied by her mother, attended the GER Headquarters at Liverpool Street where the Chairman Claud Hamilton, in the company of several officers of the company, presented the young girl with a gold watch inscribed on the back *'Alice R.E. Alger from the Directors of the Great Eastern Railway Company – for bravery – May 1916'*. The Chairman also presented Alice with a personal gift of a needlework set.

The cessation of imports of sand from abroad resulted in a great demand for home supplies, so two gravel and sandstone pits at Homersfield, with material suitable for making much-needed concrete, were opened in 1916 resulting in 35,000 tons per annum being dispatched via the branch during the remaining war years.

Despite the war economies, the painting and repairs programme to stations continued when on 1st June 1916 Vigor received the contract for work at Harleston after tendering at £228. Later in the year, on 9th October 1916, District Relief Man R. Etheridge was killed by a train at Harleston after failing to hear the approaching locomotive; but after tragedy came adulation, for on 7th December a letter was received from the General Officer commanding 62nd

Division praising Bungay station master and station staff for work involved in handling the stores and materials whilst the unit was based in the area.

The GER territory facing the German Ocean was always a prime target for Zeppelin raids as the Germans sought to attack London, the Home Counties and East Anglia. On many forays the airships followed railway routes and the first raid on Norfolk came on 19th and 20th January 1915. These continued regularly thereafter until the end of 1916 when the visits by the airships were succeeded by aircraft, which favoured raids on the Thames estuary and the Kent routes to London, with the GER affected in Essex and East London. Despite Lowestoft being bombed in Zeppelins raids on 16th April 1915 and 20th February 1916, and Yarmouth on 2nd September 1916, further inland the Waveney Valley route remained unscathed.

By December 1916 the strain of the war effort was taxing the resources of all British railways to such an extent that the Railway Executive issued an ultimatum that they could only continue if drastic reductions were made to ordinary and non-essential services from 1st January 1917; although with these economies the Waveney Valley Branch lost only one train in each direction. Thus the GER continued its essential activity giving regular passenger, freight and parcels services to the local community. It was still deemed the line was of military importance in the area, being fairly close to the East Anglian coastline which was bearing the brunt of enemy hostilities. Unfortunately the year ended on a tragic note for on 27th December 1916 Pumper T. Crisp sustained fatal injuries when run down by a train at Tivetshall.

A feature of the wartime GER was the War Relief Fund to assist servicemen and collections were made at all stations throughout the system. Donations from the Waveney Valley Branch stations showed a marked lack of benevolence as takings from Tivetshall alone for the three months ending 31st December 1917 only amounted to 12s 0d. In comparison, takings at Cockfield and Wenetham station on the Marks Tey to Bury St. Edmunds line for the same period totalled £2 5s 6d.

The GER increasingly found the constricted track layout at Beccles hindered the marshalling of military traffic and shunting movements causing unnecessary delays. After investigation, the Superintendent reported on 4th July 1918 that to obviate the problem it was necessary to remove the double-tongue trap points located in the dock siding adjacent to the Waveney Valley dock platform and also alter the retaining wall of the cattle dock. By expending an estimated £128 on these alterations the cattle dock would be available for military loading and unloading as well as serving its purpose for livestock traffic. The expenditure was readily agreed.

The end of hostilities in November 1918 was greeted with great relief and some of the branch stations were decorated with flags to celebrate the armistice. By this time seaplanes had replaced most of the coastal and SS type airships operating from Pulham airfield.

In March 1919 William Matthews, clerk at Bungay station, was presented with a solid silver cigarette case and a case of silver mounted briar pipes by Captain Surtees, supported by Captain Williams of the Royal Army Medical Corps in acknowledgement of his zealous and useful work and courtesy shown to officers, NCOs and men of the 68th Division Headquarters staff during their period at Bungay. Along the line at Earsham the station reopened for passenger traffic on 1st August 1919, while Geldeston regained station status on 14th September 1919.

After the contract was placed for the relocking of the lever frame in Tivetshall signal box it was decided to provide additional ground signals and a new crossover to facilitate the safety of shunting movements within station limits. The work, costing £1,064, was sanctioned on 1st May 1919 as the installation of the relocking was imminent. Major A. Mount conducted the BOT inspection of the new works at Tivetshall on 24th June 1920. He found a new trailing connection equipped with ground signals had been installed between the Up and Down main lines south of the signal box. The home signal had been relocated accordingly whilst a ground disc signal had been provided at the existing Up main line trailing connection at the south end of the yard. Five further ground disc signals had also been provided at the north end of the yard and at the same time the existing Up side dead-end siding had been equipped with trap points. The revised signalling and points were

Postcard illustrating the types of aircraft used on coastal patrol during World War One.
Neil Parkhouse collection

Earsham station, circa 1920. The signal box has been reduced to its foundations (near right), while the poster above the milk churns is advertising the revised train service with additional trains. The signal box was abolished in 1919 and replaced by a 3-lever ground frame to operate gate distant signals and lock the crossing gates. *John Alsop collection*

worked from the existing Tivetshall Junction signal box containing a 45-lever frame, now with 44 working and 1 spare lever. The additional interlocking was correct and the general arrangements satisfactory. However, Mount drew the attention of the railway company representative to the lack of repeater indicators in the signal box for both Up and Down distant signals. Although there was a good view of both signals, as these were located 1,300 and 1,050 yards distant respectively, the inspector considered repeat indicators were necessary to help the signalman, especially during adverse weather conditions. Mount was advised the company intended to install the repeaters as a matter of urgency.

The general feeling of elation felt by the cessation of hostilities in November 1918 was shattered by a railway strike which halted branch services from 26th September to 5th October 1919. The action undermined the patronage enjoyed by the railway as prospective passengers sought alternative modes of transport. Serious inroads were being made into the monopoly enjoyed by the GER as a local bus service was introduced. The industrial unrest began the slow decline in the freight services as farmers and growers realised for the first time that with improving roads, goods could be conveyed by motor lorry, in some cases using vehicles purchased second-hand from the military. The short journeys to local markets were possible at rates cheaper than those charged by the GER. The door-to-door services were more convenient than the double handling into and out of railway wagons. The primitive road vehicles of the day were not, however, capable of long hauls, and so middle and long distance traffic remained safely in the hands of the railway company.

Although peace had been declared the Government retained the control of the railways until 15th August 1921 as the war effort had seriously debilitated the concerns with little or minimal maintenance of infrastructure and rolling stock. In 1918 the Coalition Government had hinted at support for nationalisation, a thought that had been festering since the formation of the Railway Nationalisation League in 1895, with the later support of the railway unions and the formation of the Railway Nationalisation Society in 1908. A number of industrialists and traders were sympathetic, saying the railways should be a public corporation rather than a profit-making concern. In the event the Government fell short of full nationalisation and formed the companies into four groups. It was thus hoped the impending grouping of the railways would engender an increase in receipts as the more people took advantage to travel in East Anglia for leisure and recreation.

East Anglia experienced one of the heaviest snowfalls for years on Tuesday 3rd and Wednesday 4th January 1922, with high winds causing drifting. The branch was blocked between Harleston and Bungay, necessitating one train to turn back and the employment of the snowplough from Norwich to clear the line. Delays also occurred on the East Suffolk route and the Ipswich to Norwich main line, whilst trains were cancelled on the Southwold Railway. Further snowfalls occurred on Monday 16th January but the Waveney Valley route was kept clear by running a light engine across the branch.

As the proposed grouping of the railway approached, modified working of the Tivetshall to Beccles branch was authorised on 16th June 1922 with expenditure of £230 resulting in a saving of £1,249. Geldeston again became a staffed passenger station with effect from 2nd October 1922 whilst in the final weeks of GER ownership a contract was placed with Hipperson on 9th November 1922 for repairs and painting at Tivetshall after the firm tendered at £487. The Waveney Valley Branch had survived relatively unscathed through the recent hostilities and it was hoped the impending grouping of the railways would engender an increase in receipts as more people travelled to the East Coast for leisure.

6

Grouping

As a result of the 1921 Railways Act, on 1st January 1923 the GER amalgamated with the Great Northern, Great Central, North Eastern, North British and several smaller companies to form the London & North Eastern Railway. Initially little changed but gradually the identity on the locomotives and rolling stock working the branch services altered, with the legend L&NER on the tank and tender sides, whilst coaching and wagon stock also showed the ownership of the new company. All was not well, however, for increasing road competition forced the new ownership to accelerate the programme of economies.

The L&NER authorities also continued the programme of repairs and painting of the branch stations and on 10th May 1923 a contract was awarded to T. Carr after he tendered at £424 12s 0d to clean and paint the stations Beccles to Ditchingham inclusive provided the work was completed within six weeks. In the first year of grouping the L&NER also continued the programme of bridge renewals started by the GER and on 1st November 1923 authority was given for the renewal of the steelwork on underbridge No. 1190 at Bungay, with Boulton & Paul of Norwich receiving the contract after quoting a price of £15 15s 0d per ton.

On 31st October 1923 Arthur Offord, aged 51 years and employed by Thomas Moy Limited as chargeman at their Harleston coal depot, received injuries when the toes of his right foot were run over, which later required amputation. Amos Ford conducted the BOT inquiry into the accident and noted that Thomas Moy Limited owned a private coal yard adjoining the L&NER goods yard at Harleston, with a siding connection which was an extension of the goods shed line. On the day in question a loaded coal wagon was shunted through the goods shed to run to Moy's yard. Offord was standing near the goods shed and, thinking the wagon would come to a stand before reaching the yard, commenced to push the vehicle by the leading right-hand buffer. Whilst he was doing so two other wagons destined for the goods shed ran through the building and closed up to the slowly moving coal wagon. By the impact the coal wagon was forced forward and Offord, losing his hold, fell to the ground, the toes of his right foot being run over

'J15' Class 0-6-0 No. 65471 approaching Homersfield with a train formed of a mixture of 16-ton all steel mineral and wooden bodied open wagons with goods brake van in the rear. Note the underbridge abutments indicate the span was rebuilt in 1922. *Dr I.C. Allen*

by the wagon wheels. Ford observed that it was no part of Offord's duty to interfere with the wagon before it had entered the coal yard, and however good his intentions he should not have done so, and he later admitted his blame. The inspecting officer was also critical of railway staff for Casual Porter E.C. Norman, who was assisting with shunting operations, should have attended and brought the goods wagons to a stand in the goods shed. Had he not neglected his duty the mishap would have been avoided. It was noted at the time of the inquiry Norman was no longer in the service of the railway company.

As well as the primitive competitive bus services, renewed industrial action, culminating with a seven day railway strike from 20th January 1924, added to the decline in traffic. Competitors quickly took advantage of the stoppage and passengers who regularly patronized the railway service for short journeys turned to road transport, some never returning to use the branch line.

The London & North Eastern Railway Act 1924 (14 and 15 Geo 5), which received the Royal Assent on 1st August 1924, amongst other things authorised the company to purchase land in the borough of Beccles adjoining the railway and Station Road. Later, in the 1924 Best Kept Station Competition Tivetshall gained a third class certificate earning Station Master Thompson and his staff a £3 prize.

Some of the branch stations were due to receive the benefit of the periodic repair and repainting programme but all quotations for extensive work at Earsham and Bungay were declined on 26th March 1925. However, F.R. Hipperson was later awarded the contract on 30th April 1925 after tendering at £2,214 15s 0d.

The Chief General Manager submitted a report on 23rd April 1926 to the effect that over the past two to three years complaints had been received from farmers, traders, local councils, the National Farmers Union and other bodies regarding the lack of accommodation and facilities at certain stations for dealing with sugar beet and other produce from East Anglia. The Waveney Valley Branch was implicated by the lack of siding space at Bungay, where the estimated cost of providing additional sidings, including the purchase of additional land, amounted to £991. The matter was raised at the Traffic Committee meeting on 29th April and the expenditure sanctioned when it was revealed the additional sidings would result in an estimated net saving of £162 by concentrating loading at one point instead of overburdening goods yards at adjacent stations.

The General Strike in early May 1926 caused services to be curtailed again. Union members withdrew their labour in support of the miners and train services could not be guaranteed. The Waveney Valley services were suspended on several days; as on many other lines it was only possible for the L&NER to offer a skeletal train service by using volunteer labour. Within a week or so regular railwaymen returned to work and the volunteer labour ceased. The impact of the continuing miners strike, however, meant that coal stocks available to the railway companies were low; the L&NER authorities decided the only course of action was to reduce the train services to conserve coal supplies. From 31st May 1926, when the revised timetable was introduced, only four passenger trains ran in each direction across the Waveney Valley Branch. Later in the year matters improved and the service was enhanced as coal supplies increased.

Tivetshall station was next to receive attention for maintenance and painting when Hughes & Hughes received the contract on 26th July 1928 after tendering at £696 11s 4d against the engineer's estimate of £784, the price including works at Forncett, Flordon and Swainsthorpe on the main line as well as Norwich Victoria.

With blower on, 'F4' Class 2-4-2T No. 67158 approaches Ellingham with a Beccles to Tivetshall train in 1951; the three-coach train is formed of Gresley ex-L&NER non-gangway stock. *Dr I.C. Allen*

Forncett Junction, where Waveney Valley goods services branched left to Wymondham and through passenger services from Beccles to Norwich followed the main line to the right. This view in October 1911 looking north shows Forncett Junction signal box on the Up side of the main line. *GERS/Windwood 1283*

To permit smoother operation through Beccles station in the summer of 1928 the through road with double slip at the south end of the Up platform was removed and replaced by two new crossovers with associated minor alterations to signalling. The L&NER authorities were continually seeking ways of reducing operating costs on the branch and on 27th September 1928 the Divisional General Manager (Southern Area) submitted a proposal to withdraw the two attendants who operated the gates at Bungay Common level crossing located quarter of a mile from Bungay station. The crossing was originally provided as an occupational crossing to give access from the south side of the railway to Bungay or Outney Common, located to the north of the line. The scheme involved the erection of a gate cottage which would be occupied by a ganger and his wife, who in addition to living rent free would be paid 6s 0d per week for attending to the gates for the passage of trains. The cost was estimated at £674 with an additional annual maintenance charge of £6 offset by the saving of two gatekeepers posts equating to £217 per annum. After due discussion the Traffic Committee was not convinced by the economic argument and deferred judgement on the scheme.

Lieutenant Colonel A.H.L. Mount carried out the official inspection of the alterations at Beccles station on 2nd October 1928. He found that the through road with a double slip at the south end of the Up platform had been removed and two crossovers substituted. The permanent way was formed of 95 lbs per yard RBS rail and the necessary minor alterations to signalling effected. The connections were worked from Beccles South signal box with its existing 39-lever frame now containing 37 working and 2 spare levers, with the locking correctly installed. During his visit, Mount was concerned that the trap points of the short dead-end siding had been re-laid too near the running line, the lead of the trap of one chain radius providing only a 4 feet clearance – the toe of the points being located at the 6 feet clearance point of the siding. The L&NER representatives attending the inspection explained that the course of action was taken to give sufficient length in the siding to accommodate two tank engines. Mount duly discussed the layout with the company officers with the possibility of improving the layout by slewing or substituting a de-railer for the trap as owing to the presence of a well at the back of the buffer stops lengthening of the siding was undesirable. It was finally agreed slight improvements were possible by slewing the siding a few inches and this was considered the preferred option. The Lieutenant Colonel concluded his report:

> *In all circumstances and having regard to the fact that all up trains stop at the platform and the speed of movement in the siding is slow no extensive alterations are required. On the understanding this is an exceptional case, I recommend approval subject to the minor slewing to give as much clearance as possible.*

On 29th November 1928 the L&NER Traffic Committee authorised the provision of two additional sidings at Wymondham on the Ely to Norwich main line to assist with the marshalling of goods trains, which included traffic destined for the Tivetshall to Beccles line via the Wymondham-Ashwellthorpe-Forncett branch.

Despite rationalisation, the loss of traffic caused by various strikes and the attractions of an almost door-to-door service operated by competitive bus companies were always a source of concern to

1923	PASSENGERS	PASSENGER RECEIPTS £	PARCELS RECEIPTS £	SEASON TICKET RECEIPTS £	TOTAL RECEIPTS £
Tivetshall	19,665	1,419	1,088	148	2,655
Pulham Market	8,455	659	107	33	799
Pulham St. Mary	11,040	770	1,036	45	1,851
Harleston	34,061	3,872	1,411	140	5,423
Homersfield	16,732	1,220	1,113	12	2,345
Earsham	6,339	500	430	—	930
Bungay	29,827	3,551	958	69	4,578
Ditchingham	11,119	1,204	789	12	2,095
Ellingham	6,836	499	371	—	870
Geldeston	8,282	379	243	—	622
Beccles	148,083	12,562	2,949	n/a	15,511
Total branch stations only	132,691	12,654	6,458	311	19,513
Total including Tivetshall and Beccles	300,439	26,635	10,495	459	37,679
1924					
Tivetshall	17,574	1,326	1,154	115	2,595
Pulham Market	9,774	643	98	42	783
Pulham St. Mary	11,391	732	1,298	60	2,090
Harleston	31,145	3,679	1,563	115	5,357
Homersfield	15,278	1,092	1,127	19	2,238
Earsham	6,389	461	390	—	851
Bungay	27,101	3,153	990	95	4,238
Ditchingham	10,074	1,261	876	10	2,147
Ellingham	6,002	448	360	12	820
Geldeston	7,886	343	252	4	599
Beccles	140,156	12,221	3,097	1,217	16,535
Total branch stations only	125,040	11,812	6,954	357	19,123
Total including Tivetshall and Beccles	282,700	25,359	11,205	1,689	38,253
1925					
Tivetshall	17,022	1,281	1,313	131	2,725
Pulham Market	9,797	636	107	42	785
Pulham St. Mary	12,706	841	1,083	56	1,980
Harleston	32,253	3,429	1,949	115	5,493
Homersfield	15,795	1,072	742	34	1,848
Earsham	6,242	410	475	2	887
Bungay	26,927	3,024	1,067	223	4,314
Ditchingham	10,169	1,196	897	19	2,112
Ellingham	5,881	456	457	6	919
Geldeston	8,118	355	330	1	686
Beccles	154,551	12,943	2,676	1,125	16,744
Total branch stations only	127,888	11,419	7,107	498	19,024
Total including Tivetshall and Beccles	299,461	25,643	11,096	1,754	38,493

local L&NER officials. The decline suffered on the Waveney Valley line is evident from the receipts earned in the years 1923 to 1928 inclusive, tabulated above.

The figures were far from encouraging to the L&NER management, for Harleston dealing with 109 passengers a day in 1923 had reduced to seventy-four a day by 1928, whilst the second busiest station, Bungay with ninety-six passengers a day in 1923, reduced by over 50 per cent to forty-five a day in 1928. Of the smaller stations, Earsham and Ellingham dealt with twenty and twenty-two passengers a day respectively in 1923, reducing to twelve and fifteen respectively in 1928. Overall daily receipts from passenger and parcels traffic also reduced: Earsham earning £3 3s 2d in 1923 had reduced to £2 6s 5d by 1928, but Ellingham showed a slight upward trend with earnings of £2 15s 10d in 1923 increased to £3 0s 0d a day five years later. This upward trend was not reciprocated at the two larger stations, where Harleston's earnings

1926	Passengers	Passenger Receipts £	Parcels Receipts £	Season Ticket Receipts £	Total Receipts £
Tivetshall	15,468	1,151	1,528	124	2,803
Pulham Market	8,420	506	101	16	623
Pulham St. Mary	10,881	686	1,109	26	1,821
Harleston	27,247	2,941	1,846	99	4,886
Homersfield	13,110	916	704	31	1,651
Earsham	5,590	341	527	3	871
Bungay	20,890	2,447	1,002	198	3,647
Ditchingham	8,575	983	829	13	1,825
Ellingham	5,103	367	510	8	885
Geldeston	6,453	278	311	17	606
Beccles	138,279	11,776	2,990	1,131	15,897
Total branch stations only	106,269	9,465	6,939	411	16,815
Total including Tivetshall and Beccles	260,016	22,392	11,457	1,666	35,515
1927					
Tivetshall	16,130	1,148	1,656	147	2,951
Pulham Market	9,555	543	127	13	683
Pulham St. Mary	10,270	706	1,491	23	2,220
Harleston	27,019	2,861	1,781	105	4,747
Homersfield	12,156	901	751	30	1,682
Earsham	4,937	355	632	—	987
Bungay	18,260	2,313	1,149	166	3,628
Ditchingham	7,900	1,019	844	15	1,878
Ellingham	4,744	355	577	13	945
Geldeston	7,037	264	340	14	618
Beccles	152,864	12,208	3,113	1,000	16,321
Total branch stations only	93,878	9,317	7,692	379	17,388
Total including Tivetshall and Beccles	262,872	22,673	12,461	1,526	36,660
1928					
Tivetshall	15,215	1,042	1,634	145	2,821
Pulham Market	8,178	491	92	13	596
Pulham St. Mary	9,104	683	1,341	21	2,045
Harleston	23,098	2,580	1,602	122	4,304
Homersfield	8,407	677	790	27	1,494
Earsham	3,761	257	467	—	724
Bungay	13,900	1,859	1,099	190	3,143
Ditchingham	7,189	791	766	15	1,572
Ellingham	4,659	272	653	16	941
Geldeston	6,192	242	317	—	559
Beccles	163,544	11,759	3,068	908	15,735
Total branch stations only	84,488	7,852	7,127	404	15,378
Total including Tivetshall and Beccles	263,247	20,653	11,829	1,457	33,934

of £17 7s 6d a day in 1923 had slumped to £13 15s 10d in 1928, whilst at Bungay earnings of £14 13s 2d in 1923 had reduced to £10 1s 5d a day by 1928.

The station repair and painting programme continued in 1930 when a contract was awarded to A. Bolton on 20th February for work on Geldeston, Ellingham and Ditchingham stations at a cost of £150 17s 0d, against the engineer's estimate of £181. Steeplechase races under National Hunt rules were held each spring at Bungay and the 1930 event held on 2nd and 3rd April encouraged a large crowd. Altogether forty-eight racehorses were conveyed to the town by rail, the horseboxes filling the goods yard to capacity.

As the years progressed and freight traffic increased, so the condition of several bridges on the branch were a cause for concern to the Civil Engineer and on 4th June 1931 authority was given for the reconstruction of the superstructure of underbridge No. 1179 between Harleston and Homersfield. Estimated to cost £2,880, the contract was finally awarded to the Furness Shipbuilding Company Limited who tendered at £2,650.

For many years the loading of milk churns at Beccles had caused considerable inconvenience as the only road access was on the Down side of the line, whilst most if not all of the traffic was despatched in the Up direction to London and other centres. With increasing traffic passing through the station the L&NER authorities authorised in the autumn of 1930 the provision of a moveable timber swing bridge pivoted from the Up side island platform and capable of swinging across the Up and Down main lines to enable loaded churns to be transferred with ease across the tracks. The bridge also formed part of the Up-side platform when in the closed position.

In September 1931 the L&NER management was seeking to effect economies on lightly used services on branch lines by replacing the normal locomotive and coaching stock with a Sentinel steam railcar. Accordingly, No. 2203 *Old Blue*, which had previously worked from Guisborough in the North Eastern section and St. Margarets Edinburgh was transferred to Norwich for trials on branches between 14th and 19th September. During this period it worked at least one trip for evaluation purposes over the Waveney Valley Branch before being sent to Ipswich for two days, after which it took up trial duties at Cambridge from 21st to 25th of the month where it worked on the Mildenhall and Saffron Walden branches. Its usefulness was questioned as mixed trains ran on most branches and *Old Blue* was quickly returned to Guisborough. The decision to trial a Sentinel car is surprising, for Norwich was allocated five Clayton steam railcars between 1927 and 1937 and used them chiefly between Norwich and Lowestoft, Lowestoft and Beccles, and Wroxham to County School, but none were used between Tivetshall and Beccles.

The January 1932 edition of the *L&NER Magazine* enthused over the Beccles parcels bridge under the heading *'Novel Platform Link'*.

Since the remodelling of the station 30 years ago, which left the ramp at the south end of the up platform approximately 60 yards short of the down side with the abandonment of the level crossing, the work of transferring merchandise and luggage from one to the other proved strenuous. Large numbers of milk churns are transhipped to and from the Waveney Valley branch and together with other items have to be carried from the down side to the up side over the main lines. Eighteen months ago it was decided to install an experimental moveable goods platform, which was cheaper than lifts and stairways, to form a bridge between the two sides. This consists of a substantial wooden structure working on a centre pin set on concrete, two wheels running on steel plates also let into the concrete allowing a turning movement at one end, whilst at the extended end another two wheels carry the platform along the curved rail across the main lines. When not in use this connecting platform acts as an extended passenger platform on the up side and is locked in position by the South Box signalman. All points and signals applying to the roads affected are locked when the transfer work is in progress.

By the spring of 1932 the condition of the building on the Up platform at Bungay had deteriorated to such a degree that local passengers using the station made many complaints. The Divisional General Manager (Southern Area) duly submitted a memorandum to both the Traffic and Works committees on 12th July reporting that the station buildings on the Up platform at Bungay had been in a dilapidated condition for some years and could not be maintained unless heavy repairs were undertaken, which would entail rebuilding the structure. Bungay Urban District Council had called attention to the bad state of the premises, particularly the waiting room, and the poor condition of the station had received adverse comments in the local press. The comparatively modern buildings on the Down-side platform only accentuated the poor condition of those on the Up side. The engineer had prepared a scheme for the rebuilding of the structure on a much reduced scale and the estimated cost of £779, including demolition of the old structure, compared favourably with the £1,500 required if the building was reconstructed to the original dimensions. The cost would be offset by a reduction of £17 per annum in renewal and maintenance charges. The committees agreed the invitation to tender.

Lieutenant Colonel E.P. Anderson duly conducted the official BOT inspection of the new luggage bridge at Beccles station on 26th June 1933. The inspector found that as the only road access for vehicles bringing milk churns to the station was on the Down side of the railway, difficulties had been experienced in transferring loaded churns across the main lines to the Up platform for despatch to London, the main destination for most of the traffic. A timber swing bridge had therefore been installed at the south end of the Up main (island) platform with a width of 6 feet, housed in a recess in the platform when not in use. Fencing and a ramp were provided for the protection of passengers who used the bridge as part of the Up platform when joining a train. Anderson noted the bridge was pivoted on roller bearings at the north end and at its outer end a carrying wheel running on a curved rail fixed to the sleepers supported the structure. The bridge was normally locked in position clear of the track by a bolt which could only be released from a new 2-lever ground frame located adjacent to the bridge. The ground frame was mechanically released from Beccles South signal box and telephonic communication was also provided between the frame and the signal box, which contained a 40-lever frame now with 39 working levers and 1 spare lever. With a view to block working, the placing of the bridge across the running lines formed an obstruction and Anderson noted the following instructions had been issued for the protection of the line.

A) *For Up trains the stop signals worked by Beccles North signal box are slotted from Beccles South signal box. The slot levers are locked normal by the reversing of the lever, which released the ground frame, and in addition the special regulations require the signalman in Beccles South signal box to 'block back' before releasing the bridge.*
B) *In the Down direction the signalman at Beccles South signal box is authorised to accept a train up to the outer home signal situated 730 yards from the bridge, provided the line is clear up to the Down starting signal i.e. overrunning of about 670 yards. The outer home signal is not locked at danger by the bridge release lever. The inner home signal No. 2 situated 370 yards from the bridge and starter No. 3, 70 yards distant from the bridge, are locked at danger by the bridge lever.*

The inspector discussed at length with the L&NER company officials the desire to extend the locking to make the bridge release lever hold the outer home signal at danger but was convinced that such action could be dispensed with as the approach to the station on the Down side was on a 30 chains curve with a permanent 25 mph speed restriction and the distant signal, 1,740 yards from the bridge, was held at caution by the release of the bridge ground frame. The interlocking between the signals, points and the bridge was correctly installed.

Further stations received the benefit of the cleaning and repainting programme when J. Arundel was awarded the contract for work at Pulham Market, Pulham St. Mary, Harleston, Homersfield and Earsham on 28th June 1934 after tendering at £370 6s 6d using the spray method against the engineer's estimate of £400. During the 1930s collections were regularly made, with the full agreement of the railway management, at stations in Suffolk for the East Suffolk & Ipswich Hospital Contributory Fund. Despite being in Norfolk, Harleston station staff collected a mere 6s 0d in December 1934.

The L&NER authorities, ever seeking economies, had for some time been concerned with the increasing costs of maintenance of the permanent way on many of their branch and cross-country lines and the Waveney Valley Branch was no exception. After due investigation in the spring of 1934 it was established that savings could be made by the introduction of a motor lorry to give staff more flexibility in their day-to-day maintenance and repair programme. The matter was placed before the Works Committee at their meeting on 26th July when the Divisional General Manager Southern Area advised that it was proposed to use the road motor system of permanent way maintenance on the Tivetshall to Beccles line. The route consisted of 14 miles 50 chains of single line and 3 miles of sidings. The scheme necessitated the provision of a 2-ton motor lorry which would be stabled in the goods yard at Tivetshall and also a bicycle – the estimated cost being £244. Fourteen men maintained the railway but the introduction of the new scheme would enable maintenance to be carried out by twelve men resulting in a net saving of £73 per annum.

The breakdown of costs included:

		£	£
Wages of 2 men at £117 each			234
Less	Interest at 4 per cent on £244	9	
	Maintenance of motor lorry	31	
	Depreciation on motor lorry	26	
	Licence	30	
	Petrol	41	
	Oil, cleaning etc.	7	
	Tyres	11	
	Extra pay for driver	5	
	Maintenance and renewal of bicycle	1	
	Annual costs total	161	-161
			73

The Works Committee duly approved of the scheme. A similar one involving the Tivetshall to Trowse section of the main line was sanctioned on 20th February 1936.

For some considerable time the water pumping plant at Tivetshall had been temperamental to the extent that on some days barely enough water was available for replenishing locomotives, let alone for station use. The Divisional General Manager (Southern Area) prepared a memorandum on 27th February 1935 reporting that the consumption of water for locomotive purposes amounted to 8,000,000 gallons per annum. The water was pumped by means of a steam pump from a well, 60 feet in depth, to an overhead tank

'F3' Class 2-4-2T No. 8080 departing from Beccles with the Lowestoft portion of a Down Liverpool Street to Yarmouth express in the late 1930s. Behind the engine is the parachute water tank used to replenish locomotives on the Down main line and the Waveney Valley bay platform. The tall signal in the background is the Down starting signal with the road set for Lowestoft; the signal on the tallest post is for the Down main to Yarmouth and the signal partly obscured by the water tank is the Down main to Waveney Valley starting signal. *Author's collection*

with capacity for 8,500 gallons. One man was employed as part-time pump attendant whilst his other duties involved attendance to the level crossing gates during certain hours and also rendering assistance on station duties. It was proposed to displace the existing steam pump and replace it with a 2,500 gallons per hour centrifugal pump and motor with automatic starting gear and float switches. The subject was raised at the meeting of the Works and Traffic committees on 28th March when the gross cost was estimated at £252 offset by £10 value of recovered material, leaving a net cost of £242. Electricity was to be supplied by the East Anglian Electricity Supply Company at 2.2d per unit. The services of the pump attendant could be dispensed with but it would be necessary to employ a lad porter at Tivetshall during the winter months when staff numbers were insufficient to cover both seasonal and station work. The adoption of the scheme was expected to result in an annual net saving of £78. The committees were dubious of the savings but recommended the expenditure of £252 pending investigation into further possible economies.

However, it was to be 17th November 1936 before the Divisional General Manager (Southern Area) submitted a further memorandum regarding the water pumping plant at Tivetshall. He stressed the £252 included £75 to be paid to the East Anglian Electric Supply Company, who themselves contemplated providing an electrical supply to the parish of Tivetshall, which was the cost the L&NE Company would have to incur laying a service cable from the village to the pumping station, a distance of one mile. Shortly after the original offer was made the supply company intimated they could not get a sufficient interest to justify a public supply and that if a special supply was afforded for pumping then the cost was £500 and not £75. As this rendered the scheme unprofitable it was held in abeyance pending an offer on lower terms. The supply company was now prepared to give a supply providing the L&NE Company contributed £200 towards the initial outlay and guaranteed to pay for a period of five years not less than £50 per annum for electricity to an average of 2d per unit. These terms were considered unsatisfactory as the revised gross cost would increase from £252 to £387, with a net cost of £377, whilst the revised estimated savings would amount to £91 per annum. The scheme was subsequently aborted.

In the darkness of the early morning of 29th December 1938, Harry Albert Oakley, casual crossing keeper at Denton Level Crossing No. 58 between Homersfield and Earsham, severely injured his left hand. At the resultant inquiry J.A. Sinclair, the inspecting officer, established the crossing was operated from a 3-lever ground frame, the levers working the Up and Down gate distant signals and the gate lock. The lever frame was situated close to the track, being separated from it by a space of 5 feet 1 inch. At 6.45am Oakley was standing in the normal position, facing oncoming traffic, and was in the act of pushing forward to place the Up distant signal lever, which was the one nearest the line, to return the signal to the caution position. As he did so his foot slipped from the metal frame, which on the cold morning was coated with ice. As a result he rolled onto the four feet way of the track and had almost gained a position of safety when the Up passenger train reached him and passed over his left hand inflicting the injury. Oakley was 19 years 6 months old and at the time of the accident was booked on duty for 12 hours with a meal interval between trains of 30 minutes. At the inquiry it was agreed to erect a barrier round the frame as a guard against a similar accident. Sinclair also observed that Oakley was wearing rubber boots and in view of the slippery state of the frame due to ice this could have been a contributory cause of the accident.

Further flooding occurred on the branch in the late 1930s, especially west of Silk Factory level crossing on the Bungay side of Ditchingham; following flood damage on 26th January 1939 the

'J15' Class 0-6-0 No. 7809 passing Pulham St. Mary with a branch freight train in 1929. Note the ornate curved paint finish to the base of the signal post in the foreground. *Author's collection*

Bungay station master reported to the local newspaper that this section was *'not safe to walk over, let alone send a train over'*. On the same day a replacement bus ran into trouble in the same area and had to be towed to safety by a lorry. The branch was severed in two places each side of Bungay and through services did not resume until 31st January 1939. Although the Mid Suffolk and Framlingham branches suffered from the deluge, they reopened on 27th January.

To effect further economies, on 27th July 1939 the Southern Area Traffic Committee of the L&NER approved of the introduction of push-and-pull trains on the Waveney Valley Branch at an estimated cost of £570 with an estimated net saving of £379 by the abolition of two guards posts. Authority included the conversion of two locomotives and two 2-coach push/pull coaching stock sets augmented by a spare engine and two coaches, the latter providing maintenance cover for the Thetford to Bury St. Edmunds and Wroxham to County School branches as well as the Waveney Valley line. All such plans were, however, abandoned with the outbreak of World War Two.

Prior to the outbreak of the conflict the L&NER, together with other railway companies, came under the control of the Railway Executive Committee. Once hostilities were confirmed staff utilized shielded hand lamps to attend to train and shunting duties during the hours of darkness as a precaution against air raids. In order to hinder possible enemy invasion, station nameboards were removed and stored in lamp rooms under constant lock and key. The agricultural nature of the freight handled at all the branch stations was of the utmost importance during the war years as the vital provisions of home-grown food, vegetables, grain and sugar beet were dispatched and conveyed to markets. In addition to the outward flow of commodities, the war brought an influx of tinned fruit, dried milk and eggs for distribution to the Ministry of Food storage depots in the area.

World War Two saw the counties of Norfolk and Suffolk used as launching pads for air attacks on Europe, with the Waveney Valley line carrying much additional traffic for army and air force establishments in the area. Airfields for the United States 8th Airforce were established south-west of Bungay at Thorpe Abbots, Flixton and Metfield south of line, and Tibenham, Hardwick and Seething to the north of the branch. Thorpe Abbots was host to the B17 Flying Fortresses of Colonel Neil B. Harding's 100th group (402 Provisional Combat Bombardment Wing), whilst in 1943 Metfield fighter aerodrome based Lt Col Loren G. McCollom's 353rd Fighter Group USAAF flying P47 Thunderbolts supporting the American 491 Bomber Group flying B24s. Flixton was home to 446 Bomber Group, 93 Bomber Group and 329 Bomber Group flying B24s. Tibenham hosted 445 Bomber Group, which lost thirty aircraft in one day in September 1944; Hardwick had 310 Bomber Group and 93 Bomber Group, the latter known as the 'Travelling Circus' as they were the most travelled group in the 8th Airforce, whilst Seething was home to 448 Bomber Group. Thus, lulled from their rural somnolence, Tivetshall, Pulham Market, Homersfield, Earsham, Bungay, Ditchingham and Ellingham goods yards became strategic distribution centres for these important air bases from 1942 onwards. The airfields covered about two square miles of runways and taxing ways, incorporating 600,000 sq yards of concrete, thousands of tons of bricks, timber, corrugated iron and other materials. Aviation fuel for a typical 500-bomber raid required eight tanker wagons of fuel and 7,500 spare parts were kept in reserve. The additional traffic worked over the single line siding required an additional siding east of Pulham Market station for servicing the RAF airfield.

A number of alterations were made at Tivetshall in 1943, which became the centre for seven new airfields and where the existing goods yard sidings could only accommodate twenty-six wagons. A new facing connection from the Up main line to the Waveney Valley Branch was installed to permit Up trains from the Norwich direction gaining access to the branch from either the branch loop line or the Up main line. At the same time the trailing crossover between the Up and Down main lines was repositioned. Other works executed included the provision of a group of sidings for the Air Ministry, with a concrete roadway alongside initially for the offloading of tarmacadam for surfacing runways on new local military airfields. The associated signalling was controlled from the existing Tivetshall signal box. As well as tarmacadam came supplies of other items for personnel at the airfields including bedsteads, furniture, crockery, chairs and bicycles. Later came petrol and bombs and on one occasion Luftwaffe aircraft flew over the station when the three new sidings held a train loaded with bombs, another with petrol and a third with bitumen. American lorries with headlights full on were being loaded but fortunately the enemy passed over without making any attack.

Homersfield station served the nearby USAF airfield at Flixton and the traffic in the small goods yard doubled with wagon-loads of materials, including tarmac, concrete and other building items for the establishment of the base, then domestic supplies for the personnel and, last but not least, the delivery of bombs and armaments, As with all military traffic a Railway Transport Officer was appointed to the district to liaise between the railway company and the military. Bricks and rubble from bomb-damaged sites in London and the eastern home counties was offloaded in the goods yard for use in building the runways.

Along the line at Ditchingham the War Department took over the maltings near the railway in 1943 and converted the premises into a storage depot for the United States Army. A short siding was installed to serve the new depot and to deal with the expected increase in traffic, the original loop siding was extended 450 feet at the west end of the layout to enable goods trains to shunt clear of the main single line. The Ministry of Transport financed the work, costing £1,507. Ditchingham signal box was converted into a crossing box with Train Staff and Ticket equipment but passenger trains were not permitted to cross one another.

At Ellingham war-time improvements in 1943 included the installation of two loop sidings, one to hold a train of 100 wagons and the second as a semi-run-round loop or wagon holding siding. Financed by the Air Ministry the sidings were initially constructed with an adjacent roadway to handle quantities of tarmacadam for the surfacing of runways on adjacent airfields. Then in March 1944 a petrol depot was established at Ellingham and during the following six months it dealt with 148 trains of petroleum for the surrounding airfields, the fuel being offloaded to adjacent storage tanks before transit to the airfields.

Also in 1944 a new loop siding with capacity to hold fifty wagons and engine and brake van was installed to the west of Earsham. Financed by the Air Ministry at a cost of £2,369, the siding was built with an adjacent concrete road as an offloading point for materials and armaments destined for the nearby military airfields. So great were the number of bombs delivered that at one time stacks of bombs were stored on either side of the road leading to Hardwick, guarded by one American soldier, until they could be transported to the airfield. Other supplies were sent to a bomb dump in the nearby Earsham Hall estate before being sent to the airfields. During the war the Earsham siding handled 625 special trains formed of 21,038 wagons conveying over 200,000 tons of freight and earning the L&NER £359,100 in revenue.

Once the airfields were established they continued to be supplied with trains conveying bombs and armaments, spare parts, ground stores and, most importantly, oil. Between D-Day 6th June 1944 and early September Earsham dealt with 7,883 wagons, Ellingham 2,518 and Tivetshall 857, the Americans working twenty-four hours a day, seven days a week to transfer goods and armaments.

Special trains ran under the cover of darkness conveying armaments and bombs, which were unloaded at the various sidings and taken to ammunition dumps located at well-camouflaged sites away from the airfields. The ammunition was usually conveyed in open wagons, sheeted over to conceal the deadly cargo, although the prominent red flashed labels advised 'SHUNT WITH CARE' and 'PLACE AS FAR AWAY AS POSSIBLE FROM THE ENGINE, BRAKE VAN AND WAGONS LABELLED INFLAMMABLE'. Aviation fuel was conveyed in tank wagons.

Soon after the cessation of the war on 6th July 1945 a convoy of American lorries loaded with cluster bombs was passing over Drake's Crossing near Earsham, when some cases full of bombs fell off one of the lorries onto the track. The driver of the following lorry braked sharply, with the result that some more bomb-cases fell off the back of his lorry. He found he was stuck with bombs all over the ground in front of and behind his vehicle so that he could neither move his lorry forwards or backwards. All the bombs were fused and liable to explode at any moment and drivers and the military police directing the convoy scattered for their lives. They also shouted for Mrs Hewitt, the crossing keeper to take cover. The intrepid Mrs Hewitt, however, realising a train was approaching, ran with her red flag and some detonators down the line towards the advancing train which she succeeded in stopping. Her gallant action involved her being within the danger area for some two or three minutes and for her actions she was awarded the L&NER Medal.

After the war the ownership of the siding at Earsham remained with the Air Ministry but was utilized by the Ministry of Supply to load war scrap. In season it was also used by local farmers for loading sugar beet and at other times for storage of cripple or condemned wagons. The war-time sidings at Ditchingham and Ellingham were also used for loading of war scrap and the storage of wagons.

In 1946 military personnel were brought home by air, particularly from the Mediterranean, and Tivetshall was designated the 71st transit camp. Every day forty aircraft were scheduled to arrive, each conveying twenty men. The men arrived in the camp in the evening and after spending the night there were sent off the next morning on two trains, one destined for London and the other to the north. At the same time there was outward traffic. Much of the exercise depended on good weather but if aircraft were grounded for days an accumulation of 5,000 men would be arriving at Tivetshall camp. To clear the numbers, men were despatched 200 at a time on ordinary train services but in the event of adverse weather special trains were often cancelled resulting in an accumulation of servicemen at the camp.

In the closing days of 1946 a fatal accident occurred to a member of the permanent way gang near Geldeston during track relaying. On 11th December, B. Charge, a relayer in the engineer's department at Norwich, with but five weeks service, was standing on one of the rail wagons of a materials train during shunting operations; when the train moved to a fresh position he fell over the low end of the vehicles and was fatally injured by the following wagon. J.A. Sinclair, the inspecting officer taking the BOT inquiry, heard that the gang had commenced duty at Norwich at 7.00am and after unloading had taken place en route to Beccles the train had arrived at Geldeston at 12.55pm. Unloading of rails on the north side of the single line then commenced and the accident occurred at 1.15pm at a point 200 yards to the west of the passenger station, during a subsequent movement to a second position. Ballast Ganger Smith, who was in charge of the train, advised that he warned the men of the impending move when he was standing with the guard, on the north side of the line at the front end of the first rail unit. He sounded his whistle and shouted *'Hold Tight'* and, after an interval to allow the men on the vehicles to get a firm hold, the guard signalled the driver to move slowly ahead. As the vehicles were fitted with special couplings and buffers, the train moved away smoothly as the driver opened the regulator. The movement had just commenced when it was noticed that Charge had fallen over the trailing end of the vehicle upon which he worked and was lying across the north rail. He died later the same day as a result of the left side of his chest being crushed by the leading wheel of the following vehicle. After hearing the evidence Sinclair was of the opinion that the regulations regarding the movement of the ballast train had been properly carried out, and that Charge could not have failed to hear the warning given by Ganger Smith. He concluded:

> *It is possible that due to inexperience – this was only the second occasion that he had been out with the train – he underestimated the slight jerk which is inevitable when any train is set in motion; he had sufficient time, however, to settle himself, and take a firm hold, and the accident should be attributed to some lack of care on his part.*

After the war the railways resumed peacetime activities with run-down and life-expired rolling stock and equipment, and stations in need of maintenance. Questions were raised in Parliament regarding the deteriorating service provided by the L&NER and the poor condition of the rolling stock. The Waveney Valley Branch was no exception and frequently the company was unable to provide enough coaching stock for passenger services or provide wagons to local traders; more seriously the branch services were occasionally cancelled because Beccles or Norwich sheds were unable to provide locomotives for the booked workings. Severe weather early in 1947 with heavy snowfalls caused further delays and on more than one occasion trains were stuck in drifts and extricated by permanent way staff using nothing but shovels and muscular energy.

Despite the grim recovery from the war years the L&NER continued their Best Kept Station and Station Gardens competitions and in 1947 Homersfield was awarded a third class certificate.

The L&NER, in the final throes of existence, at long last obtained a company house at Beccles to accommodate the station master and his family, the negotiations being completed in July 1947. No. 14 Station Road was purchased from the personal representative of the deceased Mr Jessie Taylor at a cost of £1,275 plus an additional £33 15s 0d for certain fixtures and fittings making an overall total of £1,308 15s 0d. During the spring and summer availability of rolling stock improved and it was hoped the impending nationalisation of the railways would bring optimism to the future status of the line.

7

Nationalisation and Closure

THE NATIONALISATION OF THE RAILWAYS from 1st January 1948 brought few immediate changes to the Waveney Valley line, which retained its GER/L&NER atmosphere until the withdrawal of steam traction from the branch. Most stocks of L&NER tickets initially remained but those in constant demand to popular destinations were soon replaced with tickets bearing the legend 'Railway Executive' or 'British Railways'. Locomotives working the line soon lost their NE or L&NER identity in favour of the austere BRITISH RAILWAYS on side tanks or tender, and although varnished teak or brown remained on the older branch coaching stock some ex-L&NER suburban coaches began appearing in the new corporate crimson livery.

British Railways made few alterations to the timetable but market-day travel to Norwich or Ipswich was a shadow of pre-war years. As petrol rationing eased so the new management, whilst keeping a constant survey on passenger traffic, were concerned that freight traffic was also showing a steady decline as farmers and growers increasingly preferred to despatch their produce and goods by motor lorry. Livestock traffic to and from Norwich, Ipswich and other local markets in the surrounding area was sent by road, a method obviating the double handling of animals at both forwarding and receiving stations.

On 1st June 1948 Lieutenant Colonel E. Woodhouse somewhat belatedly carried out the BOT inspections of the alterations made during World War Two at Tivetshall, Earsham, Ditchingham and Ellingham. At Tivetshall he found that the alterations carried out in 1943 were to serve a group of sidings with a concrete road laid alongside constructed for the Air Ministry for unloading tarmacadam for surfacing airfield runways. The alterations comprised a facing connection from the Up line to the Beccles single line replacing a trailing connection in the Down line, a change in the positioning of the trailing crossover road and the consequential signalling alterations. The main line connections were laid with 95 lbs per yard RBS material and slag ballasted, all in accordance with the plans and signalling diagrams provided. At the time of the inspection the detection on facing points No. 13 leading to the branch and those at the Ipswich end of the crossover No. 12 over which the train leaving the branch travelled in a facing direction were a trifle slack through a slight spreading of the gauge. The altered and additional locking and related controls were correctly installed in the signal box, which contained a 41-lever frame, the detonator placers were also correct and the signalman had no criticism of the arrangements. Woodhouse noted the sidings remained the property of the Air Ministry pending a decision to their future and were used

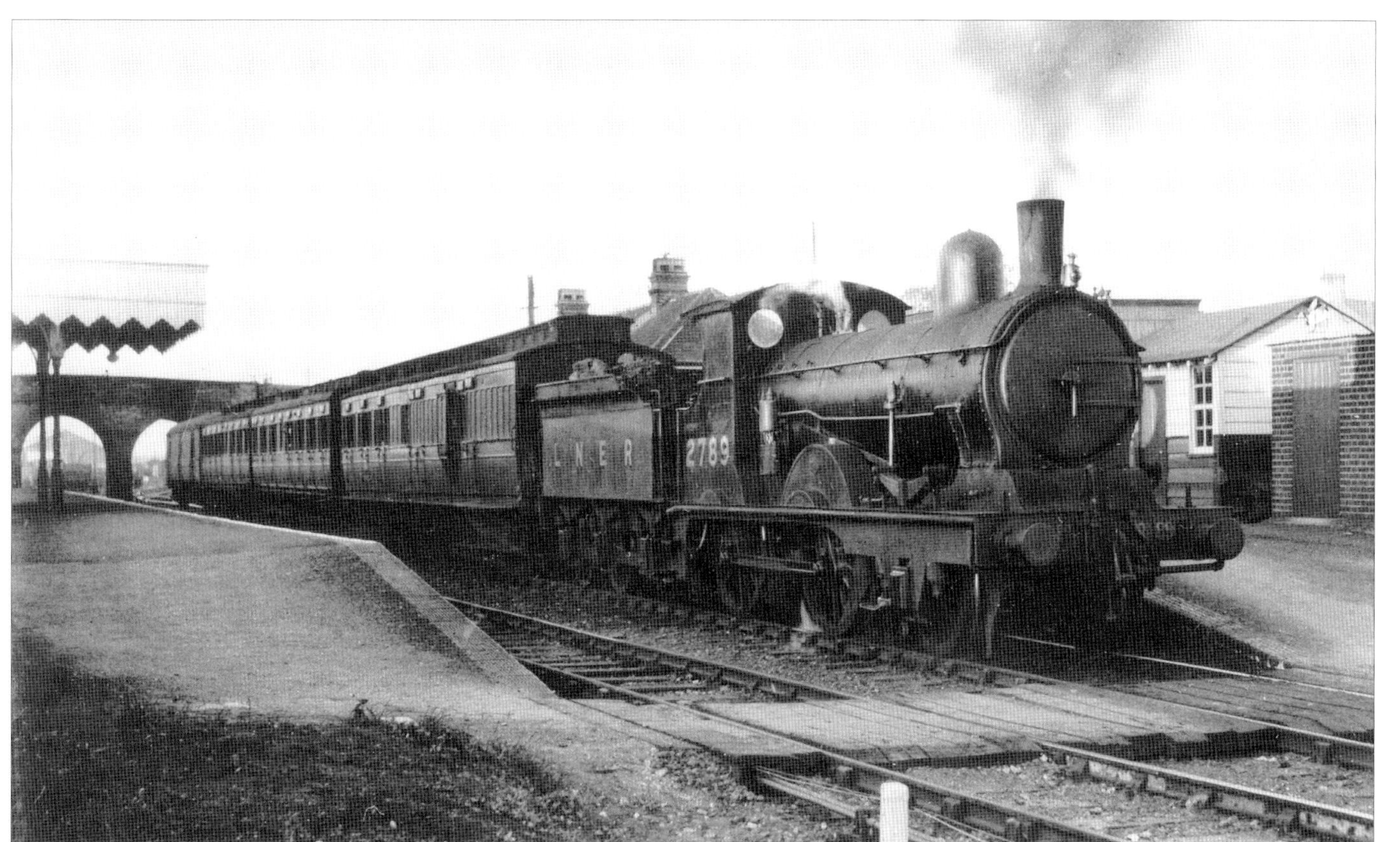

Bungay station with 'E4' Class 2-4-0 No. 2789 at the head of the 8.00pm Beccles to Tivetshall train on 16th August 1948. *W.A. Camwell*

A busy scene at Beccles on 17th May 1948 with 'F6' Class 2-4-2T No. 7231 at platform 4 with the 7.55pm departure to Lowestoft; 'D16/3' Class 4-4-0 No. 2552 is at platform 2 with the 6.22pm Ipswich to Yarmouth South Town train, whilst at platform 1 the connecting 8.00pm Waveney Valley service is hauled by 'E4' Class 2-4-0 No. 2789. *Author's collection*

for general traffic and wagon storage by arrangement. The inspector approved of the works, subject to urgent remedial attention to the facing points.

Along the line at Earsham the Lieutenant Colonel inspected a loop siding constructed in 1944 for the Air Ministry at a cost of £2,369. The siding, which could accommodate fifty wagons, was built to serve neighbouring airfields and remained the property of the Air Ministry. At the time of the visit Woodhouse was advised the siding was used by the Ministry of Supply to load war scrap, as well as for seasonal sugar beet traffic and wagon storage. The works were in accordance with the plans and signalling diagrams supplied, and the running line connections at each end of the siding were of 95 lbs per yard serviceable rail on slag ballast and were properly equipped with traps. The connections were each worked by a 2-lever ground frame released either by the single line Train Staff or Metal Ticket. The locking arrangements were correct and the works in good order.

At Ditchingham the War Department had taken over a maltings near the railway as a depot for the United States Army in 1943. As a result of the establishment of the depot, traffic had increased considerably and it had been necessary to lengthen the existing loop line by 150 yards to enable freight trains to shunt clear of the running line and provide additional signalling and telecommunications equipment in Ditchingham signal box, which previously was not a crossing station. The works was executed at a cost of £1,507 to the Ministry of Transport and at the time of Woodhouse's visit the loop was still in place but the siding connection to the maltings had been lifted. The inspector noted the new connections with the running line at the west end of the extended siding was laid with 85 lbs per yard rail on slag ballast and was properly trapped. The connection was worked from a 6-lever ground frame electrically released from Ditchingham signal box which replaced a 2-lever frame formerly used to control the gates of the adjacent level crossing. The works were in accordance with the plans and signalling diagrams supplied and the altered locking in the signal box and ground frame was found to be correct. The signalman and gatewoman in charge of the ground frame had no criticism to offer but the latter advised Woodhouse she usually worked the siding connection at least once a day.

Lastly, Woodhouse ventured to Ellingham where he found considerable new work had been made in 1943 for the Air Ministry, including the installation of two loop sidings, one to hold 100 wagons and the second to serve as a run round. The loops had road access and were originally used to receive tarmacadam and other materials for surfacing runways of neighbouring airfields, but were later used to offload petroleum and for the storage of tanks. At the time of the visit the sidings remained Air Ministry property but were used for wagon storage by arrangement. The running line connections were of serviceable 95 lbs per yard rail at one end and 85 lbs per yard at the other end, both laid on slag ballast. The inspector suggested that both sets of trap points could be improved by the addition of throw-off rails. The western connection was worked from a 2-lever ground frame released by the Train Staff or Metal Ticket. The eastern connection was worked from a 3-lever

'J15' Class 0-6-0 No. 65435 heads out of Bungay goods yard with a lengthy branch freight train in 1950, no doubt under the watchful eye of the signalman in Bungay signal box. *Dr I.C. Allen*

ground frame from which the Annett's key could be obtained after the Train Staff and Metal Ticket had been locked and thus release the western ground frame so that both could be used at the same time. The works were found to be correct and in good order and the engineer agreed to attend to the requirements for the trap points.

As wartime conditions receded so British Railways continued to run the Best Kept station and Station Garden competitions and in 1949 Bungay and Homersfield were awarded Certificates of Commendation and Pulham St. Mary a third class certificate whilst in 1950 Harleston received a Certificate of Commendation, and Homersfield and Pulham St. Mary third class certificates.

The cost-conscious Railway Executive had directed the railway regions to investigate unremunerative lines and concern over the possible withdrawal of Waveney Valley passenger services reached the House of Commons on 23rd July 1951 when Mr Baker asked the Minister of Agriculture whether, in view of the importance of the local farming industry, he would consult with the Transport Commission in an effort to prevent the closure of the passenger service on the branch railway. Mr T. Williams replied that he was satisfied that adequate facilities existed for representation to be made by any local interest likely to be affected by the closure.

The signs were ominous, however, for by the autumn of 1951 it became clear that services on the neighbouring Mid Suffolk Light Railway from Haughley to Laxfield were totally unviable in the new national railway network. The rumours of impending closure were confirmed in November when railway management officially informed members of staff and NUR and ASLEF trades unions that proposals were actively in hand. The public was informed in December and the East Anglian Transport Users Consultative Committee (TUCC) meeting was held in February to consider the arguments for retaining the passenger and goods services. All was to no avail, for complete closure of the line was advocated on and from 28th July 1952, but as no Sunday services operated the last trains ran on Saturday 26th July 1952. The publicity associated with the 'Middy' completely overshadowed the announcement of the intention to withdraw passenger services from the Wickham Market to Framlingham branch, to be followed by the confirmation that it was also the intention to withdraw passenger services from the Waveney Valley line. The same procedures followed, the local staff and trades unions were advised, followed by public announcements. Once again representations were made against closure to the TUCC but after due consideration the announcement was made that, subject to adequate alternative bus services being provided, no case could be found for the retention of passenger trains on either line. British Railways Eastern Region duly advised that passenger services would be withdrawn from the Framlingham Branch on and

In the late autumn of 1951 storms caused considerable damage to trees on the Norfolk/Suffolk border and BR was asked to assist with the removal of felled trees, some which had blocked the railway. A small travelling crane still lettered M & GN had been sent to Bungay to help clear the yard where the trees had been deposited but it was unable to cope with the influx and the Ipswich breakdown crane was summoned to load timber. 'B12/3' Class 4-6-0 No. 61535, which had failed working a Down mail train in early January 1952, made its first journey after repairs hauling the breakdown train; it reached Bungay via Tivetshall, this route having a higher route availability (RA4) than the RA3 restriction on the branch between Geldeston and Beccles which prohibited the locomotive's passage. On another occasion, sister locomotive No. 61577 and a 'D16/3' Class 4-4-0 worked a recovery train. In this view of No. 61535, the much smaller ex M&GN crane seen to the left also assisted with the loading. *B.D.J. Walsh*

'B1' Class 4-6-0 No. 61042 hurries a Norwich to Liverpool Street express through Tivetshall on 1st May 1951. The Waveney Valley Branch is in the foreground and next to that is the Up reception siding. *H.C. Casserley*

'J15' Class 0-6-0 No. 65469 rouses the echoes departing from Harleston with a Norwich to Beccles train in 1952. The train is formed of two Thompson and one Gresley non-gangway bogie coaches. *Dr I.C. Allen*

from Monday 3rd November 1952 whilst freight services would continue. Hard on the heels of this announcement came the edict that passenger services would be withdrawn from the Waveney Valley line, where the average number of passengers totalled ten persons a day, on and from Monday 5th January 1953, and in the absence of Sunday services the last train would operate on Saturday 3rd January. Freight services would be retained. The announcement was greeted with scepticism and various local bodies made half-hearted efforts to obtain a reprieve but to most the outcome was inevitable for after being used to capacity during the war years the branch had taken on a solemnity with the peace only disturbed by the brief passing of a train before calm again descended on the rural scene.

Saturday 3rd January 1953 was a cold day with a raw wind blowing and snow on the ground, which did little to deter townsfolk and villagers along the line from turning out to see the train for the last time, determined to give the line a rousing send off. The final round trip departed Beccles for Tivetshall at 6.55pm hauled by 'J15' Class 0-6-0 No. 65478 hauling five coaches, three more than usual, to cater for the expected crowds of people wishing to take a last journey on the branch. The locomotive was in the charge of Driver George Brown of 4 Neptune Street, Lowestoft, and Fireman Maurice Nash of 318 Raglan Street, Lowestoft, with Guard Walter J. Fisk of 39 Sussex Road, Lowestoft, responsible for the five well-filled coaches. With the engine running boiler first the Up journey was uneventful until Harleston where a funeral party conveying an oak coffin with a corpse attended by a widow and an undertaker dressed in Victorian costume joined the train. The coffin bore a brass plaque with the inscription *'Waveney Valley line, age 97 years. Taken from us 3. 1. 1953'.* The train reached Tivetshall a few minutes late by which time the Norwich to Ipswich main line train had arrived. Many passengers had changed from the train from Norwich, among them Arthur Harding, resplendent in a frock coat and top hat as a bygone Mayor of Beccles; he had been a ganger on the branch for many years. The departure from Tivetshall was delayed by the mock funeral procession; the 'funeral' party joined the train, the oak coffin being followed along the platform by the 'wife' of the 'corpse' in widow's weeds, an 'undertaker', and a large party of 'mourners'. The lid of the coffin lifted and the 'corpse' waved to the crowd on the platform.

The locomotive ran round the train, whilst mail was loaded into the guards van followed by the reloaded coffin. Departure was scheduled for 8.15pm but a further 5 minutes elapsed had before Guard Fisk sounded 'right away', acknowledged by the locomotive whistle, and No. 65478, now running tender first, drew away from the platform with the five coaches. After calling at the Pulhams the

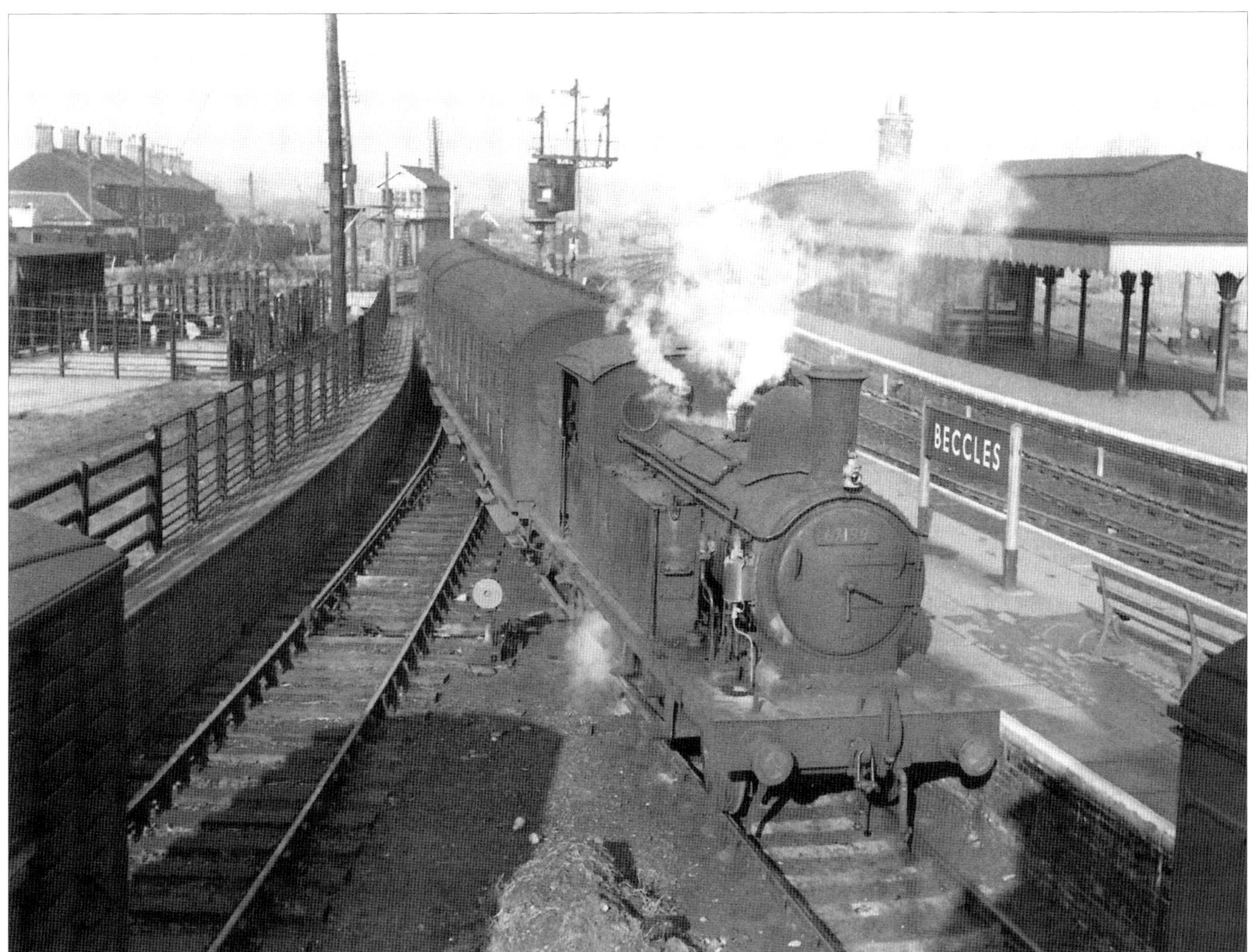

An interloper in platform 1 at Beccles: 'F5' Class 2-4-2 No. 67199 has just arrived with the push-pull shuttle from Yarmouth South Town. In the background is the Up side island platform and to the left the dock road serving the cattle pens. *Dr I.C. Allen*

train reached Harleston where a large crowd greeted the final service. Here the funeral party left the train and departed from the station accompanied by the singing of 'Abide with Me'. After further delay the train departed for Homersfield, where on arrival a laurel wreath with blue ribbons was placed on the end of the tender. Away from Homersfield to the sound of exploding detonators and the blast of a hunting horn, the train made a momentary stop at Earsham where departure was 22 minutes late.

Arrival at Bungay was greeted with great excitement for those on the train and approximately 900 people representing all walks of life were crowded on the platform. Fireworks were exploded and the civic leaders from Bungay and Beccles greeted the arrival. The Beccles 'Crazy Gang' – dressed in costumes representing the various types of passenger to use the railway, including trippers, businessmen, farmers, poachers and preachers – were escorted by the helmeted sabre-armed 'Ditchingham Dragoons'. The pride of the procession, which had earlier started from St. Johns Road and made its way to the station, was a large model engine made for the occasion by Frank Reynolds of Beccles and named 'Nutty Slack'. The party had set out at 7.30pm in crisp snow and ran the hazard of numerous snowballs hurled in the spirit of the occasion. The procession began with the twenty or so members of the 'Crazy Gang', headed by the local police sergeant D.J. Sawyer of Bungay, but every yard of the journey drew more and more people into its wake until over 200 were wending their way to the station. The hilarity of the occasion was tinged with sadness, for Station Master S.W. Clarke was serving his last day in charge before transferring to Watton, whilst Mrs Agnes Kybird, the woman porteress, was serving her last spell of duty after 10½ years at the station. Passengers joining the train included D.I. Hewitt, the Town Reeve of Bungay, and Mr and Mrs A.E. Pye, the Mayor and Mayoress of Beccles, together with members of Bungay Urban District Council and the Beccles 'Crazy Gang'.

All along the valley detonators were placed on the line at the various stations and the journey became livelier with passengers singing and a huntsman blowing his hunting horn at every opportunity. At Geldeston a laurel wreath from residents of Station Road was presented to Driver Brown. On it were flowers from the hat of 87-year-old Mrs George Fisk, whose home was near the station. Mrs Fisk was on the platform whilst her 90-year-old husband watched from the house, he having been born three months before the first train ran. A crowd of well over 1,000 cheered as the train steamed into Beccles 44 minutes late at 9.54pm with its complement of 300 passengers, having been further delayed on the approach to the station by the constant pulling of the communication cord. As soon as the train emptied it departed back to Lowestoft whilst the procession reassembled behind a loudspeaker van and marched through the town behind trumpet-blowing 'Dragoon' Nick Whistler. Returning to the station the 'Crazy Gang' party halted in mock solemnity in the blaze of light cast by the lamps above the main entrance. A top-hated member who declared himself *'The Minister for the Disposal of Ancient Rites and Privileges'* read a funeral address. The last post was sounded and black mourning cloth was draped over the model engine. After a pause, the strains of 'Auld Lang Syne' wafted over the darkened station and three rousing cheers brought the end to regular passenger services on the Waveney Valley line. Beccles station approach had been floodlit and music relayed on a loudspeaker whilst the train was awaited, and two

'F4' Class 2-4-2T No. 67176 sets a smokescreen approaching Ditchingham with a Beccles to Tivetshall train in 1952. *Dr I.C. Allen*

On the occasion when two 'J15' Class 0-6-0 tender locomotives worked an Up freight service across the branch both required replenishment from the water tank at Bungay. Because of the proximity of the bridge over the River Waveney west of the station it was thought advisable to uncouple the engines so they take water individually. Here No. 65471 is receiving attention whilst sister locomotive No. 65460 waits its turn. The photograph is being taken from the bridge. *Dr I.C. Allen*

public houses near the station were granted an extension of time so that passengers off the final train could refresh themselves or drown their sorrows!

The *Bungay & Beccles Journal* for 9th January 1953 published a requiem for the passing of the passenger train service by Victor H. Mayes.

The Waveney Train:- A Poem

Puffing, chuffing, as white steam bellows,
Past grazing cows and waving willows.
O'er marsh and river, glen and dale,
Stopping at stations on the vale.
Carrying children to the sea,
Or bringing workmen home to tea,
Bringing visitors from other lands,
Or taking us to distant sands.
Football crowds to a local game,
Rich and poor – all the same,
Mixing the sorrowful with the sad,
Girls from the town – the village lad.
Farmers, housewives, shoppers too,
Workers, shirkers, lovers true,
Soldiers coming home on leave,
Parting friends with tear on sleeve.
The Waveney train has had them all,
The fat, the thin, the short, the tall,
But now its wheels will turn no more,
No coaches three (or sometimes four),
Will ply along the Waveney Vale.
Over marsh and river, glen and dale;
Left to peace the grazing cows,
As the willows sighs and gently bows.
Alas the final trip is o'er,
And quietness reigns across the moor,
A civil journey was its last reward,
The final memories now are stored
Now it's over, gone the fuss, as we travel in an omnibus ...!

Within weeks of the withdrawal of the passenger service the branch was to become a necessary lifeline for a gale on 31st January 1953 caused by extreme weather conditions resulted in hurricane force winds channelling a surge of water some eight feet above normal level into the North Sea and down the East Coast from Lincolnshire to Kent. Added to the mixture was the exceptional high spring tide and the resultant force of wind and water slammed into the Wash with waves 16 feet high. The tsunami, having devastated North Norfolk, followed around the coast of Suffolk and Essex continuing to wreak havoc. Pertinent to the Waveney Valley line was the flooding of the lines from Yarmouth to Acle, Yarmouth to Reedham, Yarmouth South Town station, Lowestoft Central station and Lowestoft harbour. As an example, flooding at Lowestoft locomotive depot began at about 9.40pm on Saturday 31st January and the water rose so rapidly that staff were marooned until the tide ebbed at about 3.30am on the Sunday morning. With the water at a depth of three feet, engines with flooded axleboxes required attention before being rostered to work. The electricity supply failed and lighting was not restored until 5th February with other power the following day. The water softening plant was also out of action until 7th February when the town electricity supply was restored. In the aftermath, district civil engineering staff had to gauge how quickly repairs could be effected to damaged routes and, as a result of considerable scouring of embankments, supplies of heavy filling material and track ballast were required as matter of urgency. Much came from the Sheffield and Doncaster areas where trainloads of lump slag and ballast were despatched from the slag heaps and steelworks. It was also imperative to anticipate demand for extra coal, relief food and household supplies to the stricken areas. As the supplies appeared in East Anglia so the Waveney Valley line, comparatively untouched, became one of the essential access routes to the flooded coastal area, and the line remained open on a 24-hour basis for almost two weeks as relief trains passed to an fro over the single line.

After the emergency the branch freight services continued to serve all station yards and for a while all signal boxes were manned on a two-shift basis, but staff were ageing and retirements were in the offing, as a result of which on many occasions the branch could only be covered by overtime working, adding to the cost. Further savings were necessary if services were to continue in an increasingly competitive age.

Under the provisions of the Light Railways Acts of 1896 and 1912 and the Railways Act of 1921 the British Transport Commission deposited a draft order to the Ministry of Transport and Civil Aviation for the conversion of the Waveney Valley Branch to a Light Railway in January 1954. The British Transport Commission (Waveney Valley Branch) Light Railway Order sought powers to work the line as a light railway and for the removal of gates at nine level crossings. Section 5 of the statute required the provision of cattle grids at each side of the road to prevent cattle or horses from straying onto the railway. Warning posts showing the speed limit and whistle boards were to be erected on the railway approach to each ungated level crossing. On the road approach a notice board was to be erected to warn the public by day and by night of the existence of an ungated level crossing. The document also advised the Commission could not use engines, carriages or trucks bringing any weight upon the rails by any one pair of wheels exceeding such weight according to a sliding scale issued by the Ministry having regard to the authorised speed and volume of traffic carried.

Max Axle Load (in tons)	Rails Used Weigh at Least (in lbs per yard)
8 to 10	50
9 to 11	55
11 to 13	60
13 to 15	65
15 to 17	70
16 to 18 or more	75 and upwards

Clause 6 (ii) stipulated that the Commission would not run any engine or train on the light railway at any speed exceeding 20 mph and on approaching within a distance of 200 yards of any ungated crossing the speed was reduced to 10 mph. No more than four trains a day in each direction were permitted and the railway could not be used for the public conveyance of passengers without permission in writing of the Minister. Any contravention resulting in conviction would result in a penalty payment of £20 for each such offence. The level crossings, all situated in the County of Norfolk, to be converted to ungated crossings were as shown in the table below.

The second schedule of the Light Railway Order stipulated that rails should weigh at least 50 lbs per yard and on curves where the radius was less than 9 chains check rails were to be provided. If flat bottom rails and wooden sleepers were used the rails at the joints were to be secured to the sleepers by fangs or other through bolts, or by coach screws or by double dog spikes or by spring spikes on the outside of the rail with bearing plate. Rails on curves with a radius of less than 9 chains were to be secured on the outside of the outer rail to each sleeper by a fang or other through bolts, or by coach screws or by double dog spikes or by spring spikes with a bearing plate. The rails on these curves were to be tied to gauge by iron or steel ties at suitable intervals, or by any other manner as approved by the Minister of Transport.

No turntables were required on the light railway and electric communication was to be provided as directed by the Minister of Transport. Signalling was to be kept to a minimum, a home signal for each direction of travel being provided at or near the entrance points to crossing loops where trains were to pass one another. If the home signal was not visible from a distance of one quarter of a mile a distant signal was to be erected at least that distance from the

Level Crossings to be Made Ungated

Level crossing	Rural District	Parish	Road Crossed	
			From	To
No. 3 Hall Lane	Depwade	Tivetshall St. Margaret	Hall Green	Tivetshall St. Margaret
No. 4 Green Lane	Depwade	Tivetshall St. Margaret	Tivetshall St. Mary	Tivetshall St. Margaret
No. 5 Star Lane	Depwade	Tivetshall St. Margaret	Tivetshall St. Mary	Tivetshall St. Margaret
No. 24 Crossingford	Depwade	Pulham St. Mary	Garlic Street	Pulham St. Mary the Virgin
No. 41 Redenhall	Depwade	Redenhall with Harleston	Redenhall	Gawdy Hall
No. 61 Drake's	Depwade	Earsham	Earsham	Earsham Park
No. 63 Five Acre Lane	Depwade	Earsham	Earsham	Denton
No. 72 Factory Road	Loddon	Ditchingham	Bungay	Norwich.
No. 84 Bracey's	Loddon	Ellingham	Dockeney	Kirby Row

The rather remote Ellingham station viewed facing towards Tivetshall after the removal of the signal box and associated signalling.
Author's collection

entrance points. The home and distant signals were to be worked from the crossing station. All points and signals at the crossing loops were to be interlocked. Platforms were to be provided but there was no obligation for the Commission to provide shelter or conveniences at any station or stopping place.

The Light Railway Order dated 15th November 1954 allowed level crossings to be unmanned and came into operation the following January, reducing the line to a light railway with 15 mph speed limit.

Brigadier C.A. Langley inspected the level crossings detailed in the first schedule of the British Transport Commission (Waveney Valley) Light Railway Order 1954 on 12th January 1955, accompanied by A.K. Richard, the Divisional Road Engineer of British Railways Eastern Region. Langley found that suitable cattle grids in accordance with section 5 (a) of the order had been constructed on each side of the road at eight level crossings, and warning boards and whistle boards in accordance with Section 5 (b) (i) had been erected on either side of each level crossing, except that no warning boards had yet been placed at No. 84 Bracey's crossing. None of the permanent notice boards had been placed alongside the roads to give warning of the existence of level crossings without gates as specified in Section 5 (b) (ii). Langley required two notices to be fixed alongside the road on either side of the railway with the wording 'Crossing – No Gates' on the approach to the crossing and the 'Trains Cross Here' sign at the crossings; particulars of the signs being given in the Traffic Signs (Size, Colour and Type Regulations 1950). The notices when erected were to be sited to meet the requirements of the Highways Authority.

Brigadier Langley then enumerated a list of works required to improve views from the road of certain of the level crossings as required by Section 4 (i) of the order:

Crossing No. 4 Green Lane

The undergrowth on the west side of the road to the south of the railway is to be cut down for a distance of 60 yards from the crossing.

Crossing No. 5 Star Lane

The hedges on the railway property are to be trimmed to 4 feet above the road level and the undergrowth in the adjoining field to be cut down on the west side of the road to the north of the crossing.

Crossing No. 24 Crossingford

The hedge alongside the railway property on the west side of the road to the north of the railway to be trimmed to 4 feet above rail level.

Crossing No. 41 Redenhall

The hedges on both sides of the road to the south of the railway are to be replaced by fences for a distance of 60 yards from the crossing. The hedges on the east side of the road to the north of the railway are to be trimmed 4 feet above the road level for a distance of 60 yards from the crossing.

Crossing No. 61 Drake's

The trees and the undergrowth on the railway property on the east side of the road to the south of the crossing are to be cut down.

Crossing No. 84 Bracey's

The hedges on both sides of the road to the north of the railway and the western hedges to the south of the railway are to be trimmed to a height of approximately 4 feet above road level for a distance of 60 yards from the crossing.

Brigadier Langley recommended the BTC be advised of the requirements so that the Minister of Transport could withhold the removal of the level crossing gates until the remedial work was completed and relevant notices in position.

Although public passenger train services had ceased, railway enthusiast specials were operated across the branch in its declining years. The first railtour, organised by the Norfolk Railway Society on Saturday 8th September 1956, was hauled by 'E4' Class 2-4-0 tender locomotive No. 62797. Formed of three Gresley corridor coaches, the train departed Norwich Thorpe and after calling at Norwich Victoria continued up the main line to Mellis for a visit to the Eye Branch. The special then returned to Tivetshall and after reversal ran across the Waveney Valley line where after noting the old station canopy at Wortwell was used for hanging onions, passing a local football match at Earsham caused such surprise that a goalkeeper stopped to watch the train pass, allowing the opponents to score a goal. A short stop was made at Bungay so that photographers could take a picture of the engine under the arch of the bridge. Beccles was reached 15 minutes early at 5.10pm and after another reversal the train returned to Norwich Thorpe via Haddiscoe and Fleet Junction.

On Sunday 30th September 1956 the branch was visited by the Railway Enthusiasts' Club 'Suffolk Venturer' railtour train. The tour had started at Liverpool Street headed by an immaculate 'B12/3' Class 4-6-0 No. 61576 which hauled the five-coach train formed of Gresley corridor stock as far as Colchester and for the return from Ipswich to London. 'E4' Class 2-4-0 tender locomotive No. 62797 was booked to haul the train for the intermediate visits to the Hadleigh Branch, then to Snape for a tour over the goods only branch, and thence from Snape to Beccles and a run to Tivetshall. From there the train was to run to Mellis and the Eye Branch before returning to Ipswich. The committee had originally requested a 'J15' Class 0-6-0 for the tour of the branches, a request fully justified for the 'E4' ran short of steam whilst propelling the train from Hadleigh back to Bentley, and again when returning from Snape to Snape Junction. Fortunately 'J15' Class No. 65447 was on hand facing in the right direction to rescue the train from the branch and double-head the special to Beccles which was reached some 25 minutes late. Further time was lost detaching the 'E4', which ran light to Lowestoft shed, and after taking water No. 65447 departed with the special 31 minutes late at 4.23pm for a journey across the Waveney Valley line. Calls were made at Bungay from 4.43 to 4.47pm and Harleston from 5.07pm to 5.15pm before Tivetshall was reaches at 5.37pm, 5 minutes late. With recovery allowed in the timetable, Eye was reached 15 minutes before time, before the special made a return to Ipswich to hand over to 'B12/3' Class No. 61576.

There was continued grievance at the withdrawal of passenger traffic and after many written complaints in February 1957, members of Bungay Urban District Council and Harleston Chamber of Trade were invited to meet members of the Transport Users Consultative Committee at Liverpool Street to discuss the differences between *'desire and need'*. The deputation included Cecil H. Harris, chairman of Bungay UDC Highways Committee, H.F. Whyte, vice chairman

On 30th September 1956 the Railway Enthusiasts' Club ran a special train 'The Suffolk Venturer' from Liverpool Street to Colchester behind 'B12/3' Class 4-6-0 No. 61576, where it handed over to 'E4' Class 2-4-0 No. 62797 to continue to Snape and then on to Beccles and the Waveney Valley line. The 'E4' failed on the Snape Branch and the casualty, assisted by 'J15' Class 0-6-0 No. 65447, continued to Beccles where it was removed from the train and retired to Lowestoft shed. No. 65447 continued unaided and is here shown at Bungay proudly displaying an express train headcode. By this time the crossing loop had been shortened and veers away from the platform at the Tivetshall end of the station; accordingly the Up starting signal has been repositioned to the centre of the Up platform. The train, formed of Gresley corridor stock, was too long for the short platform and only the front portion could be accommodated to enable participant on the tour to inspect the station.

R.M. Casserley

Harleston station from the approach road on 30th September 1956 with 'J15' Class 0-6-0 No. 65447 standing at the platform. *R.M. Casserley*

The Railway Enthusiasts' Club special train of 30th September 1956 made a further stop at Harleston and is here seen waiting departure. Level crossing No. 34, at 6 miles 22 chains, is in the foreground. After reversing at Tivetshall, the train traversed the Mellis to Eye branch before continuing to Ipswich from where 'B12/3' Class 4-6-0 No. 61576 returned the train to Liverpool Street. *R.M. Casserley*

'J15' Class 0-6-0 No. 65471 entering the RAF Pulham airfield premises at the end of a mile long siding from Pulham Market station prior to collecting wagons, a few months before closure of the base in 1958. *Dr I.C. Allen*

of the council, John Gibbs, clerk to the council, and E.T. Moore, chairman of Harleston Chamber of Trade. The case for Bungay presented by Whyte was that since the withdrawal of passenger trains four shops had closed, a local printing firm had been unable to attract key workers, Bungay Steeplechase meeting could not be revived and the substitute bus service had been unsatisfactory. It was the opinion that diesel trains would be far more economical to run but that the trains should be run at competitive prices. A constant cause for concern was that whereas the branch train had always waited at Beccles for a late-running main line service, the bus only waited 10 minutes and any unfortunate traveller then had the additional expense of a taxi to Bungay.

For Harleston, E.T. Moore said there had been deterioration in local trade; the bus service was inadequate and was taking 1½ hours to reach Norwich, a distance of 20 miles. Light industry could not be attracted to the town without the railway, it being difficult to fetch business staff from neighbouring villages. He asked why a community of 15,000 people should be robbed of its train service when diesel trains had been introduced on so many lines. *'All we are asking for is a train service for modern times and modern demands'.*

Replying for the Committee the chairman Captain W.H. Coombs pointed out that the general branch line policy had already been laid down by Parliament and that many of the objections raised were indictments against the bus company. W.G. Hall the Traffic Manager for Eastern Counties Omnibus Company declared the company had lost *'literally hundreds and hundreds of pounds for the simple reason that the passengers are not there and they never will be there'.* The operating costs were 1s 9d per mile and on the railway replacement No. 71 service the receipts were only 10d per mile. Hall continued that when petrol rationing arrived he had been tempted to use it as an excuse to reduce the bus service but then thought otherwise. With the lack of car traffic things might have improved but that had not been the case and only fifty extra passengers per week had used the service. J. Hancock, Assistant Commercial Manager of British Railways Eastern Region, questioned: *'where can we hope to get money to make the service pay on the basis of traffic before and since 1953, and even since petrol rationing?'* He advised that *'it would cost many thousands of pounds to reinstate the track for passenger traffic; diesel railcars cost £25,000 apiece and their operating costs were 3s 8d per mile – twice the rate of the buses'.* He promised to investigate delays to commercial traffic. After hearing all the evidence the Committee unanimously agreed at the end of the two hours meeting they were unable to recommend any change in the existing transport arrangements.

The view that *'the Waveney Valley Railway would never again be reopened for passenger traffic'* was expressed by E.T. Moore when presiding at the annual general meeting of Harleston Chamber of Trade at the Magpie Hotel at the end of February. He was reporting on the meeting at Liverpool Street and although they had an extremely fair hearing the decision came as bitter disappointment. He only hoped that their efforts might result in improved goods deliveries and a better bus service!

As well as the usual agricultural commodities, coal and farm machinery conveyed by the goods services, military traffic had continued to Pulham Market but in February 1958 the RAF station was closed and the long siding serving the camp was mothballed, pending a decision on the future use of the airfield. Decline was setting in and further rationalisation was inevitable.

A reporter and photographer from the *Eastern Daily Press* visited the branch in the early summer of 1958 and duly reported their trip on the daily 'Waveney Flyer' from Tivetshall to Bungay and back in the issue of 19th June. The 'J15' Class locomotive was crewed by Driver George Burleigh and Fireman Arthur Ireson, whilst the guard for the journey was Arthur Kirby, all men based at Norwich. The reporter stated there was also a daily service between Beccles and Bungay in the sugar beet season but during the summer months the train only travelled from Beccles to Ditchingham, going on to Bungay 'as required'. The article then quoted the details of freight carried: *'In a year the line handled about 16,000 tons of sugar beet, 12,000 tons of coal, 2,000 tons of grain and seeds, 2,000 tons of malt and 2,000 tons of poultry and pig foods as well as 150 wagons of farm machinery'.* The article also gave details of the interview with Station Master W.G. Elsey of Harleston, who had assumed charge of the entire branch.

It became increasingly evident the deterioration of the freight situation could not continue, for on some days the branch trains from either end conveyed few wagons, no inward traffic and only empty vehicles away from the line. On 7th September 1959 the British Transport Commission advised Norfolk County Council and Depwade Rural District Council of the intention to close the line between Harleston (exclusive) and Bungay (exclusive) as well as Homersfield station, and to handle goods which had in the past gone from Homersfield, at either Harleston or Bungay. The document stated that in 1958, Homersfield station dealt with 2,517 tons of freight; the outgoing consisting of 1,112 tons of sugar beet, with incoming 1,405 tons of traffic consisting of roadstone chippings, fertilizer, bricks and wet pulp. At a subsequent meeting, L. England for Depwade Council stated Homersfield station was used mainly for the four months of the sugar beet campaign and during that time that station was very busy. He felt they should try and persuade the Transport Commission to keep it open for those four months of the year and not disturb the line. If the line closed it would result in more lorries on the road. England recalled that during the 1953 East Coast floods the line was used to convey ballast to the coast. W. Smith added that the proposal did not make sense when one considered how badly the alternative road twisted and turned. Their argument was weakened when it was pointed out the total amount of sugar beet moved from Homersfield station amounted to only 100 lorry loads per year, whilst another agreed and commented that spread over four months this amounted to one lorry per day! The councils thus offered no objection and freight facilities were subsequently withdrawn from the station on and from 1st February 1960, when the central section of the branch was also closed to all traffic.

However, before the branch was severed and track removed, railway enthusiasts' made final visits to the Waveney Valley when two further railtours traversed the branch. The first, on 21st May 1960 and organised by the Midland & Great Northern Joint Railway Society, was headed by an immaculate 'J15' Class 0-6-0 No. 65469 hauling five ex-L&NER Gresley corridor coaches in red and cream livery and a BR Mark 1 in crimson. The second special train followed on 8th October 1960, hauled by the same locomotive with the train formed of two Gresley corridor coaches in maroon livery, two BR Mark 1 corridor coaches also in maroon, and two BR Mark 1 vehicles in red and cream. Soon after the train had cleared the branch, buffer stops were placed across the rails at Harleston and Bungay and from late 1960 the line was worked as two separate branches, the western section from Tivetshall to Harleston and the eastern section from Beccles to Bungay. Dismantling of the track between Harleston and Bungay commenced in 1961 with

'J15' Class 0-6-0 No. 65469 waits to depart from Tivetshall on 21st May 1960 with the Midland & Great Northern Railway Society special train. Note the lower quadrant signals still in use for the branch platform and Up main line. The lowered arm denotes the road is set for the branch. The lower arm was for the use of trains using the Up loop extension to the Up main line. Tivetshall Junction signal box can be seen in the background. *Author's collection*

work starting at Redenhall Bridge (exclusive) and progressing back towards Bungay. The track was lifted in 60 feet lengths and taken with the points by train to Lowestoft permanent way depot for dismantling and possible reuse.

Freight services on the western end of the line originally commenced and finished their working from Norwich but later the branch was included in the schedule for the 5.10am goods train from Ipswich which was diverted to serve the branch. At the eastern end the train worked to and from Lowestoft with a standover at Beccles where a change of locomotive was made. The branch received the benefit of the British Railways modernisation programme from 1959, when diesel electric locomotives built by BTH/Paxman BR Class '15', BR/Sulzer Type '2' BR Class '24' and Brush Type '2', later to be Class '31/1', took over the working of the branch services between Tivetshall and Harleston. Because of weight restrictions on the timber bridges between Bungay and Beccles, only BR 204 hp diesel mechanical shunting locomotive of Class '03' and Class '05' could work the trains. Further rationalisation was also achieved when trainmen were required to open and close level crossing gates where barriers still existed. Self-locking padlocks were placed on all gates and a key attached to the single line Train Staff. Instructions were issued that after the engine or train was stopped well clear of the gates, the fireman – or guard in the case of a train or engine single manned – would open the barriers for the passage of the engine or train over the crossing. Once the engine or train was clear of the crossing the guard – or fireman in the case of a light engine – was required to close the gates and relock them. The driver was also required to ensure he had received the 'all right' signal from the guard before proceeding on the journey.

In 1963 the infamous Beeching Report was published and whilst referring specifically to passenger traffic, the map included with the report showed average freight tonnages and receipts. Stations on surviving sections of the branch provided poor results Tivetshall, Pulham Market, Pulham St. Mary and Geldeston, 0 to 5,000 tons per annum, Harleston, Bungay, Ditchingham and Ellingham 5,000 to 25,000 tons per annum and Beccles over 25,000 tons per annum – and all showing 0 to 5,000 tons per week. The continuing ailing receipts finally forced British Railways Eastern Region authorities to effect economies.

With closures taking place on many lines in the eastern counties the following comment appeared in the *Eastern Daily Press* Countryman's Notebook on 18th April 1964.

> *Rail closures continue in East Anglia. All the more curious to me is the persistence of the tiny branch line, which is in view from my window. It runs no further than Bungay, which is six miles away. It carries no passengers, but at most two dawdling goods trains per day, whose wagons mostly seem empty. They hold up two lots of road traffic to get into Beccles station. Far from being closed down, quite extensive repairs were being done to it a short while back. There is also a bridge over the Waveney to be maintained. Had Bungay some huge hidden export trade? I know only of books. Or is something hush-hush going on there – development of secret weapons, breeding of death-ray glow-worms or something? Meanwhile – there must be some reason why they are repairing the line.*

As the eastern section freight traffic continued to decline the writer of Countryman's Notes finally had his wish, for on 13th July 1964 freight facilities were withdrawn from Geldeston and Ellingham, with Bungay surviving only to 3rd August to allow for clearance of traffic from the yard and for the abandonment of a weak bridge between Ditchingham and Bungay, which had last been renewed in the 1920s. Only Beccles and Ditchingham remained open, but the latter succumbed on 19th April 1965 although it unofficially remained open until the following August

The remains of Bungay station from the Up platform facing towards Tivetshall. Only the Up line is in position terminating at buffers stops by the water tank. The Down platform is devoid of buildings and track. *Author's collection*

'03' Class 0-6-0 diesel mechanical shunting locomotive No. D2035 shunting at Ditchingham in 1964. The locomotive has run round its train which is standing on the Down loop line, whilst the wagons to the right are stabled in the station goods yard sidings. In the left background are the maltings used by the US Army as a military store during World War Two, looming above the crossing keeper's cottage beside the Norwich Road gates. *Dr I.C. Allen*

to accommodate blocks of sand trains until the new facilities at Coltishall on the Wroxham to County School branch were ready to accept the new traffic.

On the western section, freight facilities were also withdrawn from Pulham Market and Pulham St. Mary on and from 13th July 1964, but traffic continued between Tivetshall and Harleston until 18th April 1966. During this period there was an encouraging upturn in traffic, for the *Eastern Daily Press* for 23rd October 1965 published a photograph of a trainload of forty Howard Rotaspreaders at Harleston destined for Heysham, but this was an irregular consignment. Passenger train facilities were withdrawn from Tivetshall station on and from 7th November 1966 and freight facilities had been withdrawn from the junction goods yard on and from 18th April of the same year. The contract for the removal of the permanent way and other assets from the branch was awarded to A. King & Sons of Norwich; the girder bridge over the A143 at Redenhall and the section from Harleston to Tivetshall was removed in the later months of 1966.

In the meantime, work on dismantling of the eastern section of the branch continued without incident until the *Eastern Daily Press* reported in May 1966 that a party of men employed by A. King & Sons of Norwich, whilst in the process of removing part of a river bridge with the aid of a crane mounted on a lorry, suffered the ignominy of a section of the bridge collapsing under the weight of the vehicle. Fortunately the crane did not overturn and the driver was uninjured. The report surmised *'the bridge would probably best be removed by the crane on that bank with the centre section being removed with the aid of a pontoon in the river'*. In December 1966 Beccles Borough Council complained that two plots of former railway land on either side of Northgate Street level crossing had not been offered to the council before being sold privately. British Railways replied that the sale had been effected before a Government directive concerning the disposal of land to local authorities had been issued.

In 1968 suggestions had been made that the railway trackbed could be used for road improvements and by 1972 this was nearing fruition, for the route from Earsham through Bungay to Ditchingham was earmarked as the route of a by-pass taking the A143 road round the town. At that stage Bungay goods yard was used by traders and others for storage of materials and equipment, whilst the station buildings were still standing and the former station master's house used as a private dwelling.

The *Beccles & Bungay Journal* for 3rd August 1972, under the heading *'Water Tower Saved'*, reported:

The water tower, which is believed to have been at the former Bungay station on the Waveney Valley line since at least 1916, has been removed. It will be re-erected at Weybourne, a stop on the North Norfolk line, owned by the North Norfolk Railway Company Limited, and will be used to fill its locomotives. The tank, which is made of wrought iron, is 16 feet by 8 feet by 4 feet deep, holds 5,000 gallons of water and when empty weighs between 4 and 5 tons. Members of the Midland and Great Northern Joint Railway Society, who organised the move, freed the pipes the previous day.

A crane lifted the tank onto blocks and then a sling was put round it when it was lifted on a lorry. The tank will be re-erected on to a brick base or steel stilts within the next 12 months.

In October 1974 the *Eastern Daily Press* reported that work on the A143 main road had commenced during the summer at Homersfield following demolition of the station buildings but excluding the goods shed, which had been sold at auction for £2,200 in 1970 and escaped demolition. The new road was opened in sections from Redenhall and reached Ditchingham in 1983, by which time both Bungay and Ditchingham stations had been razed to the ground. Thus by September 1983 part of the WVR had been used for a section of the £2.3 million Bungay by-pass road, covering a 3.4km stretch of the trackbed between Earsham and Ditchingham. Elsewhere, in September 1984 the station buildings at Tivetshall were intact although the Down platform had been demolished. The Up-side platform was intact whilst the wooden level crossing gates were unusual in that they were modified in the form of barriers mounted on rubber wheels. Along the former trackbed the bridge adjacent to the A143 at Harleston was demolished early in December 1984.

By the winter of 1985 work began on erecting the overhead masts, cross arms and support straining arms in connection with the Norwich main line electrification, and these were in place from Tivetshall to Flordon by 8th June 1986. The Up-side front siding at Tivetshall was secured out of use on 12th May 1986 to allow masts to be erected. The north and south sidings were remodelled to form a single Up through siding on 19th May, by which time all other sidings at the former junction had been lifted, the Up through siding having been taken out of use by 13th April; the trailing crossover was secured out of use on 28th September 1986. The station buildings were demolished by 28th May and the platforms removed and demolished by 27th August; the former Junction signal box was abolished on 5th October and demolished by 28th December 1986.

In 1988 the A143 road from Bury St. Edmunds to Great Yarmouth was realigned and widened east of Harleston so as to obliterate more of the track bed of the former railway; in the course of construction the station buildings at Redenhall and Wortwell were demolished. However, the goods shed at Homersfield survived until 2004 as an industrial store as it was close to the A143 road. Careful observation will reveal remnants of the former branch but the majority who pass by speed along in their cars oblivious of the fact that many decades ago little 2-4-2 tank engines and 2-4-0 and 0-6-0 tender locomotives steamed along this by-way hauling coaches bearing the local populace to or from local towns on market days and to the seaside on weekend excursions. Beccles station, although much changed from yesteryear, is still rail served; but rail passengers travelling between Ipswich and Norwich scarcely glance out of the window as their train speeds past the site of Tivetshall station and are oblivious of the its former importance as the junction for the Waveney Valley Railway.

Line to nowhere. Bungay station looking east with buffer stops erected at the western end of the former Up loop line alongside the Up platform. The water tower and feeder pipes stand isolated and derelict, for the section of the branch between Harleston and Bungay was officially closed on 1st February 1960 and the track subsequently lifted in 1961, but only after two enthusiast special trains were allowed across the closed section on 21st May and 8th October 1960. Thereafter, until complete closure the remnants of the branch was served by freight services from each end. *Dr I.C. Allen*

8

The Route Described

BEFORE EMBARKING ON THIS CHAPTER, the reader must be made aware that anomalies were found with the mileages quoted in the working timetables compared to some engineering documents. The author has consulted over seventy documents issued by the GER, L&NER and BR(ER), as result of which the mileages shown within this chapter have been corrected and will in some cases differ from those shown in previously published works.

Tivetshall station, opened by EUR on 7th November 1849 at 100 miles 57 chains from Liverpool Street, was the junction for the Waveney Valley Branch and was originally provided with platforms on the Up and Down main lines. It served the hamlets of Tivetshall St. Mary and Tivetshall St. Margarets to the east of the railway, but after the opening of the WVR its status increased and the station was provided with three platforms; the main building was on the Down main line or westernmost platform, 280 feet in length, which could accommodate 4½ coaches of 63 feet 6 inches in length. The building, a two-storey brick structure with accommodation for the station master was probably designed by Frederick Barnes,

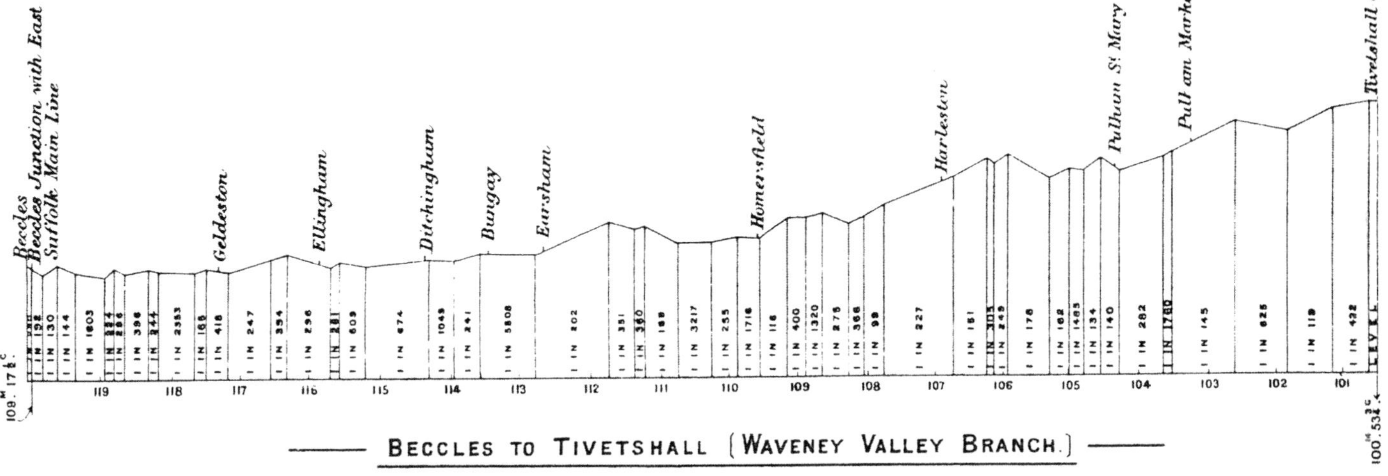

ABOVE: Gradient Chart for the line.

BELOW: Tivetshall station, 100 miles 57 chains from Liverpool Street, facing north with the Down main platform and the maltings in the background. The outer face of the island platform, 365 feet in length, was normally used by Waveney Valley line trains, with the water crane at the north end of the back road used to replenish locomotives working the branch services. *Author's collection*

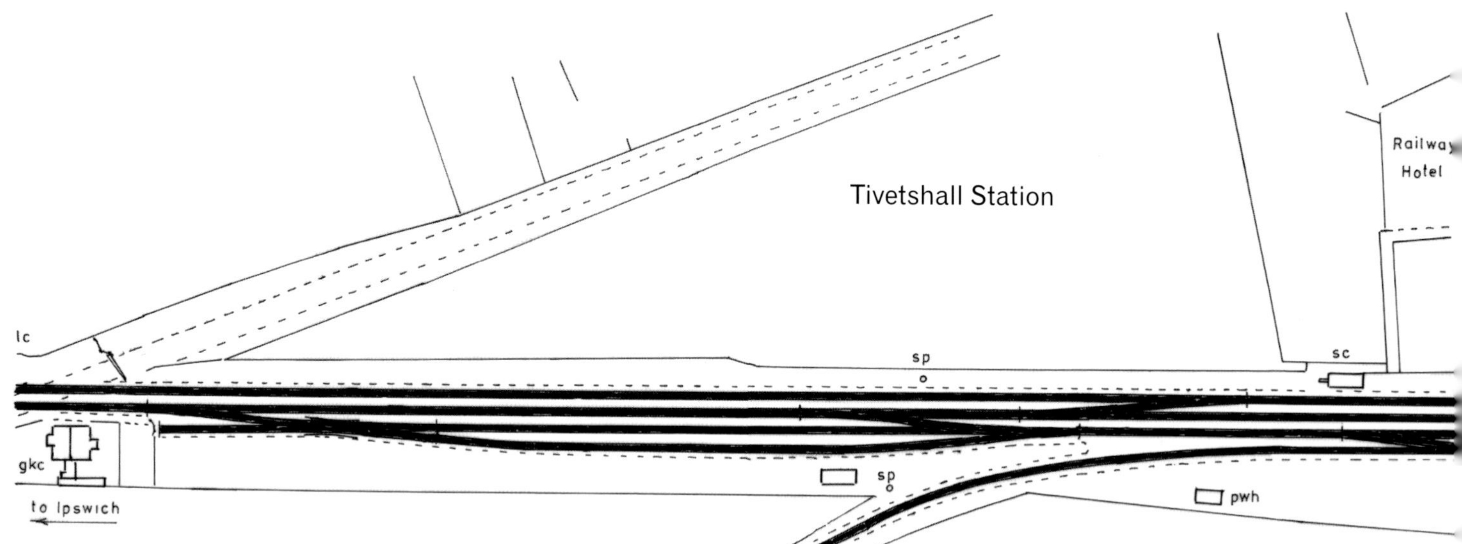

an Ipswich architect who carried out much work for the EUR. The Up-side platform was an island with the western face of 370 feet serving the Up main line and the 365 feet long eastern platform used by Waveney Valley Branch trains; each platform accommodated six coaches of 63 feet 6 inches in length. A timber waiting room with an overhanging roof and valencing provided accommodation for passengers on the Up platform. The goods yard, located on the Down side of the main line, was served by three sharply curved sidings: the 402 feet back road, 270 feet middle road and the 180 feet shed road serving the large brick-built goods shed containing a 1½-ton capacity crane. All were served from a 110 feet long headshunt alongside the Down main line. From the curved back road a connection led to the 620 feet long maltings siding, 100 feet on railway property and the remainder on private property. A number of additional sidings some 300 feet in length were installed on the Up side of the main line immediately north of the station in 1943. If required it was possible to run round fourteen bogie coaches via the Up siding and the branch platform. Signalling at the station was controlled from the brick and timber signal box with 45-lever McKenzie & Holland frame, located on the Down side of the main line south of the station at 100 miles 50½ chains. Water columns located at the south end of the Up platform, the north end of the Down-side platform and beside the north end of the branch platform line were served from a water tower on the Up side of line south of the level crossing. The station was closed for goods traffic on 18th April 1966 and for passengers on 7th November 1966. A nearby hostelry known as the Railway Tavern provided a convenient meeting place for passengers awaiting trains as well as a 'local' for the inhabitants and railway staff. Both the platforms and the Down-side station buildings were demolished at the same time as the signal box on 5th October 1986, although the timber buildings on the island platform had been demolished at an earlier date. The large and distinctive station name or running in board on the Down platform advised passengers to change for the Waveney Valley Branch, the Pulhams, Harleston, Bungay and Beccles.

Of interest on the main line were water troughs installed in 1896 at a cost of £2,923 about half a mile south of the station, used by locomotives hauling the through Cromer expresses to enable them to run non-stop from Liverpool Street to North Walsham. The troughs were removed in June 1945, although the water supply to the valve house was not disconnected until 1954.

Departing from Tivetshall, the branch train bisected the separate branch level crossing Main line No. 9 at 100 miles 53¼ chains

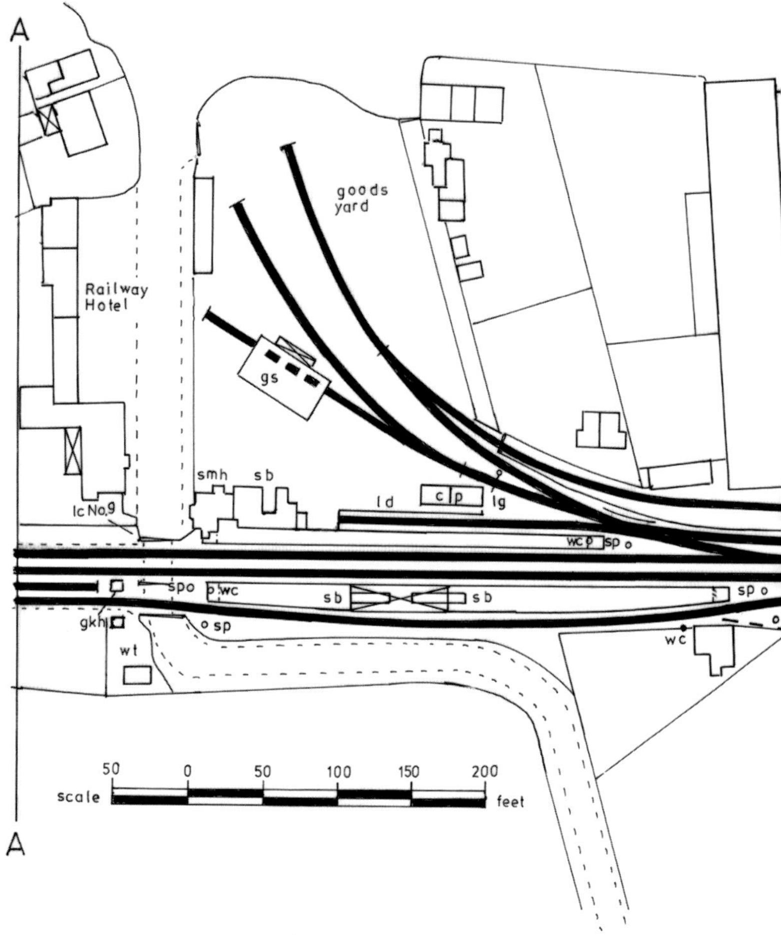

Tivetshall Junction station, 100 miles 57 chains from Liverpool Street, facing south from the Up main platform on 1st September 1951. The gates of the main line level crossing No. 9 straddle the Up and Down main lines. To the right is the 280 feet long Down main platform with station master's house and station offices by the platform ramp. To the extreme right is the road entrance to the goods yard. *H.C. Casserley*

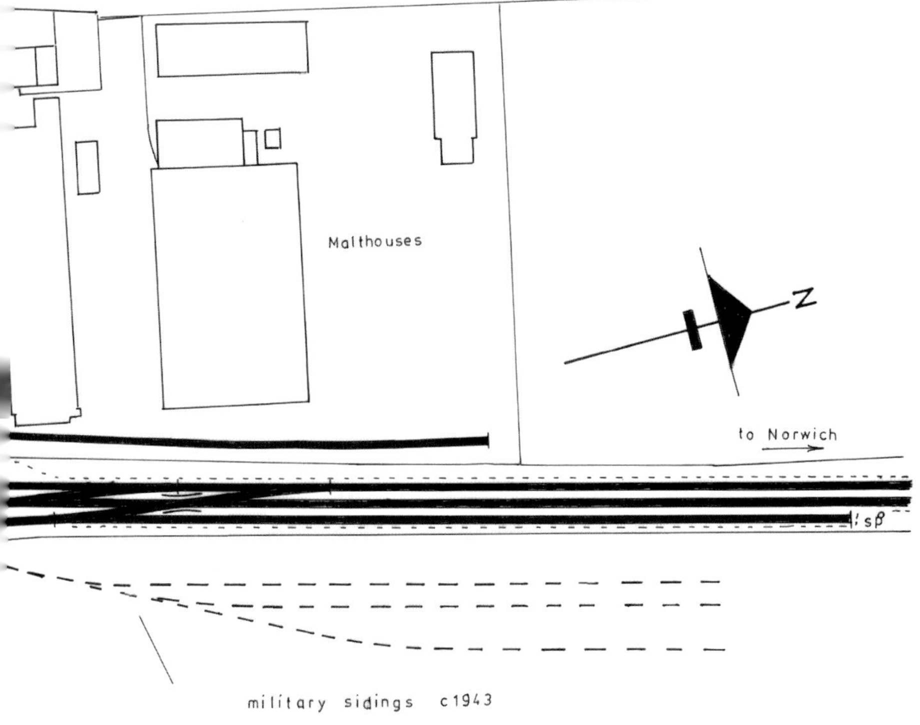

Key to Track Diagrams

BO	BOOKING OFFICE
CD	CATTLE DOCK
CP	CATTLE PENS
CS	COAL STAGE
FB	FOOTBRIDGE
FP	FOOTPATH
GKC	GATE KEEPER'S COTTAGE
GO	GOODS OFFICE
GS	GOODS SHED
LC	LEVEL CROSSING
LD	LOADING DOCK
LG	LOADING GAUGE
MP	MILE POST
OB	OVERBRIDGE
OC	OCCUPATION CROSSING
PWH	PERMANENT WAY HUT
RR	REFRESHMENT ROOM
SB	STATION BUILDINGS
SC	SIGNAL BOX
SMH	STATION MASTER'S HOUSE
SMO	STATION MASTER'S OFFICE
SP	SIGNAL POST
UB	UNDERBRIDGE
WB	WEIGHBRIDGE
WBO	WEIGHBRIDGE OFFICE
WC	WATER COLUMN
WPH	WATER PUMPHOUSE
WR	WAITING ROOM
WT	WATER TANK

from Liverpool Street and ran parallel to Up and Down main lines and Up reception siding for a short distance before swinging away on a 20 chains radius curve to the east. After passing the Up branch home signal on the Up side of the line it headed across open agricultural countryside, initially on the level and then falling at 1 in 422, skirting the hamlets of Tivetshall St. Margarets and Tivetshall St. Mary to the north and south of the branch respectively. With the small stream known as the Beck flowing on the north side, the line curved slightly to the right over bridge No. 1174 at 0 miles 44 chains with Hall Farm on the Up or south side of the railway. The 1 in 422 gave way to a 1 in 119 falling gradient as the branch then proceeded over Green Lane level crossing No. 4 at 0 miles 78½ chains before passing the 1 mile post; This was followed by another straight section where the gradient altered to rise at 1 in 625 over

The Up island platform at Tivetshall Junction on 1st September 1951, with the curved back platform used by Waveney Valley services to the right. Compared with the detailed station nameboard on the Down main platform in the background, the island platform only boasts a short running in board denoting Tivetshall. In the background are the rail-served maltings whilst at the north end of the back platform road can be seen the water crane use by locomotives on Waveney Valley services. *H.C. Casserley*

'E4' Class 2-4-0 No. 62789 departing from the back platform at Tivetshall with the 9.00am Beccles to Norwich Thorpe train on 1st September 1951. To the left is the water crane serving the back platform road whilst to the right is the one located at the north end of the Down main platform. In the background is the goods shed. *H.C. Casserley*

ABOVE: Tivetshall station facing north towards Norwich with the 280 feet long platform serving the Down main line to the left and the Up main served by the Up island platform 370 feet in length. Waveney Valley Branch trains used the outer face of the island platform, 365 feet in length. *Author's collection*

CENTRE: Tivetshall Up-side island platform looking south, with its timber and brick waiting shelter and waiting room on 30th September 1956. The Gresley corridor coaching stock of the Railway Enthusiast's special train stands at the back platform normally used by Waveney Valley services. *R.M. Casserley*

Tivetshall station was closed to passenger traffic on and from 7th November 1966 and is here shown on 10th September 1971 with the former Up island platform devoid of buildings. In the background are the Watney, Combe, Reid & Co. maltings, which were for many years rail served. *H.C. Casserley*

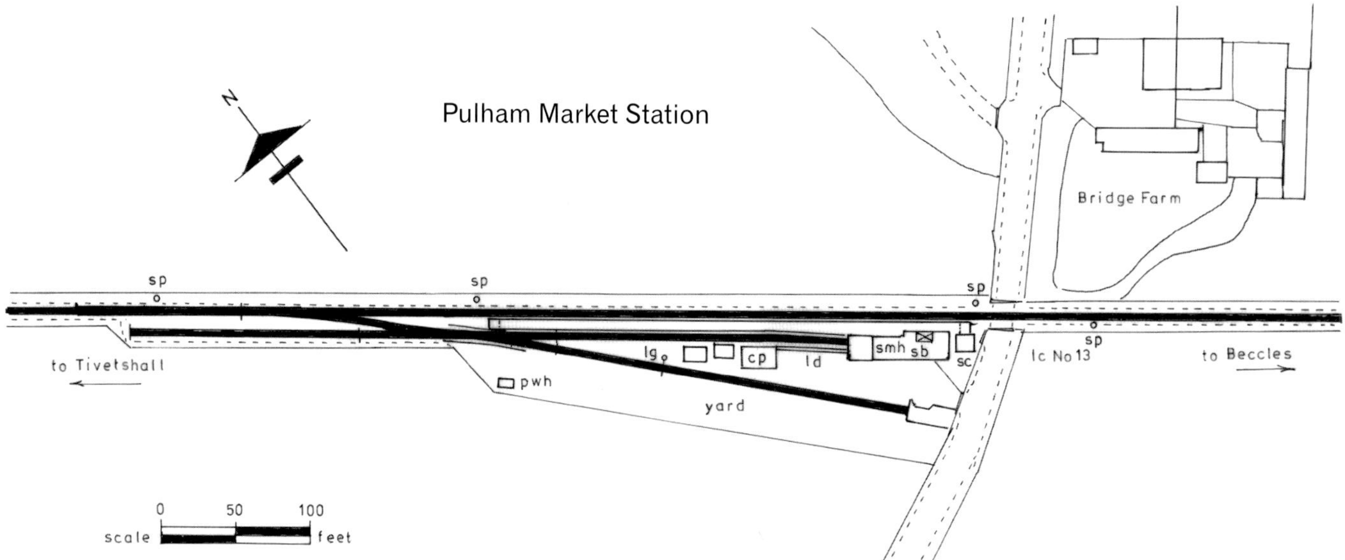

the Norwich Road (later A140) level crossing No. 8 at 1 mile 67¾ chains and then past the 2 mile post where the line fell at 1 in 145, followed by Pulham Market Down distant signal on the Down side of the railway.

With The Hall on the Up side of the line the branch passed Pulham Market Down home signal to enter **Pulham Market** station, 2 miles 52 chains from Tivetshall, located on the south side of the single line with the narrow platform 340 feet in length. The platform was originally only 99 feet in length but was extended to 130 feet in 1885 and finally to 340 feet in 1892. The platform could accommodate five coaches of 63 feet 6 inches in length. The station, with its two storey building thought to be designed by Frederick Barnes who had worked with Peter Bruff on the EUR, was originally called Pulham St. Magdalene but within a few months was renamed Pulham Market; it served the village a half mile to the north of the line. The station building, with station master's accommodation on the first floor, was virtually identical with those at Pulham St. Mary, Ditchingham, Ellingham and Geldeston; it had a gable roof, bold arches and round Italianate top windows to both floors, a shallow pitched slate roof with a central dormer either side and the ground floor extended on the platform side to form a shelter. By 1913, as a result of rationalisation of staff, the house was occupied by

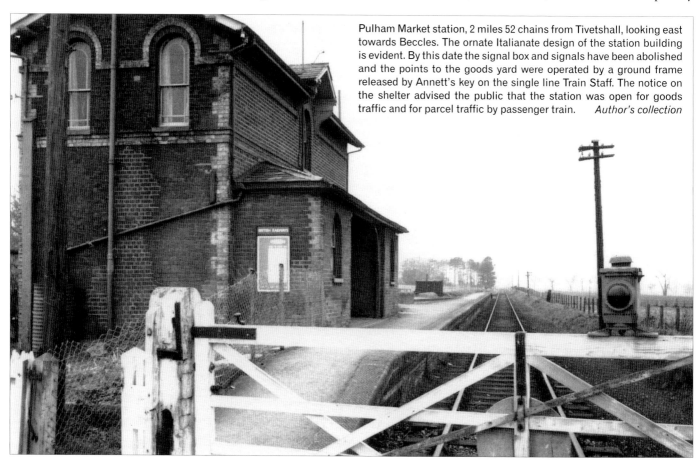

Pulham Market station, 2 miles 52 chains from Tivetshall, looking east towards Beccles. The ornate Italianate design of the station building is evident. By this date the signal box and signals have been abolished and the points to the goods yard were operated by a ground frame released by Annett's key on the single line Train Staff. The notice on the shelter advised the public that the station was open for goods traffic and for parcel traffic by passenger train. *Author's collection*

The road approach to the station building at Pulham Market showing the Italianate style of architecture with curved top to the windows. The view from across the road also shows the rear of the signal box located adjacent to the level crossing. The buildings and fencing appear to have been recently repainted as two members of the station staff pose for the cameraman. *Author's collection*

foreman-in-charge Alfred Ernest Wood paying a rental of £5 4s 0d per annum. The platform-facing frontage featured two projecting pavilions, which supported a sloping roof above a small loggia or covered waiting area. Although the line was opened in three separate sections the standard design of building was adopted on the first and last sections, with the central section between Harleston and Bungay employing a different set of designs. The design was used again a few years later on the Tendring Hundred Railway, probably as a legacy of Peter Bruff being engineer to both railways.

The small goods yard, on the Up or south side of the line west of the station, was provided with two sidings, the 280 feet coal road also serving cattle pens and the 231 feet dock road running to the back of the station platform. These were served from a 215 feet long headshunt at the west end of the layout. Points and signals at the station were worked from the Pulham Market signal box boasting a 26-lever Saxby & Farmer relock frame, located on the Up side of the line by the level crossing at the east end of platform between the road and the station building. Goods facilities were withdrawn from the station on and from 13th July 1964 and the last train passed in April 1966.

An amusing story concerning Pulham Market relates of an elderly passenger entraining at Beccles asking the guard to inform him when the station at Pulham Market was reached. Unfortunately the guard completely overlooked the request until the train was departing the station. Realising his omission he applied the emergency brake and stopped the train at the end of the platform. After dismounting onto the ballast and struggling along the track he reached the carriage to

Pulham Market station on 10th September 1971 after closure of the line and removal of the permanent way. *H.C. Casserley*

Pulham Market station facing towards Beccles, with level crossing No. 13 bisecting the line west of the 340 feet long platform. In this view the boundary between the original platform and the later extension is evident. The signal box and signalling have been abolished and the dock road at the back of the platform has been removed. *Author's collection*

Pulham Market station viewed from the platform facing towards Tivetshall. The headshunt has been removed with the signals. *Author's collection*

inform his charge, *'Out yu git. This is Pulham Market'.* To this the passenger nonchalantly replied; *'Oh I don't want tu git out here. Yu see my missus she say tu me, she say, thar'll be the time to take yar next pill just afore yu git tu Tivetshall. Thass why I arst yu tu let me know when Pullem Market wus!'*

Departing Pulham Market the line passed the Down starting signal at the end of the platform and over level crossing No. 13 at 2 miles 54¾ chains. With the Up home signal on the Up side of the railway and Bridge Farm on the Down side there were views of the square tower of Pulham St. Mary Magdalen church to the north. To the east of the station was a 770 feet long loop on the Up side of the main single line, with point connections 495 feet apart and a 152 feet long headshunt at the west end. From the east end of the loop a mile-long siding installed during World War One served **Pulham Airfield**, initially associated with the Admiralty and airships but later with the Air Ministry. Installed in 1915 and opened in 1916, entry at the west end was controlled from Pulham Market signal box whilst that at the eastern end was controlled from a ground frame released by Annett's key on the single line Train Staff. A second loop line was constructed early in 1941 to ease the movement of traffic into and out of the airfield but this was disused by 1956. The original loop and spur remained in use for traffic until late 1957, latterly used as a store by the RAF, and the base was closed in February 1958. A network of 2 feet gauge line connected the siding with airfield installations, which also served as base for R33 and R34 airships between the wars. The use of a tow rope was authorised for shunting and if required it was possible to run round eleven bogie coaches by using the Air Ministry siding.

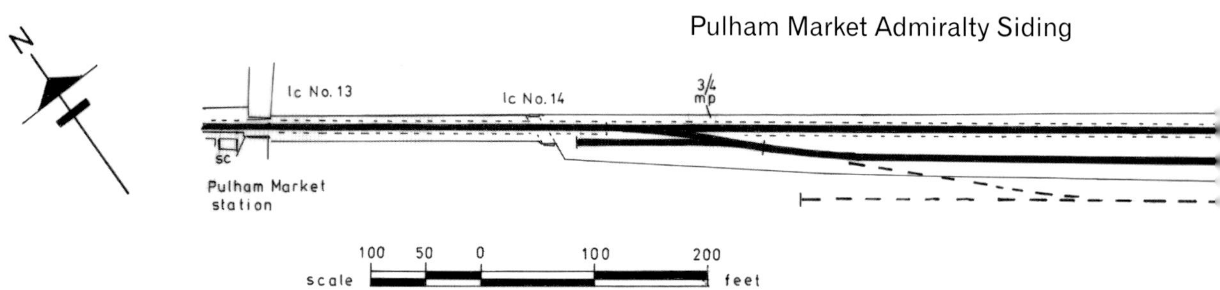

Pulham Market Admiralty Siding

'J15' Class 0-6-0 No. 65469 standing at Pulham Market prior to shunting wagons into the small goods yard, the guard is on the platform waiting to detach the wagons. Note the 231 feet dock road at the back of the platform has already been lifted. *Dr I.C. Allen*

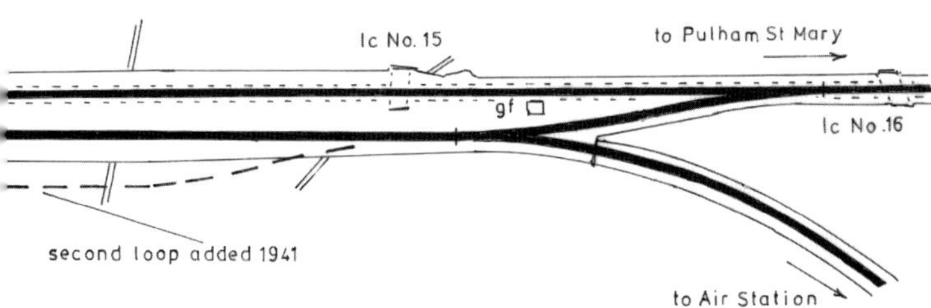

'F5' Class 2-4-2T No. 67201 pulls away from Pulham Market with a Tivetshall to Beccles train in June 1951 and is passing 'N7/3' 0-6-2T No. 69679 hauling a short freight train from Pulham Royal Air Force station; the train is travelling along the inner loop line originally installed in 1916, providing a connection to the then Royal Naval Air Station operating airships. The corridor coach on the passenger train is one vehicle of a three-coach set which after working a round trip from Beccles to Tivetshall continued to Lowestoft and finished the day as a through train from Lowestoft to Rugby. *Dr I.C. Allen*

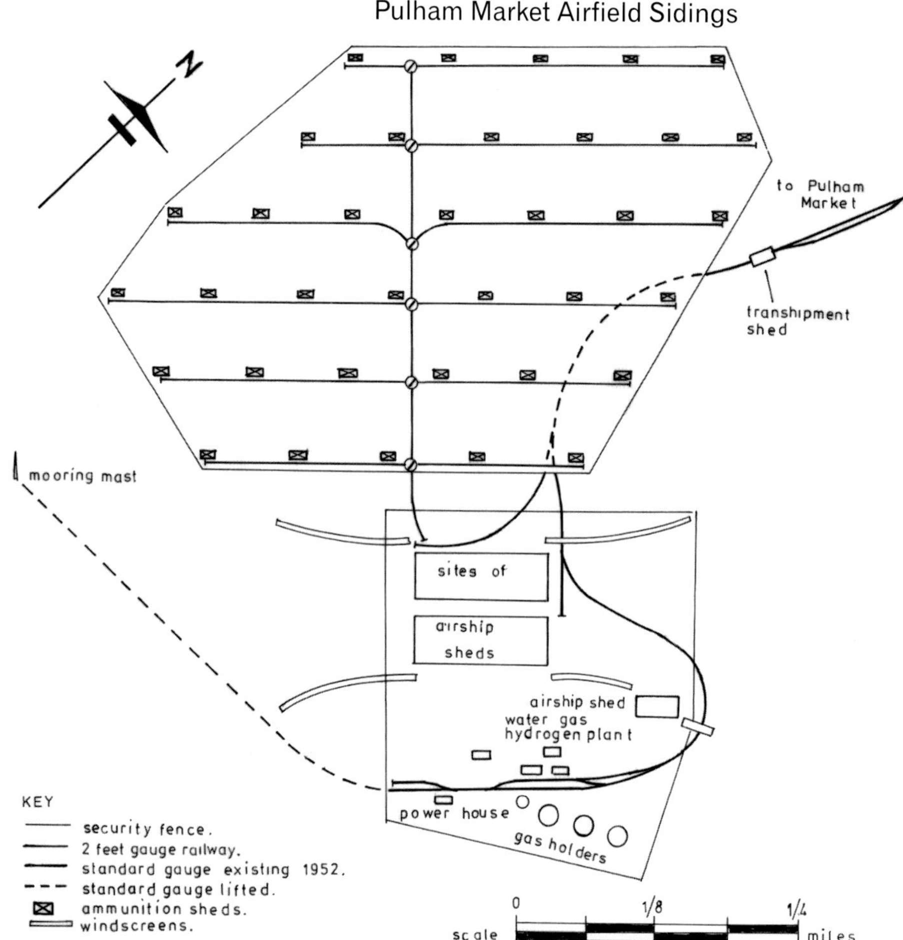

Beyond the siding the railway continued on the 1 in 145 falling gradient before a short descent of 1 in 1,760 took the line past the 3 mile post, curving left in an east-south-east direction, passing Pulham Market Up distant signal on the Up side and, very soon after, Pulham St. Mary Down distant signal on the Down side. The long raking left-hand curve continued on a 1 in 262 falling gradient with the meandering water course of the Beck on the Down side as the line straightened out passing Waveney Cottage on the Up side. A short rise of 1 in 140 brought the line past Pulham St. Mary Down home signal on the Up side of the railway and over level crossing No. 20 at 3 miles 55 chains, bisecting a minor road to enter Pulham St. Mary station 3 miles 57 chains from Tivetshall, with the Up starting signal east of the gates.

Pulham St. Mary, nearly always known as 'Pulham Mary', served the village south of the railway dominated by the church of St. Mary the Virgin. The single platform, 330 feet in length, provided on the Down or north side of the line and which could accommodate five bogie coaches, was backed by the two-storey brick-built station building in Italianate style with low pitched slated roof and arched window surrounds. The goods yard, also on the north side of

'J15' Class 0-6-0 No. 65471 prepares to depart Pulham Airfield and take the mile-long branch to Pulham Market station. The siding, dating from 1916, originally served the Royal Naval Airship Station during World War One. *Dr I.C. Allen*

'J15' Class 0-6-0 No. 65471 in December 1957, pulling into the Royal Air Force base at Pulham Market, located almost a mile from the branch line, prior to shunting the yard. The base was closed in February 1958 and the long siding removed. *Dr I.C. Allen*

the line and entered by a connection facing Up trains (i.e. towards Tivetshall), was provided with two sidings, the 320 feet long dock road at the back of the station platform and 310 feet back or coal road. From these a 230 feet headshunt alongside the main single line was provided at the east end of the yard. Two carriage bodies were located in the goods yard for storage of goods and equipment. Although Pulham St. Mary was not a staff station it was provided with a signal box boasting a 15-lever frame on the south side of the line near the level crossing. The use of a tow rope was authorised for shunting and permission was also given for a train or vehicles to be placed outside the home signal in the Down direction where there was a falling gradient steeper than 1 in 260 towards the box in rear, provided where practicable a brake van with guard in attendance was at the lower end of the train when it came to a stand. This instruction was also applicable to shunting operations at Harleston and Ditchingham.

From Pulham St. Mary the line maintained its east-south-east course climbing at 1 in 140 past the Down starting and Up home signals, both located on the Up side of the branch, to a minor summit at the 4 mile post. Curving to the right before following a straight course, the line descended at 1 in 134 over Crossingford crossing or Doctor's Lane No. 24 at 4 miles 15 chains, with the crossing keeper's cottage on the Down side of the railway west of the gates. With Pulham St. Mary Up distant signal on the Up side, the railway followed a switchback, initially climbing at 1 in 1,485 and curving to the left, passing Crossingford Farm on the Down side and over the footpath crossing leading to Crossingford Bridge which spanned the Beck on the Down side. The line then followed a straight course, first falling at 1 in 162 and then rising at 1 in 178 to bridge No. 1175 at 4 miles 69 chains, followed by a slight right-hand curve past the 5 mile post with Streamlet Farm on the

Pulham St. Mary station after closure of the line on 10th September 1971, showing details of the Italianate architecture. *R.M. Casserley*

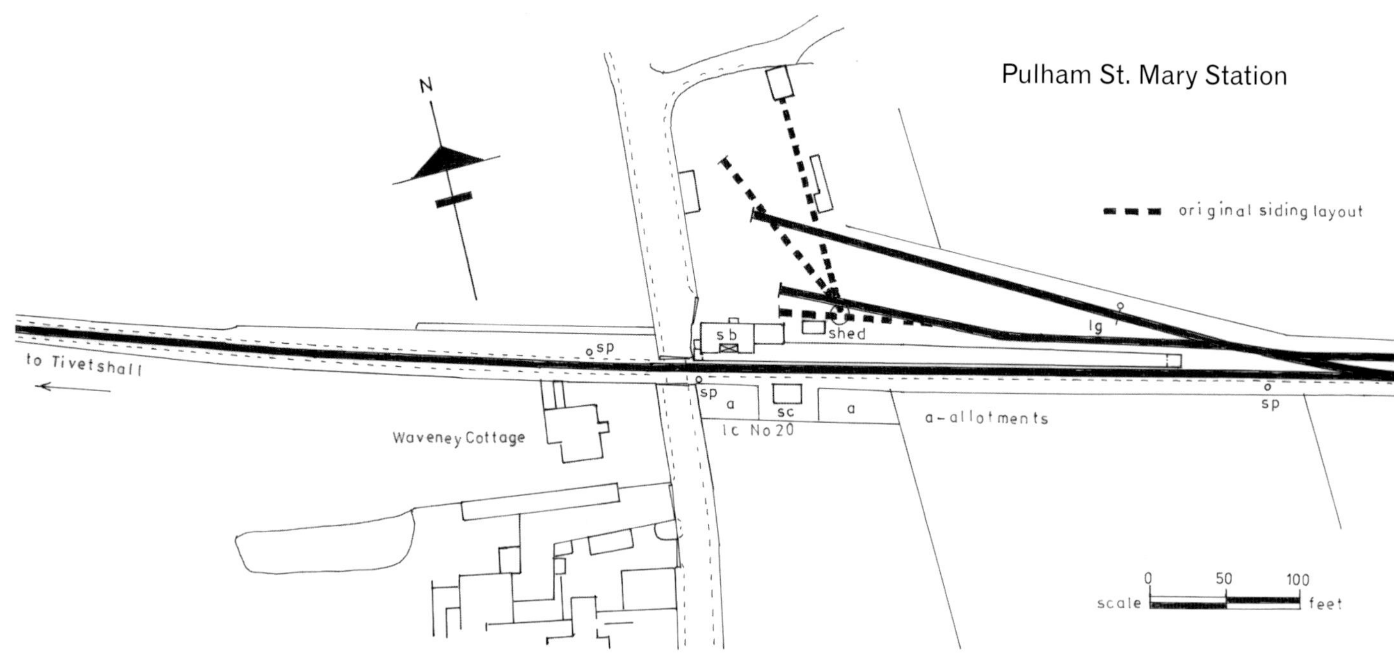

Pulham St. Mary station building on 10th September 1971 showing the platform aspect. *R.M. Casserley*

Pulham St. Mary station, 3 miles 57 chains from Tivetshall. View facing towards Beccles with the 190 feet long platform on the Down side of the line. At the far end of the platform is the connection from the main single line to the goods yard controlled from a ground frame. *Author's collection*

Down side north of the Beck. With Beck Hall also on the Down side the straight course continued, with the small stream still close at hand on the north side of line, to **Starston** or Grove Hill Road level crossing No. 31 at 5 miles 40 chains from Tivetshall. At this point a small station with a 115 feet long low platform located on the north side of the line west of the crossing was originally provided to serve a community of 485 inhabitants. As a result of rationalisation the station closed on 1st August 1866. The former two-storey station building on the Down side of the line at 5 miles 38 chains, in the same architectural style as Pulham St. Mary, was retained as a gatekeeper's accommodation. There appears to have been no raised platform at Starston, for beneath the awning of the station house were stone flags indicating that passengers were expected to climb up to the carriage footboards when joining the train, a not uncommon feature on the early railways.

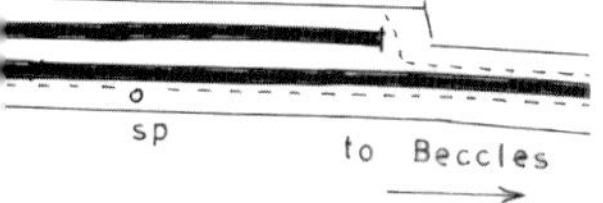

Departing Starston the line bisected Grove Hill Road or Railway Hill level crossing No. 31 at 5 miles 40 chains, with views of Grove Hill House on the Up side as the branch descended at 1 in 249 followed by a short rise of 1 on 305 before crossing over bridge No. 1176 at 5 miles 56 chains; the railway then descended at 1 in 161 with Harleston Down distant signal on the Down or north side of the line just beyond the structure. The straight course continued, passing bridge No. 1177 at 6 miles 00 chains and just beyond the

The former Starston station, 5 miles 38 chains from Tivetshall, with ornate Italianate style buildings including station offices on the ground floor and station master's accommodation on the first floor. View facing towards Beccles with Grove Hill level crossing gate No. 31 forming a barrier across the single line. Starston was opened with the branch but closed through lack of patronage as early as 1st August 1866. No platform was provided and passengers were required to clamber up or down the sideboards on the coaching stock to enter or leave the train. *Author's collection*

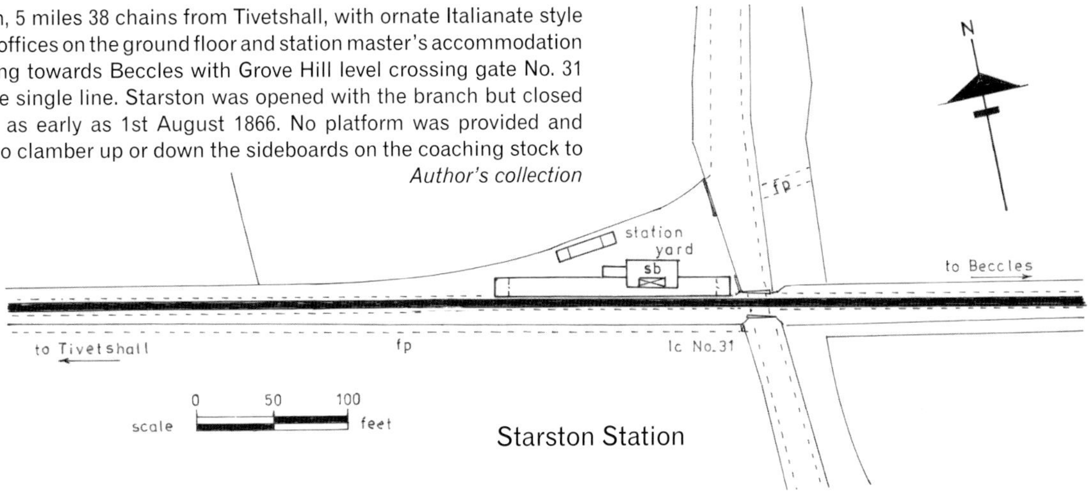

Starston Station

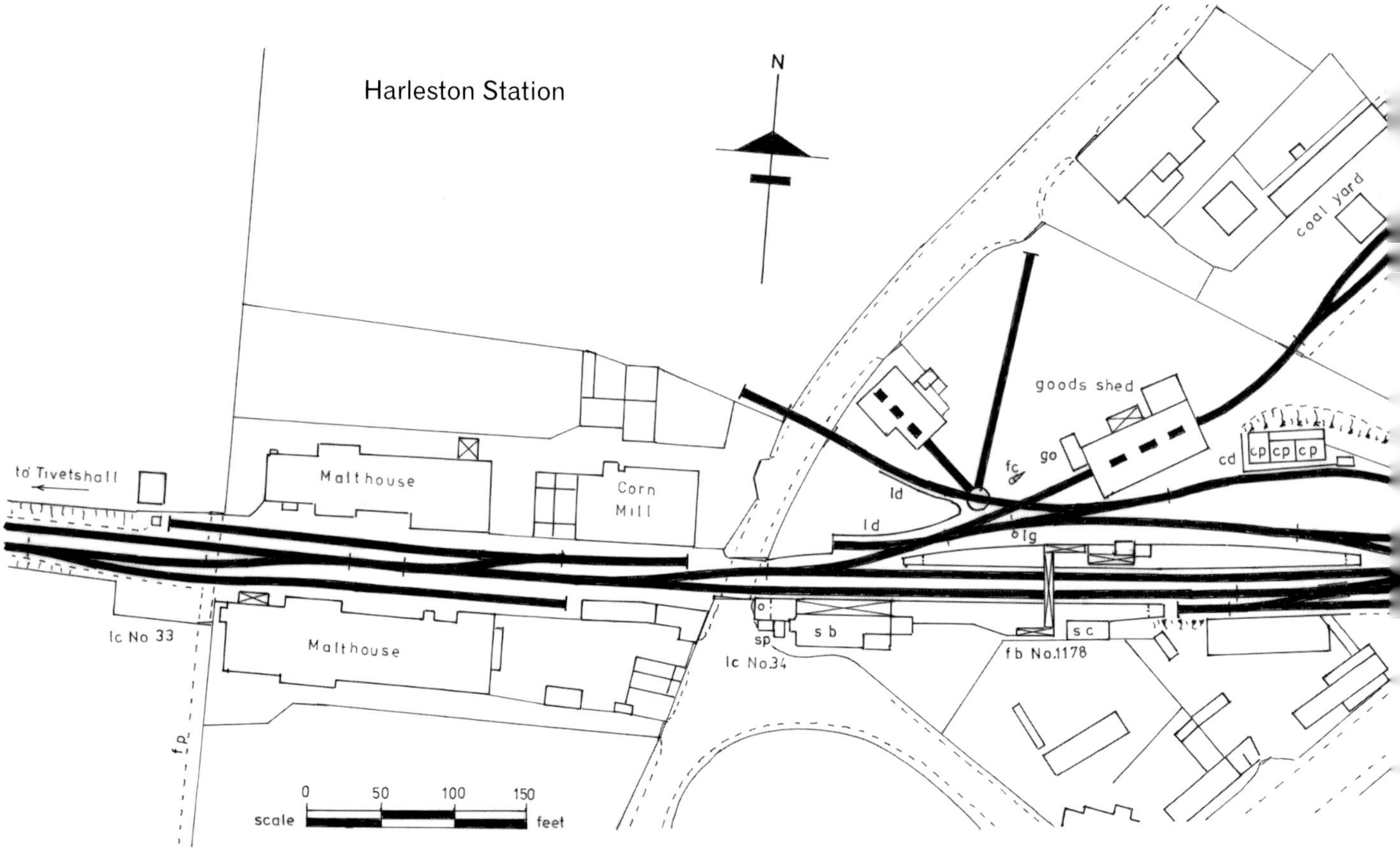

Harleston Station

Harleston station, 6 miles 25 chains from Tivetshall, with a Beccles to Norwich Up train entering, hauled by a 'Little Sharpie' Class 2-4-0 and formed of five coaches. To the left a '477' Class 0-6-0 is shunting the goods yard. Footbridge No. 1178 spans the Up and Down main lines connecting the platforms.
Author's collection

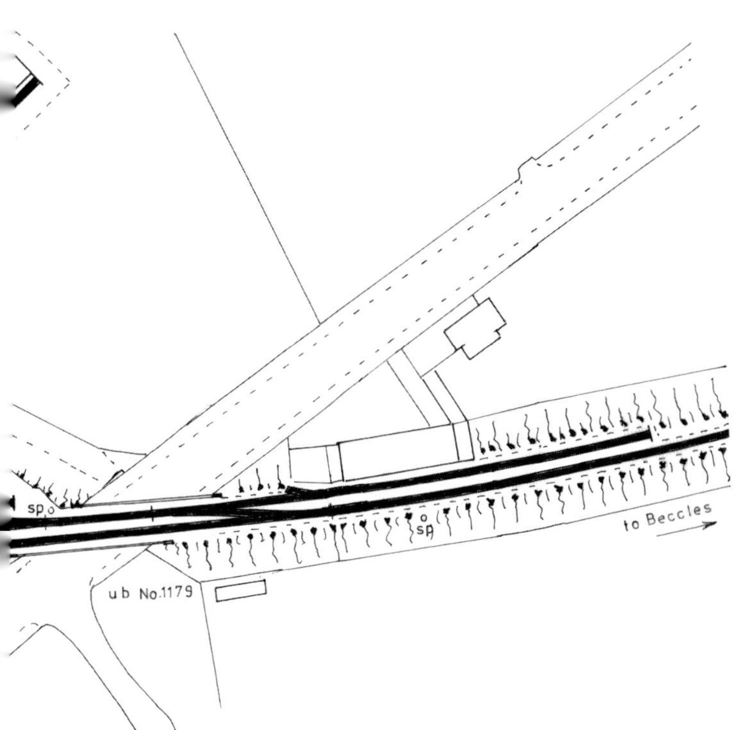

6 mile post the line curved slightly to the left with the Up advance starting signal on the Up side to the line; then falling at 1 in 227, the line approached and bisected Harleston level crossing No. 34 at 6 miles 22 chains and ran into **Harleston** station, the first passing place on the branch, 6 miles 25 chains from Tivetshall.

Originally only a single platform 210 feet in length was provided on the Up or south side of the line and conveniently situated for the small town. When the station was converted into a proper passing place by the provision of two platforms: the Up side or original platform was extended to 270 feet in length, later 300 feet; the Down platform, originally 250 feet in length, was soon extended to 300 feet, requiring track alterations culminating in an 820 feet loop serving the platforms. Both Up and Down platforms at Harleston could accommodate four coaches and if required it was possible to run round six coaches in the goods yard if certain sidings were clear of wagons. The platforms were connected by footbridge No. 1178 at 6 miles 25 chains. The station building was an elaborate structure which was probably designed by Frederick Barnes in collaboration with Peter Bruff. Harleston station was illuminated by gas throughout its life. After the withdrawal of passenger services a considerable amount of rationalisation was achieved and by 1960 the Up line had been removed and no longer served the platform, whilst the canopy had been removed from the building by 1966. The station building later achieved listed status and served as office accommodation.

The array of sidings at Harleston included the Down malthouse road of 380 feet, the 930 feet Up reception road which could accommodate forty-one wagons, engine and brake van, this with points leading to the 390 feet Up malthouse siding. On the Down side the goods yard had a 500 feet loop which led to the 415 feet shed road serving the goods shed, which ultimately continued to Moy's coal yard with its two 150 feet sidings in the form of a loop with 40 feet headshunt. From the shed road a 260 feet long siding served the cattle pens, whilst a 310 feet siding crossed the main road north of the gated level crossing to serve the corn mill. From this siding a turntable gave access to the 180 feet back road and 30 feet dock road off the goods yard loop. In 1938 the yard had five private sidings used by Watney, Combe, Reid & Company Limited, C. Marston, Thomas Moy Limited, H. Blackburn and H. Hudson. Points and signals at the station were worked from the station signal box containing a 42-lever Dutton frame, located on the Up platform.

A view of Harleston station frontage in the early years of the twentieth century, with horse-drawn traps awaiting prospective customers as passengers arrive by train. In the far background to the left are the maltings and corn mill situated on the Down side of the railway.
John Alsop collection

In the event of the non-availability of a 'J15' or 'J17' Class 0-6-0 locomotive, the Norwich shed foreman resorted to using one of the depot's allocation of 'N7' Class tank locomotive on the branch goods. Here 'N7/3' Class 0-6-2T No. 69708 shunts the train in Harleston goods yard on a frosty morning. The engine is equipped with a M&GN Tablet exchange arm near the cab. *Dr I.C. Allen*

Harleston station, 6 miles 25 chains from Tivetshall, facing west from the Down platform with the signal box containing a 42-lever Dutton frame at the east end of the Up platform. The platforms are connected by covered footbridge No. 1178, the only footbridge provided on the branch. Harleston only became a crossing station after the addition of the Down platform in 1893. *Author's collection*

The 300 feet long Down platform at Harleston viewed from the train on 1st September 1951. Originally only the Up-side platform was provided but when the station was converted to a crossing loop in 1893 the Down-side platform was added. The platform was connected to its older partner by station footbridge No. 1178 at 6 miles 25 chains. Behind the platform is the goods yard complete with goods shed and cattle pens. *H.C. Casserley*

The former Redenhall station, 7 miles 38 chains from Tivetshall, still supporting its canopy, viewed from the adjacent road in 1928. Redenhall opened for traffic in January 1861 and closed on 1st August 1866 as an economy measure. The house was occupied by a member of the permanent way staff, rent free, in return for he and his family opening and closing the gates for the passage of trains. *J.E. Kite*

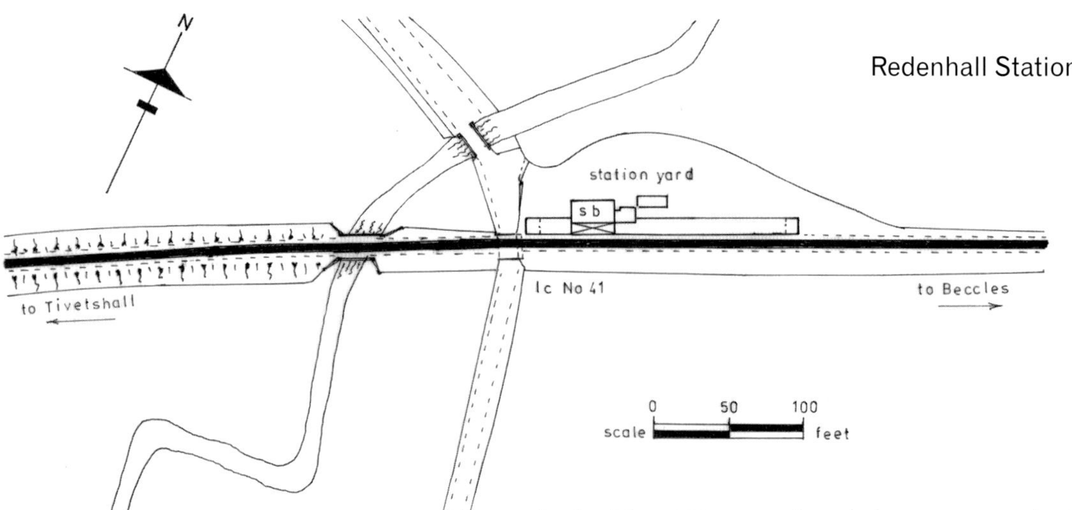

After Harleston the line continued to descend at 1 in 227 for just under half a mile, crossing the A143 main road by Harleston girder bridge No. 1179 at 6 miles 31 chains, and then on an embankment with the town located south of the line. The railway curved to the left with the main road to the north as the route turned to the north-east; it then entered a cutting with overbridge No. 1180 at 6 miles 70 chains spanning the line as the branch followed the Beck across well wooded country. The hamlet of Lushbush was to the north of the railway as the line straightened passing the 7 mile post, once more crossing the A143 main road by Redenhall girder bridge No. 1181 at 7 miles 04 chains. The branch then curved to the right over bridge No. 1183 at 7 miles 14 chains on an embankment before entering a cutting falling at 1 in 99; another straight section led over dyke bridge No. 1184 at 7 miles 34 chains and then **Redenhall** level crossing No. 41 at 7 miles 37 chains from Tivetshall. This marked the site of the long-abandoned station located on the north side of the railway at 7 miles 38 chains; opened for traffic in January 1861, like Starston it closed on 1st August 1866. The station had a 180 feet long low raised platform and the building remained in use as a gatekeeper's cottage retaining its wooden canopy for many years. Nearby were views of Redenhall church dedicated to St. Mary, with its magnificent tower built circa 1520.

Away from Redenhall the Beck continued to the north of the railway as the line fell at 1 in 368, initially following a gentle curve to the right before swinging to the left passing the copse known

The former Wortwell station, 8 miles 17½ chains from Tivetshall, with the platform on the Down side of the railway and level crossing No. 44 beyond. No siding was provided when the station opened for traffic in January 1861 and none had been provided by the closure date of 1st January 1878. As with other closed stations on the branch railway, staff occupied the building, which was extended in 1874 and was thus larger than those at Starston and Redenhall.
Author's collection

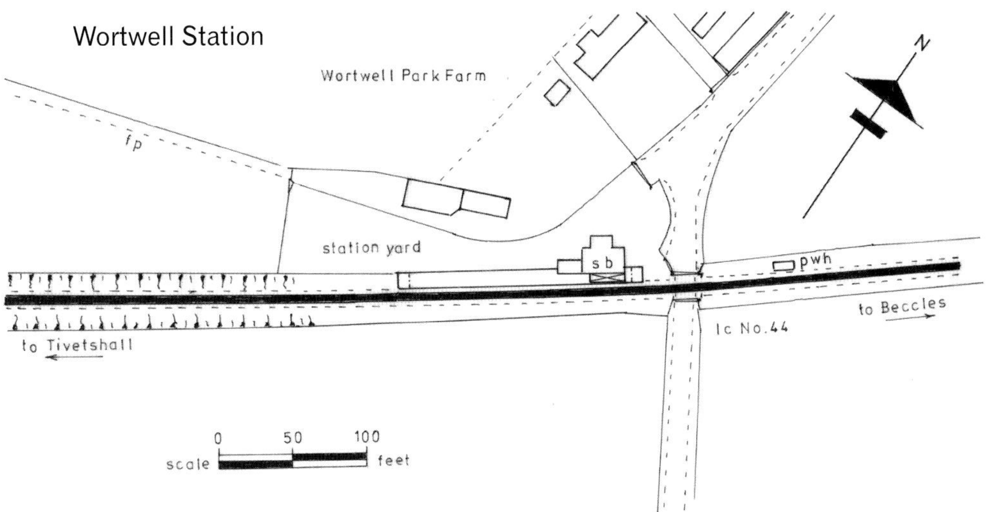

as Railway Plantation on the Down side and over occupational crossing No. 42 at 7 miles 68 chains. The line then climbed at 1 in 275 and with Mill Hill on the Up side the line straightened out past the 8 mile post continuing to **Wortwell**, 8 miles 17½ chains, located on the Down side of the line and adjacent to level crossing No. 44 at 8 miles 19 chains. The station had a 180 feet short low platform, with the same opening date of January 1861 as Redenhall, and was located close to two farms – Wortwell Park Farm and Tunbeck Farm – to the north of the railway, with the hamlet to the south of the line. An extra bedroom was added in 1874 at a cost of £55, but the station was closed as an economy measure on 1st January 1878.

Leaving Wortwell the gradient changed from 1 in 368 rising to a short 1 in 1,320 falling as it bisected level crossing No. 44 at 8 miles 19 chains carrying the minor road linking Alburgh and Wortwell across the line. The railway continued curving to the left, passing Homersfield Down distant signal on the Down side of the line and entered a shallow cutting. With the A143 main road paralleling, the line climbed a short 1 in 400, entering another straight section before falling 1 in 116 past the Congregational Chapel on the Up side and negotiating a short cutting, then an embankment. Homersfield Down home signal was passed in a shallow cutting before the line curved to the right over bridge No. 1185 at 8 miles 67 chains, where the Beck passed under the railway, and then over level crossing No. 48 at 8 miles 69 chains to arrive at **Homersfield** station, 8 miles 74 chains from Tivetshall on a 1 in 1,716 rising gradient to enter the valley of the River Waveney. Because of the winding nature of the river which formed the boundary between Norfolk and Suffolk, and its confluence with the local Beck, Homersfield station lay to the north of the river in Norfolk whilst the village was in Suffolk. The meeting of the small streams resulted in flooding on many occasions and after serious inroads in 1912 the station platform was rebuilt. In World War Two the station served the nearby Hardwick Airfield and many American servicemen arrived and departed. Homersfield station platform, 340 feet in length, was located on the Down or north side of the single line and could accommodate five bogie coaches. The station buildings were of substantial construction with booking office, booking hall, waiting rooms and toilets on the ground floor and station master's accommodation on the first floor.

The goods yard at Homersfield on the north side of the railway was formed of two main sidings and a number of short spurs. The main goods siding, 130 feet in length, was entered by a connection facing the westbound trains, this led to a wagon turntable which gave access to three radiating spur sidings, one 90 feet in length serving the goods shed, latterly rented by the Norwich-based corn merchants Woods, Sadd & Moore, the 80 feet dock road serving the cattle dock and the 50 feet yard road. The other siding, 260 feet long and serving as a headshunt, faced east-bound trains; it crossed the main goods siding and continued eastwards for a considerable distance before terminating at buffers stops. A short spur siding, 220 feet in length, extended westwards to reach a loading dock behind the passenger platform. The goods yard contained a 1 ton 10 cwt crane. In 1898 the GER Way and Works Committee authorised construction of a new granary costing £400. The use of a tow rope was authorised for shunting the yard. Points and signals at Homersfield were worked from the signal box located on the Up side of the running line and which contained a 20-lever Dutton frame.

From Homersfield the line continued on the 1 in 1,716 rising gradient on a gradual left-hand curve in a north-easterly direction, passing the 9 mile post and Up home signal on the Up side of the railway; the A143 road was on the Down side, with the River Waveney and the low-lying hinterland that was subject to flooding on the Up side and Heath Farm beyond. The line followed a 40 chains radius right-hand curve passing Homersfield Up distant signal on the Up side of the line where the gradient altered to 1 in 253 falling before following a straight course passing Low Farm on the Down side and a copse on the Up side. At the 9¾ milepost the line climbed at 1 in 3,217; Denton Wash underbridge No. 1186 at 9 miles 79 chains was crossed just before the 10 mile post with Dentonwash Farm on the Down side as the main road converged

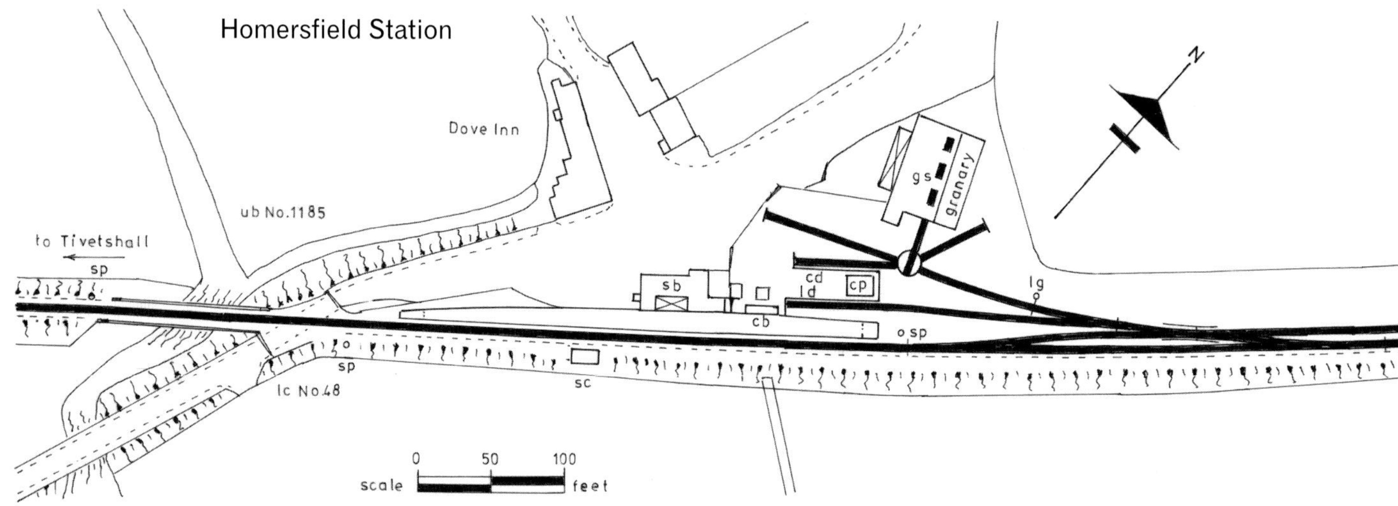

'F4' Class 2-4-2T No. 67167 departing Homersfield with an Up train in 1951, formed of an ex-GER Third Corridor Composite and ex-Great Central Railway 'Barnham' Brake Third. By this date the Up starting signal has an upper quadrant arm. *Dr I.C. Allen*

With a tender full of coal 'J15' Class 0-6-0 No. 65471 is preparing to shunt Homersfield goods yard whilst working a Down goods train to Beccles shortly before closure of the yard. *Dr I.C. Allen*

fb

to Beccles

Homersfield station 8 miles 74 chains from Tivetshall on 1st September 1951 with the 340 feet long platform on the Down side of the single line. In the background is the large goods shed capable of storing 400 quarters of grain and to the left the approach road to the station. Although Homersfield village was in Suffolk, the station was located in Norfolk. *H.C. Casserley*

Homersfield station 8 mile 74 chains from Tivetshall showing the 340 feet long platform rebuilt after flooding and the main station building with station master's accommodation on the first floor. The signal box to the right was equipped with a 20-lever Dutton frame, Note the typical droop of the Down starting signal arm. *Author's collection*

On a cold early spring morning 'J15' Class 0-6-0 No. 65471 shown soon after passing Homersfield with a Down freight train, the leading wagons conveying sugar beet destined for Cantley sugar factory. *Dr I.C. Allen*

Earsham level crossing number 64 where the road from the village to Earsham Park bisected the railway. To the left is the station and on the opposite side of the line the signal box, which contained a 7-lever Dutton frame with all levers working. The Down starting signal protects the gates. Earsham was closed as an economy measure during World War One from 1st May 1916 until 1st August 1919 as the station was just under a mile from Bungay. *Author's collection*

on the railway. Just before Denton Wash level crossing No. 58 at 10 miles 27¾ chains the gradient stiffened to 1 in 169 rising for the next half mile with Waveney Farm on the Up side before the branch negotiated a deep cutting as it sliced through Buckhills Plantation. The line then negotiated an embankment with the main road to the south of the line and the Buck Inn prominent beside the thoroughfare. A quarter mile of 1 in 360 falling brought the railway past Buck Hills with the river meandered nearer the line as it passed the 11 mile post, again climbing at 1 in 351 to another minor summit. After negotiating Drake's Lane level crossing No. 61 at 11 miles 10 chains and bridge No. 1187 at 11 miles 12 chains the railway curved away from the river and road, and descended at 1 in 202 following a straight course passing Bullocks Head Knoll on the Down side with Earsham Down distant signal on the Up side of the branch. On this section was the loop siding on the Down side of the line installed in 1944 to the orders of the Air Ministry to enable material and munitions to be offloaded for nearby airfields. The loop was worked from 2-lever ground frames at each end. At this relatively isolated spot over 200,000 tons of freight were received in 625 special trains, totalling around 21,000 wagons. Beyond the siding the straight course continued over Five Acre Lane crossing No. 63 at 11 miles 65 chains and on past the 12 mile post and the Down home signal to enter **Earsham** station, 12 miles 05 chains from Tivetshall.

Earsham for its entire existence served only as a passenger stopping point, with a 310 feet single platform on the Up or south side of the line, which could accommodate four bogie coaches. It served the village of Earsham located to the south, with access from the adjacent lane which the railway bisected to the east of the station. A 7-lever gate box controlled the level crossing gate release and associated signals; the station building was brick built with a projecting canopy. In 1884 the GER Way and Works Committee authorised the construction of a booking office and station master's house at cost of £350. The station was closed during World War One on 1st May 1916 as an economy measure but reopened on 1st August 1919. After rationalisation of staffing the station house was occupied by the foreman-in-charge and in 1913 David John Ireland was the occupant with his family paying an annual rent of £5 4s 0d. When the signal box was demolished in 1919 the level crossing gates and

Earsham Station

Earsham station 12 miles 05 chains from Tivetshall with its 310 feet long platform on the Up side of the line. This view facing towards Beccles in 1951 shows an example of the small station nameboards provided on the Waveney Valley Branch. The signal box, abolished in 1919, was located in the open space on the Down side of the line adjacent to the level crossing. *Author's collection*

Earsham station from the level crossing in 1952, viewed facing towards Tivetshall. The station was closed in World War One for economic reasons as it was located within a mile of Bungay station. No sidings were provided at the station but in World War Two a loop siding was provided to the west of the station to serve several local airfields used by the United States Air Force; many thousands of tons of armaments and bombs were off-loaded from rail wagons here and transported to the airfields by road. *Author's collection*

gate distant signals for each direction of travel were worked from a 3-lever ground frame.

Beyond Earsham the line bisected level crossing No. 64 at 12 miles 06½ chains and curved slightly still falling at 1 in 202 for a short distance before rising at 1 in 5,808 all the way to Bungay. Passing Earsham Up home signal on the Down side of the railway the curve to the right continued as the line passed the trees of The Elms estate to the south and then Earsham Up distant and Bungay Down distant signals on the Down side of the line. Just beyond the signal the branch passed over bridge No. 1188 at 12 miles 40 chains before following a straight course over bridge No. 1189 at 12 miles 50 chains and then past water meadows to run across bridge No. 1190 at 12 miles 64 chains, spanning the River Waveney to enter Bungay station 12 miles 68 chains from Tivetshall. Whereas the course of the River Waveney placed all the other stations on the branch in Norfolk, because the river made an enormous loop to the north of the town **Bungay** station was located in the county of Suffolk, requiring the construction of two bridges to span the stream, No's 1190 and 1192, within the space of half a mile. Bungay is an interesting market town with a ruined castle. Originally the station only had a platform on the Up side of the line although trains could pass by shunting. In 1893, when it became an official

The original Bungay station from the approach road in the early 1930s showing the decrepit buildings that survived until replaced by the L&NER in 1933. The location on the northern edge of the town was dictated as a result of a dispute between the railway company, the commoners of Outney Common and the townsfolk. *John Alsop collection*

Taking water at Bungay: the crews of two 'J15' Class 0-6-0 locomotives, Nos 65471 and 65460, have taken the opportunity to replenish the tender tanks before double heading a special freight train on to Tivetshall and Norwich. *Dr I.C. Allen*

'J15' Class 0-6-0 No. 65471 crossing the River Waveney on bridge No. 1190 on the approach to Bungay station. The signal is Bungay Down home. *Dr I.C. Allen*

passing place, two platforms were provided to allow passenger services to pass each other, the Up side 310 feet in length and Down platform 300 feet served by a 1,030 feet long crossing loop, the loop divided into two sections by an intermediate crossover. Both Up and Down platforms could accommodate four bogie coaches, although if required it was possible to run round thirteen bogie coaches by using platform and goods loop. The original station accommodation was far from imposing, consisting of two timber single-storey structures, but these were replaced by a brick building constructed by the L&NER in 1933, the replacement containing the booking office, waiting rooms and toilets. Bungay was the only station on the branch to have a W.H. Smith bookstall and was noted over the years for its garden floral displays. The river loop also enclosed Bungay or Outney Common, an area defined for decades before the coming of the railway, which included the site of the station approach road and forecourt for which a rent, latterly £20 annually, was paid to the Fen Reeve of Bungay Common for its use. This anomaly was finally laid to rest in 1926 when the approach road and forecourt were sold to the L&NER.

The passenger station was separated from Bungay goods yard by Outney Road overbridge No. 1191 at 12 miles 71 chains; this carried the main public access from the town to the Outney Common over the railway, where there was a golf course and racecourse. The large goods yard on the south side of the line containing five, later four, sidings, two arranged as a loop while the remaining three were dead end roads. The 620 feet loop siding located south of the

ABOVE: Bungay station looking east from Outney overbridge No. 1191 through the platforms in October 1911. Note that at this date the water tank and signal post were to the north of the track. *GERS/Windwood 1336*

The large water tank and tank house provided by the L&NER in 1931 on the Up side of the line at the Tivetshall end of the station at Bungay. The equipment replaced an earlier water tank located on the Down side of the railway at the west end of the Down platform. *J. Watling*

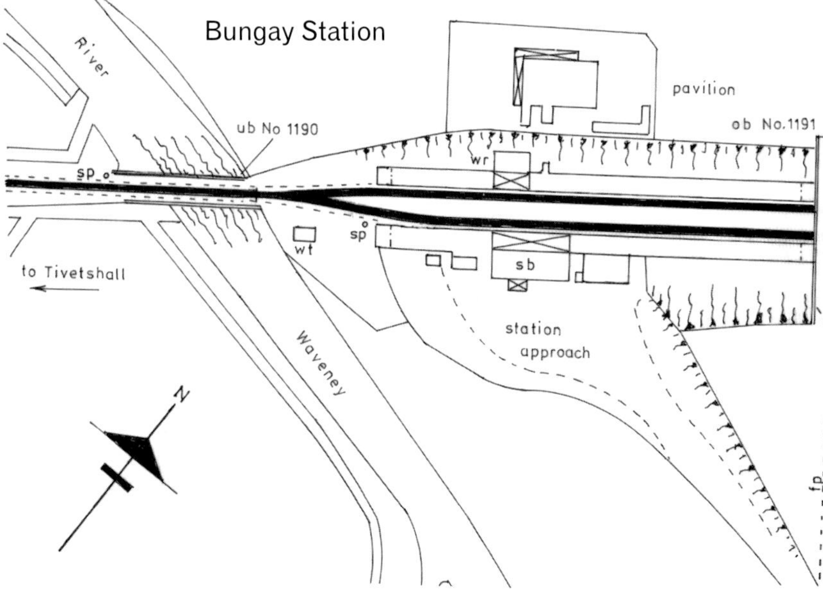

ABOVE: The Down-side platform and view of the Up-side canopy at Bungay, looking towards Tivetshall. The station loop merged into single track before crossing the River Waveney by underbridge No. 1190 west of the station. *Author's collection*

RIGHT: 'J15' Class 0-6-0 No. 65478 running light engine through the Down loop at Bungay, where the Down platform is already devoid of station buildings. *Dr I.C. Allen*

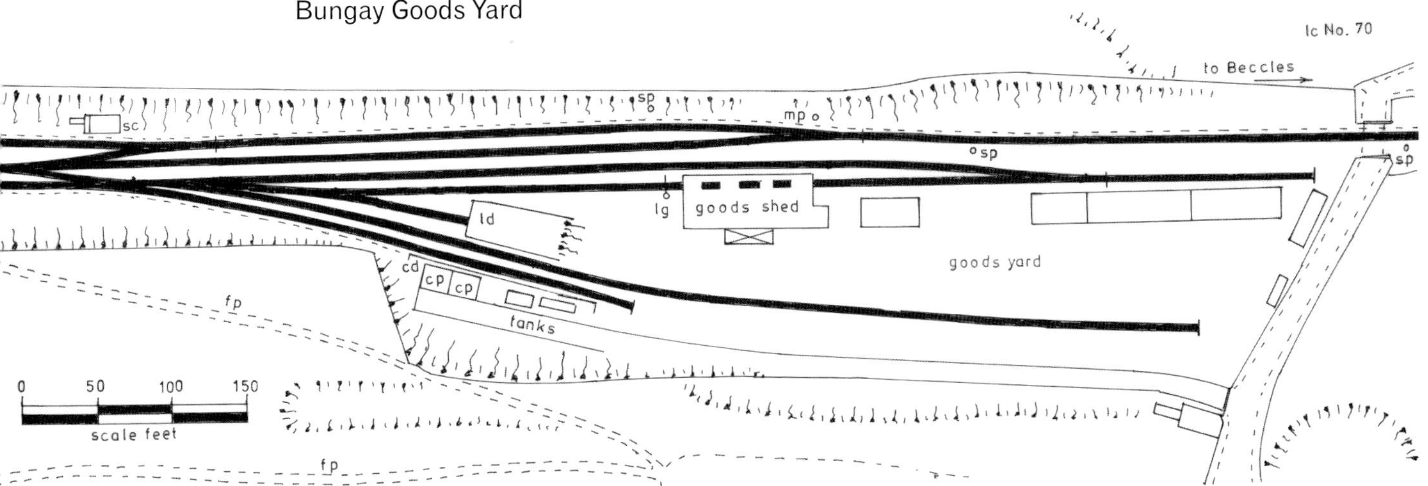

Bungay station 12 miles 68 chains from Tivetshall was made a passing place in 1893. In this view facing Beccles, to the left is the 300 feet Down platform and the right the original platform 310 feet in length hosting the main station buildings. Beyond the station is Outney Road overbridge No. 1191 at 12 miles 72 chains. *Author's collection*

Bungay station, 12 miles 68 chains from Tivetshall, facing towards Beccles with the original buildings on the Up-side platform. Note the W.H. Smith bookstall to the right and the new Down-side waiting room constructed in 1893 to the left. At the end of the platforms the three-arch Outney Common Bridge spans the double track through the station. *Author's collection*

running line was occasionally used for shunting and reception and was paralleled on the south side by the 610 feet shed road serving the goods shed equipped with a 1 ton 10 cwt capacity fixed crane with internal loading platform, the siding extended by a 150 feet headshunt. The two outermost sidings on the south side of the yard were the 760 feet coal road serving coal grounds and for wagon load traffic, and 370 feet cattle dock siding, while the fifth was a 170 feet long siding that served an end loading dock. At the end of the yard were two large sheds, the easternmost and larger of the pair occupied by W.D. & A.E. Walker, coal and grain merchants, whilst A.E. Smith occupied the smaller building. Road access to the goods yard and cattle pens was at the eastern end of the layout with gates in Broad Street. The 13 mile post was located on the Down side of the railway opposite the goods shed.

Points and signals at the station were controlled from Bungay signal box; of timber construction and located in the Down side of the line east of Outney Road bridge, it dated from February 1893 and contained a 25-lever Dutton frame which replaced an earlier structure. A water tank was originally provided at the west end on the Down platform but when the L&NER replaced the water tower

Bungay station on 30th September 1956 with 'J15' Class 0-6-0 No. 65447 at the head of the Railway Enthusiasts' Club special train. After the withdrawal of the passenger service the run round loop was shortened and the revised layout can be seen curving away from both Up and Down platforms. *R.M. Casserley*

Bungay station after the demolition of the buildings on the Down platform, the removal of the Up canopy and abolition of the signalling. View facing towards Beccles with Outney Road overbridge No. 1191 spanning the remains of the railway. *Author's collection*

in 1931 the new structure was placed at the Tivetshall end of the Up platform.

Away from Bungay, trains continued climbing at 1 in 5,808, passing over Bungay Common level crossing No. 70 at 13 miles 06 chains beyond which the railway descended at 1 in 241 to cross the River Waveney by River Crusty bridge No. 1192 at 13 miles 16 chains and re-entered Norfolk. The line then spanned Deep Dyke bridge No. 1193 at 13 miles 21 chains before curving to the right, crossing Factory bridge No. 1194 at 13 miles 32 chains and Little Factory underbridge No. 1195 at 13 miles 38 chains. Ditchingham Down home signal was passed on the Down side of the line just before Factory Road level crossing No. 72 at 13 miles 43¼ chains, where the Norwich Road A144 was bisected. The gates were controlled from a 2-lever ground frame on the west side whilst the gatekeeper's house was located north of the line and east of the road. Beside the cottage was a 6-wheel coach body built in 1895 to provide First and Third Class accommodation as well as a luggage compartment. On the opposite side a short siding was installed on 1943 to serve the former maltings which were being used as a US Army store.

RIGHT: View to the east through the arch of Outney Road bridge No. 1191 from the Up platform at Bungay in October 1911. Part of the signal box can be seen to the left whilst points from the Up loop line lead to the goods yard with its brick-built goods shed.
GERS/Windwood 1340

BELOW: View of Bungay goods yard in October 1911 looking west towards the station beyond Outney overbridge No. 1191. In the foreground is the goods shed and goods office, and to the right the Down loop line and Down starting signal.
GERS/Windwood 1338

View looking west from Bungay goods yard in October 1911 towards Outney overbridge No. 1191 and the station beyond with Bungay station signal box to the right. *GERS/Windwood 1337*

General view of Bungay goods yard looking east from the signal box. In the foreground is the Down loop and next to that the Up loop, both connected by a crossover. Alongside the Up line is the goods loop siding and parallel to that the shed road – occupied by three open wagons and a covered van – which served the goods shed with arched opening. To the right, three open wagons and two cattle wagons are stabled on the cattle dock siding. *Author's collection*

The east end of Bungay goods yard in October 1911 showing the goods yard entrance between the buildings, and Bungay Common level crossing No. 70 to the extreme left. The premises occupied by W.D. & A.E. Walker are adjacent to the crossing. *GERS/Windwood 1339*

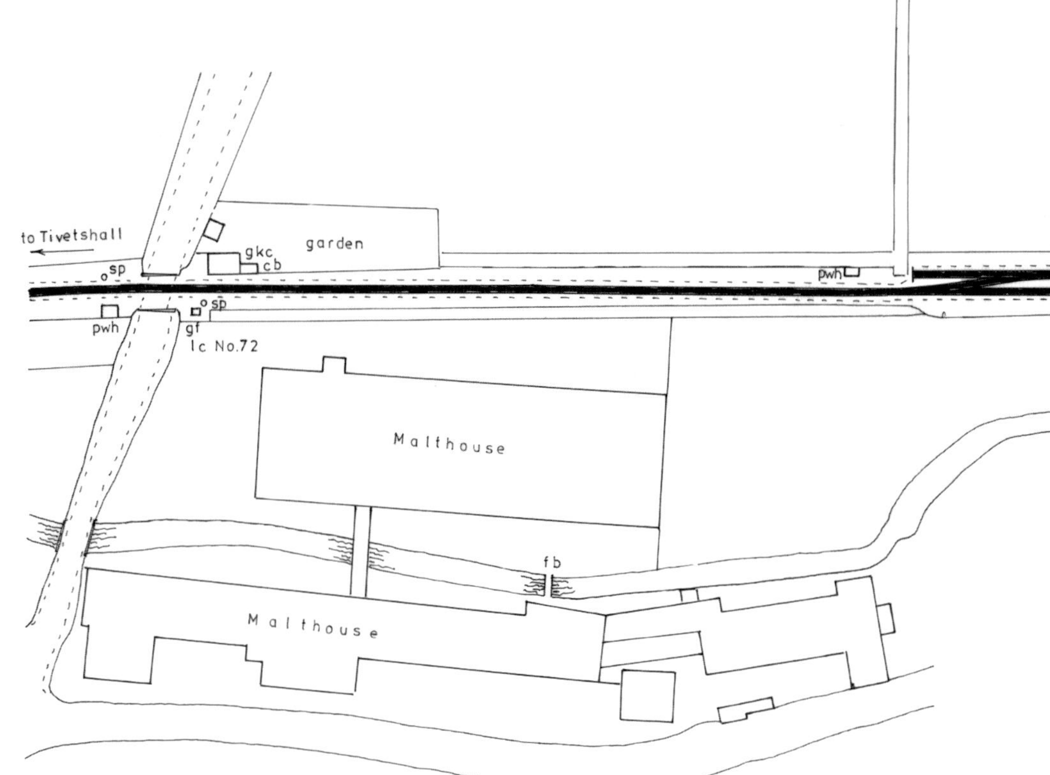

BELOW: Ditchingham station on 1st September 1951, viewed from the train, showing the small compact station nameboard which BR provided in lieu of the former GER running in board. The goods shed behind the platform is served by the 320 feet long shed road, the structure having capacity for the storage of 250 quarters of grain. In front of the shed is the 1 ton 10 cwt capacity fixed crane. *H.C. Casserley*

FACING PAGE: Ditchingham station, 13 miles 63 chains from Tivetshall, with the 310 feet long platform on the Down side of the single main line. Prominent is the brick-built goods shed served by the shed road and the 2 ton, later 1 ton 10 cwt, capacity fixed crane. By this date the siding serving the cattle dock on the Up side had been removed. *Author's collection*

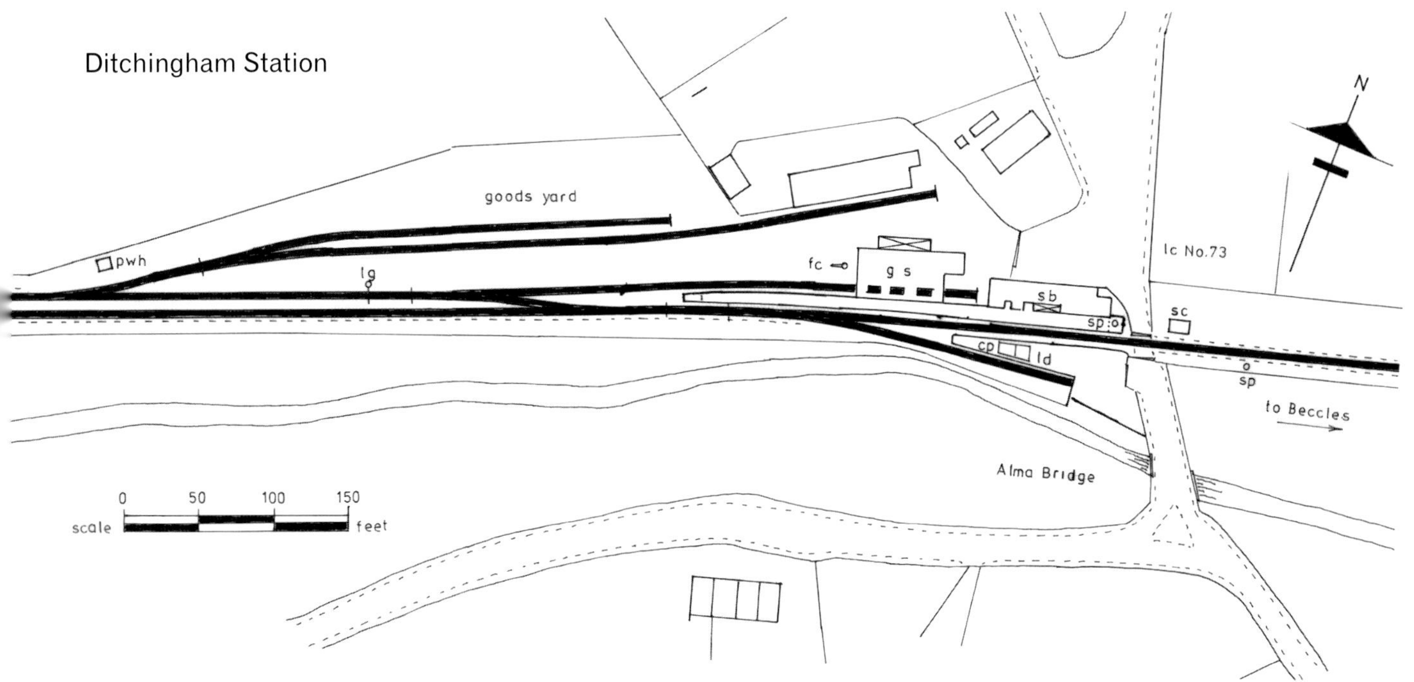

The line then climbed at 1 in 1,049 following a straight course. During World War Two the goods loop in **Ditchingham** yard was extended westward here to a length of 900 feet, just short of Factory Road level crossing, and an 8-lever, later reduced to 6, ground frame was provided to control access to the west end of the loop and also the US Army depot. The single line branch then passed the Down home and Up starting signals where the gradient altered to 1 in 674 falling, before running into Ditchingham station, 13 miles 63 chains from Tivetshall, where the single platform 310 feet in length on the Down side could accommodate five bogie coaches. Ditchingham station, serving the village to the north of the railway, had a two-storey building similar to those at Pulham Market, Pulham St. Mary and Harleston, constructed of brick with a slate roof and chimneys each end. Miniature centrally placed gables were provided at front and rear, and facing the platform a small loggia was provided between two projecting pavilions. The first floor of the building provided accommodation for the station master and his family; in 1913 Alfred James Bilham was in residence paying an annual rental of £17. A single storey extension was provided at the east end of the platform, authorised in 1912 at cost of £172 and completed the following year. One of the railway cottages at Ditchingham was occupied in 1924 by Robert William James, a permanent way supervisor, who paid an annual rental of £9 19s 4d.

The goods yard to the north side of the platform was served by the 350 feet loop siding which led to the 320 feet shed road serving the brick-built goods shed backing on to the platform, beside which stood the 1 ton 10 cwt capacity fixed yard crane. In the latter years the goods shed was rented by Silcock's for storage and distribution of animal foodstuffs. The facilities were completed by a 580 feet inner yard road and a 300 feet outer road used for coal and coke

Ditchingham station facing towards Tivetshall with, on the Up side of the line, the malthouses used by the United States Army as a storage depot in World War Two towering in the distance. The track has been removed from the cattle dock road and the points to the goods yard are operated from a ground frame released by Annett's key attached to the single line Train Staff.
Author's collection

Ditchingham level crossing No. 73 at 13 miles 65½ chains from Tivetshall, protected by the Down starting signal at the end of the platform. The ornate station building to the left is partially ivy covered whilst the entry to the cattle dock siding is on the left by the pipe smoking individual. The porter/signalman and three village youths show an interest in the photographer. *Author's collection*

traffic. The cattle dock was located on the Up side of the line opposite the station platform and by the level crossing, served by the 220 feet dock road with points facing Down trains. As stated above, during the Second World War the Down side goods loop line was extended by 470 feet to a set of points just east of Factory Road level crossing, and the signalling was amended and adjusted accordingly. It was then possible to run round eleven bogie coaches via the slip in the goods yard. Points and signals at the station were controlled by Ditchingham signal box located alongside the level crossing and containing an 18-lever Dutton frame. After closure of the line the station was demolished in October 1982 to make way for road improvements. Ditchingham was made a crossing place and Train Staff station in 1943 and served as such to shorten the single line section between Bungay and Beccles until 1949.

From Ditchingham the single line branch passed the Down starting and Up home signal flanking Purnough Street A143 level crossing No. 73 at 13 miles 65½ chains, as the 1 in 674 falling gradient continued for a mile before the line curved to the left and followed a straight course to the north-east. The branch passed Ditchingham Up distant signal before following a gradual left-hand curve over Whistle Lane level crossing No. 75 at 14 miles 16¾ chains and then skirted the village of Broome, birthplace of Thomas Manning, the first Englishman to enter the forbidden Tibetan city of Lhasa. On both sides of the line the land was liable to flooding as the railway continued on a straight course with Broome Common and the A143 road to the north as a short 1 on 609 rising and even shorter 1 in 281 falling took the line past Ellingham Marshes and the River Waveney to the south of

Ditchingham station looking west with the redundant cattle pens to the left and entry to the goods yard beyond the platform end in July 1954.
Author's collection

the railway. The line curved to the right, passing Ellingham Down distant signal and then over bridge No. 1196 at 14 miles 71 chains. The curve continued past the 15 mile post as the line climbed at 1 in 296, passing Ellingham Down home signal and goods yard on the Down side of the line and the Up starting signal on the south of the railway to enter **Ellingham** station 15 miles 23 chains from Tivetshall, with its single 310 feet long platform on the Down side serving the village to the south. The platform could accommodate five bogie coaches. The station building was another two-storey Italianate structure with low-pitched slate roof and arched window apertures, with booking office, waiting room and booking hall at platform level and station master's accommodation above. As a result of the combining of several stations under the control of one station master, the accommodation at Ellingham became vacant and in 1913 foreman-in-charge James Bishop was the occupant with his family paying an annual rent of £5 4s 0d. By 1924 the rental was £13 per annum and foreman-in-charge Robert Utting and his family were occupants. A coach body on the platform, serving as a parcels store, completed the station facilities.

The goods yard consisted of a single siding 405 feet in length on the north side entered by a connection from the main single line facing westbound trains. A short spur 200 feet in length extended eastwards from the main siding, and latterly the yard dealt with brick traffic. No goods shed or cattle loading dock was provided, although the use of a tow-rope was authorised for shunting. Points and signals were worked from Ellingham signal box, provided to control locking of the adjacent level crossing and associated signalling with its 15-lever frame with 11 working and 4 spares.

During construction of the railway the station site blocked an approach road to the village, which had to be diverted over a level crossing east of the platform. Thus on departing Ellingham the branch line bisected Ellingham station level crossing No. 81 at 15 miles 25¼ chains to continue climbing at 1 in 296 for almost half a mile, passing under overbridge No. 1197 at 15 miles 34

Ellingham station 15 miles 23 chains from Tivetshall with its 310 feet long platform on the Down side of the main single line. View facing towards Beccles with the gates of Ellingham level crossing No. 81 at the east end of the platform and the Italianate station building with accommodation for the station master on the first floor and station offices on the ground floor. *Author's collection*

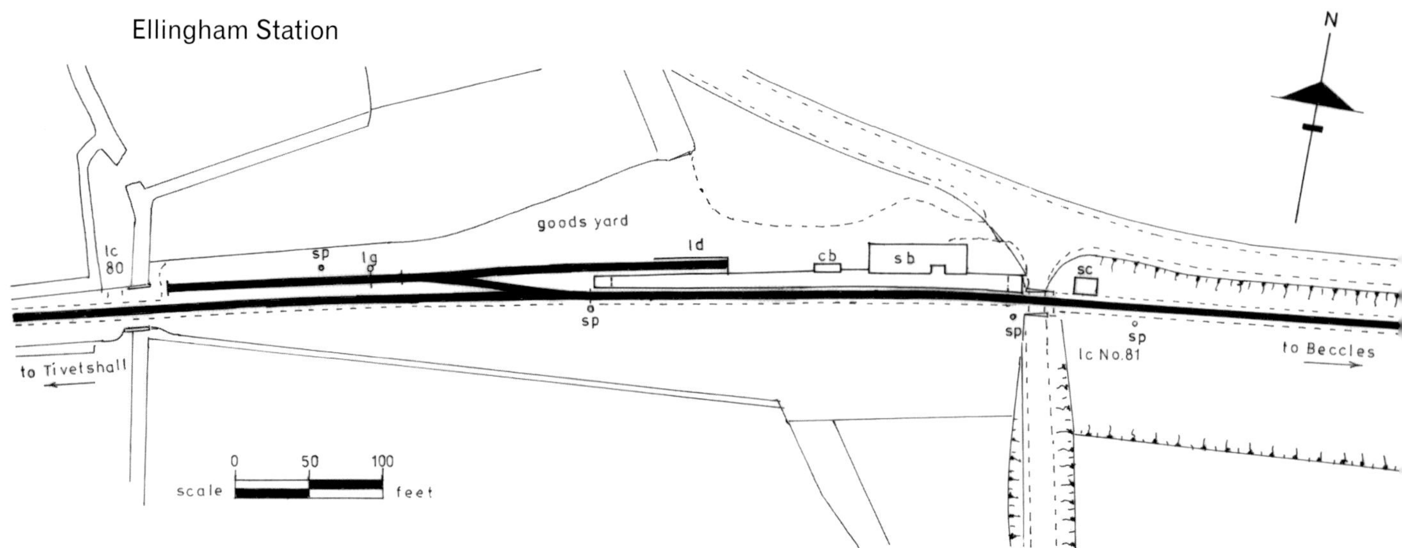

Ellingham station when it was fully operational. The oil lamp cases for night-time illumination adorn the platform whilst the Up starting signal and Down home signal are in the distance.
Author's collection

Ellingham station building from the east in the late 1950s. Despite the passenger service having been withdrawn staff are evidently still tending the climbing roses.
Author's collection

chains. Goods facilities were increased in World War Two when two additional loop sidings complete with associated storage tanks were installed in 1943 and 1944 on the Up side of the line to serve local airfields. Over 2,513 wagon-loads of bombs were received for US Army Air Force between June and September 1944; in addition, over 148 trains laden with aircraft fuel were received during six months in 1944 for the USAAF. By using these sidings it was possible to run round nineteen bogies in the sidings between Ellingham and Geldeston. Beyond the bridge the branch continued on a straight course with the main road to the south. The branch passed Ellingham Up distant signal on the Down side of the railway and beyond the distant signal the line fell at 1 in 394 for a quarter of a mile before descending at 1 in 247, continuing eastwards with a minor road running parallel on the Up side to bisect Ellingham or Brace's Lane level crossing No. 84 at 15 miles 74 chains where a minor lane crossed the railway. At the 16 milepost a minor summit was reached before the line fell at 1 in 394, passing Geldeston Marshes bordering the river to the south of the line. The straight course continued past Geldeston Down distant signal on the Down side of the line to Boor's Farm occupational crossing No. 85 at 16 miles 23 chains, with Boor's Farm to the south where the falling gradient altered to 1 in 247. The hamlet of Dockeney lay to the south of the railway as the gradient again altered to 1 in 418 rising as the line passed Geldeston goods yard on the Down side and entered **Geldeston** station, the penultimate stopping place before Beccles and 16 miles 57 chains from Tivetshall.

Geldeston station platform 330 feet in length was on the Down side of the railway and could accommodate four bogie coaches. The village lay to the north of the branch and the station building was another example of the Waveney Valley two-storey Italianate architecture containing booking office, booking hall, waiting room and lamp store with station master's accommodation on the first floor. The WVR building was virtually unaltered save for rendering of the brickwork executed during L&NER days. The front extension forming a porch gave shelter to waiting passengers. With the combining of stations under one station master, the accommodation became vacant and in 1924 James Watts the porter signalman and his family were tenants, paying £7 19s 0d per annum rental. Geldeston was closed to all traffic on 22nd May 1916 as a World War One economy but was partially reopened as an unstaffed

Geldeston station in October 1911 looking east with the brick goods shed in the Down side yard served by the 270 feet shed road, here occupied by an open wagon. The station building and signal box are largely obscured but the crossing keeper's hut stands on the Up side of the line beside the level crossing. The two signals on view are the Up home protecting the gates and the Up starting signal by the points leading to the goods yard siding.
GERS/Windwood 1366

ABOVE: Geldeston station looking east towards Beccles in October 1911, with the station buildings beyond the goods shed and the signal box beside the level crossing. The 330 feet long platform has well tended gardens. Standing guardian each side of the gates are the Down starting signal and Up home signal.
GERS/ Windwood 1368

LEFT: Geldeston station, 16 miles 57 chains from Tivetshall, view facing east showing the goods shed, capable of storing 200 quarters of grain at the back of the 330 feet long platform with the station building beyond.
Author's collection

halt on 14th September. Goods traffic resumed on 15th January 1917 but the station only became fully staffed again on and from 14th September 1919.

The connection to the goods yard faced Up trains and split the 590 feet siding, the 220 feet west end serving as a headshunt and the 270 feet east end serving the brick and slate goods shed, with sliding doors at each end, internal loading platform and a 1 ton 10 cwt capacity fixed crane. In the final decade Lever Brothers rented the goods shed for the storage of pig meal, cattle cake and chicken feed, which was delivered by rail once or twice a week and then distributed locally by road. The use of a tow-rope was authorised for shunting in the goods yard. Goods facilities were withdrawn on and from 13th July 1964. The signal box, which controlled points and signals at the station, was a brick and timber structure with a 15-lever Dutton frame. As Geldeston was not a block post in later years the signal box was usually only open as required for goods trains to work the sidings.

Away from Geldeston, trains passed over Geldeston level crossing No. 86 at 16 miles 60 chains and then past the Up home signal on the Up side of the line as the line continued climbing at 1 in 418; it then fell for a short distance at 1 in 168 before running on an embankment to pass over Geldeston or Wherry Dyke bridge No. 1198 at 16 miles 74 chains. At the 17 milepost the line negotiated a short left-hand curve before running on a straight course over bridge No. 1199 at 17 miles 24 chains, from where the gradient altered to 1 in 2,383 rising; the River Waveney curved in a long arc to pass close to the railway near bridge No. 1200 at 17 miles 34 chains, where the line crossed one of the numerous drainage dykes which drained towards the river. Railway and river ran parallel before the line curved away to the left with views of Dunburgh House to the

Geldeston station, 16 miles 57 chains from Tivetshall, in July 1954 after the withdrawal of the passenger service but before the abolition of the signalling; view facing towards Tivetshall. Note that the lights, nameboard and even the sign for the gentlemen's toilets are still present.
Author's collection

Geldeston station after the removal of the signalling, with its single 330 feet long platform located on the Down side of the main single line. This view facing west shows the goods shed and goods yard beyond the platform. The connection to the goods yard was worked by a 2-lever ground frame released by Annett's key on the single line Train Staff. Although passenger train services had long ceased, flowers and shrubbery still adorn the platform. Note the rudimentary rendering on the front of the station building.
Author's collection

Geldeston station seen from the road on 14th July 1960. Although the line was still open to goods at this date and the goods shed door is open, the station platform and trackbed are looking quite run down. *Andrew Neale*

north. A right-hand curve followed as the Waveney veered away from the railway, with the 1 in 2,383 gradient giving way to a short 1 in 244 climb. At the 18 mile post the line continued a straight course, falling at 1 in 396 over bridge No. 1201 at 18 miles 08 chains from Tivetshall. The branch then swung on a long raking left-hand curve, passing water meadows and over bridge No. 1202 at 18 miles 19 chains, after which the railway negotiated a short 1 in 296 climb to pass over bridge 1203 at 18 miles 43 chains spanning a drainage dyke for the Waveney before an equally short 1 in 224 descent. The river continued its meandering course as the railway followed a straight section on an embankment, rising at 1 in 1,603 before crossing bridge No. 1204 at 18 miles 73 chains and the River Waveney on bridge No. 1205 at 18 miles 74 chains in quick succession, and entering the outskirts of Beccles. A rising 1 in 144 took the railway over two further underbridges – one spanning a stream No. 1206 at 19 miles 00 chains, and then Northgate Street subway No. 1207 at 19 miles 03 chains – the thoroughfare being sufficiently important for a subway to be built under the line for those pedestrians not willing to wait for the passage of trains crossing Northgate Street level crossing No. 96 at 19 miles 03½ chains. As the sharp 10 chains curve continued, the railway bisected Pound Road level crossing No. 97 at 19 miles 09 chains before falling at 1 in 130 and rising again at 1 in 192/280, passing the Down branch loop and the Up branch siding to enter **Beccles** station, 19 miles 33 chains from Tivetshall. The junction points were 109 miles 27½ chains from Liverpool Street via Ipswich and the East Suffolk main line.

Beccles station, 109 miles 25 chains from Liverpool Street via Ipswich, with its staggered platforms, was opened on 4th December 1854 by the Haddiscoe, Beccles & Halesworth Railway; it was the

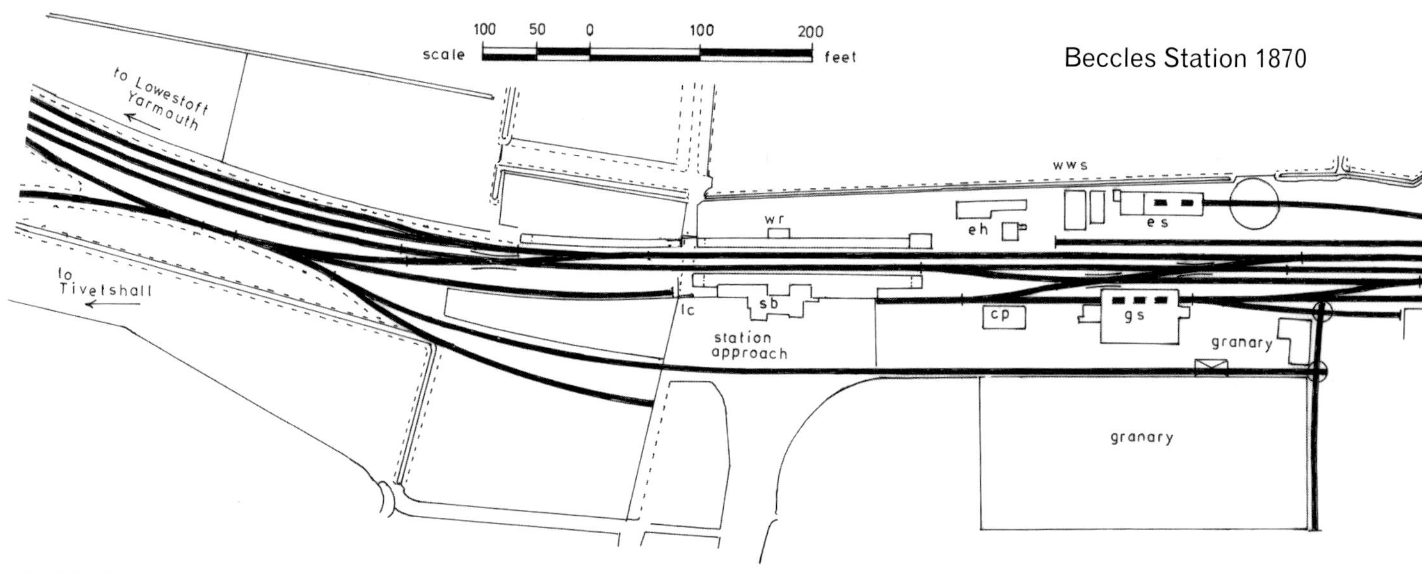

As the branch approached Beccles, the parallel River Waveney was a navigable watercourse requiring the construction of a substantial bridge, No. 1205 at 18 miles 74 chains, over the waterway. Motor cruisers and launches are berthed alongside the riverbank as the span is crossed by a Class '03' diesel mechanical shunting locomotive hauling a loaded sand train from Ditchingham. *Dr I.C. Allen*

The Waveney Valley Branch single line curving away from Beccles in October 1911, with the parallel siding to the left and Down branch reception loop line to the right. The points of the latter were controlled from the small ground-level signal box containing a 12-lever ground frame, which can be seen behind the headshunt. *GERS/Windwood 1369*

Looking north from Beccles station with the Down and Up Yarmouth and Down and Up Lowestoft routes curving away. Alongside the Down Yarmouth line is the two-road Beccles engine shed dating from 1888 which replaced an earlier structure located south of the station. To the left is the coaling stage and lines leading to the turntable, whilst goods reception and holding sidings are to the right. Note the level crossing and associated gatehouse beyond the engine shed. *GERS/Windwood 1331*

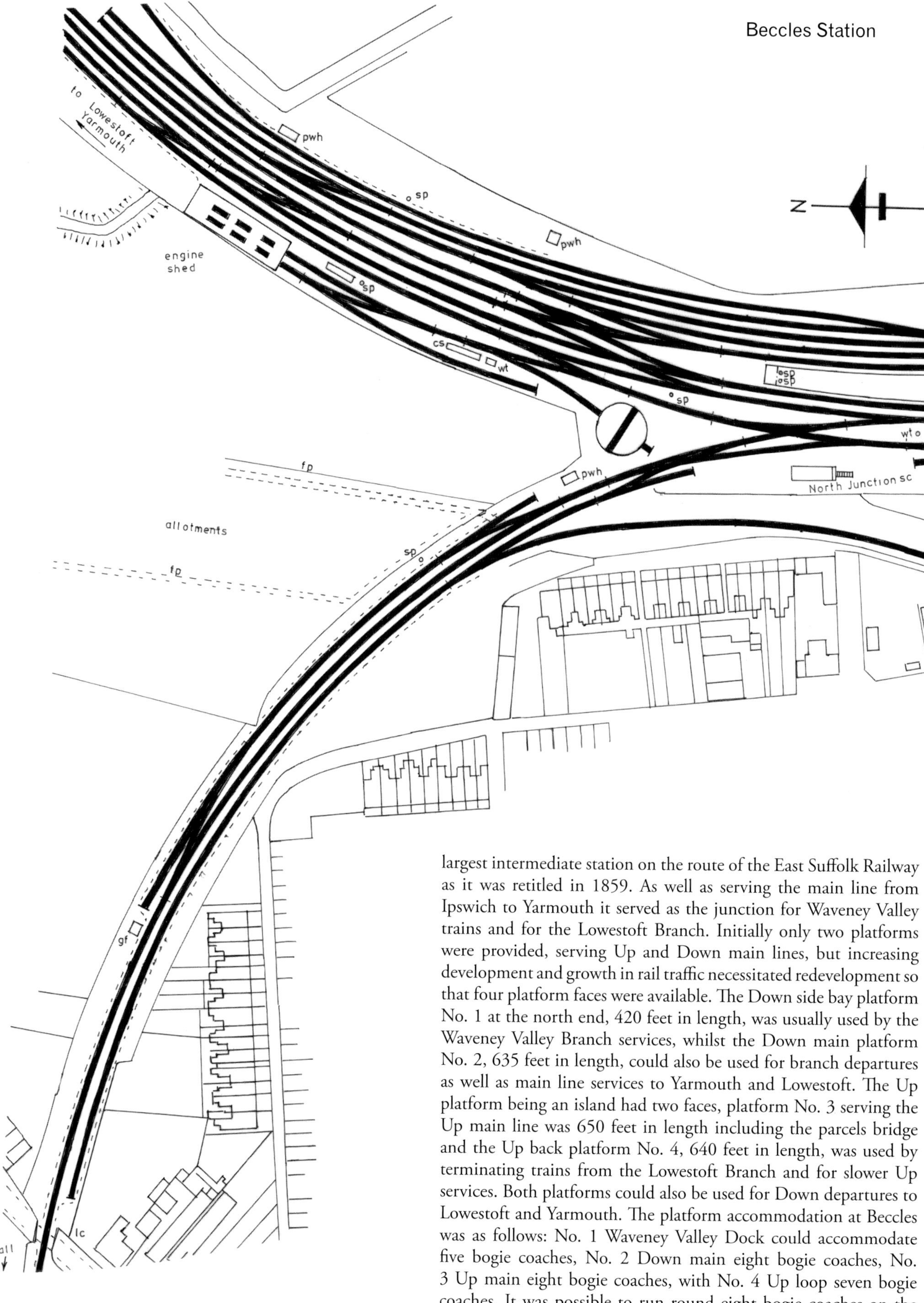

largest intermediate station on the route of the East Suffolk Railway as it was retitled in 1859. As well as serving the main line from Ipswich to Yarmouth it served as the junction for Waveney Valley trains and for the Lowestoft Branch. Initially only two platforms were provided, serving Up and Down main lines, but increasing development and growth in rail traffic necessitated redevelopment so that four platform faces were available. The Down side bay platform No. 1 at the north end, 420 feet in length, was usually used by the Waveney Valley Branch services, whilst the Down main platform No. 2, 635 feet in length, could also be used for branch departures as well as main line services to Yarmouth and Lowestoft. The Up platform being an island had two faces, platform No. 3 serving the Up main line was 650 feet in length including the parcels bridge and the Up back platform No. 4, 640 feet in length, was used by terminating trains from the Lowestoft Branch and for slower Up services. Both platforms could also be used for Down departures to Lowestoft and Yarmouth. The platform accommodation at Beccles was as follows: No. 1 Waveney Valley Dock could accommodate five bogie coaches, No. 2 Down main eight bogie coaches, No. 3 Up main eight bogie coaches, with No. 4 Up loop seven bogie coaches. It was possible to run round eight bogie coaches on the

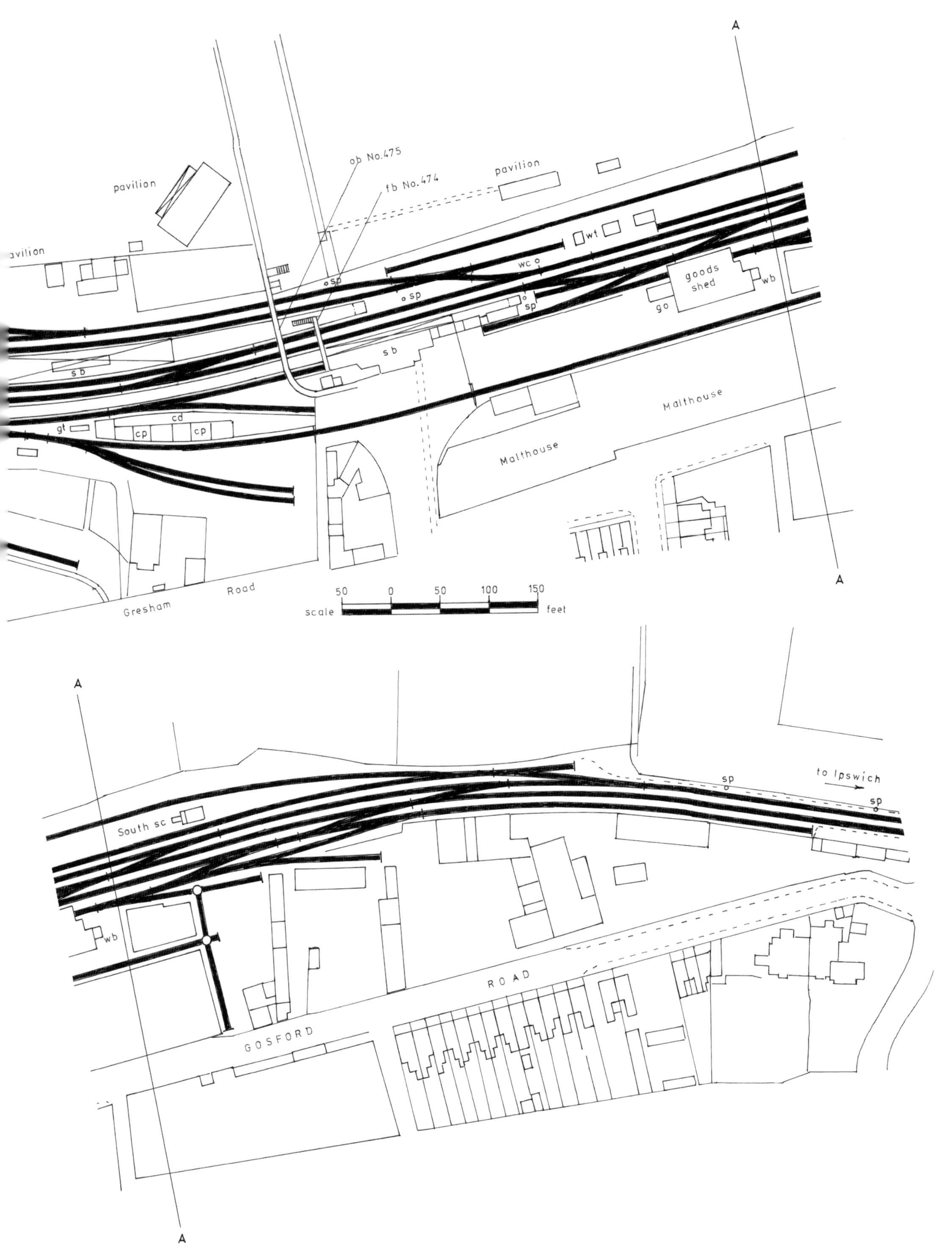
A
pavilion
ob No.475
fb No.474
pavilion
pavilion
wt
wc
sp
sp
sp
goods shed
wb
go
sb
sb
Malthouse
Malthouse
cd
gt
cp
cp
Gresham Road
scale
50 0 50 100 150
feet
A
A
South sc
to Ipswich
sp
sp
wb
ROAD
GOSFORD
A

The Waveney Valley Branch approach to Beccles station in October 1911. The 50 feet turntable in the engine shed yard is wedged into a tight space just short of the curves leading to the Down main platform and back platform; these platforms are staggered from the Up-side island platform. In the background beyond the railway is the recreation ground. Points and signals at this end of the station were controlled from Beccles North signal box, shown on the right, which at that time contained an 80-lever Saxby & Farmer duplex trigger lever frame with 77 working and 3 spare levers. *GERS/Windwood 1326*

Signal-post view of the north end of Beccles station on October 1911, with the Up side island platform in the left foreground – No. 4 serving the Up back and No. 3 the Up main line. In the centre are the Down main platform No. 2 and the Down bay No. 1 used by most Waveney Valley services. Beyond is the goods and coal yard and cattle pens. The main line to Yarmouth and Lowestoft is in the centre foreground whilst the Waveney Valley line curves sharply away to the right. The lower arm on the Down starting signal at the end of platform 3 denotes the route to Lowestoft whilst the taller arm is for the Yarmouth route. The 6-arm signal gantry at the end of platforms 1 and 2 has, from the left in this view: platform 2 – the first arm for Lowestoft, the upper arm for the Yarmouth route, with the third arm for Waveney Valley departures; platform 1 – the lower arm denoting the Lowestoft route, the taller arm the Yarmouth route and the lower arm to the right the Waveney Valley line. *GERS/Windwood 1332*

Beccles station facing south in October 1911 with the Down main platform and the Waveney Valley bay platform in the foreground, with the Up-side island platform to the left. The cattle dock and pens are located beside the bay platform road, as is gas storage tank for replenishing supplies to coaching stock. To the right a rake of 6-wheel coaches are stabled and beyond that wagons occupy the sidings. In the background the complex of maltings occupies the skyline. *GERS/Windwood 1370*

Beccles station facing south with the Waveney Valley Branch train waiting to depart for Norwich behind an 'E4' Class 2-4-0 tender locomotive. The Down main line was served by platform 2 and the Up main line served by platforms 3 and 4. Note the engine headcode for the branch service was one disc under the chimney and one disc over the left-hand buffer. *Author's collection*

Beccles station, 109 miles 25 chains from Liverpool Street and 19 miles 33 chains from Tivetshall, view facing north showing the four platforms: No. 1, the Down bay, 420 feet, used by Waveney Valley trains; platform 2, the Down main line, 635 feet; platform 3, the Up main line, 650 feet; and platform 4, the Up back road, 640 feet. Beccles North signal box is in the distance and footbridge No. 474 connects the Down side with the island platform. The line to Tivetshall curves to the left beyond the signal box. *Author's collection*

PLATFORM
3

A busy scene with 'E4' Class 2-4-0 No. 62789 standing in the Waveney Valley bay platform 1 at Beccles with a branch train to Norwich, as a '117' Class 0-6-0 passes through the Down main platform 2 with an East Suffolk line freight train and an Up passenger train waits in platform 3. Note the cattle pens and dock siding to the right. *R.E. Vincent*

'F5' Class 2-4-2T No. 67201 has just arrived with a Waveney Valley Branch train from Tivetshall and stands in the sunshine at platform 1 at Beccles. *Dr I.C. Allen*

Beccles island platform looking south with platform 4, the Up back road, and platform 3, the Up main line. In the background, 'E4' Class 2-4-0 No. 62789 waits to depart with the 9.00am train to Norwich Thorpe via the Waveney Valley line on 1st September 1951. The four-coach train is headed by a 4-compartment non-gangway suburban BSK. *H.C. Casserley*

Beccles station, photographed from the footbridge showing the Waveney Valley platform 1 and an 'F5' Class 2-4-2T passing through the Down main platform 2 with a suburban coach and goods brake van. A Lowestoft to Liverpool Street train formed of Gresley and Thompson gangway stock stands on the Up main at platform 3. *Author's collection*

Up main via the back road and five bogie coaches in the Waveney Valley carriage siding. The platforms were connected by footbridge No. 474, constructed in 1896, and the main station buildings were at the back of the Down main platform. The footbridge spanning the line at the station but independent of the railway, No. 475 leading to the Avenue, dated from 1896. The passenger station was flanked by extensive sidings on both side of the line, the main yard being on the Down side south of the platforms, whilst four sidings were located on the Up side north of the station and at the back of the Up back platform loop line The goods yard contained a large goods shed with a spacious loading platform, also a private siding connection to the private siding of John Crisp & Sons serving large maltings, J.K. & W.H. Garrod's tannery, Elliott & Garrod's Vulcan iron works, Field's agricultural implement works and Law's & Sons nurseries.

Beccles station originally had six signal boxes: Bank, South, North Junction, Lowestoft Junction, Swing Bridge South and Swing Bridge North; only two of these were involved with signalling trains to and from the Waveney valley line, located each end of the station: Beccles North and Beccles South. North box was sited near

Beccles station Up side island platform. On the right is the Up main line platform, 3, 650 feet in length, whilst the Up back platform, No. 4, 640 feet in length is on the far side. *H.C. Casserley*

Looking south from a vehicle standing in the back road platform 4 of the island platform at Beccles, often used by Lowestoft services, in October 1911. Footbridge No. 475 at 100 miles 24 chains from Liverpool Street spans the railway connecting the Avenue and golf course to the town, whilst behind it station footbridge No. 474 at 100 miles 23 chains connects the island platform to the Down main platform, which is occupied by a train. To the left is the back road run round loop whilst the signal at the end of platform 3 is the Up main starter with co-acting arm at a lower level. *GERS/Windwood 1330*

the junction with the Waveney Valley Branch, South Box was on Up side at the south end of the station. The two-road engine shed, a replacement of an earlier structure south of the station, was sited on the Down side immediately north of the Waveney Valley Branch junction.

At Tivetshall in 1875 all engines and trains from the Waveney Valley line were to come to a stand on the third line at the back of the platform clear of the Up main line. At Beccles all Up and Down trains and light engines were to stop at the station. All trains and light engines from the Waveney Valley line were to come to a stand on the branch, clear of the main line. By 1891 at Tivetshall all engines and trains from the Waveney Valley line were to come to a stand on the third line at the back of the Up platform and clear of the Up main line. At the same time trains passing through Beccles station without stopping were restricted to a speed of 5 mph raised to 15 mph by 1897. The speed limit through Beccles station in 1902 was 15 mph when passing through the station; which was still operative in 1919 but increased to 25 mph when passing through the station in 1927. Speed was also restricted to 20 later 25 mph at Beccles when passing to and from the Bungay branch, whilst in later L&NER days the speed limit on the branch was 50 mph with 20 mph when passing round the curve at Tivetshall.

In GER days at the intermediate branch stations a platform bell was rung on the approach of a train, whilst at Tivetshall and Beccles the bell was sounded on the approach of a train and again when the train was ready to depart.

Beccles station from the south in October 1911, with the main buildings on the Down platform and the Up side island platform to the right connected by footbridge No. 474. To the left, two GER open wagons are standing next the loading platform whilst some Midland Railway open wagons occupy the siding crossing the station forecourt. A water column stands beside the Up main line in the immediate foreground with brick-built lamp room to the extreme right and gas lamp standard beyond. *GERS/Windwood 1372*

The approach to Beccles station from the south on October 1911, with Down and Up main lines in the foreground. The South signal box is on the extreme right and beyond that the water tank supported by timber superstructure. The goods shed with arched entrance is on the Down side and to the immediate left are the rail served maltings. *GERS/Windwood 1352*

Looking south from the station footbridge No. 474 at Beccles in October 1911. To the right is the Down platform and Down main line with the Up main line parallel and the back platform loop road, run round and headshunt to the left. The post of the Up main starting signal is in the immediate foreground and the Down inner home signal is south of the Down platform ramp. *GERS/Windwood 1371*

The view from Beccles South signal box looking south towards Ipswich in October 1911, with Up and Down main lines curving away to the far right and shed road and maltings siding to the near right. A variety of freight rolling stock occupy the various sidings, including Coote & Warren, Peterborough open No. 1216 to the right and on the Up side a London & North Western Railway vehicle, Moy of Peterborough open No. 272 and Joseph Boam of Leicester open No. 153. Permanent way and signalling material is stored between the sidings in the foreground.

GERS/Windwood 1349

9

Permanent Way, Signalling and Staff

Permanent Way

The initial permanent way of the WVR was formed of flat bottom rails weighing between 60 and 65 lbs per yard in 21-feet lengths, secured at the joints by fishplates and four ⅞ inch jack bolts, and spiked to the intermediate sleepers by two dog spikes, each weighing 13 ounces, making four to each sleeper. The sleepers were half-rounded Baltic fir mostly measuring 9 feet by 10 inches by 5 inches laid transversely at an average distance of 3 feet apart with a minimum distance of 1 foot 9 inches at the joints. The ballast was of clean sand and gravel, said to be laid 12 inches below the underside of the sleepers.

The permanent way on the Harleston to Bungay section was for a distance of 64 chains formed of double-headed rails with an average length of 21 feet and weighing 72 lbs per yard. The rails were fixed into the chairs by compressed elm keys, the weight of the chairs at the joints being 31 lbs each and at the intermediate points 22 lbs each. The chairs were fastened to the sleepers by compressed oak trenails. The rails on the remainder of the section were flat bottom weighing 65lbs per yard in 22-feet lengths, secured at the joints by fishplates and four ⅞ inch jack bolts, and spiked down to the intermediate transverse sleepers by two dog spikes, each weighing 13 ounces, making four to each sleeper. The sleepers were half-rounded Baltic fir measuring 9 feet by 10 inches by 5 inches and 9 feet by 9 inches by 4½ inches laid transversely at an average distance of 3 feet apart, the minimum distance being 1 feet 9 inches at the joints. The ballast was formed of clean sand and gravel said to be 15 inches deep below the under side of the sleepers.

On the section from Bungay to Beccles the permanent way was formed of flat bottom rails weighing 60 lbs per yard in 24-feet lengths, secured at the joints by fishplates and fastened to the sleepers under the joints by screw bolts and nuts and washers,

'F4' Class 2-4-2T No. 67176 approaching Ellingham with a Beccles to Tivetshall train on a cold wintry day. In the foreground are the loop sidings installed in 1943 for the Air Ministry. The inner siding could accommodate 100 wagons whilst the second served as a run round. Initially used for the receipt of tarmacadam for airfield runways, they were later used for offloading petroleum and armaments. *Dr I.C. Allen*

and to the intermediate sleepers by dog spikes. The sleepers were a mixture of half-round Baltic timber, Scotch fir and larch, measuring 9 feet by 10 inches by 5 inches and 9 feet by 9 inches by 4½ inches, laid transversely under the rails at an average distance of 3 feet apart with a minimum distance of 1 feet 6 inches at the joints. The ballast was formed of clean sand and gravel stated to be 11 feet wide and 15 inches deep below the underside of the sleepers.

The permanent way only remained in use for a few years and by the late 1860s and early 1870s was extensively relaid with 77 lbs per yard bullhead rails. In the 1880s, 80 lbs per yard bullhead rails in 24 feet and 30 feet lengths were in use. These were joined by fishplates weighing 40 lbs per pair and supported on chairs weighing 38 lbs each. The chairs were secured to the sleepers by iron spikes and wooden trenails. Each sleeper was creosoted and measured 8 feet 6 inches by 10 inches by 5 inches. Around the turn of the century, 85 lbs per yard rails replaced the lighter bullhead track and these sufficed, with the replacement of worn rails, until just before grouping.

From 1923 the L&NER began replacing the remaining 24-feet lengths of rail used on the branch, with lengths of 30 and 45 feet weighing between 80 and 87 lbs per yard. Later, bullhead rails of 85, 90 and 95 lbs per yard in 45 and 60 feet lengths were installed. Of later GER and L&NER vintage, these were laid in chairs of similar origin. Further sections received 60 feet lengths as replacements became due but even so a considerable amount of 45-feet length rails remained when the branch closed. Nearly all track used on the Waveney Valley Branch was second hand, having initially served on the main line.

The original sand and gravel ballast used when the line opened was found suitable for the moderate traffic carried but within ten years the GER introduced ashes and clinker. The GER found ashes were adequate for the ballasting of many of their branch lines and supplies were readily available from the motive power depots on the system. Ashes remained the staple formation of the ballast until closure of the line. When supplies of ashes were not available from locomotive sheds, wagon loads were obtained from the Tate & Lyle sugar refinery at Silvertown and after the early 1920s from the British Sugar Corporation factories at Cantley, Bury St. Edmunds and Ipswich.

The permanent way and civil engineering activities on the branch came under the control of the district Engineer, Norwich. In GER days this was part of District 8, which came under the control of district inspector A. Mulliner. In 1897 and 1902, J.A. Radley was District Engineer at Norwich and W. Gull Permanent Way Inspector, but by 1919 the personnel were J.B. Willis District Civil Engineer and C. King Permanent Way Supervisor.

The numerous level crossings on the branch required constant manning and permanent way staff were permitted to occupy the crossing keeper's cottage rent free in return for their wife opening and closing the gates when the men were on duty. As an example, the tenants listed on the facing page were recorded on the branch in 1913 and 1924.

Families manning the crossings were allowed one day off a month, later once a fortnight, when relief crossing keepers were sent to cover. The branch train was stopped especially to pick up and set down personnel so they could attend the local town for shopping and other amenities.

The branch line was quite expensive to maintain, with each permanent way gang formed of three men. The gangs were based at each station with their allocated responsibility as follows:

The 180 feet long platform at the former Wortwell station in 1928. Opened in January 1861 the station saw little traffic and was closed as an economy measure on 1st January 1878. Thereafter railway staff occupied the station building. *Author's collection*

LEVEL CROSSING COTTAGE TENANTS		
	1913	**1924**
TIVETSHALL		
Tivetshall Hall Crossing	Arthur Chilvers	Claud Ernest Foulger George Fisher
Green Lane Gates	Albert Brown	Albert Brown
Star Crossing	Jonathan Algar	Jonathan Algar
Turnpike Gates	George Shadrake	C.K. Edwards
WAVENEY VALLEY BRANCH		
Crossingfield Crossing	Robert Gower until 30th December Ernest William Porter from 31st December	Frederick George Savoury
Starston Gates	William Moore*	H. Algar
Redenhall Crossing	Richard Gower until 24th December* John Edward Lawn from 25th December*	John Edward Lawn*
Wortwell Crossing	Bertram Greengrass*	H. Saunders* William George Farrow*
Denton Wash	Miss Algar	William Albert Catchpole*
Drake's Lane	Frederick Norman until July Thomas Runnacles from July	Frederick A. Hewitt
Five Acre Gates	William Chapman	Herbert Brinded
Silk Factory Crossing	Charles Fisk	John Harvey
Brace's Road	William Howlett	William Howlett
Pound Road	Joseph Ward	T. Hurran
BECCLES		
Black Drain Crossing	Harry Lewis	Harry Lewis
Worlington Crossing	Benjamin Jermany	Benjamin Jermany later George Goodson
North Cove	William Mayston	William Mayston
Barnaby Marshes	Robert Hardy	Robert Hardy
Hillson Road gates	Herbert James Roe	Herbert James Roe
Dawdy	William Knight	William Knight
NOTE: * Living in former station.		

Tivetshall	Tivetshall station to 1½ milepost
Pulham Market	1½ milepost to Pulham Market Up distant signal
Pulham St. Mary	Pulham Market Up distant signal to 5 milepost
Harleston	5 milepost to 7½ milepost
Homersfield	7½ milepost to 10½ milepost
Earsham	10½ milepost to 12½ milepost
Bungay	12½ milepost to 13½ milepost
Ditchingham	13½ milepost to 14¼ milepost
Ellingham	14¼ milepost to 16 milepost
Geldeston	16 milepost to 18 milepost
Beccles	18 milepost to Beccles station

After World War One the total staff was reduced by one man in each gang, and just before grouping it was again reduced to a total of fourteen men. As a result of the introduction of a road motor system of permanent way maintenance in 1934 the figure was further reduced to twelve men.

G. Howlett, foreman platelayer, J. Durrant, second man, and B. Hensey, platelayer responsible for the Geldeston length, gained an award in 1915 and 1917 for the best kept section of permanent way. Homersfield won the best kept award for tertiary length in 1945 under Ganger Farrow.

In the mists of time, records of permanent way staff serving on the branch are sparse but a few that maintained the infrastructure include Harry Self, platelayer at Tivetshall since 1883 who retired after 43 years service in June 1923, and George Goodrum, a lengthman at Tivetshall who retired on 19th October 1934. Others included W. Philpot, a ganger based at Tivetshall who retired 22nd December 1934, W. Algar, platelayer at Earsham in 1915 and later Homersfield, who after retiring died age 79 in July 1927; Jonathan Algar, lengthman at Tivetshall in 1913 who resided rent free in the Star crossing cottage, died 28th December 1935; whilst M. James, a retired platelayer formerly based at Homersfield, died on 27th April 1937. R.W. James, a ganger with the Bungay gang, died on 5th October 1938; E.G. Jarrett, a permanent way inspector with responsibilities for the branch and based at Beccles, retired on 19th December 1942. William Cutting, a retired sub-ganger at Harleston, died 20th January 1939; whilst George Norman, a retired ganger from Tivetshall, died on 6th March 1939. A. Brown and J. Aldridge, both sub gangers at Tivetshall, retired on 8th July 1939.

As well as attending to the day-to-day track maintenance, the permanent way gangs on the Waveney Valley line were responsible for cleaning the toilets at stations where no mains sewerage existed and on hot summer days, especially at harvest time, they acted as beaters to extinguish any small fires caused by stray sparks emitted by passing locomotives. They also cut the grass on the side of the embankments and cuttings, and this was used for fodder for railway horses, or during World War One was sent to London and East Anglian towns for feeding military horses.

Signalling

The original signals used on the line were a form of semaphore signal with coloured aspect glasses rotating by action of a connecting rod attached to bell crank levers. These semaphore signals were some 15 to 20 feet in height with arms conveying danger at 90 degrees to the post, caution at 45 degrees and clear when slotted in the post. At night the revolving spectacles showed red for 'danger', green for 'caution' and white for 'clear'. Pulham Market, Pulham St. Mary and Starston were each equipped with dual semaphore stop signals (stop arms for both directions of travel, mounted on one post for economy). At Tivetshall, a semaphore stop signal was provided for each direction of travel on the branch together with one auxiliary signal on the approach to the station for trains in the Up direction. At Harleston a semaphore stop signal was provided on the approach to the station, protected by an auxiliary signal. For departing trains a stop signal was provided on the same post as the Down stop signal. The auxiliary signals were positioned 800 yards in the rear of the stop signal and were kept at 'clear' or 'all right' position unless required to protect a train standing between it and the semaphore stop signal. As the line expanded the remaining stations on the branch each had station stop signals for each direction of travel together with auxiliary signals for Up and Down working, with the exception of Redenhall, Wortwell and Earsham which only had a stop signal for each direction of travel mounted on the same post. Specific instructions were issued in the event of an auxiliary signal being at danger. The driver of an approaching train having brought the train to a stand was immediately to move his train forward with great care making sure the line ahead was clear, so as to bring his train well within the protection of the signal. Drivers were especially cautioned as the failure to carry out this regulation could cause an accident which would have otherwise been avoided. If it was not practicable to draw the train far enough within the signal to afford sufficient protection from a following train, the guard was required to go back at once with hand and percussion (*sic*) signals to protect his train.

The 15-lever Dutton frame in Pulham St. Mary signal box in the 1950s had 11 working and 4 spare levers. The Tyer's single wire block instruments are evident on the block shelf above the levers but in the latter years were little used as the signal box was only 'switched in' for operational purposes when trains required to shunt the sidings. *B.D.J. Walsh*

As a result of the Regulation of Railways Act 1889, the GER authorities were required to renew most of the signalling equipment on the branch, and by 1892 the old-style semaphore signals were replaced by conventional lower quadrant home and distant signals with pitch pine posts, cedar arms and cast and wrought iron fittings. The act also required the interlocking of points and signals, and the new signals were provided to GER design. In common with GER practice, each signal arm was stamped on the reverse with the name of the controlling signal box.

Around the turn of the century modifications were made to the working distant signals on the branch. At that time the GER distant signals were painted red with a white stripe and showed red and green aspects to drivers during darkness, the same as stop signals. To avoid confusion between the stop signals and distant signals, the latter were fitted with Coligny Welch lamps which showed an additional white V at night that was actually horizontal thus > alongside the red or green light. To avoid further confusion between station distant signals and gate distant signals, the word GATE, either in cast letters or simply painted on, was shown on the approach side of each gate distant signal arm. Starting in the mid 1920s the L&NER began a programme of repainting the arms of distant signals yellow with a black chevron. Yellow spectacle plates replaced the red and the Coligny Welch lamps were removed or modified to serve as ordinary signal lamps.

Another noticeable alteration by the L&NER was the provision of upper quadrant signals where the former wooden arms or posts showed signs of rotting. It was claimed the new signals would result in economy over the cost of posts due to a restriction in height, less weight of fittings and the fact that gravity tended to bring the arm back to the danger or caution position in the case of failure of equipment, instead of reliance on balance weights. Nevertheless, many GER lower quadrant signals survived on the branch until closure of the line.

Signal Boxes

Tivetshall Junction initially controlled distant, home and starting signals on the Up and Down Norwich main line and Down starter and Up distant, home and starting signals for the

Tivetshall Junction signal box, located on the Down side of the main line south of the station and of brick and timber construction, was originally equipped with a 32-lever frame. This was later enlarged to 45 levers (with 41 working and 4 spare) using a McKenzie & Holland converted tappet frame with 4-inch centres. Note the steps are of metal construction having replaced the original wooden steps. It was finally abolished on 5th October 1986.
Author's collection

branch. A subsidiary signal on the same post as the Down branch starter authorised movements onto the Up main loop line. Later, advance starting signals were installed on both the Up and Down main lines, whilst a full-size arm mounted on the same post as the Down branch starting signal authorised movements into the Up main loop line. From 1943, after the replacement of a crossover from the branch platform to the Down main line with a crossover between the Up and Down main line and facing points from the Up main to the branch platform, the Up main home signal post also included a separate branch home authorising movements into the back platform. At the same time the Down distant signal was converted to colour light.

Pulham Market signal box was equipped with distant, home and starting signals for each direction of travel, but with the installation of the loop serving the Royal Naval Air Station sidings, distant, home and splitting starting signals were provided in the Down direction, the left-hand or upper arm of the latter serving the main single line and the right or lower arm granting access to the loop on the Up side of the railway. In the Up direction a distant arm was provided on the same post as Pulham St. Mary Down distant signal, followed by splitting outer home signals (right-hand or upper arm for the main single line and left-hand lower arm for entry to the Naval Air Station loop). An inner home signal protecting the level crossing gates was followed by the Up starting signal located west of

Pulham St. Mary station, 3 miles 57 chains from Tivetshall, in this 1952 view facing towards Beccles with the 330 feet long platform on the Down side of the main single line. In the foreground is No. 20 level crossing protected by the Up starting signal now equipped with an upper quadrant arm. Pulham St. Mary signal box containing a 15-lever Dutton frame is on the Up side of the line opposite the platform. *Author's collection*

the platform. Pulham St. Mary signal box controlled distant, home and starting signals for both Up and Down direction of travel, as did Harleston to control movements through the crossing loop. Homersfield and Bungay also possessed distant, home and starting signals for each direction of travel but Earsham signal box only controlled a distant and stop signal for each direction, the latter protecting the level crossing gates.

Initially Ditchingham signal box was provided with distant, home and starting signals for each direction of travel but from the installation of the loop on the Down side of the line west of the station in 1913, distant, home, starting and advance starting signals were provided in the Down direction and distant, home and starting signals on the Up road. With the installation of additional sidings in 1943, distant, home and starting signals were provided in the Down direction, the distant signal arm mounted on the same post as Bungay starting signal, whilst the home had a subsidiary arm for the loop on the same post. In the Up direction, distant, home and starting signals were provided, the latter having Bungay Up distant arm on the same post. Ellingham and Geldeston signal boxes were both provided with distant, home and starting signals for each direction of travel.

Beccles North signal box initially had a distant and splitting home signals on the branch, the splitting arm for the connection on to the Up main line was interlocked with Beccles South signal box, whilst the other gave access to the Down side back platform. For branch trains departing Beccles a starting signal was provided

Homersfield station, 8 miles 74 chains from Tivetshall, with the 340 feet long platform on the Down side of the line host to the main station buildings. To the right on the Up side of the main single line is the signal box, opened in 1892 and containing a 20-lever Dutton frame. Note the neat shrubbery and white stones alongside the path leading to the signal box. *Author's collection*

Bungay signal box on the Down side of the line was opened in 1892 as a replacement for an earlier structure and was provided with a 25-lever Dutton frame. Beyond the signal box is Outney Road overbridge No. 1191 and in the Down loop line an 'F4' Class 2-4-2T, No. 67186, waits at the platform with the 8.35am Tivetshall to Beccles train on 1st September 1951. *H.C. Casserley*

for both the Down main platform and the Down bay platform. By 1883 the signals for branch trains approaching Beccles were unaltered but in the Down direction the starting signal from the back platform was bracketed, the right-hand upper arm authorising movement to the Down main line whilst the left-hand lower arm authorised movements to the Waveney Valley line. The installation of the branch loop line in 1901 required signalling revisions: on the approach from the branch a splitting distant, splitting outer home signals and inner home signals gave access to the Up main line or back platform road. The basic signalling served until the rationalisation of trackwork and prior to abolition only a splitting distant and splitting home signals were provided on the approach

The divergence of the Waveney Valley Branch from Beccles station in October 1911, with Beccles North signal box on the left. Beyond the turntable the branch bracketed inner home signal protects the junction, the lower arm giving access to the bay platform and the taller arm access to the Down main platform. *GERS/Windwood 1325*

to the station. For departing branch trains a starting signal was provided at both the north end of the Down main platform and Down back platform.

The single line branch from Tivetshall to Harleston was initially worked on the One Engine in Steam or two or more coupled together principle, utilising the Train Staff only, with Train Staff stations at Tivetshall and Harleston. Train Staff working continued with the opening of the sections to Bungay and then Beccles, with both becoming Train Staff stations. The line was then divided into three sections, Tivetshall to Harleston, Harleston to Bungay and Bungay to Beccles. As traffic increased, so the Train Staff only working was proving an operational inconvenience and Train Staff and Ticket working was introduced from 23rd September 1864 under special order 1114, the first such arrangement on the GER. The Tivetshall to Harleston Train Staff was round in shape, painted green and lettered 'Harleston and Tivetshall', the Harleston to Bungay Train Staff was square, coloured yellow and inscribed 'Harleston and Bungay', whilst the Bungay to Beccles Train Staff was hexagonal in shape, coloured blue and labelled 'Bungay and Beccles'. With the opening of the Admiralty siding at Pulham Market, the station was designated a Train Staff station and an additional single line section created. The Tivetshall to Pulham Market Train Staff was triangular in shape, painted green and lettered 'Pulham Market and Tivetshall', the Pulham Market to Harleston Train Staff was round in shape, red in colour and lettered 'Pulham Market and Harleston', Harleston to Bungay Train Staff was square, coloured yellow and lettered 'Harleston and Bungay', and the Bungay and Beccles Train Staff was hexagonal, blue in colour and lettered 'Bungay and Beccles'. The paper tickets utilized the same colour as the respective Train Staffs. In 1943 yet another Train Staff station was created to ease the working of military traffic when Ditchingham was added to the list – although, like Pulham Market, passenger trains were not allowed to cross one another, only a passenger and goods train being acceded the privilege, the goods train using the respective loop whilst the passenger train used the main single line. Thus the Bungay to Beccles section became Bungay to Ditchingham and Ditchingham to Beccles. The facility was removed in 1950 and the sections reverted to Bungay to Beccles. In the final few years of operation both the Tivetshall to Harleston and Bungay, later Ditchingham, to Beccles sections were operated by One Engine in Steam method of working using a Train Staff.

Beccles South signal box on 7th May 1966. Of brick and timber construction, and dating from 1879, it contained a 40-lever frame with 37 working and 3 spare levers and was abolished on 16th February 1986. *J. Watling*

Signals

Tivetshall Junction signal box, located 100 miles 50½ chains from Liverpool Street on the Down side of the main line, was of brick and timber construction measuring 25 feet by 11 feet with the operating floor 7 feet 6 inches above rail level, replacing an earlier structure. It was initially equipped with a 32-lever McKenzie & Holland converted Tappett frame with 4-inch centres, with 30 working and 2 spare levers. After track and layout improvements the frame was enlarged to 45 levers in 1920, with 44 working and 1 spare lever. Some rationalisation took place during World War Two but after new sidings were installed for the Air Ministry in 1943 the frame was amended to 41 working and 4 spare levers. After closure of the Waveney Valley line and further rationalisation the box had 22 working and 23 spare levers by 1969, reducing still further until the signal box was abolished on 5th October 1986. A small 2-lever ground frame, later increased to 3 levers, was also in use by 1921;the Air Ministry siding ground frame leading from the branch platform road was released by Tivetshall Junction No. 23 lever.

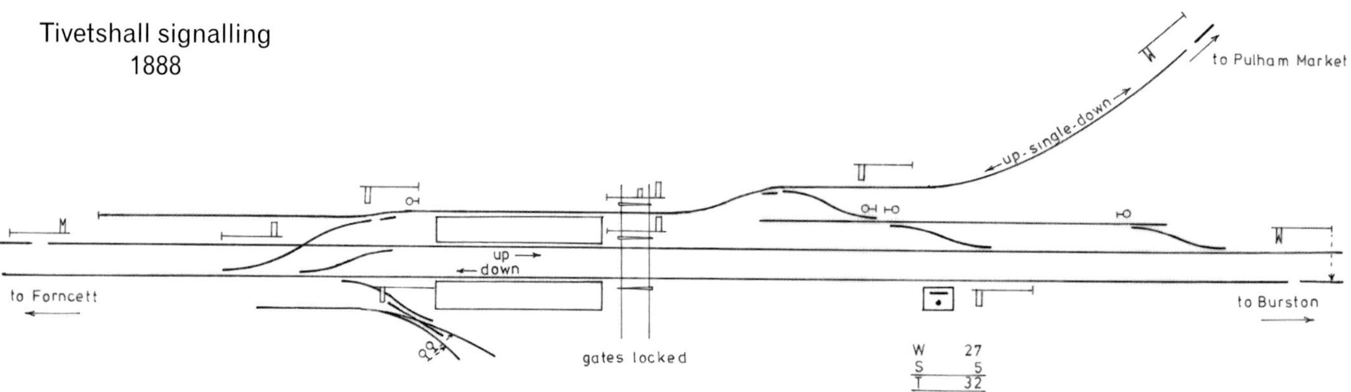

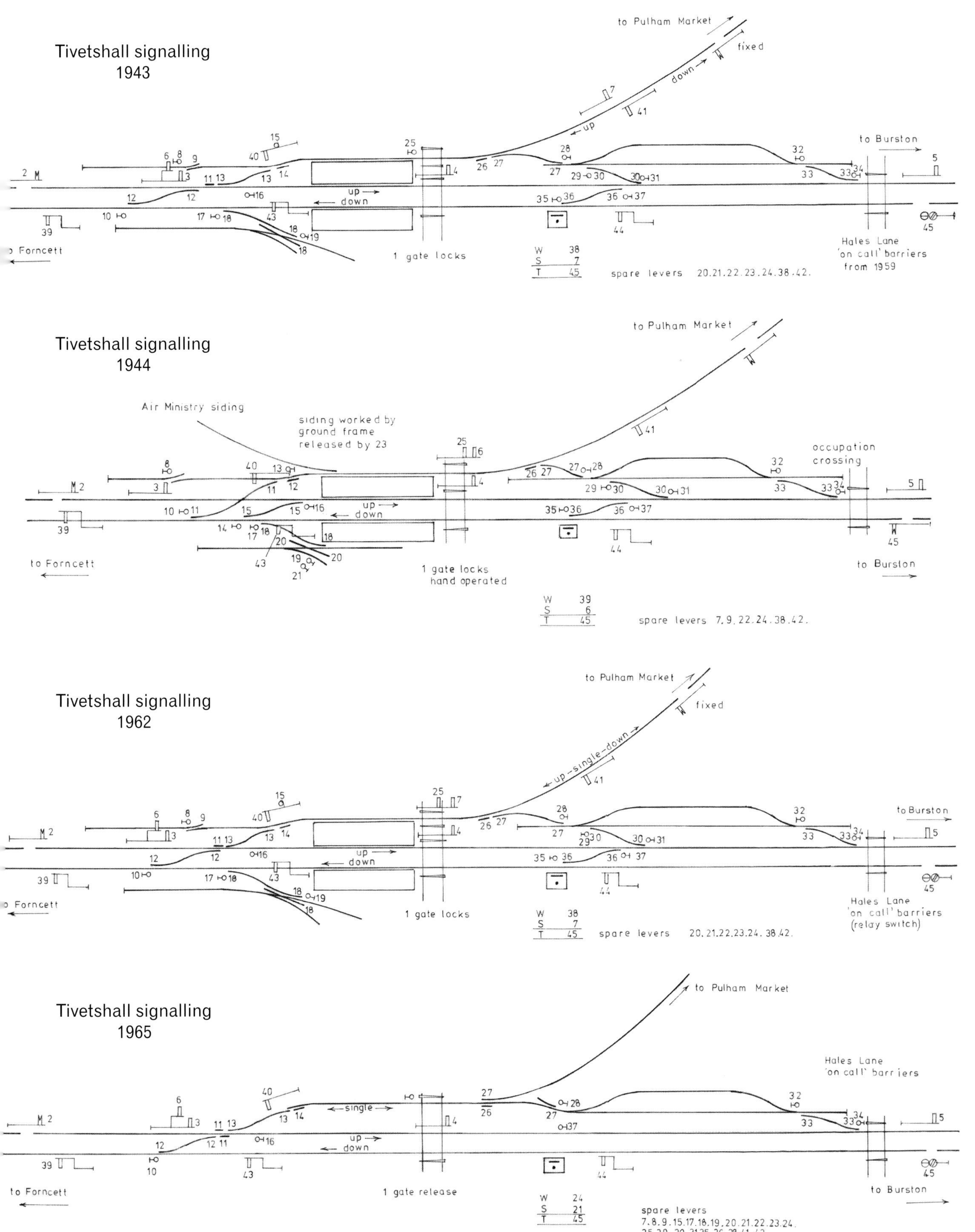
Tivetshall signalling 1943
to Pulham Market
fixed
down
up
up
down
to Burston
to Forncett
1 gate locks
W 38
S 7
T 45
spare levers 20.21.22.23.24.38.42.
Hales Lane 'on call' barriers from 1959
Tivetshall signalling 1944
to Pulham Market
Air Ministry siding
siding worked by ground frame released by 23
occupation crossing
up
down
to Forncett
to Burston
1 gate locks hand operated
W 39
S 6
T 45
spare levers 7.9.22.24.38.42.
Tivetshall signalling 1962
to Pulham Market
fixed
up-single-down
to Burston
up
down
to Forncett
1 gate locks
W 38
S 7
T 45
spare levers 20.21.22.23.24.38.42.
Hales Lane 'on call' barriers (relay switch)
Tivetshall signalling 1965
to Pulham Market
Hales Lane 'on call' barriers
single
up
down
to Forncett
1 gate release
to Burston
W 24
S 21
T 45
spare levers 7.8.9.15.17.18.19.20.21.22.23.24. 25.29.30.31.35.36.38.41.42.

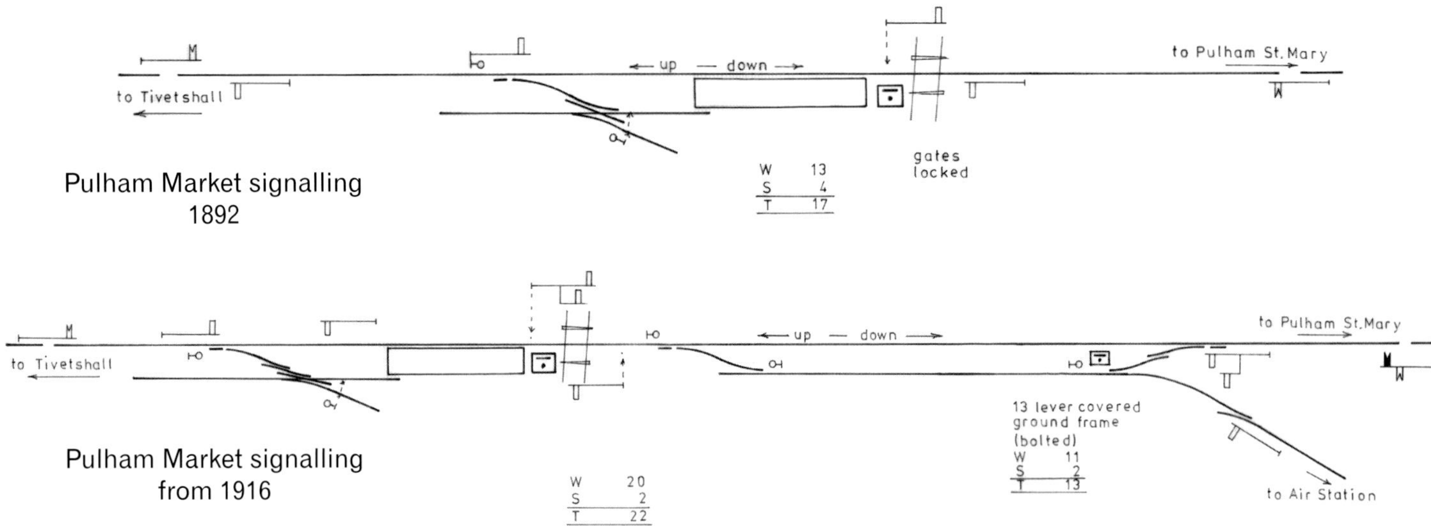

Pulham Market signalling 1892

Pulham Market signalling from 1916

Pulham Market signal box, provided in 1892, was of brick and timber construction measuring 18 feet by 11 feet 6 inches with the operating floor 7 feet above rail level. It was originally provided with a 20-lever Dutton frame having 18 working and 2 spare levers. As a result of the installation of connections to serve Pulham Market Air Base the existing frame was replaced by a 26-lever Saxby & Farmer frame with 5-inch centres containing 24 working and 2 spare levers. Subsequently the frame was relocked before the signal box was abolished in September 1958 and replaced by a ground frame to work the points to the siding. The ground frame was abolished on 31st August 1965. With the opening of the sidings to serve the air base a separate 13-lever McKenzie & Holland ground frame with 11 working and 2 spare levers was located in a covered hut at the east end of the loop. The frame was first used in February 1916 and was mechanically locked with Pulham Market signal box. By 1921 the signal box frame was relocked and with the closure of the RAF base (53MU) in February 1958 the frame was abolished, the last traffic passing into the siding in late 1957. The opening of the siding and the increase in status as a Train Staff station required revised instructions at Pulham Market. A goods train with traffic for the Naval Air Station siding could be allowed to leave Tivetshall or Harleston for Pulham Market and there be shunted clear into the Naval Air Station siding next to the main single line until it was again required to leave Pulham Market. After the goods train had arrived and been shunted clear of the main single line, a Down train or an Up train could be accepted by the Pulham Market signalman provided he was in a position to do so. After the Pulham Market signalman had accepted a Down train from Tivetshall he was not to receive an Up train from Pulham St. Mary. In a like manner if the Pulham Market signalman had accepted an Up train from Pulham St. Mary he was not to accept a Down train from Tivetshall. Likewise the signalman at Pulham St. Mary was not to accept an Up train from Harleston until he had first obtained the 'allow train to enter section' signal from Pulham Market. The Naval Air Station siding next to the main single line had to be kept clear for the reception of goods trains requiring to work it. A second loop line was added south of the original loop in 1941 to handle additional traffic. On no account were passenger trains allowed to cross one another at Pulham Market.

Along the branch at Pulham St. Mary, a timber signal box measuring 18 feet by 11 feet 6 inches with operating floor 7 feet 0 inches above rail level was provided in 1892. It contained a

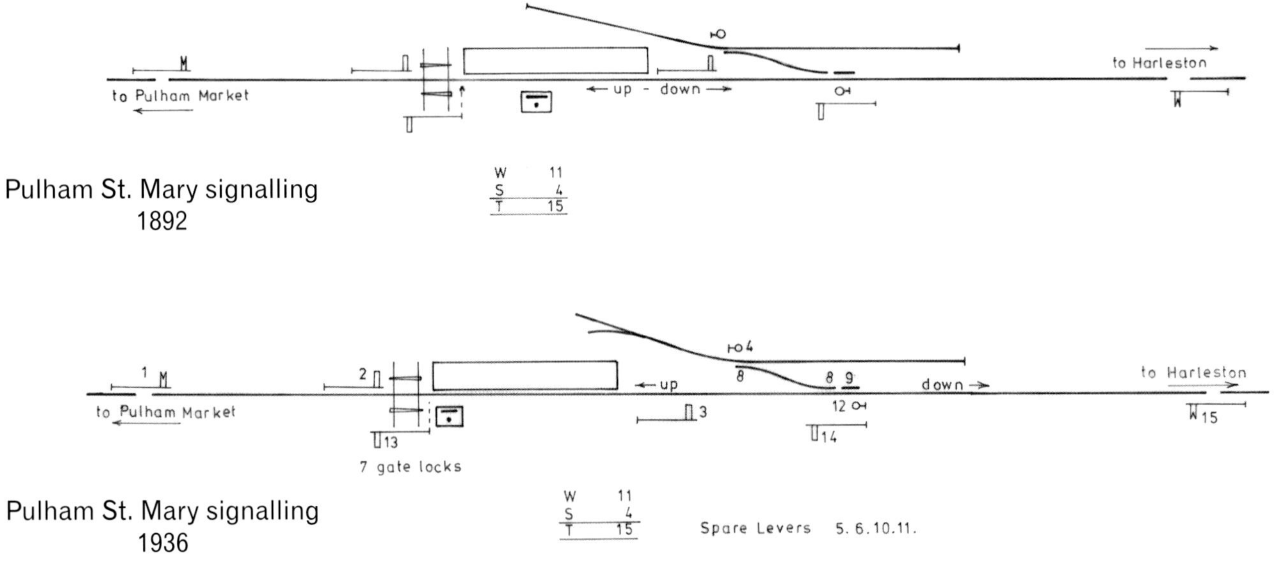

Pulham St. Mary signalling 1892

Pulham St. Mary signalling 1936

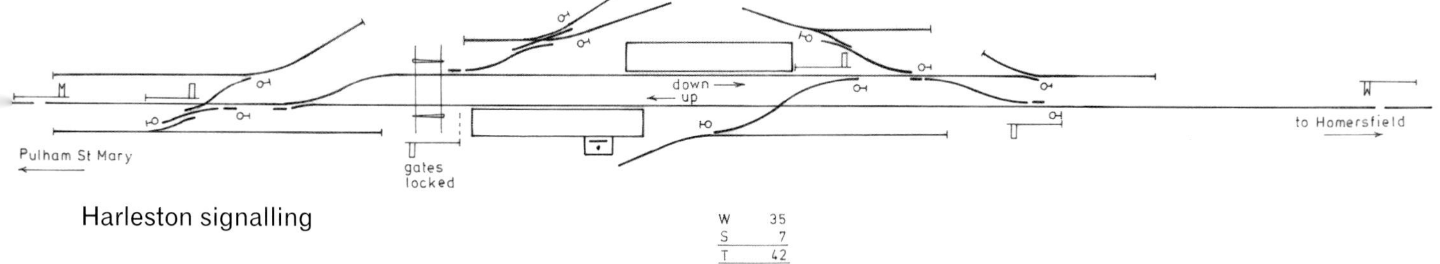

Harleston signalling

15-lever Dutton frame with 4½-inch centres with 11 working and 4 spare levers. The signal box serving as a block post was not a Train Staff station and was abolished in September 1958. The ground frame was abolished on 31st August 1965.

Harleston was one of the train crossing places on the line after 1893 as well as having a large goods yard. It was originally provided with a signal box in the 1870s, which was replaced in 1893 by a new signal box located on the Up platform. The timber structure measuring 32 feet 6 inches by 11 feet 6 inches with operating floor 8 feet 6 inches above rail level was equipped with a 42-lever Dutton frame with 4-inch centres containing 35 working and 7 spare levers. The signal box was abolished in September 1958.

Homersfield signal box, dating from July 1892, was also of all timber construction, measuring 20 feet by 11 feet 6 inches with operating floor 6 feet above rail level; it contained a 20-lever Dutton frame with 4-inch centres, with 16 working and 4 spare levers. As at Pulham Market, Homersfield signal box was a block post but not a Train Staff station and when abolished in September 1958, entry to the sidings was controlled by Homersfield East and Homersfield West ground frames, each with 2 levers operating the connections and released by Annett's key on the Train Staff or Metal Tickets. Both frames were abolished on 1st February 1960.

Between Homersfield and Earsham a double-ended siding capable of holding fifty wagons, engine and brake van was provided for the Air Ministry in 1944. Entry to the sidings was controlled by 2-lever ground frames at each end of the layout, known as 'Air Ministry

Class 'N7/3' 0-6-2T No. 69679 hauls a goods train off the RAF siding from Pulham Airfield in June 1951. The plaque on the sleeper just in front of the locomotive denotes the demarcation between the private siding and railway company property. The signal operated from the ground frame beside the Waveney Valley Branch was rarely used in the latter years, although it had an upper quadrant arm. No. 69679, allocated to Norwich, carries the Whittaker Train Staff exchange arm near the cab from the time when it worked on the Midland & Great Northern services from South Lynn to Kings Lynn. *Dr I.C. Allen*

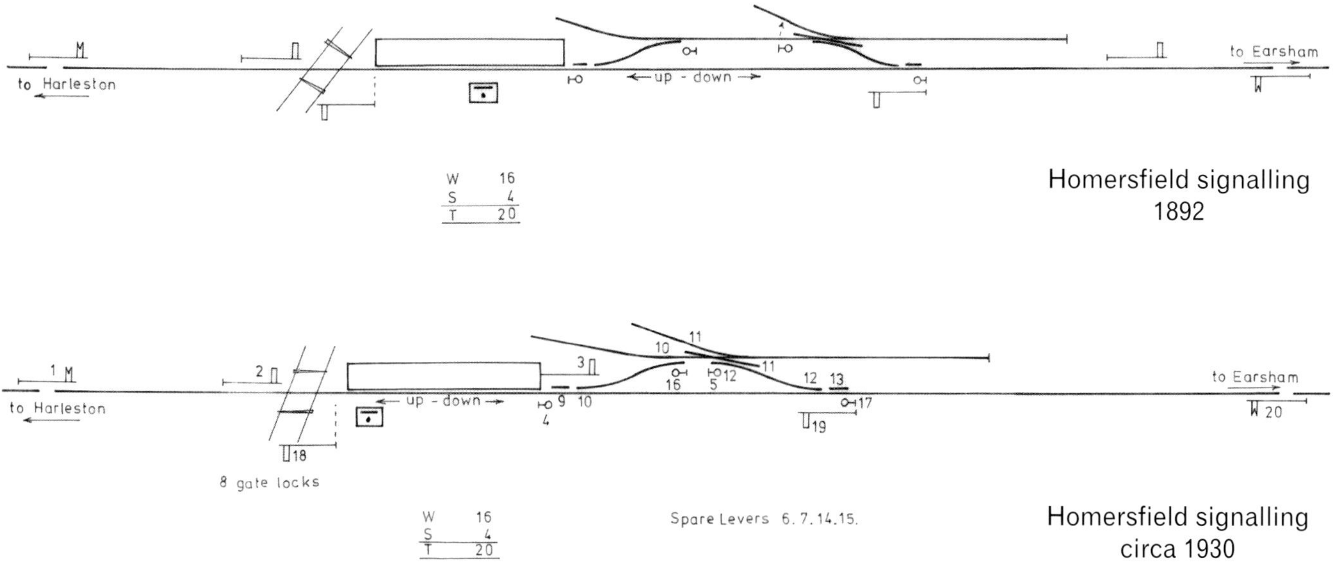

Homersfield signalling 1892

Homersfield signalling circa 1930

A busy scene at Bungay in January 1952 as 'J15' Class 0-6-0 No. 65433 approaches the signal box on the Down loop line with a rake of wagons and passes '812/3' Class 4-6-0 No. 61577 standing in the goods yard at the head of the Ipswich breakdown train whose crane was being used to load heavy baulks of timber. *Dr I.C. Allen*

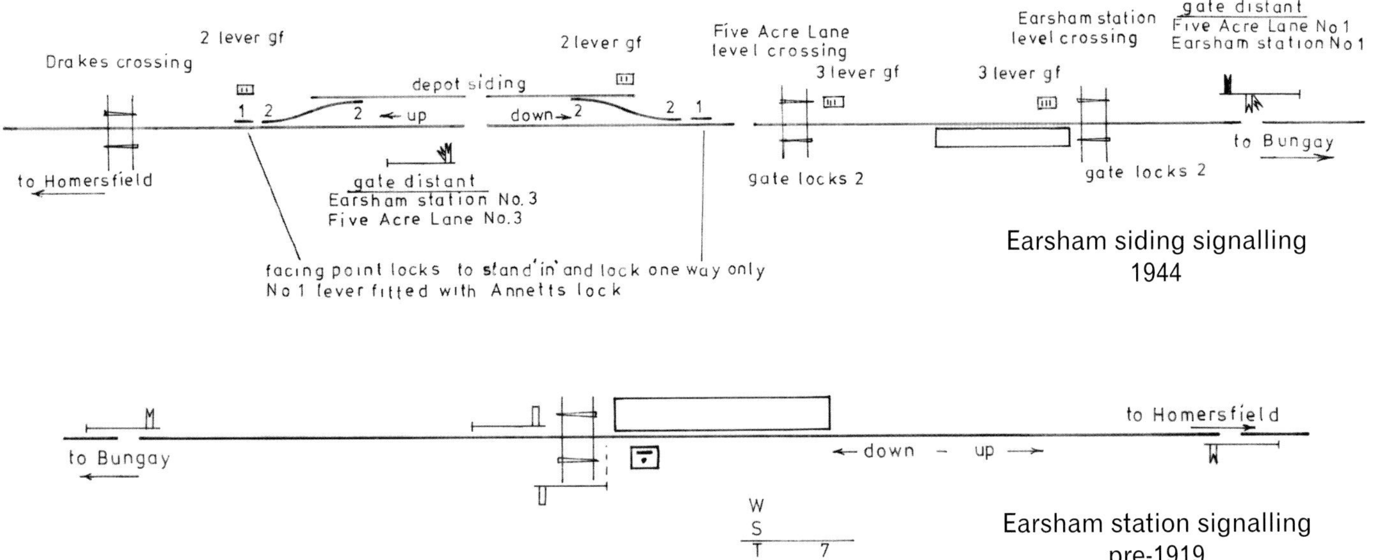

Earsham siding signalling 1944

Earsham station signalling pre-1919

East' and 'Air Ministry West', the ground frames being released by Annett's key on the Train Staff or Metal Tickets. The siding was still in situ in 1960 but the connections and ground frames were removed by 22nd July of that year.

Earsham signal box, opened in 1892, was not a block post but was essentially built to control the distant and stop signals for each direction of travel protecting the level crossing. Constructed of timber, it contained a 7-lever Dutton frame with 4-inch centres, with all levers working. The signal box was abolished in 1919 and replaced by a 3-lever ground frame to lock the level crossing gates and operate the associated gate distant signals.

A signal box was provided at Bungay in the 1870s but this was replaced in 1892 by a new timber structure measuring 22 feet by 11 feet 6 inches with operating floor 6 feet above rail level. It was equipped with a Dutton 25-lever frame with 4-inch centres, with 18 working and 7 spare levers. The signal box was abolished in September 1958 when all points were converted to hand operation. Beyond the station, Bungay Common level crossing was provided with a 2-lever ground frame, which worked the gate distant signals for each direction of travel as well as releasing the gates which were opened by hand.

Ditchingham signal box, of all timber construction, was provided in late 1891 and measured 19 feet by 11 feet 6 inches with operating floor 6 feet above rail level. It was equipped with an 18-lever Dutton frame with 4-inch centres, initially with 14 working and 4 spare levers. No block switch was initially provided but the facility was added later. By 1921 all levers were working. In 1943 the station became a crossing place for passenger and goods trains but not two passenger services and remained as such until abolition of the signal box in September 1958. As a replacement, a 2-lever ground frame known as 'Ditchingham East' was located west of the level crossing over the A143 road, this frame controlled the connection from the single line to the goods loop at the station end. A further 8-lever ground frame existed at Ditchingham West, installed in 1913 to control entry from the main single line to the maltings west of the station. The frame, with 7 working and 1 spare lever, was bolted and locked from Ditchingham signal box. In 1943 new sidings were installed for the United States Army depot and the connection at the west end was extended. A new 6-lever ground frame was installed, now also controlling the Factory Road level crossing, the levers being electrically released by levers No's 9 and 10 in Ditchingham signal box. The siding

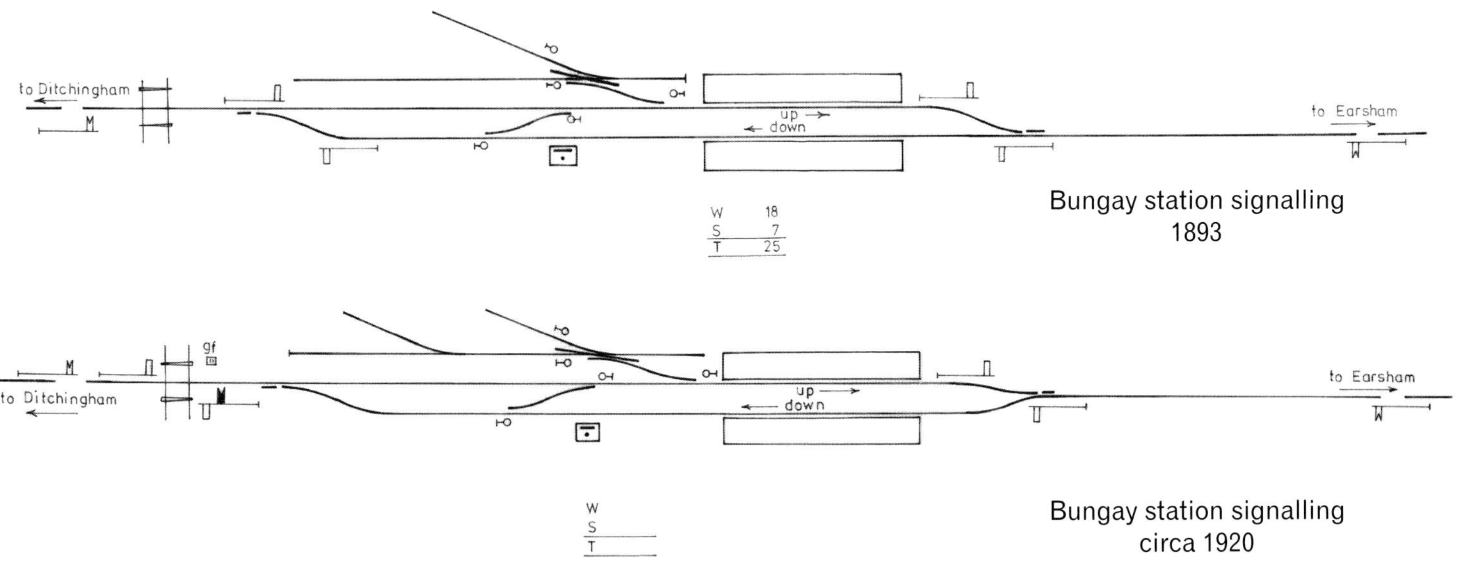

Bungay station signalling 1893

Bungay station signalling circa 1920

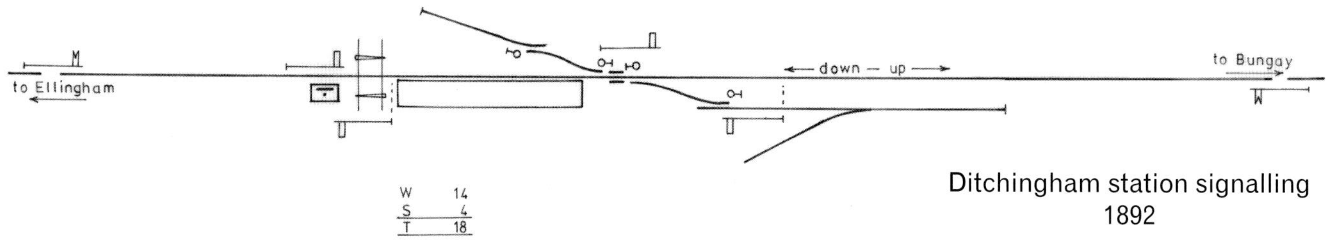

W 14
S 4
T 18

Ditchingham station signalling 1892

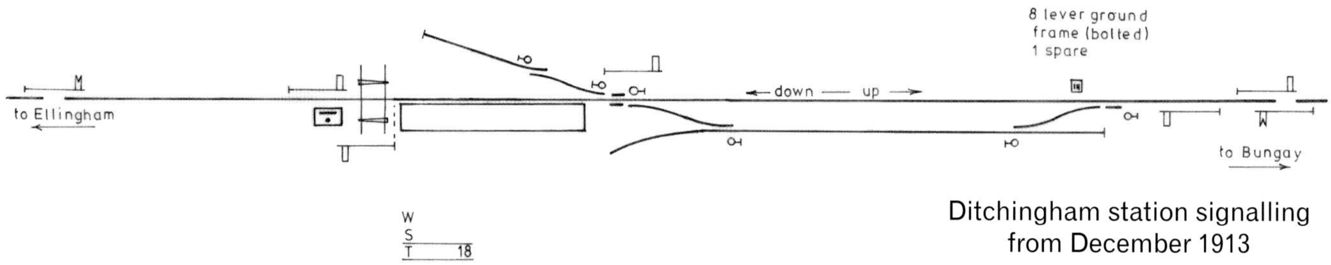

W
S
T 18

Ditchingham station signalling from December 1913

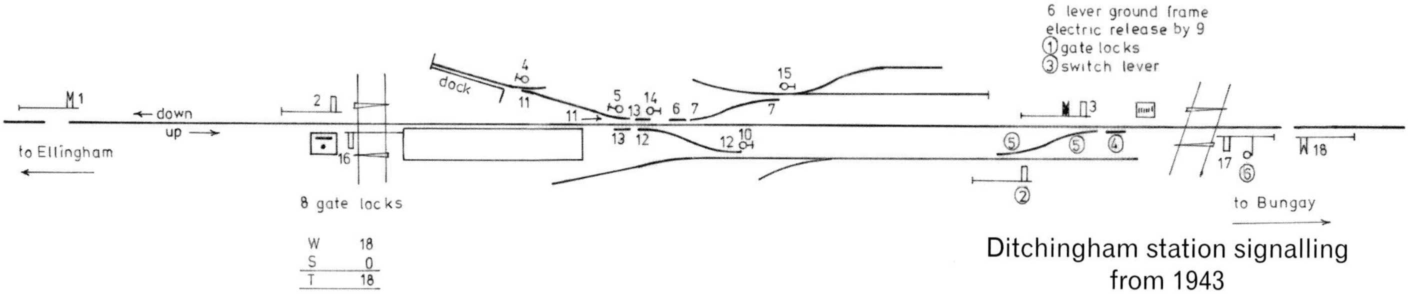

W 18
S 0
T 18

Ditchingham station signalling from 1943

was removed by 1948 and the ground frame reduced to 2 levers to control the connection from the single line to the loop at Factory Road level crossing. The level crossing on the A144 road was equipped with a 2-lever ground frame, but this was removed in 1943.

The signal box at Ellingham, provided in 1891, was of timber construction measuring 18 feet by 11 feet 6 inches with operating floor 7 feet above rail level. It was provided as a block post but was not a Train Staff station and possessed a 15-lever Dutton frame with 4-inch centres, with 11 working and 4 spare levers. A block switch was provided to allow the box to be switched out when required. Two sidings were added for the Air Ministry in 1943, including a connection to a fuel depot as well as the siding serving Ellingham Mill installed in 1877, all incorporated within the control of the 15-lever frame. The signal box was abolished in September 1958 and replaced by a 2-lever ground frame released by Annett's key on the Train Staff to control access to the sidings.

Geldeston signal box, opened in 1891, was of brick and timber construction measuring 18 feet by 11 feet 9 inches with operation floor 7 feet 9 inches above rail level. It was equipped with a 15-lever Dutton frame with 4-inch centres, with 11 working and 4 spare levers. It was a block post but not a Train Staff station and was equipped with a block switch. The signal box was abolished in September 1958.

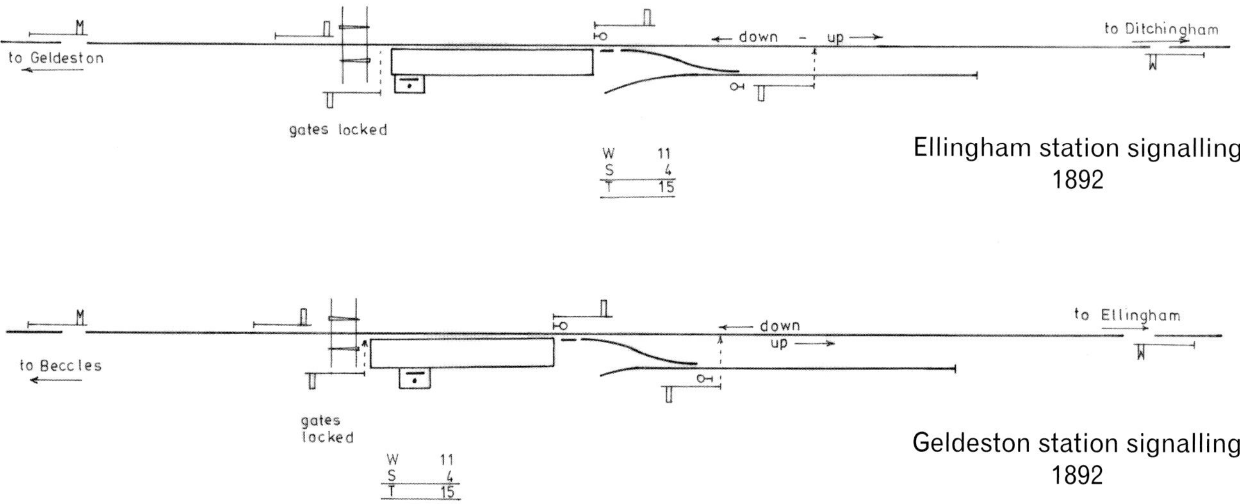

Ellingham station signalling 1892

Geldeston station signalling 1892

Looking west towards Tivetshall from the Up starting signal at Geldeston, in October 1911, with the crossover to the Down side goods yard in the foreground. The tall post at the back of the 220 feet headshunt is the Down home signal. *GERS/Windwood 1367*

'E4' Class 2-4-0 No. 62789 approaching Beccles with a through train from Norwich via Tivetshall. It is signalled into the Waveney Valley bay platform as it passes an unidentified 'J15' Class 0-6-0 shunting wagons on the Waveney Valley Branch reception siding. *Author's collection*

On the approach to Beccles, Northgate Street and Pound Street level crossings were each controlled by a 2-lever ground frame electrically released from Beccles North Junction signal box lever No. 54; both were abolished on 3rd July 1963. When new sidings were installed on the Up side of the Waveney Valley line in 1901 the connections were controlled from a 12-lever Saxby & Farmer open tappet ground frame with 5-inch centres, originally with 10 working and 2 spare levers, and bolt locked from Beccles North Junction signal box. By 1921 this had been amended to 9 working and 3 spare levers, mechanically locked by Beccles North Junction No. 66 lever. All three ground frames were taken out of use on 3rd July 1963 when the gates became trainmen operated.

The physical junction of the Waveney Valley line with the East Suffolk main line was controlled by Beccles North Junction signal box. A signal box existed at this site from the early 1870s but with no interlocking between points and signals. Interlocking was authorised in February 1879 with two new signal boxes provided – Beccles North Junction and Beccles South. The North

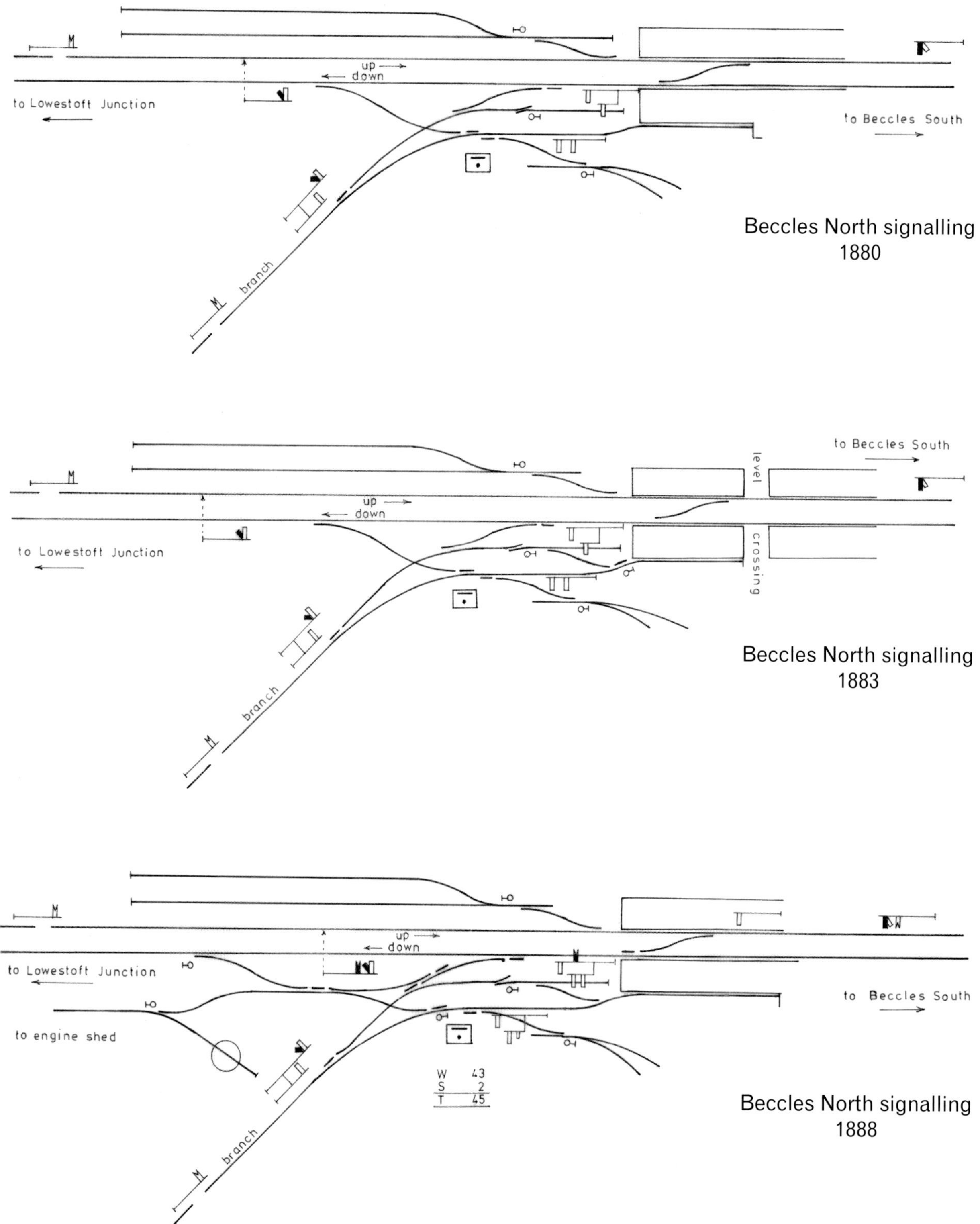

Beccles North signalling 1880

Beccles North signalling 1883

Beccles North signalling 1888

Junction, also referred to by the inspecting officer as Beccles B signal box, was originally provided with a 45-lever frame, initially with 41 working and 4 spare levers but after track alterations in 1893 this amended to 43 working and 2 spare levers. Major alterations in 1896 required a much larger signal box of brick construction to operating floor level and timber above, measuring 40 feet by 11 feet 6 inches with operating floor 12 feet above rail level. It contained an 80-lever Saxby & Farmer duplex trigger frame with 4-inch centres. Initially located alongside the old signal box it had 75 working and 5 spare levers but alterations and doubling of the Lowestoft line to Carlton Colville in 1899 resulted in it being amended to 76 working and 4 spare levers, further amended after the installation of a new loop on the Up side of the Waveney Valley line in 1901 to 77 working and 3 spare levers. The frame was subsequently enlarged to 81 levers with 79 working and 2 spare levers by 1921. As rationalisation was made, so the number of operating levers reduced until the signal box was finally abolished on 24th July 1969.

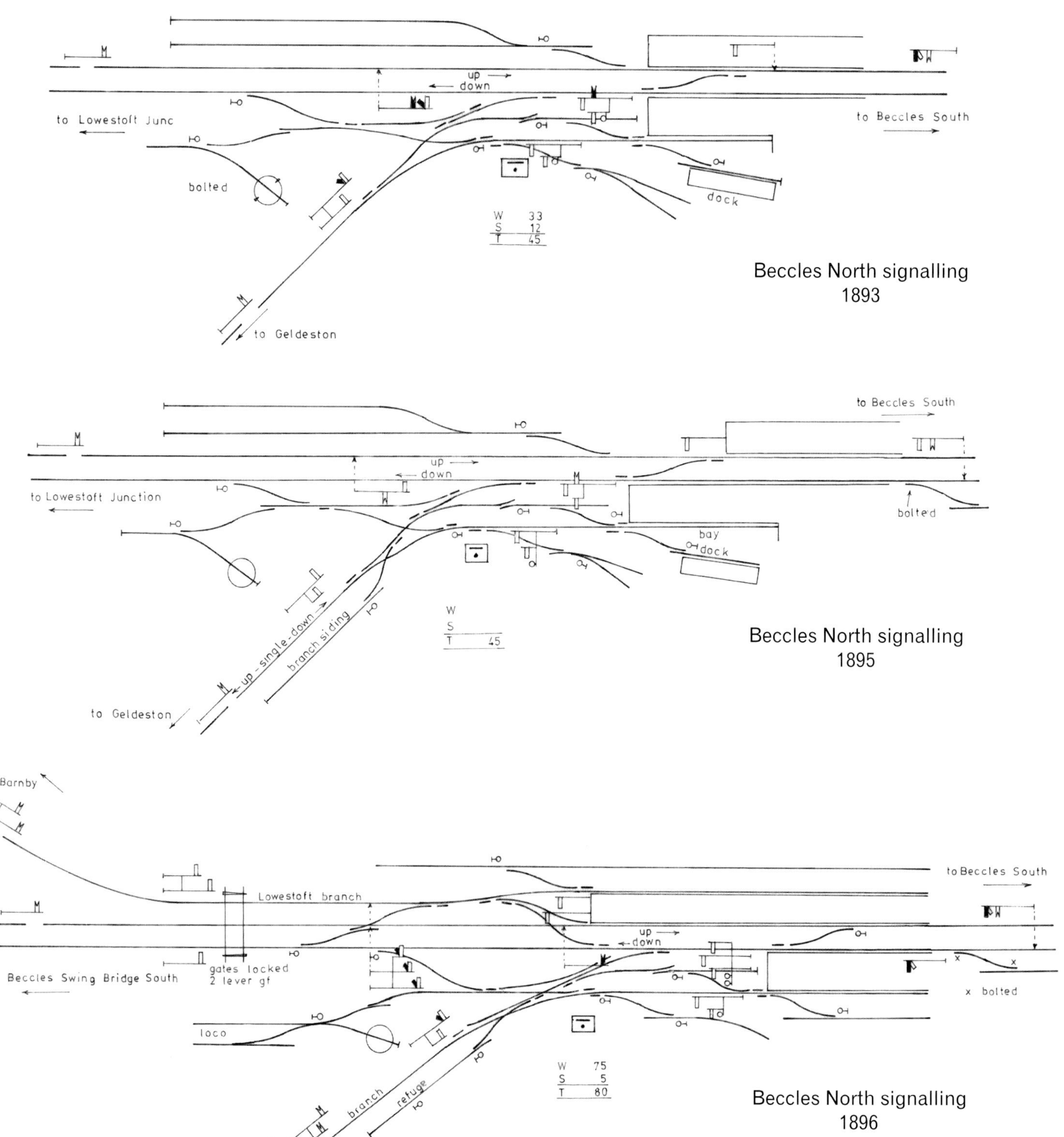

Beccles North signalling 1893

Beccles North signalling 1895

Beccles North signalling 1896

The signalman's view of the station from Beccles North signal box in October 1911. Immediately ahead is the Down or Waveney Valley bay platform, 420 feet in length, with the Down main platform and Up main platform beyond. The fine array of signals protects the junction whilst the parachute water tank to the left was provided to replenish locomotives on both the Down main line and the bay platform road. *GERS/ Windwood 1323*

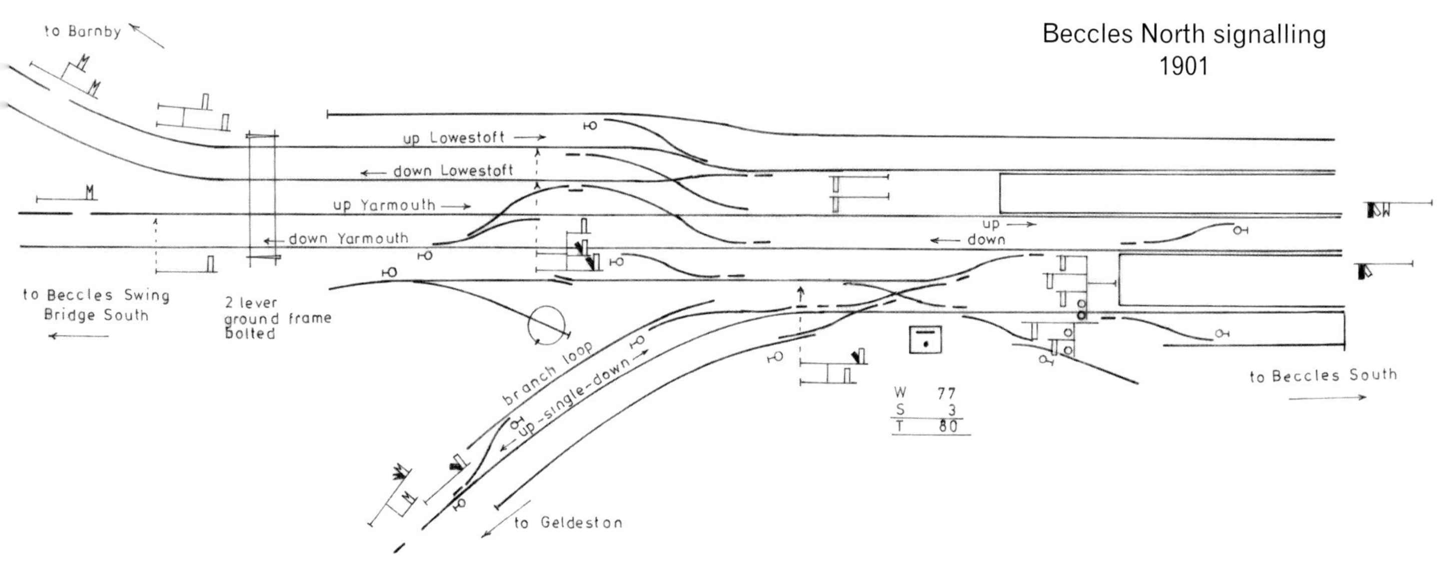
to Barnby
up Lowestoft
down Lowestoft
up Yarmouth
down Yarmouth
to Beccles Swing Bridge South
2 lever ground frame bolted
up
down
branch loop
up-single-down
to Geldeston
W 77
S 3
T 80
to Beccles South

Beccles North signalling 1901

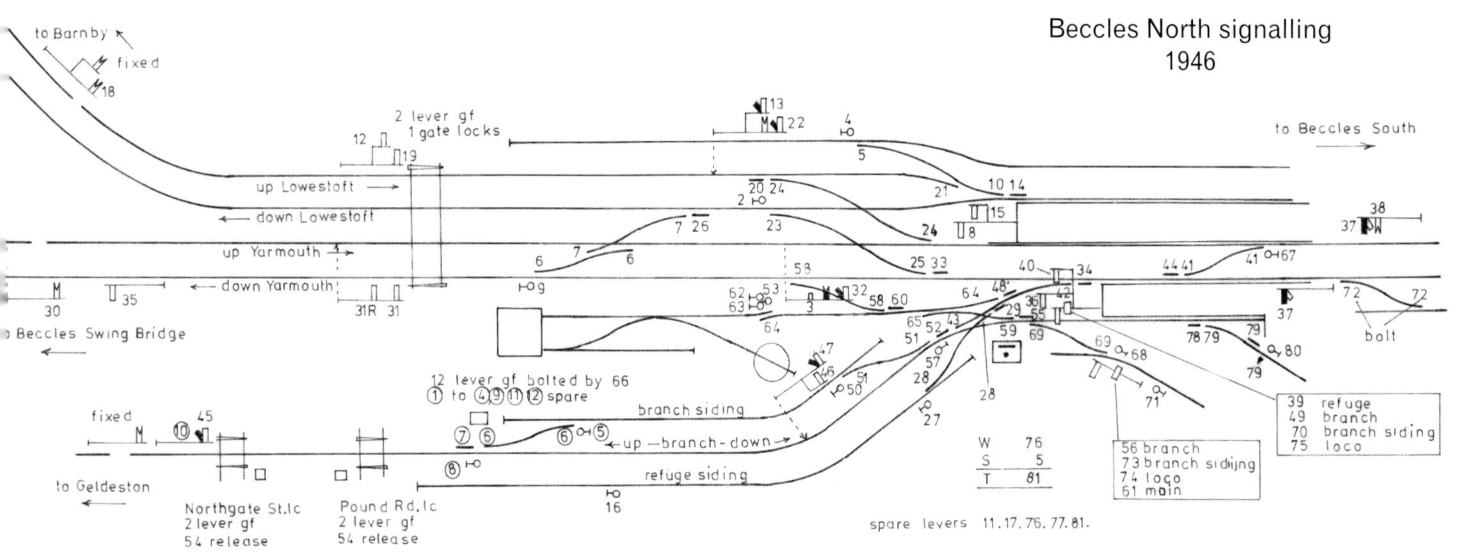
to Barnby
fixed
2 lever gf 1 gate locks
up Lowestoft
down Lowestoft
up Yarmouth
down Yarmouth
to Beccles Swing Bridge
to Beccles South
bolt
12 lever gf bolted by 66
① to ④⑨⑪⑫ spare
branch siding
up -branch- down
refuge siding
fixed
to Geldeston
Northgate St.lc
2 lever gf
54 release
Pound Rd.lc
2 lever gf
54 release
W 76
S 5
T 81
spare levers 11.17.76.77.81.
56 branch
73 branch siding
74 loco
61 main
39 refuge
49 branch
70 branch siding
75 loco

Beccles North signalling 1946

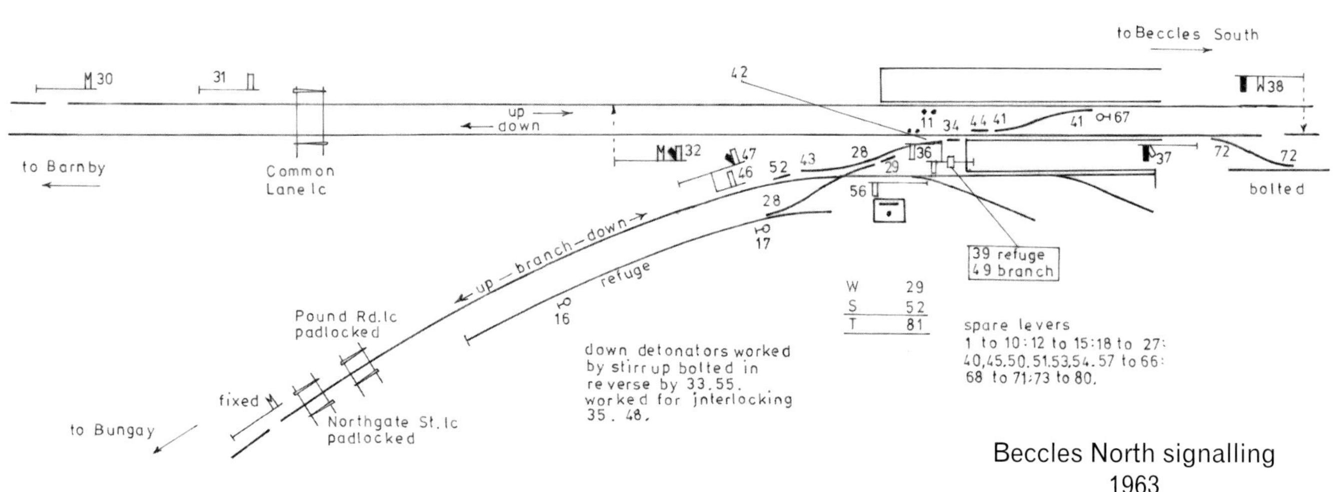
to Beccles South
up
down
to Barnby
Common Lane lc
bolted
up - branch - down
refuge
39 refuge
49 branch
Pound Rd.lc padlocked
fixed
Northgate St.lc padlocked
to Bungay
W 29
S 52
T 81
down detonators worked by stirrup bolted in reverse by 33.55. worked for interlocking 35. 48.
spare levers
1 to 10:12 to 15:18 to 27:
40,45.50.51.53.54.57 to 66:
68 to 71:73 to 80.

Beccles North signalling 1963

Beccles South signal box, of timber construction measuring 20 feet by 11 feet with operating floor 12 feet 6 inches above rail level, was provided in 1879 to control the points and signals at the south end of the station. It is uncertain as to how many levers were initially provided but a new Saxby & Farmer 38-lever duplex trigger frame with 4-inch centres and containing 34 working and 4 spare levers was provided in 1896. This frame was subsequently enlarged to 40 levers with 37 working and 3 spare levers in 1927 and then amended to 39 working and 1 spare lever in 1932 to cover control and locking of the moveable section of the Up platform which was released by No. 16 lever. The number of working levers reduced after rationalisation of facilities and the run-down of the East Suffolk line, especially after the singling of the section between Beccles and Oulton Broad North on 21st July 1985. The signal box was abolished on 16th February 1986.

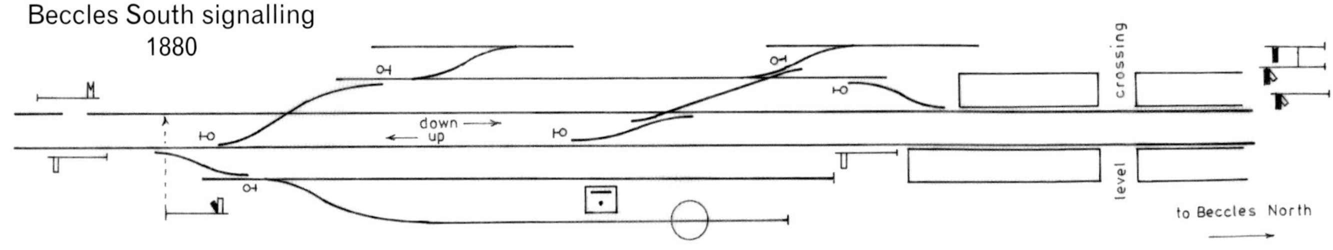

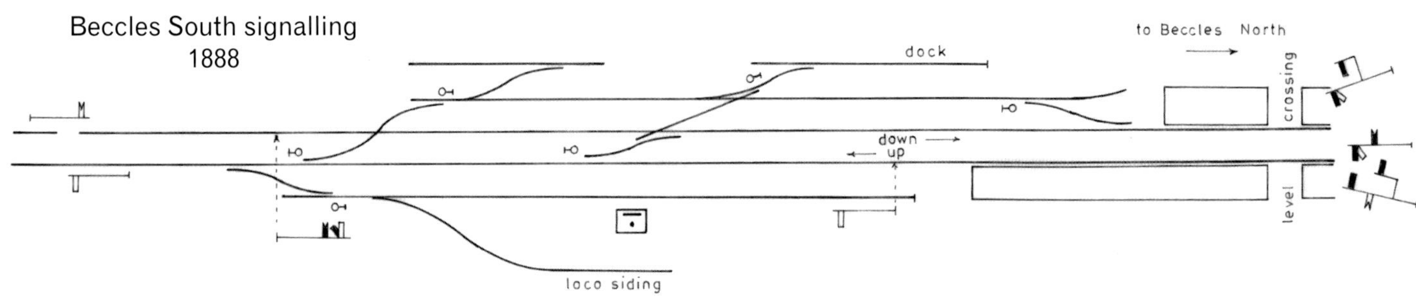

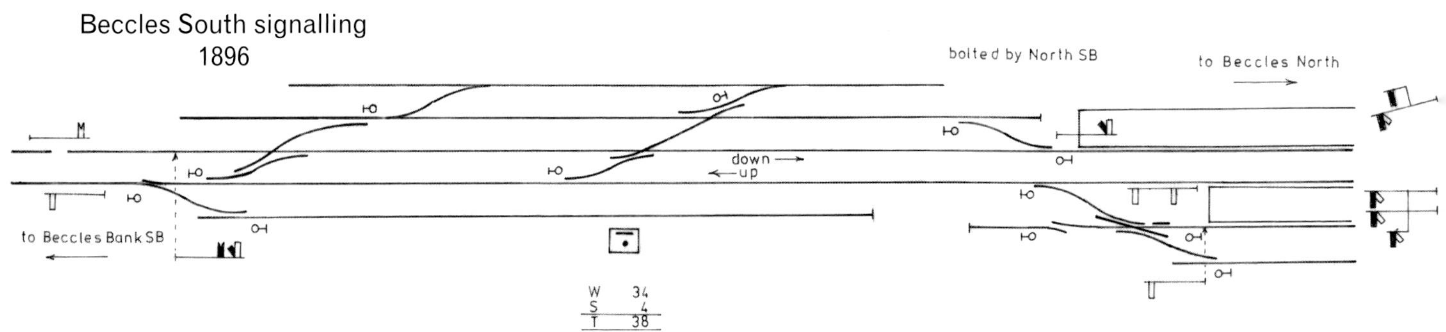

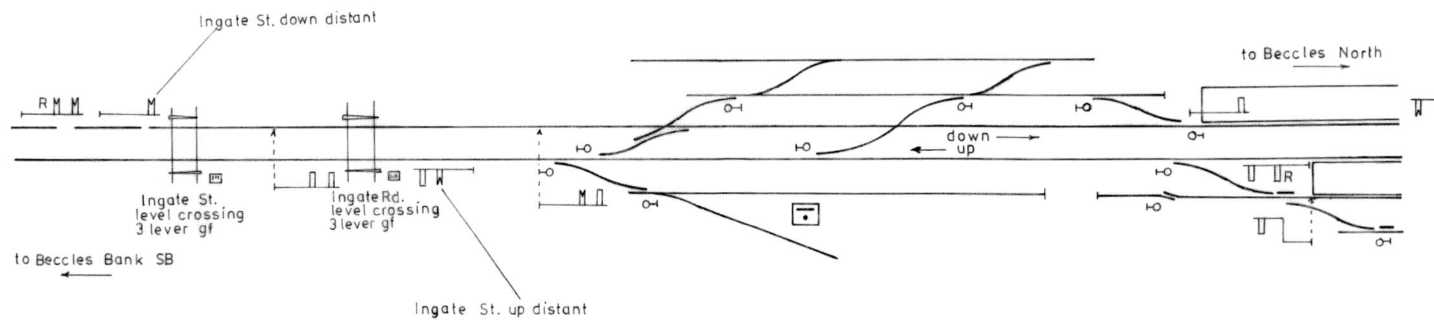

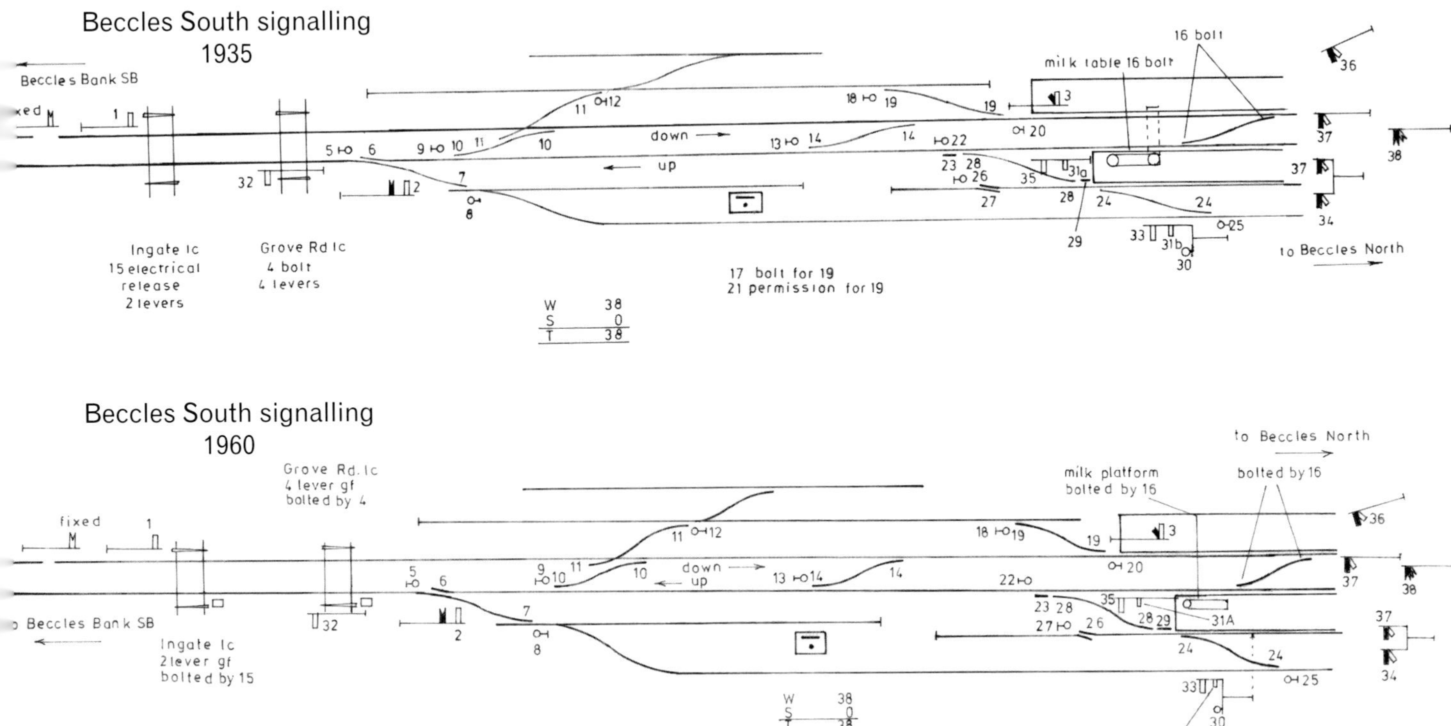

Signal Box Opening Times

In 1891 Tivetshall Station signal box was open continuously on weekdays but closed on Sundays from 6.00am until 9.00pm between the running of booked trains. On the branch, Pulham Market, Pulham St. Mary, Harleston, Homersfield, Earsham, Bungay, Ditchingham, Ellingham and Geldeston signal boxes were all closed at night and on Sundays. Beccles Station South, Beccles Station North and Beccles Junction signal boxes were open continuously. The same timings were in operation in 1897. By 1902 Tivetshall was open day and night on weekdays and closed on Sundays from 6.00am until 9.00pm between the running of booked trains; the branch station signal box timings were unchanged, whilst Beccles North Junction and Beccles South signal boxes were open day and night.

By 1919 Tivetshall signal box was open continuously from 9.00pm Sunday until 6.00am the following Sunday, and then on Sundays for the running of trains shown in the working timetable and for trains specially advised. The branch signal boxes were open for the running of trains shown in the working timetable and for trains specially advised, whilst Beccles North Junction was open continuously, with Beccles South open continuously on weekdays and for the running of trains shown in the working timetable and for trains specially advised on Sundays.

93

Stations and Signal Boxes.		Distance from Signal Box next above.		Refuge Sidings.		Opening and Closing.
Stations.	Signal Boxes.	Miles.	Chains.	Down.	Up.	
WAVENEY VALLEY LINE.						
Beccles	North Junction	...	...	41*	...	Open Day and Night. * Available for Down Main Line trains only.
Geldeston	Station	2	44	...	...	Closed at Night, and on Sundays.
Ellingham	,,	1	41	...	...	,, ,, ,,
Ditchingham	,,	1	42	...	...	,, ,, ,,
Bungay	,,	...	71	...	...	,, ,, ,,
Earsham	,,	...	67	...	...	,, ,, ,,
Homersfield	,,	3	14	...	...	,, ,, ,,
Harleston	,,	2	47	41	U	,, ,, ,,
Pulham Mary	,,	2	49	...	...	,, ,, ,,
Pulham Market	,,	1	2	...	...	,, ,, ,,
Tivetshall	,,	2	48	...	...	See Colchester Main Line.

(BLOCK.)

Hours of opening and closing of signal boxes, 1910.

WAVENEY VALLEY LINE.

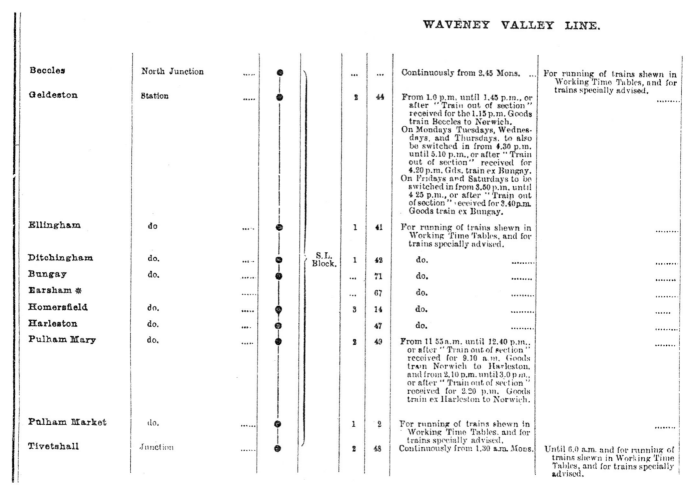

Beccles	North Junction	S.L. Block.	...	...	Continuously from 2.45 Mons.	For running of trains shewn in Working Time Tables, and for trains specially advised.
Geldeston	Station		2	44	From 1.0 p.m. until 1.45 p.m., or after "Train out of section" received for the 1.15 p.m. Goods train Beccles to Norwich. On Mondays Tuesdays, Wednesdays, and Thursdays, to also be switched in from 4.30 p.m. until 5.10 p.m., or after "Train out of section" received for 4.20 p.m. Gds. train ex Bungay. On Fridays and Saturdays to be switched in from 3.50 p.m. until 4 25 p.m., or after "Train out of section" received for 3.40 p.m. Goods train ex Bungay.	....
Ellingham	do		1	41	For running of trains shewn in Working Time Tables, and for trains specially advised.	....
Ditchingham	do.		1	42	do.	....
Bungay	do.		...	71	do.	....
Earsham *			...	67	do.	....
Homersfield	do.		3	14	do.	....
Harleston	do.			47	do.	....
Pulham Mary	do.		2	40	From 11 55 a.m. until 12.40 p.m., or after "Train out of section" received for 9.10 a.m. Goods train Norwich to Harleston, and from 2.10 p.m. until 3.0 p.m., or after "Train out of section" received for 2.20 p.m. Goods train ex Harleston to Norwich.	....
Pulham Market	do.		1	2	For running of trains shewn in Working Time Tables, and for trains specially advised.	....
Tivetshall	Junction		2	48	Continuously from 1.30 a.m. Mons.	Until 6.0 a.m. and for running of trains shewn in Working Time Tables, and for trains specially advised.

Above: Hours of opening and closing of signal boxes, 1924.

In 1927 Tivetshall Junction signal box was open continuously from 1.30am on Monday until 6.00am the following Sunday and then for trains shown in the working timetable and for trains specially advised. Pulham Market, Harleston and Bungay signal boxes were open on weekdays for the running of trains shown in the working timetable and for trains specially advised. Pulham St. Mary was open from 1.45pm until 2.40pm and from 3.55pm until 5.05pm each weekday, and then from 7.00pm until 7.40pmSX. Whenever it was necessary for either the 1.15pm goods train ex Beccles or the 3.50pm goods train ex Wymondham to stop at Pulham St. Mary to attach traffic, the station foreman at Pulham St. Mary had to arrange for the signal box to be switched in and advise the station masters at Harleston and Pulham Market accordingly. The station master at Pulham Market then advised the driver and guard of the Down train and the station master at Harleston had to advise the driver and guard of the Up train of the circumstances. Homersfield signal box was open from 9.00am until 11.00am or after 'train out of section' was received for the 4.30am goods train from Norwich to Beccles. It then opened again from 2.30pm until 3.05pm or until 'train out of section' was received for the 1.15pm goods train ex Beccles. Ditchingham signal box opened on Mondays to Thursdays from 11.00am until 2.10pm or after 'train out of section' was received for the 1.15pm goods train from Beccles to Trowse, and then again from 4.15pm until 5.00pm or after 'train out of section' was received for the 4.20pm goods train from Bungay to Beccles. On Fridays and Saturdays the afternoon opening was from 3.05pm until 4.05pm or until 'train out of section' was received for the 3.40pm Bungay to Beccles goods train. Ellingham was open from 12.15pm to 2.15pm, then from 4.15pm until 5.00pmFSX or 3.35pm until 4.20pmFSO, and from 8.15pm until 'train out of section' was received for the 7.45pmSX, 7.50pmSO passenger train from Norwich to Beccles. Geldeston signal box opened from 12.10pm until 1.45pm or until 'train out of section' was received for the 1.15pm Beccles to Trowse goods train. Beccles North Junction signal box was open continuously on weekdays and for the running of trains shown in the working timetable and for trains specially advised on Sundays. Beccles South signal box was open continuously from 2.45am on Monday, whilst on Sundays it opened for the running of trains shown in the working timetable and for trains specially advised.

By 1937, Tivetshall Junction signal box was open continuously on weekdays until 6.00am on Sunday, then for the running of trains shown in the working timetable and for trains specially advised and then again from 11.30pm. Pulham Market, Harleston and Bungay signal boxes were open on weekdays and Sundays for trains shown in the working timetable and for trains specially advised. Beccles North Junction and Beccles South were opened continuously from 4.00am on Monday until 8.15am the following Sunday, and then for the running of trains shown in the working timetable and for those specially advised. Pulham St. Mary was open on weekdays for the branch goods train as required, and from 2.55pm until 5.05pm daily and also 7.00pm to 7.45pmSX. However, whenever it was necessary for either the 11.38am goods train ex Beccles or the 3.50pmSX/5.35pmSO goods train ex Wymondham to stop at

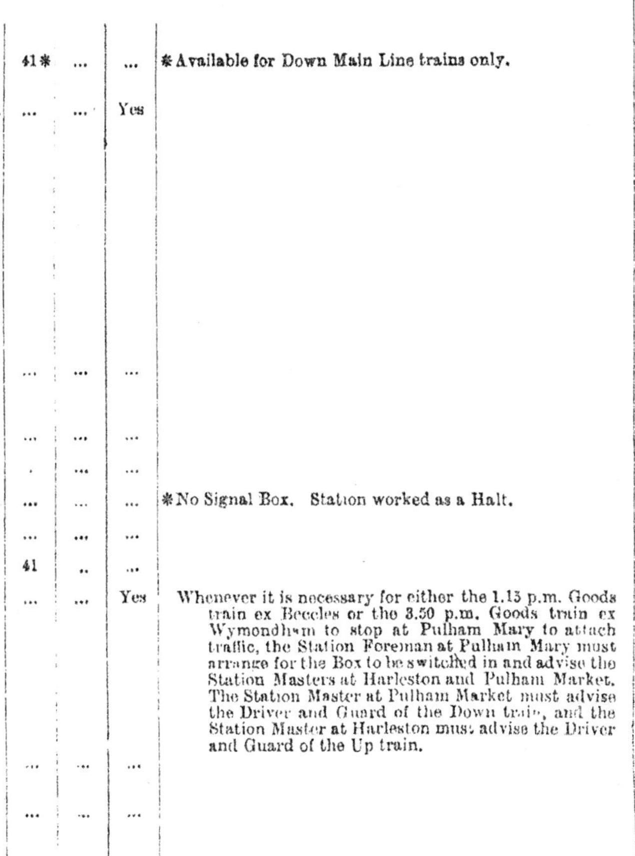

41*	...	...	*Available for Down Main Line trains only.
...	...	Yes	
...	...	...	
...	...	...	
.	...	...	
...	...	...	*No Signal Box. Station worked as a Halt.
...	...	...	
41	..	...	
...	...	Yes	Whenever it is necessary for either the 1.15 p.m. Goods train ex Beccles or the 3.50 p.m. Goods train ex Wymondham to stop at Pulham Mary to attach traffic, the Station Foreman at Pulham Mary must arrange for the Box to be switched in and advise the Station Masters at Harleston and Pulham Market. The Station Master at Pulham Market must advise the Driver and Guard of the Down train, and the Station Master at Harleston must advise the Driver and Guard of the Up train.
...	...	...	
...	...	...	

Pulham St. Mary to attach traffic the station foreman at Pulham St. Mary had to arrange for the signal box to be switched in and advise the station masters at Harleston and Pulham Market. The station master at Pulham Market was to advise the driver and guard of the Down train and the station master at Harleston to advise the driver and guard of the Up train. Homersfield signal box was to open when necessary on weekday for the 7.30am goods train ex Beccles and then from 9.00am until 11.35am or after the 'train out of section' was received for the 3.15am goods train from Norwich and then from 1.55pm until 3.30pm or after 'train out of section' was received for the 2.28pm goods train ex Norwich. It then reopened from 7.05pm until 8.30pm or after the 'train out of section' was received for the 3.50pmSX/5.35pmSO goods train ex Wymondham. At Ditchingham the box was open from 11.00am to 2.15pm or after 'train out of section' was received for the branch goods train, and then from 4.30pm until 6.25pm and again from 8.00pm until 9.20pm or until 'train out of section' was received for the 7.55pm train ex Norwich. The signal box was also to open for the 3.50pmSX/5.35pmSO goods Wymondham to Beccles when there was any traffic to attach or detach, with Bungay and Ditchingham station masters arranging as necessary. Ellingham signal box opened from 11.00am until 2.15pm or after 'train out of section' was received for the branch goods, and again from 4.30pm until 5.45pm and then from 8.15pm until 'train out of section' was received for the 7.55pm Norwich to Beccles train. Geldeston signal box was open from 11.30am until 12.30pm or after 'train out of section' was received for the branch goods, and then from 4.30pm until 6.15pm and again from 8.15pm until 9.20pm or until 'train out of section' was received for the 7.55pm Norwich to Beccles train.

In 1940 Tivetshall signal box was open from 11.30pm Sunday continuously until 5.30am the following Sunday and then for trains shown in the working timetable and for trains specially advised. On weekdays Pulham Market, Harleston and Bungay signal boxes were open for trains shown in the working timetable and for those specially advised, whilst Pulham St. Mary was open from 10.50am until 11.25am, and then from 3.55pm until 5.30pm. Along the branch Homersfield signal box was open from 8.10am until 9.45am and then from 5.25pm until 6.30pm. Ditchingham opened from 7.10am to 8.00am or after 'train out of section' was received for the branch goods, then from 7.30pm until 8.00pm or until 'train out of section' was received for the branch goods. At Ellingham the signal box opened from 6.50am to 7.30am or until 'train out of section' was received for the branch goods and then from 7.35pm until 8.10pm or after 'train out of section' was received for the branch goods. Geldeston opened from 6.20am until 7.15am or after 'train out of section' was received for the branch goods and then from 7.35pm until 8.10pm or until 'train out of section' was received for the branch goods. Beccles North Junction signal box opened continuously from 4.40am on Monday until 6.00am the following Sunday then for the running of trains shown in the working timetable or trains specially advised. On Sundays Pulham Market, Harleston and Bungay were open for trains specially advised, all other branch signal boxes being switched out. These timings continued in operation until 1943.

By 1945 Tivetshall was open continuously on weekdays and until 5.30am on Sundays, then for trains shown in the working timetable and for trains specially advised, and then from 11.30pm on Sundays. On weekdays Pulham Market, Harleston, Bungay and Ditchingham were open for the running of trains shown in the working timetable and for trains specially advised. Pulham St. Mary was open from 8.15am until 'train out of section' was received for 4.50pm train ex Harleston; Homersfield, Ellingham and Geldeston were open from 6.00am until 'train out of section' was received for 4.50pm train ex Harleston. Beccles North and Beccles South signal boxes were open continuously on weekdays and Sundays. On Sundays the branch signal boxes at Pulham Market, Harleston, Bungay, Ditchingham, Ellingham and Geldeston were only open for trains specially advised.

In 1952 Tivetshall signal box was open continuously from 6.00pm on Sunday until 'train out of section' was received for the 2.55am train ex Liverpool Street the next Sunday, and then from 8.45am until 'train out of section' was received for the 2.40am ex Norwich on Monday. It was also to be open for trains specially advised. On the branch, Pulham Market, Harleston and Bungay signal boxes were open for the running of trains shown in the working timetable Mondays to Saturdays and for trains specially advised on Sundays. Pulham St. Mary, Homersfield, Ditchingham, Ellingham and Geldeston signal boxes were only open as required for traffic purposes. Beccles North Junction signal box was open continuously whilst Beccles South was open continuously from 5.00am on Monday until 'train out of section' was received for the last booked train or trains specially advised on Sundays.

In 1961 Tivetshall signal box was open during the winter months from 4.20pm on Sunday until 'train out of section' was received for the 2.30am news train from Liverpool Street the following Sunday, then from 9.00am to 'train out of section' for the 3.00pm train ex Norwich on winter Sundays and 9.00am on Sunday until 6.00am the following Sunday during the summer months. In the same year, Beccles North Junction signal box was open during the winter months from 5.35am until 'train out of section' was received for the 9.20pm train ex Ipswich SX and 11.16pm ex Beccles SO, then from 10.07am to 'train out of section' was received for the 2.46pm ex Yarmouth and than from 6.16pm until 'train out of section' for the 7.50pm ex Ipswich on Sundays. In the summer months it was open from 5.35am until 'train out of section' was received for the 9.20pm ex Ipswich train SX, the 11.31pm ex Beccles SO and from 10.07am to 'train out of section' was received for the 9.42pm train ex Yarmouth on Sundays.

Special Instructions

By special order No. 1206 of 1st June 1904 and superseded by instruction No. 1106 of 5th September 1913 certain exemptions to Rule 99 for gates at intermediate public level crossings were permitted whereby the crossing could be kept open across the line between trains but had to be closed across the public road in sufficient time to prevent delay to trains and engines. The relevant level crossing on the branch were:

No.	Name	Located between
3	Hall Lane	Tivetshall and Pulham Market
4	Green Lane	Tivetshall and Pulham Market
5	Star	Tivetshall and Pulham Market
8	Turnpike	Tivetshall and Pulham Market
24	Crossingford	Pulham St. Mary and Harleston
31	Starston	Pulham St. Mary and Harleston
41	Redenhall	Harleston and Homersfield
44	Wortwell	Harleston and Homersfield
58	Denton Wash	Homersfield and Earsham
63	Five Acre Lane	Homersfield and Earsham
72	Factory	Bungay and Ditchingham
84	Braces Road	Ellingham and Geldeston
96	Northgate Street	Geldeston and Beccles

The maintenance of signalling and equipment on the branch was covered by staff based at Beccles and J. Riches, signal fitter, retired after 52½ years service, started in the engineering shop at Beccles in 1878 age 12½ years.

Over the years, as a result of alterations or amendments to signalling, special instructions were issued specific to certain locations. From 4th February 1904 an earlier instruction dated 1896 was superseded regarding points at Beccles station located at some distance from Beccles South signal box. A lever to work a disc indicating 'open points' or 'shut points' was located near the points leading from the Up main line to the Lowestoft back platform line and the station master was required to appoint a competent person to carry out the duty in conjunction with the signalman. After having asked the signalman to 'open points' for the purpose of: shunting a train or engine to or from the Up main line and the back platform line; or to or from the Up main line to the run round loop; or to or from the back platform line and the dead end siding; or to or from the run round road and the dead end siding, the competent person was to carefully turn the disc in the South signal box to 'shut points' immediately after the engine or vehicle had passed well clear of the respective points.

LIST OF SIGNAL BOXES,

YARMO

Description of Block System on Main Lines	SIGNAL BOX	Distance between Signal Boxes M.	Yds.	Addit Running UP
Single Line Block	Beccles North Junction	...	...	...
	Geldeston Station	2	982	...
	Ellingham Station	1	763	...
	Ditchingham Station	1	942	...
	Bungay Station	...	1561	...
	Earsham*	...	1530	...
	Homersfield Station	3	256	...
	Harleston Station	2	1041	...
	Pulham Mary Station	2	1097	...
	Pulham Market Station	1	51	...
	Tivetshall Junction	2	1065	...

Hours of opening and closing of signal boxes, 1947.

The lever also operated a gong in the signal box in conjunction with the disc and was worked by the appointed man as follows:

1	For points to or from the Up main line and back platform line	Pull lever over once
2	For points to or from the Up main line and run round road	Pull lever over twice
3	For points to and from the back platform road and dead end	Pull lever over 3 times
4	For points to and from the run round road and dead end	Pull lever over 4 times

The movement thus indicated to the signalman which points required to be operated.

During the operation the signalman in the South box was required to be careful not to move any of the points until he had received a proper indication on the gong. When the disc had been put back to 'shut points' the signalman was not to assume there was no obstruction but was required to personally confirm either himself or from the shunter that the Up main line and Lowestoft Up back platform line were clear before giving 'line clear' to the North Junction signalman or lowering any signals.

The block telegraph and signal working between Beccles South and North Junction signal boxes was the subject of a special order effective from 10th October 1904 superseding a special order of 1897. For trains in the Down direction the signalman at the South signal box was not to give 'line clear' under clause 4 of the block telegraph regulations to the signal box in the rear for a Down train

ADDITIONAL RUNNING LINES, LOOPS AND REFUGE SIDINGS

M 66

UTH S.T. AND LOWESTOFT CENTRAL VIA GORLESTON

ional Lines *	Loops and Refuge Sidings				HOURS SIGNAL BOX OPEN	REMARKS
	UP		DOWN			* Broken lines indicate lines worked by permissive or no Block Regulations
DOWN	Description †	Standage in wagons in addition to E.& V.	Description †	Standage in wagons in addition to E.& V.		† P.L.—Passenger Loop G.L.—Goods Loop R.S.—Refuge Siding
BECCLES AND TIVETSHALL (Waveney Valley Line)						
...	...	...	*RS	41	Continuously	* Available for Down Main Line trains only.
...	...	...	...	...	From 6.0 a.m. until T.O.S. received for 4.5 p.m. goods ex Harleston (M to S). For trains specially advised Sundays.	
...	...	...	...	...	From 6.0 a.m. until T.O.S. received for 4.5 p.m. goods ex Harleston (M to S). For trains specially advised, Sundays.	
...	...	...	...	...	For running of trains shown in W.T.T. (M to S) and specially advised Weekdays and Sundays.	
...	...	...	...	...	For running of trains shown in W.T.T. (M to S) and specially advised Weekdays and Sundays.	
...	...	...	...	...	... ...	* No Signal Box. Station worked as a Halt.
...	...	...	...	...	From 6.0 a.m. until T.O.S. received for 4.5 p.m. goods ex Harleston (M to S).	
...	...	...	RS	41	For running of trains shown in W.T.T. (M to S) and specially advised Weekdays and Sundays.	
...	...	...	...	...	From 8.15 a.m. until T.O.S. received for 1.20 p.m. goods ex Harleston (M to S).	
...	...	...	...	...	For running of trains shown in W.T.T. (M to S) and specially advised Weekdays and Sundays.	
...	...	...	...	...	Continuously Weekdays until 5.30 a.m. Sundays. For trains shown in W.T.T. and specially advised and from 11.30 p.m. Sundays.	

in response to a 'line clear' signal unless he had received the 'train out of section' signal from the North Junction signalman and the Down line was clear to the North Junction Down starting signal. The South signal box Down home and starting signals were slotted from the North Junction signal box and these slots normally displayed 'danger' and were only to be taken off when the Down main line was clear between the South and North Junction signal boxes for the passage of a train, care being taken to replace the slots to 'danger' when a train had arrived at the station. Discs worked from the North Junction signal box in connection with these slots were fitted in the South signal box and whenever the discs showed 'on' the signalman in the South box was to maintain his Down starting, home and distant signals at danger. In lieu of clause 5 of the Block Telegraph Regulations, amended instructions were followed. In the event of a Down train being brought to a stand at the South box Down home signal waiting 'line clear' from the North Junction signal box, the South box signalman was required to call the attention of the North Junction signalman and, having obtained it, send a special signal (2-2-2); on the receipt the North Junction signalman, if the line was clear between the signal boxes, was to respond by shifting the needle on the block instrument to 'line clear' and take his slot off the South box Down home and starting signals, after which the signalman in the South box cleared his home and starting signals for the train to proceed. Whenever the disc in the South box worked from the North Junction in conjunction with the North Junction Down distant signal showed 'on', the South box signalman had to maintain his Down starting, home and distant signals at danger until the speed of the train had been retarded to enable it to stop at the next signal in advance; when if the Down line was clear to the station and 'line clear' had been received from the North Junction, the South box signalman could lower his home and starting signals for the train to proceed as far as the line was clear. If, after the train had passed into the section between the South and North Junction signal boxes, the South box signalman had to send a 'train entering section' signal and deal with the train himself. If the train terminated and movement did not affect the signal box in advance, a 'cancelling' signal had to be sent to the North Junction signal box as soon as the line was clear to the North Junction, the signalman responding with a repeat call on the block bell.

For Up trains the signalman at Beccles North Junction was not to give 'line clear' under clause 4 of the Block Telegraph Regulations to Beccles Swing Bridge South signal box for an Up train or engine unless he had received the 'train out of section' signal from the South signal box and the Up main line was clear to the South signal box Up starting signal. The North Junction Up main and Lowestoft Branch to Up main inner home signals were slotted from the South signal box, the slot standing normally at 'danger' and was only to be taken off when the Up main line was clear between the North Junction and South signal boxes for the passage of a train. Care had to be taken to replace the slot to 'danger' when the train had arrived at the station. A disc worked from the South signal box in conjunction with the slot was fitted in the North Junction signal box and whenever the disc showed 'line blocked' the North Junction signalman was required to maintain his relevant inner home, outer home and distant signals at danger. Once an Up train had been brought to a stand at the North Junction outer home signal waiting 'line clear' from the South signal box, the outer home signal could be lowered to allow the train to proceed as far as the inner home signal. In lieu of clause 5 of the Block Telegraph Regulations the following instructions applied. In the event of an Up train being brought to a stand at the North Junction box Up home signal waiting 'line clear' from the South box, the North Junction signalman was to notify the South box and, having obtained their attention, send special signal (2-2-2) to the South box signalman who, if the line was clear between the two signal boxes, respond by moving the needle to 'line clear' and take his slot off the North Junction inner home signal to enable the train to pass into the station as far as the line was clear. Whenever the disc in the North Junction signal box worked by the South signalman in conjunction with the South signal box Up distant signal showed 'on', the North Junction signalman had to maintain his Up main and Lowestoft Branch to Up main inner, outer home and distant signals at danger until the train had been sufficiently retarded to stop at the next signal. Once 'line clear' had been received from the South signal box the North Junction signalman could lower his home signal to allow the train to proceed as far as the line was clear. If, after the train had passed into the section between the North Junction and South signal boxes, the signalman who sent 'train entering section' afterwards dealt with the train himself, he was to send the 'cancelling' signal to the signal box in advance as soon as the line was clear, the signalman receiving the call acknowledging by repeating the same number of beats on the block bell.

The working of the bolt-lock lever in the siding points operated from the South signal box required a separate instruction. The points of the connection between the Down main line and the sidings on the Bampton side of Beccles station were worked from the South box and bolt locked from the North Junction box. Whenever it was necessary for the siding points to be opened, the signalman in the South box had to work the bolt in the North Junction box asking for the points to be unlocked and the North Junction signalman, if in a position to do so, at once released the bolt lock which was indicated to the South box signalman by a disc showing 'unlocked'. After the signalman in the South box had closed the siding points he moved the disc in the North Junction signal box to the 'locked' position, after which the North Junction signalman bolt locked the points in the normal position.

Occupation of the Down main line outside of the station Down starting signal, and use of the crossover between the Down and Up main lines, required yet another instruction. Before the North Junction signalman granted occupation of the Down main line on the Bampton side of the station Down starting signal for shunting operations, or shunted an engine or vehicles through the crossover between the platforms or from the Down and Up main lines, he was required to send a 'blocking back' signal to the signalman in the South box and wait an acknowledgement; the signalman in the latter box was not to acknowledge the signal if he had accepted a Down train from the signal box in the rear under clause 4 of the Double Line Block Regulations. The signalman in the South box, after acknowledging the 'blocking back' signal received from the North Junction box, could only accept a Down train from the signal box in the rear under clause 5 of the Double Line Block Regulations. Whenever it was necessary for the South box signalman to pass an engine or vehicles on the Up main line to be afterwards passed to the Down main line through the crossover worked by the North Junction signal box he was required to send a special signal (2-1-2) to the North Junction box. The North Junction signalman, if in a position to accept the engine or vehicles, acknowledged by repeating the special signal and until the call was acknowledged no engine or vehicles were to use the crossover. The 'call attention' signal was to be used before making the special signal.

Specific instructions related to the working of the Waveney Valley Branch. The North Junction Waveney Valley Branch to the main Up home signal was slotted from the South signal box and was to be normally maintained at 'danger'; it was only to be taken off when the Up main line was clear between the North Junction and South signal boxes for the passage of a train from the Waveney Valley Branch to the Up main line, care being taken to replace the slot to 'danger' when the train had reached the station. A disc worked from the South signal box in connection with the slot was displayed in the North Junction signal box and whenever this showed 'line blocked' the North Junction signalman was to maintain his branch to main line home signal and distant signals at danger. The ordinary 'is line clear' signals were to be sent from the North Junction signal box to the South signal box for all trains and engines, but for the purpose of advising the South box signalman of Waveney Valley Branch trains destined for the Up main line platform the North Junction signalman was, immediately upon receiving 'line clear' from the South box signalman, to send a special signal (2-2-2-2) before giving 'train entering section' signal for the relevant train. When it was necessary to run a train from the Waveney Valley Branch to the Down main platform the train had to be brought to a stand at the branch home signal and piloted to the Down main platform by a competent member of staff appointed by the station master. In such cases the North Junction signalman gave a hand signal for the train to proceed to the platform; taking care that he had sent a 'blocking back' signal to the South box signalman and on obtaining his acknowledgement maintain the slot on the South box Down home signal and also maintain his Down home signals at danger. Movements in to and out of the refuge siding alongside the Waveney Valley Branch, the signalman in the North Junction signal box was forbidden to grant permission for a train to back from the refuge siding on to the Down main line until he had sent the 'blocking back' signal to the signalman in the South box and obtained his acknowledgement; such acknowledgement being withheld if he had accepted a Down train from the box in the rear. The signalman in the South box, after acknowledging the 'blocking back' signal from the North Junction box, could not give permission for a Down train to approach from the signal box in the rear until the train which was being shunted out of the refuge siding had come to a stand. When the rear of that train was well behind the Down home signal he could accept a train from the signal box in the rear under the 'section clear but station or junction blocked' signal.

The shunting of vehicles on the main line between the South and North Junction signal boxes also required special attention. In the event of an engine or vehicles being required to pass over the Down or Up main lines between the signal boxes, and the signalman initiating the shunt movement did nor work the points by which the vehicles were shunted off the main line, he was beholden, if the movement was in the right direction, to send a special signal (3-3-3) to the signalman in advance. If the signalman receiving the special signal was in a position to accept the shunt movement he was required to acknowledge by repeating the signal on his block bell. Once the shunt movement was completed and the engine or vehicles were clear of the main line the signalman controlling the operation was to send 'train out of section' to the signal box from whence the movement was initiated. If the engine or vehicles were being shunted in the wrong direction along the Down line the initiating signalman in North Junction box sent special signal (2-4) to the South signal box, and if the signalman receiving the call was in a position to accept the engine or vehicles he responded by sending a repeat signal, but if he was not in a position to accept the engine or vehicles he was not to acknowledge the signal in any way, and until the special signal had been acknowledged by repetition no shunting movement was to take place. If the shunt movement was accepted and completed, and the engine or vehicles had arrived under the control of the South box signalman and been shunted clear of the Down line, the signalman was to send special signal (4-2) to the North Junction box, the call being acknowledged by repetition. If an engine or vehicle required movement in the wrong direction along the Up line the signalman in South signal box who requested the movement had first to send special signal (2-6) to North Junction box. If the signalman in receipt of the signal was in a position to accept the engine or vehicles over the Up line he responded by repeating the special call, but if he was not in a position to accept the movement he was not to respond in any way and until the signal had been repeated no engine or vehicle was permitted to leave. When the engine or vehicles had arrived under the control of the signalman in North Junction signal box and been shunted clear of the Up main line, the receiving signalman was to send special signal (6-2) to the initiating signalman, the call being repeated as an acknowledgement. When a shunter accompanied the vehicles or engine movement, the signalman disposing of the vehicles off the main line was not to advise the line was clear until the shunter in charge of the operation or horseman had confirmed the shunting movement was completed. In the case of a light engine not accompanied by a shunter, the signalman was personally responsible for ensuring the engine was clear of the main line. All special signals had to be preceded by the 'call attention' signal.

Special instructions were also relevant to the working of the back platform line on the Up side of Beccles station. The North Junction signal box Lowestoft Branch Up home signal for the Up back platform line was slotted from the South signal box, the slot standing normally at 'danger' and was only to be taken 'off' when the Up back platform line was clear to receive a train, care being taken to replace the slot to 'danger' once the train had arrived. A disc worked from the South box in connection with this slot was fitted in the North Junction signal box and whenever the disc showed 'line blocked' the North Junction signalman was required to maintain his relevant inner and outer home signals and distant signals at danger. If the Up back platform was not clear when 'is line clear' signal was requested from the North Junction signal box, or if the South box signalman required to occupy that line before the arrival of the branch train from Lowestoft, he had to respond by sending special call (2-2-2-2) to show that was aware of the situation and be careful to maintain the disc in the North Junction signal box at 'line blocked'. On the receipt of this (2-2-2-2) signal the North Junction signalman was only to allow the train to approach from Barnby signal box or Carlton Colville station under the 'section clear but station or junction blocked' signal. If the Up back platform and Up main line platforms were both occupied and it was necessary for the signalman in the North Junction box to accept a following train from the Lowestoft Branch, whether the train was destined for the back platform or Up main platform, he had to accept the train under 'section clear but station or junction blocked' signal. When a Down train had departed the Up back platform for either Lowestoft or Yarmouth and the line was clear the North Junction signalman was required to intimate the fact to the South Box signalman by sending special signal (2-1) 'train out of section' which then had to be acknowledged. If at any time vehicles were left standing in the Up back platform after the departure of a train the signalmen in both the South and North Junction boxes were to ensure that a competent person appointed by the station master was made aware of the fact so that the man could advise when the movement of the vehicles away from the platform could be arranged. When it was necessary for the 'section clear but station or junction blocked' signal to be given to the driver of a Down train starting from the Up back platform, either for Lowestoft or Yarmouth, the signalman in the North Junction box had to obtain the sanction of the station master or foreman porter by sounding a gong located under the canopy on the Up platform. He then verbally called that the 'section was clear but station blocked' or 'section clear but swing bridge blocked' depending on the route – the instruction being passed on to the driver by the station master or foreman porter. After being notified the driver had been informed, the signalman lowered the starting signal for the train to depart.

In the event of fog or falling snow the station master was to appoint a fogsignalman at the Waveney Valley line Down distant and home signals. If the fogsignalmen were not at their posts the signalman at North Junction signal was not to give permission for a train to pass his signal box unless the branch back platform was clear or he was in a position to signal the train onto the main line. This procedure remained in force until the fogsignalmen had taken Up their respective positions. Similar arrangements were made for a train approaching from the Lowestoft Branch.

From 28th June 1906 an electric rail contact was placed 300 yards ahead of the Down main line advanced starting signal at Tivetshall. The purpose was to advise the signalman when a train had passed the signal the engine by activating the contact caused a bell to ring in the signal box. The bell continued to ring until the signalman placed the Down advanced starting signal to danger. But if the bell continued to sound after the signal was placed to danger a button was provided for the signalman to deactivate the bell. The instruction reminded the signalman that the contact and bell were provided to assist the signalman in the performance of his duties and was not intended to relieve him of keeping a good look out, neither did it supersede or interfere with Block Telegraph Regulations.

From 4th June 1907, special working was introduced at Beccles North Junction regarding trains arriving and departing on the Waveney Valley Branch. The signalman at Beccles North Junction was not to accept a train from Geldeston either under the 'allow train to enter section' signal or 'section clear but station or junction blocked' signal if he had signalled a train or vehicles to shunt from the station on to the main single line, or into the Down refuge siding on the Waveney Valley Branch, or into the siding on the north side of the Waveney Valley Branch, until the main single line was clear, or the train or vehicles had passed clear to either of the sidings. In like manner, if he had accepted a train from Geldeston under either the 'allow train to enter section' or 'station clear but station or junction blocked' signal, he was not to allow a train or vehicle to shunt from the station on to the main single line or into either of the sidings until the train from Geldeston had arrived at the station or been brought to a stand at the branch outer home signal.

For the purpose of advising the Beccles North signalman when a Down train or engine on the Waveney Valley Branch was

Pulham Mary
for Pulham Mkt
Mr Barton
" Firth
C. C. Engr
CFM
Mr Russell
" Watts
" Sedman
" Judd
Inspr Greenfield
" Rowe
" Worsted
Mr Wells
" Prytherch
MO. 24.

3/1/16

76625

INSTRUCTION
No. 1401, 1916.

Great Eastern Railway.

Chief Traffic Manager's Department,
Liverpool Street Station,
January 3rd, 1916.

PULHAM MARKET STATION.

New Siding on Beccles side of Station.

(With Points Facing Down and Up Trains.)

1. A Ground Locking Frame is fixed near to the Points at the Beccles end of the Siding. The Levers are numbered consecutively from 1 to 13. No. 1 Lever works the Signal applicable from Main Single Line to Siding; No. 2 Lever works the Facing Point Lock; No. 3 Lever works the Points in the Main Single Line; No. 4 Lever works the Points leading to and from the Siding next the Main Single Line; No. 5 Lever works the Ground Disc Signal applicable from the Siding to the Main Single Line; No. 6 Lever is the Lock on the Siding Gate; No. 7 Lever works the Signal applicable from the Naval Siding to the Siding next the Main Single Line; No. 8 Lever works the Slot on the Up Outer Home Signal; No. 9 Lever works the Slot on the Down Starting Signal; No 10 Lever locks the relative Lever in the Signal Box; No. 11 Lever works a Disc in the Signal Box shewing "Lock Points" or "Unlock Points"; and Nos. 12 and 13 Levers are spare. A Disc is also fixed in the Ground Locking Frame Hut shewing when the Points are "Locked" or "Unlocked."

2. The man appointed to work the Ground Locking Frame must pull over No. 11 Lever if an engine or vehicles are required to be shunted into or out of the Siding.

3. The Signalman must then, if in a position to do so and the Line is properly protected by the Signals, unlock the Points by the corresponding Lever in his Box, and the man in charge of the Locking Frame must then place his Slots on the Down Starting Signal and Up Outer Home Signal, after which he must pull over No. 10 Lever, which will lock the relative Lever in the Signal Box, and then pull over the Levers as required.

4. When the shunting operations are completed, the man in charge of the Locking Frame must immediately replace the Points, the Siding Gate, and the Levers in the Locking Frame, in their proper position, and when the engine or engine and vehicles have left the Locking Frame for Pulham Mary he must so advise the Signalman on the Telephone, and the Signalman must then re-lock the Locking Frame from the Signal Box.

Note.—*The Locking Frame man must not take any person's word, but must, in all cases, see for himself that the Main Single Line is clear before he takes his Slots off the Signals.*

5. The Signal, applicable from the Naval Air Station Siding to the Siding next the Main Single Line, is to stand normally **"OFF,"** and is only to be placed to Danger when shunting to and from the Main Single Line.

6. Discs, worked from the Ground Locking Frame in connection with the Slots on the Down Starting Signal and Up Outer Home Signal, are fixed in the Station Signal Box, indicating **"ON"** or **"OFF,"** as the case may be; and whenever either of the Discs shew **"ON"** the Signalman must maintain all his Signals at Danger.

7. *(a.)* In the event of the Main Single Line at the Locking Frame being obstructed from any cause, the Locking Frame man must immediately send **6 beats** on the Telephone bell to the Signalman, who must at once place or maintain all his Signals at Danger and send the **Obstruction Danger** signal to the Signal Box on each side of him, and not allow a train to approach the Ground Locking Frame until he has received the **Obstruction removed** signal, viz.: **3 beats** (thus **2—1**), from the Locking Frame man.

(b.) When the Line is again clear, the Locking Frame man must send the **Obstruction removed** signal, viz.: **3 beats** (thus **2 - 1**), to the Signalman.

8. A **Telephonic communication** is established between the Ground Locking Frame Hut and the Station Signal Box.

The Station Master will be responsible that the men appointed to work the Ground Locking Frame, and to take charge of shunting operations, are fully competent for the duty. He will also be responsible for bringing this Instruction under the special notice of all his Staff concerned, and is requested to satisfy himself, by personal enquiry and observation, that the provisions of this Instruction are being strictly carried out.

Wm. C. MAY,
Chief Traffic Manager.

F. V. RUSSELL,
Superintendent of Operation.

This Instruction will come into operation on Wednesday, 5th January, 1916.

Special Instruction No. 1401 dated 3rd January 1916 for the Naval Air Station siding at Pulham Market.

approaching, or standing at, his outer home signal at danger, a rail contact was placed in the main single line about 50 yards outside the home signal, and when the engine reached the rail contact a bell sounded in the signal box, the bell continuing to ring until the signalman either lowered the branch outer home signal, or placed a switch hook on the small button to enable him to turn the commutator on his single line block telegraph instrument. The single line block instrument was provided with a switch hook, fixed between the small button and the plunger, and when the signalman required to stop the bell ringing during the time the train or engine was detained at the branch outer home signal, he was required to place the switch hook onto the small button. The signalman was not then in a position to turn his commutator to give the 'train out of section' signal to the signal box in the rear until he had lowered his branch outer home signal and then replaced it to danger. After the signalman had replaced his signal to danger he was to remove the switch hook from the small button, and if in a position to do so, turn the commutator and give the 'train out of section' signal to the signal box in the rear. The act of removing the switch hook from the small button caused the rail contact to become reconnected ready for use for the next train. A button was fixed in the signal box in connection with the rail contact to enable the signalman to stop the ringing of the bell when an Up train depressed the rail contact. The signalman at Beccles North Junction was not to lower his branch outer home signal for the purpose of allowing a train to draw up to the inner home signal until the bell denoted the engine had depressed the rail contact. The electrical arrangement was provided for the purpose of assisting the signalman in the performance of his duties but was not intended to relieve him of the responsibility of keeping a good lookout for trains, neither did it in any way supersede or interfere with the Single Line Block Telegraph Regulations.

Special instructions also referred to the ground-locking frame located at the Bungay end of the siding on the north side of the Waveney Valley Branch. The levers were numbered consecutively from 1 to 12 and functioned as under:

No. 1	Worked a disc to Beccles North Junction signal box.
No. 2	Locked the lever in the signal box.
No. 3	Slotted the station Down starting signals applicable to the Waveney Valley Branch.
No. 4	Spare lever.
No. 5	Worked the ground disc signal applicable from the siding to the main single line.
No. 6	Worked the points.

No. 7 Worked the facing point lock.
No. 8 Worked the ground disc signal applicable from the main single line to the siding.
No. 9 Spare lever.
No. 10 Slotted the branch outer home signal.
No. 11 Spare lever.
No. 12 Slotted the branch distant signal.

The station master was required to ensure each man appointed to work the ground frame was competent for the duty and the man so appointed was required to pull over No. 1 lever if a train or engine required to be shunted into or out of the siding, thus giving an indication to the signalman of the requirement to use the siding. The signalman was then, if the line was clear and properly protected by signals, required to unlock the siding points by the corresponding lever in the signal box and the man in charge of the locking frame then placed his slots on the station starting signals applicable to the Waveney Valley Branch and on the branch outer home and distant signals. This enabled him to pull No. 2 lever, which locked the lever in the signal box. He could then work the necessary points and ground disc signals from the ground frame to enable shunting operations to begin. When shunting was completed and the main single line clear, the man in charge of the locking frame placed the points and levers in the locking frame to their proper position; the signalman then again relocked them in that position from the signal box. The man in charge of the locking frame was personally responsible for ensuring the main single line was clear before taking the slots off the signals.

A disc worked from the ground locking frame in connection with the slot on the station Down starting signals was fixed in the North Junction signal box, indicating 'on' or 'off' as the case may be; whenever this disc showed 'on' the signalman was required to maintain all the Down signals applicable to the Waveney Valley Branch at danger. In the case of a Down train on the main line destined for the Waveney Valley Branch approaching while the disc showed 'on' the signalman had to – after the train had been brought to a stand or nearly at the home signal, and the line was clear in the station – lower the home signal to admit the train as far as the starting signal. Discs worked from the ground locking frame in connection with the slots on the branch Down outer home signal and branch distant signal were fixed in the North Junction signal box, indicating either 'on' or 'off', and whenever the discs indicated 'on' the signalman was required to maintain all signals applicable from the Waveney Valley Branch at danger.

The gates at Pound Road level crossing on the Waveney Valley Branch could be kept open across the line between trains, but special signals given on the electric bell by the signalman at North Junction in no way relieved the gateman of the responsibility of keeping a good look out for trains, closing the gates across the public road in sufficient time to prevent delays to trains or engines. The special electric bell and gong communication established between the North Junction signal box and the gate hut was governed by special regulations. When a train or engine required to depart Beccles station for the Waveney Valley Branch, the signalman in North Junction signal box sent a signal of 2 beats on the bell to the gateman at the level crossing; the latter, on receipt of the call, opened the gates for rail traffic, and when completed gave 2 beats on the gong to the signalman, who then lowered the signal for the train or engine to leave the station. The gateman was not to open the gates for road traffic until the train or engine had passed over the crossing. The signalman at North Junction signal box, on receipt of the 'train entering section' signal for a Down branch train or engine from Geldeston, gave 2 beats on the electric bell to the gateman at Pound Road; the latter on receipt of the signal opened the gates for rail traffic before giving 2 beats on the electric gong to the signalman, who then lowered his signals for the approaching train or engine. The gateman was not to open the gates for road traffic until the train or engine had been brought to a stand at the outer home signal or had passed over the crossing. The signalman on no account was to lower the signals for a train or engine in either direction until he had received the signal of 2 beats on the gong from the gateman. In the event of the main single line being obstructed, or likely to become obstructed at the level crossing by an accident, the gateman was to immediately send 6 beats call on the electric gong to the signalman at North Junction signal box, who was then required to maintain all his branch signals at danger and send the 'obstruction danger' signal (6 beats) to Geldeston. Thereafter no train or engine was permitted to proceed towards the level crossing until the 'cancelling' signal 8 beats (3-5) had been received from the gateman. When the single line was again clear the gateman was required to send a 'cancelling' call of 8 beats (3-5) to the signalman at North Junction.

Station Masters

In December 1921 George Thompson, the station master at Chettisham between Ely and March, gained promotion to take charge at Tivetshall where he served until retirement on 9th August 1930. A.W. Barnes, a relief clerk in Cambridge District Superintendent's Office, was appointed to the station master's position at Tivetshall in September 1930 but his stay was relatively short for he transferred to take charge at Bramford in February 1935. The new incumbent was Edward Hannant, who gained promotion from Bartlow to Tivetshall in the same month. Hannant moved on to Shippea Hill in June 1938 and two month later Arthur Mills, formerly station master at Fambridge on the Wickford to Southminster branch, gained promotion to take charge at Tivethall.

Frederick James Borrett, station master at Pulham St. Mary, was promoted to Harleston in January 1912, Frederick Walter Wright came from Aldeby to fill the resultant vacancy. Soon after his appointment he assumed control of Pulham Market station as part of rationalisation programme. He continued to reside in the station house at Pulham St. Mary, however, and in 1913 was paying an annual rent of £16. Wright stayed for just over a decade before moving on to take charge at Brundall in February 1924. Percy George Dines, station master at East Winch on the Kings Lynn to Dereham line, gained promotion to take control of the two stations; he took up residence in the station house in 1924, paying £13 per annum. Dines remained until September 1930, when he moved on to become station master at Harleston. Later, in January 1944, R.J. Woodward, formerly station master at Middle Drove, was appointed to take charge of Pulham Market with Pulham St. Mary. At the close of the operational years, Maurice Ayres was station master at Pulham Market in 1950. Along the line at Starston, for the few years it was open for traffic John B. Rudkin was recorded as station master in 1864, but was soon replaced by H. Welkes who had transferred from Redenhall.

James Ling Wilkinson served as station master at Harleston around 1860 and was shown as unmarried in the 1861 census, when he was living at the station house with his mother; however, he transferred to Beccles when the line reached that town. As mentioned above,

Geldeston station and signal box circa 1912, with the station master and his infant daughter and two members of staff on the platform. Note the full nameboard on the signal box denoting Geldeston Station Box and the full size running in or station nameboard to the centre. *Author's collection*

Frederick James Borrett gained promotion from Pulham St. Mary to Harleston in January 1912 and in 1913 was residing in the station house for an annual rent of £13. Borrett had a short incumbency, for in April 1916 William Williamott, a relief station master in the Norwich district gained promotion to take charge at Harleston and stayed for fourteen years before transferring on promotion to Bungay; in 1924 he was paying £21 rent per annum for the station house. Percy George Dines then became station master at Harleston but passed away on 31st March 1933. For a year the position was covered by relief staff until Charles P. Lincoln, formerly station master at Somerleyton, was promoted to take charge at Harleston in March 1934. He finally retired from Harleston on 19th March 1947, after fifty years service commencing at Norwich in 1897. On 12th March at the local Magpie Hotel, local traders and farmers presented him with an electric clock and a cheque whilst the station staff presented a set of pipes and tobacco. For a short period from May 1940, Lincoln was seconded on special duties and during this period William Ward, chief clerk at Harleston, was appointed acting station master. W.G. (Bill) Elsey was station master at Harleston from 1947 and had charge of neighbouring stations Pulham Market, Pulham Mary and Homersfield during the final years of branch operation.

Daniel Smith was recorded as station master at Redenhall in 1860, superseded by H. Welkes for a few months in 1863. In 1868 the question of rent allowance was raised where no station house was available. Benjamin Smith was station master in charge of Wortwell in 1864 and is believed to have served in that capacity until closure of the station.

Along the line at Homersfield, George Realph was station master in the 1890s. In January 1913 Henry James Clarke was station master at Homersfield, residing in the station house for a rent of £16 per annum, but in January 1923 he was promoted to Bealings on the East Suffolk line; two months later Charles Taylor, a clerk at Mistley, was appointed to the vacancy. Taylor, who was paying an annual rent of £21 for the station house in 1924, was incumbent until December 1928 when he gained promotion to Southminster, ultimately retiring as station master Maldon East on 18th August 1945 after forty-five years' service. Taylor's replacement was near at hand, for H.A. Havers, who had spent twenty-four years in the booking office at Halesworth, was appointed station master in February 1928. His tenure was short for in July 1929 John Moss transferred from Laxfield to become station master at Homersfield, where he stayed for nearly four years until in February 1933 he transferred to take charge at Lakenheath. John Shead, a clerk at Liverpool Street, took charge at Homersfield in June 1933 but was promoted to Billericay in November 1938. P. Stimpson, a clerk at Pulham Market became the next station master at Homersfield in January 1939, but his stay was short for R. Wilson, a relief clerk from Ipswich, was appointed acting station master at Homersfield in September 1941. Geoffrey Chapel was then transferred from Eye to take charge at Homersfield during World War Two, where he supervised the transfer of munitions and other traffic to and from local USAAF airfields including nearby Flixton; before the end of hostilities, however, he gained promotion to Harling Road. John (Jack) Mayhew was the last station master and was made redundant when the line closed to passenger traffic.

On the Waveney Valley Branch at Earsham, in 1868 Rudkin was in charge, earning an annual salary of £54 12s 0d and receiving an additional £6 10s 0d to rent accommodation locally. Frederick Charles Foulger, station master at Earsham until the station was taken under the control of Bungay, retired and passed away in July 1928, aged 81 years.

The initial station master at Bungay was Lovell Lawlor Allshorn, who departed sometime in 1865 to be succeeded by Norman Seeley, who was earning the magnificent salary of £110 per annum in 1868 with an additional £20 for housing allowance as there was no accommodation provided at the station. Then in the mid-1880s Joseph William Norman was appointed to the post, but by 1891 he had been replaced by John Haythorpe. From 14th June 1897 Arthur John Mann became station master until his retirement in April 1923; during his tenure he assumed control of Earsham and in October 1922 his responsibilities increased when he took charge of Ditchingham. The new incumbent at Bungay was Henry Howard, who transferred from Middle Drove in March 1923 and served at the station until he retired on 30th September 1930. At his retirement he was presented with an umbrella from staff at Bungay and Earsham, and a pipe and pouch of tobacco from staff at Ditchingham; he subsequently passed away on 29th January 1936. William Williamott, formerly station master at Harleston, was then appointed until he retired on 31st December 1935, subsequently passing away on 7th February 1944. A fortnight later, on 15th January 1936, Frederick William Mann, formerly station master at Conisborough on the Great Central & Midland Joint line, became station master until he retired on 14th May 1939; his retirement was short for he died on 3rd December 1939. A.H.G. Flunder arrived on 30th August 1939 and served at the station in the early war years until November 1943 when he was promoted to Halesworth; on 30th September he was presented with a smoker's stand and chrome plated cigarette box by G. Bedwell signalman, G.C. High, signalman, and A.E. Linner, chief goods clerk. Flunder was succeeded by Henry W.G. Taylor, formerly in charge at Glemsford; he remained during the rest of the hostilities until his promotion away on 11th August 1946. On 10th October 1946 B.E. Tuck took charge of the station and remained in the post until November 1950, to be replaced by Stanley W. Clarke who stayed for a short period until December 1952. The last station master to serve at Bungay, Maurice Evans, arrived in January 1953 just as the passenger service was withdrawn and remained in charge until June 1956 when the post was withdrawn. He had served earlier at Pulham Market and Pulham St. Mary. He moved on to Brandon and then gained promotion to Melton Constable. During the life of the branch the stationmaster at Bungay also assumed control of Earsham from 1920, followed by Ditchingham from June 1922, and then Ellingham and Geldeston in 1950.

At the next station on the branch, England Barnes was station master at Ditchingham in 1885, having transferred from a clerical job at Reedham; he gained promotion to take charge at Harling Road in 1891. Arthur Aldis, in charge in the early years of the twentieth century, gained promotion to Acle in January 1905. By 1913, Alfred James Bilham was station master residing in the station house at an annual rent of £17. In the years to December 1918, H.G. Wooltorton was station master at Ditchingham, including Ellingham and Geldeston, when he was promoted to take charge at Wickford. His replacement from December 1918 was H. Margetson, relief clerk in the London district, promoted to station master Ditchingham including Ellingham and Geldeston. Margetson then transferred to station master Elsenham and the Thaxted Light Railway in April 1922. He was presented with a silver-plated teapot by local station staff before his departure.

When the line opened from Bungay to Beccles, H. Welkes of Ipswich was delegated to ride on the special train from Ipswich on 1st March 1863, to be left in charge of Ellingham station for a few days before being transferred to Redenhall where he remained for a few months before going on to Starston. P.R. Souter was appointed to the post of station master at Geldeston including Ellingham in 1905; residing in the station house he served for seven years before gaining promotion to Lea Bridge. On leaving in May 1912 he was presented with a gold and pearl tie-pin from station staff. His replacement at Geldeston was Henry Hammond, but his stay was short-lived for in October 1913 he transferred to take charge at Lakenheath; in a balancing move John Thomas Kimm of Lakenheath was appointed to Geldeston, where he served until September 1916 before transferring to take charge at Foulsham on the Wroxham to County School line. Both Hammond and Kimm resided in the station house for an annual rental in 1913 of £16. As mentioned above, Ditchingham, Ellingham and Geldeston stations were combined under one station master.

In October 1863 James Ling Wilkinson married Amelia Agnes Flint at Redenhall Church when he was station master at Beccles after the WVR was extended beyond Bungay. He remained at Beccles until retirement in 1895 and died after a long retirement on 13th August 1923. Joseph Butters was promoted from Thetford, but only remained in the post until 1896 when he gained further promotion as station master at Wells. After Frederick Clarke became station master at Beccles in 1907, he also from 1916 assumed control of Geldeston and Ellingham stations before retiring on 22nd June 1929, aged 65; he died on 21st April 1938. Clarke had commenced his railway career as a clerk at Bishop's Stortford before becoming station master at Elsenham in 1894; he then moved on to Broxbourne in 1900. On his retirement he was presented with a Jacobean smoker's cabinet on behalf of his staff by Mr Lincoln, chief goods clerk. V.E. Turner, a subsequent station master at Beccles, retired on 24th May 1946 and was succeeded by B.E. Tuck.

Traffic Staff

Unfortunately, with the mists of time, only a few staff can be readily identified. Of the many, a few sacrificed their lives serving with the armed forces during World War One. Frank Henry Smith – who was porter signalman at Beccles, joined the Norfolk Regiment and was reported missing in August 1915 aged 22 years – started on the railway as porter at Flordon in June 1910. James Benjamin Edwards, who enlisted with the Suffolk Regiment in February 1916, died as a result of his injuries in Southwark Military Hospital aged 21 years; he had commenced his railway career as lad porter at Earsham in April 1912 before gaining promotion to porter at Lowestoft in November 1914 and subsequently signalman at Haddiscoe. Oliver James Payne, who joined the Royal Engineers (Railway Operating Division) in December 1916, was drowned in the Mediterranean on 31st December 1917 aged 20 years; he had commenced his railway career as lad porter at Spooner Row in April 1914 before being promoted as porter at Bungay the following year; he subsequently transferred as porter signalman at Middleton in September 1916. Charles William Minns, gate lad at Harleston who enlisted with the Norfolk Regiment, was killed in action on 19th August 1918 aged 21 years. His brother Harry Edward Minns, who was employed as porter at Dunham and then Beccles, and who served in the same regiment, was killed on 11th August 1917. Although not on active service, Thomas Baden Potter, clerk at Homersfield station, died on 14th September 1917 aged 17 years, after four years service with the GER; at his funeral floral tributes were received from staff at Homersfield, Beccles and Tivetshall stations.

In the early years, clerical staff were employed at each station and many went on to gain promotion. P.H. Simpson, clerk at Pulham Market, was presented with a wedding present from staff at Pulham Market and Pulham St. Mary stations by Mr Dines, the station master in 1927. W.J. Hood started his railway career as clerk at Harleston in October 1881 and finished as station master at North Elmham; he died on 29th June 1929 aged 63 years. H. Rackham, another clerk at Harleston, was appointed station master at Somerleyton in April 1934, whilst C. Barrett, clerk Pulham Market, gained promotion to station master Branston and Heighington on the former GN & GE Joint line in March 1940. Fred Coleman was booking clerk at Harleston during the last years of passenger operation.

Each of the stations had signalmen initially on duty for the entire period of train service operation; later, with the rearrangement of employment, they were on early and late turns, but many were employed as porter signalmen as a result of rationalistion so that they could be employed on general station duties. H. Green, porter signalman at Geldeston from July 1890, had transferred from

Homersfield where he was goods porter, but his stay was short for he moved on to Cantley as signalman in 1891. J.H. Myhill, signalman at Homersfield from June 1892 until transferring to Yaxham in October 1897, had started his railway career at Wendling in December 1889 and retired in March 1934. George Clark started as porter at Harleston in March 1876 and was promoted to signalman at Tivetshall in August 1879; his tenure was short for he transferred to Dereham in March 1880. William Philpot, porter signalman at Ditchingham, resided in a company cottage in 1913 paying an annual rent of £7 16s 0d. William Cubitt, porter signalman on the other turn at Ditchingham in 1913 and also residing in a company cottage for which he paid £5 4s 0d per annum, was replaced by Frederick Thomas Myall in June of that year. H. Clarke, a long-serving signalman at Tivetshall, retired on 28th March 1927 but did not have a long sojourn for he died in September of the same year, aged 60 years. E.W. Steward, signalman at Bungay, retired on 7th June 1930 after forty-seven years' service. R.M. Guyton, signalman for forty-one out of his fifty years' career at Tivetshall, retired on 22nd November 1930 and died on 10th September 1935; he had started as a lad at Belton. Edward Kerridge, porter signalman at Ditchingham who was renting one of the cottages near the station for £7 7s 4d per annum in 1924, retired on 14th March 1934; whilst H.F. Canham, porter signalman at Geldeston, died on 28th July 1935. L.H. Taylor, porter signalman at Homersfield, retired in July 1930; he had been presented with an eight-day clock on occasion of his wedding on 19th May 1930. C. Bedwell, signalman at Bungay, retired in January 1947 and was presented with an oak smoker's cabinet by station master B.E. Tuck in behalf of colleagues. W. Sampher, a retired signalman from Bungay, died on 11th February 1939. John Bird, signalman at Harleston, received a clock as parting gift from staff on his promotion to Stowmarket in 1930. Walter Jensen, a signalman for forty-three years at Beccles, retired on 7th March 1931; he had started with the GER as porter at Middleton on the Kings Lynn to Dereham line in 1880. Engine driver Richard Pegg retired after forty-eight years service from Stratford shed in June 1912; he commenced his career at Beccles as a porter in 1863, then became a relief signalman, where he recalled he had to walk to the signal posts to operate the equipment. J.J. Skouling, a retired signalman at Beccles, died on 20th June 1943.

Of the other grades to serve on the branch, mention can only be made of a few. William Clarke started as guard on the Waveney Valley line on 1st January 1864 and remained as passenger guard at Beccles; he passed away after twenty years retirement in January 1929 aged 89 years. S.J. Chalker, a checker at Harleston, retired on 26th January 1935; whilst David John Ireland, the station foreman at Earsham and then Homersfield, retired on 12th February 1927. He resided in the station house at Earsham, paying an annual rental of £7 7s 4d in 1924. W.B. Wiseman, a crossing keeper at Tivetshall, retired 11th April 1936, followed by J.H. Harris, retired gatekeeper at Beccles, who died on 8th July 1939. Thomas Hinsley, known as 'Tifler Tom', another crossing keeper at Beccles, retired 8th February 1930 age 65 years; he started as horseman at Beccles in October 1891 before being promoted to guard in March 1912. Owing to ill health he became crossing keeper in January 1920 and was presented with an umbrella by Mr Bloom, the station master, at a short ceremony on 21st March 1930. W.J. Hadingham, parcels porter at Bungay, transferred to Oulton Broad in March 1937; whilst John Cook, who commenced his railway career at Pulham Market on 12th June 1876, later transferring to Brandon, retired 29th April 1927 as inspector at Norwich. George Beckett was porter/signalman when the passenger service was withdrawn, when he was transferred to Barnby near Oulton Broad.

George Gooch, a goods supervisor at Beccles in the first decade of the twentieth century, occupied the crossing cottage at Mutford Lock where he and his family lived rent free as his wife acted as gatekeeper. In the latter years of the Waveney Valley Branch, porter signalmen Baldrey and Savery served at Pulham Market in 1950, Mrs Savery was crossing keeper at Crossingford gates and Mr and Mrs Kybird were porters at Bungay.

Staff employed on the branch were a close-knit community and many social gatherings were held in the halcyon days before rationalisation. At one such event, Harleston staff held their annual staff dinner at the Swan Hotel on 4th April 1911, when James Stone the station master presided. Not to be outdone, in June 1912 the annual dinner for staff on the Bungay to Beccles section of the Waveney Valley Branch was revived and held at the Fleece Hotel Bungay; it was hoped to be annual event. Waveney Valley staff also held first aid classes at Bungay in 1931.

The Pulham Market station staff are joined on the platform by the three-man permanent way gang in shirtsleeves and waistcoats in 1910. The signal box at that time containing a 20-lever Dutton frame is to the left whilst the covered way in front of the station building is adorned with various posters, the most prominent advising train service alterations from May 1910 above an enamel advertisement for Sutton's seeds. *Author's collection*

10

Timetables and Traffic

When the EUR opened for traffic on 7th November 1849 there was no connecting road service to the Pulhams or Harleston, but by 1851 a road coach ran to and from Tivetshall to connect with the morning Up train to London and also to meet passengers arriving on the 4.45pm Up train from Norwich. The Waveney Valley Railway was built essentially as a feeder line to both the Eastern Union main line with its connection to Norwich and London, and the East Suffolk line with its connection to Lowestoft and Great Yarmouth. This it achieved and it was hoped the new line would help expand trade and thereby generate an increase in the population of the towns and villages served. Like many other routes built or absorbed by the GER, however, the area served was formed of large agricultural estates with the majority of the populace employed on the land. Local industry was focussed on Harleston and Bungay where the railway over the years helped to halt a decline in trade, but passenger traffic tended to be spasmodic and long distance, with the regular traffic only conveyed on market days – Wednesday at Harleston and Lowestoft, Thursday at Bungay, and Friday at Beccles, and to a lesser extent on Saturday at Norwich and Yarmouth, and Tuesday at Ipswich. Thus in the lifespan of the branch the population of the area steadily declined, except during World War Two when a huge influx of servicemen and women temporarily swelled the ranks but such increase did not register in the census figures shown below.

The initial timetable from 1st December 1855 showed a total of five trains in each direction SX and six each way including one goods train SO, the latter running direct from Harleston to Norwich.

Timetable From 1st December 1855

						SO	
	Classes	123P	123	123P	12	123P	3
		am	am	pm	pm	pm	pm
Tivetshall	dep	6.35	9.30	1.20	3.55	6.12	8.38
Pulham St. Magdalene	dep	6.45	9.38	1.28	4.03	6.20	8.46
Pulham St. Mary	dep	6.50	9.43	1.33	4.08	6.25	8.51
Starston	dep	7.00	9.50	1.40	4.15	6.32	8.58
Harleston	arr	7.10	9.55	1.50	4.20	6.37	9.05

						SO	
	Classes	123P	123	123	12	gds	3
		am	am	am	pm	pm	pm
Harleston	dep	5.50	9.00	11.20	3.00	4.35	7.40
Starston	dep	5.53	9.03	11.23	3.03		7.43
Pulham St. Mary	dep	5.58	9.08	11.28	3.08		7.48
Pulham St. Magdalene	dep	6.03	9.12	11.32	3.12		7.52
Tivetshall	arr	6.15	9.20	11.40	3.20		8.00
Norwich	arr					5.20	

The ECR working timetable for 1856 showed four mixed trains in each direction, Saturdays excepted departing from Harleston at 7.35am, 11.25am, 3.20pm and 7.35pm, and returning from

Population Figures

Year	1861	1871	1881	1891	1901	1911	1921	1931	1951	1961
Tivetshall St. Margaret	375	343	339	303	342	400	354	345	311	277
Tivetshall St. Mary	362	287	299	368	263	247	242	198	238	267
Pulham Market	1,279	1,187	1,127	1,082	1,014	1,001	964	882	875	866
Pulham St. Mary	863	886	822	831	784	738	841	701	682	636
Wortwell	466	454	416	477	393	357	340	316	341	419
Starston	481	492	510	516	493	444	430	391	393	340
Harleston^	1,302	1,267	1,731	2,003	2,001	1,882	1,789	1,645	1,709	1,809
Homersfield	208	178	144	160	139	144	143	140	125	168
Earsham	697	643	608	572	560	603	581	578	606	622
Bungay	3,805	3,807	3,579	3,560	3,314	3,359	3,103	3,100	3,535	3,582
Ditchingham	1,100	974	1,075	1,083	1,110	1,137	997	942	1,141	1,059
Ellingham	386	388	340	342	322	286	302	277	362	363
Geldeston	345	325	292	318	310	295	305	365	328	338
Beccles	4,266	4,844	5,721	6,669	6,898	7,139	7,085	6,545	6,870	7,332
Total*	10,932	10,601	10,644	10,944	10,440	10,246	9,795	9,336	10,097	10,202
Total+	15,935	16,075	17,003	18,284	17,943	18,032	17,476	16,425	17,516	18,078

Notes: * Total branch stations only
+ Total including Tivetshall and Beccles
^ with Redenhall

Harlestone Branch.

Down.---Week Days. (Single Line). Up.---Week Days.

Dist.	FROM	1	2 Eng.	3	4	5	6
		a.m.	a.m.	p.m.	p.m.	p.m.	p.m.
—	Tivetshall	8 10	10 50	1 25	4 0	5 35	8 25
2¾	Pulham Market	*	...	*	*	*	*
3¾	Pulham St. Mary	*	...	*	*	*	*
5½	Starston	*	...	*	*	*	*
6¼	Harlestone	8 35	11 10	1 50	4 25	6 0	8 50

FROM	1	2	3	4	5	6
	a.m.	a.m.	a.m.	p.m.	p.m.	p.m.
Harlestone	7 35	10 15	11 25	3 20	5 0	7 35
Starston	*	*	*	*	*	*
Pulham St. Mary	*	*	*	*	*	*
Pulham Market	*	*	*	*	*	*
Tivetshall	8 0	10 40	11 50	3 45	5 25	8 0

N.B.—These Train carry both Goods and Passengers. Nos. 2 and 5 Up and Down Saturdays only. No Trains over this Branch on Sundays. * Trains will only call at the Stations marked thus * when required.
No. 1 Up on Mondays will start at 5.50 a.m. and will be an extra trip—returning from Tivetshall at 6.25 a.m.

ECR working timetable 1856.

Tivetshall at 8.10am, 1.25pm, 4.00pm and 8.25pm. On Mondays only, an additional mixed train ran in each direction departing Harleston at 5.50am before returning from Tivetshall at 6.25am. On Saturdays only, two additional Up trains departed Harleston at 10.15am and 5.00pm, but in the Down direction only one additional mixed train operated, departing Tivetshall at 5.35pm. To balance the working, the branch engine, after hauling the 10.15am Up train, returned light to Harleston to work the 11.25am departure. All mixed trains were allowed 25 minutes running time for the 6½ miles journey and calls were made at Pulham Market, Pulham St. Mary and Starston only when required. No Sunday services were provided.

Little alteration was made to the timetable when the line was extended to Bungay. Five trains ran in each direction on weekdays only, with services calling at Earsham, Wortwell and Redenhall only if required. The 11.00am Up service from Bungay was replaced by the 11.10am through train to Norwich Victoria arriving at 12.40pm, conveying passengers for Norwich Market.

The initial timetable for the extended service between Tivetshall and Beccles from 2nd March 1863 showed that trains to or from Norwich Thorpe or Norwich Victoria only called at Harleston, Homersfield and Bungay, with trains calling at other stations only when required to take up or set down passengers. Passengers wishing to alight were requested to advise the guard at the preceding stopping place. Trains departed Beccles at 8.35am, 12.15pm, 2.50pm and 7.10pm, returning from Tivetshall at 10.35am, 1.30pm, 4.10pm and 8.25pm, and were allowed between 55 and 70 minutes for the journey.

Waveney Valley Branch.
Single Line.

The Trains on this Branch are to be worked under the Train Staff and Train Ticket arrangements, as laid down in Special Order, No. 1114, dated September 23rd, 1864.
No Engine or Train is to be run on this Branch without a Train Staff or Train Ticket.

Down. Week Days.

Miles from Tivetshall	FROM	1 A Pass. 1 2 3	2 Mxd 1 2	3 Cars.	4 Parly 1 2 3	5 N Pass. 1 2	6 S Mkt. 1 2 3	7 Pass. 1 2 3	8	9	10
		a.m.	a.m.	a.m.	p.m.	p.m.	p.m.	p.m.			
	Tivetshall	8 0	9 0	10 45	1 35	4 10	5 45	8 20	...	...	...
2½	Pulham Market	...	*	...	*	*	*	*	...	...	...
3¾	Pulham Mary	*	*	...	*	*	*	*	...	...	...
5½	Starston	...	*	...	*	*	*	*	...	...	...
6¼	Harleston arr.	...	9 35	...	...	...	...	...	...	...	...
	Harleston dep.	8 15	9 45	10 59	1 53	4 28	6 3	8 37	...	...	...
7¼	Redenhall	...	*	Saturdays only.	*	*	*	*	...	...	...
8¼	Wortwell	...	*		*	...	*	*	...	...	..
8¾	Homersfield	8 23	10 5		2 3	4 38	6 13	8 47	...	...	...
12	Earsham	...	*		*	...	*	*	...	...	...
12¾	Bungay arr.	...	10 20		...	...	...	...	...	...	...
	Bungay dep.	8 30	10 30	11 13	2 13	4 48	6 23	8 52	...	...	...
13¾	Ditchingham	*	*	...	*	*	*	*	...	...	...
15¼	Ellingham	...	*	...	*	*	*	*	...	...	...
16¾	Geldeston	*	*	...	*	*	*	*	...	...	...
19¼	Beccles	8 52	11 15	11 30	2 35	5 10	6 45	9 20	...	...	...

Up. Week Days.

Miles from Beccles.	FROM	1 M Pass. 1 2	2 Pass. 1 2	3 S Mkt. 1 2 3	4 Pass 1 2 3	5 PL Pass. 1 2 3	6 Gds.	7 Cars.	8 Pass. 1 2 3	9	10
		a.m.	a.m.	a.m.	a.m.	p.m.	p.m.	p.m.	p.m.		
	Beccles	5 25	7 0	9 15	11 50	2 40	2 55	...	7 0	...	...
2½	Geldeston	....	...	*	*	*	*	...	*	...	...
4	Ellingham	...	...	*	*	*	*	...	*	...	...
5½	Ditchingham	...	...	*	*	*	*	...	*	...	...
6½	Bungay arr.	...	...	...	...	...	3 35	...	...	...	...
	Bungay dep.	5 40	7 15	9 35	12 10	3 0	3 40	5 0	7 20	...	...
7¼	Earsham	...	...	*	*	*	*	Saturdays only.	*	...	...
10½	Homersfield	5 48	7 23	9 45	12 20	3 10	3 55		7 30	...	...
11	Wortwell	...	...	*	...	*	*		*	...	...
11¾	Redenhall	...	...	*	*	*	*		*	...	...
13	Harleston arr.	...	...	...	...	...	4 20		...	...	...
	Harleston dep.	5 58	7 33	9 55	12 30	3 25	4 35	5 15	7 42	...	...
13¾	Starston	...	...	*	...	*	*	...	*	...	...
15½	Pulham Mary	*	*	*	*	*	*	...	*	...	...
16¾	Pulham Market	...	...	*	*	*	*	...	*	...	...
19½	Tivetshall	6 17	7 52	10 20	12 56	3 50	5 15	5 30	8 5	...	...

A No. 1. Not exceeding six Spring Buffer Trucks of Perishable Goods may be worked from Tivetshall by this Train.
N The 4.10 p.m. Train ex Tivetshall to Beccles will not run beyond Bungay on Saturdays.
No. 2 runs from Ipswich to Lowestoft, and on Saturdays to await at Harleston arrival of No. 3 Up Market Train.
No. 5 Down and No. 6 Up Trains to pass at Harleston.
S No. 6 runs on Saturdays only.

M No. 1 runs on Mondays only.
No. 2 does not run on Mondays.
S No. 3 runs on Saturdays only.
No. 6 Up runs from Lowestoft to Ipswich.
No. 6 Up and No. 5 Down Trains to pass at Harleston.
No. 8. A limited number of Trucks may be attached to this Train, if required.
P L Parliamentary from Waveney Valley District to London and intermediate Stations.

* Will call when required.

63

September 1, 1865.

GER working timetable 1865.

72

The Trains on this Branch are worked under the Train Staff and Train Ticket arrangements, as laid down in Special Order, No. 1114, dated September 23rd, 1864.
No Engine or Train is to be run on this Branch without a Train Staff or Train Ticket.

WAVENEY VALLEY BRANCH.

Single Line.

Down Trains. Week Days.

Miles from Tivetshall	FROM	1	2	3	4	5	6	7	8	9	10	11	12
		A Pass. 1 2 3	B Mxd 1 2	Cars.	Parl. 1 2 3	C Pass. 1 2	Mkt. 1 2 3	Pass. 1 2 3					
		a.m.	a.m.	a.m.	p.m.	p.m.	p.m.	p.m.					
—	**Tivetshall** ....dep.	8 0	8 50	10 45	1 35	4 10	5 45	8 20	...	...	...	...	...
2½	Pulham Market............	...	*	...	*	*	*	*	...	...	...	...	...
3¾	Pulham Mary............	*	*	..	*	*	*	*	...	...	...	...	...
6¼	**Harleston** .... arr.	8 14	9 25	10 58	1 52	4 27	6 2	8 36	...	...	...	...	...
	dep.	8 15	9 35	10 59	1 53	4 28	6 3	8 37	...	...	...	...	...
8¼	Wortwell	...	*	Saturdays only.	*	...	*	*	...	...	...	...	...
8¾	Homersfield	8 23	9 55		2 3	4 38	6 13	8 47	...	...	...	...	...
12	Earsham............	...	*		*	...	*	*	...	...	...	...	...
12¾	**Bungay** .... arr.	8 29	10 10		2 12	4 47	6 22	8 56	...	...	...	...	...
	dep.	8 30	10 50	11 13	2 13	4 48	6 23	8 57	...	...	...	...	...
13¾	Ditchingham	*	*	...	*	*	*	*	...	...	...	...	...
15½	Ellingham	...	*	...	*	*	*	*	...	...	...	...	...
16¾	Geldeston	*	*	...	*	*	*	*	...	...	...	...	...
19¼	**Beccles** ....arr.	8 52	11 25	11 30	2 35	5 10	6 45	9 20	...	...	...	...	...
							Satur						

A No. 1. Not exceeding six Buffer Trucks of Perishable Goods may be worked from Tivetshall by this Train.
B No. 2 runs from Ipswich to Lowestoft. See No. 1 Train, page 48, and No. 3 Down Train page 71.
C No. 5 does not run on Saturdays.

Up Trains. Week Days.

Miles from Beccles.	FROM	1	2	3	4	5	6	7	8	9	10	11	12
		Pass. 1 2	E Pass. 1 2	Mkt. 1 2 3	F Pass. 1 2	Pass. 1 2	G Pass. 1 2 3	H Gds.	I Pass. 1 2 3				
		a.m.	a.m.	a.m.	a.m.	a.m.	p.m.	p.m.	p.m.				
—	**Beccles** ....dep.	5 25	7 0	9 15	10 30	11 50	2 40	3 0	7 0	...	...	...	...
2½	Geldeston	...	...	*	*	*	*	*	*	...	...	...	...
4	Ellingham	...	...	*	*	*	*	*	*	...	...	...	...
5½	Ditchingham	...	...	*	*	*	*	*	*	...	...	...	...
6½	**Bungay** .... arr.	5 39	7 14	9 34	10 50	12 9	2 59	3 40	7 19	...	...	...	...
	dep.	5 40	7 15	9 35	10 53	12 10	3 0	3 45	7 20	...	...	...	...
7¼	Earsham............	...	...	*	*	*	*	*	*	...	...	...	...
10½	Homersfield	5 48	7 23	9 45	11 3	12 20	3 10	4 0	7 30	...	...	...	...
11	Wortwell	...	...	*	...	*	*	*	*	...	...	...	...
13	**Harleston** .... arr.	5 57	7 32	9 54	11 13	12 29	3 24	4 20	7 41	...	...	...	...
	dep.	5 58	7 33	9 55	11 15	12 30	3 25	4 35	7 42	...	...	...	...
15½	Pulham Mary	*	*	*	*	*	*	*	*	...	...	...	...
16¾	Pulham Market............	...	...	*	*	*	*	*	*	...	...	...	...
19¼	**Tivetshall** ....arr.	6 17	7 52	10 20	11 40	12 50	3 50	5 15	8 5	...	...	...	...
		Mondays only.		Saturdays only.		Saturdays only.							

E No. 2 does not run on Mondays.
F No. 4 does not run on Saturdays.
G No. 6 Parliamentary from Waveney Valley District to London and intermediate Stations.
H No. 7 from Lowestoft to Ipswich. See No. 5 Up Train page 71, and No. 52 Up Train page 58.
I No. 8. A limited number of Trucks may be attached to this Train, if required.

* Will call when required.

October 1, 1866.

GER working timetable 1866.

The working timetable for 1866 offered four passenger and one mixed train in the Down direction on weekdays only, augmented by a set of cars (ECS) running on Saturdays only. The first Down train 8.00am ex Tivetshall was permitted to convey not exceeding six buffer trucks of perishable goods from Tivetshall and made mandatory calls at Harleston, Homersfield and Bungay, called at Pulham Mary, Ditchingham and Geldeston only when required, and omitted calling at Pulham Market, Wortwell, Earsham and Ellingham. The mixed train conveying First and Second Class passengers only was a through train from Ipswich (departing 6.00am) to Lowestoft (arriving at 12.15pm) and entered the branch at Tivetshall at 8.50am, making mandatory calls at the three important stations and all other stations only if required. The 1.35pm ex Tivetshall conveyed Parliamentary fare paying passengers, whilst the 4.10pmSX ex Tivetshall, conveying First and Second Class passengers only, omitted calls at Wortwell and Earsham; it was replaced on Saturdays by the 5.45pm market day train. In the Up direction the service consisted of four SX and five SO passengers trains, and a goods service. Of the passenger services, the 5.25am ex Beccles ran MO whilst the 7.00am departure ran MX. Both of these services conveyed only First and Second Class passengers, calling at Bungay, Homersfield and Harleston, and Pulham Market only if required. The 9.15amSO and 11.50am SO ex Beccles conveyed First and Second Class passengers only, the former omitting the Wortwell stop. The 10.30amSX, 2.40pm and 7.00pm ex Beccles made mandatory calls at Bungay, Homersfield and Harleston, but only called at the other stations if required, the latter train being permitted to convey a limited number of trucks if required. The solitary goods train serving the branch was a through working from Lowestoft (departing 2.15pm) to Ipswich and after shunting and reversing at Beccles from 2.40pm until 3.00pm called at all stations if required, arriving at Tivetshall at 5.15pm. After reversal the train departed at 5.40pm, arriving at Ipswich at 7.50pm. Both the Down mixed train from Ipswich and Up goods service from Lowestoft were worked by an Ipswich engine and men.

The timetable for 1867 showed a service of five trains in each direction and by 1869 the service shown overleaf operated on weekdays only.

The 1870 working timetable showed a service of four passenger trains MThO and three passenger trains on the other weekdays in the Down direction. The 7.45amMThO ex Tivetshall called at Harleston, Homersfield and Bungay, with stops at Pulham St. Mary, Ditchingham and Geldeston only if required. The mixed train, 8.45am ex Tivetshall, was a through service from Norwich Thorpe (depart 6.45am) to Lowestoft (arriving at 12.15pm) and was booked 15 minutes at Harleston and 30 minutes at Bungay for shunting purposes. A mandatory call was made at Homersfield but the other stations were only served if required. The 1.13pm ex Tivetshall conveyed Parliamentary fare paying passengers from the London side of Ipswich and like other service made mandatory calls at Harleston, Homersfield and Bungay, with conditional stops at the other branch stations. However, the 4.20pmSX ex Tivetshall omitted calling at Wortwell, whilst the 5.45pm market train ex Tivetshall ran on Saturdays only and started back at Norwich Victoria at 5.00pm. The last Down service, 8.20pm ex Tivetshall, arrived at Beccles 9.20pm. In the Up direction a service of four passenger services operated MThO and three on the other weekdays. The first train of the day, 5.35am ex Beccles, only called at Bungay, Homersfield and Harleston, with an additional call at Pulham St. Mary if required. The mixed train 7.35am ex Beccles was a through

Timetable for 1867

Down			A Mxd	B Parl		
		am	am	pm	pm	pm
Tivetshall	dep	8.00	8.50	1.35	4.10	8.20
Pulham Market	dep		*	*	*	*
Pulham Mary	dep	*	*	*	*	*
Harleston	dep	8.15	9.35	1.53	4.28	8.37
Wortwell	dep		*	*		*
Homersfield	dep	8.23	9.55	2.03	4.38	8.47
Earsham	dep		*	*		*
Bungay	dep	8.30	10.20	2.13	4.43	8.57
Ditchingham	dep	*	*	*	*	*
Ellingham	dep		*	*	*	*
Geldeston	dep	*	*	*	*	*
Beccles	arr	8.52	11.00	2.35	5.10	9.20

Additional train departs Tivetshall at 5.45pm SO to Beccles in connection with the 5.00pm market train from Norwich.
Notes: A Through train from Ipswich to Lowestoft.
B Train terminates at Bungay on Saturdays only.
* Trains only call when required to take up or set down passengers. Passengers wishing to alight are requested to intimate to the guard at the previous stopping station.

Up		MO	MX	SX	SO		
		am	am	am	am	pm	pm
Beccles	dep	5.25	7.00	10.30	11.50	2.40	7.00
Geldeston	dep			*	*	*	*
Ellingham	dep			*	*	*	*
Ditchingham	dep			*	*	*	*
Bungay	dep	5.40	7.15	10.53	12.10	3.00	7.20
Earsham	dep			*	*	*	*
Homersfield	dep	5.48	7.23	11.03	12.20	3.10	7.30
Wortwell	dep			*	*	*	
Harleston	dep	5.58	7.33	11.15	12.30	3.25	7.42
Pulham Mary	dep	*	*	*	*	*	*
Pulham Market	dep			*	*	*	*
Tivetshall	arr	6.17	7.52	11.40	12.50	3.50	8.05

Additional train departs Beccles at 9.15amSO to Tivetshall to connect with the market train due at Norwich at 11.15am.
Notes: * Trains only call when required to take up or set down passengers. Passengers wishing to alight are requested to intimate to the guard at the previous stopping station.

Timetable for 1869 Weekdays Only

Down		MO			SX	SO	
		am	am	pm	pm	pm	pm
Tivetshall	dep	7.45	8.55	1.05	4.15	5.45	8.35
Pulham Market	dep		*	*	*	*	*
Pulham Mary	dep	*	*	*	*	*	*
Harleston	dep	8.05	9.45	1.25	4.35	6.05	8.55
Wortwell	dep		*	*		*	*
Homersfield	dep	8.14	10.05	1.34	4.44	6.14	9.04
Earsham	dep		*	*		*	*
Bungay	dep	8.24	10.50	1.44	4.54	6.25	9.14
Ditchingham	dep	*	*	*	*	*	*
Ellingham	dep		*	*	*	*	*
Geldeston	dep	*	*	*	*	*	*
Beccles	arr	8.45	11.25	2.05	5.15	6.45	9.35

Up		MO	SO	SX		
		am	am	am	pm	pm
Beccles	dep	5.20	9.00	10.30	2.30	7.05
Geldeston	dep	*	*	*	*	*
Ellingham	dep	*	*	*	*	*
Ditchingham	dep	*	*	*	*	*
Bungay	dep	5.34	9.21	10.51	2.55	7.27
Earsham	dep	*	*	*	*	*
Homersfield	dep	5.44	9.31	11.01	3.06	7.38
Wortwell	dep	*	*	*	*	*
Harleston	dep	5.51	9.40	11.10	3.23	7.48
Pulham Mary	dep	*	*	*	*	*
Pulham Market	dep	*	*	*	*	*
Tivetshall	arr	6.11	10.00	11.30	3.43	8.08

Note: * Calls only when required; passengers wishing to be taken up to be at the station 5 minutes before the times shown, those wishing to be set down must give notice to the guard at the preceding stopping station.

service from Lowestoft (departing at 5.50am) to Norwich Thorpe (arriving 9.45am) with mandatory calls at Bungay, Homersfield and Harleston, and stops at Ditchingham and Pulham St. Mary only if required. The 9.00amSO market train called at the important stations and served Geldeston, Ellingham, Ditchingham, Earsham, Wortwell, Pulham St. Mary and Pulham Market by request. The 10.35amSX ex Beccles followed the same stopping pattern except it omitted the Wortwell stop. Parliamentary fare paying passengers were conveyed by the 2.30pm ex Beccles which served Bungay, Homersfield and Harleston, and other stations only if required, and was permitted to work perishable and other important brake goods; on SO this train ran through to Norwich Victoria arriving at 4.15pm. The last passenger train of the day, the 7.00pm Beccles to Tivetshall, was permitted to attach a limited number of trucks if required. In the Up direction, a goods train, the 2.15pm from Lowestoft, departed Beccles at 3.05pm each weekday calling at Bungay, Homersfield and Harleston, and at all other stations if required, with arrival at Tivetshall at 5.05pm before continuing to Norwich Thorpe arriving at 7.00pm.

The working timetable for 1877 showed a weekdays-only service of five MThO and four MThX passenger trains and one goods train in the Down direction. Of these, the 7.12am ex Tivetshall ran MThO whilst the 5.45pm ex Tivetshall market train ran SO. The 9.00am ex Tivetshall was a through train to Yarmouth arriving at 10.55am after reversing at Beccles and was permitted to convey locally a few trucks of perishable goods or cattle, whilst the 12.55pm

68

The Trains on this Branch are worked under the Train Staff and Train Ticket arrangements, as laid down in Special Order, No. 1114, dated September 23rd, 1864.
No Engine or Train is to be run on this Branch without a Train Staff or Train Ticket The Train Staff Stations are Tivetshall, Harleston, Bungay, and Beccles

WAVENEY VALLEY BRANCH

Single Line.

Down Trains. Week Days.

Miles from Tivetshall	FROM	1	2	3	4	5	6	7	8	9	10	11	12
		A Pass. 1 2 3	B Mxd. 1 2 3	C Parl. 1 2 3	D Pass. 1 2	E. Mkt. 1 2 3	Pass. 1 2 3						
		a.m.	a.m.	p.m.	p.m.	p.m.	p.m.						
—	**Tivetshall** ....dep.	7 45	8 45	1 13	4 20	5 45	8 20	...	...	...	...	...	...
2½	Pulham Market..................	...	*	*	*	*	*	...	...	...	...	...	...
3¾	Pulham Mary.....................	*	*	*	*	*	*	...	...	...	...	...	...
6¼	**Harleston** .... arr.	8 4	9 20	1 32	4 39	6 4	8 39	...	...	...	...	...	...
	dep.	8 5	9 35	1 35	4 40	6 5	8 40	...	...	...	...	...	...
8¼	Wortwell	...	*	*	...	*	*	...	...	...	...	...	...
8¾	Homersfield	8 14	10 0	1 42	4 49	6 14	8 49	...	...	...	...	...	...
12	Earsham..........................	...	*	*	...	*	*	...	...	...	...	...	...
12¾	**Bungay** .... arr.	8 25	10 25	1 53	5 0	6 25	9 0	...	...	...	...	...	...
	dep.	8 26	10 55	1 54	5 1	6 26	9 1	...	...	...	...	...	...
13¾	Ditchingham	*	*	*	*	*	*	...	...	...	...	...	...
15¼	Ellingham	...	*	*	*	*	*	...	...	...	...	...	...
16¾	Geldeston	*	*	*	*	*	*	...	...	...	...	...	...
19¼	**Beccle** ....arr.	8 45	11 30	2 15	5 20	6 45	9 20	...	...	...	...	...	...
		Mondays and Thursdys				Saturdays only.							

Up Trains. Week Days.

Miles from Beccles.	FROM	1	2	3	4	5	6	7	8	9	10	11	12
		Pass. 1 2	F Mxd. 1 2 3	Mkt. 1 2 3	G Pass. 1 2	H Pass. 1 2 3	I Gds. 1 2 3	K Pass. 1 2 3					
		a.m.	a.m.	a.m.	a.m.	p.m.	p.m	p.m.					
—	**Beccles** ....dep.	5 35	7 35	9 0	10 35	2 30	3 5	7 0	...	...	...	...	...
2½	Geldeston	...	...	*	*	*	*	*	...	...	...	...	...
4	Ellingham	...	...	*	*	*	*	*	...	...	...	...	...
5½	Ditchingham.....................	...	*	*	*	*	*	*	...	...	...	...	...
6½	**Bungay** .... arr.	5 48	7 55	9 20	10 55	2 50	3 40	7 21	...	...	...	...	...
	dep.	5 49	8 0	9 21	10 56	2 55	3 50	7 22	...	...	...	...	...
7¼	Earsham..........................	...	...	*	*	*	*	*	...	...	...	...	...
10½	Homersfield	6 0	8 13	9 31	11 8	3 8	4 5	7 36	...	...	...	...	...
11	Wortwell	...	...	*	...	*	*	*	...	...	...	...	...
13	**Harleston** .... arr.	6 7	8 21	9 40	11 16	3 17	4 20	7 46	...	...	...	...	...
	dep.	6 8	8 25	9 42	11 17	3 20	4 35	7 47	...	...	...	...	...
15½	Pulham Mary	*	*	*	*	*	*	*	...	...	...	...	...
16¾	Pulham Market....................	...	...	*	*	*	*	*	...	...	...	...	...
19¼	**Tivetshall** ....arr.	6 27	8 45	10 0	11 35	3 40	5 5	8 5	...	...	...	...	...
		Mondays and Thursdys		Saturdays only.									

A No. 1 to pass No. 2 Up Train at Bungay.
B No. 2 runs from Norwich to Lowestoft. See No 22 Train, page 54, and No. 3 Down Train page 67. On Saturdays to await at Harleston arrival of No. 3 Up Train.
C No. 3 Parliamentary from Stations London side of Ipswich.
D No. 4 does not run on Saturdays.
E No. 5 runs from Norwich. See No. 55 Train, page 56.

F No. 2 runs from Lowestoft to Norwich. See No. 2 Up Train, page 67, and No. 4 Train, page 48. On Mondays to pass No 1 Down Train at Bungay.
G No. 4 does not run on Saturdays.
H No. 5 Parliamentary from Waveney Valley District to London and intermediate Stations. To work Perishable and other important Break Goods. On Saturdays to run through to Norwich. See No. 27 Train, page 49.
I No. 6 runs from Lowestoft to Norwich. See No. 6 Up Train page 67, and No. 37 Train page 50.
K No. 7. A limited number of Trucks may be attached to this Train, if required.

* Will call when required.

October 1, 1870.

GER working timetable 1870.

126

The Trains on this Single Line are worked by Train Staff and Train Staff Ticket, according to the " Train Staff Regulations " contained in pages 132 and 133 of this Working Time Book. No Engine or Train is to be run on this Branch without a Train Staff or Train Staff Ticket. The Train Staff Stations are Tivetshall, Harleston, Bungay, and Beccles.

WAVENEY VALLEY BRANCH.—*Single Line.*

Down Trains—Week Days.

Miles from Tivetshall.	FROM	1	2	3	4	5	6	7	8	9	10	11	12	13
		Pass.	A Pass.	Gds.	B Parl.	C Pass.	Mkt.	Pass.						
		a.m.	a.m.	a.m.	p.m.	p.m.	p.m.	p.m.						
	Norwich ....dep.	.....	.....	6 0	12 25	.....	.....	7 50	.....	.....	.....	.....	.....	.....
—	**Tivetshall** ....dep.	7 12	9 0	9 10	1 8	4 15	5 45	8 30	...	...	...	...	...	...
2½	Pulham Market	*	*	*	*	*	*	*	.....	.....	.....	.....	.....	.....
3¾	Pulham Mary	*	*	*	*	*	*	*	...	...	...	...	...	...
6¼	Harleston.............. arr.	7 31	9 19	9 50	1 27	4 34	6 4	8 40	.....	.....	.....	.....	.....	.....
	dep.	7 32	9 20	10 10	1 28	4 35	6 27	8 50	...	...	...	...	...	...
8¼	Wortwell	*	*	.....	*	.....	*	*	.....	.....	.....	.....	.....	.....
8¾	Homersfield	7 41	9 29	10 35	1 37	4 44	6 37	8 59	...	...	...	...	...	...
12	Earsham.......................	*	*	...	*	*	*	*	.....	.....	.....	.....	.....	.....
12¾	Bungay.................. arr.	7 52	9 40	10 50	1 48	4 55	6 48	9 10	...	...	...	...	...	...
	dep.	8 0	9 41	11 40	1 49	4 56	6 49	9 11	.....	.....	.....	.....	.....	.....
13¾	Ditchingham..................	*	*	*	*	*	*	*	...	...	...	...	...	...
15¼	Ellingham	*	*	*	*	*	*	*	.....	.....	.....	.....	.....	.....
16¾	Geldeston	*	*	*	*	*	*	*	...	...	...	...	...	...
19¼	**Beccles** ....arr.	8 20	10 0	1 10	2 10	5 15	7 10	9 30	.....	.....	.....	.....	.....	.....
	Yarmouth ....arr.	...	10 55	...	...	...	...	...	...	...	...	...	...	...
		Mondays and Thursdays only.	See page 122.	See page 108.	See page 109.	Does not run on Saturdays.	Saturdys only.	See page 111.						

Up Trains—Week Days.

Miles from Beccles.	FROM	1	2	3	4	5	6	7	8	9	10	11	12	13
		Pass.	Gds.	Pass.	Pass.	C Pass.	D Gds.	E Pass.						
		a.m.	a.m.	a.m.	a.m.	p.m.	p.m.	p.m.						
	Lowestoft ....dep.	...	5 0	..	...	...	...	...	...	...	...	...	...	...
	Yarmouth	.....	.....	.....	.....	.....	.....	5 0	.....	.....	.....	.....	.....	.....
—	**Beccles** ....dep.	5 35	6 0	7 32	9 20	2 30	2 40	5 45	...	...	...	...	...	...
2½	Geldeston	.....	*	*	*	*	*	*	.....	.....	.....	.....	.....	.....
4	Ellingham	...	*	*	*	*	*	*	...	...	...	...	...	...
5½	Ditchingham....................	.....	*	*	*	*	*	*	.....	.....	.....	.....	.....	.....
6½	Bungay .... arr.	5 48	6 40	7 52	9 40	2 50	3 25	6 5	...	...	...	...	...	...
	dep.	5 49	7 0	7 53	9 41	2 54	3 45	6 6	.....	.....	.....	.....	.....	.....
7¼	Earsham.........................	...	...	*	*	*	*	*	...	...	...	...	...	...
10½	Homersfield	6 0	7 20	8 3	9 51	3 6	4 5	6 16	.....	.....	.....	.....	.....	.....
11	Wortwell	...	...	*	*	*	*	*	...	...	...	...	...	...
13	Harleston.............. arr.	6 7	7 30	8 13	10 0	3 15	4 25	6 26	.....	.....	.....	.....	.....	.....
	dep.	6 8	7 45	8 14	10 2	3 17	4 40	6 27	...	...	...	...	...	...
15½	Pulham Mary	*	.....	*	*	*	*	*	.....	.....	.....	.....	.....	.....
16¾	Pulham Market	*	*	*	*	*	D	*	...	...	...	...	...	...
19¼	**Tivetshall** ....arr.	6 28	8 20	8 35	10 20	3 35	5 20	6 45	.....	.....	.....	.....	.....	.....
	Norwich ....arr.	...	9 55	...	11 3	...	6 50	7 25	...	...	...	...	...	...
		Mondays and Thursdays only.	Not on Mondays. See pages 125 and 100.		See page 100.		See page 102.	See page 123.						

A No. 2 may work locally a few Trucks of Perishable Goods and Cattle only.

B No. 4 Parliamentary from Stations London side of Ipswich. A limited number of Trucks may be attached at Tivetshall if required.

C No. 5. Cattle may be worked from Harlestone by this Train when required.

C No. 5 Parliamentary from Waveney Valley District to London and intermediate Stations. To work Perishable and other important Break Good's.

D No. 6 calls at Pulham Market for Break Goods and Cattle only, except on Saturdays when it will work any description of Traffic.

E No. 7. A limited number of Trucks may be attached to this Train if required.

GER working timetable 1877.

ex Norwich to Beccles departed Tivetshall at 1.08pm, conveying Parliamentary fare paying passengers from stations the London side of Ipswich. It could also convey a limited number of trucks from Tivetshall for branch stations. The 4.15pmSX ex Tivetshall was permitted to work cattle traffic forward from Harleston but ran at the later time of 5.45pmSO. The last Down train of the day, the 7.50pm ex Norwich to Beccles, departed Tivetshall at 8.30pm. All passenger trains only called at Pulham Market, Pulham St. Mary, Wortwell, Earsham, Ditchingham, Ellingham and Geldeston if required. The solitary goods train departed Norwich at 6.00am and after serving stations on the main line departed Tivetshall at 9.10am with a four-hours timing to Beccles, making mandatory calls at Harleston, Homersfield and Bungay, and serving the other stations with the exception of Wortwell and Earsham only if required. Five MThO and four MThX passenger trains ran in the Up direction, augmented by one MO and two MX goods trains. The 9.20am ex Beccles passenger train was a through service to Norwich, as was the 5.00pm ex Yarmouth, which departed Beccles at 5.45pm. The 5.35am ex Beccles omitted calling at Geldeston, Ellingham, Ditchingham and Wortwell, and called only if required at Pulham Mary and Pulham Market; all other passenger services called at these stations only if required. The 2.30pm ex Beccles conveyed Parliamentary fare paying passengers from the Waveney Valley district destined for London and intermediate stations, and could also work perishable and other important brake goods, whilst the 5.00pm ex Yarmouth could attach a limited number of trucks from the branch stations. The branch was served by the 5.00amMX ex Lowestoft goods train, which departed Beccles at 6.00am, and the 2.45pm ex Beccles. The 5.00amMX goods ex Lowestoft served Bungay, Homersfield and Harleston, but only called at Geldeston, Ellingham, Ditchingham and Pulham Market if required and omitted calling at Earsham and Pulham Mary. The 2.45pm goods ex Beccles served all important stations but only called at Geldeston, Ellingham, Earsham and Pulham Mary if required, and called at Pulham Market for brake goods and cattle traffic only, except on Saturdays when any traffic could be collected.

The timetable for 1882 had the weekdays only passenger service illustrated below.

The working timetable for 1883 showed a service of six passenger trains MThSO and five passenger trains TuWFO in the Down direction, augmented by an excursion train from Norwich to Yarmouth via the Waveney Valley running on Mondays only. The 7.30am ex Tivetshall ran MThO whilst the 8.30am ex Tivetshall was a through train to Yarmouth calling at all stations on the branch except Earsham. The 10.38am from Tivetshall was a through train from Wymondham to Ipswich via Beccles, whilst the 12.05pm passenger train ex Norwich (12.42pm ex Tivetshall) terminated at Beccles. The 3.36pm from Tivetshall was permitted to convey not

Timetable for 1882 Weekdays Only

Down		MThO				SX	SO	WO	
		am	am	am	pm	pm	pm	pm	pm
Tivetshall	dep	7.30	8.55	10.36	12.45	3.35	5.30		8.25
Pulham Market	dep	*	*	*	*	*	*		*
Pulham Mary	dep	*	*	*	*	*	*		
Harleston	dep	8.00	9.15	10.52	1.05	3.56	5.50	6.50	8.45
Homersfield	dep	8.07	9.22	10.59	1.12	4.03	5.57	*	8.52
Earsham	dep	*	*	*	*	*	*	*	*
Bungay	dep	8.20	9.36	11.09	1.24	4.15	6.24	7.30	9.04
Ditchingham	dep	*	*	*	*	*	*	*	*
Ellingham	dep	*	*	*	*	*	*	*	*
Geldeston	dep	8.34	9.51	11.22	1.39	4.30	6.40	*	9.19
Beccles	arr	8.40	9.57	11.28	1.45	4.36	6.46	8.10	9.25
Up		MThO							
		am	am	am	pm	pm			
Beccles	dep	6.15	7.20	9.15	2.00	6.05			
Geldeston	dep		*	*	*	*			
Ellingham	dep	*	*	*	*	*			
Ditchingham	dep	*	*	*	*	*			
Bungay	dep	6.28	7.41	9.38	2.21	6.26			
Earsham	dep	*	*	*	*	*			
Homersfield	dep	6.38	7.51	9.49	2.31	6.36			
Harleston	dep	6.45	8.00	10.00	2.40	6.45			
Pulham Mary	dep	*	*	*	*	*			
Pulham Market	dep	*	*	*	*	*			
Tivetshall	arr	7.05	8.20	10.20	2.59	7.04			

Notes: * Stops by signal to take up and set down on informing the guard at the preceding stopping place.
MThO Runs Monday and Thursday only.
WO Runs Wednesday only.

220

The Trains on this Single Line are worked by Train Staff and Train Staff Ticket, according to the "Train Staff Regulations" contained in the "Appendix" to this Working Time Book. No Engine or Train is to be run on this Branch without a Train Staff or Train Staff Ticket. The Train Staff Stations are Tivetshall, Harleston, Bungay, and Beccles.

WAVENEY VALLEY BRANCH.—*Single Line.*

Down Trains.—Week Days.

Miles from Tivetshall.	FROM	1 Pass.	2 A Exc.	3 Pass.	4 B Brk. Gds.	5 Pass.	6 C Parl.	7 D Pass.	8 Mkt.	9 E Gds.	10 Pass.	11	12	13
		a.m.	a.m.	a.m.	a.m.	a.m.	noon	p.m.	p.m.	p.m.	p.m.			
	Norwich ....dep.	...	6 50	...	6 0	...	12 5	...	...	...	7 50	...	...	...
—	**Tivetshall** ....arr.	.....	7 40	.....	8 30	9 27	12 34	.....	.....	5 40	8 20	.....	.....	.....
	dep.	7 30	7 41	8 50	9 5	10 38	12 42	3 36	5 30	6 0	8 25	...	...	...
2¼	Pulham Market ...... „	7 37	7 48	8 56	*	10 44	12 48	3 42	5 37	*	8 31	.....	.....	.....
3¾	Pulham Mary .... „	*	7 52	*	*	...	*	*	*	*	*	...	...	...
6¼	Harleston...............arr.	7 49	7 58	9 7	9 45	10 53	12 59	3 53	5 40	6 30	8 42	.....	.....	.....
	dep	7 54	8 10	9 8	10 15	10 54	1 0	3 54	5 50	6 50	8 43	...	...	...
8¾	Homersfield .... „	8 1	8 20	9 15	10 40	11 1	1 7	4 1	5 57	*	8 50	.....	.....	.....
12	Earsham.................. „	*	...	*	...	...	*	*	*	E	*	...	...	...
12¾	Bungay ....arr.	8 12	8 30	9 28	10 55	11 10	1 18	4 12	6 8	7 15	9 1	.....	.....	.....
	dep.	8 13	8 35	9 30	11 40	11 11	1 19	4 13	6 24	7 30	9 2	..	...	...
13¾	Ditchingham........... „	*	8 39	*	*	.....	*	*	*	*	*	.....	.....	.....
15¾	Ellingham .... „	*	8 44	*	*	*	*	*	*	*	*	...	...	...
16¾	Geldeston ....arr.	8 26	8 48	9 42	*	11 22	1 32	4 26	6 37	*	9 14	.....	.....	.....
	dep	8 28	8 40	9 44	...	11 24	1 34	4 28	6 40	...	9 16	...	...	...
19¼	**Beccles** ....arr	8 34	8 57	9 50	12 45	11 30	1 40	4 35	6 46	8 10	9 22	.....	.....	.....
	Yarmouth ....arr.		9 40	10 40	.....	.....	.....	.....	.....	.....	.....	.....	.....	.....
	Ipswich .... „		...	...	...	1 21	...	...	...	...	...	...	...	...
		Mondays and Thursdays only.	Mondays only.	See page 213	See page 196	See page 221 and 215	See page 197		Saturdays only.	See No. 6 Up Train, page 221.	See page 199			

A No. 2 to cross No. 3 Up Train at Harleston.
B No. 4. To shunt at Bungay for No. 5 Down Passenger Train. On Saturdays not to leave Bungay until No. 5 Up Passenger Train arrives.
C No. 6 Parliamentary from Stations London side of Ipswich. Not exceeding 4 Trucks may be attached at Tivetshall if required; also not exceeding 2 Trucks of Beer for Bungay may be attached at Norwich.
D No. 7 may work not exceeding 4 Trucks Cattle from Harleston when required.
E No. 9. On Mondays not to leave Bungay until No. 9 Up Train arrives. On Wednesdays, 4th and 18th July, to leave Tivetshall at 6.10 p.m. (on arrival of 5.45 p.m. from Harleston) not call at Pulham Market or Pulham Mary, and be due at Harleston at 6.30 p.m. On Wednesdays is a Mixed Train between Harleston and Beccles and calls at Earsham if required. On Thursdays a Carriage is to be attached to this Train for the conveyance of Passengers from Bungay to Beccles and intermediate Stations.

Up Trains.—Week Days.

Miles from Beccles.	FROM	1 Pass.	2 F Gds.	3 G Pass.	4 H Pass.	5 I Pass.	6 K Parl.	7 ‡ Brk. Gds.	8 L Pass	9 M Exc.	10	11	12	13
		a.m.	a.m.	a.m.	a.m.	a.m.	p.m.	p.m.	p.m.	p.m.				
	Lowestoft ....dep.	.....	.....	.....	.....	.....	.....	.....	.....	.....	.....	.....	.....	.....
	Yarmouth .... „	...	...	..	...	...	...	...	5 10	6 45	...	...	...	...
—	**Beccles** ....dep.	6 15	6 20	7 13	9 10	11 37	2 0	2 20	6 5	7 22	...	...	...	...
2½	Geldeston .... „	.....	.....	*	*	*	*	*	*	7 28	.....	.....	.....	.....
4	Ellingham .... „	...	...	*	*	*	*	*	*	7 33	...	...	...	...
5½	Ditchingham............ „	.....	*	*	*	*	*	*	*	7 38	.....	.....	.....	.....
6½	Bungay ....arr.	6 27	6 50	7 33	9 30	11 56	2 20	2 55	6 24	7 42	...	...	...	...
	dep.	6 28	7 10	7 34	9 38	11 57	2 21	3 10	6 26	7 44	.....	.....	.....	.....
7¼	Earsham.................. „	...	...	*	*	*	*	...	*	...	...	...	...	...
10½	Homersfield .... „	6 38	*	7 46	9 49	12 8	2 32	*	6 38	7 54	.....	.....	.....	.....
13	Harleston...............arr.	6 44	7 40	7 52	9 58	12 14	2 39	3 35	6 44	8 0	...	...	...	...
	dep.	6 45	8 20	7 53	10 0	12 15	2 40	4 0	6 45	8 2	.....	.....	.....	.....
15½	Pulham Mary .... „	*	...	*	*	*	*	*	*	8 11	...	...	...	...
16¾	Pulham Market ...... „	6 58	.....	8 4	10 11	12 26	2 51	*	6 56	8 16	.....	.....	.....	.....
19¼	**Tivetshall** ....arr.	7 5	8 40	8 10	10 17	12 32	2 57	4 30	7 2	8 22	...	...	...	...
	dep.	.....	9 10	.....	10 22		2 58	4 55	7 5		.....	.....	.....	.....
	Norwich ....arr.	.....	.....	.....	10 53	.....	To Forncett	5 55	7 33	9 10	.....	.....	.....	.....
		Mondays and Thursdays only.	See No. 2 Down Train, page 221.		See page 190	Saturdays only.	See page 190	See page 191	See page 215 and 191	Mondays only.				

F No. 2. To shunt at Harlestone for No. 3 Passenger Train.
G No. 3. On Mondays not to leave Harleston until No. 2 Down Train has arrived.
H No. 4. Two Trucks of London Goods for Ditchingham and Bungay may be worked from Beccles by this Train. Not exceeding 2 Trucks of Pigs may be worked from Pulham Market by this Train.
I No. 5 to cross No. 4 Down Train at Bungay.
K No. 6 Parliamentary from Waveney Valley District to London and intermediate Stations.
L No. 8. Not exceeding 6 Trucks may be attached to this Train if required.
M No. 9 to cross No. 9 Down Train at Bungay.

‡ *No. 7. On Wednesdays, 4th and 18th July, the Engine, &c., of this Train to return from Tivetshall to Harleston at 4.50 p.m., and leave Harleston for Norwich with Cattle at 5.45 p.m., be due at Tivetshall at 6.5., depart 6..20 p.m., and be due at Norwich at 7.10 p.m.*

ABOVE: GER working timetable 1883.

BELOW: GER public timetable 1884.

WAVENEY VALLEY BRANCH.

Junctions with Colchester Main Line at Tivetshall, and with East Suffolk Main Line at Beccles.

FROM	WEEK DAYS. mrn	morn	morn	mrn	morn	even.	even.
LONDON (Liverpool Street) ....dep.	Mondays only.	...	5 10	Saturdays only.	10 0	...	3 20
Ipswich................ „		...	7 8		11 52	...	5 6
Woodbridge .... „		...	7 32		12 16	...	5 24
Saxmundham...... „		...	7 59		12 41	...	5 51
Halesworth......... „		...	8 20		1 2	...	6 11
Beccles ....arr.		...	8 35		1 16	..	6 25
Yarmouth (S. T.) dep.		6 15	8 15	...	1 10	6 15	6 5
Lowestoft............ „		6 20	8 17	...	12 50	5 45	...
Beccles ....arr.		6 47	8 42	...	1 43	6 3	6 40
Beccles ....dep.	6 15	7 5	9 0	1135	2 0	6 4	6 45
Geldeston .... „	...	7 12	9 7	1141	2 7	6 10	6 54
Ellingham .... „	...	7 17	9 12	1146	2 12	6 15	6 59
Ditchingham .... „	...	7 22	9 17	1151	2 17	6 20	7 4
Bungay .... „	6 28	7 26	9 28	1155	2 21	6 25	7 8
Earsham .... „	...	7 29	9 31	1158	2 24	6 28	7 11
Homersfield .... „	6 38	7 38	9 38	12 5	2 32	6 36	7 19
Harleston .... „	6 45	7 45	9 50	1212	2 40	6 44	7 27
Pulham Mary .... „	6 53	7 52	9 57	1218	2 47	6 51	7 35
Pulham Market ...... „	6 58	7 56	10 1	1222	2 51	6 55	7 39
Tivetshall..............arr.	7 5	8 2	10 7	1228	2 57	7 1	7 45
Tivetshall ....dep.	...	8 9	10 12	1232	2 58	7 3	7 48
Forncett ....arr	...	8 19	10 22	1240	3 6	7 10	7 55
Dereham .... „	...	9 7	11 28	1 38	..	8 19	...
Norwich (Vic.) ... „	...	8 53	10 45	1 8	3 55	7 33	...
Norwich (Thorpe) „	...	8 45	...	1 10	...	8 5	8 25
Tivetshall ....dep.	7 10	...	10 37	...	2 58	7 15	...
Diss ....arr.	7 27	...	10 51	...	3 34	7 29	...
Bury .... „	8 24	...	12 25	...	5 36	8 30	...
Ipswich.................. „	8 32	...	11 53	...	4 16	8 35	...
LONDON (Liverpool Street) ....arr.	1030	...	2 10	...	6 0	...	...

FROM	WEEK DAYS. mrn	morn	morn	morn	noon		even.		even.	Mixd even	evn.	
LONDON (Liverpool Street) ....dep.	Mondys only.	5 10	...	9 3	12 0		...		3 20	...	3 5	...
Ipswich................ „		7 3	...	11 21	2 10		...		5 2	Thursdays only.	6 53	...
Bury .... „		7 3	...	10 38	2 10		...		...		6 53	...
Diss .... „		8 9	...	12 18	3 11		...		5 57		7 56	...
Tivetshall ....arr.		8 23	...	12 32	3 25		...		6 7		8 12	...
Norwich (Thorpe) dep.	...	8 0	10 0	...	2 55	Saturdays only Market.	...	Wednesdays only.	...		...	...
Norwich (Vic.) ... „	6 40	...	10 0	12 5			4 50		...		7 50	...
Dereham .... „		...	8C26	10 48	2 38		...		...		5 40	...
Forncett .... „	7 2	8 28	10 28	12 27	3 26		5 15		...		8 13	...
Tivetshall............arr.	7 10	8 35	10 37	12 34	...		5 20		Mixd		8 20	—
Tivetshall ....dep.	7 25	8 40	10 38	12 38	3 36		5 30		6 8	...	8 25	...
Pulham Market ...... „	7 32	8 46	10 44	12 44	3 42		5 37		*	...	8 31	...
Pulham Mary .... „	7 37	8 51	10 48	12 48	3 47		5 42		*	...	8 36	...
Harleston .... „	7 46	8 58	10 55	12 55	3 54		5 50		7 30	...	8 43	...
Homersfield .... „	7 55	9 5	11 2	1 2	4 1		5 57		*	...	8 50	...
Earsham.................. „	8 3	9 14	11 10	1 10	4 9		6 5		*	...	8 58	...
Bungay .... „	8 7	9 20	11 14	1 14	4 13		6 23		8 5	8 5	9 2	...
Ditchingham .... „	8 10	9 23	11 17	1 18	4 17		6 27		*	*	9 6	...
Ellingham .... „	8 15	9 28	11 22	1 23	4 22		6 32		*	*	9 10	...
Geldestone.............. „	8 23	9 34	11 28	1 29	4 28		6 39		*	*	9 16	...
Beccles ....arr.	8 30	9 40	11 34	1 35	4 35		6 45		8 45	8 45	9 22	—
Beccles ....dep.	8 41	9B15	11 57	1 45	6D5		8 23		...	...	...	...
Lowestoft............arr.	9 20	10 11	12 23	2 11	6 58		8 41		...	...	...	...
Yarmouth (S. T.) „	9 20	10 30	12 32	2A22	6 40		9 2		...	...	...	...
Beccles ....dep.	8 48	...	11 50	2 52	6 17		7 2		...	...	...	...
Halesworth ....arr.	9 3	...	12 11	3 9	7 21		7 21		...	...	...	...
Saxmundham ...... „	9 21	...	12 31	3 28	7 39		7 39		...	...	...	...
Woodbridge......... „	9 50	...	1 2	3 51	8 7		8 7		...	...	...	...
Ipswich................ „	10 10	...	1 28	4 10	7 15		8 30		...	...	...	...
LONDON (Liverpool Street) ....arr.	12 7	...	3 25	6 0	9 5		...		...	...	...	...

A Not to Yarmouth on Saturdays.
B Leaves Beccles for Yarmouth at 11.7 a.m. on Saturdays.
C Not from Dereham on Mondays.
D On Saturdays leaves Beccles at 4.42 p.m., due at Yarmouth at 5.17 p.m. On Fridays due at Lowestoft at 5.13 p.m.
* Will call *only* when required to take up or set down Passengers. Passengers wishing to alight must intimate the same to the Guard at the preceding *stopping* Station.

exceeding four cattle trucks from Harleston when required. The 5.30pm from Tivetshall market train ran SO, whilst the last Down train of the day, the 7.50pm ex Norwich (8.25pm ex Tivetshall), terminated at Beccles. All passenger services called at Pulham St. Mary, Earsham, Ditchingham and Ellingham only if required, although the 10.38 am ex Tivetshall also omitted calling at Earsham and Ditchingham. Of the two goods trains in the Down direction, the 6.00am ex Norwich which entered the branch at 9.05am made mandatory calls at Harleston, Homersfield and Bungay, and served the other stations only if required, arriving at Beccles at 12.45pm. The afternoon Down goods train, 6.00pm ex Tivetshall, also only served the smaller stations if required; on Wednesdays it ran as a mixed train between Harleston and Beccles calling at Earsham only if required; on Thursdays a carriage was attached to this train for the conveyance of passengers from Bungay and intermediate stations to Beccles. In the Up direction the branch was served on weekdays by five passenger trains MThSO and four TuWFO, augmented by the return excursion train from Yarmouth to Norwich via Beccles. The 6.15am MThO train omitted calling at Geldeston, Ellingham, Ditchingham and Earsham, and served Pulham St. Mary only if required. The 7.15am Beccles to Tivetshall and 9.10am Beccles to Norwich served Geldeston, Ellingham, Ditchingham, Earsham and Pulham St. Mary only if required, the latter reaching Norwich at 10.33am. The 11.31am ex Beccles ran SO, whilst the 2.00pm ex Beccles Parliamentary train operated through to Forncett. The 5.10pm Yarmouth to Tivetshall and 8.05pm ex Beccles, the last booked service across the branch, like the other passenger services called at Geldeston, Ellingham, Ditchingham, Earsham and Pulham St. Mary only if required; the latter train was permitted to take not exceeding six cattle trucks. The 6.45pmMO Yarmouth to Norwich via the branch excursion train called at all stations except Earsham, arriving at its destination at 9.10pm. The two goods services in the Up direction departed Beccles at 6.20am, making mandatory calls at Bungay and Harleston, and called at Ditchingham and Homersfield only if required. The second train, the 2.20pm ex Beccles, was a through service to Norwich arriving at 5.55pm, making mandatory calls at Bungay, Homesfield and Harlestion, and other stations only if required.

By 1886 the passenger services shown opposite were operated on weekdays only. By 1887 the timetable had been modified, the table reproduced here shows the passenger services running on weekdays only. Calls at the intermediate stations were by request.

By 1892 the weekdays-only working timetable showed six passenger trains MWSO and five on other days in the Down direction, augmented by two goods trains. The 7.35amMO ex Tivetshall served all stations, as did the 8.45am ex Tivetshall, which was a through train to Yarmouth, arriving Beccles at 9.40am and its destination at 10.25am. The 10.40am ex Tivetshall was a through working from Norwich (departing 8.05am) which arrived at the junction at 8.40am, from where after the prolonged wait it arrived at Beccles at 11.31am. The 12.03pm ex Norwich to Beccles departed Tivetshall at 12.40pm and was permitted to attach four trucks at the junction for conveyance across the branch. This train could also take not exceeding two trucks of beer from Norwich to Bungay, and on Mondays departed Tivetshall at 12.47pm running 7 minutes later throughout. The next Down passenger train, the 3.34pm ex Tivetshall, started back at Forncett at 3.20pm where it provided a cross-country connection for the branch train from Wymondham and Ashwellthorpe. The 5.10pmSO Norwich to Beccles entered the branch at Tivetshall at 5.40pm and like other services called at

244

The Trains on this Single Line are worked by Train Staff and Train Staff Ticket, according to the "Train Staff Regulations" contained in the "Appendix" to this Working Time Book. No Engine or Train is to be run on this Branch without a Train Staff or Train Staff Ticket. The Train Staff Stations are Tivetshall, Harleston, Bungay, and Beccles.

WAVENEY VALLEY BRANCH.—*Single Line.*

Down Trains.—Week Days.

Miles from Tivetshall.	FROM	1	2	3	4	5	6	7	8	9	10	11	12	13
		Pass.	Pass.	A Pass.	B Brk. Gds.	Pass.	D Pass.	E Pass.	Mkt.	F Gds.	Pass.			
		a.m.	a.m.	a.m.	a.m.	a.m.	p.m.	p.m.	p.m.	p.m.	p.m.			
	Norwich ....dep.	6 45	6 45	...	6 0	...	12 5	...	...	...	7 50	...	...	...
	Forncett .... „	7 13	7 13	.....	*	.....	12 27	3 56	.....	5 40	8 13	.....	.....	.....
—	**Tivetshall** ....arr.	7 20	7 20	.....	8 20	.....	12 34	4 3	.....	5 50	8 20	.....	.....	.....
	dep.	7 25	7 25	8 40	9 0	10 38	12 42	4 6	5 30	6 5	8 25	...	...	...
2¼	Pulham Market ...... „	7 32	7 32	8 46	*	10 44	12 48	4 12	5 37	F	8 31	.....	.....	.....
3¾	Pulham Mary .... „	7 37	7 37	8 51	*	...	12 52	4 17	5 42	*	8 36	...	...	...
6¼	Harleston...............arr.	7 43	7 43	8 57	9 40	10 53	12 58	4 23	5 49	6 30	8 42	.....	.....	.....
	dep	7 48	7 55	8 58	10 15	10 54	12 59	4 24	5 50	7 30	8 43	...	...	...
8¾	Homersfield .... „	7 55	8 5	9 5	10 40	11 1	1 6	4 31	5 57	*	8 50	.....	.....	.....
12	Earsham.................. „	8 3	8 14	9 14	...	...	1 14	4 39	6 5	F	8 58	...	...	...
12¾	Bungay ....arr.	8 6	8 17	9 18	10 55	11 10	1 17	4 42	6 8	7 55	9 1	.....	.....	.....
	dep.	8 7	8 20	9 20	11 40	11 11	1 18	4 43	6 23	8 5	9 2	..	...	...
13¾	Ditchingham............ „	8 10	8 24	9 23	*	.....	1 22	4 47	6 27	*	9 5	.....	.....	.....
15½	Ellingham .... „	8 15	8 30	9 28	*	11 18	1 27	4 52	6 32	*	9 10	...	...	...
16¾	Geldeston ....arr.	8 20	8 35	9 32	*	11 22	1 31	4 56	6 36	*	9 14	.....	.....	.....
	dep	8 23	8 37	9 34	...	11 24	1 33	4 58	6 39	...	9 16	...	...	...
19¼	**Beccles** ....arr	8 30	8 44	9 40	12 45	11 30	1 40	5 5	6 45	8 45	9 22	.....	.....	.....
	Yarmouth ....arr.		9 32	10 30	.....	.....	.....	.....	.....	.....	.....	.....	.....	.....
	Ipswich .... „			...	...	...	...	...	...	...	...	...	...	...
		Tuesdays, Wednesdays, Fridays, and Saturdays.	Mondays and Thursdays only	See page 237	See page 217	See page 217	See page 218	See page 219	Saturdays only.	See No. 6 Up Train, page 245.	See page 221			

A No. 3. Not exceeding 2 Trucks of Cattle may be worked from Harleston to Beccles by this Train.
B No. 4. To shunt at Bungay for No. 5 Down Passenger Train. On Saturdays not to leave Bungay until No. 5 Up Passenger Train arrives.
D No. 6. Not exceeding 4 Trucks may be attached at Tivetshall if required; also not exceeding 2 Trucks of Beer for Bungay may be attached at Norwich.
E No. 7 may work not exceeding 4 Trucks Cattle from Harleston when required.
F No. 9. On Wednesdays to leave Tivetshall at 6.8 p.m. and be a Mixed Train between Tivetshall and Beccles calling at Pulham Market, and Earsham if required. On Thursdays a Carriage is to be attached to this Train for the conveyance of Passengers from Bungay to Beccles and intermediate Stations.

Up Trains.—Week Days.

Miles from Beccles.	FROM	1	2	3	4	5	6	7	8	9	10	11	12	13
		Pass.	G Gds.	Pass.	H Pass.	I Pass.	Pass.	K Brk. Gds.	Pass.	L Pass.				
		a.m.	a.m.	a.m.	a.m.	a.m.	p.m.	p.m.	p.m.	p.m.				
	Lowestoft ....dep.	.....	.....	.....	.....	.....	.....	.....	.....	.....	.....	.....	.....	.....
	Yarmouth .... „	...	...	..	...	...	...	...	5 15	6 5	...	...	...	...
—	**Beccles** ....dep.	6 15	6 20	7 5	9 0	11 35	2 0	2 20	6 4	6 47	...	...	...	...
2½	Geldeston .... „	.....	.....	7 12	9 7	11 41	2 7	*	6 10	6 54	.....	.....	.....	.....
4	Ellingham .... „	...	...	7 17	9 12	11 46	2 12	*	6 15	6 59	...	...	...	...
5½	Ditchingham............ „	.....	*	7 22	9 17	11 51	2 17	*	6 20	7 4	.....	.....	.....	.....
6½	Bungay ....arr.	6 27	6 50	7 25	9 20	11 54	2 20	2 55	6 23	7 7	...	...	...	...
	dep.	6 28	7 10	7 26	9 28	11 55	2 21	3 10	6 25	7 8	.....	.....	.....	.....
7½	Earsham.................. „	...	...	7 29	9 31	11 58	2 24	...	6 28	7 11	...	...	...	...
10½	Homersfield .... „	6 38	*	7 38	9 39	12 5	2 32	*	6 36	7 19	.....	.....	.....	.....
13	Harleston...............arr.	6 44	7 35	7 44	9 48	12 11	2 39	3 35	6 43	7 25	...	...	...	...
	dep.	6 45	8 10	7 45	9 50	12 12	2 45	4 25	6 44	7 27	.....	.....	.....	.....
15½	Pulham Mary .... „	6 53	...	7 52	9 57	12 18	2 52	*	6 51	7 35	...	...	...	...
16¾	Pulham Market ...... „	6 58	.....	7 56	10 1	12 22	2 56	*	6 55	7 39	.....	.....	.....	.....
19¼	**Tivetshall** ....arr.	7 5	8 30	8 2	10 7	12 28	3 2	4 55	7 1	7 45	...	...	...	...
	dep.	.....	9 10	.....	10 12		3 3	5 10	7 3	7 48	.....	.....	.....	.....
	Forncett ....arr.	...	9 20	...	10 19	...	3 11	*	7 9	7 54	...	...	...	...
	Norwich .... „	.....	.....	.....	10 45	.....	.....	6 10	7 33	8 25	.....	.....	.....	.....
			See No. 4 Down Train, page 245.		See page 209	Saturdays only.	See page 209	See page 210	See page 239 and 211	See page 211				

G No. 2. To shunt at Harleston for No. 3 Up Passenger Train.
H No. 4. Two Trucks of London Goods for Ditchingham and Bungay may be worked from Beccles by this Train. Not exceeding 2 Trucks of Pigs may be worked from Pulham Market by this Train.
I No. 5 to cross No. 4 Down Train at Bungay.
K No. 7. On Wednesdays to leave Harleston at 4.30 p.m. and be due at Tivetshall at 5.0, depart 5.20 p.m., Norwich arrive 6.20 p.m.
L No. 9. Not exceeding 6 Trucks may be attached to this Train if required.

GER working timetable 1885.

Timetable for 1886 Weekdays Only											
Down		MThO					SX	SO	WO	ThO	
		am	am	am	pm	pm	pm	pm	pm	pm	pm
Tivetshall	dep	7.25	8.40	10.38	12.42	3.20	4.35	5.30	6.08		8.25
Pulham Market	dep	7.32	8.46	10.44	12.48	3.26	4.41	5.37	*		8.31
Pulham Mary	dep	7.37	8.51		12.52	3.31	4.46	5.42	*		8.36
Harleston	dep	7.45	8.58	10.54	12.59	3.38	4.53	5.50	7.30		8.43
Homersfield	dep	7.52	9.05	11.01	1.06	3.43	5.00	5.57	*		8.50
Earsham	dep	8.00	9.14		1.14	3.53	5.08	6.05	*		8.58
Bungay	dep	8.05	9.20	11.11	1.18	3.57	5.12	6.23	8.05	8.05	9.02
Ditchingham	dep	8.08	9.23		1.22	4.01	5.16	6.27	*	*	9.05
Ellingham	dep	8.13	9.28	11.18	1.27	4.06	5.21	6.32	*	*	9.10
Geldeston	dep	8.19	9.34	11.24	1.33	4.13	5.28	6.39	*	*	9.16
Beccles	arr	8.25	9.40	11.30	1.40	4.20	5.35	6.45	8.45	8.45	9.22
Up		MThO									
		am	am	am	am/pm	pm	pm	pm			
Beccles	dep	6.15	7.05	9.00	11.35	2.00	6.04	6.50			
Geldeston	dep		7.12	9.07	11.41	2.07	6.10	6.59			
Ellingham	dep		7.17	9.12	11.46	2.12	6.15	7.04			
Ditchingham	dep		7.22	9.17	11.51	2.17	6.20	7.09			
Bungay	dep	6.28	7.26	9.28	11.55	2.21	6.25	7.13			
Easham	dep		7.29	9.31	11.58	2.24	6.28	7.16			
Homersfield	dep	6.38	7.38	9.39	12.05	2.32	6.36	7.24			
Harleston	dep	6.45	7.45	9.50	12.12	2.40	6.44	7.32			
Pulham Mary	dep	6.53	7.52	9.57	12.18	2.47	6.51	7.40			
Pulham Market	dep	6.58	7.56	10.01	12.22	2.51	6.55	7.44			
Tivetshall	arr	7.04	8.02	10.07	12.28	2.57	7.01	7.50			
Note: * Stops when required to pick up or set down passengers											

all stations, whilst the last Down service, 7.50pm from Norwich, 8.25pm ex Tivetshall on Saturdays, could work not exceeding four trucks of cattle from Norwich Victoria to Waveney Valley Branch destinations. Two short workings operated in connection with local markets, the 5.25pmWO Harleston to Beccles and the 5.41pmThO Bungay to Beccles, both permitted to take not exceeding four trucks of cattle. Freight traffic across the branch was handled by the 7.00am brake goods train from Norwich, which after spending 35 minutes at the junction departed Tivetshall at 8.55am, serving Pulham Market and Pulham St. Mary only if required before calling at all other stations with arrival at Beccles at 12.55pm. The afternoon freight service was the 4.30pm ex Wymondham, which departed

Passenger Timetable for 1887 Weekdays Only							
Down		MThO					
		am	am	am	pm	pm	pm
Tivetshall	dep	7.30	8.45	10.40	12.42	3.20	8.25
Harleston	dep	7.50	9.05	10.56	12.58	3.36	8.41
Homersfield	dep	7.56	9.11	11.02	1.04	3.42	8.47
Bungay	dep	8.06	9.21	11.12	1.14	3.52	8.57
Beccles	arr	8.25	9.40	11.31	1.33	4.11	9.16
Up		MThO					
		am	am	am	pm	pm	pm
Beccles	dep	6.20	7.10	9.02	2.05	6.05	6.32
Bungay	dep	6.33	7.28	9.34	2.24	6.23	7.10
Homersfield	dep	6.41	7.38	9.44	2.34	6.33	7.20
Harleston	dep	6.47	7.45	9.50	2.41	6.39	7.31
Tivetshall	arr	7.02	8.00	10.05	2.56	6.54	7.46

304

WAVENEY VALLEY BRANCH.—*Single Line.*

The Trains on this Single Line are worked by Train Staff and Train Staff Ticket, according to the "Train Staff Regulations" contained in the "Appendix" o this Working Time Book. No Engine or Train is to be run on this Branch without a Train Staff or Train Staff Ticket. The Train Staff Stations are Tivetshall, Harleston, Bungay, and Beccles.

Down Trains.—Week Days.

Miles from Tivetshall.	FROM	1	2	3	4	5	6	7	8	9	10	11	12	13	14
		Pass.	A Pass.	B Brk. Gds.	C Pass.	D Pass.	Pass.	E Pass.	F Pass.	Mkt. Pass.	G Gds.	H Pass.			
		a.m.	a.m.	a.m.	a.m.	p.m.	p.m.	p.m.	p.m.	p.m.	p.m.	p.m.			
	Norwich ....dep.	...	...	7 0	8 5	12 3	...	...	...	5 10	...	7 50	...	...	...
	Wymondham ... „	...	...	...	...	...	...	...	...	...	4 30	...	...	...	...
	Forncett .... „	...	...	8 10	8 33	12 25	3 26	...	...	5 28	5 40	8 13	...	...	...
—	Tivetshall ....arr.	...	...	8 20	8 40	12 31	3 22	...	...	5 35	5 50	8 20	...	...	...
	Tivetshall ....dep.	7 35	8 45	8 55	10 40	12 40	3 34	...	...	5 40	6 5	8 25	...	...	...
2¾	Pulham Market ...... „	7 41	8 51	*	10 46	12 46	3 40	...	...	5 46	...	8 31	...	...	...
3¾	Pulham Mary .... „	7 44	8 54	*	10 49	12 49	3 43	...	...	5 49	*	8 34	...	...	...
6¼	Harleston..............arr.	7 49	8 59	9 35	10 54	12 54	3 48	...	...	5 54	6 30	8 39	...	...	...
	Harleston..............dep	7 55	9 5	10 5	10 56	12 56	3 50	5 25	...	5 56	7 33	8 41	...	...	...
9	Homersfield .... „	8 1	9 11	10 40	11 2	1 2	3 56	5 31	...	6 2	*	8 47	...	...	...
12	Earsham.................. „	8 7	9 17	...	11 8	1 8	4 2	5 37	...	6 8	...	8 53	...	...	...
12¾	Bungay ....arr.	8 9	9 19	10 55	11 10	1 10	4 4	5 39	...	6 11	7 55	8 55	...	...	...
	Bungay ....dep.	8 11	9 21	11 52	11 12	1 12	4 6	5 41	5 41	6 25	8 5	8 57	...	...	...
13¾	Ditchingham............ „	8 15	9 25	12 5	11 16	1 16	4 10	5 45	5 45	6 29	*	9 1	...	...	...
15¼	Ellingham .... „	8 19	9 29	12 25	11 20	1 20	4 14	5 49	5 49	6 33	*	9 5	...	...	...
16¾	Geldeston ....arr.	8 22	9 32	12 35	11 23	1 23	4 17	5 52	5 52	6 36	*	9 8	...	...	...
	Geldeston ....dep.	8 24	9 34	12 45	11 25	1 25	4 19	5 54	5 54	6 38	...	9 10	...	...	...
19¼	Beccles ....arr	8 30	9 40	12 55	11 31	1 31	4 25	6 0	6 0	6 44	8 35	9 16	...	...	...
	Yarmouth ....arr.	...	10 25	...	...	...	...	...	...	...	...	...	...	...	...
		Mondays only.	See page 297	See page 270	See page 270	See page 271	See page 273	Wednesdays only.	Thursdays only.	Saturdays only.	See page 305 and 274	See page 275			

A No. 2. May work not exceeding 2 Trucks of Cattle from Harleston to Beccles.
B No. 3. To shunt at Bungay for No. 4 Passenger Train.
D No. 5. Not exceeding 4 Trucks may be attached at Tivetshall if required; also not exceeding 2 Trucks of Beer for Bungay may be attached at Norwich. On Mondays leaves Tivetshall at 12.47 p.m. and runs 7 minutes later.
E No. 7. May work not exceeding 4 Trucks of Cattle from Harleston to Beccles.
F No. 8. May work not exceeding 4 Trucks of Cattle from Bungay to Beccles.
G No. 10. This Train is to call at Pulham Mary, Ditchingham, Ellingham, and Geldeston to attach Traffic for Yarmouth, Lowestoft, and London. Ditchingham, Ellingham, and Geldeston to advise Bungay what Trucks they have to go forward by this Train. Bungay to arrange load accordingly. Traffic worked by this Train for Ditchingham, Ellingham, and Geldeston to be left at Bungay; that Station to send forward next day by the 7.0 a.m. Goods Train Norwich to Beccles.
H No. 11. **On Saturdays** not exceeding 4 Trucks of Cattle for he W. V. Line may be worked from Norwich (Victoria) by this Train.

Up Trains.—Week Days.

Miles from Beccles.	FROM	1	2	3	4	5	6	7	8	9	10	11	12
		Pass.	Pass.	I Gds.	K Pass.	Pass.	Pass.	Brk. Gds.	Cars.	Cars.	Pass.	M Pass.	
		a.m.	a.m.	a.m.	a.m.	a.m.	p.m.	p.m.	p.m.	p.m.	p.m.	p.m.	
	Yarmouth ....dep.	...	...	...	...	...	...	...	...	...	5 15	6 7	...
—	Beccles ....dep.	6 30	7 15	7 22	9 2	11 35	2 5	2 12	4 45	4 50	6 5	6 55	...
2½	Geldeston .... „	...	7 21	...	9 8	11 41	2 11	*	...	...	6 11	7 1	...
4½	Ellingham .... „	...	7 25	...	9 12	11 45	2 15	*	...	...	6 15	7 5	...
5¾	Ditchingham............ „	...	7 29	7 50	9 16	11 49	2 19	*	...	...	6 19	7 9	...
6½	Bungay ....arr.	6 42	7 32	7 55	9 19	11 52	2 22	2 45	...	5 3	6 22	7 12	...
	Bungay ....dep.	6 43	7 33	8 20	9 42	11 53	2 24	3 0	4 57	...	6 23	7 13	...
7½	Earsham.................. „	...	7 36	...	9 45	11 56	2 27	...	...	...	6 26	7 16	...
10½	Homersfield .... „	6 51	7 43	*	9 52	12 3	2 34	*	...	...	6 33	7 23	...
13½	Harleston..............arr.	6 56	7 49	8 45	9 57	12 8	2 39	3 25	5 10	...	6 38	7 28	...
	Harleston..............dep.	6 57	7 50	10 5	9 58	12 9	2 41	4 0	...	...	6 39	7 31	...
15¾	Pulham Mary .... „	7 3	7 56	*	10 4	12 15	2 47	*	...	...	6 45	7 37	...
16½	Pulham Market ...... „	7 6	7 59	...	10 7	12 18	2 50	*	...	...	6 48	7 40	...
19½	Tivetshall ....arr.	7 12	8 5	10 30	10 13	12 24	2 56	4 40	...	...	6 54	7 46	...
	Tivetshall ....dep.	...	...	11 10	10 25	12 25	2 58	5 0	...	...	6 56	7 48	...
	Forncett ....arr.	...	...	11 20	10 31	...	3 5	*	...	...	7 2	7 54	...
	Wymondham ... „	...	...	11 40	...	...	...	...	...	...	...	...	...
	Norwich .... „	...	...	...	10 55	12 50	...	6 0	...	...	7 26	8 25	...
		Mondays only.		See page 261 and 305	See page 261	Saturdays only.	See page 262	See page 264	Wednesdays only.	Thursdays only.	See page 299 and 264	See page 299 and 264	

I No. 3. To shunt at Harleston for No. 4 Passenger Train. Load to be limited to 30 Trucks between Bungay and Harleston.

K No. 4. Two Trucks of London Goods for Ditchingham and Bungay may be worked from Beccles by this Train. Not exceeding 2 Trucks of Pigs may be worked from Pulham Market by this Train.

M No. 11. Not exceeding 6 Trucks may be attached to this Train if required.

GER working timetable 1892.

Tivetshall at 6.05pm, making mandatory calls at Harleston and Bungay before reaching Beccles at 8.35pm. This train was to call at Pulham St. Mary, Ditchingham, Ellingham and Geldeston to attach traffic for Yarmouth, Lowestoft or London; the latter stations were to advise Bungay what trucks they had to go forward by this service, with Bungay arranging accordingly. Traffic worked by this train destined for Ditchingham, Ellingham and Geldestion was to be left at Bungay for forwarding the next day by the 7.00am Norwich to Beccles train. In the Up direction the branch was served by six passenger trains MSO and five passenger trains every other weekday, augmented by two empty stock workings. The first train of the day, 6.30amMO ex Beccles, called at Bungay, Homersfield and then all stations, arriving at Tivetshall at 7.12am, whilst the 7.15am ex Beccles called at all stations on the branch. The next service, the 9.02am ex Beccles, was a through train to Norwich arriving at 10.55am; with a 12-minute stand at Tivetshall, it also served Forncett. Two trucks of London goods from Ditchingham and Bungay could be worked by this train together with not exceeding two trucks of pigs from Pulham Market. The 11.35amSO ex Beccles was a through train to Norwich arriving at 12.50pm, whilst the 2.05pm ex Beccles calling all stations to Tivetshall terminated at Forncett to provide connections to Ashwellthorpe and Wymondham. The return train from Yarmouth, departing 5.15pm, was a through train to Norwich calling at all the branch stations from Beccles, departing 6.05pm to Tivetshall (arriving 6.54pm and departing at 6.56pm), then Forncett. The final train of the day was also a through service from Yarmouth, departing 6.07pm to Norwich (arriving at 8.25pm), serving all stations on the branch as well as Forncett, and was permitted to take nor exceeding six trucks of merchandise. The empty coaching stock workings departed 4.45pmWO ex Beccles to Harleston and 4.50pmThO to Bungay, both forming Down trains. Two goods trains catered for the branch freight traffic; the first departed Beccles at 7.22am calling at Ditchingham, Bungay and Harleston, with 'Q', as and when required, calls at Homersfield and Pulham St. Mary, arriving at Tivetshall where 40 minutes were allowed for shunting before departure at 11.10am to Wymondham, arriving at 11.40am. The loading of this train was limited to thirty trucks between Bungay and Harleston. The later freight train, conveying brake goods, departed Beccles at 2.12pm making mandatory calls at Bungay and Harleston, and conditional stops if required at Geldeston, Ellingham, Ditchingham, Homersfield, Pulham St. Mary and Pulham Market. After spending 20 minutes at Tivetshall the train departed the junction at 5.00pm arriving at Norwich at 6.00pm.

Five years later, in 1897, the working timetable showed a service of eight passenger trains MThO and six on other weekdays in the Down direction, augmented by two goods trains. The first service, the 7.26am ex Tivetshall, ran MThO calling at all stations, whilst the 8.45am ex Tivetshall was formed by either ECS departing Norwich at 7.55am, arriving at Tivetshall at 8.27amMThO, or on the other days as the 8.05am passenger train from Norwich calling at Forncett arriving at Tivetshall at 8.40am. This train was permitted to work one truck of cattle only from either Tivetshall or Harleston to Beccles if the truck was fitted with Westinghouse brake pipes, the stations masters at Tivetshall and Harleston arranging locally so that no more than one truck of cattle was accepted on any one day. The next service to traverse the branch was the 8.05am excursion ex Norwich, which departed Tivetshall at 8.55am, calling all stations to Beccles (arriving at 9.55am) and on to Yarmouth, arriving at 10.37am. Three further services from

362

WAVENEY VALLEY BRANCH.—*Single Line.*

The Trains on this Single Line are worked by Train Staff and Train Staff Ticket, according to the "Train Staff Regulations" contained in the "Appendix" to this Working Time Book. No Engine or Train is to be run on this Branch without a Train Staff or Train Staff Ticket. The Train Staff Stations are Tivetshall, Harleston, Bungay, and Beccles.

Down Trains.—Week Days.

Miles from Tivetshall	FROM	1	2	3	4	5	6	7	8	9	10	11	12	13	14	15	16	17	18	19	20	21	22	23	24	25	26	27	28	29	30
		Pass.	Cars.	Pass.	B Pass.	Exc.	C Gds.		Pass.	Pass.	Pass.	Pass		Mkt. Pass.	F Gds.	G Gds.	Pass.														
		a.m.	a.m.	a.m.	a.m.	a.m.	a.m.		a.m.	p.m.	p.m.	p.m.		p.m.	p.m.	p.m.	p.m.														
	Norwich .... dep.	...	7 55	8 5	...	8 5	7 0	...	9 48	12 8	2 50	...	...	5 10	.	...	7 50	...	...	...	...	...	...	...	...	...	...	...	...	...	...
	Wymondham .... ,,	.....	.....	.....	.....	.....	.....	.....	.....	.....	.....	.....	.....	.....	5 20	4 30	.....	.....	.....	.....	.....	.....	.....	.....	.....	.....	.....	.....	.....	.....	.....
	Forncett .... ,,	...	...	8 33	...	8 33	...	...	10 15	12 30	3 12	4 10	...	5 33	5 40	6 25	8 13	...	...	...	...	...	...	...	...	...	...	...	...	...	...
—	Tivetshall .... arr.	.....	8 27	8 40	.....	8 40	8 20	.....	10 21	12 36	3 18	4 17	.....	5 40	5 50	6 35	8 20	.....	.....	.....	.....	.....	.....	.....	.....	.....	.....	.....	.....	.....	.....
	Tivetshall .... dep.	7 26	...		8 45	8 55	8 55	...	10 25	12 50	3 21	4 20	...	5 45	6 5	7 0	8 25	...	...	...	...	...	...	...	...	...	...	...	...	...	...
2¼	Pulham Market .... ,,	7 32			8 51	9 2	*	.....	10 31	12 56	3 27	4 26	.....	5 51	F	G	8 31	.....	.....	.....	.....	.....	.....	.....	.....	.....	.....	.....	.....	.....	.....
3¼	Pulham Mary .... ,,	7 35			8 54	9 6	*	...	10 34	12 59	3 30	4 29	...	5 54	F	...	8 34	...	...	...	...	...	...	...	...	...	...	...	...	...	...
6½	Harleston .... arr.	7 40			8 59	9 11	9 35	.....	10 39	1 4	3 35	4 34	.....	5 59	6 30	7 25	8 39	.....	.....	.....	.....	.....	.....	.....	.....	.....	.....	.....	.....	.....	.....
	Harleston .... dep.	7 50			9 2	9 13	10 5	...	10 41	1 6	3 37	4 36	...	6 1	7 35	7 45	8 41	...	...	...	...	...	...	...	...	...	...	...	...	...	...
9	Homersfield .... ,,	7 56			9 8	9 19	10 33	.....	10 47	1 12	3 48	4 42	.....	6 7	*	8 10	8 47	.....	.....	.....	.....	.....	.....	.....	.....	.....	.....	.....	.....	.....	.....
13	Earsham .... ,,	8 2			9 14	9 26	...	~	10 53	1 18	3 49	4 48	...	6 13	...	...	8 53	...	...	...	...	...	...	...	...	...	...	...	...	...	...
13¼	Bungay .... arr.	8 4			9 16	9 28	10 50	.....	10 55	1 20	3 51	4 50	.....	6 16	8 0	8 20	8 55	.....	.....	.....	.....	.....	.....	.....	.....	.....	.....	.....	.....	.....	.....
	Bungay .... dep.	8 6			9 21	9 33	12 5	...	10 57	1 22	3 53	4 52	...	6 25	8 10	8 35	8 57	...	...	...	...	...	...	...	...	...	...	...	...	...	...
13¾	Ditchingham .... ,,	8 10			9 25	9 38	12 30	.....	11 1	1 26	3 57	4 56	.....	6 29	*	G	9 1	.....	.....	.....	.....	.....	.....	.....	.....	.....	.....	.....	.....	.....	.....
15¼	Ellingham .... ,,	8 14			9 29	9 43	12 45	...	11 5	1 30	4 1	5 0	...	6 33	F	...	9 5	...	...	...	...	...	...	...	...	...	...	...	...	...	...
16¼	Geldeston .... ,,	8 18			9 33	9 49	1 5	.....	11 9	1 34	4 5	5 4	.....	6 37	F	.....	9 9	.....	.....	.....	.....	.....	.....	.....	.....	.....	.....	.....	.....	.....	.....
[illegible]	Beccles .... arr.	8 24			9 39	9 55	1 15	...	11 15	1 40	4 11	5 10	...	6 43	8 45	9 0	9 15	...	...	...	...	...	...	...	...	...	...	...	...	...	...
	Yarmouth .... arr.	.....			10 20	10 37	.....	.....	.....	.....	.....	.....	.....		Not Sats.	Sats only.		.....	.....	.....	.....	.....	.....	.....	.....	.....	.....	.....	.....	.....	.....
		Mondays and Thursdays.	Mondays and Thursdays. To work No. 4 Down.	Tuesdays, Wednesdays, Fridays, and Saturdays. To work No. 4 Down.	See page 352	Mondays and Thursdays.	See page 319		See page 320	See page 321	See page 322	Not on Saturdays.		Saturdays only.	See page 361 & 324	See page 361 & 324	See page 325														

B No. 4. May work 1 Truck of Cattle only from either Tivetshall or Harleston to Beccles if the Truck is fitted with Brake pipes. The Tivetshall and Harleston Station Masters to arrange so that not more than 1 Truck of Cattle is accepted for this Train on any one day.

C No. 6. **To shunt at Bungay for No. 8 Passenger Train.** On Mondays and Thursdays to follow No. 5 Excursion Train from Tivetshall.

F No 14. This Train is to call at Pulham Mary, Ellingham, and Geldeston to attach Traffic for Yarmouth, Lowestoft, and London. Ellingham, and Geldeston to advise Bungay what Trucks they have to go forward by this Train. Bungay to arrange load accordingly. Traffic worked by this Train for Ellingham and Geldeston to be left at Bungay; that Station to send forward next day by the 7.0 a.m. Goods Train Norwich to Beccles. On Mondays and Thursdays to leave Harleston at 7.58 p.m., on arrival of No. 13 Up Excursion, and be due at Beccles at 9.0 p.m.

G No. 15. **To call at Pulham Market and Ditchingham to leave Cattle only.**

N.B.—Traffic in Trucks, fitted with Brake pipes, may only be worked by Passenger Trains which start **direct** from Tivetshall or Beccles, and only from and to these points, except in the case provided for in foot note **B** on this page.

WAVENEY VALLEY BRANCH.—*Single Line.*

The Trains on this Single Line are worked by Train Staff and Train Staff Ticket, according to the "Train Staff Regulations" contained in the "Appendix" to this Working Time Book. No Engine or Train is to be run on this Branch without a Train Staff or Train Staff Ticket. The Train Staff Stations are Beccles, Bungay, Harleston, and Tivetshall.

Up Trains.—Week Days.

FROM	1	2	3	4	5	6	7	8	9	10	11	12	13	14	15	16	17	18	19	20	21	22	23	24	25	26	27	28	29	30	31
	A Pass.	Pass.		C Gds.	Pass.	Pass.	E Pass.	Pass.	Brk. Gds.		Pass.	Pass.	F Exc.																		
	a.m.	a.m.		a.m.	a.m.	a.m.	p.m.	p.m.	p.m.		p.m.	p.m.	p.m.																		
Yarmouth .... dep.	...	...	...	...	...	...	...	...	...	...	5 10	...	6 40	...	...	...	...	...	...	...	...	...	...	...	...	...	...	...	...	...	...
Beccles .... dep.	6 30	7 10	.....	7 30	9 2	11 45	2 0		2 10	.....	6 7	7 0	7 17	.....	.....	.....	.....	.....	.....	.....	.....	.....	.....	.....	.....	.....	.....	.....	.....	.....	.....
Geldeston .... ,,	...	7 14	...	...	9 8	11 51	2 6		*	...	6 13	7 6	7 24	...	...	...	...	...	...	...	...	...	...	...	...	...	...	...	...	...	...
Ellingham .... ,,	.....	7 20	.....	.....	9 12	11 55	2 10		*	.....	6 17	7 10	7 29	.....	.....	.....	.....	.....	.....	.....	.....	.....	.....	.....	.....	.....	.....	.....	.....	.....	.....
Ditchingham .... ,,	...	7 24	...	7 55	9 16	11 59	2 14		*	...	6 21	7 14	7 34	...	...	...	...	...	...	...	...	...	...	...	...	...	...	...	...	...	...
Bungay .... arr.	6 41	7 27	.....	8 0	9 19	12 2	2 17		2 45	.....	6 24	7 17	7 37	.....	.....	.....	.....	.....	.....	.....	.....	.....	.....	.....	.....	.....	.....	.....	.....	.....	.....
Bungay .... dep.	6 43	7 28	...	8 20	9 30	12 3	2 19		3 0	...	6 25	7 18	7 38	...	...	...	...	...	...	...	...	...	...	...	...	...	...	...	...	...	...
Earsham .... ,,	A	7 31	.....	.....	9 33	12 6	2 22		.....	.....	6 28	7 21	7 42	.....	.....	.....	.....	.....	.....	.....	.....	.....	.....	.....	.....	.....	.....	.....	.....	.....	.....
Homersfield .... ,,	6 51	7 38	...	*	9 40	12 13	2 29		*	...	6 35	7 28	7 50	...	...	...	...	...	...	...	...	...	...	...	...	...	...	...	...	...	...
Harleston .... arr.	6 56	7 43	.....	8 45	9 45	12 18	2 34		3 25	.....	6 40	7 33	7 55	.....	.....	.....	.....	.....	.....	.....	.....	.....	.....	.....	.....	.....	.....	.....	.....	.....	.....
Harleston .... dep.	6 57	7 44	...	9 55	9 46	12 19	2 36		3 35	...	6 41	7 34	7 58	...	...	...	...	...	...	...	...	...	...	...	...	...	...	...	...	...	...
Pulham Mary .... ,,	7 3	7 50	.....	.....	9 52	12 25	2 42		*	.....	6 47	7 40	8 5	.....	.....	.....	.....	.....	.....	.....	.....	.....	.....	.....	.....	.....	.....	.....	.....	.....	.....
Pulham Market .... ,,	7 6	7 53	...	...	9 55	12 28	2 45		*	...	6 50	7 43	8 9	...	...	...	...	...	...	...	...	...	...	...	...	...	...	...	...	...	...
Tivetshall .... arr.	7 12	7 59	.....	10 15	10 1	12 34	2 51		4 15	.....	6 56	7 49	8 15	.....	.....	.....	.....	.....	.....	.....	.....	.....	.....	.....	.....	.....	.....	.....	.....	.....	.....
Tivetshall .... dep.		8 0	...	11 0	10 3	12 35	2 53		5 0	...	6 58	7 51	8 17	...	...	...	...	...	...	...	...	...	...	...	...	...	...	...	...	...	...
Forncett .... arr.	.....	8 6	.....	11 10	10 9	12 41	3 0	3 1	.....	.....	7 4	7 57	8 24	.....	.....	.....	.....	.....	.....	.....	.....	.....	.....	.....	.....	.....	.....	.....	.....	.....	.....
Wymondham .... ,,	...	...	...	11 50	...	...	...	...	...	...	...	...	...	...	...	...	...	...	...	...	...	...	...	...	...	...	...	...	...	...	...
Norwich .... ,,	.....	8 30	.....	.....	10 38	1 5	.....	3 23	5 46	.....	7 28	8 27	8 55	.....	.....	.....	.....	.....	.....	.....	.....	.....	.....	.....	.....	.....	.....	.....	.....	.....	.....
	Mondays and Thursdays.	See page 308		See page 310 and 361	See page 309	See page 310	See page 311	Saturdays only. From Beccles. See No. 7. See page 311	See page 312		See page 351 and 315	See page 313	Mondays and Thursdays.																		

A No. 1. To call at Earsham when required to take up London Passengers.

C No. 4. To shunt at Harleston for No. 5 Passenger Train.

E No. 7. On Saturdays runs to Norwich Victoria as shewn in No. 8 column.

F No. 13. To cross No. 14 Down Goods Train at Harleston.

N.B.—Traffic in Trucks, fitted with Brake pipes, may only be worked by Passenger Trains which start direct from Tivetshall or Beccles, and only from and to these points, except in the case provided for in foot note **B**, page 362.

363

GER working timetable 1897.

Norwich, departing at 9.48am, 12.08pm and 2.50pm, called at Forncett before serving all stations on the branch, with arrival at Beccles at 11.15am, 1.40pm and 4.11pm respectively, followed by the 4.10pmSX Forncett to Beccles train. This was balanced by the 5.10pmSO market train from Norwich, which after calling at Forncett continued all stations to Beccles arriving at 6.43pm. The last Down passenger train to serve the Waveney Valley departed Norwich at 7.50pm, then Tivetshall at 8.25pm, with arrival at Beccles at 9.15pm. Two goods trains also served the branch; the 7.00am ex Norwich, which served Pulham Market and Pulham St. Mary only if required, and then all stations to Beccles, arriving at 1.15pm. The afternoon goods service departed Wymondham at 5.20pmSX and 4.30pmSO, and after calling at Forncett departed Tivetshall at 6.05pmSX and 7.00pmSO. Mandatory calls were made at Harleston and Bungay, with arrival at Beccles at 8.45pmSX and 9.00pmSO. The SX service called at Homersfield and Ditchingham only if required, and Pulham St. Mary, Ellingham and Geldeston to attach traffic for Yarmouth, Lowestoft or London. Ellingham and Geldestion were to advise Bungay what trucks were to go forward, with Bungay arranging accordingly. Traffic worked by this train for Ellingham and Geldeston was to be left at Bungay for forwarding by the 7.00am Norwich to Beccles goods train the following day. On MThO the train was retimed to reach Beccles at 9.00pm. The SO service also called at Pulham Market and Ditchingham to leave cattle traffic. In the Up direction the branch was served by eight passenger trains MThO and seven on all other weekdays, together with two goods trains. The first train of the day, the 6.30amMThO, called at Bungay, Earsham when required to take up London passengers, Homersfield and than all stations to Tivetshall, arriving at 7.12am. The 7.10am ex Beccles called all stations to Tivetshall, then Forncett, to terminate at Norwich at 8.30am. The 9.02am and 11.45am ex Beccles also served all stations on the branch, arriving at Tivetshall at 10.03am and 12.35pm respectively before continuing to Forncett and then Norwich, arriving at 10.35am and 1.05pm. The 2.00pm ex Beccles also served all stations to Forncett, arriving at 3.00pm, but on Saturdays continued to Norwich Victoria arriving at 3.23pm. The return train from Yarmouth departed the coastal town at 5.10pm and Beccles at 6.07pm, calling all stations to Tivetshall, arriving at 6.56pm before continuing to Forncett and Norwich, arriving at 7.28pm. The 7.00pm ex Beccles followed the same pattern, arriving at Norwich at 8.27pm. The 6.40pmMThO excursion from Yarmouth, after departing Beccles at 7.17pm also called all stations to Tivetshall, arriving at 8.16pm before continuing to the cathedral city, arriving at 8.55pm. Of the goods services, the 7.30am ex Beccles served Ditchingham, Bungay, Homersfield only if required, Harleston and then Tivetshall from 10.15am until 11.00am, before continuing to Forncett and terminating at Wymondham at 11.50am. The afternoon freight service conveying brake goods departed Beccles at 2.10pm, making mandatory stops at Bungay, Harleston and Tivetshall, arriving at 4.15pm, serving Geldeston, Ellingham, Homersfield, Pulham St. Mary and Pulham Market only if required. Departing Tivetshall at 5.00pm the train continued to Norwich arriving at 5.46pm. Traffic in trucks fitted with Westinghouse brake pipes were only to be worked by passenger trains which started direct from Tivetshall or Beccles, and only from and to these points.

In 1907 a weekdays-only service of eight passenger trains ran in the Down direction MThO, six SO and five TuWFO, augmented by an SO set of empty coaching stock. All passenger trains called at all stations with the initial 7.16am ex Tivetshall running on MThO. All other services commenced their journey at Norwich; the 8.05am (8.44am ex Tivetshall) being a through train to Yarmouth, arriving at 10.20am. This train was permitted to work a truck of cattle from either Tivetshall or Harleston to Beccles if the vehicles were fitted with Westinghouse brake pipes, with the respective station master arranging locally so that no more than one truck of cattle

Wymondham station, where for many years the daily freight train from Beccles and the Waveney Valley line terminated and started back after connecting with cross-country services. This view from the east of October 1911 shows the vast array of cattle pens to the left and covered coal drops to the right, with the goods shed beyond. The station building on the Down side dominates the skyline. *GERS/Windwood 1289*

166

WAVENEY VALLEY BRANCH.—*Single Line.*

The Trains on this Single Line are worked by Train Staff and Train Staff Ticket, according to the "Train Staff Regulations" contained in the "Appendix" to this Working Time Book. No Engine or Train is to be run on this Branch without a Train Staff or Train Staff Ticket. The Train Staff Stations are Tivetshall, Harleston, Bungay, and Beccles.

Down Trains.—Week Days.

Miles from Tivetshall.	FROM	1	2	3	4	5	6	7	8	9	10	11	12	13	14	15	16	17	18	19	20	21	22	23	24	25	26	27	28	29	30
		Pass.		A Pass.		C Gds.	Pass.	Gds.	Pass.	Pass.	Pass.		Mkt. Pass.	F Gds.	G Gds.	Pass.															
		a.m.		a.m.		a.m.	a.m.	a.m.	p.m.	p.m.	p.m.		p.m.	p.m.	p.m.	p.m.															
	Norwich ... dep.	...	...	8 5	...	7 0	9 48	8 30	12 10	2 50	...	...	5 20		...	7 50	...	...	...	...	...	...	...	...	...	...	...	...	...	...	...
	Wymondham ... "	...	...	...	...	...	...	...	...	...	...	...	...	4 30	5 20	...	...	...	...	...	...	...	...	...	...	...	...	...	...	...	...
	Forncett ... "	...	...	8 33	...	...	10 15	10 40	12 33	3 12	4 3	...	5 43	5 40	6 20	8 13	...	...	...	...	...	...	...	...	...	...	...	...	...	...	...
—	Tivetshall ... arr.	...	...	8 40	...	8 10	10 21	10 50	12 39	3 18	4 13	...	5 50	5 50	6 30	8 20	...	...	...	...	...	...	...	...	...	...	...	...	...	...	...
	Tivetshall ... dep.	7 15	...	8 45	...	8 55	10 28	11 20	12 50	3 21	4 30	...	5 55	6 5	7 5	8 25	...	...	...	...	...	...	...	...	...	...	...	...	...	...	...
2¾	Pulham Market ... "	7 21	...	8 51	...	C	10 31	11 40	12 56	3 27	4 36	...	6 1	F	G	8 31	...	...	...	...	...	...	...	...	...	...	...	...	...	...	...
3¾	Pulham Mary ... "	7 24	...	8 54	...	C	10 37	11 55	12 59	3 30	4 39	...	6 4	F	...	8 34	...	...	...	...	...	...	...	...	...	...	...	...	...	...	...
6¼	Harleston ... arr.	7 29	...	8 59	...	9 35	10 42	12 5	1 4	3 35	4 44	...	6 9	6 30	7 30	8 39	...	...	...	...	...	...	...	...	...	...	...	...	...	...	...
	Harleston ... dep	7 55	...	9 2	...	10 5	10 44	12 35	1 6	3 37	4 46	...	6 11	7 35	7 45	8 41	...	...	...	...	...	...	...	...	...	...	...	...	...	...	...
9	Homersfield ... "	8 1	...	9 8	...	C	10 50	1 0	1 12	3 43	4 52	...	6 17	F	8 10	8 47	...	...	...	...	...	...	...	...	...	...	...	...	...	...	...
12	Earsham ... "	8 7	...	9 14	...	...	10 56	...	1 18	3 49	4 58	...	6 23	...	...	8 53	...	...	...	...	...	...	...	...	...	...	...	...	...	...	...
12¾	Bungay ... arr.	8 9	...	9 16	...	10 50	10 58	1 10	1 20	3 51	5 0	...	6 26	7 55	8 20	8 55	...	...	...	...	...	...	...	...	...	...	...	...	...	...	...
	Bungay ... dep.	8 11	...	9 21	...	12 10	11 0	...	1 22	3 53	5 2	...	6 30	8 10	8 35	8 57	...	...	...	...	...	...	...	...	...	...	...	...	...	...	...
13¾	Ditchingham ... "	8 15	...	9 25	...	12 45	11 4	...	1 26	3 57	5 6	...	6 34	*	G	9 1	...	...	...	...	...	...	...	...	...	...	...	...	...	...	...
15¼	Ellingham ... "	8 19	...	9 29	...	1 0	11 8	...	1 30	4 1	5 10	...	6 38	F	...	9 5	...	...	...	...	...	...	...	...	...	...	...	...	...	...	...
16¾	Geldeston ... "	8 23	...	9 33	...	1 20	11 12	...	1 34	4 5	5 14	...	6 42	F	...	9 9	...	...	...	...	...	...	...	...	...	...	...	...	...	...	...
19¼	Beccles ... arr.	8 29	...	9 39	...	1 30	11 18	...	1 40	4 11	5 20	...	6 48	8 45	9 0	9 15	...	...	...	...	...	...	...	...	...	...	...	...	...	...	...
	Yarmouth ... arr.	...	...	10 20	...	...	...	...	...	...	...	...	...	Not Sats.	Sats only.	...	...	...	...	...	...	...	...	...	...	...	...	...	...	...	...
		Mondays only.		See page 156		See page 122	See page 124	See page 124	See page 125	See page 127	Not on Saturdays.		Saturdays only.	See page 168 & 129	See page 168 & 180	See page 131															

A No. 3. May work 1 Truck of Cattle only from either Tivetshall or Harleston to Beccles if the Truck is fitted with Brake pipes. The Tivetshall and Harleston Station Masters to arrange so that not more than 1 Truck of Cattle is accepted for this Train on any one day.

C No. 5. To shunt at Bungay for No. 6 Passenger Train. To call at Pulham Market, Pulham Mary, and Homersfield to detach Cattle and leave Brake Goods, and to attach Trucks and take in Brake Goods for Stations beyond Bungay only.

F No 13. This Train is to call at Pulham Market, Pulham Mary, Ellingham, and Geldeston to attach Traffic for Yarmouth, Lowestoft, and London. Ellingham, and Geldeston to advise Bungay what Trucks they have to go forward by this Train. Bungay to arrange load accordingly. Traffic worked by this Train for Ellingham and Geldeston to be left at Bungay; that Station to send forward next day by the 7.0 a.m. Goods Train Norwich to Beccles. To call at Homersfield to detach or attach Cattle only.

G No. 14. To call at Pulham Market and Ditchingham to leave Cattle only.

N.B.—Traffic in Trucks, fitted with Brake pipes, may only be worked by Passenger Trains which start direct from Tivetshall or Beccles, and only from and to these points, except in the case provided for in foot note **B** on this page.

WAVENEY VALLEY BRANCH.—*Single Line.*

The Trains on this Single Line are worked by Train Staff and Train Staff Ticket, according to the "Train Staff Regulations" contained in the "Appendix" to this Working Time Book. No Engine or Train is to be run on this Branch without a Train Staff or Train Staff Ticket. The Train Staff Stations are Beccles, Bungay, Harleston, and Tivetshall.

Up Trains.—Week Days.

FROM	1	2	3	4	5	6	7	8	9	10	11	12	13	14	15	16	17	18	19	20	21	22	23	24	25	26	27	28	29	30	31
	A Pass.	B Pass.		C Gds.	Pass.	Pass.	D Pass.	Pass.	E Gds.	Brk. Gds.		Pass.	Pass.																	
	a.m.	a.m.		a.m.	a.m.	a.m.	p.m.	p.m.	p.m.	p.m.		p.m.	p.m.																	
Yarmouth ... dep.	...	...	...	...	...	...	...	...	...	...	...	5 10	...	...	...	...	...	...	...	...	...	...	...	...	...	...	...	...	...	...
Beccles ... dep.	6 20	6 56	...	7 30	9 2	11 45	2 0	...	...	2 30	...	6 12	7 0	...	...	...	...	...	...	...	...	...	...	...	...	...	...	...	...	...
Geldeston ... "	...	7 2	...	...	9 8	11 51	2 6	Saturdays only. From Beccles. See No. 7.	...	*	...	6 18	7 6	...	...	...	...	...	...	...	...	...	...	...	...	...	...	...	...	...
Ellingham ... "	...	7 6	...	...	9 12	11 55	2 10		...	*	...	6 22	7 10	...	...	...	...	...	...	...	...	...	...	...	...	...	...	...	...	...
Ditchingham ... "	...	7 10	...	7 55	9 16	11 59	2 14		...	*	...	6 26	7 14	...	...	...	...	...	...	...	...	...	...	...	...	...	...	...	...	...
Bungay ... arr.	6 32	7 13	...	8 0	9 19	12 2	2 17		...	3 35	...	6 29	7 17	...	...	...	...	...	...	...	...	...	...	...	...	...	...	...	...	...
Bungay ... dep.	6 34	7 14	...	8 20	9 30	12 3	2 19		2 25	4 0	...	6 31	7 18	...	...	...	...	...	...	...	...	...	...	...	...	...	...	...	...	...
Earsham ... "	A	7 17	...	...	9 33	12 6	2 22				...	6 34	7 21	...	...	...	...	...	...	...	...	...	...	...	...	...	...	...	...	...
Homersfield ... "	6 41	7 24	...	*	9 39	12 13	2 29		2 50	4 25	...	6 41	7 28	...	...	...	...	...	...	...	...	...	...	...	...	...	...	...	...	...
Harleston ... arr.	6 46	7 29	...	8 45	9 44	12 18	2 34		3 0	4 35	...	6 46	7 33	...	...	...	...	...	...	...	...	...	...	...	...	...	...	...	...	...
Harleston ... dep.	6 47	7 30	...	9 55	9 46	12 19	2 36		3 37	5 0	...	6 48	7 34	...	...	...	...	...	...	...	...	...	...	...	...	...	...	...	...	...
Pulham Mary ... "	6 53	7 36	...	...	9 52	12 25	2 42		E	...	...	6 54	7 40	...	...	...	...	...	...	...	...	...	...	...	...	...	...	...	...	...
Pulham Market ... "	6 56	7 39	...	C	9 55	12 28	2 45		*	...	...	6 57	7 43	...	...	...	...	...	...	...	...	...	...	...	...	...	...	...	...	...
Tivetshall ... arr.	7 2	7 45	...	10 20	10 1	12 34	2 51		4 20	5 20	...	7 3	7 49	...	...	...	...	...	...	...	...	...	...	...	...	...	...	...	...	...
Tivetshall ... dep.		7 47	...	11 0	10 3	12 58	2 53	...	5 5	6 30	...	7 5	7 51	...	...	...	...	...	...	...	...	...	...	...	...	...	...	...	...	...
Forncett ... arr.	Mondays only.	7 53	...	11 10	10 9	1 4	3 0	3 1	...	...	...	7 11	7 57	...	...	...	...	...	...	...	...	...	...	...	...	...	...	...	...	...
Wymondham ... "			...	11 50	...	...	...			...	...	...	...	...	...	...	...	...	...	...	...	...	...	...	...	...	...	...	...	...
Norwich ... "		8 15	...	...	10 33	1 28	...	3 23	6 15	7 10	...	7 35	8 27	...	...	...	...	...	...	...	...	...	...	...	...	...	...	...	...	...
		See page 106		See page 108 and 168	See page 107	See page 109	See page 110	See page 110	See page 112	See page 112		See page 160 and 112	See page 113																	

A No. 1. To call at Earsham when required to take up London Passengers.

B No. 2. This Train runs to Norwich Thorpe Station, except on Saturdays when it runs to Norwich Victoria, returning as a Carriage Train from Norwich Victoria to Norwich Thorpe at 9.10 a.m.

C No. 4. To shunt at Harleston for No. 5 Passenger Train. To call at Pulham Market when required to attach N.C. Traffic.

D No. 7. On Saturdays runs to Norwich Victoria as shown in No. 8 Column.

E No. 9. To call at Pulham Mary for Meat and Brake Goods only.

N.B.—Traffic in Trucks, fitted with Brake pipes, may only be worked by Passenger Trains which start direct from Tivetshall or Beccles, and only from and to these points, except in the case provided for in foot note **B**, page 166.

167

GER working timetable 1901.

166

WAVENEY VALLEY BRANCH.—*Single Line.*

The Trains on this Single Line are worked by Train Staff and Train Staff Ticket, according to the "Train Staff Regulations" contained in the "Appendix" to this Working Time Book. No Engine or Train is to be run on this Branch without a Train Staff or Train Staff Ticket. The Train Staff Stations are Tivetshall, Harleston, Bungay, and Beccles.

Down Trains.—Week Days.

Miles from Tivetshall	FROM	1	2	3	4	5	6	7	8	9	10	11	12	13	14	15	16	17	18	19	20	21	22	23	24	25	26	27	28	29	30
		Pass.	A Cars.	B Pass.	A Exc.	C Gds.	Pass.	Gds.	Pass.	Pass		E Pass.	Mkt. Pass.	F Gds.	G Gds.	Pass.	Cars.														
		a.m.	a.m.	a.m.	a.m.	a.m.	a.m.	a.m.	p.m.	p.m.		p.m.	p.m.	p.m.	p.m.	p.m.	p.m.														
	Norwich ... dep.	...	7 55	8 5	...	7 0	9 48	8 35	12 10	2 45	...	...	5 20	...	...	7 50	...														
	Wymondham ... "	...	...	...	...	...	...	...	...	...	...	...	...	4 30	5 20	...	...														
	Forncett ... "	...	8 20	8 33	8 49	...	10 15	10 50	12 33	3 6	...	4 0	5 43	5 40	6 45	8 18	...														
—	Tivetshall ... arr.	...	...	8 40	8 47	8 10	10 21	11 0	12 39	3 12	...	4 7	5 50	5 50	6 55	8 20	Saturdays only.														
	Tivetshall ... dep.	7 16	...	8 45	8 55	8 55	10 26	11 25	12 58	3 16	...	4 25	5 55	6 5	7 5	8 25															
2¼	Pulham Market ... "	7 22	Mondays and Thursdays. To work No. 4 Excursion.	8 51	9 2	C	10 32	11 45	1 4	3 22	...	4 31	6 1	F	G	8 31															
3¾	Pulham Mary ... "	7 25		8 54	9 6	C	10 35	12 0	1 7	3 25	...	4 34	6 4	F	...	8 34															
6½	Harleston ... arr.	7 30		8 59	9 11	9 35	10 40	12 10	1 12	3 30	...	4 39	6 9	6 30	7 30	8 39															
	Harleston ... dep.	7 55		9 2	9 13	10 5	10 42		1 14	3 32	...	4 41	6 11	6 50	7 45	8 41	10 55														
9	Homersfield ... "	8 1		9 8	9 19	10 40	10 48	...	1 20	3 38	...	4 47	6 17	F	8 10	8 47	...														
12	Earsham ... "	8 7		9 14	9 20	...	10 54	...	1 26	3 44	...	4 53	6 23	...	...	8 53	...														
12¾	Bungay ... arr.	8 9		9 16	9 28	10 50	10 56	...	1 28	3 46	...	4 55	6 26	7 10	8 20	8 55	...														
	Bungay ... dep.	8 11		9 21	9 35	12 10	10 58	...	1 32	3 48	...	4 57	6 28	7 35	8 35	8 57	11 7														
13½	Ditchingham ... "	8 15		9 25	9 40	12 45	11 2	...	1 36	3 52	...	5 1	6 32	8 0	G	9 1	...														
15¼	Ellingham ... "	8 19		9 29	9 45	1 0	11 6	...	1 40	3 56	...	5 5	6 36	8 15	...	9 5	...														
16¾	Geldeston ... "	8 23		9 33	9 51	1 20	11 10	...	1 44	4 0	...	5 9	6 40	8 30	...	9 9															
19¾	Beccles ... arr.	8 29		9 39	9 57	1 30	11 16	...	1 50	4 6	...	5 15	6 46	8 40	9 0	9 15	11 20														
	Yarmouth ... arr.	...	...	10 20	10 35	...	...	...	...	...	...	...	...	Not Sats.	Sats only.	...	...														
		Mondays and Thursdays.		See page 156	Mons. & Thurs. See page 156.	See page 122	See page 124	See page 124	See page 125	See page 127		Not on Saturdays.	Saturdays only.	See page 169 & 130	See page 169 & 130	See page 132															

A *Nos. 2 and 4. Will not run after Thursday, 12th September.*

B No. 3. May work 1 Truck of Cattle only from either Tivetshall or Harleston to Beccles if the Truck is fitted with Westinghouse Brake pipes. The Tivetshall and Harleston Station Masters to arrange so that not more than 1 Truck of Cattle is accepted for this Train on any one day.

C No. 5. To shunt at Bungay for No. 6 Passenger Train. To call at Pulham Market and Pulham Mary to detach Cattle and leave Brake Goods, and to attach Trucks and take in Brake Goods for Stations beyond Bungay only. On Mondays and Thursdays to follow No. 4 Excursion from Tivetshall.

E *No. 11. From 1st to 12th July, and 16th to 30th September inclusive will leave Tivetshall at 4.30 p.m. and run 5 minutes later.*

F No 13. This Train is to call at Pulham Market and Pulham Mary to attach traffic for Yarmouth, Lowestoft and London. To call at Homersfield to detach or attach Cattle only. On Mondays and Thursdays to cross No. 14 Up Excursion at Bungay.

G No. 14. To call at Pulham Market and Ditchingham to leave Cattle only.

N.B.—Traffic in Trucks, fitted with Westinghouse Brake pipes, may only be worked by Passenger Trains which start direct from Tivetshall or Beccles, and only from and to these points, except in the case provided for in foot note **B** on this page.

WAVENEY VALLEY BRANCH.—*Single Line.*

The Trains on this Single Line are worked by Train Staff and Train Staff Ticket, according to the "Train Staff Regulations" contained in the "Appendix" to this Working Time Book. No Engine or Train is to be run on this Branch without a Train Staff or Train Staff Ticket. The Train Staff Stations are Beccles, Bungay, Harleston, and Tivetshall.

Up Trains.—Week Days.

FROM	1	2	3	4	5	6	7	8	9	10	11	12	13	14	15	16	17	18	19	20	21	22	23	24	25	26	27	28	29	30	31
	A Pass.	B Pass.	C Gds.	Pass		Pass.	E Pass.	Pass.	F Gds.	G Brk. Gds.		Pass.	Pass.	H Exc.	Pass.																
	a.m.	a.m.	a.m.	a.m.		a.m.	p.m.	p.m.	p.m.	p.m.		p.m.	p.m	p.m.	p.m.																
Yarmouth ... dep.	...	...	...	...	...	...	...	...	...	...	...	5 10	...	6 55	...																
Beccles ... dep.	6 22	6 56	7 30	9 2	...	11 40	2 0	...	...	2 30	...	6 10	7 0	7 20	10 10																
Geldeston ... "	...	7 2	...	9 8	...	11 46	2 6	Saturdays only. From Beccles. See No. 7.	...	*	...	6 16	7 6	7 27	10 16																
Ellingham ... "	...	7 6	...	9 12	...	11 50	2 10		...	*	...	6 20	7 10	7 32	10 22																
Ditchingham ... "	...	7 10	7 55	9 16	...	11 54	2 14		...	*	...	6 24	7 14	7 37	10 26																
Bungay ... arr.	6 34	7 13	8 0	9 19	...	11 57	2 17		...	3 35	...	6 27	7 17	7 40	10 29																
Bungay ... dep.	6 35	7 14	8 20	9 30	...	11 58	2 19		...	3 55	...	6 29	7 18	7 41	10 31																
Earsham ... "	A	7 17	...	9 33	...	12 1	2 22		...	...	...	6 32	7 21	7 45	10 34																
Homersfield ... "	6 43	7 24	*	9 39	...	12 8	2 29		...	4 20	...	6 39	7 28	7 53	10 41																
Harleston ... arr.	6 48	7 29	8 45	9 44	...	12 13	2 34		...	4 30	...	6 44	7 33	7 58	10 46																
Harleston ... dep.	6 49	7 30	9 55	9 46	...	12 14	2 36		3 37	5 0	...	6 46	7 34	8 1	...																
Pulham Mary ... "	6 55	7 36	...	9 52	...	12 20	2 42		F	G	...	6 52	7 40	8 8	Saturdays only.																
Pulham Market ... "	6 58	7 39	C	9 55	...	12 23	2 45		*	...	...	6 55	7 43	8 12																	
Tivetshall ... arr.	7 4	7 45	10 20	10 1	...	12 29	2 51		4 20	5 20	...	7 1	7 49	8 18																	
Tivetshall ... dep.	...	7 47	11 0	10 8	...	12 30	2 53	...	4 55	6 30	...	7 5	7 51	8 20																	
Forncett ... arr.	...	7 53	C	10 9	...	12 36	3 0	3 1	...	...	...	7 9	7 57	8 27																	
Wymondham ... "	...	...	11 50	...	...	...	...	...	...	...	...	...	...																		
Norwich ... "	...	8 15	...	10 33	...	1 0	...	3 23	5 45	7 10	...	7 33	8 17	8 58																	
	Mondays and Thursdays.	See page 106	See page 108 and 169	See page 107		See page 109	See page 110	See page 110	See page 112	See page 112		See page 160 and 113	See page 114	Mons. & Thurs. See page 114																	

A No. 1. To call at Earsham when required to take up London Passengers.

B No. 2. This Train runs to Norwich Thorpe Station, except on Saturdays when it runs to Norwich Victoria, returning as a Carriage Train from Norwich Victoria to Norwich Thorpe at 9.10 a.m. On Mondays and Thursdays to await at Harleston arrival of No. 1 Down Passenger Train.

C No. 3. To shunt at Harleston for No. 4 Passenger Train. To call at Pulham Market when required to attach N.C. Traffic, and at Forncett to attach only.

E No. 7. On Saturdays runs to Norwich Victoria as shewn in No. 8 Column.

F No 9. To call at Pulham Mary for Meat and Brake Goods only.

G No. 10. To call at Pulham Mary to leave traffic from Ditchingham.

H *No. 14. Will not run after Thursday, 12th September.*

N.B.—Traffic in Trucks, fitted with Brake pipes, may only be worked by Passenger Trains which start direct from Tivetshall or Beccles, and only from and to these points, except in the case provided for in foot note **B**, page 166.

167

GER working timetable 1907.

was accepted. This service was followed by the 8.40am Forncett to Yarmouth train, the stock having departed Norwich at 7.55am; Beccles was reached at 9.57am and Yarmouth at 10.33am. Other services departed Norwich at 9.48am, 12.10pm and 2.45pm, calling at all stations on the branch and arriving at Beccles at 11.16am, 1.50pm and 4.06pm respectively. The next train across the branch was the 4.00pmSX ex Norwich, calling all stations to Beccles, which was replaced on a Saturday by the later running 5.20pm market train ex Norwich departing Tivetshall at 5.55pm, whilst the final train of the day was the 7.55pm ex Norwich to Beccles which entered the branch departing Tivetshall at 8.25pm. The passenger service was augmented by the 10.55pmSO ECS from Harleston to Beccles. Freight traffic was handled by the 7.00am goods ex Norwich, which served all stations on the branch after departing Tivetshall at 8.55am. This train called at Pulham Market and Pulham St. Mary to detach cattle and leave brake goods, and attach trucks and take in brake goods for stations beyond Bungay. A second goods train departed Norwich at 8.35am and, after spending 25 minutes at Tivetshall from 11.00am to 11.25am, served all stations and terminated at Harleston. The final goods train departed Wymondham 4.30pmSX and 5.20pmSO. This train served all stations; at Pulham Market and Pulham St. Mary it was to attach traffic for Yarmouth, Lowestoft and London, and at Homersfield to detach or attach cattle wagons only. In the Up direction a service of eight passenger trains MThO and seven on other weekdays operated. The 6.22amMThO ex Beccles called all stations from Bungay to Tivetshall, calling at Earsham only if required to take up passengers for London. All other services called all stations on the branch; the 6.50am ex Beccles, running as a through train to Norwich Thorpe SX and to Norwich Victoria SO, returning as ECS from Norwich Victoria to Norwich Thorpe at 9.10am. The 9.02am and 11.40am ex Beccles were through trains to Norwich, arriving at 10.33am and 1.00pm respectively; the 2.00pm ex Beccles terminated at Forncett arriving 3.00pmSX, but continued to Norwich Victoria SO arriving at 3.23pm. The 5.10pm ex Yarmouth departed Beccles at 6.10pm, calling all stations to Tivetshall arriving 7.01pm, then Forncett and on to Norwich arriving 7.33pm. This was followed by the 7.00pm ex Beccles arriving Norwich at 8.37pm. The return excursion, 6.59pm ex Yarmouth, followed across the branch, arriving at Tivetshall at 8.18pm before continuing to Norwich arriving at 8.58pm. On SO a late train departed Beccles at 10.10pm, calling all stations to Harleston arriving at 10.46pm. Of the goods services, the 7.30am ex Beccles called at Ditchingham, Bungay, Homersfield if required and Harleston, before departing Tivetshall at 11.00am for Wymondham, arriving at 11.50am. This train called at Pulham Market when required to attach North Country traffic and also at Forncett to attach only. A short goods working departed Harleston at 3.57pm, calling at Pulham St. Mary for meat and brake goods traffic only, and Pulham Market, if required, and with 35 minutes allowed for shunting at Tivetshall it continued to Norwich arriving at 5.45pm. The final goods service of the day departed Beccles at 2.30pm, calling at Geldeston, Ellingham and Ditchingham only if required, then mandatory stops at Bungay, Homersfield and Harleston, before calling at Pulham St. Mary to leave traffic for Ditchingham, arriving at Tivetshall at 5.20pm; the train departed the junction at 6.30pm

Forncett station, view looking south towards Tivetshall and Ipswich in October 1911, was frequently used by Waveney Valley Branch trains en route to and from Norwich. Both platforms were constructed of timber and were connected by station footbridge No. 331. Note also the timber barrow crossing in front of the signal box. *GERS/Windwood 1279*

with Norwich reached 40 minutes later. Traffic with trucks fitted with Westinghouse brake pipes were only to be worked by passenger trains which started direct from Tivetshall or Beccles, and only from and to those points.

By 1916 the working timetable showed a service of nine passenger and four goods trains serving the branch in the Down direction, together with a short goods working from Tivetshall to Pulham Market to serve the recently opened Admiralty siding. At this time both Earsham and Geldeston stations were closed as a wartime economy. Most trains commenced their journey at Norwich, departing at 8.25am, 9.47am, 12.52pm, 2.32pm, 4.08pm, 5.10pm, 8.04pmSX and 8.07pmSO, serving all stations on the branch before terminating at Beccles. The exceptions were the 7.27am ex Tivetshall, arriving Beccles at 8.18am, and the 9.22am Harleston

WAVENEY VALLEY BRANCH.—

Ref.	DOWN TRAINS.	WEEK DAYS.														
		morn	morn	morn		morn	morn	morn	even.		Mkt even.		even.			
106	LONDON (L'pl St.) dep	...	5 5	...	...	6 38	9 20	11 45	...	...	Saturdays only.		5 0	...	...	...
112	Ipswich „	—	7 1	—	—	9 8	11K32	1 48	—	—			6 50	—	—	—
99	Stowmarket „	...	7 23	...	...	9 35	11K55	2 15	...	...			7 17	...	...	...
	Bury St. Edmund's „	—	6B42	—	—	8 28	11B8	1 54	—	—			6 58	—	—	—
	Haughley „	...	...	...	...	9 41	11I31	2 25	...	...			7 25	...	...	...
106	Diss „	—	7 51	—	—	10 4	12K25	2 48	—	—			7 49	—	—	—
112	Tivetshall arr.	...	F	...	...	10 17	12K42	3 2	...	...			8 3	...	...	...
113	Norwich Thorpe dep	—	8 5	8 5	Mondays and Thursdays only. Will not run after 8th September.	9 48	12 23	...	—	—	—	Saturdays only.	...	—	—	—
119	Norwich Victoria „	6 45	...	...		...	12 10	2 45	3 50	...	5 20		7 50	...	...	...
132	Dereham „	—	7J4	7J4		9 1	10 50	—	2 57	—	4 17		5 51	—	—	—
113	Forncett „	7 6	8 33	8 40		10 15	12 44	3 6	4 12	...	5 43		8 13	...	...	...
119	Tivetshall arr	7 13	8 40	8 47		10 21	12 52	3 12	4 20	—	5 50		8 20	—	—	—
	TIVETSHALL dep	7 16	8 45	8 55		10 26	12 58	3 16	4 25	Not on Saturdays.	5 55		8 25	...	...	...
	Pulham Market	7 22	8 51	9 2		10 32	1 4	3 22	4 31		6 1		8 31	—	—	—
	Pulham St. Mary	7 25	8 54	9 6		10 35	1 7	3 25	4 34		6 4		8 34	...	...	...
	Harleston	7A55	9 2	9 13		10 42	1 14	3 32	4 41		6 11		8 41	—	—	—
	Homersfield	8 1	9 8	9 19		10 48	1 20	3 38	4 47		6 17		8 47	...	...	...
	Earsham	8 7	9 14	9 25		10 54	1 26	3 44	4 53		6 23		8 53	—	—	—
	Bungay	8 11	9 21	9 35		10 58	1 32	3 48	4 57		6 28		8 57	...	...	...
	Ditchingham	8 15	9 25	9 40		11 2	1 36	3 52	5 1		6 32		9 1	—	—	—
	Ellingham	8 19	9 29	9 45		11 6	1 40	3 56	5 5		6 36		9 5	...	...	...
	Geldeston	8 23	9 33	9 51		11 10	1 44	4 0	5 9		6 40		9 9	—	—	—
	BECCLES arr.	8 29	9 39	9 57		11 16	1 50	4 6	5 15		6 46		9 15	...	...	...
	Beccles dep	8 37	9U54	10 5		11 48	2 0	4 11	6 4	—	6 51 / 7 56		10 18 / 10 48	—	—	—
131	Lowestoft (Central) arr.	9 0	10 11	10 37		12 18	2 23	4 28	6 34	...	7 8 / ...		10 35 / ...	...	...	...
108/112	Yarmouth (S.T.) „	9 14	10U30	10 37		12 27	2 33	4 45	6 30	—	/ 8 24		— / 11 14	—	—	—
	Beccles dep.	8 52	10 43	10 43		11 25	2 55	4 25	6 44	...	Saturdays only. / 7 11		10T10 / T	...	...	...
113	Halesworth arr.	—	11 6	11 6		11 47	3 14	4 48	7 4	—	7 31		10T32	—	—	—
10?	Saxmundham „	9 17	11 27	11 27		12 9	3 32	4 53	7 50	...	7 50		10T48	...	...	...
119	Woodbridge „	—	12 3	12 3		12 41	3 59	5 37	8 22	—	8 22		—	—	—	—
	Ipswich „	9 51	12 31	12 31		1 6	4 16	6 4	7 49	...	8 45		... / ...	...	...	...
	LONDON (L'pl St.) arr.	11 35	2 23	2 23		3 30	5 55	6 52	9 27	—	11 21		— / —	—	—	—

A Arrives at Harleston at 7.30 a.m. **B** Passengers from Bury by this Train travel via Stowmarket.
F Passengers by this Train from London, Diss, &c., join the Branch Train at Forncett.
I Passengers for Haughley and Bury St. Edmund's by these Trains travel via Stowmarket.
J From Dereham on Mondays only. **K Commencing 12th September** will run 3 mins. earlier.
L On Saturdays due at Norwich (Victoria) at 8.13 a.m.
M Passengers by these Trains for Diss, London, &c., join the Up Train at Forncett.

Junctions with Colchester Main Line at Tivetshall, and with East Suffolk Main Line at Beccles.

UP TRAINS.	WEEK DAYS.												
	morn		morn	morn	morn	morn	even	even.	even.		even			
LONDON (L'pl St.) dep	...		...	5 5	6 38	10 27	3 24	...	...	...	...	...	...	...
Ipswich „	—		—	7 7	8 50	12 17	5 6	5 11	—	—	—	—	—	—
Woodbridge „	...		...	7 27	9 13	12 35	...	5 32	...	...	...	...	...	...
Saxmundham „	—		—	7 55	9 38	1 0	—	6 0	—	—	—	—	—	—
Halesworth „	...		...	8 16	9 58	1 26	5O25	6 23	...		...	...	...	...
Beccles arr.	—		—	8 33	10 11	1 43	6 0	6 40	—		—	—	—	—
Yarmouth (S.T.) dep	...		6 5	8 20	10 55	1 12	5 10	6 15	6 50	Mondays and Thursdays only. Will not run after 8th September.	9 50	...	...	...
Lowestoft (Central) „	—		6 18	8 27	10 58	1 3	5 42	6 38	—		9 45	—		—
Beccles arr.	...		6 37	8 45	11 20	1 45	5 59	6 55	7 15		10 2	...	...	...
BECCLES dep	6 22		6 56	9 2	11 40	2 0	6 10	7 0	7 18		10 10	—	—	—
Geldeston	...		7 2	9 8	11 46	2 6	6 16	7 6	7 27		10 16	...	...	...
Ellingham	—		7 6	9 12	11 50	2 10	6 20	7 10	7 32		10 22	—	—	—
Ditchingham	...		7 10	9 16	11 54	2 14	6 24	7 14	7 37		10 26	...	...	...
Bungay	6 35		7 14	9 20	11 58	2 19	6 29	7 19	7 41		10 31	—	—	—
Earsham	P		7 17	9 33	12 1	2 22	6 32	7 22	7 45		10 34	...	...	...
Homersfield	6 43		7 24	9 39	12 8	2 29	6 39	7 29	7 53		10 41	—	—	—
Harleston	6 49		7 30	9 46	12 13	2 36	6 46	7 36	8 1		10 45	...	...	...
Pulham St. Mary	6 55		7 36	9 52	12 20	2 42	6 52	7 42	8 8		Saturdays only.	—	—	—
Pulham Market	6 58		7 39	9 55	12 23	2 45	6 55	7 45	8 12		...	...	...	...
TIVETSHALL arr.	7 4		7 45	10 1	12 29	2 51	7 1	7 51	8 18		—	—	—	—
Tivetshall dep	...		7 47	10 3	12 30	2 53	7 3	7 53	8 20			...	...	...
Forncett arr.	—		7 55	10 11	12 37	3 0	7 11	8 0	8 28			—	—	—
Dereham „	...		8 59	11 29	1 47	...	8 6	...	...			...	...	...
Norwich Victoria „	—		8L35	10 33	1 0	3S33	7 33	8 35	—			—	—	—
Norwich Thorpe „	...		8N15	10 50	1K24	M	7 52	8 27	9 0			...	...	...
Tivetshall dep	7 16	Mons. only.	7M47 / 9 21	10 39	12 52	2 53	7 21	—	—			—	—	—
Diss arr.	7 30		6 24 / 9 30	10 54	1 5	1 5	7 38	...	...			...	...	...
Haughley „	7 57		— / 9 46	12I6	1 28	5 1	8 4	—	—	—	—	—	—	—
Bury St. Edmund's „	8 27		9I16 / 11V5	12I32	2 58	5 23	10I24	...	...	...	...	...	...	...
Stowmarket „	8 4		8 46 / 9 52	11 26	1 35	4 23	8 11	—	—	—	—	—	—	—
Ipswich „	8 38		9 4 / 10 10	11 48	1 53	4 43	8 40	...	...	...	...	...	...	—
LONDON (L'pl St.) „	10 33		10 45 / 12 27	2 13	3 43	6 35	11 21	—	—	—	—	—	—	...

N On Saturdays due at Norwich Thorpe at 8.37 a.m. **O** From Halesworth on Tuesdays only.
P Calls at Earsham at 6.37 a.m. when required to take up London Passengers.
R Passengers from Haughley travel via Stowmarket.
S On Saturdays arrives at Norwich Victoria at 3.23 p.m.
T From Beccles to Halesworth and Saxmundham on Thursdays only.
U On Mondays and Thursdays leaves Beccles at 9.45 a.m. and arrives Yarmouth at 10.10 a.m.
V Except on Wednesdays Passengers for Bury St. Edmund's travel via Stowmarket.

GER public timetable 1910.

WAVENEY VALLEY BRANCH.—*Single Line.*

The Trains on this Single Line are worked by Train Staff and Train Staff Ticket, according to the "Train Staff Regulations" contained in the "Appendix" to this Working Time Book. No Engine or Train is to be run on this Branch without a Train Staff or Train Staff Ticket. The Train Staff Stations are Tivetshall, Harleston, Bungay, and Beccles.

Down Trains.—Week Days.

Miles from Tivetshall M.	C.	FROM		1	2	3	4	5	6	7	8	9	10	11	12	13	14	15	16	17	18	19	20	21	22	23	24	25	26	27	28	29	30
				Pass.	A Cars. Mondays and Thursdays. To work No. 5 Excursion.	B Gds.	C Pass.	A Exc.	Pass.	D Gds.	Pass.	Pass	Gds.	Pass.	Runs 11th July to 13th September inclusive.	Pass.	Runs 1st to 10th July and 15th to 30th September.	Mkt. Pass.	F Gds.	G Gds.	Pass.	Cars. Saturdays only.											
				a.m.	a.m.	a.m.	a.m.	a.m.	a.m.	a.m.	p.m.	p.m.	p.m.	p.m.		p.m.		p.m.	p.m.	p.m.	p.m.	p.m.											
		Norwich	dep.	...	7 55	5 40	8 5	...	9 48	8 25	12 10	2 53	...	...		...		5 22	...	...	7 50	...											
		Wymondham	,,	-----	-----	-----	-----	-----	-----	-----	-----	-----	-----	-----		-----		-----	4 30	5 20	-----	-----											
		Forncett	,,	...	8 20	...	8 33	8 40	10 15	10 50	12 33	3 14	...	3 57		3 57		5 45	5 40	6 45	8 18												
—	—	Tivetshall	arr.	-----		6 50	8 40	8 47	10 22	11 0	12 39	3 20	-----	4 4		4 4		5 52	5 50	6 55	8 20												
			dep.	7 16		7 50	8 45	8 55	10 28	11 25	12 58	3 25	...	4 20		4 25		5 57	6 5	7 5	8 25												
2	51	Pulham Market	,,	7 22		B	8 51	9 2	10 32	11 45	1 4	3 31	-----	4 26		4 31		6 3	F	G	8 31												
3	53	Pulham Mary	,,	7 25		B	8 54	9 6	10 35	12 0	1 7	3 34	...	4 29		4 34		6 6	F	...	8 34												
6	20	Harleston	arr.	7 30		8 6	8 52	9 11	10 40	12 10	1 12	3 39	-----	4 34		4 39		6 11	6 30	7 30	8 38	-----											
			dep	7 55		8 30	9 2	9 13	10 42	...	1 14	3 41	...	4 36		4 41		6 13	6 50	7 45	8 41	10 55											
8	71	Homersfield	,,	8 1		8 50	9 8	9 19	10 48	-----	1 20	3 47	-----	4 42		4 47		6 19	F	8 10	8 47	-----											
12	3	Earsham	,,	8 7		B	9 14	9 26	10 54	...	1 26	3 53	...	4 48		4 53		6 25	...	...	8 53	...											
12	66	Bungay	arr.	8 9		9 5	9 16	9 28	10 56	-----	1 28	3 55	-----	4 50		4 55		6 28	7 10	8 20	8 56	-----											
			dep.	8 11		9 40	9 21	9 35	10 58	...	1 32	3 57	4 1	4 52		4 57		6 30	7 45	8 35	8 57	11 7											
13	60	Ditchingham	,,	8 15		B	9 25	9 40	11 2	-----	1 36	4 1	4 15	4 56		5 1		6 34	8 10	G	9 1	-----											
15	22	Ellingham	,,	8 19		B	9 29	9 45	11 6	...	1 40	4 5	4 30	5 0		5 5		6 38	F	...	9 5	...											
16	63	Geldeston	,,	8 23		B	9 33	9 51	11 10	-----	1 44	4 9	4 50	5 4		5 9		6 42	F	-----	9 9	-----											
19	34	Beccles	arr.	8 29	...	10 25	9 39	9 57	11 16	...	1 50	4 15	5 0	5 10		5 15		6 48	8 45	9 0	9 15	11 20											
		Yarmouth	arr.	-----	-----	-----	10 31	10 37	-----	-----	-----	-----	-----	-----		-----		Saturdays only.	Not Sats.	Sats only.	-----	-----											
						See page 138	See page 176	Mons & Thurs. See page 176.	See page 140	See page 140	See page 141	See page 143		Not on Saturdays.		Not on Saturdays.		See page 14d.	See page 192 & 146	See page 192 & 147	See page 148												

A Nos. and 5. *Will not run after Thursday, 11th September.*

B No. 3. To shunt at Bungay for No. 4 Passenger and No. 5 Excursion Trains. To call at Pulham Market and Pulham Mary to detach Cattle and leave Brake Goods, and to attach Trucks and take in Brake Goods for Stations beyond Bungay only. To call at Homersfield and Ditchingham when required to detach Traffic or to attach Cattle and leave or pick up Brake Goods, and call at Ellingham and Geldeston to detach Traffic and leave or pick up Brake Goods.

C No. 4. May work 1 Truck of Cattle only from either Tivetshall or Harleston to Beccles if the Truck is fitted with Westinghouse Brake pipes. The Tivetshall and Harleston Station Masters to arrange so that not more than 1 Truck of Cattle is accepted for this Train on any one day.

D No. 7. On Saturdays to leave Tivetshall at 11.15 a.m. and run 10 minutes earlier to Harleston.

F No 16. This Train is to call at Pulham Market and Pulham Mary to attach traffic for Yarmouth, Lowestoft and London. To call at Homersfield to detach or attach Cattle only, and at Ellingham and Geldeston when required to detach or leave Brake Goods only. On Mondays and Thursdays to cross No. 15 Up Excursion at Bungay.

G No. 17. To call at Pulham Market and Ditchingham to leave Cattle only.

N.B.—Traffic in Trucks, fitted with Westinghouse Brake pipes, may only be worked by Passenger Trains which start direct from Tivetshall or Beccles, and only from and to these points, except in the case provided for in foot note C on this page.

WAVENEY VALLEY BRANCH.—*Single Line.*

The Trains on this Single Line are worked by Train Staff and Train Staff Ticket, according to the "Train Staff Regulations" contained in the "Appendix" to this Working Time Book. No Engine or Train is to be run on this Branch without a Train Staff or Train Staff Ticket. The Train Staff Stations are Beccles, Bungay, Harleston, and Tivetshall.

Up Trains.—Week Days.

FROM		1	2	3	4	5	6	7	8	9	10	11	12	13	14	15	16	17	18	19	20	21	22	23	24	25	26	27	28	29	30	31
		A Pass.	B Pass.	Pass.	C Gds. Sats. only. From Beccles. See No. 5.	D Gds.		Pass.	Gds.	F Pass.	Pass. Saturdays only. From Beccles. See No. 9.	G Gds.	H Brk. Gds.	Pass.	Pass.	I Exc.	Pass. Saturdays only.															
		a.m.	a.m.	a.m.	a.m.	a.m.		a.m.	a.m.	p.m.	p.m.	p.m.	p.m.	p.m.	p.m.	p.m.	p.m.															
Yarmouth	dep.	...	...	...		...	...	...	...	...	...	...	...	5 10	...	6 50	...															
Beccles	dep.	6 22	6 56	9 1		10 50	-----	11 40	11 53	2 0	-----	-----	2 40	6 12	7 0	7 20	10 10															
Geldeston	,,	...	7 2	9 8		...	...	11 46	12 10	2 6		...	H	6 18	7 6	7 27	10 16															
Ellingham	,,	-----	7 6	9 12		-----	-----	11 50	12 30	2 10		-----	H	6 22	7 10	7 32	10 22															
Ditchingham	,,	...	7 10	9 16		...	...	11 54	1 5	2 14		...	3 25	6 26	7 14	7 37	10 26															
Bungay	arr.	6 34	7 13	9 19		10 50	...	11 57	1 10	2 17		-----	3 30	6 29	7 17	7 40	10 29															
	dep.	6 35	7 14	9 30		11 2[illegible]	..	11 58	...	2 19		...	3 58	6 31	7 19	7 41	10 31															
Earsham	,,	A	7 17	9 33		-----	-----	12 1	-----	2 22		-----	-----	6 34	7 22	7 45	10 34															
Homersfield	,,	6 43	7 24	9 39		D	...	12 8	...	2 29		...	4 20	6 41	7 29	7 53	10 41															
Harleston	arr.	6 48	7 29	9 44	11 50	11 50	-----	12 13	-----	2 34		-----	4 30	6 46	7 34	7 58	10 46															
	dep.	6 49	7 31	9 46	12 20	1 20	...	12 14	...	2 36		3 42	5 0	6 48	7 36	8 1	...															
Pulham Mary	,,	6 55	7 37	9 52	-----	-----	-----	12 20	-----	2 42		G	H	6 54	7 42	8 8	-----															
Pulham Market	,,	6 58	7 40	9 55	C	D	...	12 23	...	2 45		*	H	6 57	7 45	8 12	...															
Tivetshall	arr.	7 4	7 46	10 1	12 45	1 50	..	12 29	-----	2 51		4 18	5 20	7 3	7 51	8 18																
	dep.	...	7 47	10 3	1 15	2 10	...	12 30	..	3 8	...	5 0	6 30	7 5	7 53	8 20																
Forncett	arr.	-----	7 53	10 [illegible]	1 25	2 20	-----	12 36	----	3 15	3 16	-----	-----	7 11	7 59	8 21																
Wymondham	,,	...	...	...	2 15	3 5	...	...	...	...	...	...	...	...	...	...																
Norwich	,,	-----	8 15	10 38	-----	-----	-----	1 0	-----	-----	3 38	5 45	7 10	7 35	8 27	9 0																
			See page 118	See page 120	See page 192	See page 123 and 192		See page 171		See page 123	See page 123	See page 126	See page 126	See page 181 and 127	See page 127	Mons. and Thurs. See page 128																

A No. 1. To call at Earsham when required to take up London Passengers.

B No. 2. This Train runs to Norwich Thorpe Station, except on Saturdays when it runs to Norwich Victoria, returning as a Carriage Train from Norwich Victoria to Norwich Thorpe at 9.10 a.m.

C No. 4. To shunt at Harleston for No. 7 Passenger Train. To call at Pulham Market, if required, to attach Cattle for Tufnell Park. Pulham Market to advise Harleston what to go on. Harleston to arrange. Not to detach traffic at Tivetshall and attach traffic only for Wymondham and Wells branch stations. Load not to exceed 23 Trucks and Brake from Pulham Market.

D No. 5. On Saturdays runs from Harleston as shewn in No. 4 Column. To shunt at Harleston for No. 7 Passenger Train. To call at Homersfield to attach N.C. Traffic and at Pulham Market when required to attach N.C. Cattle.

F No. 9. On Saturdays runs to Norwich Victoria as shewn in No. 10 Column.

G No 11. To call at Pulham Mary for Meat and Brake Goods only.

H No. 12. To call at Geldeston and Ellingham to attach Up Road Traffic and leave or take in Brake Goods, at Pulham Mary, if required, to detach traffic from Ditchingham or to attach malt Traffic and at Pulham Market for Meat and Market Goods and if required to attach or detach Cattle.

I No. 15. *Will not run after Thursday, 11th Sept.* To cross No. 16 Down Goods at Bungay.

N.B.—Traffic in Trucks, fitted with Brake pipes, may only be worked by Passenger Trains which start direct from Tivetshall or Beccles, and only from and to these points, except in the case provided for in foot note C page 190.

GER working timetable 1913.

to Beccles due at 9.58am. The 8.25am ex Norwich was permitted to work one truck of cattle from either Tivetshall or Harleston to Beccles if the truck was fitted with the Westinghouse brake pipes, the Tivetshall and Harlestion station masters liaising so that only one truck was accepted for this train on any given day. The 4.10am goods train from Norwich was allowed 50 minutes for shunting at Tivetshall from 5.30am to 6.20am before proceeding across the branch with mandatory calls at Harleston, Homersfield and Bungay; the train also called at Pulham Market and Pulham St. Mary to detach cattle traffic and brake goods, Tivetshall advising those stations if the train was to call. Similar calls were made at Homersfield and Ditchingham, when the train was required to detach traffic or attach cattle wagons and leave or pick up brake goods. Ellingham was only served if required. The war years resulted in much change in the goods handled and military traffic was on the increase. The 6.45am goods train ex Norwich, arriving at Tivetshall at 7.50am to attach traffic for the Admiralty siding and departing at 8.40am, arrived at Pulham Market at 8.50am to service the air station. The next working, the 7.25am ex Norwich, was booked 40 minutes at Tivetshall (10.10am to 10.50am) before calling at Pulham Market and Pulham St. Mary, terminating at Harleston at 12.35pm. On SO the train departed Tivetshall at the later time of 11.50am, calling at the intemediate stations before terminating at Harleston at 12.35pm. The final Down freight working was the 4.12pmSX ex Wymondham, which spent from 6.40pm until 7.00pm shunting at Tivetshall before making mandatory calls at Harleston and Bungay with arrival at Beccles at 9.00pm. This train also called at Pulham Market, at Pulham St. Mary to attach traffic for Yarmouth, Lowestoft and London, at Homersfield to detach or attach cattle traffic only and at Ditchingham to detach important traffic. On Saturdays the train departed Wymondham at 4.55pm and, as well as making the mandatory stops at Harleston and Bungay, called only if required at Pulham Market, Homersfield and Ditchingham to detach cattle traffic, with arrival at Beccles at 9.00pm. In the Up direction all branch trains commenced their journey at Beccles and the services offered consisted of eight SX and nine SO passenger trains, together with three goods workings. All passenger services called at all stations on the branch and ran through to Norwich, with the exception of the 6.28am ex Beccles which called at Bungay then all stations terminating at Tivetshall at 7.12am, and the 8.40am ex Beccles which was a short working to Harleston terminating at 9.14am. The 7.08am Beccles to Norwich was permitted to work one truck of London goods to Bungay off the 11.20pm ex Spitalfields if the truck was Westinghouse brake fitted; similar arrangements were allowed on the 8.40am Beccles to Harleston train. The 10.35am Beccles to Norwich ran SO whilst the remaining trains from Beccles – 12.07pm, 1.30pm, 3.16pm, 5.56pm and 7.51pm – called all stations. Of the freight services, the 9.15amSO Beccles to Wymondham made mandatory calls at Bungay and Harleston, and called at Homersfield when required to attach wagons and Pulham Market to attach cattle traffic for Tufnell Park; Pulham Market advising Harleston when there was traffic to forward. When calling at Tivetshall between 11.35am and 1.35pm it was not permitted to detach traffic but only attach traffic for Wymondham and the Wells branch; the loading of this train was not to exceed twenty-three wagons and a brake van from Pulham Market. On SX the train departed Beccles at 10.27am with mandatory calls at Bungay and Harleston, also Homersfield and Pulham Market only if required to attach North Country traffic. The Down special working to Pulham Market for Admiralty traffic returned Up road at 12.00 noon and after a 10-minute call at Tivetshall continued to Norwich. Another short working, the 12.15pm ex Beccles, called at Ellingham and Ditchingham before terminating at Bungay, whilst the 3.20pm goods ex Harleston called at Pulham St. Mary for meat and brake goods only, and at Pulham Market only if required, arriving Tivetshall at 3.55pm and departing 60 minutes later for Trowse yard. The final goods working departed Beccles 2.40pm with mandatory calls at Ditchingham, Bungay, Homersfield and Harleston, with stops at Ellingham and Pulham St. Mary only if required: at Ellingham to attach Up road traffic and leave or take up brake goods; at Pulham St. Mary if required to detach traffic from Ditchingham or to attach malt traffic, and Pulham Market for meat and market goods and if required to attach or detach cattle traffic. After arrival at Tivetshall at 5.25pm the train shunted and departed at 6.35pm for Trowse yard.

By 1917 the increasing demands of war resulted in a slight reduction of passenger services as freight traffic increased. Six passenger services operated in the Down direction on weekdays only, with four starting from Norwich and two from Tivetshall. The first Down train, the 7.27am ex Tivetshall, called at all stations including Geldeston, which had reopened the previous October. The next train, the 8.25am ex Norwich, was detained at Tivetshall from 8.59am until 9.28am, before continuing to Beccles arriving at 10.17am. The early afternoon train departed Tivetshall at 1.45pm, followed by the 2.32pm ex Norwich, which departed Tivetshall at 3.03pm. The final Down passenger services of the day departed Norwich at 5.05pm and 8.04pm, arriving at Beccles at 6.33pm and 9.34pm respectively. The first Down goods train to serve the branch departed Norwich at 4.10am and, after shunting at Tivetshall from 5.30am to 6.10am, served all stations on the branch to Bungay (arriving at 8.35am and departing at 11.05am), then calling at Ditchingham, Ellingham and Geldeston only if required, with Beccles reached at 11.50am. Norwich Thorpe was required to make up and attach daily for this train a direct brake goods truck especially for Pulham St. Mary. This was followed by the 6.20am ex Norwich, which paused at Tivetshall from 7.40am until 8.20am, where traffic for the Admiralty siding was attached for conveyance to Pulham Market, arriving at 8.30am. After the necessary shunting and outsorting of wagons, this train returned to Norwich in a special 'Q' path 'as and when ready'. The 6.55am goods train ex Norwich arrived at Tivetshall at 8.40am and, after shunting and outsorting, departed the junction at 10.00am, calling at Pulham Market, Harleston and Homersfield, and terminated at Bungay at 1.45pm. The return working from Bungay to Beccles, serving Ditchingham and Ellingham only, departed at 6.20pm and terminated at the junction at 7.10pm. The final Down freight service of the day was the 4.12pmSX, 4.55pmSO ex Wymondham, departing Tivetshall at 7.00pmSX and 5 minutes later SO, mandatory calls were made at Harleston and Bungay, with arrival at Beccles at 9.00pm. The SX train called at Pulham Market and Pulham St. Mary to attach traffic for Yarmouth, Lowestoft and London, at Homersfield to detach or attach cattle traffic, and Ditchingham to leave cattle traffic only. The SO train called at Pulham Market, Pulham St. Mary and Homersfield to leave cattle only. A new innovation was a Sunday freight service from Norwich, departing 6.20am and running to Pulham Market with traffic for the Admiralty air station, the train returning to Norwich as a special in a 'Q' path. In the Up direction the branch was served by six SX and seven SO passenger trains, all commencing their journey at Beccles, with four SX and five SO working through to Norwich, whilst the 6.23am and 12.13pm ex

TIVETSHALL AND BECCLES

See page		WEEK DAYS.														
		morn		morn	morn		morn		even.		even.		even.			
8 to 10	**LONDON (L'pool St.)** dep.	—	—	5 10	—	—	10 15	—	—	—	12 30	—	5A23	—	—	—
	Colchester "	...	...	6 37	...	...	11 32	...	...	...	1 12	...	5A21	...	...	...
	Ipswich "	—	—	7 12	—	—	12 4	—	—	—	2 18	—	7A 0	—	—	—
	Tivetshall arr.	...	...	8 23	...	...	1 19	...	...	...	3 38	...	8A19	...	...	...
11 to 13	Norwich (Thorpe) dep.	6 43	—	8 22	8 53	—	1 9	—	2 31	—	5 2	—	7 44	—	—	—
	Trowse "	6 48	...	8 27	8 58	...	1 14	...	2 36	...	5 7	...	7 49	...	...	...
	Swainsthorpe "	6 58	—	8 37	—	—	1 21	—	—	—	5 17	—	7 59	—	—	—
	Flordon "	7 5	...	8 41	...	...	1 31	...	...	...	5 24	...	8 6	...	...	...
	Forncett "	7 11	—	8 52	9 15	—	1 37	—	2 52	—	5 30	—	8 12	—	—	—
	Tivetshall arr	7 21	...	8 59	9 24	...	1 47	...	2 59	...	5 37	...	8 19	...	...	...
	TIVETSHALL dep.	7 24	...	9 28	...	...	1 50	...	3 3	...	5 41	...	8 24	...	...	...
	Pulham Market "	7 30	—	9 34	—	—	1 56	—	3 9	—	5 48	—	8 30	—	—	—
	Pulham St. Mary "	7 33	...	9 37	...	...	1 59	...	3 12	...	5 51	...	8 33	...	...	...
	Harleston "	7 41	—	9 43	—	—	2 5	—	3 18	—	5 59	—	8 41	—	—	—
	Homersfield "	7 47	...	9 49	...	...	2 11	...	3 24	...	6 5	...	8 47	...	...	...
	Bungay "	8B15	...	9 59	...	...	2 21	...	3 34	...	6T20	...	8 57	...	...	...
	Ditchingham "	8 19	—	10 3	—	—	2 25	—	3 38	—	6 24	—	9 1	—	—	—
	Ellingham "	8 23	...	10 7	...	...	2 29	...	3 42	...	6 28	...	9 5	...	...	...
	Geldeston (Halt) "	8 27	—	10 11	—	—	2 33	—	3 46	—	6 32	—	9 9	—	—	—
	BECCLES arr.	8 33	...	10 17	...	...	2 39	...	3 52	...	6 38	...	9 15	...	...	...
14	**Beccles** dep.	8 56	—	10 20	—	—	3 31	—	4 14	—	6 49	—	11 11	—	—	—
	Yarmouth (S.T.) arr.	9 31	...	10 55	...	...	3 55	...	4 49	...	7 23	...	11 36	...	...	...
14	**Beccles** dep.	9 0	—	10 35	—	—	3 35	—	4 19	—	6 57	—	11 15	—	—	—
	Lowestoft (Central) arr.	9 18	...	10 52	...	...	3 52	...	4 36	...	7 14	...	11 30	...	...	...
15	**Beccles** dep.	8 55	...	10 31	...	...	2 56	—	4 2	—	6 56	—	—	—	—	—
	Ipswich arr.	9 57	—	12 15	—	—	4 16	...	5 37	...	7 57	...	...	...	...	...
	Colchester "	10 58	...	12 46	...	...	5 17	—	6 31	—	8 38	—	—	—	—	—
	LONDON (L'pool St.) "	11 30	—	1 58	—	—	5 55	...	7 48	...	9 58	...	...	...	...	...

A Passengers from or to London, Colchester and Ipswich travel via Forncett.
B Arrives Bungay 7.55 a.m.

MO Mondays only.
NS Not Saturdays.

(WAVENEY VALLEY LINE.)

See page		WEEK DAYS.														
		morn		morn	morn		SO morn		morn		morn		even.		even.	
14	**LONDON (L'pool St.)** dep.	—	—	5 10	—	—	—	—	8 15	—	10 15	—	3 15	—	3 22	—
	Colchester "	...	...	6 37	...	...	*7 40*	...	9 40	...	11 32	...	3 53	...	4 36	...
	Ipswich "	—	—	7 17	—	—	*8 45*	—	10 32	—	12 15	—	4 56	—	5 6	—
	Beccles arr.	...	...	8 52	...	...	*10.12*	...	12 3	...	1 35	...	5 51	...	6 43	...
15	Lowestoft (Central) dep.	—	—	8 25	—	—	*9 53*	—	11 43	—	2 28	—	5 24	—	6 23	—
	Beccles arr.	...	...	8 42	...	...	*10 10*	...	12 0	...	2 45	...	5 41	...	6 40	...
15	Yarmouth (S.T.) dep.	—	—	8 25	—	—	*9 54*	—	—	—	2 24	—	5 35	—	6 26	—
	Beccles arr.	...	...	8 49	...	...	*10 28*	...	...	...	2 50	...	5 59	...	6 50	...
	BECCLES dep.	6 23	—	9 6	—	—	*10 35*	—	12 14	—	3 16	—	6 2	—	7 10	—
	Geldeston (Halt) "	6 29	...	9 12	...	...	*10 41*	...	12 20	...	3 22	...	6 8	...	7 16	...
	Ellingham "	6 33	—	9 16	—	—	*10 45*	—	12 24	—	3 26	—	6 12	—	7 20	—
	Ditchingham "	6 37	...	9 20	...	...	*10 49*	...	12 28	...	3 30	...	6 16	...	7 24	...
	Bungay "	6 41	—	9 26	—	—	*10 55*	—	12 33	—	3 35	—	6 23	—	7 31	—
	Homersfield "	6 51	...	9 36	...	...	*11 5*	...	12 43	...	3 45	...	6 33	...	7 41	...
	Harleston "	6 57	—	9 44	—	—	*11 11*	—	12 49	—	3 51	—	6 40	—	7 50	—
	Pulham St. Mary "	7 3	...	9 50	...	...	*11 17*	...	12 55	...	3 57	...	6 46	...	7 57	...
	Pulham Market "	7 6	—	9 53	—	—	*11 20*	—	12 58	—	4 0	—	6 49	—	8 1	—
	TIVETSHALL arr.	7 12	...	9 59	...	...	*11 26*	...	1 4	...	4 6	...	6 55	...	8 7	...
8 to 10	**Tivetshall** dep.	8 23	...	10 1	10 12	...	*11 27*	...	1 19	...	4 8	...	6 58	...	8 9	...
	Forncett arr.	8 31	—	—	10 20	—	—	—	1 27	—	4 15	—	7 5	—	8 16	—
	Flordon "	8 37	...	...	10 26	...	...	...	1 33	...	4 21	...	7 11	...	8 22	...
	Swainsthorpe "	8 44	—	—	10 33	—	—	—	1 40	—	4 28	—	7 18	—	8 29	—
	Trowse "	8 53	...	...	10 42	...	...	...	1 49	...	4 37	...	7 27	...	8 38	...
	Norwich (Thorpe) "	8 58	—	10 22	10 46	—	*11 49*	—	1 53	—	4 42	—	7 31	—	8 42	—
11 to 13	**Tivetshall** dep.	7 21	...	11 0	...	...	...	...	1 47	...	4 24	...	7 36	...	...	...
	Ipswich arr.	8 35	—	12 11	—	—	—	—	3 0	—	5 43	—	8 44	—	—	—
	Colchester "	9 14	...	12 46	...	...	...	...	4 5	...	6 31	...	9 24	...	...	...
	LONDON (L'pool St.) "	10 28	—	1 58	—	—	—	—	5 0	—	7 48	—	11 15	—	—	—

SO Saturdays only.
T Arrives Bungay 6.13 p.m.

GER public timetable 1919.

Beccles terminated at Tivetshall at 7.12am and 1.03pm respectively. Of the goods services the 12.20pm ex Beccles called all stations and terminated at Bungay at 1.30pm whilst the 2.25pm ex Harleston served all stations to Tivetshall arriving at 4.35pm and departed 20 minutes later en route to Trowse yard. The 2.40pm ex Beccles conveyed brake goods and called at Ditchingham, Bungay, Harleston, Pulham Market and Tivetshall arriving at 5.25pm and departing at 6.35pm for Trowse yard. This train called at Pulham St. Mary if required to detach traffic from Ditchingham or to attach malt traffic. Traffic for Homersfield was to be taken through to Harleston and worked by the 4.12pm Down train ex Wymondham. Beccles was to make up and attach daily a brake goods truck for Bungay to be worked by this train. When required the engine working the 12.20pm ex Beccles after shunting at Bungay worked light to Ditchingham at 3.55pm to perform shunting returning at 5.00pm to Bungay to work the 6.20pm Down train to Beccles. On Sundays a goods service departed Beccles at 8.00am serving Ditchingham, Bungay, Homersfield, Harleston, Pulham St. Mary and Pulham Market arriving at Tivetshall at 2.05pm; this train was to perform shunting as required at all stations. The train returned at 3.15pm ex Tivetshall, calling all stations except Ellingham and Geldeston, carrying out shunting as required and arriving at Beccles at 6.00pm.

By 1920 little had changed, and in the Down direction six passenger and three freight trains served the branch on weekdays only. Four of the passenger trains ran from Norwich Thorpe to Beccles and two – the 7.27am and 1.50pm ex Tivetshall – were self-contained to the branch. Trains departed Norwich at 8.23am, 2.26pm, 5.00pm and 7.45pm, and as before all passenger service called at all stations; specific instructions were issued and empty vehicles were not to be attached to the 5.00pm ex Norwich. Down freight services commenced with the 5.00am ex Norwich, which called at Tivetshall between 6.30am and 7.30am to collect traffic destined for the Admiralty siding at Pulham Market; after arrival at 7.40am the train shunted the connection to the air station before departing Up road at 10.30am with outgoing traffic, arriving at Tivetshall 10 minutes later. The engine having reformed the train, returned across the branch departing at 11.25am and, after calling at Pulham Market to shunt ordinary traffic, continued to Pulham St. Mary where Up road traffic was collected and taken through to Harleston where the train terminated at 12.40pm. The next goods service departed Norwich at 6.30am and after spending 40 minutes at Tivetshall departed at 8.20am, calling at Pulham Market, Harleston, Homersfield and Bungay, also Ditchingham, Ellingham and Geldeston only if required, with arrival at Beccles at 11.50am. The 3.50pmFSO Bungay to Beccles working also called at Ditchingham, Ellingham and Geldeston only if required, with arrival at the junction at 4.25pm. The last Down freight working, 4.00pmSX or 5.00pmSO ex Wymondham, arrived at Tivetshall 5.55pmSX and 6.40pmSO, departing at 7.00pmSX and 7.05pmSO, making mandatory calls at Harleston and Bungay with arrival at Beccles at 8.40pm. The SX working called at Pulham Market, at Pulham St. Mary to attach traffic for Yarmouth, Lowestoft and London, at Homersfield to detach or attach cattle traffic and at Ditchingham to detach important traffic. On SO the train called at Pulham Market, Homersfield and Ditchingham to leave cattle traffic only. In the Up direction the branch was served by six SX and seven SO passenger trains: the 8.23am and 12.14pm ex Beccles terminated at Tivetshall; the 9.06am, 10.35amSO, 3.10pm, 5.57pm and 7.10pm ex Beccles were through trains to Norwich Thorpe. All trains called at all stations. Of the goods services, mention has been made of the backworking of the 5.10am ex Norwich returning to Tivetshall after shunting the Admiralty siding at Pulham Market. The later goods service, departing Beccles 10.30amSX and 10.41amSO, served Bungay, Harleston and Pulham Market, with the SX train also calling at Homersfield; the train arrived at Tivetshall at 12.02pm and departed 8 minutes later for Wymondham. At 12.30pm a short goods working to Ditchingham and Bungay departed Beccles, followed by the 1.15pm Beccles to Trowse, which called at all stations with the exception of Pulham St. Mary, with arrival at Tivetshall at 4.25pm; thirty minutes were allowed for shunting before the train continued its journey. The afternoon train departing from Harleston at 4.10pm called at Pulham St. Mary, if required to attach important traffic, and Pulham Market before departing Tivetshall at 5.30pm for Trowse yard.

After grouping, the L&NER made few alterations and the 1924 working timetable showed a weekdays only service of six passenger and three freight trains in each direction, augmented by a short goods working from Beccles to Bungay and return. All passenger trains called at all stations on the branch and in the Down direction four trains – the 8.24am, 2.26pm, 5.08pm and 7.45pmSX or 7.50pmSO – commenced their journey at Norwich Thorpe, with the remaining two – the 7.47am and 1.38pmMFSO or 1.47pmTuWThO – starting at Tivetshall. The 8.24am ex Norwich was allowed three minutes recovery time between Geldeston and Beccles, whilst the 5.08pm was not permitted to convey empty vehicles attached to the formation. Of the Down goods services the 5.40am ex Norwich called at Trowse, Flordon to leave mail bags, Forncett, then Tivetshall between 7.00am and 8.00am. This train was required to work the London to Harleston brake goods truck forward and called at Pulham Market and Pulham St. Mary to leave London brake goods only. Loaded trucks from these stations were taken through to Beccles and returned on the 1.15pm Up goods train. Mandatory calls were made at Harleston, Homersfield and Bungay, calls were made at Ditchingham and Ellingham only if required, and at Geldeston with brake goods only, with Beccles reached at 11.50am. The 9.10am Norwich to Harleston goods train called at Trowse and Flordon, then spent 40 minutes shunting at Tivetshall before departing at 11.10am. This train worked traffic to and from the Air Ministry siding at Pulham Market when required, with Tivetshall advising when there was any traffic, before it continued to Pulham St. Mary and terminated at Harleston at 12.40pm. The short goods working from Beccles to Bungay returned at 3.40pmFSO and 4.20pmFSX, calling when required for shunting at the intermediate stations. The late branch goods departed Wymondham 3.50pmSX and 5.05pmSO, with mandatory calls at Harleston and Bungay only. The SX train served other stations only if required, and at Pulham Market and Pulham St. Mary to attach traffic for Yarmouth, Lowestoft and London, at Homersfield to detach or attach cattle wagons only, and at Ditchingham to detach important traffic. On SO the train called at Pulham Market, Homersfield and Ditchingham to leave cattle traffic only. The train arrived at Beccles at the uniform time of 8.45pm. In the Up direction the 6.15am and 12.18pm passenger services ex Beccles terminated at Tivetshall, whilst the 9.08am, 3.12pm, 5.41pm and 7.12pm departures were through trains to Norwich. As before, all trains called at all stations. The 9.30am Up goods train ex Beccles called at Bungay, Homersfield, Harleston and Pulham Market only, before spending 30 minutes (12.05pm to 12.35pm) at Tivetshall and continuing to Wymondham arriving at 1.10pm. The 12.30pm goods train ex Beccles was the short working to Bungay, calling at Ellingham and Ditchingham, with arrival at 1.40pm. The 2.20pm train ex Harleston to Trowse called at Pulham St. Mary if required to attach important traffic and for brake goods only. The final Up freight train of the day departed Beccles at 1.15pm, calling all stations to Harleston then Pulham Market and Tivetshall, arriving at 4.25pm. Departing at 4.50pm it then called at Forncett to attach cattle traffic and terminated at Trowse at 5.20pm. This train was to work brake goods only to Ellingham and after picking up wagons at Homersfield outsorted the wagons at Harleston for onward conveyance.

The protracted miners strike in 1926 resulted in a shortage of coal supplies and train services were reduced to conserve fuel. The Waveney Valley line was no exception and from 31st May 1926 only four trains ran each way, weekdays only, departing Beccles at 9.06am, 3.09pm, 6.05pm and 7.10pm, and from Tivetshall at 9.23am, 2.57pm, 5.46pm and 8.24pmSX or 8.29pmSO.

The working timetable for 1935 showed a weekdays only service of six passenger trains and two freight trains in the Down direction, together with an SO ECS working commencing 6th June, whilst

TIVETSHALL AND BECCLES

See page	WEEK DAYS.	morn		morn	morn		morn		even.		even.		NS even.	SO even.	
18 to 20	**LIVERPOOL STREET** — dep.	—	—	5 0	—	—	10 12	—	—	—	12 33	—	5A18	5 18	—
	Colchester ,,	...	...	6 23	...	...	11 35	...	...	...	1 46	...	5A22	5 22	...
	Ipswich ,,	—	—	6 54	—	—	12 8	—	—	—	2 22	—	6A58	7 10	—
	Tivetshall arr.	...	...	8 5	...	...	1 26	...	...	...	3 39	...	8A19	8 24	...
21 to 23	Norwich (Thorpe) dep.	6 43	—	8 23	8 50	—	12 54	—	2 25	—	5 7	—	7 44	7 49	—
	Trowse ,,	6 48	...	8 28	8 55	...	12 59	...	2 30	...	5 12	...	7 49	7 54	...
	Swainsthorpe ,,	6 58	—	8 38	—	—	1 9	—	—	—	5 22	—	7 59	8 4	—
	Flordon ,,	7 5	...	8 45		...	1 16	...	...	...	5 29	...	8 6	8 11	...
	Forncett ,,	7 11	—	8 52	9 12	—	1 23	—	2 46	—	5 35	—	8 12	8 17	—
	Tivetshall arr	7 21	...	8 59	9 21	...	1 33	...	2 53	...	5 42	...	8 19	8 24	...
	TIVETSHALL dep.	7 47	...	9 23	...	...	1 38	...	2 57	...	5 46	...	8 24	8 29	...
	Pulham Market ,,	7 53	—	9 30	—	—	1 44	—	3 3	—	5 53	—	8 30	8 35	—
	Pulham St. Mary ,,	7 56	...	9 34	...	...	1 47	...	3 6	...	5 56	...	8 33	8 38	...
	Harleston ,,	8 3	—	9 42	—	—	1 57	—	3 12	—	6 5	—	8 41	8 46	—
	Homersfield ,,	8 9	...	9 50	...	...	2 3	...	3 18	...	6 11	..	8 47	8 52	...
	Earsham ,,	8 15	—	9 56	—	—	2 9	—	3 24	—	6 17	—	8 53	8 58	—
	Bungay ,,	8 19	...	10 1	...	...	2 16	...	3 30	...	6 22	...	8 57	9 2	...
	Ditchingham ,,	8 23	—	10 6	—	—	2 20	—	3 34	—	6 26	—	9 1	9 6	—
	Ellingham ,,	8 27	...	10 10	...	...	2 24	...	3 38	...	6 30	...	9 5	9 10	...
	Geldeston ,,	8 31	—	10 14	—	—	2 28	—	3 42	—	6 34	—	9 9	9 14	—
	BECCLES arr.	8 37	...	10 25	...	...	2 34	...	3 48	...	6 40	...	9 15	9 20	...
24, 25	**Beccles** dep.	8 46	—	10 26	—	—	3B27	—	3 57	—	6 52	—	10P 0	10R 0	—
	Yarmouth (South Town) arr.	9 20	...	11 0	...	...	3B50	...	4 22	...	7 26	...	10P32	10R32	...
24, 25	**Beccles** dep.	8 56	—	10 37	—	—	3D 0	—	4 6	—	6 58	—	—	—	—
	Lowestoft (Central) arr.	9 13	...	10 54	...	...	3D17	...	4 23	...	7 15	...	...	...	...
26, 27	**Beccles** dep.	8 54	...	10 33	...	...	2 56	—	4 2	—	6 56	—	—	—	—
	Ipswich arr.	9 57	—	12 11	—	—	4 17	...	5 37	...	7 57	...	...	...	...
	Colchester ,,	11 1	...	12 48	...	...	5 17	—	6 36	—	8 38	—	—	—	—
	LIVERPOOL STREET ,,	11 30	—	2 3	—	—	5 56	...	7 51	...	10 0	...	...	...	...

A Passengers travel via Forncett.
B Commences 17th September.

(WAVENEY VALLEY LINE.)

See page	WEEK DAYS.	morn		morn	morn		morn		morn		even.		even.		
24, 25	**LIVERPOOL STREET** — dep.	—	—	5 0	—	—	8 15	—	10 20	—	3 15	—	3 18	—	—
	Colchester ,,	...	...	6 23	...	...	9 40	...	11 43	...	3 53	...	4 35	...	...
	Ipswich ,,	—	—	7 7	—	—	10 37	—	12 30	—	4 57	—	5 6	—	—
	Beccles arr.	...	...	8 42	...	...	12 7	...	1 56	...	5 52	...	6 46	...	...
26, 27	Lowestoft (Central) — dep.	—	—	8 25	—	—	11 40	—	2 28	—	5 30	—	6 25	—	—
	Beccles arr.	...	...	8 42	...	...	11 57	...	2 45	...	5 47	...	6 42	...	...
26, 27	Yarmouth (South Town) — dep.	—	—	8 24	—	—	11 30	—	2 24	—	5 22	—	6 24	—	—
	Beccles arr.	...	...	8 48	...	...	12 4	...	2 50	...	5 57	...	6 50	...	...
	BECCLES dep.	6 23	—	9 6	—	—	12 15	—	3 12	—	6 4	—	7 10	—	—
	Geldeston ,,	6 29	...	9 12	...	...	12 24	...	3 18	...	6 10	...	7 16	...	...
	Ellingham ,,	6 33	—	9 16	—	—	12 28	—	3 22	—	6 14	—	7 20	—	—
	Ditchingham ,,	6 37	...	9 20	...	...	12 32	...	3 26	...	6 18	...	7 25	...	...
	Bungay ,,	6 41	—	9 26	—	—	12 40	—	3 31	—	6 23	—	7 31	—	—
	Earsham ,,	6 44	...	9 29	...	...	12 43	...	3 34	...	6 26	...	7 34	...	...
	Homersfield ,,	6 51	—	9 36	—	—	12 50	—	3 41	—	6 33	—	7 43	—	—
	Harleston ,,	6 57	...	9 43	...	...	1 0	...	3 47	...	6 40	...	7 52	...	...
	Pulham St. Mary ,,	7 3	—	9 49	—	—	1 6	—	3 53	—	6 46	—	8 0	—	—
	Pulham Market ,,	7 6	...	9 52	...	...	1 9	...	3 56	..	6 49	...	8 4	...	...
	TIVETSHALL arr.	7 12	—	9 58	—	—	1 15	—	4 2	—	6 55	—	8 10	—	—
18 to 20	**Tivetshall** dep.	8 5	...	9 59	10 12	...	1 26	...	4 4	...	7 0	...	8 12	...	...
	Forncett arr.	8 13	—	—	10 20	—	1 34	—	4 11	—	7 7	—	8 19	—	—
	Flordon ,,	8 19	...	...	10 26	...	1 40	...	4 17	...	7 13	...	8 25	...	...
	Swainsthorpe ,,	8 26	—	—	10 33	—	1 47	—	4 24	—	7 20	—	8 32	—	—
	Trowse ,,	8 35	...	10 18	10 42	...	1 56	...	4 33	...	7 29	..	8 41	...	...
	Norwich (Thorpe) ,,	8 43	—	10 22	10 46	—	2 0	—	4 37	—	7 33	—	8 46	—	—
21 to 23	**Tivetshall** dep.	7 21	...	10A12	11 0	...	1 33	...	4 23	...	7 39	...	...	...	...
	Ipswich arr.	8 37	—	11A32	—	—	3 0	—	5 43	—	8 47	—	—	—	—
	Colchester ,,	9 14	...	...	12 48	...	4 5	...	6 36	...	9 25	...	...	...	...
	LIVERPOOL STREET ,,	10 30	—	1A20		—	4 58	—	7 51	—	11 16	—	—	—	—

D Commencing 17th September leaves Beccles 3.31 and arrives Lowestoft 3.50 p.m.
NS Not Saturdays.
P Wednesdays only. **Not after 12th September.**
R Not after 15th September.
SO Saturdays only.

L&NER public timetable 1923.

in the Up direction the service was six SX and seven SO passenger services together with two freight trains; commencing on 31st May, two passenger services operated on Sundays. As in former years, four of the passenger services – 8.24am, 2.23pm, 5.14pm and 7.55pm – commenced their journey at Norwich Thorpe, with the 7.47am and 1.53pm operating from Tivetshall. The 8.24am was not permitted to work empty stock and was allowed two minutes extra running time between Geldeston and Beccles for recovery of time lost by exceptional circumstances. The 7.55pm provided a connection at Forncett for branch passengers travelling on the 7.00pm Down main line train from Ipswich, which did not call at Tivetshall. Of the Down freight services, the 3.15am ex Norwich Thorpe served all stations on the branch, with a prolonged journey of 12 hours 35 minutes before reaching Beccles at 5.50pm. Extensive time was spent shunting at Harleston and Bungay. In the early stages of the journey on the main line it worked Eastern Union traffic to Forncett to go forward by the 1.35am Whitemoor to Stowmarket goods train, and from Tivetshall it was booked to take forward the London to Harleston brake goods wagon. This train in the later stages of the journey only called at Geldeston if required. The later train (3.50pmSX and 5.05pmSO ex Wymondham) served Tivetshall departing at 7.05pm, then Harleston and Bungay, arriving at Beccles at 8.55pm. The SX train called at Pulham Market and Pulham St. Mary to attach traffic for Yarmouth, Lowestoft and London, at Homersfield to detach or attach cattle traffic, and at Ditchingham to detach important traffic. The train on SO called at Pulham Market, Homersfield and Ditchingham to leave cattle traffic. In the Up direction, the 6.20am and 12.20pm passenger services ex Beccles terminated at Tivetshall; the former, omitting Earsham, was allowed four minutes extra recovery time between Pulham Market and the junction. The 9.04am, 3.08pm, 6.09pm and 7.10pm ex Beccles passenger services were through trains to Norwich Thorpe. The 6.09pm on Fridays was permitted to work not exceeding four wagons of cattle from Beccles through to Norwich provided the vehicles were fitted with automatic brakes. On SO the 9.34pm ex Yarmouth South Town offered local townsfolk and

NORWICH THORPE, TIVETSHALL, HARLESTON, BUNGAY AND BECCLES.

Single Line between Tivetshall and Beccles.

42

Miles from Norwich T. (M. C.)	DOWN WEEK DAYS.		2	5	7	9	11	13	15	17	18	19	22	23	SUNDAYS 24	26
			Pass.	Gds.	Pass.	Gds.	Pass.	Pass.	Gds.	Pass.	Gds.	Gds.	Pass.	Cars	Pass.	Pass.
	See page										41	41		C 51	C 51	C 51
											SX	SO		SO		
			a.m.	a.m.	a.m.	a.m.	p.m.	p.m.	p.m.	p.m.	p.m.	p.m.	p.m.	p.m.	a.m.	p.m.
— —	Norwich Thorpe	dep.		3 15	8 24			2 28		5 15			7 55		10 20	
1 0	Trowse	arr.	—	3 20	8 27	—	—	2 31	—	5 18	—	—	7 58	—	—	—
		dep.		3 35	8 28			2 32		5 19			7 59			
5 23	Swainsthorpe	arr.	—	3 55	8 36	—	—	—	—	5 27	—	—	8 7	Commences 4th June.		Commences 29th May.
		dep.		4 15	8 37					5 28			8 8			
8 21	Flordon	arr.	—	4 28	8 43	—	—	—	—	5 34	—	—	8 14		10 37	
		dep.		4 38	8 44					5 35			8 15		10 38	
— —	Wymondham	"	—	—	—	—	—	—	—	—	3 50	5 35			—	
10 71	Forncett	arr.		4 50	8 48			2 47		5 39	4 30	6 0	8 19		10 42	
		dep.	—	5 48	8 49	See Col. 5.	—	2 48	—	5 40	5 50	6 30	8 20		10 43	
14 31	Tivetshall (S)	arr.		6 3	8 55			2 54		5 46	6 5	6 45	8 26		10 49	
		dep.	7 49	7 55	9 24		1 53	2 58	—	5 50	7 5	7 5	8 30	—	10 53	—
17 4	Pulham Market (S) (see note)	arr.	7 54	8 5	9 29		1 58	3 3		5 55	**	**	8 35		10 58	
		dep.	7 55	8 20	9 31		1 59	3 4	See Col. 9.	5 56	7 15	7 15	8 36	—	10 59	—
18 6	Pulham Mary	"	7 58	8 40	9 35		2 2	3 7		6 0	**		8 39		11 2	
20 53	Harleston (S)	arr.	8 3	8 50	9 40	8 50	2 7	3 12		6 5	7 35	7 25	8 44	—	11 7	—
		dep.	8 4	1 0	9 43	1 0	2 9	3 13		6 7	7 55	7 55	8 45	10 42	11 8	1 43
23 24	Homersfield	"	8 10	—	9 50	1 45	2 15	3 19		6 13	**	**	8 51	—	11 14	—
26 36	Earsham (NB)	"	8 16	See Col. 9.	9 56		2 21	3 25		6 19					11 20	
27 16	Bungay (S)	arr.	8 18		9 58	1 56	2 23	3 27	1 56	6 21	8 15	8 15	8 57	—	11 23	1 53
		dep.	8 20		10 0	4 30	2 25	3 30	4 30	6 27	8 25	8 25	8 59	10 52	11 25	1 54
28 14	Ditchingham	"	8 24		10 4	See Col. 15.	2 28	3 33	4 50	6 30	**	**	9 2	—	11 29	1 57
29 55	Ellingham	"	8 28		10 8		2 32	3 37	5 5	6 34			9 6		11 34	
31 17	Geldeston	"	8 32		10 12		2 36	3 41	*	6 38	—	—	9 10	—	11 38	—
33 67	Beccles (S)	arr.	8 38		10 20		2 42	3 47	5 50	6 44	8 55	8 55	9 16	11 7	11 44	2 6
		dep.	—	—	—	—	—	—	—	—	—	—	—	11 12	11 52	2 15
— —	Yarmouth S.T.	arr.												11 37	12 12	2 40

(Columns 1, 3, 4, 6, 8, 10, 12, 14, 16, 20, 21, 25 and 27 carry no trains.)

5 & 9 To work Eastern Union Line traffic to Forncett to go forward by 1.35 a.m. (1.30 a.m. MO) Whitemoor to Stowmarket. This traffic to be marshalled for attaching at Forncett in one shunt. To work from Tivetshall the London to Harleston brake goods wagon. To perform station shunting at Harleston and Bungay. Homersfield arr. 1.10 p.m.

=7 Not to work empty stock. Due Pulham Mary 9.33, Homersfield 9.48, and Ditchingham 10.2 a.m. Is allowed 2 minutes extra between Geldeston and Beccles for recovery of time lost by exceptional circumstances.

=17 Pulham Mary arr. 5.58 p.m.

18 To call at Pulham Market and Pulham Mary to attach traffic for Yarmouth, Lowestoft, and London. To call at Homersfield to detach or attach cattle only, and at Ditchingham to detach important traffic.

19 To call at Pulham Market, Homersfield, and Ditchingham to leave cattle only.

=22 In connection at Forncett with 7.0 p.m. ex Ipswich.

=24 Commences 29th May.

BECCLES, BUNGAY, HARLESTON, TIVETSHALL AND NORWICH THORPE.

Single Line between Beccles and Tivetshall.

Miles from Beccles (M. C.)	UP WEEK DAYS.		1	4	6	8	10	14	16	20	22	23	SUNDAYS 24	27
			Pass.	Gds.	Pass.	Pass.	Gds.	Pass.	Gds.	Pass.	Pass.	Pass.	Pass.	Pass.
												SO		
			a.m.	a.m.	a.m.	p.m.	p.m.	p.m.	p.m.	p.m.	p.m.	p.m.	p.m.	p.m.
— —	Yarmouth S.T.	dep.										9 30	12 45	7 50
— —	Beccles (S)	arr.	—	—	—	—	—	—	—	—	—	9 58	1 9	8 13
		dep.	6 22	7 30	9 4	12 20	12 30	3 10	12.30 p.m. ex Beccles	6 9	7 10	10 7	1 14	8 23
2 50	Geldeston	"	6 28	—	9 10	12 26	12 46	3 16		6 15	7 16	10 13	—	8 30
4 12	Ellingham	"	6 32		9 14	12 30	1 15	3 20		6 19	7 20	10 17		8 35
5 53	Ditchingham	"	6 36	—	9 18	12 34	1 55	3 25		6 23	7 26	10 21	—	8 40
6 48	Bungay (S)	arr.	6 39	7 50	9 21	12 37	2 0	3 28		6 26	7 29	10 24	1 24	8 43
		dep.	6 40	8 35	9 24	12 39	2 30	3 31	See Col. 10.	6 29	7 31	10 25	1 25	8 46
7 31	Earsham (NB)	"			9 27	12 42		3 34		6 32	7 34			8 49
10 33	Homersfield	"	6 48	**	9 34	12 49	3 0	3 41		6 39	7 41	10 31	—	8 57
13 14	Harleston (S)	arr.	6 53		9 39	12 54	3 10	3 46	3 10	6 44	7 46	10 36	1 34	9 2
		dep.	6 54	9 0	9 42	12 55	4 20	3 47	4 20	6 47	7 48	—	—	9 5
15 61	Pulham Mary	"	7 0		9 48	1 1	See Col. 16.	3 54	4 40	6 53	7 55			9 12
16 63	Pulham Market (S) (see note)	arr.	7 2	9|10	9 50	1 3		3 56	4 45	6 55	7 57	Commences 4th June.		9 14
		dep.	7 8	10 0	9 51	1 4		3 57	5 10	6 56	7 59			9 16
19 36	Tivetshall (S)	arr.	7 13	10 10	9 57	1 10	—	4 3	5 20	7 2	8| 5		Commences 29th May.	9 22
		dep.		11 5	9 58			4 5	6 35	7 5	8 45			9 25
22 76	Forncett	arr.	—	11 20	10 4	—	—	4 10	6 42	7 10	8 51			9 31
		dep.		11 30	10 5			4 11	6 52	7 11	8 52			9 32
— —	Wymondham	arr.	—	12 20	—	—	—	—	—	—	—			—
25 46	Flordon	arr.						4 16		7 16				9 37
		dep.	—	—	—	—	—	4 17	—	7 17	—	—	—	9 38
28 44	Swainsthorpe	arr.						4 22		7 22				B
		dep.	—	—	—	—	—	4 23	—	7 23	—	—	—	
32 66	Trowse	arr.			10 20			4 30	7 20	7 30				pass
		dep.	—	—	10 21	—	To Trowse.	4 31		7 31	—	—	—	9 52
33 67	Norwich Thorpe	arr.			10 26			4 35		7 35	9 15			9 56
	See page			41								C 54	C 55	C 55

(Columns 2, 3, 5, 7, 9, 11, 12, 13, 15, 17, 18, 19, 21, 25 and 26 carry no trains.)

=1 Due Homersfield 6.46 a.m. Allowed 4 minutes extra between Pulham Market and Tivetshall for recovery.

4 To call at Homersfield when required to detach empty wagons.

10 Traffic to be attached rough at Homersfield arr. 2.40 p.m. and marshalled on arrival at Harleston.

=14 Due Ditchingham 3.23, Pulham Mary 3.52 p.m.

16 Calls at Forncett to attach traffic for transfer at Trowse to 10.0 p.m. ex Norwich.

=20 On Fridays may work not exceeding 4 wagons cattle from Beccles to Norwich T. if wagons are fitted.

=22 Due Ditchingham 7.23, and Pulham Mary 7.53 p.m. On Sats. Norwich arr. 9.16 p.m.

=27 Commences 29th May.

43

L&NER working timetable 1937.

villagers a late return from the coast to Harleston: the train departing Beccles at 9.58pm and calling all stations except Earsham, arriving at its destination at 10.34pm; the engine returned with the ECS to Yarmouth, departing Harleston at 10.40pm. The Up road freight train serving the branch departing Beccles at 7.30am called at Bungay, Homersfield if required to detach empty wagons, Pulham Market, then Tivetshall from 10.10am until 11.15am, before continuing to Wymondham arriving 12.20pm. The 12.30pm Beccles to Trowse goods train served all stations to Bungay, Homersfield and Harleston, where 70 minutes were allowed for shunting before continuing to Pulham St. Mary, Pulham Market and Tivetshall, where another 70 minutes were allowed; this train collected wagons from Homersfield and outsorted them at Harleston prior to onward transit; it finally completed its journey at 7.20pm. From 31st May 1935 the L&NER operated two passenger services to Yarmouth South Town from the branch stations. The 10.20am ex Norwich Thorpe called all stations on the branch and, after reversal at Beccles 11.44am to 11.52am, arrived at Yarmouth South Town at 12.12pm. This was followed by the 1.45pm ex Harleston, which called at Bungay and Ditchingham only before reversal at Beccles 2.07pm to 2.15pm, and arrived at the coastal resort at 2.46pm. The later train was the return working of the 12.45pm ex Yarmouth South Town to Harleston which, after reversal at Beccles 1.09pm to 1.14pm, served Bungay only, with arrival at Harleston at 1.34pm. The return train to Norwich departed Yarmouth South Town at 8.00pm and called all stations across the branch, departing Beccles at 8.34pm and Tivetshall at 9.33pm, with arrival at Norwich Thorpe at 9.56pm.

The working timetable for 1939 showed six SX and seven SO passenger trains in the Down direction, augmented by a single freight working. Two passenger trains commenced their journey at Tivetshall (at 7.49am and 1.38pmMFSO or 1.53pmTuWThO), whilst four SX and five SO trains started at Norwich Thorpe, departing at 8.24am, 12.05pmSO, 2.28pm, 5.10pm and 7.55pm. The 8.24am was not permitted to work empty stock attached to the formation and was allowed two minutes recovery time between Geldeston and Beccles. The 12.05pmSO ex Norwich was formed of Third Class stock only, whilst the 5.10pm was, like the earlier train, not permitted to convey empty coaching stock. The freight traffic for the branch was handled by the 3.00pm goods train ex Forncett which called all stations to Bungay, and then served Ditchingham, Ellingham and Geldeston only if required, with arrival at Beccles at 8.10pm. A goods train also departed Tivetshall 4.50pmWO for Harleston, arriving at 5.10pm in a 'Q' 'as and when required' path, worked by the engine off the 7.10am goods ex Ipswich specifically to clear all livestock traffic from Harleston, returning Up road at 5.30pm, calling at Pulham Market with arrival at Tivetshall at 6.10pm. In the Up direction, six passenger services operated SX increasing to eight SO and nine SO in August. Two services (6.22am, 12.22pmSX or 12.25pmSO ex Beccles) terminated at Tivetshall whilst the 9.04am, 3.10pm, 6.02pm, 7.10pm and 8.02pmSO ex Beccles were through trains to Norwich Thorpe, augmented by the 9.30pmSO ex Yarmouth South Town (10.07pm ex Beccles) to Harleston which operated during August, only arriving at 10.38pm. For freight traffic the branch was served by the 6.30am goods train ex Beccles which called all stations, arriving at Tivetshall at 12.00 noon and departed at 12.45pm for Forncett, arriving at 1.00pm. Sunday passenger services were operated in high summer season, commencing with the 10.20am ex Norwich Thorpe which called at all stations on the main line except Swainsthorpe and, with a four minutes stand at Tivetshall, departed at 10.53am calling all stations to Beccles, arriving at 11.44am. After reversal the train continued to Yarmouth South Town, arriving at 12.12pm. The stock then returned at 12.45pm hauled by a fresh locomotive to Harleston, calling at Beccles and Bungay en route; arriving at 1.34pm, the engine ran round the stock and the train departed at 1.42pm for Beccles and Yarmouth South Town, arriving at 2.40pm after calling at Homersfield, Bungay and Ditchingham. In the evening the 7.40pm ex Yarmouth South Town called all stations to Bungay, arriving at 8.34pm, before the engine and stock returned as the 8.55pm to Yarmouth South Town arriving at 9.47pm. A later Up train departed Yarmouth at 8.05pm and, after reversal at Beccles 8.25pm to 8.35pm, called at Bungay and all stations to Tivetshall arriving 9.24pm during the month of August, and all stations to

'F5' Class 2-4-2T No. 67216 departing Beccles with the Tivetshall branch train in December 1951. The train is unusually formed of two Gresley coaches, a corridor Brake Third and an Open Third, followed by an ex-GER corridor coach. On return to Beccles the set of stock would go forward to Lowestoft to work a through train to Rugby later the same day. *Author's collection*

Tivetshall arriving 9.28pm during the other summer months. The stock then returned to Crown Point yard, departing Tivetshall at 9.50pm and arriving at 10.15pm.

On 2nd October 1939 the L&NER drastically reduced operations and introduced an emergency timetable when the passenger service on the Waveney Valley line was reduced to two trains in each direction on weekdays only, working from Beccles to Norwich and return. After the initial scare of imminent enemy attack had passed, the service was increased to five passenger trains in each direction, with the 1940 timetable and connections as shown below.

The freight train working timetable of 1944 (overleaf) is typical of the service offered when the military offensive from the local airfields was at its height. The branch was served by the 5.50am from Wensum Junction worked by a Norwich locomotive. This train spent considerable time at Forncett (6.35am to 9.10am), collecting traffic from the Midlands routed via Wymondham and Ashwellthorpe, before spending another 80 minutes at Tivetshall (9.25am to 10.45am). A short run was made to Pulham Market, where the train served the Air Ministry siding and was looped for an Up train to pass. Departing Pulham Market at 11.50am, a run of 5 minutes found the train at Pulham St. Mary, where another 55 minutes was spent shunting before final arrival at Harleston at 1.00pm. The engine then shunted the yard and outsorted traffic arriving from Beccles, before propelling the brake van on a 'Q' 'as and when required' path back to Pulham St. Mary at 3.00pm (actually the eastern end of the Air Ministry sidings where military

Emergency Timetable from 2nd October 1939

		am	pm
Liverpool Street	dep	8.12	4.00
Norwich Thorpe	dep	11.15	7.15
Forncett	dep	11.29	7.29
Tivetshall	dep	11.50	7.50
Pulham Market	dep	11.56	7.56
Pulham St. Mary	dep	11.59	7.59
Harleston	dep	12.06	8.06
Homersfield	dep	12.12	8.12
Earsham	dep	12.18	8.18
Bungay	dep	12.22	8.22
Ditchingham	dep	12.26	8.26
Ellingham	dep	12.30	8.30
Geldeston	dep	12.34	8.34
Beccles	arr	12.40	8.40
Lowestoft C	arr	2.27	
Yarmouth S T	arr	2.40	9.20
Liverpool Street	arr		

		am	am/pm
Liverpool Street	dep		10.00*
Yarmouth S T	dep	8.12	1.38
Lowestoft C	dep	8.05	3.05
Beccles	dep	9.00	3.25
Geldeston	dep	9.06	3.31
Ellingham	dep	9.10	3.35
Ditchingham	dep	9.14	3.39
Bungay	dep	9.19	3.44
Earsham	dep	9.22	3.47
Homersfield	dep	9.29	3.54
Harleston	dep	9.35	4.00
Pulham St. Mary	dep	9.41	4.05
Pulham Market	dep	9.44	4.09
Tivetshall	arr	9.50	4.15
Forncett	arr	10.02	4.24
Norwich Thorpe	arr	10.25	4.47
Liverpool Street	arr	1.40	7.40

Note: * Depart Liverpool Street 12.20pmSO.

Timetable 1940

		T	T		T	
		am	am	pm	pm	pm
Liverpool Street	dep		8.12	10.00	1.00	4.00
Norwich Thorpe	dep	7.02	11.15	1.21	4.55	7.10
Tivetshall	dep	7.36	11.50	2.00	5.29	7.50
Pulham Market	dep	7.42	11.56	2.06	5.35	7.56
Pulham St. Mary	dep	7.45	11.59	2.09	5.38	7.59
Harleston	dep	7.51	12.06	2.16	5.44	8.07
Homersfield	dep	7.57	12.12	2.22	5.50	8.13
Earsham	dep	8.03	12.18	2.28	5.56	8.19
Bungay	dep	8.07	12.22	2.32	6.00	8.24
Ditchingham	dep	8.11	12.26	2.36	6.04	8.27
Ellingham	dep	8.15	12.30	2.40	6.08	8.31
Geldeston	dep	8.19	12.34	2.44	6.12	8.35
Beccles	arr	8.26	12.40	2.50	6.18	8.41
Lowestoft C	arr	8.50	2.27	3.35	6.52	9.10
Yarmouth S T	arr	9.04	2.37	3.30	6.52	9.20
Liverpool Street	arr	11.35	5.03	6.51	9.41	

		T		T		T
		am	am	pm	pm	pm
Liverpool Street	dep	4.40	8.12	12S20	3.40	4.00
Yarmouth S T	dep	8.15	9.00	2.40	6.10	7.00
Lowestoft C	dep	8.08	11.05	2.48	6.10	7.15
Beccles	dep	9.00	12.00	3.30	6.35	8.06
Geldeston	dep	9.06	12.06	3.36	6.41	8.12
Ellingham	dep	9.10	12.10	3.40	6.45	8.16
Ditchingham	dep	9.14	12.14	3.41	6.49	8.20
Bungay	dep	9.19	12.21	3.49	6.53	8.26
Earsham	dep	9.22	12.24	3.52	6.56	8.29
Homersfield	dep	9.29	12.31	3.59	7.03	8.36
Harleston	dep	9.35	12.37	4.05	7.09	8.42
Pulham St. Mary	dep	9.41	12.43	4.11	7.15	8.48
Pulham Market	dep	9.44	12.46	4.14	7.18	8.51
Tivetshall	arr	9.50	12.52	4.20	7.24	8.57
Norwich Thorpe	arr	10.25	2.10	4.52	8.11	9.29
Liverpool Street	arr	1.40	5.03	7.18	12.55	

Notes: T Through train Norwich to Beccles or Beccles to Norwich.
S Saturdays only.

traffic was shunted). The engine then hauled a train back to Harleston at 3.45pm on a 'Q' path, arriving 10 minutes later. After more shunting the train departed Harleston at 4.50pm en route to Norwich Thorpe yard, calling a Pulham St. Mary for 15 minutes and Pulham Market 5.25pm to 6.05pm to collect empty wagons from the Air Ministry siding and to allow a Down passenger service to pass. An hour was spent shunting at Tivetshall, from 6.15pm to 7.15pm to pick up vehicles from the military sidings, before the train set off for a non-stop run to Trowse, where 15 minutes were allowed for shunting, and final arrival at Norwich at 8.10pm. From the eastern end the branch was served by the 6.20am goods from Beccles to Forncett, worked by a Lowestoft engine, which called at Geldeston and Ellingham only if required before spending 30 minutes at Ditchingham from 6.45am to 7.15am. The train then continued to Bungay where considerable time was spent shunting and to allow a Down passenger train to pass. Continuing to

NORWICH THORPE, TIVETSHALL, HARLESTON, BUNGAY AND BECCLES. (NO SUNDAY SERVICE)

Single Line between Tivetshall and Beccles.

Miles from Norwich T.	DOWN WEEK DAYS		1	2	3	4	5	6	7	8	9
			Pass.		Pass.		Pass.		Pass.		Pass.
M. C.			a.m.		a.m.		p.m.		p.m.		p.m.
— —	Norwich Thorpe	dep.	6 55	....	11 5	....	....	....	4 55	....	....
5 23	Swainsthorpe	arr.	7 5	—	11 15	—	—	—	5 5	—	—
		dep.	7 6	....	11 16	....	....	....	5 6	....	....
8 21	Flordon	arr.	7 12	—	11 22	—	—	—	5 12	—	—
		dep.	7 13	....	11 23	....	....	....	5 13	....	....
10 71	Forncett	arr.	7 18	—	11 28	—	—	—	5 18	—	—
		dep.	7 19	....	11 29	....	....	....	5 19	....	....
14 31	Tivetshall (S)	arr.	7 25	—	11 35	—	—	—	5 25	—	—
		dep.	7 29	....	11 40	....	1 55	....	5 29	....	7 55
17 4	Pulham Market (S)	arr.	7 34	—	11 45	—	2 0	—	5 34	—	8 0
	(see note)	dep.	7 35	....	11 46	....	2 1	....	5 35	....	8 1
18 6	Pulham Mary	"	7 38	—	11 49	—	2 4	—	5 38	—	8 4
20 53	Harleston (S)	arr.	7 43	....	11 54	....	2 9	....	5 43	....	8 9
		dep.	7 45	—	11 56	—	2 13	—	5 44	—	8 11
23 24	Homersfield	"	7 51	....	12 2	....	2 19	....	5 50	....	8 17
26 36	Earsham (NB)	"	7 57	—	12 8	—	2 25	—	5 56	—	8 23
27 16	Bungay (S)	arr.	7 59	....	12 10	....	2 27	....	5 58	...	8 25
		dep.	8 1	—	12 12	—	2 32	—	6 0	—	8 27
28 14	Ditchingham	"	8 5	....	12 16	....	2 36	....	6 4	....	8 30
29 55	Ellingham	"	8 9	—	12 20	—	2 40	—	6 8	—	8 34
31 17	Geldeston	"	8 13	....	12 24	....	2 44	....	6 12	....	8 38
33 67	Beccles (S)	arr.	8 20	—	12 30	—	2 50	—	6 18	—	8 44

9 Forms 9.0 p.m. to Lowestoft.

Miles from Beccles.	UP WEEK DAYS		10	11	12	13	14	15	16	17	18
			Pass.		Pass.		Pass.	Pass.		Pass.	Pass.
M. C.			a.m.		a.m.		p.m.	p.m.		p.m.	p.m.
— —	Beccles (S)	dep.	5 10	....	9 0	....	12 35	3 30	....	6 36	8 6
2 50	Geldeston	"	—	—	9 6	—	12 41	3 36	—	6 42	8 12
4 12	Ellingham	"	....	....	9 10	....	12 45	3 40	....	6 46	8 16
5 53	Ditchingham	"	5 24	—	9 14	—	12 49	3 44	—	6 50	8 20
6 48	Bungay (S)	arr.	5 27	....	9 17	...	12 52	3 47	....	6 53	8 23
		dep.	5 29	—	9 19	—	12 55	3 49	—	6 54	8 26
7 31	Earsham (NB)	"	....	....	9 22	....	12 58	3 52	....	6 57	8 29
10 33	Homersfield	"	5 39	—	9 29	—	1 5	3 59	—	7 4	8 36
13 14	Harleston (S)	arr.	5 44	....	9 34	....	1 10	4 4	....	7 9	8 41
		dep.	5 46	—	9 35	—	1 11	4 5	—	7 11	8 42
15 61	Pulham Mary	"	5 52	....	9 41	....	1 17	4 11	....	7 17	8 48
16 63	Pulham Market (S)	arr.	5 54	—	9 43	—	1 19	4 13	—	7 19	8 50
	(see note)	dep.	5 55	....	9 44	....	1 20	4 14	....	7 20	8 51
19 36	Tivetshall (S)	arr.	6 1	—	9 50	—	1 26	4 20	—	7 26	8 57
		dep.	6 5	....	9 53	....		4 22	....		8 59
22 76	Forncett	arr	6 11	—	9 59	—	—	4 28	—	—	9 5
		dep	6 12	....	10 0	....	....	4 29	....	....	9 6
25 46	Flordon	arr.	—	—	10 5	—	—	4 34	—	—	9 11
		dep.	....	....	10 6	....	....	4 35	....	....	9 12
28 44	Swainsthorpe	arr.	B	—	10 12	—	—	4 41	—	—	9 18
		dep.	....	....	10 13	....	....	4 42	....	....	9 19
33 67	Norwich Thorpe	arr.	6 35	—	10 25	—	—	4 52	—	—	9 30

Passenger trains must not be allowed to cross each other at Pulham Market station.

81

L&NER working timetable; passenger 1943.

120

NORWICH T., TIVETSHALL, BUNGAY AND BECCLES.

Single Line between Tivetshall and Beccles.

Miles from Norwich T. M. C.	DOWN WEEK DAYS.		1	2	3	4	5	6	7	8	9	10	11	12	13	14
				Gds.				Gds.	Q Gds.		G Gds.					
				a.m.				p.m.	p.m.		p.m.					
	Norwich Thorpe...	dep.	—	—	—	—	—	—	—	—	—	—	—	—	—	—
— —	Wensum Jc. Sdgs. ...	dep.		5 50												
1 1	Trowse..................	arr.	—	pass	—	—	—	—	—	—	—	—	—	—	—	—
		dep.		6 5												
5 23	Swainsthorpe	arr.	—	—	—	—	—	—	—	—	—	—	—	—	—	—
		dep.														
8 21	Flordon	arr.	—	—	—	—	—	—	—	—	—	—	—	—	—	—
		dep.														
10 71	Forncett	arr.	—	6 35	—	—	—	—	—	—	—	—	—	—	—	—
		dep.		9 10							3 10					
14 31	**Tivetshall** .... Ⓢ	arr.	—	9 25	—	—	—	—	—	—	3 25	—	—	—	—	—
		dep.		10 45							3 50					
17 4	Pulham Market ...... Ⓢ	arr.	—	10 55	—	—	—	—	—	—	4 0	—	—	—	—	—
		dep.		11 50							5 40					
18 6	Pulham Mary	arr.	—	11 55	—	—	—	—	—	—	5 45	—	—	—	—	—
		dep.		12 50					3 45		6 10					
20 53	Harleston .... Ⓢ	arr.	—	1 0	—	—	—	—	3 55	—	6 20	—	—	—	—	—
		dep.						2 20			7 18					
23 34	Homersfield	"	—	—	—	—	—	3 0	—	—	7 38	—	—	—	—	—
26 36	Earsham .... (NB)	"						*			—					
27 19	Bungay .... Ⓢ	arr.	—	—	—	—	—	3 30	—	—	7 50	—	—	—	—	—
		dep.						3 50			8 20					
28 14	Ditchingham........... Ⓢ	arr.	—	—	—	—	—	—	—	—	—	—	—	—	—	—
	(See note)	dep.						4 20								
29 55	Ellingham	"	—	—	—	—	—	—	—	—	—	—	—	—	—	—
31 17	Geldeston	"														
33 67	Beccles .... Ⓢ	arr.		—	—	—	—	4 40	—	—	8 40	—		—	—	—

6 To Lowestoft C. A brake to be each end of train. To convey a load of empties from Beccles to Lowestoft C.

9 Engine to shunt Beccles Yard and return to Lowestoft at 1.30 a.m.

Miles from Beccles. M. C.	UP WEEK DAYS.		1	2	3	4	5	6	7	8	9	10	11	12	13	14	15
					Gds.	Gds.			Eng. & Brke.			Gds.					
					G a.m.	a.m.			Q p.m.			G p.m.					
— —	**Beccles**......... Ⓢ	dep.			6 20	10 0											
2 50	Geldeston	"	—	—	*	10 15	—	—	—	—	—	—	—	—	—	—	—
4 12	Ellingham	"			*	10 40											
5 53	Ditchingham... Ⓢ	arr.	—	—	6 45	10 50	—	—	—	—	—	—	—	—	—	—	—
	(See note)	dep.			7 15	11 50											
6 48	Bungay .... Ⓢ	arr.	—	—	7 21	11 55	—	—	—	—	—	—	—	—	—	—	—
		dep.			8 40	1 10											
7 31	Earsham......... (NB)	"	—	—		*	—	—	—	—	—	—	—	—	—	—	—
10 33	Homersfield	"			9 5	2 0											
13 14	Harleston ...... Ⓢ	arr.	—	—	9 15	2 10	—	—	—	—	—	—	—	—	—	—	—
		dep.			11 15				3 0			4 50					
15 61	Pulham Mary	arr.	—	—	...	—	—	—	3 8	—	—	5 5	—	—	—	—	—
		dep.			11 30							5 20					
16 63	Pulham Market Ⓢ	arr.	—	—	11 35	—	—	—	—	—	—	5 25	—	—	—	—	—
		dep.			12 15							6 5					
19 35	**Tivetshall** ... Ⓢ	arr.	—	—	12 25	—	—	—	—	—	—	6 15	—	—	—	—	—
		dep.			1 15							7 15					
22 76	Forncett	arr.	—	—	1 30	—	—	—	—	—	—	—	—	—	—	—	—
		dep.															
25 46	Flordon	arr.	—	—	—	—	—	—	—	—	—	—	—	—	—	—	—
		dep.															
28 44	Swainsthorpe.....	arr.	—	—	—	—	—	—	—	—	—	—	—	—	—	—	—
		dep.															
32 66	Trowse..............	arr.	—	—	—	—	—	—	—	—	—	7 50	—	—	—	—	—
		dep										8 5					
33 67	**Norwich T.**	arr.	—	—	—	—	—	—	—	—	—	8 10	—	—	—		

3 Homersfield arr. 8.52 a.m.

4 Geldeston arr. 10.9, Ellingham arr. 10.21. To be worked by engine of 9.5 a.m. ex Lowestoft.

7 Eng. and Brake off 5.50 a.m. ex Wensum. Engine to propel brake.

DITCHINGHAM.

Passenger trains must not be permitted to cross each other at Ditchingham, but a goods train may be shunted into the siding to allow a passenger train or another goods train to cross.

L&NER working timetable; freight 1944.

Homersfield, where 13 minutes was allowed for shunting the yard, the train continued to Harleston where two hours (from 9.15am to 11.15am) allowed ample time for shunting and for a Down train to cross. The service next called at Pulham Market where 40 minutes was allowed to shunt the Air Ministry siding and local yard, and also for a Down passenger train to cross. After arriving at Tivetshall, 50 minutes was allowed for shunting the local yard and military sidings, and to drop off Up road traffic before the train continued to Forncett, arriving at 1.30pm. The return working departed with traffic from the Midlands and North routed via Wymondham and Ashwellthorpe at 3.10pm, with 25 minutes allowed at Tivetshall from 3.25pm until 3.50pm where military consignments were shunted. A 16-minute run to Pulham Market, arriving at 4.06pm and a departure at 5.40pm, allowed ample time for shunting wagons to and from the Admiralty siding, and for an Up passenger train to pass. Twenty-five minutes were permitted at Pulham St. Mary from 5.45pm until 6.10pm, followed by a 10-minute run to Harleston where 58 minutes were allowed for shunting and to allow another Up passenger train to pass. Departing at 7.18pm with a momentary stop at Homersfield gave the service 30 minutes to shunt the yard at Bungay from 7.50pm to 8.20pm. The train then ran non-stop to Beccles, arriving at 8.40pm, before the engine shunted Beccles yard and returned to Lowestoft shed at 1.30am. A second goods train departed Beccles at 10.00am and called all stations to Harleston, with 60 minutes allowed at Ditchingham from 10.50am to 11.50am, and 75 minutes at Bungay for shunting the yard and for a Down passenger train to cross. The military siding at Earsham was served on an as and when required basis and Harleston was reached at 2.10pm. The return working departed at 2.20pm, serving Homersfield, Earsham as and when required, and Bungay from 3.30pm until 3.50pm to cross an Up working. With a call at Ditchingham if required, the train arrived back at Beccles at 4.40pm. This working stipulated a brake van was to be provided at each end of the train and was to convey empty wagons from Beccles to Lowestoft. At this period additional trains conveying armaments operated across the branch at short notice.

The working timetable for passenger trains in 1945 showed a service of three through trains from Norwich Thorpe (departing 6.38am, 11.05am and 4.55pm) to Beccles, serving Swainsthorpe, Flordon, Forncett and Tivetshall before calling at all stations on the branch and arriving at the Suffolk town at 8.11am, 12.30pm and 6.18pm respectively. This trio of services was augmented by two trains from Tivetshall, departing at 2.15pm and 8.12pm, again calling at all stations, with arrival at Beccles at 3.10pm and 9.06pm, the latter forming the 9.15pm service to Lowestoft. In the Up direction an equal number of services ran from Beccles (departing at 9.00am, 3.25pm and 7.57pm) as through services to Norwich. The 9.00am called at all stations on the branch and departed Tivetshall at 9.53am, running non-stop to Norwich Thorpe and arriving at 10.13am; the other services called all stations on the branch as well as Forncett, Flordon and Swainsthorpe, with arrival at Norwich Thorpe at 5.03pm and 9.27pm. The remaining services (12.35pm and 6.48pm ex Beccles) served all stations to Tivetshall, arriving at 1.27pm and 7.43pm respectively.

The working timetable for 1949 was basic in the extreme, much of the military traffic had diminished and thus freight services were reduced and worked from each end with no through service, whilst six passenger trains ran in each direction weekdays only, all trains

'E4' Class 2-4-0 No. 62789 makes a spirited approach to Harleston with a Down branch train from Norwich to Beccles in 1951. *Dr I.C. Allen*

M 51

TIVETSHALL AND BECCLES (NO SUNDAY SERVICE)

Single Line

DOWN — WEEKDAYS

Miles from Tivetshall		1	2	3	4	5	6	7	8	9	10	11	12	13	14	15
	Description	OP					OP		OP				OP		OP	
	Class			D							B					
	Departs from	Norwich T. 6.55 a.m.		Wensum 8.0 a.m.			Norwich T. 10.53 a.m.						Norwich T. 5.0 p.m.			
	Previous Times on Page	L 49		L 49			L 50						L 52			
M. C.		am		am			am		WSO PM		PM		PM		PM	
— —	Tivetshall	7 17		9 22			11 23						5 30			
— —	TIVETSHALL (S)	7 19		9 55			11 25		2 0				5 32		8 15	
2 53	Pulham Market } See (S)	7 24		10 5			11 30		2 5				5 37		8 20	
— —	Pulham Market } note	7 25		10 15			11 31		2 6				5 38		8 21	
3 55	Pulham St. Mary	7 28		11 15			11 34		2 9				5 41		8 24	
6 22	Harleston (S)	7 33		11 25			11 39		2 14				5 46		8 29	
— —	Harleston	7 35					11 41		2 17		4 5		5 47		8 36	
8 73	Homersfield	7 41					11 47		2 23		4 30		5 53		8 42	
12 5	Earsham	7 47					11 53		2 29				5 59		8 48	
12 65	Bungay (S)	7 49					11 55		2 31		4 55		6 1		8 50	
— —	Bungay	7 52					11 57		2 36		5 20		6 3		8 52	
13 63	Ditchingham { See (S)	7 55					12 0		2 39		5 25		6 6		8 55	
— —	Ditchingham { note	7 57					12 1		2 41		5 45		6 7		8 56	
15 24	Ellingham	8 1					12 5		2 45		*		6 11		9 0	
16 66	Geldeston	8 5					12 9		2 49		*		6 15		9 4	
19 36	BECCLES (S)	8 11					12 15		2 55		6 10		6 21		9 10	

3 Pulham St. Mary arr. 10.20 a.m.
6 Engine to be used for shunting at Beccles as required prior to working 10 up.
10 Homersfield arr. 4.15 p.m. 12 Advertised to arr. Beccles 6.23 p.m.
14 Forms 9.20 p.m. to Lowestoft.

UP — WEEKDAYS

Miles from Beccles		1	2	3	4	5	6	7	8	9	10	11	12	13	14	15
	Description			OP				OP			OP		OP		OP	
	Class					D			D							
M. C.				am		am		WSO PM	PM		PM		PM		PM	
— —	BECCLES (S)			9 0		10 0		12 35			3 25		6 56		8 0	
2 50	Geldeston			9 6		10 15		12 41			3 31		7 2		8 6	
4 12	Ellingham			9 10		10 35		12 45			3 35		7 6		8 10	
5 53	Ditchingham { See (S)			9 13		10 40		12 48			3 38		7 9		8 13	
— —	Ditchingham { note			9 14		11 20		12 49			3 39		7 10		8 14	
6 48	Bungay (S)			9 17		11 25		12 52			3 42		7 13		8 17	
— —	Bungay			9 19		1 10		12 55			3 44		7 15		8 20	
7 31	Earsham			9 22		*		12 58			3 47		7 18		8 23	
10 33	Homersfield			9 29		1 38		1 5			3 54		7 25		8 30	
13 14	Harleston (S)			9 34		1 48		1 10			3 59		7 30		8 35	
— —	Harleston			9 35				1 12	1 20		4 1		7 34		8 40	
15 61	Pulham St. Mary			9 41				1 18	1 40		4 7		7 40		8 46	
16 63	Pulham Market } See (S)			9 43				1 20	1 45		4 9		7 42		8 48	
— —	Pulham Market } note			9 44				1 21	2 45		4 10		7 43		8 49	
19 36	TIVETSHALL (S)			9 50				1 27	2W55		4 18		7 49		8 55	
— —	Tivetshall			9 52					3 7		4 26				8 56	
	Arrives at			Norwich T. 10.16 a.m.					Trowse 4.0 p.m.		Norwich T. 4.58 p.m.				Norwich T. 9.31 p.m.	
	Forward Times on Page			L 39					L 42		L 42				L 43	

5 Homersfield arr. 1.23 p.m. 8 Pulham St. Mary arr. 1.30 p.m.

Passenger trains must not be permitted to cross each other at **Ditchingham**, but an ECS or goods train may be shunted into the goods yard to allow a passenger train or another goods train to cross.

Passenger trains must not be allowed to cross each other at **Pulham Market Station.**

L&NER working timetable 1947.

M 49

TIVETSHALL AND BECCLES (NO SUNDAY SERVICE)

Single Line

DOWN — **WEEKDAYS**

Miles from Tivetshall		1	2	3	4	5	6	7	8	9	10	11	12	13	14	15
	No.	1	2	3	4	5	6	7	8	9	10	11	12	13	14	15
	Description	OP	OP				OP		OP				OP		OP	
	Class				D						B					
	Departs from	Norwich T. 6.55 a.m.			Wensum 8.50 a.m.		Norwich T. 10.53 a.m.						Norwich T. 5.3 p.m.			
	Previous Times on Page	L 61			L 61		L 62						L 64			
M. C.		am	am		am		am		PM		PM		PM		PM	
— —	Tivetshall	7 17			10 12		11 23						5 33			
— —	**TIVETSHALL** (S)	7 19	8 35		10 32		11 25		2 0		..		5 36		8 15	
2 53	Pulham Market } See (S)	7 24	8 40		10 42		11 30		2 5				5 41		8 20	
— —	Pulham Market } note	7 25	8 41		10 47		11 31		2 6		..		5 42		8 21	
3 55	Pulham St. Mary	7 28	8 44		11 15		11 34		2 9				5 45		8 24	
6 22	Harleston (S)	7 33	8 49		11 25		11 39		2 14		..		5 50		8 29	
— —	Harleston	7 36	8 56				11 41		2 17		4 5		5 51		8 36	
8 73	Homersfield	7 42	9 2				11 47		2 23		4 30		5 57		8 42	
12 5	Earsham	7 48	9 8				11 53		2 29				6 3		8 48	
12 65	Bungay (S)	7 50	9 10				11 55		2 31		4 55		6 5		8 50	
— —	Bungay	7 52	9 20				11 56		2 32		5 20		6 7		8 51	
13 63	Ditchingham { See (S)	7 55	9 23				11 59		2 35		5 25		6 10		8 54	
— —	Ditchingham { note	7 57	9 24				12 0		2 37		5 45		6 11		8 55	
15 24	Ellingham	8 1	9 28				12 4		2 41		*		6 15		8 59	
16 66	Geldeston	8 5	9 32				12 8		2 45		*		6 19		9 3	
19 36	**BECCLES** (S)	8 11	9 38				12 14		2 51		6 10		6 25		9 9	

2 Forms 10.0 a.m. to Lowestoft C. **4** Pulham St. Mary arr. 10.52 a.m
6 Engine to be used for shunting at Beccles as required prior to working 10 up.
10 Homersfield arr. 4.15 p.m.
14 Forms 9.20 p.m. to Lowestoft C.

UP — **WEEKDAYS**

Miles from Beccles		1	2	3	4	5	6	7	8	9	10	11	12	13	14	15
	No.	1	2	3	4	5	6	7	8	9	10	11	12	13	14	15
	Description	OP		OP				OP			OP		OP		OP	
	Class					D			D	D						
M. C.		am		am		am		PM	PM	am	PM		PM		PM	
— —	**BECCLES** (S)	7 0		9 0		10 0		12 35			3 18		6 54		8 2	
2 50	Geldeston	7 6		9 6		10 15		12 41	..	See	3 24		7 0		8 8	
4 12	Ellingham	7 10		9 10		10 35		12 45		Col.	3 28		7 4		8 12	
5 53	Ditchingham { See (S)	7 13		9 13		10 40		12 48	..	5	3 31		7 7		8 15	
— —	Ditchingham { note	7 14		9 14		11 20		12 49			3 32		7 8		8 16	
6 48	Bungay (S)	7 17		9 17		11 25		12 52	..	11 25	3 35		7 11		8 19	
— —	Bungay	7 19		9 19		1 10		12 53		1 10	3 37		7 12		8 20	
7 31	Earsham	7 22		9 22		..		12 56	..	*	3 40		7 15		8 23	
10 33	Homersfield	7 29		9 29				1 3		1 38	3 47		7 22		8 30	
13 14	Harleston (S)	7 34		9 34		See		1 8	..	1 48	3 52		7 27		8 35	
— —	Harleston	7 35		9 35		Col.		1 10	1 20		3 54		7 29		8 40	
15 61	Pulham St. Mary	7 41		9 41		9		1 16	1 40	..	4 0		7 35		8 46	
16 63	Pulham Market } See (S)	7 43		9 43				1 18	1 45		4 2		7 37		8 48	
— —	Pulham Market } note	7 44		9 44		..		1 19	2 45	..	4 3		7 38		8 49	
19 36	**TIVETSHALL** (S)	7 50		9 50				1 25	2W55		4 11		7 44		8 55	
— —	Tivetshall	..		9 52		..		..	3 7	..	4 21		..		9 0	
	Arrives at			Norwich T. 10.16 a.m.					Trowse 4.5 p.m.		Norwich T. 4.53 p.m.				Norwich T. 9.31 p.m.	
	Forward Times on Page			L 53					L 55		L 56				L 57	

8 Pulham St. Mary arr. 1.30 p.m. **9** Homersfield arr. 1.23 p.m.

Passenger trains must not be permitted to cross each other at **Ditchingham**, but an ECS or goods train may be shunted into the goods yard to allow a passenger train or another goods train to cross.

Passenger trains must not be allowed to cross each other at **Pulham Market Station.**

L&NER working timetable 1949.

calling at all stations. By this time only three services operated to and from Norwich, with the remainder running between Tivetshall and Beccles or vice versa. The first Down passenger train of the day, the 6.55am from Norwich, stopped at Tivetshall 7.17am to 7.19am, with arrival at Beccles at 8.11am. The next train (8.35am ex Tivetshall), on arrival at Beccles at 9.38am formed the 10.00am departure to Lowestoft. The 10.35am ex Norwich entered the branch at Tivetshall at 11.25am and on arrival at Beccles the engine was used for shunting as required before working the 3.18pm Up working to Norwich via Tivetshall. The 5.03pm ex Norwich departed Tivetshall at 5.36pm, whilst the other Down workings (2.00pm and 8.15pm ex Tivetshall) were self-contained to the branch; the latter on arrival at Beccles at 9.09pm formed the 9.20pm departure to Lowestoft. In the Up direction the 7.00am, 12.35pm and 6.54pm ex Beccles all terminated at Tivetshall at 7.50am, 1.25pm and 7.44pm respectively, whilst the 9.00am, 3.18pm and 8.02pm from Beccles were through trains to Norwich Thorpe, arriving at 10.16am, 4.53pm and 9.31pm respectively. The 8.50am Class 'D' freight train ex Wensum yard called at all stations to Harleston, where the train terminated at 11.25am before returning Up road at 1.20pm as a Class 'D', again calling all stations to Tivetshall, from where it departed at 3.07pm for Trowse yard arriving at 4.05pm. The 10.00am Class 'D' goods train ex Beccles served all stations to Bungay, arriving at 11.25am. After yard shunting it departed at 1.10pm, calling at Earsham sidings if required for the removal of obsolete military materials or other goods, then Homersfield, to terminate at Harleston at 1.48pm. The working returned as a Class 'B' goods train departing Harleston 4.05pm, calling at all stations to Ditchingham except Earsham, and then Ellingham and Geldeston only if required, arriving at Beccles at 6.10pm.

The following year, 1950, six passenger trains continued each way, the only occasion of the passing of two passenger services occurred at Bungay when the 8.35am train from Tivetshall crossed the 9.00am train from Beccles. The stock of the 8.35am train consisted of more modern corridor coaches as the vehicles formed a Lowestoft to Rugby train later the same day. The freight timetable was identical to the previous year.

The point-to-point running times of passenger trains in the early 1950s before the withdrawal of services was:

From	To	Mileage M	Ch	Start to Stop Minutes
Down				
Tivetshall	Pulham Market	2	53	5
Pulham Market	Pulham St. Mary	1	02	2
Pulham St. Mary	Harleston	2	47	5
Harleston	Homersfield	2	51	5
Homersfield	Earsham	3	12	5
Earsham	Bungay	0	60	2
Bungay	Ditchingham	0	78	3
Ditchingham	Ellingham	1	41	4
Ellingham	Geldeston	1	42	3
Geldeston	Beccles	2	50	6
Up				
Beccles	Geldeston	2	50	5
Geldeston	Ellingham	1	42	3
Ellingham	Ditchingham	1	41	3
Ditchingham	Bungay	0	78	3
Bungay	Earsham	0	60	2
Earsham	Homersfield	3	12	6
Homersfield	Harleston	2	51	5
Harleston	Pulham St. Mary	2	47	6
Pulham St. Mary	Pulham Market	1	02	2
Pulham Market	Tivetshall	2	53	6

The working timetable with effect from 15th September 1952 was the last to include passenger services and showed a similar number of trains to those scheduled in 1949, with in some cases minor adjustments in timing. The chief alterations were with the goods workings, for in the Down direction the Class 'D' goods train departed Wensum yard at 8.00am, arriving at Tivetshall at 9.26am.

The Waveney Valley Branch train from Norwich Thorpe to Beccles passing Thorpe Junction signal box on 11th August 1952, hauled by 'E4' Class 2-4-0 No. 62789. *Canon Charles Bayes*

M 52

TIVETSHALL AND BECCLES (NO SUNDAY SERVICE)

Single Line

DOWN — WEEKDAYS

Miles from Tivetshall	No.	1	2	3	4	5	6	7	8	9	10	11	12	13	14	15
	Class	B	B		K		B		B		K		B		B	
	Description															
	Departs from	Norwich T. 6.55 a.m.			Wensum Jc. 8.0 a.m.		Norwich T. 10.54 a.m.						Norwich T. 5.3 p.m.			
	Previous Times on Page	L 61			L 61		L 62						L 64			
M. C.		am	am		am		am		PM		PM		PM		PM	
— —	**Tivetshall**	7 15			9 26		11 24						5 33			
— —	**TIVETSHALL** (S)	7 19	8 35		10 0		11 25		1 55				5 36		8 15	
2 53	Pulham Market } See (S)	7 24	8 40		10 10		11 30		2 0				5 41		8 20	
— —	Pulham Market } note	7 25	8 41		10 20		11 31		2 1				5 42		8 21	
3 55	Pulham St. Mary	7 28	8 44		10 50		11 34		2 4				5 45		8 24	
6 22	Harleston (S)	7 33	8 49		11 0		11 39		2 9				5 50		8 29	
— —	Harleston	7 36	8 56				11 41		2 12		4 5		5 51		8 36	
8 73	Homersfield	7 42	9 2				11 47		2 18		4 30		5 57		8 42	
12 5	Earsham	7 48	9 8				11 53		2 24				6 3		8 48	
12 65	Bungay (S)	7 50	9 10				11 55		2 26		4 55		6 5		8 50	
— —	Bungay	7 52	9 20				11 56		2 27		5 15		6 7		8 51	
13 63	Ditchingham	7 55	9 23				11 59		2 30		5 20		6 10		8 54	
— —	Ditchingham	7 57	9 24				12 0		2 31		5 40		6 11		8 55	
15 24	Ellingham	8 1	9 28				12 4		2 35		*		6 15		8 59	
16 66	Geldeston	8 5	9 32				12 8		2 39		*		6 19		9 3	
19 36	**BECCLES** (S)	8 11	9 38				12 14		2 45		6 5		6 25		9 9	

2 Forms 9.55 a.m. to Lowestoft C. 4 Pulham St. Mary arr. 10.25 a.m

6 Engine to be used for shunting at Beccles as required prior to working 10 Up.

10 Homersfield arr. 4.25 p.m.

UP — WEEKDAYS

Miles from Beccles	No.	1	2	3	4	5	6	7	8	9	10	11	12	13	14	15
	Class	B		B		K		B	K	K	B		B		B	
	Description															
M. C.		am		am		am		PM	PM	am	PM		PM		PM	
— —	**BECCLES** (S)	7 0		9 0		9 45		12 35			3 25		6 55		8 2	
2 50	Geldeston	7 6		9 6		10 0		12 41		See	3 31		7 1		8 8	
4 12	Ellingham	7 10		9 10		10 20		12 45		Col.	3 35		7 5		8 12	
5 53	Ditchingham	7 13		9 13		10 25		12 48		5	3 38		7 8		8 15	
— —	Ditchingham	7 14		9 14		11 5		12 49			3 39		7 9		8 16	
6 48	Bungay (S)	7 17		9 17		11 10		12 52		11 10	3 42		7 12		8 19	
— —	Bungay	7 19		9 19		1 10		12 53		1 10	3 44		7 13		8 20	
7 31	Earsham	7 22		9 22				12 56		*	3 47		7 16		8 23	
10 33	Homersfield	7 29		9 29				1 3		1 38	3 54		7 23		8 30	
13 14	Harleston (S)	7 34		9 34		See		1 8		1 48	3 59		7 28		8 35	
— —	Harleston	7 35		9 35		Col.		1 9	1 20		4 1		7 30		8 40	
15 61	Pulham St. Mary	7 42		9 42		9		1 16	1 40		4 8		7 37		8 47	
16 63	Pulham Market } See (S)	7 44		9 44				1 18	1 45		4 10		7 39		8 49	
— —	Pulham Market } note	7 45		9 45				1 19	2 45		4 11		7 40		8 50	
19 36	**TIVETSHALL** (S)	7 51		9 51				1 25	2W55		4 19		7 46		8 56	
— —	**Tivetshall**			9 52					3 12		4 23				9 0	
	Arrives at			Norwich T. 10.16 a.m.					Trowse 4.10 p.m.		Norwich T. 4.53 p.m.				Norwich T. 9.28 p.m.	
	Forward Times on Page			L 53					L 56		L 56				L 57	

8 Pulham St. Mary arr. 1.30 p.m. 9 Homersfield arr. 1.23 p.m.

Pulham Market Station. — Passenger trains must not cross.

BR(ER) working timetable 1952.

After shunting and outsorting of wagons the train departed at 10.00am, calling all stations and terminating at Harleston at 11.00am. The train returned to Trowse yard, departing Harleston at 1.20pm. On the Up road the goods services departed Beccles at the earlier time of 9.45am, but with 15 minutes less shunting time at Bungay, then ran in the same times as shown in 1949.

By 1953 the point-to-point and starting and stopping allowance timings shown below were in force for freight trains.

It was permissible for an engine to assist Up and Down freight trains across the branch providing the assisting engine was coupled to the train; it was also permissible to propel a train not exceeding thirty wagons in the Up direction between Pulham St. Mary and Pulham Market.

After the withdrawal of passenger services in 1953 the freight train working timetable showed the branch served by two services meeting and exchanging traffic if necessary at Harleston. The eastern end of the line was served by the 10.35am Class 'K' train from Beccles to Harleston, returning at 1.20pm, and the western end by the 9.38am Class 'K' Tivetshall to Harleston, which returned from Harleston to the junction at 3.30pm; these timings continued the following year.

In 1955 the branch was served by two freight services, the western end by the 8.04am Class 'K' from Wensum Junction which, after spending 20 minutes shunting at Tivetshall from 8.56am to 9.16am, departed for Bungay serving all stations except Homersfield, where the train only called if required. After arriving at 11.49am the train departed in the Up direction at 12.30pm, spending 40 minutes shunting at Harleston from 1.20pm until 2.00pm, calling at Pulham St. Mary only of required, and then Pulham Market from 2.35pm until 2.55pm before clearing the branch at Tivetshall at 3.15pm. The 10.30am Class 'K' train from Beccles served the eastern end of the branch, calling all stations to Ditchingham, arriving at 11.22am.

From	To	Timing Allowances 1953		
		Starting Minutes	Stopping Minutes	Passing Minutes
Down				
Tivetshall	Pulham Market	3	2	5
Pulham Market	Pulham St. Mary	2	2	1
Pulham St. Mary	Harleston	3	2	5
Harleston	Homersfield	3	2	5
Homersfield	Earsham	3	2	7
Earsham	Bungay	2	2	1
Bungay	Ditchingham	2	2	1
Ditchingham	Ellingham	3	2	2
Ellingham	Geldeston	3	2	2
Geldeston	Beccles	3	2	5

From	To	Timing Allowances 1953		
		Starting Minutes	Stopping Minutes	Passing Minutes
Up				
Beccles	Geldeston	3	2	5
Geldeston	Ellingham	3	2	2
Ellingham	Ditchingham	3	2	2
Ditchingham	Bungay	2	2	1
Bungay	Earsham	2	2	1
Earsham	Homersfield	3	2	7
Homersfield	Harleston	3	2	7
Harleston	Pulham St. Mary	3	2	5
Pulham St. Mary	Pulham Market	2	2	1
Pulham Market	Tivetshall	3	2	6

TIVETSHALL AND BECCLES — WEEKDAYS

DOWN

Mileage M	Mileage C			K		K	
				8.4 am from Wensum Jn.			
				am		am	
		TIVETSHALL	arr	8 56			
0	0		dep	9 16	..	..	..
2	53	Pulham Market	arr	9 36			
			dep	9 46	..	..	..
3	55	Pulham St. Mary	arr	9 51			
			dep	10 4	..	..	..
6	22	Harleston	arr	10 24			
			dep	10 54	..	..	..
8	73	Homersfield	arr	R			
			dep	..	..	..	..
12	65	Bungay	arr	11 49			
			dep	..	..	..	..
13	63	Ditchingham	arr				
			dep	..	..	11 45	..
15	24	Ellingham	arr			R	
			dep	..	..	..	..
16	66	Geldeston	arr			R	
			dep	..	..	..	..
19	36	BECCLES	arr			12 10	

UP

Mileage M	Mileage C			K		K	
						To Trowse	
				am		PM	
0	0	BECCLES	dep	10 30			
2	50	Geldeston	arr	10 40	..	..	..
			dep	10 50			
4	12	Ellingham	arr	10 57	..	..	..
			dep	11 15			
5	53	Ditchingham	arr	11 22	..	..	..
			dep				
6	48	Bungay	arr	..	..	..	..
			dep			12 30	
10	33	Homersfield	arr	..	..	..	..
			dep				
13	14	Harleston	arr	..	..	1 20	..
			dep			2 0	
15	61	Pulham St. Mary	arr	..	..	R	..
			dep				
16	63	Pulham Market	arr	..	..	2 35	..
			dep			2 55	
19	36	TIVETSHALL	arr	..	..	3 15	..
			dep			3 17	

BR(ER) working timetable; freight 1955.

The return service running as Class 'K' departed at 11.45am, calling only if required at Ellingham and Geldeston, with arrival back at Beccles at 12.10pm. By 1956 the Norwich train via Tivetshall ran as far as Bungay, while the train from Beccles terminated at Ditchingham. In 1963 a Class 'K' freight service departed Lowestoft and was booked to shunt at intermediate stations before arrival at Bungay at 2.07pm; it then departed at 2.35pm and was allowed 30 minutes to cover the 6 miles back to Beccles. As the train crew were required to open and close several crossing gates en route the train often arrived late. Little alteration was made to the timings at the western end of the branch before closure.

Excursions

During the early years the excursions offered from the branch stations usually required passengers to change into main line trains at either Tivetshall or Beccles, although in some cases through coaches were attached to forwarding services at the junction stations which made for easier travelling. As well as London, destinations included Ipswich, Felixstowe, Harwich, Clacton and Walton. In September 1862 a special train conveyed passengers from Bungay to Tivetshall where the through coaches were added to the train from Norwich destined for London for the Hyde Park Exhibition. Departure at a very early hour failed to deter would-be passengers from the 4-hour journey. Nine hours were offered in the capital before the return train conveyed the weary passengers home.

London excursions were always popular and in 1865 passengers from the branch stations joined a train conveying over 600 passengers from Beccles and East Suffolk line stations. Generally special traffic was slow to materialise and patronage varied according to the season, destination and, not least, the weather. When the line opened the wages of agricultural workers were low, so it was to the middle and upper classes that the railway excursion appealed most. Gradually alterations were made and the introduction of paid holidays and additional leisure periods brought the price of the railway excursion within the pockets of most inhabitants served by the line. During the 1870s and 1880s the most popular destinations were Yarmouth and Lowestoft, and to a lesser degree Felixstowe and Cromer. Shorter half-day excursions were offered to Norfolk and Suffolk resorts but for longer excursions through coaches from the branch were attached and detached at the junction stations. In the event of a late return, a special train connected at either Beccles or Tivetshall to convey passengers back to the branch stations. The popularity of Yarmouth found the GER, and later the L&NER and BR, working a through train or trains from Norwich via Tivetshall and all stations to Beccles with a return service in the evening each weekday during the summer months and on Sundays during July and August.

For many years the GER offered facilities for travelling to London on Saturdays, returning on the following Monday, by issuing cheap return tickets available for travel by any train on the day of issue and any train on the Monday. On the branch, tickets were

A Sunday excursion from Norwich Thorpe to Yarmouth South Town hauled by 'E4' Class 2-4-0 No. 62789 and 'J15' Class 0-6-0 No. 65471 makes a smoky approach to Ellingham. The train is composed of ex-L&NER Gresley corridor stock and, being eight coaches in length, was considered too heavy for single locomotive haulage. Norwich men who worked these trains, as well as enjoying the bonus of Sunday pay, were booked off duty after disposing of the locomotives, allowing them to spend a few hours by the sea, often with their families, before resuming duty to work the return service. The first post-war excursion was composed of two quint-art sets displaced by the recent London suburban electrification, these were extremely uncomfortable for passengers, who complained bitterly, hence the provision if eight corridor coaches on subsequent trains.
Dr I.C. Allen

A Norwich to Great Yarmouth Sunday excursion formed of Gresley gangwayed coaches headed by 'E4' Class 2-4-0 No. 62789 and 'J15' Class No. 65471 approaching Ellingham on a fine day. Although formed of corridor stock the engine correctly displays the stopping passenger headcode of one white disc at the base of the chimney as the train called in the course of its journey called at all stations on the branch. These excursions were popular and had to be double-headed as the load was too great for one locomotive. *Dr I.C. Allen*

'E4' Class 2-4-0 No. 62789 and 'J15' Class 0-6-0 No. 65471 depart Ellingham with another 8-coach Sunday excursion train from Norwich to Great Yarmouth, this time including BR Mark 1 corridor coaches. Most of the train is formed of ex London Midland & Scottish Railway corridor stock. The pair were used on numerous occasions and appeared to be firm favourites with the engine crews. *Dr I.C. Allen*

available at Tivetshall, Harleston, Bungay and Beccles, and in 1884 the fares were:

	First Class s	d	Second Class s	d	Third Class s	d
Tivetshall	18	8	14	4	8	5½
Harleston	19	10	15	2	8	11½
Bungay	21	1	16	0	9	6
Beccles	20	3	15	6	9	2

Later, fortnightly tickets were available for return within fifteen days of issue, whilst Friday or Saturday to Tuesday tickets were available for return on the Sunday, Monday or Tuesday following date of issue.

These were the halcyon days for the excursion programme and cheap fares were available to many exhibitions in London, including the annual Smithfield show. As well as running special trains, the GER and L&NER provided facilities for private parties to travel by rail. The 27th September 1930 is typical of many others, when 186 schoolchildren from council schools at Diss, Forncett, Tivetshall, Pulham Market and Pulham St. Mary accompanied by fifty-six adults travelled by rail to London.

Between the two world wars the excursion programme available to residents included the usual East Anglian destinations, with Aldeburgh and Thorpeness added, and in addition Spalding and Peterborough, although later the choice of destinations was reduced. In the years before and after World War Two cheap fares were offered to Norwich for the home games of Norwich City Football Club.

Saturday, 13th August.

TIVETSHALL, BECCLES AND YARMOUTH S.T.

(Evening excursion. For particulars of fares, etc., see public bills.)

		297 Vac. p.m.
Norwich Thorpe	dep.	4†15
Tivetshall	arr.	4†45
	dep.	5 0
Pulham Market	arr.	5 6
	dep.	5 7
Pulham Mary	"	5 12
Harleston	arr.	5 17
	dep.	5 19
Homersfield	"	5 26
Earsham	"	5 33
Bungay	arr.	5 36
	dep.	5 38
Ditchingham	"	5 44
Ellingham	"	5 51
Geldeston	"	5 56
Beccles	arr.	6 3
	dep.	6 15
Yarmouth S.T.	arr.	6 35

		297 Vac. p.m.
Yarmouth S.T.	dep.	10 35
Beccles	arr.	10 55
	dep.	11 5
Geldeston	"	11 12
Ellingham	"	11 17
Ditchingham	"	11 22
Bungay	arr.	11 26
	dep.	11 28
Earsham	"	11 32
Homersfield	"	11 40
Harleston	arr.	11 46
	dep.	11 49
Pulham Mary	"	11 57
Pulham Market	arr.	12 0
	dep.	12 2
Tivetshall	arr.	12 10
	dep.	12†15
Norwich Thorpe	arr.	12†45

Collect on alighting.

Formation:—
Engine.
1 T.C.B.
8 T.C. } 6-wheel.
1 T.C.B.
—
10
—

Cross at Pulham Market 4.20 p.m. goods ex Harleston.

6.2 p.m. ex Beccles to await there arrival of this special.

Left: Special train notice for evening excursion from Tivetshall to Yarmouth South Town and return on Saturday 13th August 1938 using 6-wheel coaching stock.

Below: Special train notice for British Legion juvenile party from Bungay to Lowestoft and return on Saturday 13th August 1938, using 6-wheel Westinghouse brake fitted coaching stock. By the time these excursions were operated only fifteen 6-wheel Thirds (excluding conductor guard stock) were still in service, so it appears twelve of these vehicles were used on that day!

Saturday, 13th August.

LOWESTOFT, BECCLES AND BUNGAY.

(Bungay British Legion juvenile party. 100 adults, 200 juveniles.)

		293 a.m.	294 p.m.
Bungay	dep	9 30	7†45
Ditchingham	arr.	9 34	...
	dep.	9 35	...
Ellingham	arr.	9 39	...
	dep.	9 40	...
Beccles	arr.	9 50	8 0
	dep.	9 57	8 10
Lowestoft C.	arr.	10 15	8†30

		295 a.m.	296 p.m.
Lowestoft C.	dep.	7†59	6 20
Beccles	arr.	8 16	6 36
	dep.	8 40	6 45
Ellingham	arr.	...	6 54
	dep.	...	6 55
Ditchingham	arr.	...	6 59
	dep.	...	7 0
Bungay	arr.	8†55	7 3

293—Await at Bungay arrival of 9.4 a.m. ex Beccles.

295 { Await at Beccles arrival of 7.49 a.m. ex Tivetshall. Forms 9.30 a.m. special to Lowestoft.

Formation:—
Engine.
1 T.C.B.
6 T.C.
—
7 Westinghouse (six-wheel).
—

Fares

The initial fares charged on the Waveney Valley line from 1855 are shown below, alongside those from Liverpool Street to the branch stations and locally from Norwich in 1884 (giving evidence of the anomaly in the GER pricing policy) and from Liverpool Street in 1947.

Fares, 1855	First Single £ s d	Second Single s d	Third Single s d	Parliamentary Single s d
London Bishopsgate to				
Pulham St. Magadalene	1 4 8	19 0	14 1	8 6½
Pulham St. Mary	1 4 10	19 2	14 3	8 7½
Starston	1 5 3	19 4	14 4	8 9½
Harleston	1 5 3	19 6	14 5	8 10
Harleston to				
Starston	4	3	2	½
Pulham St. Mary	6	4	3	2½
Pulham St. Magdalene	9	6	4	3½
Tivetshall	1 3	1 0	8	6
Norwich	3 6	2 6	2 0	1 7½
Ipswich	7 9	6 3	4 8	3 2

Fares, 1884	Single			Return		
	First Class s d	Second Class s d	Third Class s d	First Class s d	Second Class s d	Third Class s d
Liverpool Street to						
Tivetshall	18 8	14 4	8 5½	28 8	22 8	16 11
Pulham Market	19 2	14 9	8 8	29 0	23 3	17 4
Pulham St. Mary	19 4	14 10	8 9	29 4	23 6	17 6
Harleston	19 10	15 2	8 11½	30 0	24 0	17 11
Homersfield	20 4	15 6	9 2½	30 6	24 8	18 5
Earsham	21 0	16 0	9 5½	31 6	25 2	18 11
Bungay	21 1	16 0	9 6	31 10	25 6	19 0
Ditchingham	21 3	16 3	9 7½	32 0	25 8	19 3
Ellingham	21 2	16 0	9 6	31 10	25 6	19 0
Geldeston	20 10	15 10	9 4½	31 3	25 2	18 9
Beccles	20 3	15 6	9 2	30 6	24 5	18 4
Norwich To						
Tivetshall	2 7	2 0	1 1½	3 11	3 1	2 3
Pulham Market	3 2	2 5	1 4	4 9	3 10	2 8
Pulham St. Mary	3 4	2 7	1 5	5 0	4 0	2 10
Harleston	3 8	2 10	1 7½	5 6	4 5	3 3
Homersfield	3 3	2 6	1 10½	5 6	3 10	3 3
Earsham	3 0	2 6	1 9	5 0	3 10	2 11
Bungay	3 0	2 6	1 9	5 0	3 10	2 11
Ditchingham	3 3	2 8	1 10	5 6	4 0	3 0
Ellingham	3 6	2 11	2 1	5 9	4 6	3 6
Geldeston	3 10	3 2	2 0½	6 3	5 0	3 9
Beccles	4 0	3 0	1 9½	5 6	3 10	3 3

Goods Traffic

Before the coming of the railway, the local carriers' carts were a common sight on the roads linking the villages and towns of the area with the larger centres of Norwich, Ipswich, Lowestoft and Yarmouth. As the branch developed so the carriers provided an essential link from outlying villages and hamlets to the railhead,

Fares, 1947												
	Single						Monthly Return					
	First Class			Third Class			First Class			Third Class		
	£	s	d	£	s	d	£	s	d	£	s	d
Liverpool Street to												
Tivetshall	1	9	8		17	11	1	15	8	1	3	9
Pulham Market	1	10	7		18	4	1	16	11	1	4	7
Pulham St. Mary	1	10	9		18	7	1	17	5	1	4	11
Harleston	1	11	7		18	11	1	17	11	1	5	3
Homersfield	1	12	4		19	4	1	18	11	1	5	11
Earsham	1	13	3		19	11	2	0	0	1	6	10
Bungay	1	13	5	1	0	1	2	0	6	1	7	0
Ditchingham	1	13	8	1	0	4	2	1	0	1	7	4
Ellingham	1	13	5	1	0	1	2	0	6	1	7	0
Geldeston	1	13	0		19	11	1	19	11	1	6	7
Beccles	1	12	4		19	4	1	18	11	1	5	11

bringing goods for onward despatch by rail and delivering commodities brought by train to the branch station goods yards. The railway company failed to gain the monopoly, for as late as the 1890s carriers still operated from Beccles: Laws travelling from the White Horse, New Market Place to Bungay on Mondays, Wednesdays and Fridays; Flegg travelled from the King's Head Hotel to Norwich on Wednesdays and Saturdays. From Bungay, Gardner's van ran to Norwich daily at 7.00am, returning from the Lamb, Haymarket at 4.30pm.

The initial freight handled by rail confirmed the optimistic views of the promoters, as barley, hay, wheat, straw and vegetable traffic were transferred from farm and carriers' carts for rapid transit to and from Norwich, Ipswich, Lowestoft, Yarmouth, Colchester and London markets as well as those in the Midlands. In addition to these basic commodities, vegetable crops including potatoes, swedes, carrots, parsnips, turnips and mangold wurzels were sent by rail. From the early 1920s sugar beet was grown increasingly in Suffolk and Norfolk. The growing of sugar beet in the United Kingdom could be traced back to 1835 but in East Anglia the first factory was erected at Lavenham in the 1860s. This was small and unsuccessful and it was not until 1912 that the first modern factory opened at Cantley, followed in 1920 by one at Kelham, near Norwich, and a third at Colwick near Nottingham in 1924. The passing of the Sugar Beet (Subsidy) Act of 1925 marked a considerable step forward and five new factories were erected in 1925: at Ely, Ipswich, Bury St. Edmunds, Wissington near Downham and Kidderminster in Worcestershire, to be followed in 1926 by Felstead and Peterborough, and in 1927 by Kings Lynn amongst others. Thus the growing of sugar beet was quickly established on the lands served by the Waveney Valley Branch and continued almost to the time that freight traffic was withdrawn. Considerable loads were transferred from horse-drawn waggons to railway wagons at the various sidings, which in season created an animated scene as loads were required to be sent as programmed by the sugar processing factory. Incoming commodities included seed potatoes from Scotland, animal foodstuffs and fertilizers, agricultural machinery and smalls traffic for local shops; specific items included Lyons cakes, Walls ice cream, John Player's and Churchman's tobacco and cigarettes, general merchandise and returned luggage.

Another important commodity conveyed on the branch was barley en route to the maltings and breweries established at Tivetshall, Harleston, Ditchingham and Beccles. Traffic was considerable, with malt being sent to local breweries as well as further afield to Burton and London; the maltings received barley by rail and in return despatched sacks of malt to many breweries in East Anglia as well as to the larger towns. From the latter part of the 19th century until the end of World War One, truck-loads of hay and straw were loaded at the branch stations and sent to London, Ipswich and Norwich for use in the many stables in those towns and cities, a greater need being required during the World War One when the commodity was required for military stables.

Mention must be made of the conveyance of manure for local farms, a much-maligned commodity detested by railway staff because of the pungent smell, which took time to clear from wagons and required the thorough cleaning of rolling stock. Building materials, including bricks, cement and timber, were offloaded at most stations but the traffic all but disappeared after World War Two when it was conveyed by road. The opening of two gravel and stone pits at Homersfield in 1916 containing material especially suited to the making of concrete resulted in an annual 35,000 tons being conveyed by rail for the much needed war effort.

Fruit from various farms, smallholdings and nurseries was loaded at Harleston and Bungay for conveyance to Spitalfields and Covent Garden markets in London, with smaller tonnages being sent to local markets at Norwich and Ipswich as well as Harleston, Bungay and Beccles. Apples and pears were loaded into crates and placed into covered vans, whilst summer fruits grown from June to August were initially loaded into 7 lb baskets or 12 lb sieves, but after World War One the fruit was packed in baskets, trays or tubs varying in weight according to size; they were then loaded into vans for onward transit. Most of this traffic had transferred to road haulage by the late 1940s.

Milk was regularly sent from all stations on the branch and conveyed to dairies at Beccles, Ipswich and Norwich in the familiar 17-gallon churns. Two loads were despatched during the summer months, the first by the early morning service and again in the late afternoon. Milk was only forwarded on the early morning train in the winter months. In the early years smaller quantities of milk were also sent to dairies at Harleston and Bungay, and occasionally to Yarmouth and Lowestoft. The area served by the branch was not noted for its dairy farming and the relatively small amounts were quickly lost to road transport in the late 1930s when most milk churns were collected from the farms and delivered direct to the dairies.

Eggs became another significant commodity conveyed by rail from the branch stations and in October 1916 the GER Egg and Poultry Train was exhibited at Harleston station as part of an East Anglian tour to promote higher yields for the war effort. From the early 1930s most of the conveyance of eggs had been transferred to road haulage and the railway saw little if any traffic thereafter.

Before the coming of the railway, drovers herded animals along the roads to and from markets and prices fluctuated according to the condition of the beasts. The arrival of the railway meant animals could be conveyed relatively quickly to local and London markets, arriving in much fresher condition and therefore gaining a higher price. From the outset livestock handled at the branch stations was two-way traffic. The potential of the railway for the speedy transportation was quickly realised and horses were regularly conveyed in wagons or horseboxes attached to passenger trains. Until World War Two hunting horses were conveyed to or from hunt meetings on 24 hours' notice being given to the forwarding station. Cattle wagons were a common feature until the early 1950s and the branch was used to convey livestock to Ipswich and Norwich markets as well as to the local markets at Beccles, Bungay and Harleston. Certain passenger trains were permitted to convey cattle wagons and this was especially useful on market days at Ipswich (Tuesday), Norwich (Wednesday and Saturday), Beccles (Friday), Bungay (Thursday) and Harleston (Wednesday). Pigs and sheep were also conveyed by the branch freight service but trade declined with the relaxation of petrol rationing after World War Two, when nearly all livestock traffic was lost to road transport. The conveyance of cattle traffic required the cattle vans as well as the pens at the stations to be limewashed to prevent disease. The pens constructed of timber were originally painted white but the continuing white finish as depicted in photographs was usually limewash.

Coal and coke traffic was regularly received at all stations on the branch, with consignments for local fuel merchants from various collieries including Sherwood, Newstead, Kirkley, Bestwood, Hucknall, Sheepbridge, Stanton, Shirebrook, Clipstone, Worksop, Gedling and Blidworth. The wagons from the coal pits usually travelled via Peterborough where the Stanground sidings acted as a clearing-house for empty wagons returning to the collieries or loaded ones destined for the branch stations. Other traffic came on the Great Northern & Great Eastern Joint line via Spalding and March. The coal loaded in colliery private owner wagons was then routed via Ely and Norwich, although to save congestion at Norwich consignments were later routed via Wymondham, Ashwellthorpe and Forncett and thence to Tivetshall, the wagons returning the same way. In the 1920s and 1930s coke was also conveyed for horticultural purposes but after World War Two this commodity was taken by road. Local coal and coke merchants receiving fuel by rail included Thomas Moy and the Co-operative Society.

In the late 1920s and early 1930s many of the roads in Suffolk and Norfolk remained unmetalled, dust tracks in summer and muddy quagmires in winter. Both county councils undertook a rolling programme of road improvements, which involved levelling the surface before covering it in granite chippings and tarmacadam. Much of this material was delivered by rail to the branch station goods yards from where the material was offloaded and taken to site by horse and waggon. The granite and tarmacadam was then levelled by steamroller.

During World War Two the Ministry of Food established cold storage depots local to the branch and a considerable tonnage of meat, dried egg powder, dried milk and other food stuffs was conveyed to the depots, both during and after the hostilities. Mention has also been made of the considerable contribution made by the branch in the conveyance of military equipment and armaments to airfields, initially in World War One and later during World War Two; it is not repeated here.

Sand and gravel handled at Ditchingham after World War Two continued until 19th April 1964 (but extended to August 1965). Pointers provided sand traffic originally using 16-ton all-steel mineral wagons but latterly conveyed in SNCF French Railways

Forncett station looking south towards Tivetshall and Ipswich in October 1911 with Forncett Station signal box on the Down side alongside a carriage body serving as a store located at the end of the Down refuge siding. Many of the through services from Norwich to Beccles called at Forncett, whilst a few local Waveney Valley Branch services were extended to terminate and start back from the station. *GERS/Windwood 1282*

'J15' Class 0-6-0 No. 65478 works a Down branch goods train and crosses one of the many timber underbridges between Geldeston and Beccles in 1952. *Dr I.C. Allen*

wagons (of which the company had a fleet of seventy-five vehicles) from Ditchingham to Beccles and then to Ipswich for onward transit to Beddington Lane on the Southern Region. When Pointers transferred their traffic flow from Coltishall on the Wroxham to County School branch, the facility at Ditchingham ceased production and the eastern end of the branch closed to all traffic.

From 1902 Beccles station was permitted to hold two horseboxes and two carriage trucks for exceptional traffic originating from stations to Yarmouth South Town, Halesworth and from the Waveney Valley Branch.

The following private sidings were located at the branch stations:

Tivetshall
- E. Packard & Company Limited
- T.M. Read
- Watney, Combe, Reid & Company Limited

Pulham Market
- Admiralty, later Air Ministry

Harleston
- Charles Marston (Bungay) Limited
- H. Blackburn
- H. Hudson
- T. Moy Limited
- Stanton & Company
- Watney, Combe, Reid & Company Limited
- W.D. & A.E. Walker Limited

Bungay
- W.D. & A.E. Walker Limited
- W.A. Warnes

Beccles
- Co-operative Society
- John Crisp & Sons
- Elliott & Garrood Limited
- H.G. Rose
- Beccles Model Laundry Company Limited
- Beccles Working Men's Co-op Association

The following goods facilities were available at the branch stations:

Tivetshall
- Loading gauges
- Loading dock
- Cattle dock
- 2 paved Cattle pens
- Watering supply for animals in transit
- Fixed crane, 2 tons, later 1 ton 10 cwt capacity
- Weighing machine, 1 ton 2 cwt capacity
- Goods shed with storage capacity for 50 quarters of grain
- Lock up for small packages
- Facility for loading vans and furniture vans on wheels, also round timber
- Latest time for same day forwarding:
  4.30pm Up road
  1.00pm Down road

Pulham Market
- Loading gauge
- Loading dock
- Paved cattle pen
- Weighing machine, 2 tons 2 cwt capacity
- Facility for loading vans
- Wagon turntable (removed by 1905)
- Lock up for small packages
- Latest time for same day forwarding:
  3.15pm Mon-Fri
  1.00pm Saturday

Pulham St. Mary
- Loading gauge
- Loading dock
- Weighing machine, 8 cwt capacity
- Facility for loading vans
- Lock up for small packages
- Latest time for same day forwarding:
  3.30pm Up road Mon-Fri
  5.00pm Down road Mon-Fri
  3.00pm Saturdays

Harleston

Loading gauges
Loading dock
Cattle dock
3 paved Cattle pens
Watering facilities for animals in transit
Fixed crane, 10 tons, later 8 tons, then 5 tons capacity
Duckhams weighbridge, 8 tons capacity
Weighing machine, 1 ton 2 cwt capacity
Goods shed with storage capacity for 150 quarters of grain
Wagon turntable
Facility for loading vans and furniture vans on wheels, also round timber
Cartage by railway company
Latest time for same day forwarding:
3.00pm Up road
6.00pm Down road

Homersfield

Loading gauge
Loading dock
Cattle dock
Paved Cattle pen
Fixed crane, 1 ton, later 1 ton 10 cwt capacity
Weighing machine, 15 cwt, later 1 ton 2 cwt capacity
Goods shed with storage capacity for 400 quarters of grain
Wagon turntable
Lock up for small packages
Facility for loading vans and furniture vans on wheels
Latest time for same day forwarding:
3.30pm Up road Mon-Fri
10.00am Down road Mon-Fri
3.00pm Saturdays

Earsham

Weighing machine, 10 cwt capacity
Lock up for small packages

Bungay

Loading gauges
Loading dock
Cattle dock
2 paved Cattle pens
Watering facilities for animals in transit
Fixed crane, 1 ton 10 cwt capacity
Weighing machine, 1 ton 10 cwt capacity
Goods shed with storage capacity for 50 quarters of grain
Wagon turntable (removed by 1905)
Lock up for small packages
Facilities for loading vans and furniture vans on wheels, also round timber
Cartage by railway company
Latest time for same day forwarding:
2.00pm Up road Mon-Fri
11.00am Down road Mon-Fri
3.00pm Saturdays

Ditchingham

Loading gauge
Loading dock
Cattle dock
2 paved cattle pens
Fixed crane, 2 tons, later 1 ton 10 cwt capacity
Weighing machine, 1 ton 2 cwt capacity
Goods shed with storage capacity for 250 quarters of grain
Lock up for small packages
Facilities for loading vans and furniture vans on wheels (also round timber for immediate forwarding in limited quantities)
Latest time for same day forwarding:
1.45pm Up road Mon-Fri
11.30am Down road Mon-Fri
3.00pm Saturdays

The wagon turntable at Homersfield dating from 1860 enabled several sidings to be accommodated in the cramped space. It was used until goods facilities were withdrawn from the station on and from 1st February 1960 and is shown here in May 1962 before demolition. The top right-hand siding led to the goods shed. *J. Watling*

Assorted views of the fixed yard crane at Harleston on 3rd June 1966. The crane was manufactured by Harwood & Turner of St. Peter's Foundry, Ipswich and had capacity for lifting 10 tons, later reduced to 8 tons and then 5 tons. The makers details of Harwood & Turner of St. Peter's Foundry are cast of the side panel, although the lifting capacity has been chiselled off (*below right*). *J. Watling*

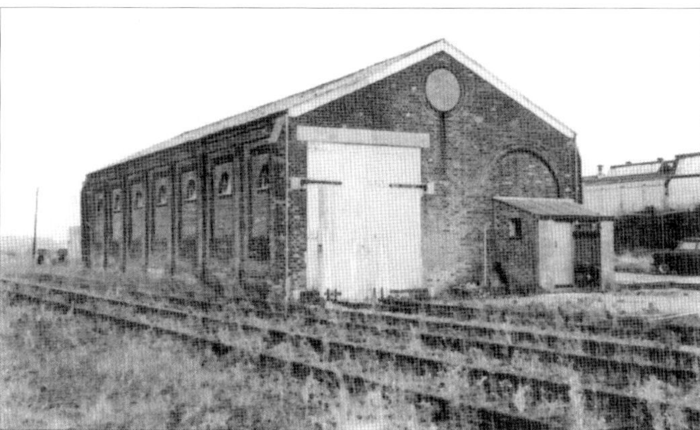

The large goods shed in Bungay goods yard which when operational had capacity for 50 quarters of grain. This scene on 25th September 1965 presents a sad sight after the withdrawal of the freight service but before the weed infested permanent way was lifted. On the left is the west end, whilst the east end and associated goods office can be seen on the right. *J. Watling*

Ellingham

Loading gauge
Loading dock
Weighing machine, 1 ton, later 10 cwt capacity
Lock up for small packages
Facility for loading vans and furniture vans on wheels
Latest time for same day forwarding:
1.30pm Up road
11.45am Down road

Geldeston

Loading gauge
Loading dock
Fixed crane, 1 ton 10 cwt capacity
Weighing machine, 5 cwt capacity
Goods shed with storage capacity for 200 quarters of grain
Lock up for small packages
Facility for loading furniture vans on wheels
Latest time for same day forwarding:
1.15pm Up road
12.00 noon Down road

Beccles

Loading gauges
Loading dock
Cattle dock
3 paved Cattle pens
Watering facilities for animals in transit
Fixed crane, 1 ton, later 6 tons capacity
Duckhams, 12 tons capacity
Wagon weighbridge, 20 tons capacity
Weighing machine, 16 cwt capacity
Goods shed with storage capacity for 100 quarters of grain
2 Wagon turntables giving access to Malthouse
Lock up for small packages
Facility for loading vans and furniture vans on wheels, also round timber
Cartage by railway company
Latest time for same day forwarding:
via Waveney Valley and via Norwich 1.30pm
6.00pm Down road
3.00pm Saturdays

In 1865 the permitted load of the branch engine was not to exceed twenty-five trucks and regular goods trains thirty trucks, but from 1870 specific loadings were stipulated, with three empty trucks considered as equal to two loaded.

Locomotive Class	Goods Trucks Loaded		Coal Trucks Loaded		Gross	Net
	Down	Up	Down	Up	tons	tons
Four-wheel coupled Second Class engines	30	30	25	25	300	200
Third Class engines	25	25	21	21	252	160
Fourth Class engines	22	22	20	20	220	140

By 1891 the loading allowed for goods engines on the branch was:

Locomotive Class	Goods Trucks Loaded		Coal Trucks Loaded		Gross	Net
	Down	Up	Down	Up	tons	tons
Second Class engines	30	30	25	25	300	200
Third Class engines	25	25	21	21	252	160

The permitted loading limit to be hauled by goods engines on the Waveney Valley route in 1897 was:

Locomotive Class	Goods Trucks Loaded		Coal Trucks Loaded	
	Down	Up	Down	Up
First Class engine	—	—	—	—
Second Class engine	30	30	25	25
Third Class engine	25	25	21	21

After the turn of the century the loads for goods engines were revised as under.

Class of Locomotive	Minerals		Goods	
	Down	Up	Down	Up
A	35	35	35	35
B	33	33	35	35
C	29	29	35	35
D	27	27	35	35
E	26	26	35	35
F	25	25	35	35
G	21	21	30	30
H	20	20	28	28

The following locomotives, regularly allocated to work the Waveney Valley services, were classified as follows.

GER Class	L&NER Class	Type	Classified
Y14	J15	0-6-0	C
M15	F4	2-4-2T	D
M15R	F5	2-4-2T	D
G69	F6	2-4-2T	D
C32	F3	2-4-2T	E
417	—	0-6-0	F
477	—	0-6-0	F
T26	E4	2-4-0	F
E22	J65	0-6-0T	H

When the L&NER reissued the loads book, freight trains on the Waveney Valley line were not to exceed fifty-two wagons on both the Down and Up run between Tivetshall and Bungay, and sixty wagons in both directions between Bungay and Beccles, with individual loadings as follows.

ENGINE	MINERALS	GOODS	EMPTIES
TIVETSHALL TO BUNGAY			
Class 1	29	43	52
Class 2	32	48	52
Class 3	35	52	52
BUNGAY TO BECCLES			
Class 1	32	48	60
Class 2	36	54	60
Class 3	40	59	60
BECCLES TO BUNGAY			
Class 1	27	40	54
Class 2	30	45	59
Class 3	33	49	60
BUNGAY TO TIVETSHALL			
Class 1	27	40	52
Class 2	30	45	52
Class 3	33	49	52

A Class '3' goods engine was a 'J15' Class 0-6-0 tender locomotive. 'F3', 'F4', 'F5' and 'F6' Class 2-4-2 tank locomotives were to convey six mineral wagons less than the load shown for a No. 1 freight engine.

British Railways maintained the length limit of trains on the branch but made slight amendments to the individual loadings for Class 'J' and Class 'K' freight trains as under.

ENGINE	MINERALS	GOODS	EMPTIES
TIVETSHALL TO BUNGAY			
Class 1	26	46	52
Class 2	29	51	52
Class 3	31	52	52
Class 4	34	52	52
BUNGAY TO BECCLES			
Class 1	29	51	58
Class 2	32	57	60
Class 3	36	60	60
BECCLES TO BUNGAY			
Class 1	24	42	48
Class 2	27	48	54
Class 3	30	53	60
BUNGAY TO TIVETSHALL			
Class 1	24	42	48
Class 2	27	48	52
Class 3	30	52	52
Class 4	33	52	52

'J15' Class 0-6-0 No. 65460 makes for Beccles with a train composed of a mixture of open wagons including 16-ton all-steel mineral and ex-private owner wooden bodied vehicles conveying sugar beet, ultimately destined for Cantley sugar processing factory. No. 65460 tender is equipped with a back plate to protect footplate crews in the winter months as many of the branch line duties involved tender-first working in one direction. *Dr I.C. Allen*

The following were the load groups for the various classes that worked across the Waveney Valley line.

Tender	Group 1	Class 'D15'* Class 'D16'* Class 'E4'+
	Group 2	Class 'J15'
	Group 3	Class 'B12/3'
	Group 4	Class 'J17'
Tank	Group 1	Class 'F3'+ Class 'F4'+ Class 'F5'+ Class 'F6'+
Notes: * These classes to convey three heavy wagons or equivalent less than the loads shown for Group 1 engines. + These classes to convey five heavy wagons or equivalent less that the loads shown for Group 1 engines.		

Following dieselisation of freight services a load limit of fifty-two wagons was permitted on the branch services between Tivetshall and Harleston, with the undermentioned load limit for individual classes of locomotive.

Class of Train	4,5,6	7	8,9
Class '15' 800 hp	25	32	40
Class '21' 1,100 hp	36	34	42
Class '24' 1,160 hp	38	36	44
Class '31' 1,250/1,365 hp	42	40	50

Between Beccles and Bungay the load limit was thirty wagons, with only BR/Gardner '2/1' class (later Class '03'), Drewry Gardner '2/13' and '2/13A' classes (later Class '04') and Hunslet/Gardner '2/15' and '2/15A' classes (later Class '05') 204 hp diesel mechanical shunting locomotives permitted to haul a maximum load of thirty wagons in each direction.

Hunslet 204 hp Class '05' diesel mechanical shunting locomotive No. 02559 pulls out of the western end of the Down loop, which was extended in World War Two as a continuation of Ditchingham station Down reception siding. The shunter is operating the 6-lever ground frame prior to opening the gates of Norwich Road (a.k.a. Factory Road) level crossing No. 72 at 13 miles 43¼ chains. The scene is completed by the two-storey gate keeper's cottage and a grounded coach body. *Dr I.C. Allen*

A Brush Type '2' Class '31' diesel electric locomotive working a short branch freight train from Harleston halts at London Road level crossing No. 8 at 1 mile 67¾ chains from Tivetshall for the trainman to open the gates. Despite being the busy main A140 road between Ipswich and Norwich, no traffic lights were installed to stop road traffic as at Capel, where the Hadleigh Branch bisected the A12. Railmen frequently complained that they were forced to take risks to close the gates because of speeding motorists trying to beat the barriers.

11

Locomotives and Rolling Stock

Like many routes in East Anglia the relatively light construction of the permanent way on the Waveney Valley Railway precluded the use of locomotives with heavy axle loading, so only those with light or medium axle loading were permitted. The ECR, EUR and later GER possessed ample engines of low route availability to work the branch. The GER prohibited the use of locomotives No's 725, 776, 778, 1000 and 1001, 1140 to 1249, 1260 to 1269, 1500 to 1505, 1507 to 1540 and 1790 to 1900 across the line; later the L&NER initially permitted only 'E4' Class 2-4-0 and 'J15' Class 0-6-0 tender locomotives together with 'F4' and 'F7' Class 2-4-2, 'J65', 'J67' and 'J70' 0-6-0 tank classes as well as Y1, Y3, Y5, Y6 and Y10 sentinel shunting engines. As the permanent way was improved the L&NER, and later BR, classified the branch to Route Availability 4 (RA4) with additional classes 'C12' and 'C13' 4-4-2Ts, 'D1', 'D15', 'D16' 4-4-0s, 'F2' 2-4-2T, 'J19' and 'J27' 0-6-0s and 'N7' 0-6-2T with higher route availability. In later years the Beccles to Bungay section was designated RA3, with only 204 hp of classes 'D2/1', 'D2/13', 'D2/13A', 'D2/15' and 'D2/15A' permitted, whilst Tivetshall to Harleston was classified RA4 with classes '10/4', '11/1', '11/4', '12/2', '13/2' and '16/2' of higher route availability 6 and 7 permitted, all classes being restricted to a speed limit of 25 mph by the fact the line was downgraded to the status of a light railway.

The EUR and ECR 2-2-2 Tender Engines

During the inspection of the Harleston to Bungay section of line in October 1860, Colonel Yolland was concerned that until the WVR commenced independent operation of their railway the EUR and ECR had resorted to using tender locomotives on services despite the absence of turntables, so that locomotives had to work tender first in one direction. For the period from 1st December 1855 until independent operation, the line was probably worked initially by one of the twenty-six locomotives owned by the EUR, usually with high mileage and ready for shops. The most numerous class of thirteen were the standard type of 2-2-2 built by Sharp Brothers of Manchester; six were constructed in 1846 receiving the following numbers and names: No. 1 *Ipswich*, No. 2 *Bury*, No. 3 *Colchester*, No. 4 *Diss*, No. 5 *Stowmarket* and No. 6 *Haughley*. A further six were delivered the following year receiving the numbers 14 to 19 inclusive, whilst a thirteenth, No. 26, was delivered in 1849. The leading dimensions were:

Cylinders		15 ins x 20 ins	
Boiler	Max diameter	3 feet 6 ins	
	Barrel length	10 feet 0 ins	
Firebox		3 feet 8 ins	
Heating surface			
	Tubes	147 x 1⅝ ins	704.7 sq feet
	Firebox		63.2 sq feet
	Total		767.9 sq feet
Grate area		10.8 sq feet	
Leading wheels		3 feet 6 ins	
Driving wheels		5 feet 6 ins	
Trailing wheels		3 feet 6 ins	
Wheelbase		12 feet 8 ins	
Weight in working order		18 tons 12 cwt	
Max axle loading		9 tons 8 cwt	

Another class of single-driver 2-2-2 tender locomotive built for the EUR came from Stothert, Slaughter & Company in 1846 and numbered 7, 8, 20 and 21. The principal dimensions were:

Cylinders		15 ins x 22 ins
Boiler	Barrel length	10 feet 6 ins
Firebox		4 feet 2½ ins
Leading wheels		3 feet 6 ins
Driving wheels		5 feet 0 ins
Trailing wheels		3 feet 6 ins

They were rebuilt into 2-4-0s by the ECR with the added dimensions:

Wheelbase	14 feet 3½ ins
Weight in working order	34 tons 19 cwt
Max axle loading	13 tons 0 cwt

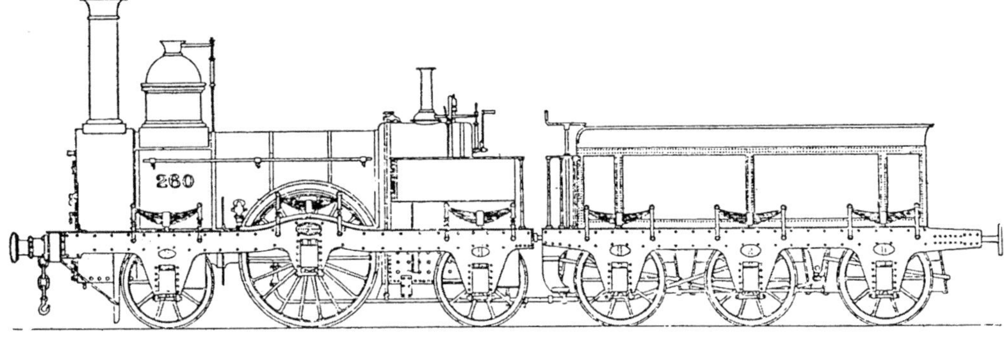

EUR No. 1 built by Sharp Brothers in 1846 and originally named *Ipswich*, is shown here after renumbering to 260 by the ECR.

The same company built a further six tender engines in 1847, with 0-4-2 wheel arrangement and outside framing, and these were numbered 9, 10 and 22 to 25 inclusive; No. 9 was named *Suffolk* and No. 10 *Essex*. The principal dimensions were:

Cylinders		15 ins x 22 ins
Boiler	Barrel length	10 feet 6 ins
Firebox		4 feet 2½ ins
Driving wheels		5 feet 0 ins
Trailing wheels		3 feet 6 ins
Wheelbase		13 feet 4 ins

The final three tender locomotives delivered in the same year, No's 11, 12 and 13, were built by R. & W. Hawthorn & Company with 2-2-2 wheel arrangement. The leading dimensions were:

Cylinders		15 ins x 20 ins
Boiler	Barrel length	11 feet 6 ins
Firebox		4 feet 0 ins
Leading wheels		3 feet 8 ins
Driving wheels		6 feet 0 ins
Trailing wheels		3 feet 8 ins
Wheelbase		14 feet 7½ ins
Weight in working order		20 tons 6 cwt
Max axle loading		10 tons 10 cwt

All the EUR locomotives were said to have carried names but unfortunately only the first six and No's 9 and 10 were definitely recorded. When the ECR took over the working of the EUR all the locomotives were renumbered, and these and subsequent scrapping dates if known are given below.

Sharp Brothers 2-2-2

EUR No.	ECR No	Withdrawn
1	260, later 2600	December 1879
2	261	October 1874
3	262, later 2620	December 1879
4	263	January 1873
5	264, later 2640	August 1877
6	265	March 1874
14	266	July 1875
15	267, late 2670	August 1880
16	268	March 1874
17	269	March 1874
18	270	February 1873
19	271, later 116	June 1867
20	272, later 117	February 1875

ECR No. 205, originally EUR No. 7, built by Stothert, Slaughter & Co. in 1846 as a 2-2-2, rebuilt as a 2-4-0 in 1852. No tender shown.

Storthert, Slaughter 2-2-2, later converted to 2-4-0 by the ECR

EUR No.	ECR No	Withdrawn
7	205	
8	206	June 1867
20	209	
21	210	February 1868

Stothert, Slaughter 0-4-2

EUR No.	ECR No.	Withdrawn
9	207	
10	208	
22	211	June 1867
23	212	
24	213	
25	214, later 204	June 1867

R. & W. Hawthorn 2-2-2

EUR No.	ECR No.	Withdrawn
11	273	
12	274, later 271	
13	275, later 272	

The ECR 2-4-0 Tender Engines

Another class employed in the early years were 2-4-0 tender locomotives supplied to the ECR by E. & B. Wilson and built between December 1848 and February 1849. By the time the Waveney Valley line opened the eight members of the class, No's 193 to 200, had been relegated to secondary duties and at least two members of the class were employed on the branch services in their final years of operation. No's 194 and 195 were withdrawn in

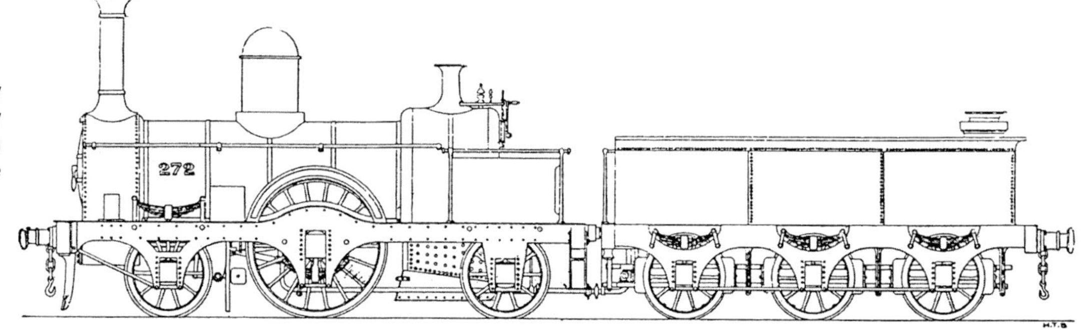

ECR 2-2-2 No. 272, originally supplied to the Ipswich & Bury Railway by R. & W. Hawthorn in 1846 and numbered 13 in the EUR fleet.

ECR 2-4-0 No. 200 built by E. & B. Wilson.

November 1868, No's 193 and 198 in April 1869, No's 197 and 199 in January 1870 and No's 196 and 200 in February 1871. In service the locomotives were supplied with 6-wheel tenders. The leading dimensions of the class were:

Cylinders		15 ins x 22 ins	
Boiler	Barrel length	10 feet 10 ins	
	Diameter	3 feet 6¾ ins	
Firebox		4 feet 2¾ ins	
Heating surface			
	Tubes	150 x 1⅞ ins	863.8 sq feet
	Firebox		81.3 sq feet
	Total		945.1 sq feet
Grate area		12.6 sq feet	
Leading wheels		3 feet 8 ins	
Coupled wheels		5 feet 0 ins	
Wheelbase Engine		14 feet 8½ ins	
Weight in working order		24 tons 3 cwt	
Max axle loading		10 tons 15 cwt	

The EUR and ECR 2-2-2 Tank Engines

The working of the Waveney Valley line between Tivetshall and Harleston with tender engines was wasteful of time and resources and the absence of turntables at each end meant tender-first running in one direction, which was unpopular with engine crews. When the WVR took over operation from 15th September 1860 a tank locomotive worked the line, and indeed the inspecting officer stipulated the extension from Harleston to Bungay and on to Beccles was to be worked by a tank engine. Thus it is almost certain an EUR locomotive was outbased at Harleston and then Bungay to work the line. In 1849 the EUR had taken delivery of a 2-2-2 tank locomotive built by Sharp Brothers of Manchester (Maker's No. 595). It initially carried the number 27 and undoubtedly worked the Bentley to Hadleigh branch at some time in its early career. When the ECR took over the running of the EUR they renumbered the engine to No. 16 and it was during this period that it took turns on the Waveney Valley line, working turn and turn about with the other three Sharp tank engines before being scrapped in February 1871. The leading dimensions of No. 27 were:

Cylinders		14 ins x 18 ins	
Boiler	Barrel length	10 feet 0 ins	
Firebox		3 feet 6 ins	
Heating surface			
	Tubes	147 x 1⅝ ins	704.7 sq feet
	Firebox		63.2 sq feet
	Total		767.9 sq feet
Grate area		10.8 sq feet	
Leading wheels		3 feet 6 ins	
Driving wheels		5 feet 6 ins	
Trailing wheels		3 feet 6 ins	
Wheelbase		12 feet 8 ins	

It is almost certain the Waveney Valley services were also worked by one of the trio of EUR 2-2-2 tank locomotives built by Sharp Brothers of Manchester in 1854 (Maker's No's 765, 766 and 768). They were allocated No's 29, 30 and 31 by the EUR but it is doubtful if these numbers were actually carried for they were delivered after the ECR had taken over the operation of the line. The new owner renumbered the 2-2-2Ts to 13, 14 and 15 and although slightly smaller than 2-2-2T No. 16 they were well equipped to handle both passenger and freight traffic on the branch. All three were withdrawn for scrapping in November 1871.

The leading dimensions were:

Cylinders		14 ins x 18 ins	
Heating surface			
	Tubes	122 x 2 ins	507.62 sq feet
	Firebox		54.00 sq feet
	Total		561.62 sq feet
Leading wheels		3 feet 0 ins	
Driving wheels		5 feet 0 ins	
Trailing wheels		3 feet 0 ins	
Wheelbase		13 feet 0 ins	
Weight on working order		19 tons 0 cwt	
Max axle loading		8 tons	

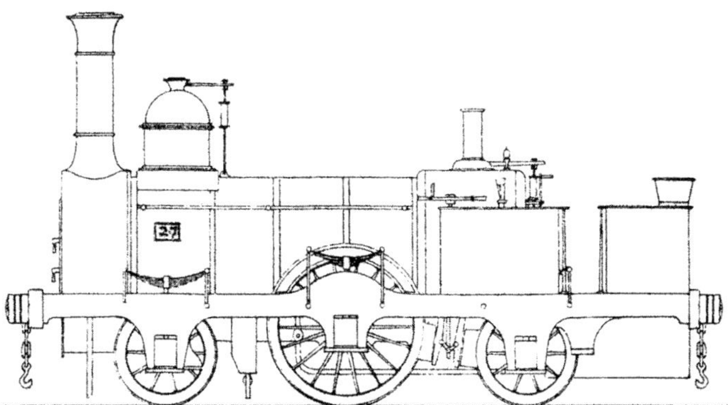

EUR 2-2-2 tank locomotive No. 27.

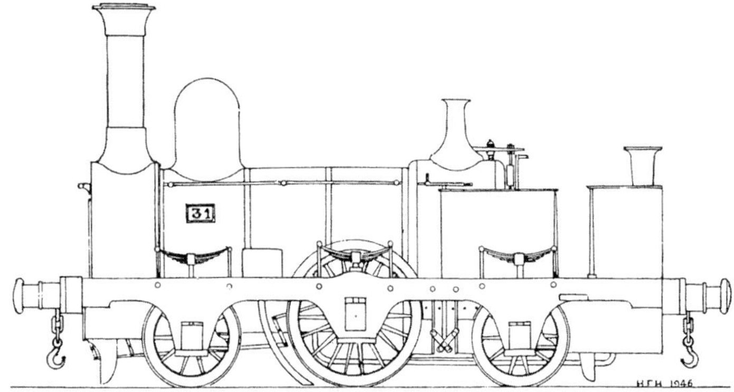

EUR 2-2-2 tank locomotive No. 31.

The WVR 2-2-2 Engine

In their bid to run the line independently the Waveney Valley Company ordered a 2-2-2 tank locomotive from Sharp, Stewart & Company of Manchester in 1861, as the ECR was reluctant to loan a locomotive, let alone carry out repairs at Harleston or Bungay. The engine (Maker's No. 1228 to order E391 for Mr Peter Bruff) entered service the same year, operating between Tivetshall and Bungay. According to Sharp, Stewart records the locomotive was delivered bearing the name *Perseverance*. When the line from Bungay to Beccles was completed and opened on 1st March 1863 the line became vested in the GER and the locomotive entered GER stock from the same date, receiving the number 30. Sinclair, the Locomotive Superintendent, quickly realised its performance left much to be desired and transferred the engine away. Being of an unusual design with a single driving axle, side tanks and outside cylinders, boiler with a flush barrel with dome over the firebox and no slide bars to guide the pistons rods, the latter perforce to work through a guide in a suspended bracket, the engine was rife for modification. The locomotive was subsequently altered to a 2-4-0 well tank by replacing the small trailing wheels with a pair 5 feet 6 ins in diameter coupled to the existing driving wheels. The side tanks were also removed and a well tank placed under the bunker, and standard chimney and splashers fitted. The engine as rebuilt was released into traffic but did not return to the Norfolk/Suffolk border line and spent much of is time in the Stratford area where it was recorded derailed with three wagons on 14th December 1864. The locomotive survived for a further fifteen years and was broken up in November 1881.

The original dimensions of the locomotive were:

Cylinders		15 ins x 22 ins	
Boiler	Max diameter	4 feet 3 ins	
	Length	9 feet 5 ins	
Firebox		5 feet 0 ins	
Heating surface			
	Tubes	164 x 1⅞ ins	778.0 sq feet
	Firebox		72.0 sq feet
	Total		850.0 sq feet
Grate area		15.0 sq feet	
Leading wheels		3 feet 6 ins	
Driving wheels		5 feet 6 ins	
Trailing wheels		3 feet 6 ins	
Length over buffers		23 feet 3 ins	
Wheelbase		14 feet 0 ins	

The alterations as rebuilt were:

Max axle loading	11 tons 11 cwt
Weight in working order	31 tons 10 cwt

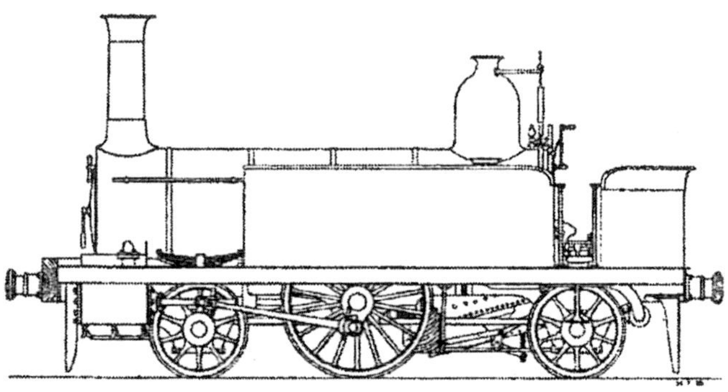

WVR 2-2-2 tank locomotive *Perseverance*, built by Sharp, Stewart & Co. in 1861 and used by the company for independent operation.

Former WVR 2-2-2 tank locomotive as rebuilt by the GER as a 2-4-0 and numbered 30.

Sinclair 'Y' Class 2-4-0 tender locomotives in their declining years were used on the branch freight services. No. 396, by this time on the duplicate list as No. 0396, seen standing at Norwich on 3rd November 1895, is typical of the class. *Author's collection*

Sinclair 'Y' Class 2-4-0 tender locomotive.

THE SINCLAIR 'Y' CLASS

As earlier locomotives were scrapped, Sinclair's celebrated 'Y' Class 2-4-0 freight engines, introduced into service between July 1859 and August 1866, operated goods and some of the passenger services. One hundred and ten locomotives were provided by a variety of makers: Neilson & Company building No's 307 to 326, Robert Stephenson & Company No's 327 to 341, R. & W. Hawthorn No's 342 to 356, Kitson & Company No's 357 to 381, Vulcan Foundry No's 382 to 406 and Schnider et Cie of Creusot No's 407 to 416. Each batch had detailed differences and locomotive No. 327 was displayed at the Exhibition held in Hyde Park, London in 1862. The engines worked all over the GER system on passenger, mixed and goods trains. Over the years most were rebuilt and a number were converted into 4-4-0 locomotives for passenger work. Scrapping of the class commenced in 1882 and after 1888 surviving engines were placed on the duplicate list by having the prefix 0 placed before the running number. The final batch of four locomotives was condemned in 1894.

The principal dimensions of the 327 to 356 batch of locomotives as built were:

Cylinders		17 ins x 24 ins	
Motion		Stephenson with slide valves	
Boiler	Max dia. outside	4 feet 0 ins	
	Length	11 feet 5¾ ins	
Firebox		4 feet 8 ins	
Heating	Tubes	192 x 1⅞ ins	968.52 sq feet
	Firebox		72.36 sq feet
	Total		1,040.88 sq feet
Grate area		13.75 sq feet	
Boiler pressure		120 psi	
Leading wheels		3 feet 7 ins	
Coupled wheels		6 feet 1 in	
Tender wheels		3 feet 7 ins	
Wheelbase			
	Engine	15 feet 1 in	
	Tender	11 feet 5 ins	
Weight in working order			
	Engine	30 tons 16 cwt	
	Tender	21 tons 15 cwt	
	Total	52 tons 11 cwt	
Water capacity		1,600 gallons	

THE NEILSON 2-4-0 TENDER ENGINES

After the line was opened throughout to Beccles the utilisation of tank locomotives was found restrictive and an operational inconvenience so workings of these engines tended to be confined to between Beccles and Tivetshall because of the necessity to top up side tanks with water after each journey. Once through workings were introduced from Norwich to Beccles and Lowestoft tender locomotives were the preferred motive power. Initially when Samuel Johnson became Locomotive Superintendent he found the locomotive stock was insufficient to meet immediate requirements as many older engines were past repair. He thus ordered five 2-4-0 tender locomotives from Neilson & Company of Glasgow, built to the same drawings as twelve engines being built for the North British Railway, which he had put in hand when he was Locomotive Superintendent of that company. To further hasten matters he arranged, with the sanction of the NBR, for five of those actually in hand to be delivered to the GER, with the GER order going to the NBR. The GER engines were No's 125 to 129 inclusive (Maker's No's 1294, 1295, 1296, 1300 and 1301) delivered in February, April and May 1867, all equipped with 4-wheel tenders. No's 126 and 128 were recorded working the Waveney branch services, with the possibility of the others also being utilised. The former disgracing itself by colliding with the buffer stops at Lowestoft on 31st August 1880 and in another collision at Norwich Thorpe on 21st January 1881. None of the class were rebuilt or fitted with continuous brakes and being a precursor of Johnson's famous 'No. 1' Class were withdrawn at an early date: No. 128 being scrapped in 1884, No's 125 and 127 in February 1885 and No's 126 and 1290 (renumbered from 129 in July 1885) in February 1886.

The principal dimensions of the class were:

Cylinders		16 ins x 20 ins	
Motion		Stephenson with slide valves	
Boiler	Barrel length	10 feet 0 ins	
	Diameter	4 feet 3 ins	
Firebox		5 feet 0 ins	
Heating surface			
	Tubes	147 x 2⅛ ins	840.0 sq feet
	Firebox		85.0 sq feet
	Total		925.0 sq feet
Grate area		14.9 sq feet	
Boiler pressure		140 psi	
Leading wheels		3 feet 11½ ins	
Driving wheels		6 feet 0½ ins	
Length	Engine	22 feet 11⅜ ins	
Wheelbase			
	Engine	15 feet 0 ins	
	Tender	8 feet 11 ins	
Weight in working order			
	Engine	30 tons 9 cwt	
	Tender	18 tons 1 cwt	
	Total	48 tons 10 cwt	
Max axle loading		10 tons 16 cwt	

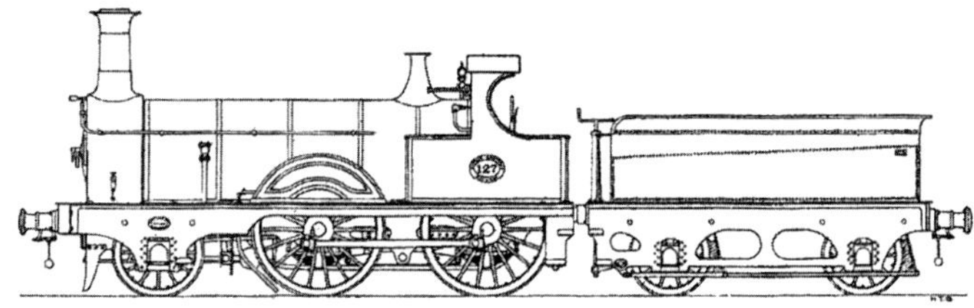

GER 2-4-0 tender locomotive No. 127, built by Neilson & Company of Glasgow.

The 'Little Sharpies'

From introduction Samuel Johnson's No. 1 Class (nicknamed 'Little Sharpies', as Sharp, Stewart & Company built thirty of the forty locomotives) were used on the through trains from Norwich to the branch. These 2-4-0 tender locomotives were built between October 1867 and August 1872, and during the years 1889 and 1893 the whole class was rebuilt when most were then allocated to cross-country and branch line duties. Engines allocated to Norwich and Lowestoft, the latter sub-shedded at Beccles, appeared on these branch workings. In the final years most of the 'Little Sharpies' were transferred to work out their days on branch lines in Norfolk, when occasional visits were still made to the Waveney Valley line. The following were known to have worked the branch services.

GER No.	GER Duplicate No.	Date Duplicated	Withdrawn
1	01	1911	1913
6			1904
26*			1913
31			1902
33			1913
34			1903
48			1911
49			1903
105	0105	1905	1913
107	0107	1905	1913
Note: * Renumbered 30 in 1898.			

Locomotive No. 0107 differed from others of the class by having a steel firebox with the safety valve carried on the second boiler ring. Owing to the forward position, which left the spring lever in a more prominent position, the engine was thereafter referred to as the 'monkey tail' engine by footplatemen.

The principal dimensions of the 'Little Sharpies' were:

Cylinders		16 ins x 22 ins	
Motion		Stephenson with slide valves	
Boiler	Max diameter	4 feet 2 ins	
	Length	9 feet 1 inch	
Firebox		4 feet 6 ins	
Heating surface			
	Tubes	223 x 1⅝ ins	881.24 sq feet
	Firebox		78.00 sq feet
	Total		959.24 sq feet
Grate area		12.4 sq feet	
Boiler pressure		140 psi	
Leading wheels		3 feet 8 ins	
Coupled wheels		5 feet 8 ins	
Tender wheels		3 feet 8 ins	
Weight in working order			
	Engine	30 tons 15 cwt	
	Tender	18 tons 6 cwt	
	Total	49 tons 1 cwt	
Max axle loading		10 tons 10 cwt	
Water capacity		1,184 gallons	

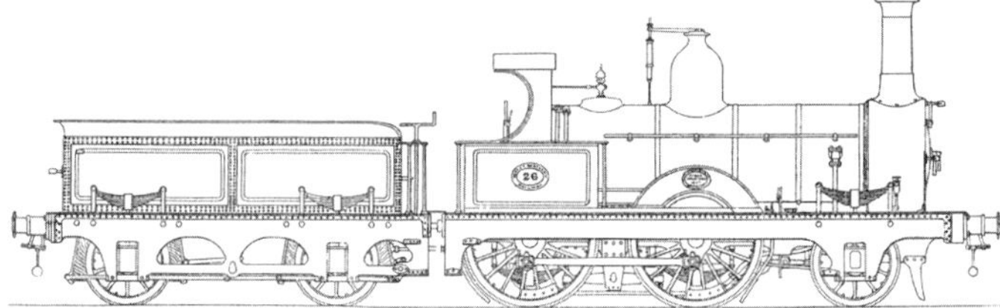

Johnson's 'Little Sharpie' 2-4-0 tender locomotive.

Johnson 'Little Sharpie' 2-4-0 No. 107 built by Sharp Stewart in 1871 was later rebuilt and, in its final form on the duplicate list as No. 0107, regularly worked across the branch on Norwich to Beccles trains. Note the 4-wheel tender. No. 0107 was withdrawn in 1913. *Author's collection*

The 'T26'/'E4' Tender Engines

In 1891 Holden introduced ten 2-4-0 tender locomotives into service. In the next ten years a further ninety of these 'T26' Class engines were built and nicknamed 'Intermediates'. Both Norwich and Lowestoft shed received an allocation and, as well as working main line services, the class members were diagrammed for through trains from Norwich to Beccles and Lowestoft via the Waveney Valley route. One round trip was regularly rostered for 'light work' men from Norwich on an out and back basis, which involved a number of separately timed trains, constituting a full shift for the locomotive men. The L&NER reclassified the 'T26s' to Class 'E4' but soon after grouping many were withdrawn from service and thereafter visits to the branch were not so regular. From 1942 only eighteen remained in service, mostly at Cambridge and Norwich, and the Norfolk based engines were still rostered for passenger excursion work on the Waveney Valley until withdrawal from service. Locomotives known to have worked across the branch are listed below.

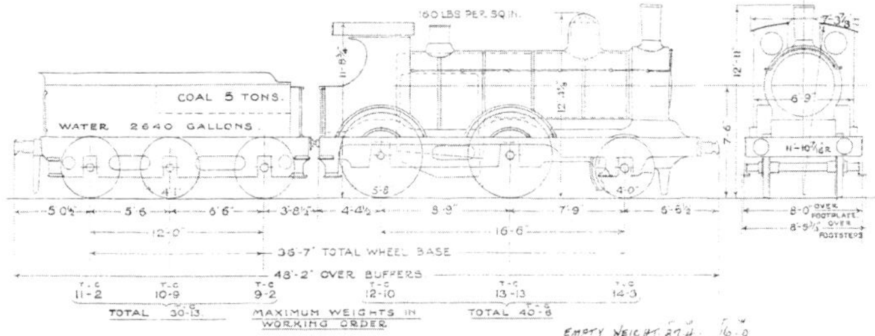

Holden GER 'T26' Class, later L&NER 'E4' Class, 2-4-0 tender locomotive.

The principal dimensions of the 'E4' Class were:

Cylinders	2 inside	17½ ins x 24 ins	
Motion		Stephenson with slide valves	
Boiler	Max diameter	4 feet 4 ins	
	Barrel length	10 feet 0 ins	
Firebox		6 feet 0 ins	
Heating surface			
	Tubes	242 x 1⅝ ins	1,063.8 sq feet
	Firebox		100.9 sq feet
	Total		1,164.7 sq feet
Grate area		18.0 sq feet	
Boiler pressure		160 psi	
Leading wheels		4 feet 0 ins	
Driving wheels		5 feet 8 ins	
Tractive effort		14,700 lbs	
Length over buffers		48 feet 2 ins *	
Wheelbase		36 feet 7 ins *	
Weight in working order		40 tons 6 cwt	
Max axle loading		14 tons 3 cwt	
Tender			
	Wheelbase		12 feet 0 ins
	Wheel diameter		4 feet 1 in
	Weight in working order		30 tons 13 cwt
	Water capacity		2,640 gallons
	Coal capacity		5 tons

Note: * Engine and tender.

GER No.	L&NER 1924 No.	L&NER 1946 No.	BR No.	Withdrawn	GER No.	L&NER 1924 No.	L&NER 1946 No.	BR No.	Withdrawn
407	7407	2792	62792	June 1956 (1)	451	7451	—	—	February 1929
408	7408	2793	62793	February 1955	452	7452	—	—	September 1929
413	7413	—	—	October 1931	453	7453	—	—	March 1935
415	7415	—	—	June 1937	466	7466	2782	62782	November 1954 (2)
416	7416	2797	62797	March 1958	472	7472	—	—	May 1938
420	7420	—	—	March 1927	474	7474	—	—	April 1929
423	7423	—	—	July 1926	484	7484	—	—	March 1936
426	7426	—	—	October 1926	485	7485	—	—	January 1940
428	7428	—	—	May 1929	486	7486	—	—	January 1931
429	7429	—	—	October 1929	487	7487	—	—	December 1929
439	7439	—	—	August 1927	489	7489	—	—	March 1936
440	7440	—	—	June 1929	490	7490	2785	62785	December 1959
442	7442	—	—	December 1927	491	7491	—	—	January 1935
443	7443	—	—	October 1931	492	7492	2786	62786	July 1956
445	7445	—	—	January 1927	493	7493	—	—	July 1929
446	7446	—	—	April 1926	494	7494	2787	62787	November 1956
447	7447	—	—	September 1926	495	7495	—	—	May 1928
448	7448	—	—	January 1930	496	7496	2788	62788	March 1958 (3)
449	7449	—	—	February 1930	497	7497	2789	62789	December 1957
450	7450	—	—	May 1927					

Notes:

1. 7407 became 7791 in the L&NER 1942 renumbering scheme.
2. 7466 became 7802 in the L&NER 1942 renumbering scheme.
3. 7496 became 7805 in the L&NER 1942 renumbering scheme.

'E4' Class 2-4-0 No. 7415 fitted with a stovepipe chimney, wooden cab roof and coupled to a watercart tender is shown at Stratford in April 1932. This locomotive was regularly employed on Norwich to Beccles services via the Waveney Valley but was withdrawn from traffic in June 1937.
Author's collection

Samuel Johnson's 0-4-4 Tank Engines

The extension of lines in the north-east London suburban district – opened from Bethnal Green to Stoke Newington on 27th May 1872, Hackney Downs to Copper Mill Junction on 22nd June 1872, Stoke Newington to Edmonton Junction on 22nd July 1872 and Clapton through Hall Farm Junction and on to Chingford on 17th November 1873 – and the subsequent growth in traffic necessitated an increase in locomotives. Samuel Johnson designed a 0-4-4 class of tank locomotive for these duties, fifteen coming from Neilson & Company between November 1872 and April 1873 (Maker's No's 1707 to 1716 and 1736 to 1740) and fifteen from the Avonside Engineering Company between October 1872 and September 1873 (Maker's No's 917 to 926 and 978 to 982). The Neilson engines were numbered 134 to 139 and 162 to 170 by the GER, whilst the Avonside engines received the numbers 186 to 199. Initially only straight weatherboards were provided for the protection of footplate crews but later they were fitted with a small cab for forward running. As built, a hand brake activated wooden blocks on all four coupled wheels, but the entire class was equipped with the Westinghouse brake when rebuilt at Stratford Works between 1885 and 1894. After the class was displaced from the London suburban services the majority of engines were transferred to the Norwich district, with others going to Cambridge and Ipswich. During this period both Norwich and Lowestoft engines worked the Waveney Valley Branch services, including No's 165, 169, 186, 192, 193, 195 and 199. Several of the class were transferred to the duplicate list by having the prefix 0 added to the running number. No. 0165 worked the first train from Lowestoft to Yarmouth and return on the opening of the new line of the Norfolk & Suffolk Joint Committee on 13th July 1903, whilst others were involved in serious mishaps, including No's 186 and 192 which collided head on at Barnby between Beccles and Lowestoft on a foggy Christmas Eve 1901. Fortunately no mishaps were recorded when the class were working the Waveney Valley services. No. 0165 was withdrawn in 1905, 0169 and 186 in 1907, 0192 and 193 in 1902, and 0195 and 0199 in 1904.

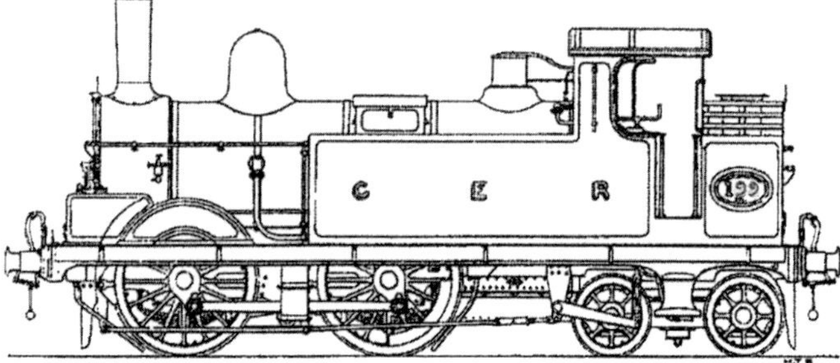

Johnson 0-4-4 tank locomotive No. 199, which worked the Waveney Valley line after displacement from the London suburban services.

The leading dimensions of the class were:

Cylinders	2 inside	17 ins x 24 ins	
Motion		Stephenson with slide valves	
Boiler	Max diameter	4 feet 0 ins	
	Length	10 feet 0 ins	
Firebox		5 feet 5 ins	
Heating surface			
	Tubes	247 x 1½ ins	1,000.9 sq feet
	Firebox		100.0 sq feet
	Total		1,100.9 sq feet
Grate area		16.62 sq feet	
Boiler pressure		140 psi	
Driving wheels		5 feet 4 ins	
Trailing wheels		2 feet 10 ins	
Wheelbase		21 feet 0 ins	
Weight in working order			
	No's 186 to 189	46 tons 18 cwt	
	Remainder	45 tons 9 cwt	
Max axle loading			
	No's 186 to 189	17 tons 8 cwt	
	Remainder	16 tons 11 cwt	
Water capacity			
	No's 186 to 189	1,080 gallons	
	Remainder	960 gallons	

Samuel Johnson's 0-4-4T No. 193, one of a class of thirty locomotives used on London suburban services before being relegated to work country branch lines. No. 193 was used on Waveney Valley services and here supports a half cab, which was later replaced by a full cab. It was withdrawn in 1902. *Author's collection*

The 'C32'/ 'F3' Class

The fifty 'C32' Class 2-4-2 tank locomotives designed by James Holden and built between 1893 and 1902 at Stratford works then took over some of the branch services. When initially introduced into traffic they worked the principal longer distance semi-fast services from Liverpool Street to Bishop's Stortford and later from Liverpool Street to Southend and Southminster. Soon after the turn of the century many were displaced and sent to GER country depots, when Beccles and Norwich sheds received a selection of the class for Waveney Valley diagrams. The 'C32's were reclassified 'F3' by the L&NER after grouping and remained

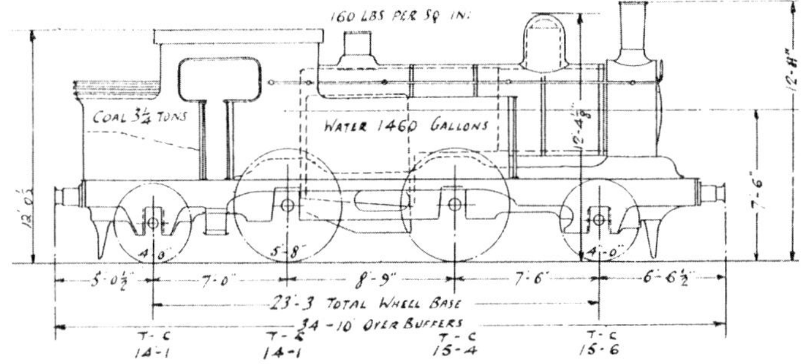

GER 'C32' Class, later L&NER 'F3' Class 2-4-2 tank locomotive.

'F3' Class 2-4-2T No. 8095 was one of a number of the class used on local Tivetshall to Beccles passenger services. It became No. 7117 under the L&NER 1946 renumbering scheme and was withdrawn from traffic in May 1948. *Author's collection*

the mainstay on the branch services for many years. Locomotives known to have worked the line included:

GER No.	L&NER 1924 No.	L&NER No.	BR No.	WITHDRAWN
1040	8040	7141	—	May 1948
1045	8045	7146	—	August 1947
1047	8047	7148	—	July 1947
1048	8048	7149	67149	July 1949
1049	8049	7150	—	October 1949
1061	8061	7134	—	May 1948
1067	8067	7139	—	December 1950
1078	8078	7126	—	January 1950
1079	8079	7127	67127	April 1953
1080	8080	—	—	December 1938
1086	8086	—	—	April 1938
1087	8087	—	—	October 1938
1088	8088	7131	—	November 1947
1089	8089	7132	—	November 1947
1091	8091	—	—	July 1938
1092	8092	7114	—	March 1948
1093	8093	7115	—	May 1948
1094	8094	7116	—	November 1947
1095	8095	7117	—	May 1948
1096	8096	7118	—	August 1947
1097	8097	7119	—	February 1948
1098	8098	—	—	December 1937
1099	8099	7120	—	December 1947

The leading dimensions of the 'F3' Class were:

Cylinders	2 inside	17½ ins x 24 ins	
Motion		Stephenson with slide valves	
Boiler	Max diameter	4 feet 4 ins	
	Barrel length	10 feet 0 ins	
	Firebox length	6 feet 0 ins	
Heating surface			
	Tubes	242 x 1⅝ ins	1,063.8 sq feet
	Firebox		100.9 sq feet
	Total		1,164.7 sq feet
Grate area		18.0 sq feet	
Boiler pressure		160 psi	
Leading wheels		4 feet 0 ins	
Coupled wheels		5 feet 8 ins	
Trailing wheels		4 feet 0 ins	
Tractive effort		14,700 lbs	
Length over buffers		34 feet 10 ins	
Wheelbase		23 feet 3 ins	
Weight in working order		58 tons 12 cwt	
Max axle load		15 tons 6 cwt	
Water capacity		1,460 gallons	
Coal capacity		3 tons 5 cwt	

'F3' Class 2-4-2T No. 8067, also used on Waveney Valley services, became 7139 in the L&NER 1946 renumbering scheme before withdrawal in December 1950. *Author's collection*

The 'M15'/'F4' and 'M15R'/'F5' Classes

Working turn and turn about with the 'F3' Class were some of the 'F4' Class 2-4-2 tank engines. The initial forty members of the 'M15' Class entered service between 1884 and 1887 to the design of T.W. Worsdell. Between 1903 and 1909 a further 120 locomotives were built, and from 1911 to 1920 the GER rebuilt thirty engines with higher boiler pressure and designated these M15R. The earliest built locomotives were all condemned by 1929, whilst the L&NER reclassified the 'M15's to Class 'F4' and the rebuilt engines to Class 'F5'. They were nicknamed 'Gobblers' because the original engines fitted with Joy's valve gear had a voracious appetite for coal and although improvements were made the name persisted. The following 'F4' and 'F5' Class engines travelled across the branch from Tivetshall to Beccles – chiefly on passenger turns but were not unknown to haul the occasional freight train, although care had to be taken with maintaining water supplies.

'F4' Class

GER No.	L&NER 1924 No.	L&NER 1946 No.	BR No.	Withdrawn
74	7074	7182	67182	January 1953
76	7076	7184	67184	December 1952
78	7178	7186	67186	July 1953
171	7171	7167	67167	September 1952
180	7180	7174	67174	December 1954
185	7185	7176	67176	July 1953
186	7186	7177	67177	March 1951
187	7187	7178	67178	August 1952
219	7219	7163	67163	December 1951
232	7232	7165	67165	January 1951
233	7233	7166	67166	April 1952
579	7579	7156	—	November 1950
584	7584	7158	67158	January 1953
654	7654	—	—	November 1927
666	7666	—	—	March 1926
677	7677	—	—	April 1925
678	7678	—	—	November 1929

'F5' Class

GER No.	L&NER 1924 No.	L&NER 1946 No.	BR No.	Withdrawn
179	7179	7216	67216	December 1956
788	7788	7201	67201	December 1956

The leading dimensions of the 'F4' Class were:

Cylinders	2 inside	17½ ins x 24 in	
Motion		Stephenson with slide valves	
Boiler	Max dia. outside	4 feet 2 ins	
	Barrel length	10 feet 2½ ins	
Firebox outside length		5 feet 5 ins	
Heating surface			
	Tubes	227 x 1⅝ ins	1,018.0 sq feet
	Firebox		98.4 sq feet
	Total		1,116.4 sq feet
Grate area		15.3 sq feet	
Boiler pressure		160 psi	
Leading wheels		3 feet 9 ins	
Coupled wheels		5 feet 4 ins	
Trailing wheels		3 feet 9 ins	
Tractive effort		15,618 lbs	
Length over buffers		34 feet 10 ins	
Wheelbase		23 feet 0 ins	
Weight in working order		51 tons 11 cwt	
Max axle loading		14 tons 18 cwt	
Water capacity		1,200 gallons	
Coal capacity		3 tons 10 cwt	

The detail differences of the 'F5' Class were:

Heating surface			
	Firebox		96.7 sq feet
	Total		1,114.7 sq feet
Grate area		15.2 sq feet	
Boiler pressure		180 psi	
Tractive effort		17,571 lbs	
Weight in working order		53 tons 19 cwt	
Max axle loading		16 tons 0 cwt	

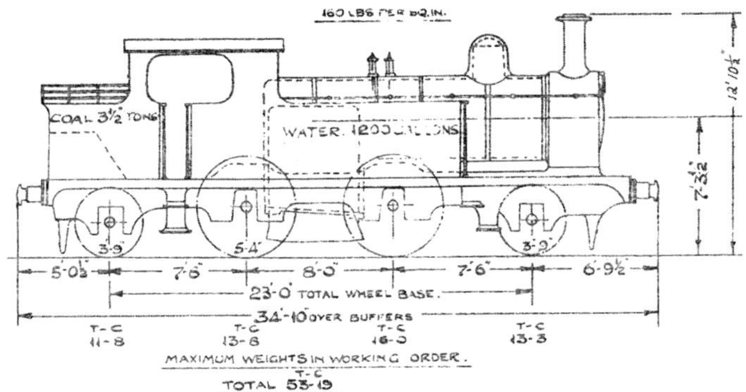

GER 'M15' Class, later L&NER 'F4' Class, 2-4-2 tank locomotive.

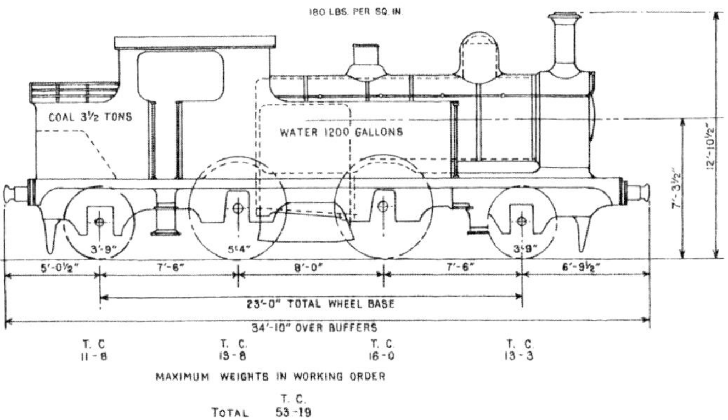

GER 'M15R' Class, later L&NER 'F5' Class, 2-4-2 tank locomotive.

'F4' Class 2-4-2T No. 7219, later renumbered by the L&NER in the 1946 scheme to 7163, regularly worked on the Waveney Valley Branch. It was renumbered to 67163 by BR and was withdrawn from service in December 1951. *Author's collection*

The '9G'/'F2' Class

In 1898 Harry Pollitt introduced ten of his '9G' Class 2-4-2 tank locomotives for suburban work on the Great Central Railway, all being built by Beyer, Peacock. When new the engines were allocated to Altrincham, Gorton and Lincoln sheds but later they served time at Walton-on-the-Hill and Gorton. The L&NER reclassified the class as 'F2' and in 1936 four were auto fitted for push-pull working and transferred to East Anglia to replace five Clayton steam railcars which had proved unsuccessful in the Norwich area: No's 5778, 5783 and 5784 at Norwich and No. 5781 at Lowestoft. No's 5781 and 5784 later went to Yarmouth South Town shed in November 1940 and for the next nine years worked the Yarmouth to Beccles service. In 1941 two of the Norwich locomotives were transferred to Stratford for use on the Epping to Ongar line. The four locomotives had their weight redistributed to allow them to pass over RA3 routes and, although it usually worked the Lowestoft to Beccles service, in August 1937 No. 5781 was noted hauling a Waveney Valley train on a Lowestoft diagram involving a through working from Lowestoft to Tivetshall and return, with the engine running round the train at Beccles. Then in March 1942 No. 5784 was borrowed to work the Waveney Valley service, a further sighting being made later in the war years.

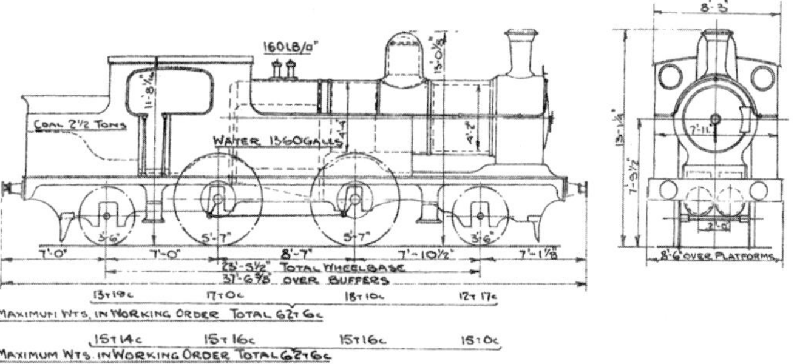

GCR '9G' Class 2-4-2, later L&NER 'F2' Class, 2-4-2 tank locomotive.

GCR No.	L&NER 1924 No.	L&NER 1946 No.	BR No.	Withdrawn
781	5781	7109	—	November 1949
784	5784	7112	—	May 1949

The principal dimensions of the 'F2' Class were:

Cylinders	2 inside	18 ins x 26 ins	
Motion		Stephenson with slide valves	
Boiler	Max dia. outside	4 feet 4 ins	
	Barrel length	10 feet 8⅛ ins	
Firebox	Length outside	6 feet 0 ins	
Heating surface			
	Tubes	190 x 1¾ ins	964.0 sq feet
	Firebox		99.0 sq feet
	Total		1,063.0 sq feet
Grate area		18.3 sq feet	
Boiler pressure		160 psi	
Leading wheels		3 feet 6 ins	
Coupled wheels		5 feet 7 ins	
Trailing wheels		3 feet 6 ins	
Tractive effort		17,100 lbs	
Length over buffers		37 feet 6⅝ ins	
Wheelbase		23 feet 5½ ins	
Weight in working order		62 tons 6 cwt	
Max axle loading		15 tons 16 cwt	
Water capacity		1,360 gallons	
Coal capacity		2 tons 10 cwt	

Sentinel Steam Railcar

In September 1931 the L&NER authorities arranged for a twin-engine 6-cylinder gear-driven 200 hp Sentinel steam railcar to work trials in the Norwich area with a view to possible replacement of steam locomotives and hauled coaches on lightly used services, thereby effecting economies. The vehicle chosen was No. 2203 *Old Blue* (Works No. 7823), built to diagram 98, which entered service on 17th October 1930, painted green and cream. Initially allocated to Guisborough on the former North Eastern section of the L&NER, the car spent six months at St. Margarets, Edinburgh before working five days of trials at Norwich from 14th to 19th September during which it was evaluated on the Tivetshall to Beccles service. *Old Blue* then moved on to Ipswich on 19th and 20th of the month before completing trials at Cambridge from 21st to 25th. The vehicle then returned to Guisborough from where it was withdrawn on 8th September 1941. The leading dimensions of *Old Blue* were:

Cylinders	(2 x 6)	6 ins x 7 ins
Horsepower nominal		200 hp
Transmission		Gear and cardan shaft
Boiler pressure		300 psi
Bogie wheels		3 feet 1 inch
Wheelbase	Front bogie	7 feet 0 ins
	Rear bogie	7 feet 0 ins
	Total	52 feet 6 ins
Length over body		61 feet 6 ins
Width over body		9 feet 0 ins
Length over buffers		65 feet 8 ins
Seating		54
Weight without coal and water		42 tons 12 cwt

The 'C2'/'C12' Class

In 1935 former Great Northern Railway Ivatt 'C2' Class, L&NER 'C12' Class, 4-4-2 tank locomotive No. 4016 made several appearances on the Waveney Valley services deputizing for the normal 'F3' Class 2-4-2 tank engine during its wanderings in the Norwich and Ipswich districts. The locomotive was not popular with local crews and finally settled at Parkeston shed. The class was introduced between 1898 and 1907 for use on the GNR London suburban services and also in the West Riding of Yorkshire. On being displaced on the services from Kings Cross by the Ivatt and Gresley 0-6-2 tank locomotives, later L&NER 'N1' and 'N2' classes, many 'C2's were dispersed to country depots and it is thought that after grouping No. 4016 was sent to the former GER section for evaluation. In later years after nationalisation four of the class worked on the Saffron Walden Branch whilst others saw service on the Bury St. Edmunds to Long Melford and Thetford to Swaffham services. For a short while in the early 1950s, No. 67387, allocated to Yarmouth South Town shed and fitted with push-pull gear, also worked shuttle services to Lowestoft as well as Beccles and Saxmundham over the East Suffolk line. During that time it was 'borrowed' by Beccles on one occasion to work a round trip to Tivetshall, covering for a failed engine.

GNR No.	L&NER 1924 No.	L&NER 1946 No.	BR No.	Withdrawn
1016	4016	7355	—	March 1948
1537	4537	7387	67387	February 1955

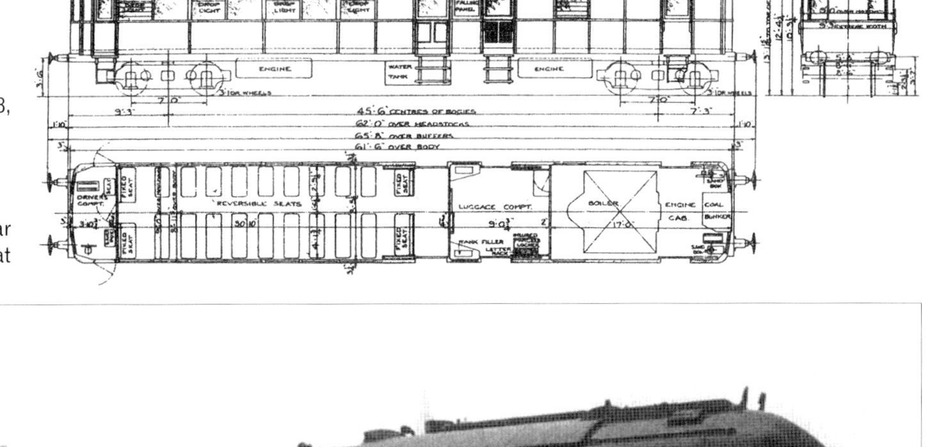

Right: Sentinel steam railcar to diagram 98, No. 2283 *Old Blue*.

Below: Sentinel twin engine 6-cylinder gear driven car No. 2203 *Old Blue* to diagram 98 at Middlesbrough in 1932.

The leading dimensions of the 'C12' Class were:

Cylinders	2 inside	18 ins x 26 ins	
Motion		Stephenson with slide valves	
Boiler	Max diameter	4 feet 5 ins	
	Barrel length	10 feet 1 in	
Firebox		5 feet 6 ins	
Heating surface			
	Tubes	213 x 1¾ ins	1,016.0 sq feet
	Firebox		103.0 sq feet
	Total		1,119.0 sq feet
Grate area		16.25 sq feet	
Boiler pressure		170 psi	
Leading wheels		3 feet 8 ins	
Coupled wheels		5 feet 8 ins	
Trailing wheels		3 feet 8 ins	
Tractive effort		17,900 lbs	
Length over buffers		36 feet 9¼ ins	
Wheelbase		27 feet 3 ins	
Weight in working order		62 tons 6 cwt	
Water capacity		1,350 gallons	
Coal capacity		2 tons 5 cwt	

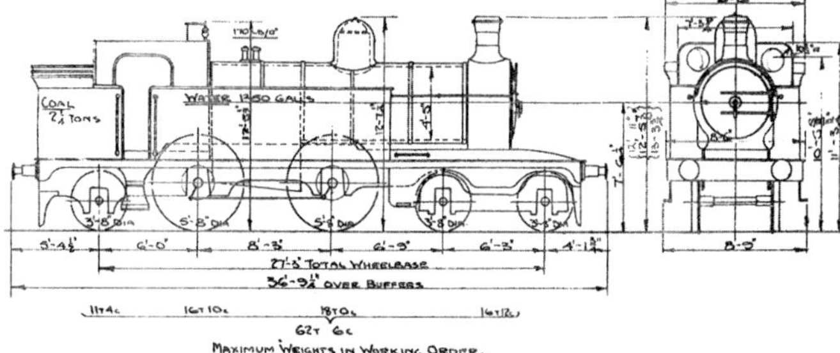

GNR 'C2' Class, later L&NER 'C'12 Class, 4-4-2 tank locomotive.

The 'N7' Class

Gresley's 'N7' Class 0-6-2 tank locomotives, based on A.J. Hill's GER design, made occasional visits to the branch in the later years working special trips to Pulham Market in connection with the delivery or removal of military traffic from Pulham airfield as well as goods diagrams. The Norwich based engines were popular with enginemen on such tasks because of their enclosed cab and high tractive effort. Those known to have appeared on such workings were:

L&NER No.	Built	Class No.	L&NER 1946 No.	BR No.	Withdrawn
2639	Gorton	N7/3	9679	69679	January 1961
2604	Doncaster	N7/3	9706	69706	December 1960
2605	Doncaster	N7/3	9707	69707	April 1961
2606	Doncaster	N7/3	9708	69708	January 1961
2607	Doncaster	N7/3	9709	69709	November 1960

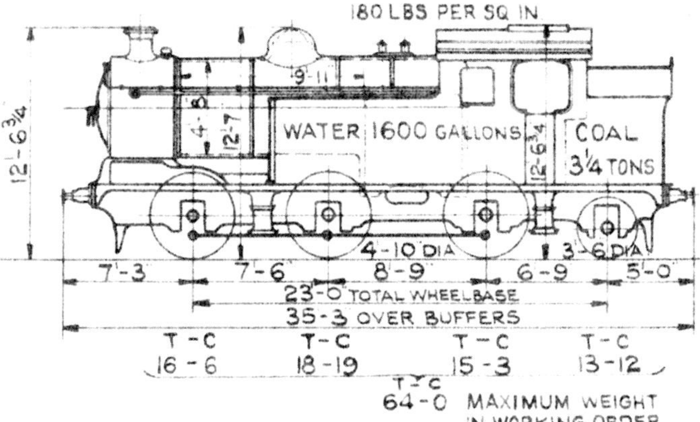

Gresley L&NER 'N7/3' Class 0-6-2 tank locomotive.

'N7/3' Class 0-6-2T No. 69679 approaching Pulham Market with a short freight train along the siding from Pulham RAF station in June 1951. The main single Waveney Valley Branch is to the left. *Dr I.C. Allen*

The principal dimensions of the 'N7/3' Class were:

Cylinders	2 inside	18 ins x 24 ins	
Motion		Walschaerts with 9-in piston valves	
Boiler	Max diameter	4 feet 8 ins	
	Barrel length	9 feet 7 ins	
	Firebox	6 feet 0 ins	
Heating surface			
	Tubes	132 x $1\frac{3}{4}$ ins	599.6 sq feet
	Flues	18 ins x 5 ins	232.2 sq feet
	Firebox		107.3 sq feet
	Total evaporative		938.1 sq feet
	Superheater	18 x $1\frac{3}{32}$ ins	134.2 sq feet
	Total		1,072.3 sq feet
Grate area		17.7 sq feet	
Boiler pressure		180 psi	
Coupled wheels		4 feet 10 ins	
Trailing wheels		3 feet 6 ins	
Length over buffers		35 feet 3 ins	
Tractive effort		20,512 lbs	
Wheelbase		23 feet 0 ins	
Weight in working order		64 tons 0 cwt	
Max axle loading		18 tons 19 cwt	
Coal capacity		3 tons 5 cwt	
Water capacity		1,600 gallons	

The 'B12/3' Class

In the years following World War Two, Gresley's rebuild of Holden's 'S69' Class 4-6-0 tender locomotives, the L&NER 'B12/3' Class were occasionally used on the branch, usually on engineering trains after the withdrawal of the passenger services but especially when the Ipswich breakdown crane was required to assist in the removal of timber from Bungay yard in 1952. Even then they were restricted from working between Bungay and Beccles. The locomotives were first introduced in 1911 when the GER authorities were finding the Claud Hamilton 'D15' and 'D16' Class 4-4-0 tender locomotives struggling with ever increasing heavy trains. Known as the '1500's from the number of the initial engine, a total of seventy-one were built to 1921, although one of these was totally written off after a fatal crash at Colchester. After grouping the locomotives were allocated to Class 'B12' and a further ten engines were introduced. With the introduction of the Gresley 'B17' Class 3-cylinder 4-6-0

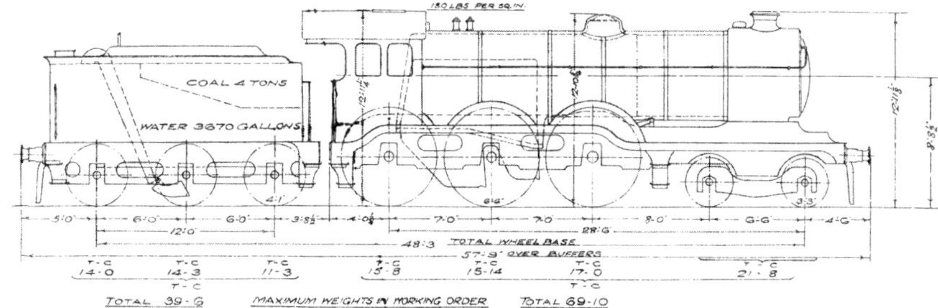

S.D. Holden GER 'S69' Class, later L&NER 'B12/3' Class, 4-6-0 tender locomotive.

'B12/3' Class 4-6-0 No. 61535 standing with the Ipswich breakdown crane in Bungay yard early in 1952 during a campaign to load and remove many tons of damaged trees brought down by gale force winds. *Dr I.C. Allen*

tender locomotives from 1928 and a general improvement in motive power availability, the L&NER found several 'B12's could be made available for use on other sections of their system. Accordingly, between 1931 and 1942 several of the class migrated to the Great North of Scotland section, working trains from Aberdeen to Keith and Elgin. Most of the class that remained on the GE section were subsequently rebuilt between 1932 and 1944 with a larger boiler and other alterations and were designated to Class 'B12/3'. Norwich and Ipswich depots had a large allocation and it was from these that the occasional forays were made over the Waveney Valley line; those known to have entered the branch were:

GER No.	L&NER 1924 No.	L&NER 1948 No.	BR No.	WITHDRAWN
1535	8535*	1535	61535	December 1959
	8577*	1577	61577	December 1959
Note: *	In the 1942 renumbering scheme 8535 became 7449 and 8577 became 7491.			

The leading dimensions of the 'B12/3' Class were:

Cylinders	2 inside	20 ins x 28 ins	
Motion		Stephenson with 10-in piston valves	
Boiler	Max diameter	5 feet 6 ins	
	Barrel length	12 feet 7½ ins	
Firebox	Outside length	10 feet 1½ ins	
Heating surface			
	Tubes	143 x 2 ins	979.0 sq feet
	Flues	24 x 5¼ ins	426.0 sq feet
	Firebox		154.0 sq feet
	Total evaporative		1,559.0 sq feet
	Superheater	24 x 1 7/32 ins	315.0 sq feet
	Total		1,874.0 sq feet
Grate area		31.0 sq feet	
Boiler pressure		180 psi	
Tractive effort		21,969 lbs	
Leading wheels		3 feet 3 ins	
Coupled wheels		6 feet 6 ins	
Tender wheels		4 feet 1 in	
Length over buffers		57 feet 9 ins	
Wheelbase			
	Engine	28 feet 6 ins	
	Tender	12 feet 0 ins	
	Total	48 feet 3 ins	
Weight in working order			
	Engine	69 tons 10 cwt	
	Tender	39 tons 6 cwt	
	Total	108 tons 16 cwt	
Max axle loading		17 tons 0 cwt	
Coal capacity		4 tons 0 cwt	
Water capacity		3,670 gallons	

THE 'D16/3' CLASS

The L&NER 'D14', 'D15' and 'D16' Class 4-4-0 tender locomotives made sporadic visits to the branch but only on special workings and in the latter years working freight services, although their 7 feet 0 inches driving wheels were most unsuitable for yard shunting when they were deputising for a failed 'J15' or 'J17' Class 0-6-0. Even then the classes were restricted from working the eastern end of the branch because of weak timber bridges. The 111 GER 'S46' and 'D56' classes, later L&NER 'D14' and 'D15' classes dated from 1900 and were built at Stratford, with the last ten emerging as Class 'D16' in 1923. Throughout the years many were rebuilt and the majority that survived into BR ownership formed the 'D16/3' sub-class. Locomotive known to have strayed on to the Waveney Valley Branch were:

GER No.	L&NER 1924 No.	L&NER 1946 No.	BR No.	WITHDRAWN
1871	8871	2522	62522	August 1958
1869	8869	2540	62540	August 1959
1841	8841	2552	62552	October 1955
1814	8814	2585	62585	April 1955
1802	8802	2593	62593	October 1957
1781	8781	2612	62612	November 1959

The leading dimensions of the 'D16/3' Class were:

Cylinders	2 inside	10 ins x 26 ins	
Motion		Stephenson with slide valves	
Boiler	Max diameter	5 feet 1⅛ ins	
	Barrel length	11 feet 9 ins	
	Firebox	7 feet 0 ins	
Heating surface			
	Tubes	172 x 1¾ ins	957.1 sq feet
	Flues	21 x 5¼ ins	346.3 sq feet
	Firebox		126.0 sq feet
	Total evaporative		1,429.4 sq feet
	Superheater	21 x 1¼ ins	302.5 sq feet
	Total		1,731.9 sq feet
Grate area		21.0 sq feet	
Boiler pressure		180 psi	
Leading wheels		3 feet 9 ins	
Coupled wheels		7 feet 0 ins	
Tender wheels		4 feet 1 in	
Length over buffers		53 feet 2 ins	
Weight in working order			
	Engine	53 tons 19 cwt	
	Tender	39 tons 5 cwt	
	Total	95 tons 3 cwt	
Max axle loading		18 tons 14 cwt	
Water capacity		3,450 gallons	
Coal capacity		5 tons 0 cwt	

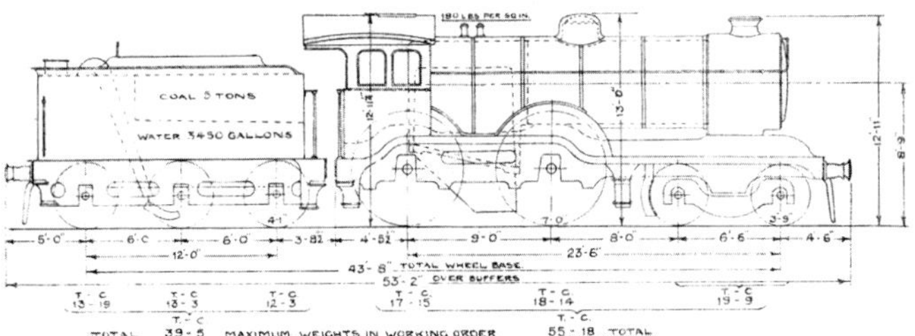

LEFT: L&NER 'D16/3' 4-4-0 tender locomotive.

'D16/3' Class 4-4-0 No. 62540 pulls out of Harleston goods yard with a special freight train en route to Norwich conveying consignments to the Midlands. The 7 feet diameter driving wheels of these main line engines was not conducive to shunting, especially when the rails were damp, and on the few occasions when a member of the class was diagrammed to work the branch goods train in the absence of a 'J15' or 'J17' Class 0-6-0, footplate crews threatened to refuse to take the locomotives. However, gentle persuasion by the shed foreman with an offer of overtime usually solved the crisis. *Dr I.C. Allen*

Stephenson's 'Long Boiler' Freight Engines

In the mists of time it is uncertain which locomotives worked the freight services across the branch at the outset. Certainly in the early years the through services from Norwich to Ipswich were hauled by R. Stephenson's 'Long Boiler' 2-4-0 tender locomotives delivered to the ECR between March and September 1847. Numbered in the series 71 to 77 they regularly worked the East Suffolk line in the first decade after opening. They were the subject of several modifications and rebuilding, No's 71 and 77 receiving new boilers in 1860 whilst No's 72 and 75 were rebuilt in June 1867. Several were placed on the duplicate list, No's 71, 72 and 75 becoming 710, 720 and 750 respectively in 1876. The locomotives were scrapped as follows: No. 710 in May 1878, No. 720 in September 1877, No. 73 in November 1869, No. 74 in April 1859, No. 750 in April 1881, No. 76 in July 1868 and No. 77 in August 1871. The leading dimensions of the class as modified by Robert Sinclair, the locomotive superintendent of the ECR and GER from 1856 to 1866, were:

Cylinders		15 ins x 22 ins	
Boiler	Max diameter	3 feet 8 ins	
	Length	13 feet 8½ ins	
Firebox		4 feet 2 ins	
Heating surface			
	Tubes	123 x 1⅞ins	838.5 sq feet
	Firebox		67.6 sq feet
	Total		906.1 sq feet
Grate area		10.8 sq feet	
Boiler pressure		110 psi	
Leading wheels		3 feet 6 ins	
Coupled wheels		6 feet 0 ins	
Wheelbase Engine		11 feet 7 ins	

Robert Stephenson 'Long Boiler' 2-4-0 tender locomotive.

Six-Coupled Goods Engines

Between 1854 and 1855 John V. Gooch, Locomotive Superintendent of the ECR from 1850 to 1856, introduced into service five 6-coupled goods engines with fairly new boilers taken from five large Crampton singles which were scrapped through lack of adhesion. The five 0-6-0 tender locomotives, numbered 233 to 237, were built at Stratford Works and had outside bearings. They served at Ipswich and Norwich for a while, working the East Suffolk line and main line pick up freight services, during which time they were diagrammed for the branch freight services. New boilers designed by Sinclair were fitted to No's 234 and 236 in October 1867, whilst Johnson rebuilt the remaining three engines in 1869 and 1870. The five engines were placed on the duplicate list in 1880 by having a cipher added to their running number but they only survived for a few more years in service, No. 234 being scrapped in April 1882, No's 233 and 235 in January 1883, No. 237 in October 1883 and No. 236 in November 1884.

The leading dimensions of the Johnson rebuilt engines were:

Cylinders		16 ins x 24 ins	
Motion		Stephenson with slide valves	
Boiler	Max dia. outside	4 feet 0 ins	
	Length	9 feet 11¼ ins	
Firebox		5 feet 1¾ ins	
Grate area		15.5 sq feet	
Heating surface			
	Tubes	157 x 2 ins	841.5 sq feet
	Firebox		89.65 sq feet
	Total		931.15 sq feet
Boiler pressure		140 psi	
Driving wheels		5 feet 0 ins	
Wheelbase			
	Engine	14 feet 6 ins	
	Tender	10 feet 2 ins	
Weight in working order			
	Engine	27 tons 7 cwt	
	Tender	17 tons 1 cwt	
	Total	44 tons 8 cwt	
Max axle loading		10 tons 15 cwt	

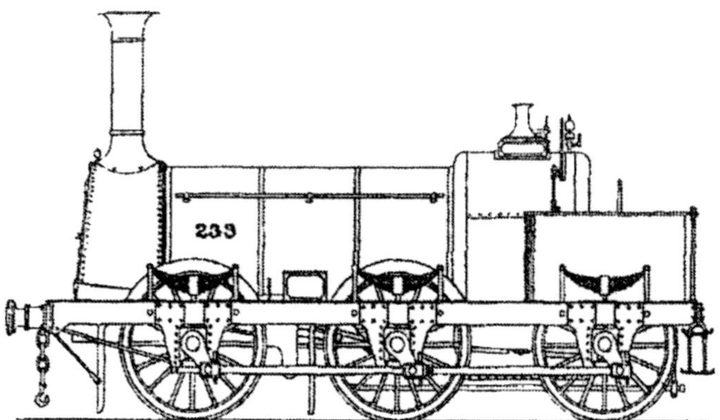

Gooch 6-coupled tender locomotive No. 233.

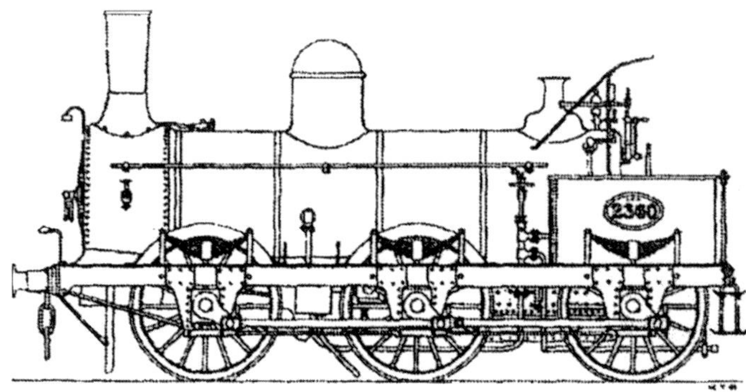

Gooch 6-coupled tender locomotive No. 2360.

Johnson's '417' and '477' Class 0-6-0 tender locomotives were used on freight workings across the Waveney Valley line after displacement from main line duties. The '477' Class was an improved '417' Class and was coupled to a 6-wheel tender. Here '477' Class No. 512 stands beside a GER 3-plank open wagon fitted with dumb buffers and sacking protection over the axleboxes. *Author's collection*

The '417' Class

From the 1880s a variety of 0-6-0 tender locomotives were used on the daily freight services. The first of these was the '417' Class 0-6-0s designed by S.W. Johnson and built between 1867 and 1869 by Neilson & Company and the Worcester Engine Company. The sixty members of the class were numbered 417 to 476 inclusive and initially worked main line goods trains, but on the introduction of the '477' Class and 'Y14' Class 0-6-0 tender locomotives they were relegated to pick-up freights and branch line work. The various members of the class allocated to Norwich and Lowestoft depots worked out their last years on the Waveney Valley goods services. The first of the class was withdrawn in 1888 and scrapping continued every year, with the exception of 1897, until 1899. The survivors after 1891 were placed on the duplicate list by having a prefix 0 added to the number.

The principal dimensions of the '417' Class were:

Cylinders	2 inside	16½ ins x 24 ins	
Motion		Stephenson with slide valves	
Boiler	Max dia. outside	4 feet 2 ins	
	Length	10 feet 0 ins	
Firebox		5 feet 5 ins	
Heating surface			
	Tubes	203 x 1¾ ins	957.6 sq feet
	Firebox		94.9 sq feet
	Total		1,052.5 sq feet
Grate area		15.27 sq feet	
Boiler pressure		140 psi	
Driving wheels		5 feet 3 ins	
Tender wheels		3 feet 7 ins	
Wheelbase			
	Engine	15 feet 3 ins	
	Tender	9 feet 0 ins	
Weight in working order			
	Engine	30 tons 15 cwt	
	Tender	21 tons 17 cwt	
	Total	52 tons 12 cwt	
Max axle loading		11 tons 5 cwt	
Water capacity		1,740 gallons	

The '477' Class

The larger '477' Class, numbered 477 to 526, came from a variety of builders: Beyer, Peacock; Robert Stephenson; Dübs; Nasmyth, Wilson, and the Yorkshire Engine Company. They were originally introduced to cope with the rapidly increasing goods traffic and the need for a locomotive which could provide greater hauling capacity and more effective braking power than the '417' Class. After the introduction of the 'Y14' Class, the '477's were, like their smaller sisters, relegated to more menial tasks, those allocated to Norwich often making appearances on the Waveney Valley Branch with special goods trains. The '477' Class was withdrawn between 1897 and 1902.

The leading dimensions of the class were:

Cylinders	2 inside	17 in x 24 in	
Motion		Stephenson with slide valves	
Boiler	Max diameter	4 feet 2 ins	
	Barrel length	10 feet 0 ins	
Firebox	Outside length	5 feet 5 ins	
Heating surface			
	Tubes	223 x 1⅝ in	980.0 sq feet
	Firebox		94.9 sq feet
	Total		1,074.9 sq feet
Grate area		15.27 sq feet	
Boiler pressure		140 psi	
Coupled wheels		5 feet 2 ins	
Tender wheels		3 feet 8 ins	
Wheelbase			
	Engine	15 feet 6 ins	
	Tender	12 feet 0 ins	
Weight in working order			
	Engine	32 tons 13 cwt	
	Tender	26 tons 5cwt	
	Total	58 tons 18 cwt	
Max axle loading		12 tons 6 cwt	
Water capacity		2,038 gallons	

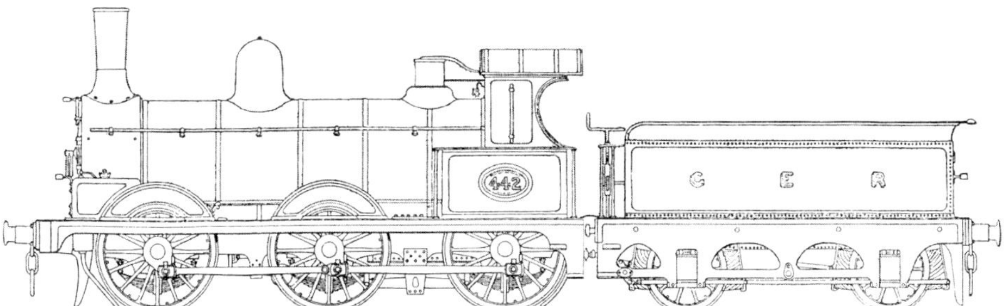

Above: Johnson '417' Class 0-6-0 tender locomotive.

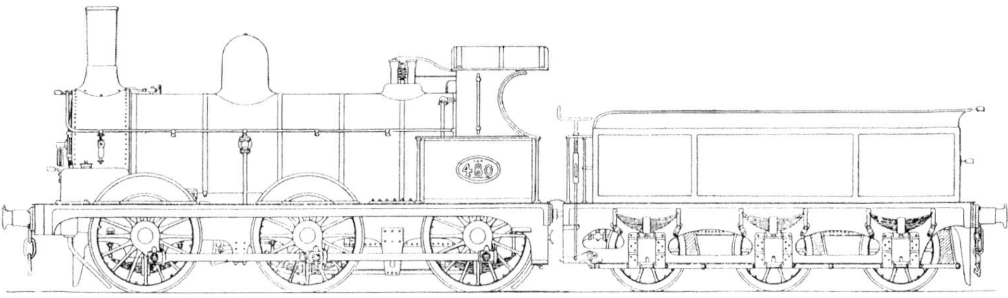

Right: Johnson '477' Class 0-6-0 tender locomotive.

The 'Y14'/'J15' Class

After the withdrawal of the '477' Class 0-6-0 tender locomotives, the freight traffic was placed in the hands of the GER 'Y14' Class 0-6-0 tender locomotives designed by T.W. Worsdell. Introduced in 1883, these small engines were later classified 'J15' by the L&NER. Such was the success of the design the building continued until 1913 with all except nineteen of the class of 289 built at Stratford Works, the others being constructed by Sharp, Stewart & Company. Because of their low RA1 route availability, the ubiquitous class was ideal for branch line traffic, excursion trains and in the latter years they often deputized on Waveney Valley passenger services, including the last steam hauled passenger train, when No. 65478 worked the 8.15pm train from Tivetshall to Beccles. Thereafter 'J15's often worked the branch freight traffic until the demise of steam traction. No. 65469 hauled a special train on 21st May 1960 formed of six ex-L&NER and BR standard corridor coaches organised by the Midland & Great Northern Railway Preservation Society, and then again on 8th October 1960 with a 6-coach train.

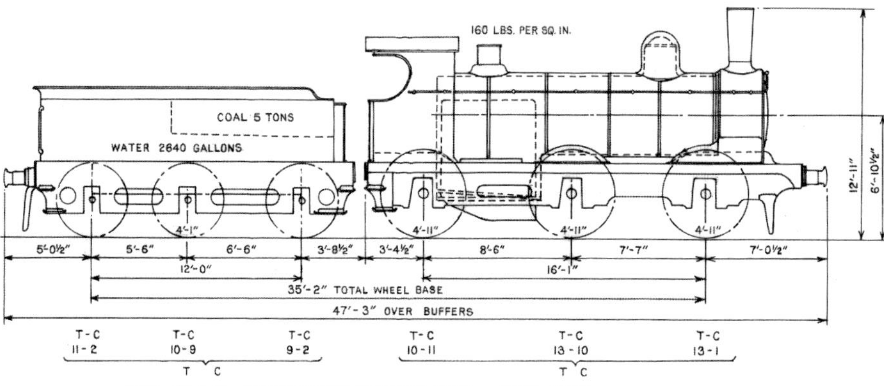

GER 'Y14' Class, later L&NER 'J15' Class, 0-6-0 tender locomotive.

Locomotives known to have worked Waveney Valley services included those listed below.

GER No.	L&NER 1924 No.	L&NER 1946 No.	BR No.	Withdrawn	GER No.	L&NER 1924 No.	L&NER 1946 No.	BR No.	Withdrawn
119	7119	—	—	September 1929	639	7639	—	—	June 1928
120	7120	—	—	February 1928	807	7807	—	—	March 1929
121	7121	—	—	March 1933	809	7809	—	—	August 1936
122	7122	—	—	January 1930	810	7810	—	—	January 1929
124	7124	—	—	July 1933	812	7812	—	—	February 1929
514	7514	5433	65433	January 1958	813	7813	5350	—	February 1951
516	7516	5435	65435	October 1956	815	7815	—	—	June 1936
530	7530	5355	—	February 1951	816	7816	—	—	January 1930
542	7542	5470	65470*	December 1959	817	7817	—	—	March 1936
543	7543	5471	65471*	June 1960	818	7818	—	—	November 1938
544	7544	5472	65472*	December 1959	819	7819	—	—	April 1938
550	7550	5478	65478*	October 1961	820	7820	—	—	July 1928
551	7551	5479	65479*	August 1960	821	7821	5351	—	May 1949
562	7562	5460	65460*	September 1962	824	7824	—	—	January 1936
564	7564	5462	65462*	September 1962	825	7825	5352	—	May 1948
565	7565	5463	65463*	November 1959	828	7828	5353	—	December 1949
566	7566	5464	65464*	September 1962	829	7829	—	—	August 1936
571	7571	5469	65469*	August 1962	830	7830	5358	—	August 1947
610	7610	—	—	October 1929	848	7848	5367	—	January 1950
611	7611	—	—	August 1926	855	7855	5373	—	October 1950
612	7612	—	—	January 1932	866	7866	5377	—	February 1951
613	7613	—	—	June 1931	883	7883	5388	65388	May 1959
614	7614	—	—	September 1926	886	7886	5389	65389	April 1960
615	7615	—	—	October 1926	887	7887	5390	65390*	December 1958
616	7616	—	—	July 1929	894	7894	5394	—	May 1948
617	7617	—	—	October 1926	901	7901	5398	65398	February 1952
620	7620	—	—	October 1926	906	7906	5401	—	September 1951
629	7629	—	—	September 1926	910	7910	5404	65404	October 1956
630	7630	—	—	June 1929	915	7915	5408	65408	December 1951
631	7631	—	—	December 1933	921	7921	5411	—	April 1948
633	7633	—	—	August 1926	928	7928	5417	65417	August 1956
634	7634	—	—	January 1929	937	7937	5422	65422	July 1955
638	7638	—	—	June 1936	943	7943	5426	65426	May 1951

Note: * Westinghouse and vacuum brake fitted for working passenger trains

As there was no freight traffic, 'J15' Class 0-6-0 No. 65469 hurries a former Southern Railway goods brake van along an open section of the branch between Earsham and Homersfield in 1955, with the trees of Buckhills Plantation in the background. *Dr I.C. Allen*

The leading dimensions of the 'J15' Class were:

Cylinders	2 inside	17½ ins x 24 ins	
Motion		Stephenson with slide valves	
Boiler	Max dia. outside	4 feet 4 ins	
	Barrel length	10 feet 0 ins	
Firebox	Outside length	6 feet 0 ins	
Heating surface			
	Tubes	242 x 1⅝ ins	1,063.8 sq feet
	Firebox		105.5 sq feet
	Total		1,169.3 sq feet
Grate area		17.9 sq feet	
Boiler pressure		160 psi	
Coupled wheels		4 feet 11 ins	
Tender wheels		4 feet 1 in	
Tractive effort		16,942 lbs	
Length over buffers		47 feet 3 ins*	
Wheelbase			
	Engine	16 feet 1 in	
	Tender	12 feet 0 ins	
	Total	35 feet 2 ins	
Weight in working order			
	Engine	37 tons 2 cwt	
	Tender	30 tons 13 cwt	
	Total	67 tons 15 cwt	
Max axle loading		13 tons 10 cwt	
Water capacity		2,640 gallons	
Coal capacity		5 tons	

NOTE: * Engine and tender.

THE 'G58'/'J17' CLASS

In the latter years of steam haulage of the branch freight services Norwich shed foremen occasionally resorted to the use of 'J17' 0-6-0 tender locomotives if a 'J15' Class was not available, although they were restricted from working between Bungay and Beccles because of the weak timber bridges. The introduction of 8-coupled heavy goods locomotives on the Whitemoor to Temple Mills and other main line freight services from the 1930s gradually released the 0-6-0 tender classes for cross-country and branch line freight workings. The sixty 'J17's built to the design of James Holden were originally introduced from 1900 as GER Class 'F48' with round-topped fireboxes, with a further batch of thirty engines produced with Belpaire fireboxes as Class 'G58' from 1905 to 1911. Thereafter some of the earlier engines were rebuilt with Belpaire fireboxes and reclassified. After grouping the 'F48's became L&NER Class 'J16' and the 'G58's L&NER Class 'J17', but by 1932 all the round-topped firebox locomotives had been rebuilt with Belpaire fireboxes as Class 'J17' and the Class 'J16' became extinct. Locomotives known to have worked over the branch included those listed overleaf.

'J17' Class 0-6-0s were generally diagrammed for working goods services from the Tivetshall end of the line as far as Bungay, as they were restricted thence to Beccles. Here No. 65513, equipped with a small 2,640-gallon tender, is engaged in shunting the yard at Harleston. *Dr I.C. Allen*

GER No.	L&NER 1924 No.	L&NER 1946 No.	BR No.	WITHDRAWN
1157	8157	5507	65507	September 1961
1160	8160	5510	65510	March 1955
1162	8162	5512	65512	December 1959
1163	8163	5513	65513	March 1961
1174	8174	5524	65524	March 1955
1184	8184	5534	65534	March 1958
1203	8203	5553	65553	April 1959
1218	8218	5568	65568	September 1958
1219	8219	5569	65569	February 1955
1220	8220	5570	65570	April 1960
1224	8224	5574	65574	April 1955

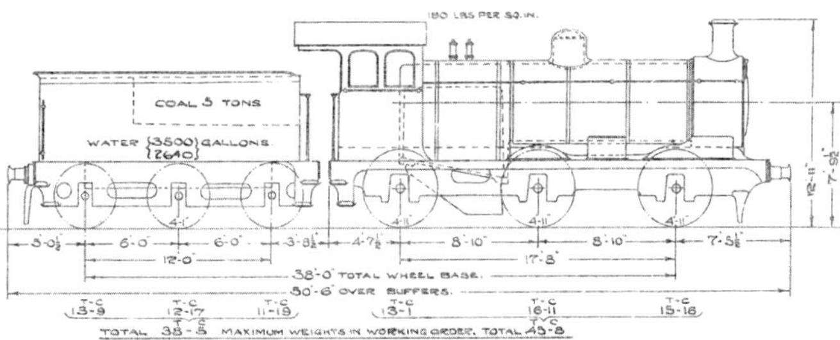

GER 'G58' Class, later L&NER 'J17' Class, 0-6-0 tender locomotive.

The leading dimensions of the 'J17' Class were:

Cylinders	2 inside	19 ins x 26 ins	
Motion		Stephenson with slide valves	
Boiler	Max dia. outside	4 feet 9 ins	
	Barrel length	11 feet 9 ins	
Firebox outside length		7 feet 0 ins	
Heating surface			
	Tubes	156 x 1¾ ins	863.5 sq feet
	Flues	18 x 5 ins	282.7 sq feet
	Firebox		117.7 sq feet
	Total evaporative		1,263.9 sq feet
	Superheater	18 x 1³⁄₃₂ ins	154.8 sq feet
	Total		1,418.7 sq feet
Grate area		21.24 sq feet	
Boiler pressure		180 psi	
Coupled wheels		4 feet 11 ins	
Tender wheels		4 feet 1 in	
Tractive effort		24,340 ins	
Length over buffers		50 feet 6 ins*	
Wheelbase			
	Engine	17 feet 8 ins	
	Tender	12 feet 0 ins	
	Total	38 feet 0 ins	
Weight in working order			
	Engine	45 tons 8 cwt	
	Tender	38 tons 5 cwt	
	Total	83 tons 13 cwt	
Max axle loading		16 tons 11 cwt	
Water capacity		3,500 gallons	
		2,640 gallons	
Coal capacity		5 tons	

NOTE: * Engine and tender.

THE 'E72'/'T77'/'J19' CLASS

A.J. Hill designed ten 'E72' Class 0-6-0 goods locomotives which were introduced into traffic in 1912, followed by twenty-five 'T77' Class built between 1916 and 1920. They were used on main line freight workings until displaced by larger and more modern locomotives in the 1930s. Between 1934 and 1939 all thirty-five were rebuilt with larger boilers and round-topped fireboxes similar to the rebuilt 'Claud Hamilton' 'D16/3' 4-4-0 tender locomotives. Known in the rebuilt form as Class 'J19/2', the suffix /2 was usually ignored. Initially they were prohibited from working between Tivetshall and Beccles but then special dispensation was given for their use. This was critical in 1953 when, as a result of the disastrous East Coast floods, the Yarmouth to Beccles and Lowestoft to Beccles routes were inundated and it was the necessary to work train loads of ballast across the Waveney Valley Branch to assist with repair work. It was during this period that the two 'J19's allocated to Norwich, No's 64644 and 64674, were utilised to good effect on these trains because of their superior tractive effort.

GER No.	L&NER 1924 No.	L&NER 1946 No.	BR No.	WITHDRAWN
1244	8244	4644	64644	July 1959
1274	8274	4674	64674	January 1961

The principal dimensions of the 'J19' Class were:

Cylinders	2 inside	20 ins x 28 ins	
Motion		Stephenson with 10 in piston valves	
Boiler	Max dia. outside	5 feet 1½ ins	
	Barrel length	11 feet 9 ins	
Firebox	Outside length	7 feet 0 ins	
Heating surface			
	Tubes	172 x 1¾ ins	957.1 sq feet
	Flues	21 x 5¼ ins	346.3 sq feet
	Firebox		126.0 sq feet
	Total evaporative		1,429.4 sq feet
	Superheater	21 x 1¼ ins	302.5 sq feet
	Total		1,731.9 sq feet
Grate area		21.4 sq feet	
Boiler pressure		160 psi	
Coupled wheels		4 feet 11 ins	
Tender wheels		4 feet 1 in	
Tractive effort		25,817 lbs	
Length over buffers		52 feet 4 ins*	
Wheelbase			
	Engine	17 feet 8 ins	
	Tender	12 feet 0 ins	
	Total	38 feet 7 ins	
Weight in working order			
	Engine	50 tons 7 cwt	
	Tender	38 tons 5 cwt	
	Total	88 tons 12 cwt	
Max axle loading		18 tons 15 cwt	
Water capacity		3,500 gallons	
Coal capacity		5 tons 0 cwt	

NOTE: * Engine and tender.

THE '03' CLASS DIESEL SHUNTER

With the withdrawal of steam traction from the line, BR utilised two diesel mechanical shunting locomotive classes on the sand trains between Beccles and Ditchingham. The first of these, the Class '03' 204 hp locomotives, numbered in the range D2000 to D2142 and allocated to Norwich depot, were permitted over the branch as heavier diesel classes were not allowed. Locomotives known to have hauled the trains included D2019 (originally No. 11206) and D2032 to D2039 inclusive. The leading dimensions of the locomotives were:

Weight in working order	30 tons 4 cwt
Tractive effort	15,300 lbs
Wheelbase	9 feet 0 ins
Wheel diameter	3 feet 7 ins
Width overall	8 feet 6 ins
Length overall	26 feet 0 ins
Height overall	12 feet 2⁷⁄₁₆ ins
Minimum curve negotiable	2 chains
Maximum speed	28½ mph
Fuel tanks	300 gallons
Brakes	Compressed air, vacuum and hand
Sanding	Compressed air operated
Power equipment	8-cylinder diesel engine – Gardner 8L3 type 204 hp at 1,200 rpm
Transmission	Fluid coupling – Vulcan Sinclair type 23, capacity 8½ gallons
Gearbox	Wilson Drewry CA5 R7 compressed air operated
Reverse gear and final drive	Type RF11

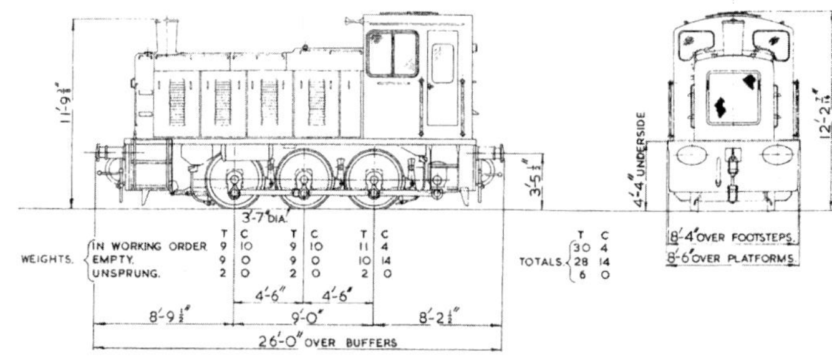

BR Class '03', 204 hp 0-6-0 diesel mechanical shunting locomotive.

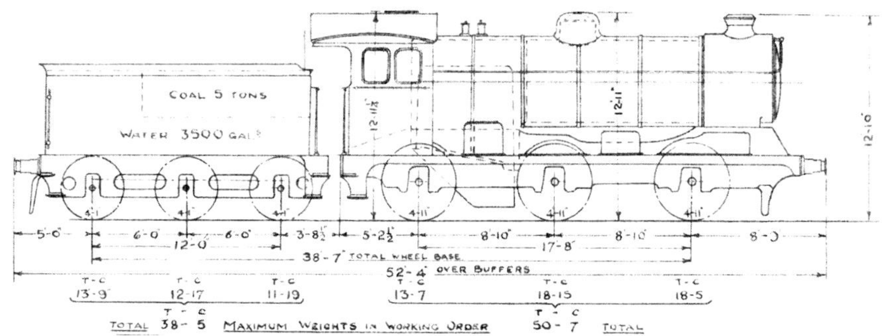

A.J. Hill GER 'E72/T77' Class, later L&NER 'J19' Class, 0-6-0 tender locomotive.

'03' Class 0-6-0 diesel mechanical shunting locomotive No. D2033 trundles a train of empty wagons along the branch near Ditchingham in 1965, shortly before total closure of the line between Ditchingham and Beccles. *Dr I.C. Allen*

The Hunslet 'D2/15A' ('05') Class Diesel Shunter

The second class of diesel mechanical shunting locomotive used on the branch was built by Hunslet and introduced into service in 1955. Of 204 hp, the locomotives were allocated to Norwich and Lowestoft depots for maintenance and repairs and received the classification 'D2/15A' by British Railways. Initially numbered in the series commencing at 11136, under the standard BR numbering scheme the class received the numbers from D2550 onwards and later became Class '05'. Locomotives known to have worked across the branch included:

Old Number	New Number	Old Number	New Number
11139	D2553	11169	D2566
11141	D2555	11170	D2567
11161	D2558	11171	D2568
11162	D2559	11172	D2569
11165	D2562	11173	D2570
11166	D2563	11176	D2573
11168	D2565		

Four of the class survive in preservation, including D2554 which was exiled to the Isle of Wight for use on ballast and engineering trains between Ryde Pierhead and Shanklin. While at Ryde (RY) shed No. D2554 was renumbered 05001 before being transferred to departmental stock as 97803. On being replaced by a Class '03' shunting locomotive, the '05' locomotive was purchased for preservation by the Isle of Wight Steam Railway at Haven Street.

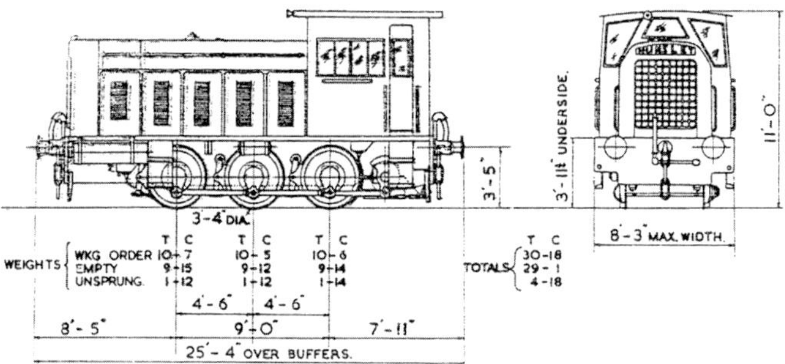

Hunslet BR Class '05', 204 hp diesel mechanical shunting locomotive.

The leading dimensions of the 'D2/15A' class were:

Weight in working order		30 tons
Tractive effort	1st gear	14,500 lbs
	2nd gear	9,070 lbs
	3rd gear	5,700 lbs
	4th gear	3,640 lbs
Wheelbase		9 feet 0 ins
Wheel diameter		3 feet 4 ins
Width overall		8 feet 3 ins
Length overall		21 feet 10 ins
Height overall		11 feet 0 ins
Minimum curve negotiable		1.8 chains
Maximum speed	1st gear	4.48 mph
	2nd gear	7.14 mph
	3rd gear	11.37 mph
	4th gear	17.80 mph
Fuel oil capacity		300 gallons
Cooling water		50 gallons
Lubricating oil sump		8 gallons
Brakes	Compressed air and hand operated	
Sanding	Compressed air operated	
Power equipment	8-cylinder diesel engine – Gardner 8L3 type 204 hp at 1,200 rpm	
Transmission	Hunslet pattern friction main clutch and automatically operated shaft brake to reduce the output shaft speed during gear change	
Gearbox	Hunslet 4 speed	
Reverse gear	Bevel gears incorporated in gearbox	
Final drive	Jackshaft and coupling rods	

The Brush '13/2' ('31/1') Class

At the western end of the severed branch the goods services were worked by Brush Type '2' diesel electric locomotives, later Class '31/1', allocated to Norwich and Ipswich. As well as working main line passenger and freight services they also worked the various branch lines. The principal dimensions of the Brush '13/2' Class locomotives were:

Type		A1A–A1A
Weight in working order		
Mirlees engine		104 tons
English Electric engine		106 tons
Tractive effort maximum		42,000 lbs
Wheelbase		42 feet 10 ins
Wheel diameter		3 feet 7 ins
Bogie wheelbase		14 feet 0 ins
Bogie centres		28 feet 10 ins
Width overall		8 feet 9 ins
Length overall		56 feet 9 ins
Height overall		12 feet 7½ ins
Minimum curve negotiable		4½ chains
Max permissible speed		
D5520–D5534		80 mph
D5535–D5699		90 mph
D5800–D5862		90 mph
Fuel tank capacity		550 gallons
Brakes		Compressed air and handbrakes on locomotive. Vacuum brake equipment giving proportional air braking on the locomotive.
Power equipment		
Mirlees		12-cylinder diesel engine JVs 12T 1,250 hp at 900 rpm
English Electric		Diesel engine 12SVT 1,470 hp at 850 rpm
Traction motors	4	Brush DC type TM 73-68 4-pole force ventilated

The details given are those extant at the time the '13/2' Class operated on the Waveney Valley line. Many alterations were subsequently made.

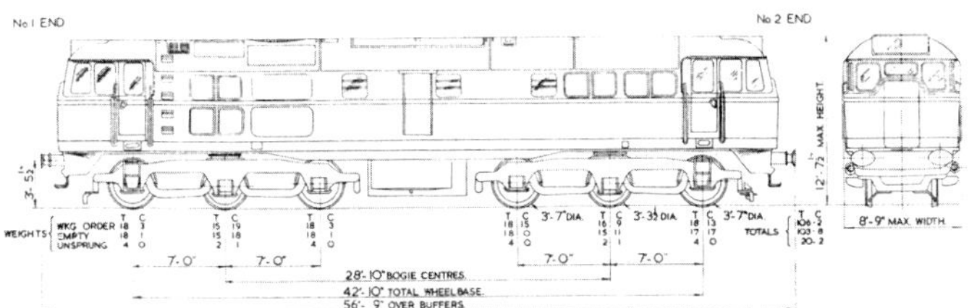

Brush Type '2', BR Class '31/1', diesel electric locomotive.

The BTH/AEI '8/5' ('15') Class

Working turn and turn about with the Brush Type '2' Class were the BTH/AEI 800 hp '8/5' Class Bo-Bo diesel electric locomotives, later BR Class '15'. The principal dimensions were

Type		Bo–Bo
Weight in working order		68 tons
Tractive effort – maximum		38,000 lbs
Wheelbase		31 feet 0 ins
Wheel diameter		3 feet 3½ ins
Bogie wheelbase		8 feet 6 ins
Bogie pivot centres		22 feet 6 ins
Width overall		9 feet 2 ins
Length overall		42 feet 3⅜ ins
Height overall		12 feet 6 ins
Minimum curve negotiable		4 chains
Maximum permitted speed		60 mph
Fuel tank capacity (main tank)		400 gallons
Brakes		Oerlikon/Davies & Metcalfe compressed air brake and hand brakes on locomotive. Vacuum brake equipment giving proportional air braking on the locomotive.
Power equipment		16-cylinder diesel engine Davey-Paxman type 16 YHXL 800 hp at 1,250 rpm
Traction motors	4	D8200-10 GEC forced ventilated type 137 AZ D8211-43 GEC forced ventilated type 137 BZ

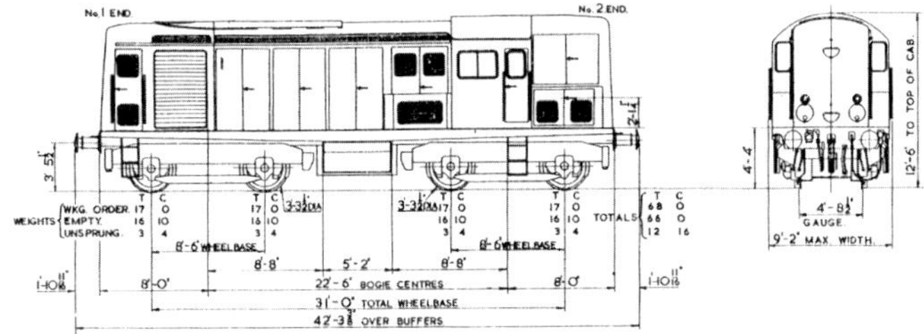

BTH/Paxman 800 hp, later BR Class '15', diesel electric locomotive.

RIGHT: Hunslet Class '05' 0-6-0 diesel mechanical shunting locomotive No. 02559 standing on the Down loop line between Ditchingham and Silk Factory level crossing; the extension of the reception siding in the goods yard at Ditchingham was installed in 1943 to serve the US Air Force depot in the converted maltings. The shadow in the foreground is cast by these former maltings, which towered over the railway. After the official closure date for freight facilities, on and from 19th April 1965, block trainloads of sand continued to operate between Ditchingham and Beccles until August 1965; new workings were excavated at Coltishall on the North Walsham to County School branch. *Dr I.C. Allen*

Facilities

An engine shed was established at Beccles to coincide with the opening of the WVR, the single-road building located at the south end of the station on the Up side of the line, measuring some 65 feet in length, was served by access directly off a connection from the 38 feet diameter turntable, later extended to 41 feet 9 inches. All was not well, for by 4th July 1870 the Way and Works Committee reported that the water supply was *'very bad and doing serious injury to the locomotive boilers'.* Two locomotives had been stopped on account of the water incrustation blocking the tubes. The Locomotive Superintendent Samuel Johnson was informed that the provision of a well 20 to 25 feet deep would improve the water supplies and obviate the problem. One, and later two, locomotives were initially allocated, outbased from Lowestoft; this was increased to four by the mid-1880s, at which point the building was considered too small and cramped. Thus authority was given on 5th April 1887 for a new engine shed at an estimated cost of £2,150 and the contract was duly placed with Bennett Brothers of Cambridge in April 1888 after the firm had tendered at the reduced price of £1,676, with the proviso work was to be completed by 1st September 1888. The new brick structure, measuring 110 feet in length by 30 feet, was located north of the station on the Down side of the Down main line. It contained two roads, with associated coal stage, water tank and replacement 50 feet diameter turntable. Subsequently the old shed was demolished and the new shed, now with an allocation of four locomotives, came under the supervision of the locomotive foreman at Lowestoft. The shed establishment consisted initially of two sets of footplatemen and a labourer, but gradually increased to five sets with two passed cleaners, two coalmen and two cleaners. The shed remained operational covering main line as well as Lowestoft and Waveney Valley Branch traffic, but by the mid 1930s the allocation of engines was reduced to three and, although still in operation throughout World War Two, was closed in 1945. The shed building was used as an abattoir until 1986 when it was demolished.

Much to the chagrin of the Board of Trade inspectorate, no turntables were provided for the opening of the line from Tivetshall to Harleston, despite the EUR working the branch with tender locomotives. For the opening of the second section of line from Harleston to Bungay, the use of tank engines was stipulated, an instruction which continued with the opening to Beccles. Although no turntable was installed at Tivetshall, soon after the takeover by the GER the 38 feet diameter turntable was installed at Beccles and, as recorded above, was later extended to 41 feet 9 inches before being replaced by the 50 feet 0 inches diameter turntable to accommodate larger and longer locomotives.

Water for locomotives at Tivetshall was hand pumped, later mechanised, from the local stream to the water tank located on the east side of the station. This fed water to the jib crane located at the south end of station for the Up main line, a jib crane at the north end of station for the Down main line, and the jib crane at the north end of the back platform to replenish the branch engines. At Bungay a tank house was originally located at the west end of

The north end of Beccles station in October 1911 with the divergence of the Waveney Valley Branch to the left and Yarmouth and Lowestoft routes beyond the end of the Up island platform to the right and the engine shed in the middle distance. Note also the connection from the bay platform to the engine shed and the Down Yarmouth line. *GERS/Windwood 1324*

the Down platform and later at the west end of the Up platform, serving a water crane at the Tivetshall end of the Up platform for the Up loop line. The water, which was hand pumped, was initially for emergency use only. At Beccles water was pumped from a well by pumping engine and serviced the jib water crane at the south end of station for the Up main line, the parachute tank at the north end of station for the Down main line and the branch platform, and the water crane in the engine shed yard.

Headcodes

Initially the locomotive working the booked branch services carried no headlamp by day and only one white light at the base of the chimney by night, special trains only carried lights at night with the engine displaying a white light at the base of the chimney and another light on the buffer beam, if fitted with a lamp bracket, or if not presumably attached to the coupling. By 1875 the headcode for ordinary trains was the same but special trains carried a white disc at the base of the chimney by day and two white lights at night. The headcode carried by locomotives hauling the branch train in later GER days was a red light at the top of the smokebox by the chimney and a white light on the buffer beam. During daylight hours a circular red disc with white rim was carried under the chimney. Special trains carried an additional white light by night or a white disc by day on the buffer beam. By 1890 a red disc with white rim was carried under the chimney by day and a red light under the chimney and a white light on the left hand end of the buffer beam by night. Special trains then carried a red disc with white outer rim under the chimney and a white disc in the centre of the buffer beam by day, whilst at night a red lamp under the chimney and a white light on the left and right hand ends of the buffer beam were stipulated. In 1903 the headcode for single line working was again changed to a red disc, with white outer rim under the chimney during daylight hours and a red lamp under the chimney and a green lamp on the left hand end of the buffer beam by night. From 1910 ordinary and special trains carried the same code, red disc with white outer rim or red lamp under the chimney and a green disc with white outer rim or green lamp over the left hand end of the buffer beam. After grouping the L&NER phased out the green lights and discs as a possible source of danger and replaced them with a purple light or purple disc with white outer rim. From 1925 the standard stopping passenger train code of a white light or disc at the base of the chimney was used on the Waveney Valley services. Freight trains on the branch then carried the appropriate Railway Clearing House class headcode.

In 1891 a unique headcode had to be provided on Up ordinary or special Waveney Valley passenger trains commencing their journey at Beccles, destined for Norwich, which from Tivetshall became Down trains on the main line. After leaving the branch one white light or lamp or white disc over the left hand buffer as viewed from the locomotive cab, had to be placed in position on the lamp iron but only from Forncett. By 1902 an Up branch train destined for Norwich carried the same headcode when working in the Down direction on the main line, the headlamp or disc being place on the

locomotive at Tivetshall. By 1919 the headcode had changed to a green disc with white outer rim or green headlamp on both the top of the smokebox and on the left hand buffer, the headlamp or disc being placed at Tivetshall.

Whistle Codes

The engine whistle codes to be sounded at **Tivetshall** were: 1 distinct sound for an engine or train on the main line, 2 distinct sounds to or from the Waveney Valley line and the back platform line, 3 distinct sounds from the back platform line to the Down main line and 4 distinct sounds to or from the Up main line and the back platform line.

At **Beccles Station North signal box** the whistle codes were:

Main Line	1 distinct sound
Waveney Valley Branch to or from the main line	2 distinct sounds
Waveney Valley Branch to or from the dock line	3 distinct sounds
Waveney Valley dock to the main line	4 distinct sounds
Engine Shed road to or from the main line	1 crow
Engine Shed road to or from the dock line	5 distinct sounds
Lowestoft Branch to or from the main line	2 short and 1 long
Lowestoft Branch to or from the Up back platform line	3 short and 1 long
Up back platform line to Down main line	2 given twice
Down main line to refuge siding on the Waveney Valley Branch	6 distinct sounds

And at **Beccles South signal box**:

Main Line	1 distinct sound
Up back platform line to Up main line	1 long and 2 short

By 1902 the whistle code at Beccles had been amended:

Beccles North Junction signal box:

Main Line	1 distinct sound
Waveney Valley Branch to or from Main Line	2 distinct sounds
Waveney Valley line to or from Down Back Platform Line	3 distinct sounds
Waveney Valley Dock to Main Line	4 distinct sounds
Engine Turntable to or from Main Line	1 crow
Engine Turntable to or from Waveney Valley Dock Line	5 distinct sounds
Lowestoft Branch to or from the Main Line	2 short, 1 long
Lowestoft Branch to or from Up Back Platform line	3 short, 1 long
Up Back Platform Line to Down Main Line	2 given twice
Down Main Line to Refuge siding on Waveney Valley Branch	6 distinct sounds
To or from Waveney Valley Branch Dock and Siding on Waveney Valley Branch	2 long, 2 short
To or from Down Main Line and Siding on Waveney Valley Branch	3 long, 3 short

Beccles South signal box:

Main Line	1 distinct sound
Up Back Platform Line to Up Main Line	1 long and one short

Between Beccles and Geldeston:

Two 'Whistle Boards', one for Down trains and the other for Up trains, each 300 yards from Dunburgh House Foot Crossing	1 distinct sound

By 1927 the L&NER altered the whistle codes to:

Tivetshall Junction signal box:

To or from Branch and Back Platform	2 short
Back Platform to Down Main	3 short
To or from Up Main and Back Platform	4 short

Beccles North Junction signal box:

To or from Waveney Valley Branch and Down Back Platform	3 short
From Down Back Platform to Down Main	4 short
To or from Waveney Valley Dock and Engine Turntable	5 short
To or from Up Back Platform and Lowestoft Branch	3 short, 1 long
Up Back Platform to Down Main	2 short
Down Main to Refuge Siding on Waveney Valley Branch	6 short
To or from Down Main and Siding on Waveney Valley Branch	3 long, 3 short
To or from Waveney Valley Branch Dock and Siding on Waveney Valley Branch	2 long, 2 short

Beccles South signal box:

Up Back Platform to Up Main	1 long, 2 short

These remained unaltered in 1942, but a decade later on 27th April 1952 the whistle codes were altered at Tivetshall and Beccles as under:

Tivetshall Junction signal box:

To or from Branch and back Platform	4 short, 1 long
Back platform to Down Main	3 short, 1 long
To or from the Up Main and Back Platform	6 short

Beccles North Junction signal box:

To or from Waveney Valley Branch and Down Back Platform	2 short, 1 long
To or from Waveney Valley Dock and Engine Turntable	2 short, pause, 4 short
To or from Up Back Platform and Lowestoft Branch	4 short, 1 long
Up Back Platform to Down Main	3 short, 1 long
Down Main to Refuge Siding on Waveney Valley Branch	6 short
To or from Down Main and Siding on Waveney Valley Branch	3 long, 3 short
To or from Waveney Valley Branch Dock and Siding on Waveney Valley Branch	2 short, pause, 5 short

Staff

William Wenham, a driver at Beccles, commenced his footplate career on the London & South Western Railway before transferring to the GER at Norwich in 1878. In the same year he transferred to Beccles, from where he retired in 1913. Frederick William Crisp was 14 years old when he joined the GER as a lad in Beccles refreshment room. He soon transferred to the locomotive department as an engine cleaner and by March 1917, when he was called up for military service, had gained promotion as acting fireman. Initially he served with the 5th Lancers but was transferred to the King's Liverpool 8th Irish Battalion before being killed in action on 11th September 1918 aged 20 years. Driver F.G. Brown of Beccles retired on 13th May 1939.

The working of the Waveney Valley Branch was usually entrusted to Norwich (later coded 32A by BR) and Beccles (a sub-shed of Lowestoft, coded 32C) depots, but in the early years Ipswich covered a few turns of duty and in later years Lowestoft depot increasingly covered some diagrams. As an example, in 1925 Norwich No. 24 engine and men worked from Norwich to Beccles and back after working a round trip from Norwich to Cromer and another to Yarmouth Vauxhall; Norwich No. 27 diagram worked the branch service after two round trips from Norwich to Yarmouth Vauxhall; Norwich No. 34 diagram engine and men worked across the branch before a round trip from Norwich to Lowestoft; finally, Norwich No. 36 diagram worked the goods service from Norwich to Harleston and Beccles before returning to Trowse yard. Beccles No. 1 engine and men were responsible for working some

NORWICH DEPOT—Continued.

WEEK DAYS.

No. 24.

	arr.		dep.	
	a.m.		a.m.	
		On Duty		E P
		Loco'	2 0	L
		Norwich	2 15	
	3 [illegible]0	Yarmouth Vx.	8 34	
			p.m.	
	9 15	Norwich PP	12 45	TWTh
	p.m.			
TWTh	1 35	Cromer	2 20	ATWTh
ATWTh	3 17	Norwich	5- 8	
	6 41	Beccles	7 12	
	8 47	Norwich	L	
		Loco'		

Second set on duty 4.5 p.m. **M F S**
E P 12.30 p.m. **TWTh**, and relieve on arrival 8.47 p.m.

No. 27

arr.		dep.	
a.m.		a.m.	
	On Duty	5 50	
	Loco'	6 35	L
	Norwich	6 50	
7 39	Yarmouth Vx.	8 43	
9 29	Norwich	10 4	
10 48	Yarmouth Vx.	11 55	
p.m.		p.m.	
12 40	Norwich	2 26	
3 48	Beccles	6 5	
7 35	Norwich	L	
	Loco'		

Second set on duty 1.25 p.m.

No. 34.

	arr.		dep.	
	a.m.		a.m.	
		On Duty	7 54	E P
		Loco'	8 9	L
		Norwich	8 24	
	9 58	Bungay	10 1	
			p.m.	
	10 23	Beccles	12 18	
	p.m.			
	1 15	Tivetshall	1 38 / 1 47	M F S / T W Th
M F S / T W Th	2 34 / 2 37	Beccles	3 9	
	4 37	Norwich	6 20	
	7 21	Lowestoft	9 0	
	9 52	Norwich	L	
		Loco'		

First set change footplates at Bungay with Beccles men working 9.30 a.m. goods ex Beccles, and work that train forward to Wymondham, thence travel passengers to Norwich by 3.47 p.m. ex Wymondham.

Beccles men work 3.9 p.m. Beccles to Norwich, and return working 7.45 p.m. **S X** 7.50 p.m. **S O** Norwich to Beccles with engine of No. 1 diagram.

Second set Norwich men work 6.20 p.m. Norwich to Lowestoft.

No. 36.

arr.		dep.	
a.m.		a.m.	
	On Duty	4 40	
	Loco'	5 25	L
	Norwich	5 40	G
9 30	Harleston	9 50	G
		p.m.	
11 50	Beccles	1 15	G
p.m.			
5 30	Trowse	L	
	Loco'		

First set change footplates at Harleston with men of 9.6 a.m. ex Beccles, and work forward to Norwich.

See Beccles No. 1 diagram.

Second set travel passengers from Norwich to Beccles to work 1.15 p.m.

Above Left: Locomotive and enginemen's workings, Norwich depot 1925.

Right: Locomotive and enginemen's workings, Beccles depot 1925.

BECCLES DEPOT.

WEEK DAYS.

No. 1.

	arr.		dep.	
	a.m.		a.m.	
		On Duty	5 20	
		Loco'	6 5	L
		Beccles	6 15	
	7 9	Tivetshall	7 47	
	8 37	Beccles	9 6	
			p.m.	
	10 22	Norwich	12 38	MFS from 17th July
	p.m.			
MFS	12 41	Trowse	12 55	EMFS from 17th July
MFS	1 0	Norwich	4 26	
	5 13	Yarmouth V.	5 43	
	6 32	Norwich	7 45 / 7 50	S X / S O
S X / S O	9 15 / 9 20	Beccles	10 0	W S O
W SO	10 32	Yarmouth S.T.	11 0	W SO
W SO	11 32	Beccles	L	
		Loco'		

First set Beccles men change footplates at Harleston with men working 5.40 p.m goods ex Norwich diagram No. 36. Norwich men take charge Norwich 12.0 noon and work until relieved by Beccles men.

Second set Beccles men work 3.9 p.m. Beccles to Norwich with Norwich engine of diagram No. 34 and return working 7.45 p.m. **S X** 7.50 p.m. **SO** as above.

GOODS ENGINE.

arr.		dep.	
a.m.		a.m.	
	On Duty	6 45	
	Loco'	7 30	L
	Beccles G.P.	9 30	
9 50	Bungay	11 0	
p.m.		p.m.	
1 10	Wymondham	3 50	SX 5 5SC
7 25	Harleston	7 55	
8 45	Beccles G.P.	L	
	Loco'		

First set change footplates at Bungay with Norwich men working 8.24 a.m. ex Norwich. diagram No. 34. Norwich men passengers to Wymondham by 3.10 p.m. ex Norwich to work 3.50 p.m. **SX** 5.5 p.m. **SO**. Goods Wymondham to Harleston and return home passengers.

Second set Beccles men passengers to Harleston by 7.12 p.m. ex Beccles to work forward 3.50 p.m. **SX** 5.5 p.m. **SO**. Goods ex Wymondham and on arrival at Beccles to perform shunting as required.

NORWICH DEPOT—*continued*

Eng. Diagram No.	Engine M.P. Class	Engine Diagram			Days Run	Train Class	Reference to Trainmen's Workings: Enginemen	Reference to Trainmen's Workings: Guards
112	4	a.m.	Norwich (W)	a.m. 8 0	EWD	K	NOR 11	NOR 22
		11 0	Harleston	p.m. 1 20		K	NOR 11	NOR 22
		p.m. 4 10	Norwich (Trowse)					

LOWESTOFT DEPOT—*continued*

Eng. Diagram No.	Engine M.P. Class	Engine Diagram			Days Run	Train Class	Reference to Trainmen's Workings: Enginemen	Reference to Trainmen's Workings: Guards
110	2	a.m.	Lowestoft Cen.	a.m. 9 28 L	EWD		LOW 6	—
		9 48	Beccles	10 35		K	BCL 1	BCL 1
		p.m. 2 31	Harleston	p.m. 3 30		K	BCL 1	BCL 1
		6 25	Beccles	7 20		H	LOW 10	NOR 23
		7 40	Haddiscoe	8 40		J	LOW 10	NOR 23
		9 5	Lowestoft Cen.					

Locomotive and enginemen's workings, Norwich and Lowestoft depots 1953.

of the trains across the branch with an interlude working from Norwich to Yarmouth Vauxhall, whilst the Beccles goods engine worked the freight service to Tivetshall and on to Wymondham and back.

In 1953 Norwich No. 112 diagram locomotive – booked for a Class '4', 'J17' Class engine, but invariably a 'J15' Class engine – worked the 8.00am Norwich to Harleston Class 'K' freight train, arriving at 11.10am and departing for the return working at 1.20pm, arriving back at Trowse yard at 4.10pm. Norwich diagram 11 men manned the engine throughout, with Norwich diagram 22 guard in charge of the train. The eastern end of the branch was worked by Lowestoft No. 110 diagram locomotive booked for a 'J15' Class 0-6-0, departing Lowestoft light engine at 9.28am to Beccles arriving at 9.48am, where Lowestoft diagram 6 men handed over to Beccles diagram 1 men to work the 10.35 am Class 'K' goods train to Harleston arriving at 2.31pm. Here goods was exchanged with the freight working from Norwich via Tivetshall together with yard shunting before the return Class 'K' train departed at 3.30pm, arriving back at Beccles at 6.25pm. Lowestoft diagram 10 men relieved the Beccles men before working forward with the 7.20pm Class 'H' to Haddiscoe and Lowestoft. On the branch the train was in charge of Beccles diagram 1 guard.

Breakdown Vehicles

In the event of a mishap or breakdown, the Norwich breakdown vans – later breakdown vans and crane – initially covered the entire branch, but later Lowestoft breakdown vans were also involved, the branch then being divided for coverage at Earsham. Under the L&NER, new breakdown arrangements were introduced, Tivetshall to Beccles being covered by Norwich when the Train Staff was at the Tivetshall end of the line or by Lowestoft 5-ton hand crane when the Train Staff was at the Beccles end. By then Norwich were using 15-ton capacity breakdown crane No. 961604, built by Cowans, Sheldon & Company Limited of Carlisle (Works No. 2246) in 1899 for the Great Northern Railway where it was numbered 150A. After 1938 it was allocated to Norwich, paired with match truck 961658, but by November 1947 it had been transferred to Colchester and was finally withdrawn in 1954. Norwich used 35-ton steam crane No. 131 for the section Tivetshall to Earsham. This crane, built in 1932 by Ransomes & Rapier of Ipswich (Works No. D4648), was numbered 961601 by the L&NER in 1938 and was paired with match wagon 961652. It was originally allocated to Cambridge and then Stratford in 1947, before moving to Norwich. It was renumbered 131 by British Railways and was withdrawn in March 1970. At this period Lowestoft tool vans covered Lowestoft to Beccles and Bungay. Ipswich 20-ton capacity crane No. 132 was prohibited from working between Beccles and Bungay because of weight restrictions on the timber viaducts.

Coaching Stock

The ECR and GER placed no weight or loading gauge restrictions for coaching stock on the Waveney Valley line and conventional stock was utilised. Initially coaching stock was very primitive 4-wheel vehicles, with First, Second, Third and Parliamentary accommodation offered, the latter travelling in Third Class. The First Class vehicles had fully upholstered seats in the compartments, whilst at the other end of the spectrum the Third Class and Parliamentary passengers were subjected to sitting on bare wooden boards, often receiving splinters in the nether regions as the boards wore down or received the attention of vandals. Until the early 1900s, coaching stock was exclusively 4-wheeled, provided with oil lighting and only latterly equipped with the Westinghouse brake.

During the 1860s and 1870s, the stock allocated to the branch was of Sinclair's design for the ECR, with 4-compartment First/Second Composites to diagram 33, 5-Compartment Thirds to diagram 34, both with 24 feet body, and Full Brake to diagram 39 with a 21 feet body. The branch train usually comprised four or five vehicles with one or two Composites, two Full Thirds and one Brake Van as the normal formation. On Norwich, Ipswich and Beccles market days, an additional Full Third was attached. The leading dimensions of these vehicles were:

GER Diagram No.	33	34	39
Type	4-wheel Composite	4-wheel Third	4-wheel Full Brake
Length over body	24 ft 0 ins	24 ft 0 ins	21 ft 0 ins
Body height	6 ft 1¾ ins	6 ft 5¾ ins	6 ft 2½ ins
Wheelbase	13 ft 6 ins	13 ft 6 ins	12 ft 0 ins
Seating			
First Class	16	—	—
Third Class	20*	50	—
Weight empty	8 tons 2 cwt	7 tons 5 cwt	7 tons 17 cwt
Note: * Second or Third Class.			

From the early 1880s, the GER began drafting in 4-wheel vehicles, 27 feet in length, originally built for main line services during the 1870s. Trains were usually formed of up to five coaches, two being Third Class, one Second Class, one First Class or Composite and a

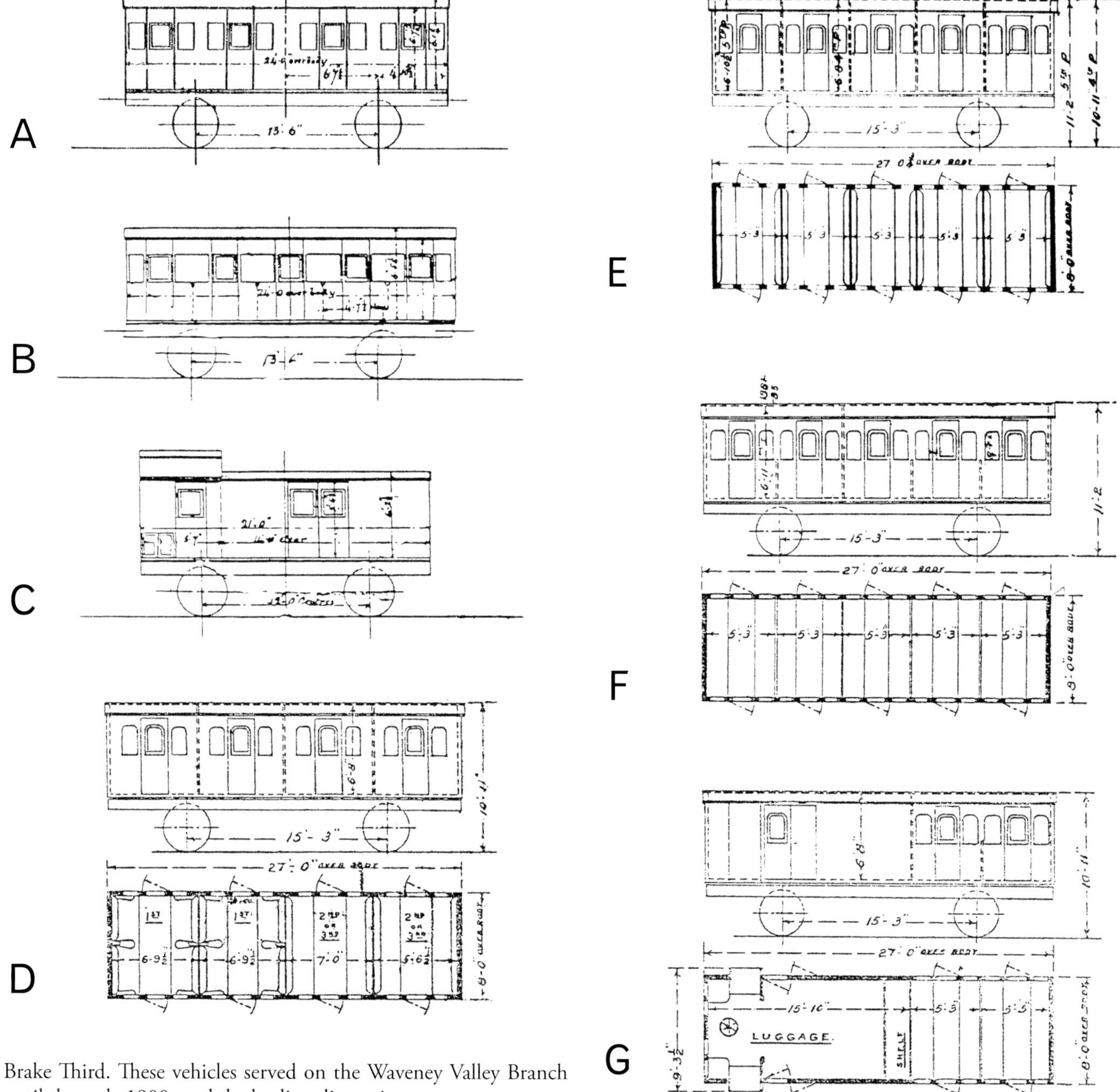

Brake Third. These vehicles served on the Waveney Valley Branch until the early 1900s and the leading dimensions were:

Diagram	217	302	402	504
Type	4-wheel Composite	4-wheel Second	4-wheel Third	4-wheel Brake/Third
Length over body	27 ft 0 ins	27 ft 0¾ ins	27 ft 0 ins	27 ft 0 ins
Max height	10 ft 11 ins	10 ft 11 ins#	11 ft 2 ins	10 ft 11 ins
Body height	6 ft 8 ins	6 ft 8¼ ins	6 ft 11 ins	6 ft 8 ins
Max width	8 ft 0 ins	8 ft 0 ins	8 ft 0 ins	9 ft 3½ ins+
Wheelbase	15 ft 3 ins	15 ft 3 ins	15 ft 3 ins	15 ft 3 ins
Seating				
First Class	16	—	—	—
Second Class	20	30	—	—
Third Class	*	—	30	20
Weight empty	8 tons 15 cwt	9 tons 18 cwt	9 tons 8 cwt	9 tons 12 cwt

Notes: # also 11 feet 2 ins.
\+ over guard's lookout.
* also 16 x First, 20 x Third.

(A) 4-wheel Composite to diagram 33.

(B) 4-wheel Third to diagram 34.

(C) 4-wheel Full Brake to diagram 39.

(D) 4-wheel Composite to diagram 217.

(E) 4-wheel Second to diagram 302.

(F) 4-wheel Third to diagram 402.

(G) 4-wheel Brake Third to diagram 504.

The introduction of bogie stock on the principal GER trains from the late 1890s was a gradual process and the use of 4-wheel coaching stock outside the London suburban area continued for many years. When replacement of stock was finally made on the branch, the 6-wheel vehicles dated from 1879 onwards and varied in length from 32 feet for a Full Brake to 34 feet 6 inches for a 6-compartment Third. The branch train was then usually formed of a Composite, two Thirds and a Brake Third, strengthened on market days and other busy periods by either a Composite or a Full Third vehicle. During the early years of the 20th century trains were formed of a mixture of 4- and 6-wheel stock. The principal dimensions of the 6-wheel coaching stock used on the Waveney Valley services were:

DIAGRAM	219	404	422
Type	6-wheel Composite	6-wheel Third	6-wheel Third
Length over buffers	35 ft 1½ ins 37 ft 7½ ins	37 ft 4½ ins	37 ft 7½ ins
Length over body	32 ft 0 ins	34 ft 6 ins	34 ft 6 ins
Height overall	11 ft 2 ins	11 ft 3 ins	11 ft 7 ins
Body height	6 ft 11 ins	7 ft 0 ins	7 ft 4 ins
Width over body	8 ft 0 ins	8 ft 0 ins	8 ft 0 ins
Width over guard's lookout	—	—	—
Wheelbase	20 ft 0 ins	21 ft 0 ins	22 ft 6 ins
Seating			
First Class	12	—	—
Third Class	20	60	60
Luggage	15 cwt	—	—
Weight empty	12 tons 16 cwt	13 tons 3 cwt	18 tons 3 cwt

DIAGRAM	514	108	208
Type	6-wheel Brake/Third	6-wheel First	6-wheel Composite
Length over buffers	37 ft 7½ ins	34 ft 10½ ins	37 ft 4½ ins 37 ft 7½ ins
Length over body	34 ft 6 ins	32 ft 0 ins	34 ft 10 ins
Height overall	11 ft 3 ins	11 ft 7 ins	11 ft 7 ins
Body height	7 ft 0 ins	7 ft 4 ins	7 ft 4 ins
Width over body	8 ft 0 ins	8 ft 0 ins	8 ft 0 ins
Width over guard's lookout	9 ft 3½ ins	—	—
Wheelbase	20 ft 0 ins	20 ft 0 ins	22 ft 6 ins
Seating			
First Class	—	22	10
Third Class	30	—	20
Luggage	2 tons	—	10 cwt
Weight empty	12 tons 16 cwt	13 tons 15 cwt	13 tons 19 cwt

DIAGRAM	511	532
Type	6-wheel Brake/Third	6-wheel Full Brake
Length over buffers	35 ft 1½ ins	35 ft 1½ ins
Length over body	31 ft 6 ins	32 ft 0 ins
Height overall	11 ft 2 ins	11 ft 7 ins
Body height	6 ft 11 ins	7 ft 4 ins
Width over body	8 ft 0 ins	8 ft 6 ins
Width over guard's lookout	9 ft 0 ins	9 ft 4 ins
Wheelbase	20 ft 0 ins	22 ft 6 ins
Seating		
First Class	—	—
Third Class	30	—
Luggage	2 tons	4 tons
Weight empty	12 tons 18cwt	12 tons 2 cwt

From about 1937 a variety of 50 feet long bogie stock fully replaced the remaining 6-wheel stock on the Waveney Valley Branch, usually formed of a three-coach set. These included 8-compartment Thirds to diagram 430 or 439, Composites to diagram 226 from the

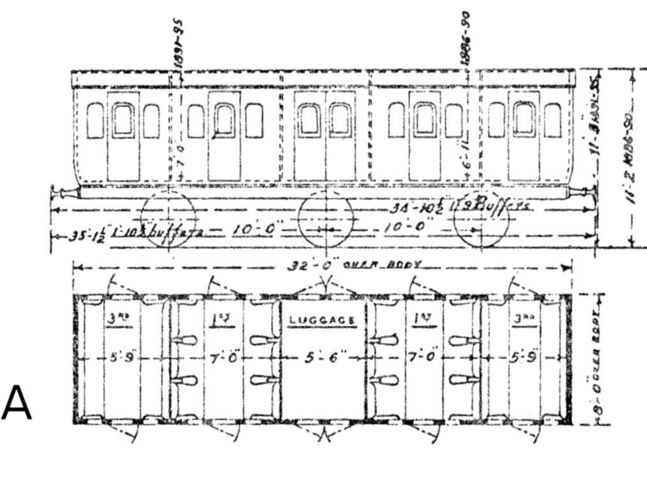

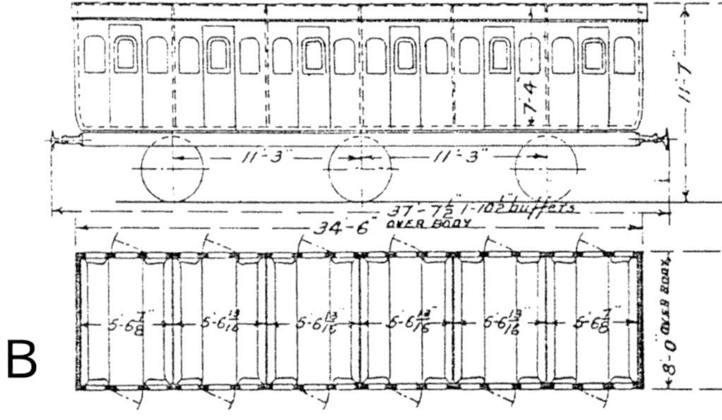

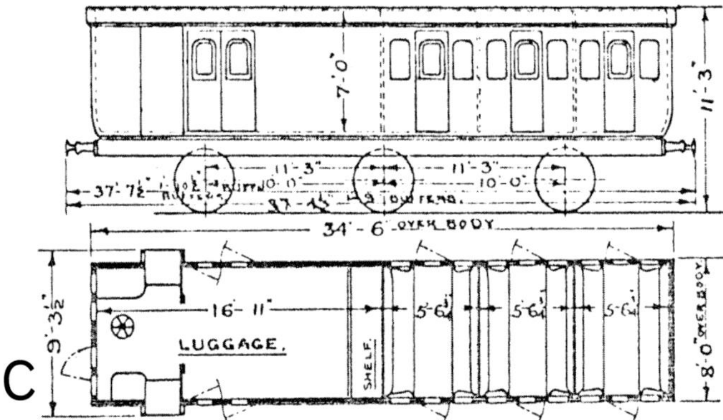

(A) 6-wheel Composite to diagram 219.
(B) 6-wheel Third to diagram 422.
(C) 6-wheel Brake Third to diagram 514.

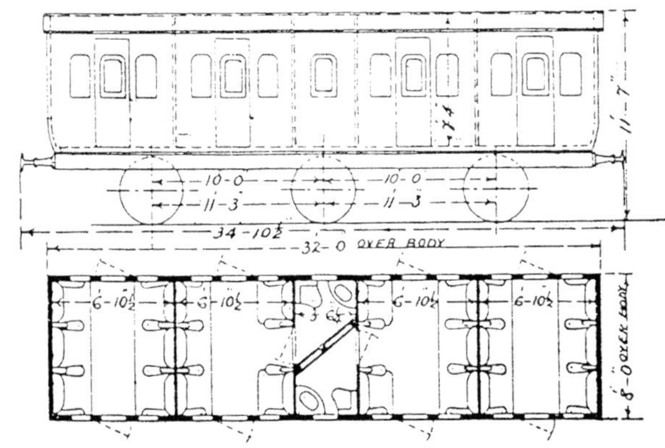

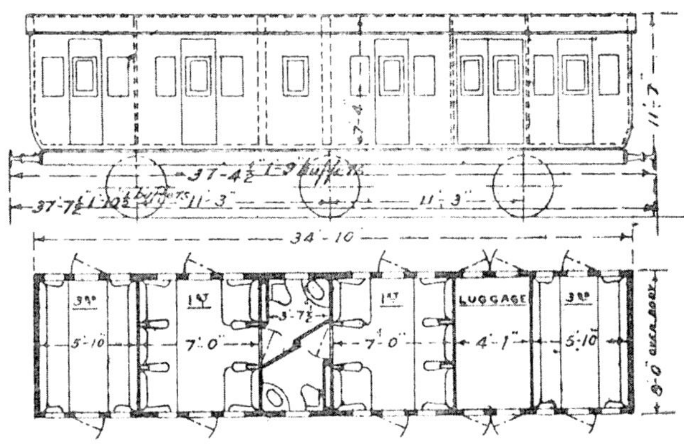

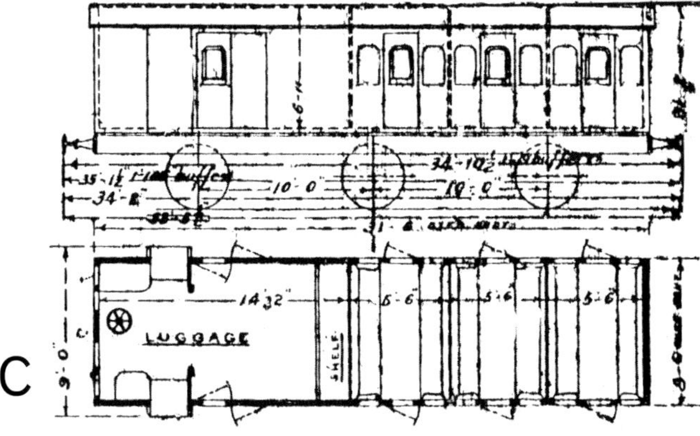

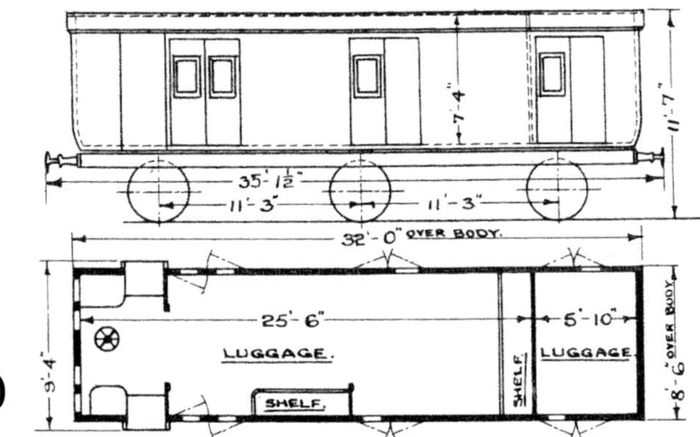

Norfolk Coast Express or 227 to the same design, and Brake Thirds to diagram 541. The stock was often interchanged and other ex-GER vehicles were supplemented or replaced by former North Eastern Railway bogie coaches, and even an ex-Great Central 'Barnum' Brake Third. The leading dimensions of the ex GER vehicles were:

Diagram	226	227	430
Type	Bogie Composite	Bogie Composite	Bogie Third
Length over buffers	53 ft 1½ ins	53 ft 1½ ins	53 ft 1½ ins
Length over body	50 ft 0 ins	50 ft 0 ins	50 ft 0 ins
Height overall	12 ft 5 ins	12 ft 5 ins	12 ft 5 ins
Body height	8 ft 2¼ ins	8 ft 2¼ ins	8 ft 2¼ ins
Width over body	8 ft 9 ins	8 ft 9 ins	8 ft 9 ins
Width over guard's lookout	—	—	—
Wheelbase	43 ft 0 ins	43 ft 0 ins	43 ft 0 ins
Bogie wheelbase	8 ft 0 ins	8 ft 0 ins	8 ft 0 ins
Seating			
First class	12	12	—
Third class	32	38	80
Luggage	—	—	—
Weight empty	26 tons 12 cwt	26 tons 12 cwt	24 tons 7 cwt

Diagram	439	541
Type	Bogie Third	Bogie Brake/Third
Length over buffers	57 ft 1½ ins	53 ft 1½ ins
Length over body	54 ft 0 ins	50 ft 0 ins
Height overall	12 ft 5 ins	12 ft 5 ins
Body height	8 ft 2¼ ins	8 ft 2¼ ins
Width over body	8 ft 10 ins	8 ft 9 ins
Width over guard's lookout	—	9 ft 1 in
Wheelbase	45 ft 0 ins	43 ft 0 ins
Bogie wheelbase	8 ft 0 ins	8 ft 0 ins
Seating		
First class	—	—
Third class	96	24
Luggage	—	3½ tons
Weight empty	27 tons 11 cwt	26 tons 14 cwt

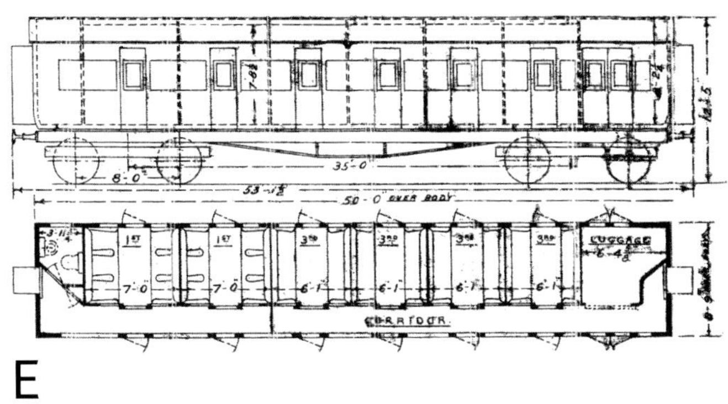

(A) 6-wheel First to diagram 108.
(B) 6-wheel Composite to diagram 208.
(C) 6-wheel Brake Third to diagram 511.
(D) 6-wheel Full Brake to diagram 532.
(E) Bogie Composite to diagram 226.

Varieties of L&NER suburban bogie coaches later appeared on the branch, including Gresley panelled non-corridor stock. These were augmented by ex-GER bogie Composites to diagram 212 and 231, which had two First and four Third Class compartments with corridors to separate toilets plus a luggage locker, standard 3-compartment Brake Thirds to diagram 547 dating from 1920, and ex-North Eastern Railway Thirds to diagram 503 transferred to the GE area from 1936 both before and after hostilities.

Diagram	212	231
Type	Bogie Composite	Bogie Composite
Length over buffers	51 ft 4½ ins	51 ft 4½ ins
Length over body	48 ft 3 ins	48 ft 3 ins
Height overall	12 ft 8 ins	12 ft 8 ins
Body height	8 ft 5 ins	8 ft 5 ins
Width over body	8 ft 6 ins	8 ft 6 ins
Width over guard's lookout	—	—
Wheelbase	40 ft 3 ins	40 ft 3 ins
Bogie wheelbase	8 ft 0 ins	8 ft 0 ins
Seating		
First Class	9	9
Third Class	33	33
Luggage	—	—
Weight empty	25 tons 9 cwt	25 tons 9 cwt

Diagram	503	547
Type	Bogie Third	Bogie Brake/Third
Length over buffers	55 ft 8 ins	57 ft 1½ ins
Length over body	52 ft 0 ins	54 ft 0 ins
Height overall	12 ft 7 ins	12 ft 5 ins
Body height	8 ft 2¼ ins	
Width over body	8 ft 0 ins	8 ft 9 ins
Width over guard's lookout	9 ft 0 ins	9 ft 1 in
Wheelbase	44 ft 6 ins 41 ft 3 ins	45 ft 0 ins
Bogie wheelbase	8 ft 0 ins	8 ft 0 ins
Seating		
First Class	—	—
Third Class	50	24
Luggage	2 tons	3½ tons
Weight empty	23 tons 3 cwt	27 tons 12 cwt

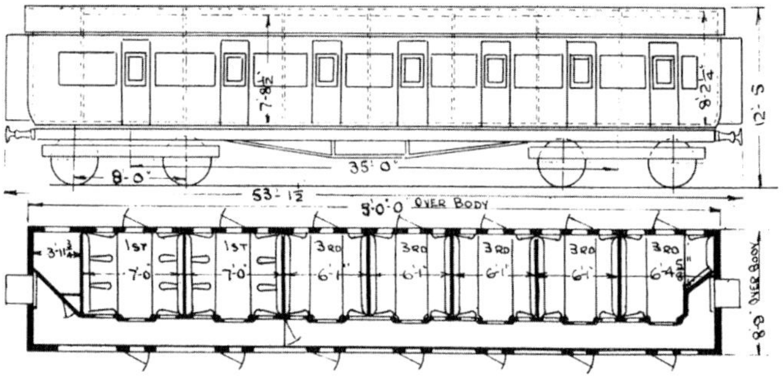

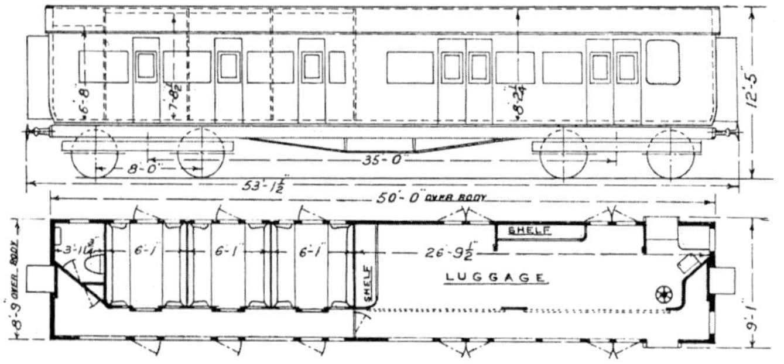

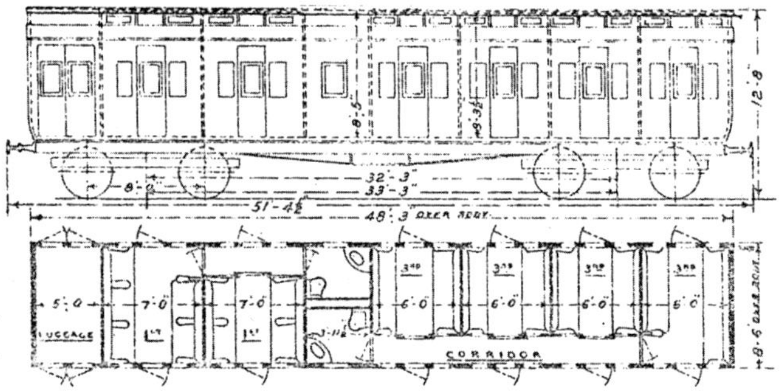

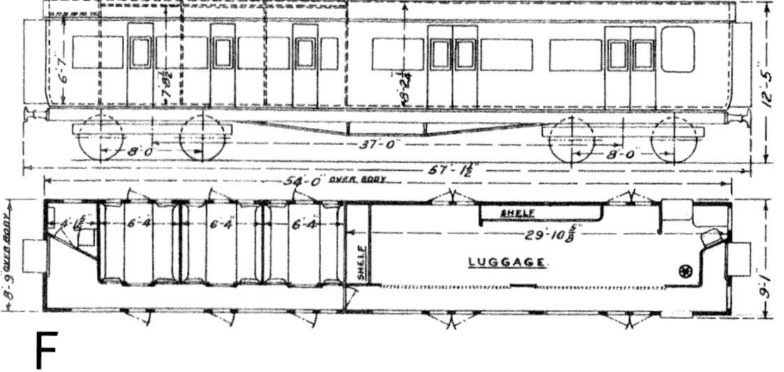

(A) Bogie Composite to diagram 227.
(B) Bogie Third to diagram 430.
(C) Bogie Third to diagram 439.
(D) Bogie Brake Third to diagram 541.
(E) Bogie Composite to diagram 212 and 235.
(F) Bogie Brake Third to diagram 547.

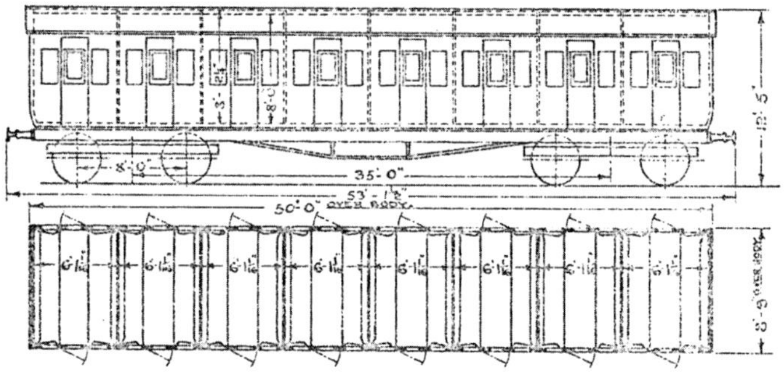

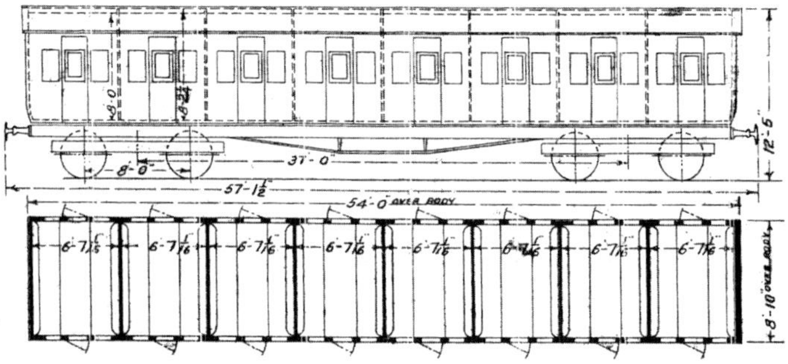

The L&NER vehicles were:

Diagram	37	64	65
Type	Gresley Bogie Brake/Third Corridor	Gresley Bogie Brake/Third Non-Vestibule	Gresley Bogie Brake/Third Non-Vestibule
Length over body	61 ft 6 ins	51 ft 1½ ins	51 ft 1½ ins
Width over body	9 feet 3 ins	9 ft 0 ins	9 ft 3 ins
Seating			
First Class	—	—	—
Third Class	40	40	40

Diagram	215	244
Type	Gresley Bogie Composite Non-Vestibule	Gresley Bogie Composite Non-Vestibule
Length over body	51 ft 1½ ins	51 ft 1½
Width over body	9 ft 3 ins	9 ft 3 ins
Seating		
First Class	20	13
Third Class	60	41

The L&NER diagram 244 Composite dating from 1936 was the equivalent of GER diagrams 212 and 231 and was unique to East Anglia having five Third Class compartments instead of four.

In 1950 the branch was served by two carriage diagram sets. The first set, No. 52, was formed of a three-coach branch set consisting of non-gangway Third Lavatory (TL), Composite Lavatory (CL) and a Brake Third (BT), in total weighing 76 tons and seating 13 First Class and 136 Third Class passengers. Alternatively, another non-gangway three-coach set was provided formed of Third Lavatory (TL), Composite Lavatory (CGL) and Brake Third (BT), also weighing 76 tons with accommodation for 13 First and 128 Third Class passengers. Of especial interest was the four-coach set 116, which formed the 7.00am Beccles to Tivetshall train and 8.35am return working. On alternate days it was formed of Eastern Region or London Midland Region gangway stock starting at Lowestoft at 5.55am and finishing the day working the 12.55pm Lowestoft to Rugby via March and Peterborough East. The set returned from Rugby to Lowestoft the next day on diagram 111 but not via the Waveney Valley. The set was formed of a Brake Third (BTKBS), Composite (CKBS), Full Third (TKBS) and another BTKBS, weighing 108 tons and with accommodation for 12 First and 142 Third Class passengers (BS denoted British Standard gangway).

In the latter years excursions trains were formed of Gresley corridor stock augmented after nationalisation by BR Mark 1 corridor stock, and after the closure of the line to passenger traffic the railway enthusiast special trains were formed of similar stock.

The day-to-day maintenance and inspection of the coaching stock used on the branch services was carried out by a carriage inspector based at Beccles and staff from the Carriage and Wagon department at Norwich.

Wagon Stock

The wagons used by the WVR, EUR and ECR were wooden open vehicles with side doors and fitted with dumb buffers. Where grain, straw or merchandise traffic was susceptible to wet weather a tarpaulin sheet was utilised to cover the contents of the wagon. The brake van at the tail of the train would have been a 10-ton vehicle. In the years prior to the turn of the century the GER utilised 4-plank bodied, open wagons with wooden frames dating from 1882 for the conveyance of general merchandise and minerals. From 1887, these wagons were gradually superseded by 5-plank 9-ton capacity (later 10-ton) opens, to diagram 16 with 9 feet 6 inch wheelbase and measuring 15 feet 0 inches over headstocks. Later 10-ton, 7-plank open wagons to diagram 17, with a length of 15 feet over headstocks and 9 feet 0 inches wheelbase

1 to 62 G.E. BRANCH SETS.

TL (8), CL (2-5), BT (3)=3 Vehs. (13 F, 136 T) 76 tons
or TL (8), CGL (2-4), BT (3)=3 Vehs. (13 F, 128 T) 76 tons.

WEEKDAYS

Attach	Station	Arr.	Dep.	Detach
	52			
		a.m.	a.m.	
	Norwich Thorpe		6 55	
	Beccles	8 11	9 0	
	Norwich	10 16	10 53	
		p.m.	p.m.	
	Beccles	12 14	12 35	
	Tivetshall	1 25	2 0	
	Beccles	2 51	3 18	
	Norwich	4 53	5 3	
	Beccles	6 25	6 55	
	Tivetshall	7 44	8 15	
	Beccles	9 9	9 20	
106	Lowestoft	9 35	9 50	
	Norwich Thorpe	10 54		106
	Works Daily.			

110 & 111 MR & ER stock alternate days.

BTKBS (3), CKBS (2-5), TKBS (7), BTKBS (3) = 4 Vehs
(12 F, 142 T.) 108 tons.

Attach	Station	Arr.	Dep.	Detach
	110			
		a.m.	a.m.	
	Lowestoft		5 55	
	Beccles	6 12	7 0	
	Tivetshall	7 50	8 35	
	Beccles	9 38	10 0	
	Lowestoft	10 15	p.m.	
112	Lowestoft	p.m.	12 35	
	March	3 38	3 45	
	Peterboro' East	4 5	4 15	112
	Rugby			
	Works 111 next day.			

Coaching stock workings for the Waveney Valley Branch 1950.

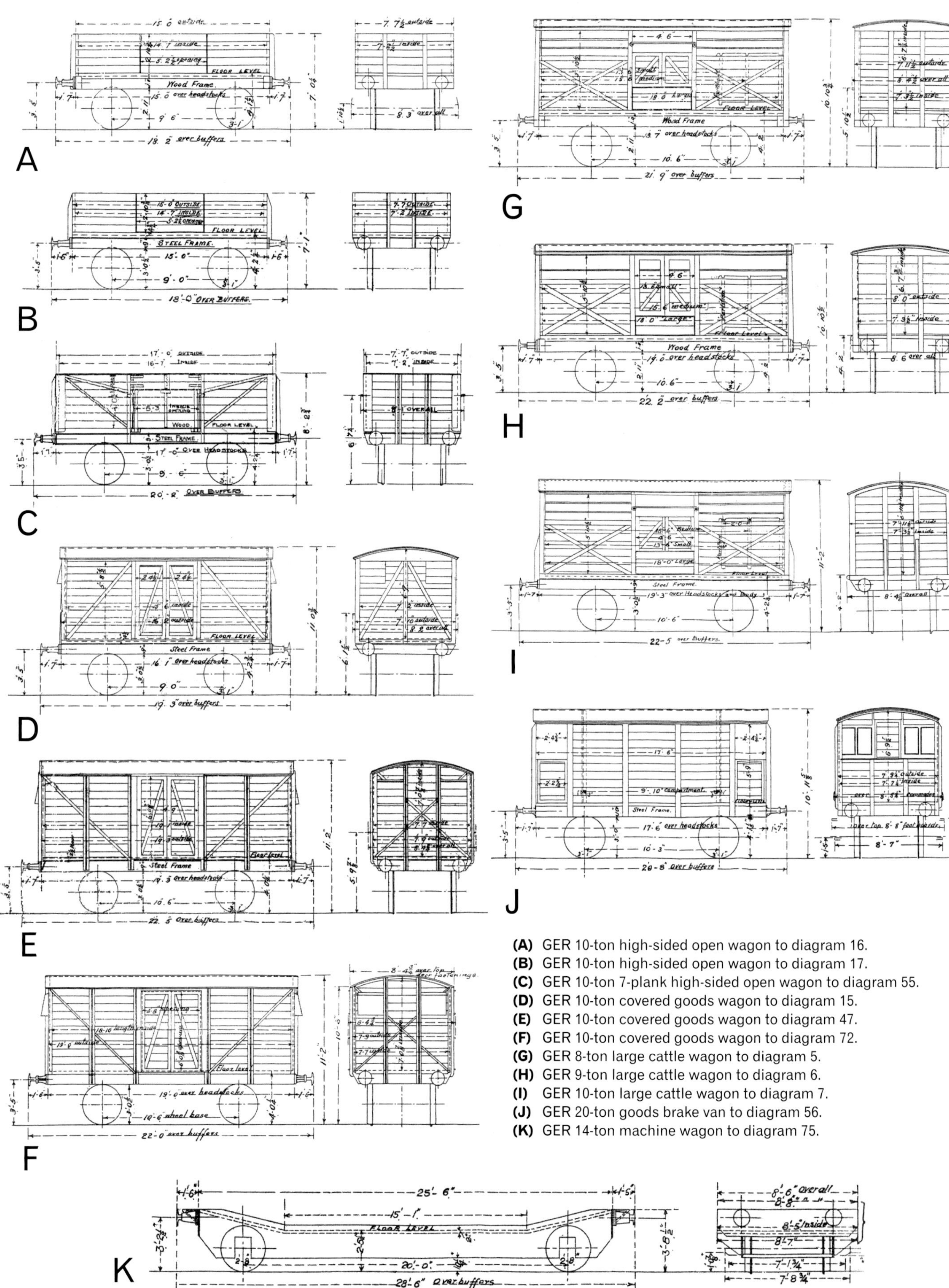

(A) GER 10-ton high-sided open wagon to diagram 16.
(B) GER 10-ton high-sided open wagon to diagram 17.
(C) GER 10-ton 7-plank high-sided open wagon to diagram 55.
(D) GER 10-ton covered goods wagon to diagram 15.
(E) GER 10-ton covered goods wagon to diagram 47.
(F) GER 10-ton covered goods wagon to diagram 72.
(G) GER 8-ton large cattle wagon to diagram 5.
(H) GER 9-ton large cattle wagon to diagram 6.
(I) GER 10-ton large cattle wagon to diagram 7.
(J) GER 20-ton goods brake van to diagram 56.
(K) GER 14-ton machine wagon to diagram 75.

Hunslet BR Class '05' diesel mechanical shunting locomotive No. D2558 hauls a sand train from Ditchingham just east of Ellingham station a few days before the traffic ceased in August 1965 and complete closure of the line. The sand traffic was conveyed after official closure between Ditchingham and Beccles to fulfil a contract and to allow the transfer of traffic to Coltishall on the Wroxham to County School cross-country branch. *Dr I.C. Allen*

were also used. Another variation was the use of 10-ton 7-plank opens to diagram 55, measuring 17 feet 0 inches over headstocks and 9 feet 6 inches wheelbase for vegetable and root traffic. For fruit and perishable traffic, 10-ton ventilated vans to diagram 15 were provided, measuring 16 feet 1 inch over headstocks, with 9 feet 0 inches wheelbase and overall height of 11 feet 0¾ inches. Covered goods vans to diagram 47 were later also utilised; they measured 17 feet 3 inches over headstocks, had a wheelbase of 10 feet 6 inches and were 11 feet 2 inches in height. A third variation was the 10-ton capacity covered goods wagon to diagram 72, which measured 19 feet 0 inches over headstocks whilst maintaining a 10 feet 6 inches wheelbase.

The extensive cattle traffic, conveyed to the various local markets would have entailed the use of three types of cattle wagons on the branch. The first, of 8 tons capacity, was to diagram 5 and was 18 feet 7 inches over headstocks, had a 10 feet 6 inches wheelbase and was 10 feet 10¾ inches in height. The second, to diagram 6, was of 9 tons capacity and measured 19 feet 0 inches over headstocks with a 10 feet 6 inches wheelbase and overall height of 11 feet 2 inches. The third GE variant of cattle wagon, to diagram 7, was of 10 tons capacity, 19 feet 3 inches over headstocks with 10 feet 6 inches wheelbase and overall height of 11 feet 2 inches. At the tail of the train was usually a 20-ton 4-wheel goods brake van to diagram 56, measuring 17 feet 6 inches over headstocks, a 10 feet 3 inches wheelbase and 3 feet 1 inch diameter wheels. In addition, many wagons owned by other railway companies were used to deliver and collect agricultural and livestock traffic, whilst coal and coke supplies came in private owner wagons. These fell into two categories: those belonging to the collieries consigning the coal, and merchants and coal factors wagons which were loaded at the collieries. These included W. Fowler who operated 5-plank opens with side doors only painted red oxide and white letters shaded black, later taken over by Charrington's.

After grouping the GER wagons continued in use but gradually L&NER standard designed wagons made an appearance. The most numerous were probably the 12-ton, 5-plank opens with 8 feet 0 inches wheelbase to code 2, and 12-ton 6-plank opens with 10 feet 0 inches wheelbase to code 91 built after 1932. Later variations included a 13-ton 7-plank open wagon to code 162 measuring 16 feet 6 inches over headstocks and with a 9 feet 0 inches wheelbase. All were used on vegetable and sugar beet traffic. Fitted and unfitted 12-ton, 9 feet 0 inches wheelbase covered vans to code 16 conveyed perishable goods, fruit and malt, and later some were designated for fruit traffic only. From 1934, 12-tons capacity vans to code 171, with steel underframes and pressed corrugated steel ends were introduced, whilst at the same time the wheelbase was extended to a length of 10 feet 0 inches. Specific fruit vans with both 9 feet 0 inches and 10 feet 0 inches wheelbase saw service on the branch for malt traffic. Agricultural machinery destined for local farms was delivered on 12-ton 'Lowfit' wagons, with 10 feet 0 inches wheelbase and overall length over headstocks of 17 feet 6 inches. Larger machinery would have been conveyed on one of the ex-GER 14-ton, 25 feet 6 inches 'Mac K2' machinery wagons to diagram 75 and later L&NER builds. L&NER brake vans provided for branch traffic included 20-ton 'Toad B' to code 34 and 'Toad E' to code 64 vehicles, with 10 feet 6 inches wheelbase and measuring 22 feet 5 inches over buffers. Later 'Toad D' brake vans to code 61 with 16 feet wheelbase and measuring 27 feet 5 inches over buffers were employed. After nationalisation many of the older wooden wagons were scrapped and much of the traffic was conveyed in open wagons in the standard 16-ton all steel mineral vehicles. Malt traffic was conveyed in 20-ton bulk grain wagons.

In GER days the body, solebars and headstocks of the open wagons were painted slate grey, whilst the ironwork below solebar level, buffer guides, buffers, drawbars, drawbar plates and couplings were black. The L&NER wagon livery was grey for non-fitted wagons and covered vans, whilst all vehicles with automatic brakes, including brake vans, were painted red oxide, which changed to bauxite around 1940. Similar liveries were carried in BR days.

The wagon repair shops at Ipswich or Norwich carried out the maintenance of wagon stock used on the branch. In the event of the failure or defect of a wagon on the branch, a travelling wagon repairer based at Beccles attended to the vehicle.

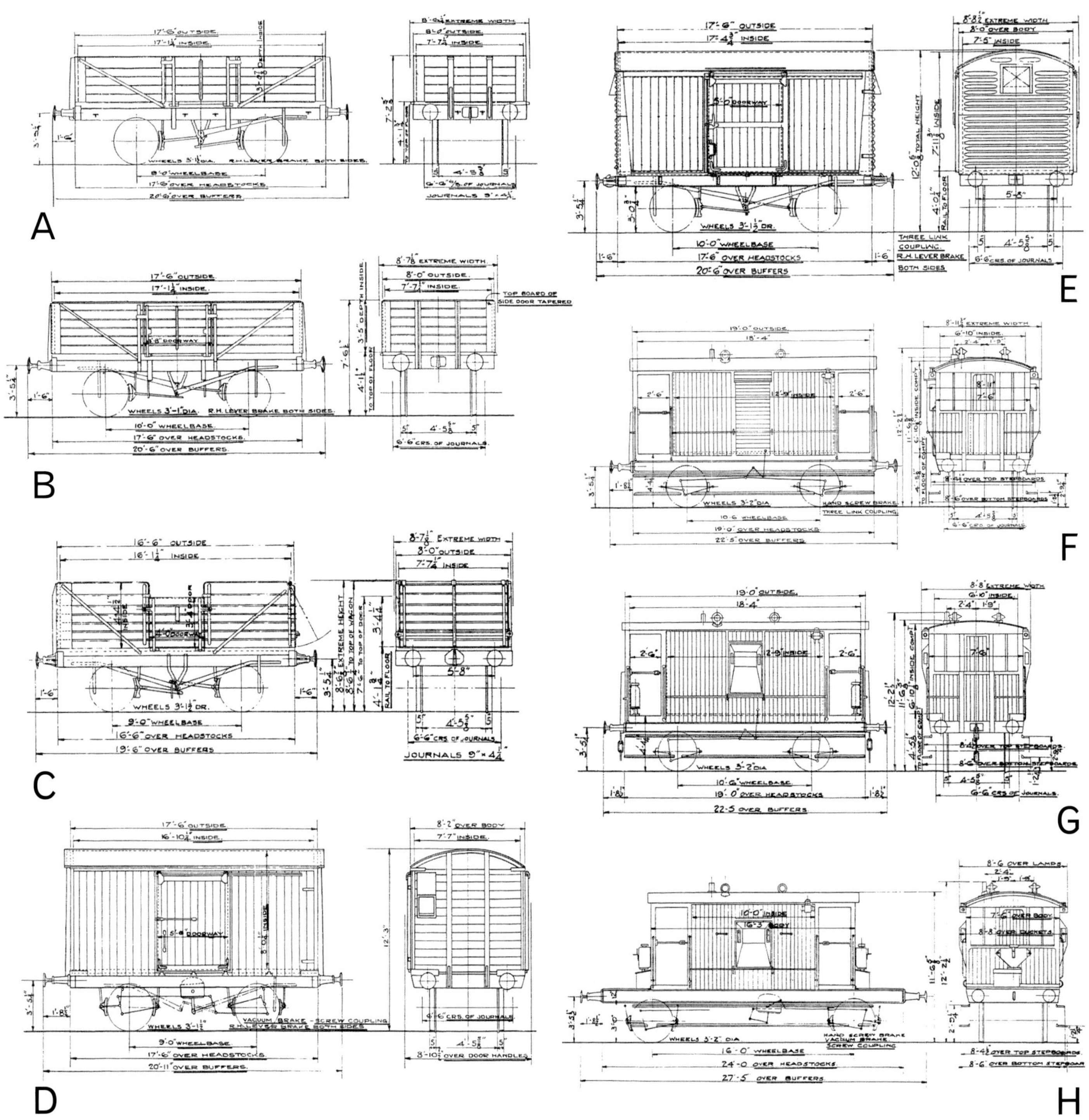

(A) L&NER 12-ton open goods wagon to code 2.
(B) L&NER 12-ton open goods wagon to code 91.
(C) L&NER 13-ton open goods wagon to code 162.
(D) L&NER 12-ton covered goods wagon to code 16.
(E) L&NER 12-ton covered goods wagon with steel ends to code 171.
(F) L&NER 20-ton goods brake van 'Toad B' to code 34.
(G) L&NER 20-ton goods brake van 'Toad E' to code 64.
(H) L&NER 20-ton goods brake van 'Toad D' to code 61.

Appendix 1

Level Crossings

No	Location	Mileage M Ch	Local Name	Status	Type
Main Line		From Liverpool St			
9	**Tivetshall Station**	100 53¼	Tivetshall Station	Public Road	Gates
Branch		From Tivetshall			
1	Tivetshall & Pulham Mkt	0 44¾		Occupation	Gates
2	Tivetshall & Pulham Mkt	0 50		Occupation	Gates
3	Tivetshall & Pulham Mkt	0 67¼	Hall Lane	Public Road	Gates*
4	Tivetshall & Pulham Mkt	0 78½	Green Lane	Public Road	Gates*
5	Tivetshall & Pulham Mkt	1 19¼	Star Lane	Public Road	Gates*
6	Tivetshall & Pulham Mkt	1 38		Occupation	Gates
7	Tivetshall & Pulham Mkt	1 45		Occupation	Gates
8	Tivetshall & Pulham Mkt	1 67¾	Norwich Road (Turnpike), also known as Roman Road	Public Road	Gates+
9	Tivetshall & Pulham Mkt	2 07		Occupation	Gates
10	Tivetshall & Pulham Mkt	2 21½		Occupation	Gates
11	Tivetshall & Pulham Mkt	2 27½		Occupation	Gates
11A	Tivetshall & Pulham Mkt	2 35½		Footpath	Stile
12	Tivetshall & Pulham Mkt	2 44		Occupation	Gates
	Pulham Market Station	2 52			
13	Pulham Mkt & Pulham St. Mary	2 54¾	Pulham Market Station	Public Road	Gates+
14	Pulham Mkt & Pulham St. Mary	2 58½		Occupation	Gates
15	Pulham Mkt & Pulham St. Mary	2 72½		Occupation	Gates
16	Pulham Mkt & Pulham St. Mary	2 77½		Occupation	Gates
17	Pulham Mkt & Pulham St. Mary	3 31¾		Occupation	Gates
18	Pulham Mkt & Pulham St. Mary	3 35		Footpath	Gates
19	Pulham Mkt & Pulham St. Mary	3 43		Occupation	Gates
20	Pulham Mkt & Pulham St. Mary	3 55	Pulham St. Mary Station	Public Road	Gates+
	Pulham St. Mary Station	3 57			
21	Pulham St. Mary & Harleston	3 68¾		Occupation	Gates
22	Pulham St. Mary & Harleston	3 74½		Occupation	Gates
23	Pulham St. Mary & Harleston	4 01¼		Occupation	Gates
24	Pulham St. Mary & Harleston	4 15	Crossingford, also known as Doctor's Lane	Public Road	Gates*
25	Pulham St. Mary & Harleston	4 24¼		Occupation	Gates
26	Pulham St. Mary & Harleston	4 38½	Crossingford Farm	Occupation	Gates
27	Pulham St. Mary & Harleston	4 69		Occupation	Gates
28	Pulham St. Mary & Harleston	5 02¼		Occupation	Gates
29	Pulham St. Mary & Harleston	5 09¾		Occupation	Gates
30	Pulham St. Mary & Harleston	5 25¾		Occupation	Gates
	Starston Station	5 38	(Closed 1st August 1866)		

No	Location	Mileage M	Ch	Local Name	Status	Type
31	Pulham St. Mary & Harleston	5	40	Grove Hill Road, also known as Starston Station	Public Road	Gates⁺
32	Pulham St. Mary & Harleston	5	70¼		Occupation	Gates
33	Pulham St. Mary & Harleston	6	16	Malthouse	Occupation	Gates (a)
34	Pulham St. Mary & Harleston	6	22	Harleston Station	Public Road	Gates
	Harleston Station	6	25			
35	Harleston & Homersfield	6	42¾		Occupation	Gates
36	Harleston & Homersfield	6	50½		Footpath	Stile
37	Harleston & Homersfield	6	51		Occupation	Gates
38	Harleston & Homersfield	7	02¾		Occupation	Gates
39	Harleston & Homersfield	7	19		Occupation	Gates
40	Harleston & Homersfield	7	27¾		Occupation	Gates
41	Harleston & Homersfield	7	37	Redenhall	Public Road	Gates*
	Redenhall Station	7	38	(Closed 1st August 1866)		
42	Harleston & Homersfield	7	68	Railway Plantation	Occupation	Gates
43	Harleston & Homersfield	8	01		Occupation	Gates
	Wortwell Station	8	17½	(Closed 1st January 1878)		
44	Harleston & Homersfield	8	19	Wortwell	Public Road	Gates
45	Harleston & Homersfield	8	36¾		Occupation	Gates
46	Harleston & Homersfield	8	37		Footpath	Gates
47	Harleston & Homersfield	8	64¾		Occupation	Gates
48	Harleston & Homersfield	8	69	Homersfield Station	Public Road	Gates
	Homersfield Station	8	74			
49	Homersfield & Earsham	8	78¾		Occupation	Gates
50	Homersfield & Earsham	9	24¾		Occupation	Gates
51	Homersfield & Earsham	9	58¼		Occupation	Gates
52	Homersfield & Earsham	9	59		Occupation	Gates
53	Homersfield & Earsham	9	66¼		Occupation	Gates
54	Homersfield & Earsham	9	71½		Occupation	Gates
55	Homersfield & Earsham	9	79		Occupation	Gates
56	Homersfield &Earsham	10	05½		Occupation	Gates
57	Homersfield & Earsham	10	20½		Occupation	Gates
58	Homersfield & Earsham	10	27¾	Denton Wash	Public Road	Gates
59	Homersfield & Earsham	10	30½		Occupation	Gates
60	Homersfield & Earsham	10	75¼		Occupation	Gates
61	Homersfield & Earsham	11	10	Drakes Lane	Public Road	Gates*
62	Homersfield & Earsham	11	47		Occupation	Gates
63	Homersfield & Earsham	11	65	Five Acre Lane	Public Road	Gates*
	Earsham Station	12	05			
64	Earsham & Bungay	12	06½	Earsham Station	Public Road	Gates
65	Earsham & Bungay	12	22¼		Footpath	Gates
66	Earsham & Bungay	12	25		Occupation	Gates
67	Earsham & Bungay	12	26½		Occupation	Gates
68	Earsham & Bungay	12	34¼		Occupation	Gates
69	Earsham & Bungay	12	54¼		Occupation	Gates
	Bungay Station	12	68			
70	Bungay & Ditchingham	13	06	Bungay Common	Public	Gates

No	Location	Mileage M Ch	Local Name	Status	Type
71	Bungay & Ditchingham	13 31		Occupation	Gates
72	Bungay & Ditchingham	13 43¼	Factory Road	Public Road	Gates
	Ditchingham Station	13 63			
73	Ditchingham & Ellingham	13 65½	Ditchingham Station, also known as Purnough Street	Public Road	Gates
74	Ditchingham & Ellingham	13 78¾		Occupation	Gates
75	Ditchingham & Ellingham	14 16¾	Whistle Lane	Public Road	Gates
76	Ditchingham & Ellingham	14 28¼		Occupation	Gates
77	Ditchingham & Ellingham	14 45½		Occupation	Gates
78	Ditchingham & Ellingham	14 58¾		Occupation	Gates
79	Ditchingham & Ellingham	15 06		Occupation	Gates
80	Ditchingham & Ellingham	15 18½		Occupation	Gates
	Ellingham Station	15 23			
81	Ellingham & Geldeston	15 25¼	Ellingham Station	Public Road	Gates+
82	Ellingham & Geldeston	15 48½		Occupation	Gates
83	Ellingham & Geldeston	15 64¼	Church Farm	Occupation	Gates
84	Ellingham & Geldeston	15 74	Ellingham/Brace's Lane, also known as Bracey's	Public Road	Gates*
85	Ellingham & Geldeston	16 23	Boor's Farm	Occupation	Gates
	Geldeston Station	16 57			
86	Geldeston & Beccle	16 60	Geldeston Station	Public Road	Gates+
87	Geldeston & Beccles	17 12		Occupation	Gates
88	Geldeston & Beccles	17 19¼		Occupation	Gates
89	Geldeston & Beccles	17 22½		Occupation	Gates
90	Geldeston & Beccles	17 31½		Occupation	Gates
91	Geldeston & Beccles	17 43½		Occupation	Gates
92	Geldeston & Beccles	17 60	Dunburgh House	Footpath	Gates
93	Geldeston & Beccles	17 74		Occupation	Gates
94	Geldeston & Beccles	18 23¼		Occupation	Gates
95	Geldeston & Beccles	18 60¼		Occupation	Gates
96	Geldeston & Beccles	19 03½	Northgate Street	Public Road	Gates+
97	Geldeston & Beccles	19 09	Pound Road	Public Road	Gates+
	Beccles Station	19 33			

Notes:

(a) Crossing No. 33: Closed 31st October 1938.
* Converted to level crossing without gates 1954.
\+ Crossing No. 81: Train crew operated from 16th September 1963.
Crossing No. 86: Train crew operated from 16th September 1963.
Crossing No. 96: Train crew operated from 3rd July 1963.
Crossing No. 97: Train crew operated from 3rd July 1963.
Crossing No. 8: Train crew operated from 13th July 1964.
Crossing No. 13: Train crew operated from 13th July 1964.
Crossing No. 20: Train crew operated from 13th July 1964.
Crossing No. 31: Train crew operated from 13th July 1964.

Appendix 2

Bridges and Culverts

Bridge No	Location	Mileage M Ch	Local Name	Under or Over	Type	Spans between Abutments or Supports	Span FT IN	Width FT IN	Length FT IN	Distance from Road or Surface of Water to Rail FT IN	Construction
	Tivetshall Stn	0 00									
1174	Tivetshall & Pulham Market	0 44	Hall Farm	Under	Occup'n	1	11 10	13 8	24 0	8 9	Brick abutments, timber superstructure. Renewed 1882; later RSJs and concrete.
	Pulham Market Stn	2 52									
	Pulham St. Mary Stn	3 57									
1175	Pulham St. Mary & Harleston	4 69		Under	Occup'n	1	11 10	13 11	27 0	8 4	Brick abutments, timber superstructure. Renewed 1879; later RSJs and concrete.
	Starston Stn	5 38									
1176	Pulham St. Mary & Harleston	5 56		Under	Occup'n	1	11 10	13 8	25 0	9 8	Brick abutments, timber superstructure. Later RSJs and concrete.
1177	Pulham St. Mary & Harleston	6 00		Over	Public Road	1	19 0	26 0	72 0	18 0	Brick abutments, brick arch & parapets.
	Harleston Stn	6 25									
1178	Harleston Station	6 25	Station footbridge	Over	Footbridge	1	38 3	– –	00 4	14 9	Cast iron columns, wrought iron superstructure.
1179	Harleston & Homersfield	6 31	Harleston Girder	Under	Public Road	1 3	25 2 12 3	33 5	167 5	19 0	Brick abutments, brick arches and parapets.
1180	Harleston & Homersfield	6 70	Lushbush	Over	Occup'n	1	25 8	16 0	74 0	19 0	Brick abutments, brick arch & parapet.
1181	Harleston & Homersfield	7 04	Redenhall Girder	Under	Public Road	1	25 3	11 1	86 0	16 6	Brick abutments, wrought iron girders.
1182	Harleston & Homersfield	7 10	Beck No. 1	Under	Culvert	1	16 0	– –	50 8	20 6	Brick abutments, brick arch & girders.
1183	Harleston& Homersfield	7 14		Under	Occup'n	1 2	12 7 12 2	11 9	56 0	17 0	Brick abutments, brick arch & parapets.

Bridge No	Location	Mileage M Ch	Local Name	Under or Over	Type	Spans between Abutments or Supports	Span FT IN	Width FT IN	Length FT IN	Distance from Road or Surface of Water to Rail FT IN	Construction
1184	Harleston& Homersfield	7 34	Beck No. 2	Under	Dyke	1	21 9	15 3	33 5	7 7	Timber piles, timber superstructure.
	Redenhall Stn	7 38									
	Wortwell Stn	8 17½									
1185	Harleston & Homersfield	8 67		Under	Dyke	1 4	13 6 12 6	13 0	91 0	8 10	Timber piles, timber superstructure. Rebuilt 1881.
	Homersfield Stn	8 74									
1186	Homersfield & Earsham	9 79	Denton Wash	Under	Dyke	1	20 0	14 10	28 4	6 8	Brick abutments, timber superstructure. Rebuilt 1882.
1187	Homersfield & Earsham	11 12		Under	Dyke	1	13 0	12 2	40 0	12 0	Brick abutments, brick arch & parapets.
	Earsham Stn	12 05									
1188	Earsham & Bungay	12 40	Temple Bar	Under	River	1 1	16 2 14 8	11 5	35 8	5 6	Timber piles, timber superstructure. Rebuilt 1878.
1189	Earsham & Bungay	12 50		Under	River	1	35 0	11 2	57 0	6 0	Brick abutments, wrought iron girders. Rebuilt 1877.
1190	Earsham & Bungay	12 64	Waveney	Under	River	5 1	16 0 14 0	15 9	102 7	6 0	Timber piles, timber superstructure. Rebuilt 1922 with iron superstructure on concrete piling
	Bungay Stn	12 68									
1191	Bungay & Ditchingham	12 71	Outney	Over	Occup'n	3	15 0	22 6	100 6	20 8	Brick abutments, brick arch & parapets.
1192	Bungay & Ditchingham	13 16	River Crusty	Under	River	1 5	16 0 14 6	13 4	109 6	5 0	Timber piles, timber superstructure. Rebuilt 1881 and 1920.
1193	Bungay & Ditchingham	13 21	Deep Dyke	Under	Water	3	14 0	11 6	61 0	5 0	Timber piles, timber superstructure.
1194	Bungay & Ditchingham	13 32	Factory	Under	Water	4	14 6	13 0	69 6	4 0	Timber piles, timber superstructure. Rebuilt 1882.
1195	Bungay &	13 38	Little Factory	Under	Water	1	15 0	13 11	21 0	4 0	Timber piles, timber superstructure.

Bridge No	Location	Mileage M Ch	Local Name	Under or Over	Type	Spans between Abutments or Supports	Span ft in	Width ft in	Length ft in	Distance from Road or Surface of Water to Rail ft in	Construction
	Ditchingham										Rebuilt 1882.
	Ditchingham Stn	13 63									
1196	Ditchingham & Ellingham	14 71	Langford	Under	Water	3	12 0	13 6	40 0	4 0	Timber piles, timber superstructure. Rebuilt 1881.
	Ellingham Stn	15 23									
1197	Ellingham & Geldeston	15 34	St Mary's	Over	Public	1	16 0	20 0	71 0	17 6	Brick abutments, brick arch & parapets.
	Geldeston Stn	16 57									
1198	Geldeston & Beccles	16 74	Wherry Dyke	Under	Water	2 1	20 0 18 0	13 0	64 0	9 0	Timber piles, timber superstructure. Rebuilt 1881.
1199	Geldeston & Beccles	17 24		Under	Water	1	13 0	10 6	16 0	3 6	Timber piles, timber superstructure. Rebuilt 1881.
1200	Geldeston & Beccles	17 34		Under	Water	1	11 0	12 6	16 0	3 6	Timber piles, timber superstructure. Rebuilt 1881.
1201	Geldeston & Beccles	18 08		Under	Water	1	13 0	11 6	18 0	5 6	Timber piles, timber superstructure.
1202	Geldeston & Beccles	18 19		Under	Water	1 2	15 0 14 0	15 0	50 0	5 6	Timber piles, timber superstructure. Rebuilt 1877.
1203	Geldeston & Beccles	18 43		Under	Water	1	13 6	13 6	18 0	4 6	Timber piles, timber superstructure. Rebuilt 1881.
1204	Geldeston & Beccles	18 73		Under	Water	1	11 6	11 6	16 6	10 6	Timber piles, wrought iron girders.
1205	Geldeston & Beccles	18 74	River Waveney	Under	Water	2 1	72 0 15 6	13 0	207 9	12 6	Timber piles, timber superstructure. Rebuilt 1880.
1206	Geldeston & Beccles	19 00		Under	Water	No details					Timber piles, timber superstructure.
1207	Geldeston & Beccles	19 03	Ravensmere	Under	Public Road	2 1	12 0 23 0	12 6	29 6	10 6	Brick abutments, wrought iron girders, brick wing walls & parapets.
	Beccles Stn	19 33									

Bibliography

General Works

Aldrich, C., *GER Locomotives*

Allan, C.J., *The Great Eastern Railway*, Ian Allan

Gordon, D.I., *Regional History of the Railways of Great Britain*, Volume 5, David & Charles

Periodicals

Bradshaw's Railway Guide

Bradshaw's Railway Manual

British Railways, Eastern Region Magazine

Buses Illustrated

East Anglian Magazine

Great Eastern Railway Magazine

Herepath's Journal

Locomotive Carriage & Wagon Review

L&NER Magazine

Railway Magazine

Railway World

Railway Year Book

Trains Illustrated

Newspapers

Beccles Weekly News

Diss Express and Norfolk & Suffolk Journal

Diss, Harleston, Bungay & Eye Journal

Diss, Harleston, Bungay, Beccles & Eye Journal

East Anglian Daily Times

Eastern Daily Press

East Suffolk Gazette

Norfolk News

Norfolk & Suffolk Journal and Diss Express

Other Sources

The minute books of the Waveney Valley Railway (extracts)

The minute books of the Eastern Counties Railway

The minute books of the Eastern Union Railway (extracts)

The minute books of the Great Eastern Railway

The minute books of the London & North Eastern Railway

Working timetables
ECR, GER, L&NER and BR (ER)

Appendices to the working timetables
GER, L&NER and BR (ER)

Miscellaneous working instructions
ECR, GER, L&NER and BR (ER)

'J15' Class 0-6-0 No. 65460 rounding a curve towards Bungay with a Down freight train, the leading open wagons loaded with sugar beet. *Dr I.C. Allen*

Acknowledgements

The publication of this history would not have been possible without the assistance of many people. In particular I should like to thank:

The late A.R. Cox
The late W. Fenton
The late W. Blois
The late G. Woodcock
The late Dr I.C. Allen
The late Bernard Walsh
The late Canon C. Bayes
The late G. Pember
The late P. Proud
The late R.C. (Dick) Riley
The late Ted Vaughan
The late Ken Riley
John Watling
Dave Hoser
John Petrie
Alan Keeler
The late R.H.N. (Dick) Hardy
Peter Webber
Les Wood
Chris Cock } for signalling matters.
Michael Back }

Also staff at the former Ipswich, Norwich and Lowestoft motive power depots, Ipswich wagon repair depot and the many retired railway staff of the Norwich and Ipswich districts, some of whom worked on the Waveney Valley Branch.

Thanks are also due to the National Archives, British Railways (Eastern Region), the House of Lords' Record Office, the British Museum Newspaper Library, Norfolk County Record Office at Norwich, Suffolk County Record Offices at Ipswich and Bury St. Edmunds, and many members of the Great Eastern Railway Society.

'F5' Class 2-4-2T No. 67199 arriving at the Up main platform 3 at Beccles with the push-pull shuttle service from Yarmouth South Town. On at least two occasions the push-pull service penetrated to Bungay on special workings when No. 67199 was the diagrammed engine. *Dr I.C. Allen*

Index

'J15' Class 0-6-0 No. 65471 with brake van spins along the Waveney Valley line midway between Earsham and Bungay in 1951. *Dr I.C. Allen*

'F5' Class 2-4-2T No. 67216 departs from Ellingham with a Beccles to Tivetshall service formed of an ex-GE Corridor Third and Gresley ex-L&NER Corridor Brake Composite. *Dr I.C. Allen*

GER 'T26' Class, later L&NER 'E4' Class, 2-4-0 tender locomotives were the mainstay of through services from Norwich to Beccles via the Waveney Valley line. No. 7416 was regularly employed on these services until transferred to the North Eastern area in 1935. *Author's collection*

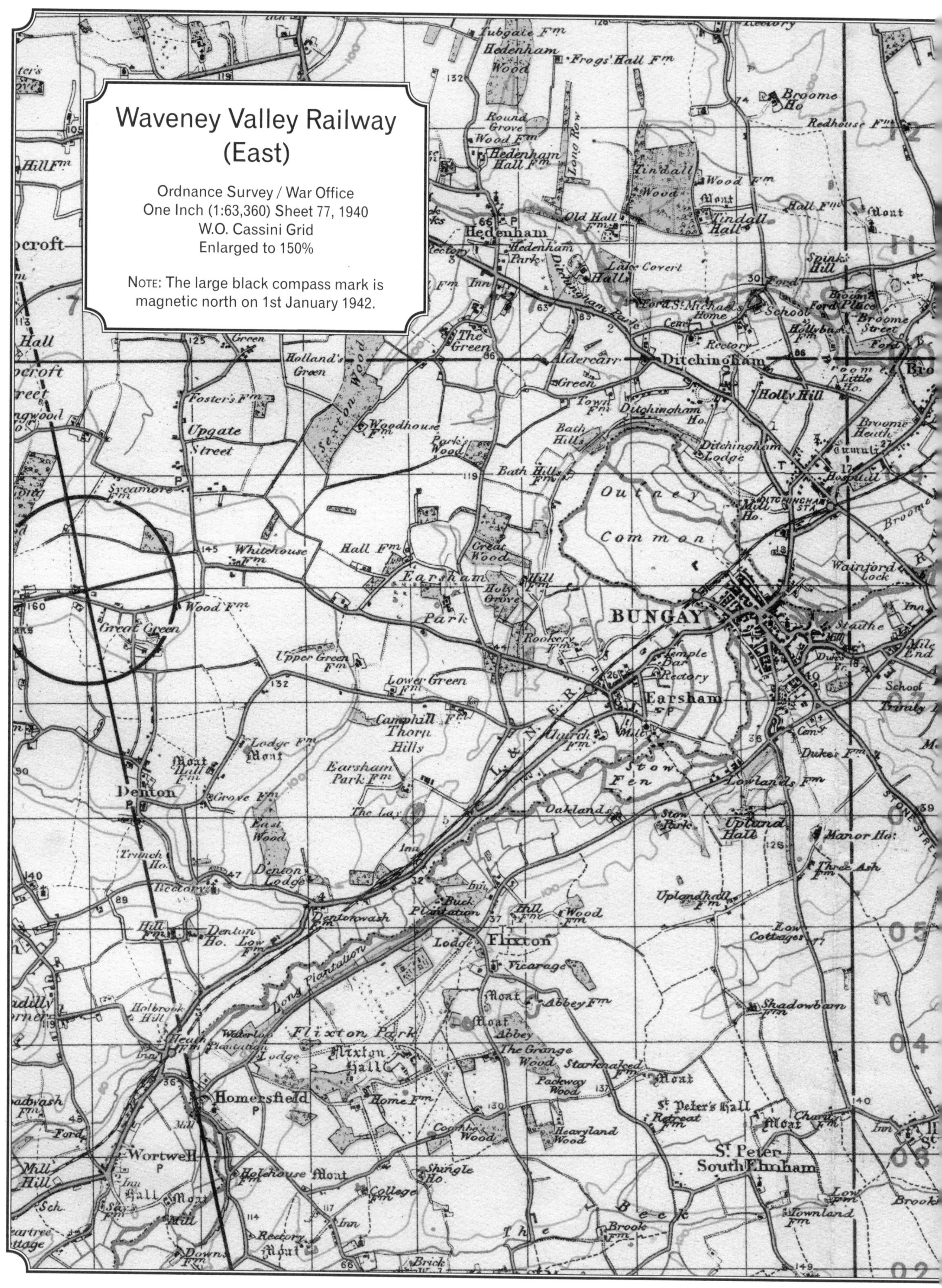
Waveney Valley Railway (East)
Ordnance Survey / War Office
One Inch (1:63,360) Sheet 77, 1940
W.O. Cassini Grid
Enlarged to 150%
NOTE: The large black compass mark is magnetic north on 1st January 1942.
Hedenham
Ditchingham
BUNGAY
Earsham
Denton
Flixton
Homersfield
Wortwell
St. Peter South Elmham